Emotional Problems of Childhood and Adolescence

A MULTIDISCIPLINARY PERSPECTIVE

EDITED BY

Betty C. Epanchin
Wright School, The North Carolina Re-Education Center and
University of North Carolina at Chapel Hill

AND

James L. Paul
University of North Carolina at Chapel Hill

Merrill Publishing Company
A Bell & Howell Information Company
Columbus London Toronto Melbourne

Cover Photo: Students from N.E.T.C. art classes;
Carol Cosgrove, instructor.

Published by Merrill Publishing Company
A Bell & Howell Information Company
Columbus, Ohio 43216

This book was set in Palatino and Optima.

Administrative Editor: Vicki Knight
Production Coordinator: Molly Kyle
Cover Designer: Cathy Watterson
Text Designer: Martha Morss

Library of Congress Catalog Card Number:
86-63012
International Standard Book Number:
0-675-20566-2
Printed in the United States of America
1 2 3 4 5 6 7 8 9 — 92 91 90 89 88 87

Preface

THE STUDY OF human behavior is one of the most challenging and complex areas of science. It has been the focus of great minds from the fields of theology, literature, history, and science. While there have been major advances in the social, psychological, and neurosciences, however, no one has yet proposed a definitive explanation of behavior disorders.

Science enables us to explain variances in behavior and, thus, to make predictions about it. In the human sciences, variability is explained by developmental theories that focus on the child's neurobehavioral and social history and on adaptive, cognitive, behavioral, and affective skills. Variability is also explained by factors concurrent with the behavior, including expectations and the reinforcement characteristics of the environment in which the behavior occurs. Scientists generally accept the view that most human behavior is best understood as an interaction of the developmental characteristics of the child and the setting in which the behavior occurs.

There are several well-developed bases of knowledge about human behavior in the behavioral, social, and neurosciences. A scientific understanding of behavior disorders in children that informs practitioners—teachers, therapists, social workers, child care workers, group home staff, and others—must draw from each of these areas and integrate that knowledge to guide assessment, diagnosis, and clinical management.

Several important issues add to the complexity of the task of understanding and working effectively with children who have behavior disorders and with their families. One issue is the difference among disciplines of those who work with these children. Knowledge bases and language vary considerably.

The issue of communication among disciplines is also important. A clinician who is interested primarily in a child's observable behavior may use concepts and language very different from those of a clinician who is primarily interested in the child's inner life—feelings, attitudes, and values.

Another major issue has to do with the inherent limitations of science in understanding human behavior. Different scientific philosophies view reality differently and thus have different views of the appropriate domain and methods of scientific inquiry. Whether all behavior is lawful and can ultimately be understood scientifically or whether much is a function of free will, so that choices can never be predicted with certainty, is a philosophical question to which scientists and scholars give very different answers.

We believe that human behavior has meaning and can be understood only with some understanding of the person and of the culture in which the behavior and the responses to it occur. The human sciences provide an important foundation for such understanding. The humanities—the arts, philosophy, literature, religion, and history—provide another important and necessary foundation. Therefore, the many clinical and pedagogical decisions one must make in working with children with behavior disorders must be culturally as well as scientifically informed. Those who work with children need a strong educational foundation in the liberal arts as well as in the human sciences. Neither poetic sensitivity nor scientific rigor alone is sufficient to guide clinical practice. While the clinical and pedagogical practice of a teacher, psychotherapist, medical doctor, or others who work with children must be based on the best science available, a creative understanding of human problems and the uses of science in treatment and education are, in the broadest sense, artistic in nature.

The contributors to this text present current research and state-of-the-arts practice used in the treatment and education of children with behavior disorders. The general theoretical lens of human ecology is used to look at behavior as an interaction of psychological and social variables. The limitations of the human sciences in explaining and predicting variability in human behavior and the value of the humanities are recognized in the art of psychological and educational practice.

This text introduces the interdisciplinary nature of the problem of children's behavior disorders and the broad foundations that support professional practice. It is written for teachers, social workers, psychologists, child care workers, and others who need current philosophical perspectives and a synthesis of the research on behavior disorders from different fields as applied to clinical and pedagogical practice.

ACKNOWLEDGEMENTS

We are grateful to many people who helped us in developing this book and are pleased to acknowledge their contributions. Their commitment and patience made our work possible.

First, to those who contributed chapters, we owe a special debt. In every instance the final product was what we sought in terms of quality of scholarship and the fit of the contributor's viewpoint with the perspective we were developing.

Several people read the manuscript at various stages of its development and their suggestions improved the book substantially. These included Scott Bryant-Comstock, Michael Owen, Debbie Simmers, Elaine Fields, Mary Sue Reynolds, Pam DiValore, and Greg Olley. We also wish to thank Jerry Dillard, University of Alabama; Dr. Robert Cohen, Department of Health and Mental Retardation, Virginia Treatment Center, Richmond; Steve McCarney, University of Missouri—Columbia; Carl Smith, Buena Vista College; Frank Wood, University of Minnesota at Minneapolis; George Griffin, University of North Carolina; Dr. Patrick Fowler, University of Virginia Medical Center, Charlottesville; and Sharon Morgan, University of Texas at El Paso.

To Vicki Knight and Molly Kyle at Merrill Publishing, who provided invaluable information, feedback, and encouragement, we are especially grateful.

We wish to thank the children—our teachers—who contributed the art used in the book.

Finally, to our families and dear friends, who have gracefully tolerated our periods of being preoccupied with the book rather than attending to them and who have also provided us with support and good humor when we tired of the project, we offer our deepest appreciation.

B. C. E.

J. L. P.

Contents

SECTION ONE

Philosophical and Technical Foundations

Children's behavior disorders are a complex area of study and clinical practice. Researchers' and clinicians' views increasingly reflect an integration of the perspectives and knowledge bases of developmental psychology and the study and treatment of psychopathology. This integration improves our understanding and the effectiveness of interventions with behavior disordered children.

Section One presents knowledge about behavior disorders in children in a historical and cultural context. An understanding of the philosophical and cultural, as well as the scientific, foundations of behavior disorders is necessary to adequately guide teachers and clinicians in their work with these children and their families.

This integrative perspective provides the framework for defining behavior disorders and assessing a child's needs. Diagnosis of a behavior disorder should reflect an understanding of the child's social and developmental context and guide the development of a plan for intervention. We will discuss the philosophical and developmental foundations for child study and describe the processes of defining, assessing, and diagnosing behavior disorders in children.

It is only with the heart that one sees rightly. What is essential is invisible to the eye.

THE LITTLE PRINCE

This picture was drawn by a 9-year-old border-line psychotic boy who had an abusive and chaotic background. Asked to describe the picture, the boy said "the title is a man riding a horse." His teacher felt the picture was like the child—beautiful, but distorted and chaotic.

CHAPTER ONE

Understanding Behavior Disorders in Children

James L. Paul
UNIVERSITY OF NORTH CAROLINA
AT CHAPEL HILL

Several problems have limited the development of a common understanding of behavior disorders among child behavior specialists. These include the difficulty in defining "normal" behavior in a multicultural society, communication problems between and among disciplines concerned with children's behavior disorders, and the imperfect science that guides professional practices.

Research on behavior disorders is limited by the complexity of the field, moral constraints on research, researchers' philosophical predispositions, ethical issues involved in identification, and barriers to multidisciplinary communication.

Factors such as socialization, central nervous system pathology, temperament, and learning disabilities play varying roles in behavior disorders. The fact that behavior disorders are sometimes related to social, medical, psychological, and/or legal problems has contributed to the failure to centralize administrative responsibility for children with behavior disorders into a single service delivery system.

As sources of knowledge about human behavior, the humanities are necessary to complement the views and methods of the sciences. History, philosophy, literature, and the arts are especially helpful in increasing awareness of the values, preconceptions, and cultural images that are embedded in our views of behavior disorders and in offering alternatives.

Sensitivity to the needs of children with behavior disorders and of their families requires understanding of basic ethical issues, philosophical problems, and inherent limitations in clinical work and research.

BILLY, JOEY, RAYMOND, and Kathryn are children with behavior disorders. They are very different from each other, however, and illustrate the range of problems that can be labelled "behavior disordered." These brief descriptions suggest the complexity of the interaction between these children and their school environments.

Billy is very aggressive. He is smart enough to succeed in his academic work with relatively little effort, but always seems angry. Billy's teacher dreads his coming into the room in the morning because she knows there will probably be some negative encounter with him. She knows that if she ignores him, he will persist in distracting other children and doing things that he knows annoy her. She knows when she disciplines him, he will curse her and say something obscene, embarrassing her and the rest of the class. He makes her angry every day. His parents are also exasperated. They are reluctant to take him with them to any social gathering because he always gets into trouble with someone.

Joey is a quiet child; he seems almost afraid to be in the world. His academic work is erratic, and he never participates in class discussions and activities. Joey seems so vulnerable and so helpless that his teacher is at times overcome with sadness. "Why is this child so hurt? Why can't I reach him? Why doesn't he trust me?" His parents cannot get him involved in any community activities. He has no friends, and his parents feel hurt.

Raymond tries to be a good student and desperately wants to please his teacher, yet his behavior is often unacceptable. Despite the teacher's repeated efforts, he is out of his seat a lot at inappropriate times. He constantly interrupts the teacher when she is talking, has great difficulty waiting his turn during class activities, and rarely does his homework correctly. His academic work is marginal.

Kathryn has difficulty with her schoolwork. At age ten, she has never learned to read. Her attention span is short, and she sometimes seems to have difficulty understanding and successfully participating in social situations. Her social and physical development have been slightly delayed; she has accomplished most developmental tasks a year or more later than her older sisters. The pediatrician has commented on the possibility that the difficulties Kathryn's mother had during both pregnancy and delivery may have resulted in Kathryn's having some neurological damage. Kathryn's behavior is usually normal except that she is phobic about furry animals and is excessively concerned about cleanliness. She keeps everything in her room in perfect order, allowing no one to move anything from its place. She also has frequent nightmares and wakes up terrified.

Children with behavior disorders often disturb us and make us uncomfortable. Sometimes they offend us because they do not play by the rules. They may say hurtful and inappropriate things to their teachers and parents. Their feelings can bother us when they are so intense and seem out of control. Some children make us anxious and, perhaps, more aware of our own angers and tenuous control over them. Their vulnerability can touch our existential apprehensions about our welfare in the world. Their sadness can be contagious when we are carrying unresolved grief of our own.

Sometimes we know things about the children's biological or social history that suggest the possible origins of their difficulties; sometimes we have nothing to go on to explain their problems. Mostly we are limited to describing the problems and trying to fit those descriptions to a model or view of behavior that will suggest a way to understand what is going on with the child and how to plan an intervention.

Any approach to describing the condition, and any model we choose to guide our understanding, is based on assumptions about reality and the ways of studying or knowing what is real. We also assume certain values or qualities of life as normative or acceptable. Our understanding of behavior is thus always limited, imperfect, and one among several possible views.

How then do we approach an understanding of behavior disorders? Among the major challenges to professionals in understanding and providing services for children with behavior disorders, these issues have been especially problematic: the role of values in defining normalcy and the standards for acceptable behavior; the communication problems and the often poorly-defined responsibilities among the different service systems that provide special education and treatment; and the imperfect science that guides professional practices.

RESEARCH ISSUES

Behavior disorders in children are one of the most interesting and complex areas of study in psychology and special education, and must be understood in the context of the rapidly evolving psychological and biological sciences. Equally important is the changing sociocultural context within which the norms for acceptable and expectable behavior are defined. To understand behavior disorders in children, it is necessary to understand both the psychobiological and the sociocultural aspects of normal growth and development.

The normative frame of reference is necessary and important, but it is also problematic, because our knowledge about human behavior in general, and child development in particular, is limited. Kagan points out that "although children have been scurrying under the watchful eyes of interested and intelligent adults for a very long time, we have a less satisfying explanation of human psychological development than of the life cycle of the fruit fly, which has been an object of

study for less than 100 years" (Kagan, 1984, p. xi).

Kagan notes four reasons for the limitations on our knowledge of human development. First, the topics in which we are interested, such as thought, emotion, and intention, are more complex and more difficult to study than topics like eating, reproduction, or movement. Second, moral limitations on scientific investigations of human behavior necessarily limit the kinds of research designs and procedures we can use and, therefore, slow the process of acquiring knowledge. Third, research on children is affected by researchers' personal philosophies about human nature. Fourth, "the combination of invisible events, limitations on experiments, and preferred interpretations have prevented agreement on concepts and methods . . ." (p. xi). If these factors limit research on human development, research on behavior disorders in children is even more limited, because the issues may in some respects be magnified in attempts to understand children.

Even though scientific research on children, rooted in the efforts of European scholars, is more than a century old, we have not had many years of systematic and integrated research on children with behavior disorders. Several problems have plagued this area. One problem has been the lack of communication among the different disciplines that have legitimate vested interests in research on children with behavior disorders. These include, for example, psychiatry, psychobiology, anthropology, sociology, genetics, psychology, education, and neurology. These different areas of study have different foci in their research and function at different levels of inquiry, ranging from brain chemistry to social skills and adaptation. Our discussion of the different views of children's behavior disorders and the professional, technical, and ethical issues associated with clinical interventions and education will reflect the communication problems among different disciplines and the fundamental philosophical differences among professionals.

HUMAN SERVICES ISSUES

Historically, responsibility for treating emotionally disturbed children rested with the mental health system. Hospitalization for the most severely disturbed and treatment in mental health clinics for those who could function in the community were primary strategies.

Emotional problems in children may be associated with basic social problems, such as poverty and/or family violence; medical problems, such as central nervous system disorders; psychological problems, such as intellectual deficits and/or learning disabilities; and legal problems, such as those involved in juvenile delinquency. Children often have more than one problem, and the primary responsibility for treating different problems or responding to different needs may rest with different agencies or service systems, such as mental health, social services, medical, legal-correctional, and/or educational. (For a thorough review of the history and nature of these and other systems see Rhodes & Head, 1974.)

Differences in definition, perspectives, semantics, and legal mandates make communication among these systems problematic. Because children and families often need more than one kind of service, and agencies may fail to coordinate sufficiently to respond at the needed time, children often "fall into the cracks." This problem was addressed directly in P.L. 88–164, passed in 1963, which called for continuity and comprehensiveness of care.

Part of the difficulty in providing appropriate services for children with behavior disorders, then, is the nature of service delivery systems, as well as the clinical and social nature of the problems. These difficulties continue, and human services integration remains more a goal than a reality. Computer-aided information processing has helped and will certainly improve coordination of clinical services in the future. The more fundamental conceptual and philosophical problems, however, and the political problems associated with the bureaucracies of caregiving, are likely to continue as barriers to integration of services. And while technical solutions such as those offered by rapid information processing will help, they will not solve the more basic problems of understanding and providing services for children with behavior disorders.

PHILOSOPHICAL ISSUES: SCIENCE AND THE HUMANITIES

Each of the many different social scientific views of human behavior rests on the assumption that scientific methods are appropriate to the study of behavior. These methods are important and necessary, yet we must recognize that limitations in the scientific approach limit the extent to which human behavior can be fully understood, as we see when we compare scientific views of behavior to the views and methods of the humanities.

Kerlinger (1979) argues that there is no conflict between science and the humanities. They are simply different, dealing with different areas of reality altogether. If they are indeed different, then it is useful for someone concerned with essentially human questions, such as the nature of behavior disorders, to understand what is appropriately the object of scientific study and what is outside the domain of social science.

Some views of psychology would place it as much in the humanities as in science. In adding to the understanding of society, Rappaport (1977) suggests that Community Psychology, for example, may be more like history, philosophy, and literature than like physics.

Addressing the question, What is psychology about? D.O. Hebb observes:

It is to the literary world, not to psychological science, that you go to learn how people live with people, how to make love, how not to make enemies; to find out what grief does to people, or the stoicism that is possible in the endurance of pain, or how if you're lucky you may die with dignity; to see how corrosive the effects of jealousy can be, or how power corrupts or does not corrupt. For such knowledge and understanding of the human species, don't look in my textbook of psychology (or anyone else's), try *Lear* and *Othello* and *Hamlet*. (Hebb, 1974, p. 74)

Science is one system for viewing the world that works well for the natural sciences, perhaps less well for the social sciences (Rappaport, 1977). There are many ways outside science "to help humanity view itself." A writer such as Kafka, Rappaport argues, may say as much about us as a scientist studying alienation. The social sciences may be a new way of viewing things already known. "Does Shakespeare's literature say any less about us than Freud or Skinner? The choice between methods of understanding lies in a leap of faith to science, religion, art or some other system. Once the leap is made, each has its own logic. Today most psychologists believe in science" (Rappaport, 1977, p. 28).

THE HUMANITIES: UNDERSTANDING AND TREATING BEHAVIOR DISORDERS

The arts, history, philosophy, and religion are sources of wisdom about the nature of humankind. The images of life depicted in stories of our origins and our past and celebrated in ritual arts are important cultural products. Whether truth is in our perception of it (that is, the order, purpose, and meaning we bring to reality) or in the reality itself, which we continue to discover and perceive only in part, our views change, and our reality, or truth, changes.

It seems reasonable to consider both creation and discovery as necessary activities in the growth and development of humankind. What we ceremonially dance or sing or paint or play is no less a product of our imagination, no less evidence of our evolved nature, no less true, than is the knowledge of science. The perspectives provided by the humanities not only change the lenses through which we view behavior, they call attention to the lenses—that is, to the fact that our views of reality are constrained or limited in particular ways. The humanities are not an alternative to the social sciences, but another source of information in the study of the complex phenomenon of behavior disorders.

Scientific knowledge has increased our power to predict and control events, but it has not substantially contributed to knowledge about our own nature. We know little more of human nature than we knew before the scientific revolution. Wars confirm the worst suspicions, and charitable outpourings, like the international famine relief, keep hope alive. By some views, people are relatively unfree victims of culture; we are what we have learned to be. By others' views we are victims of biology, of drives and needs that we learn to inhibit or satisfy in ways that please us without offending the culture. Whether we are inherently good or inherently evil, whether we are products of socialization or innovators and creators of society, whether we are students of the culture's view of the purpose of life or creators/discovers of our own life's meaning, human nature remains a mystery. To recognize that we are both creator and created only emphasizes the paradox and mystery of life.

In this discussion, we will analyze some philosophical and historical issues that help us understand behavior disorders, to complement the predominantly social scientific perspective in the chapters that follow.

History

Coleman, Butcher, and Carson (1984) distinguish between popular and scientific views of abnormal behavior. Reviewing cases of mental disorders from literature and history, they note that popular views about abnormal behavior tend to be based on unscientific descriptions of the unusual or atypical case. Euripides, for example, described the "phrenzy of Hercules." Hercules was said to froth at the mouth, roll his eyes, become violent, and attack people. He would fall, writhe, and slip into a deep sleep. When he awakened, he would have no memory of his seizure, although he was reported to have killed two of his own children, two of his brother's children, his best friend, and his teacher. Socrates, Alexander the Great, and Julius Caesar, among other notables of Greece and Rome, appear to have suffered from mental disorders. Jean Jacques Rousseau, the French philosopher, became paranoid in his later years, obsessed with fears that others were waging war against him. He believed that his enemies caused him to be physically ill.

Coleman et al. list many other philosophers, painters, writers, and musicians who were emotionally disturbed. Keats had spells of uncontrollable laughter and crying. Van Gogh cut off one of his ears and sent it to a prostitute. It is believed he did this during "a state of clouded consciousness resulting from his epileptic condition" (Coleman et al., 1984, p. 9). Schopenhauer, Chopin, and John Stewart Mill had attacks of depression; Rabelais, Samuel Butler, Burns, Byron, and Poe were excessive users of alcohol. (Coleman et al. note that they are in some measure viewing these behaviors as mental disorders based on present-day concepts.)

The public's images of mental disorders have also been influenced by literature. Shakespeare created several characters who fit clinical patterns of behavior disorders—for example, Lady MacBeth's obsessive-compulsive behavior, King Lear's paranoia, Ophelia's depression, and Othello's paranoid jealousy. Coleman et al. go on to review contemporary literature that has contributed to the public's view of behavior disorders. *Three Faces of Eve* and *Sybil* vividly describe the problem of multiple personalities. Mark Vonnegut's *The Eden Express* is an autobiographical account of a schizophrenic breakdown; Hannah Green's *I Never Promised You a Rose Garden* describes her treatment as a schizophrenic patient. Many have argued that *A Mind That Found Itself*, an autobiographical account of Clifford Beers's own psychosis and institutionalization in a psychiatric hospital in the late 1890s, started the mental health movement in this country. Mary Jane Ward's *The Snake Pit* and Ken Kesey's *One Flew Over the Cuckoo's Nest* provide vivid and disturbing accounts of the dehumanization of patients in psychiatric hospitals.

The Importance of Literature

Freud was very much aware of the value of literature as a source of information about human variance: "Imaginative writers are valuable colleagues. . . . In the knowledge of the human heart they are far ahead of us common folk, because they draw on sources that we have not yet made accessible" (Stone & Stone, 1966).

In the introduction to his elegant study of enchantment, Bettelheim (1977) makes clear the important role literature in general, and fairy tales in particular, can have in helping children find meaning in their lives in the context of their own culture. In his discussion of his work as an educator and therapist of severely disturbed children, Bettelheim notes that his primary task was "to restore meaning to their lives"; he observed, "regarding this task, nothing is more important than the impact of parents and others who take care of the child; second in importance is our cultural heritage, when transmitted to the child in the right manner. When children are young, it is literature that carries such information best" (Bettelheim, 1977, p. 4).

The child needs help in bringing coherence and sense to his feelings. "He needs ideas on how to bring his inner house into order, and on that basis be able to create order in his life. He needs . . . a moral education which subtly, and by implication only, conveys to him the advantages of moral behavior, not through abstract ethical concepts but through that which seems tangibly right and therefore meaningful to him." Bettelheim quotes Schiller, the German poet, who expressed a similar view: "Deeper meaning resides in the fairy tale told to me in my childhood than in the truth that is taught by life" (Bettelheim, 1977, p. 5).

Bettelheim argues that in our culture, particularly where children are concerned, we tend to deny the existence of the dark side of man, believing rather in "an optimistic meliorism." Bettelheim suggests some distortion of the role of psychoanalysis in our culture, observing that:

Psychoanalysis itself is viewed as having the purpose of making life easy—but this is not what its founder intended. Psychoanalysis was created to enable man to accept the problematic nature of life without being defeated by it, or giving in to escapism. Freud's prescription is that only by struggling courageously against what seem like overwhelming odds can man succeed in wringing meaning out of his existence. (Bettelheim, 1977, p. 8)

It is in this context that Bettelheim argues for the value of fairy tales for children. Fairy tales convey the unavoidable struggle against life's difficulties, a condition of human existence. There is value in the struggle and in mastering obstacles, some of which are unjust. In Bettelheim's view, the fairy tale is a unique art form that both entertains and enlightens the child about himself. It enriches the child's life and fosters his personality development.

The Importance of the Arts

Art has long been recognized as a medium for the diagnosis and treatment of persons with behavior disorders. There are many approaches to art therapy, a relatively new aspect of therapeutic work. Once viewed primarily as a diagnostic tool, art therapy has been used successfully in working with disturbed children and many other persons with psychiatric disorders. Fuller, noting that art therapy is rooted in educational, aesthetic, and psychological disciplines, describes the traditional psychoanalytic view of art. Freud distinguished between secondary processes (that is, verbal, rational, and analytic thought) and primary processes (that is, imaginative, symbolic, nonverbal, and nondiscursive modes). Freud, Fuller argues, associated primary processes in adults with regression, neurosis, and ill health, and "was never able to free himself entirely from the view that art was on the side of illness—or, at best, an uneasy defense against it" (Fuller, 1984, p. x).

D. W. Winnicot, a British analyst, described the need throughout life for an area of human experiencing that commingles both the objective secondary processes and the subjective primary processes. Winnicot called this "the location of cultural experience" (Fuller, 1984, p. x).

Social scientists and artists alike have noted the interplay between behavior disorders and culture. This interplay or connection can be dramatically evident in art, as Jean Dubuffet recognized when, in 1945, he collected art created by mental patients, maladjusted individuals, and others who live outside the cultural mainstream. Dubuffet believed that in this art, "creation shines in its pure state, free of all the compromises which alter the mechanisms in professionals' productions" (Coleman et al., 1984, p. i). Dubuffet's art collection, now housed in the Château de Beaulieu in Lausanne, Switzerland, "provides an extraordinary glimpse into the inner lives and private visions of cultural outsiders . . . considered to be abnormal" (p. i).

Margaret Naumberg, a pioneer of art therapy in the U.S., describes art as a way to bring clarity and order to mixed or poorly understood feelings. "The process of art therapy is based on the recognition that man's most fundamental thoughts and feelings, derived from the unconscious, reach expression in images rather than words" (Naumberg, 1958).

The notion that we can learn something about one's perceptions, feelings, and thoughts by examining that person's paintings, music, or prose is not new. What may be more recent is the idea that the assumptions, values, and images of human personality we use to understand others' creative work may be changed by that work. The norms, values, and preconceptions that shape the clinical sciences should themselves be changed, as well as the clinical interventions we use to change human behavior. The behavioral sciences help us with the latter, i.e. changing others'; the humanities are our teachers and help us with the former, i.e. understanding ourselves and the nature of science.

POPULAR MISCONCEPTIONS OF BEHAVIOR DISORDERS

Coleman et al. describe some of the popular misconceptions of mental disorders that have been shaped by superstition, ignorance, and fear. One misconception is that abnormal behavior is always bizarre. History, literature, and now the mass media tend to focus on extreme behavior. Coleman et al. point out that most abnormal behavior is so labeled not because it is dangerous or bizarre, but because it is self-defeating and maladaptive.

Another false belief is that "normal" and "abnormal" behavior are different in kind. When considering human behavior, there is no clear demarcation between normal and abnormal; rather, adjustment is a matter of degree. Adjustment falls along a more or less normal pattern of distribution; most people are moderately well adjusted and fall in the middle of the distribution, and a small percentage of the population is spread out at the extremes. That is, a relatively small number of people are so emotionally disturbed that they require hospitalization, and an equally small number are relatively free from any maladaptive patterns of behavior. In the presence of serious stressors such as divorce or physical illness, any individual in the distribution of normal to abnormal behavior may shift position in terms of the adequacy of coping behavior. "Both normal and abnormal behavior patterns are now seen as attempts to cope with life's problems as the individual perceives them. Although people have different adaptive resources, use different methods of coping, and have differing degrees of success, the same general principles apply to both normal and abnormal behavior, however unusual the latter may be" (Coleman et al., 1984, p. 12).

Another popular misconception is that former mental patients are unstable and dangerous. The corollary to this view is that mental disorders are "incurable," but research does not generally support this view; fewer than one percent of all psychiatric patients released from hospitals or clinics are dangerous and are more likely to be dangerous to themselves than to others.

Unfortunately, the popular belief that mental disorder is something to be ashamed of persists in our society. A mental disorder should be as acceptable as a physical disorder, since both represent adaptive difficulties.

Another unfounded belief is that a mental disorder is magical or awe-inspiring. Even in contemporary society, there have been those who idealize psychological problems and criticize any therapeutic interventions, viewing the abnormal as closer to the "truth." But as Coleman points out, "they ignore the reality that many people who show 'odd behavior' are not simply expressing their individuality but rather are unhappy, confused, and incapacitated by their behavior" (Coleman et al., 1984, p. 14).

Another problem with popular misconceptions is confusing feelings of anxiety, irrational fantasies, and lack of self-confidence—relatively common experiences—with symptoms of mental disorder. The universality of such feelings may help us see people with serious emotional disorders as less strange, but it is important to maintain perspective on one's usually irrational fear that these feelings will necessarily lead to mental disorders. "A realization that other people have the same worries and self-doubts as we have can help reduce the feelings of isolation and of being 'different' that often play a part in personal fears of mental disorders" (Coleman et al., 1984, p. 14).

It is important to note in this context that not all children with behavior disorders exhibit the symptoms of classical mental illness. The boundaries between behavior problems and serious mental disorders are not always clear, and even professionals often disagree. Intensity and duration of behavior problems are among the qualitative criteria professionals use, but their subjective nature makes it difficult for even trained clinicians to agree.

VIEWS OF BEHAVIOR DISORDERS IN THE SOCIAL SCIENCES

Coleman and his colleagues also provide a conceptual account of abnormal behavior as social scientists see it. A major issue in abnormal psychology is the need to define "normal" and "abnormal," specifying criteria to differentiate one from the other. Noting the difficulties in defining abnormal behavior, Coleman et al. describe two general perspectives within which the distinction between normal and abnormal has been made. One perspective suggests that "abnormal" is the deviation from social norms—that is, behavior that differs from social expectations. This cultural relativist position described by Ullmann and Krasner (1975), for example, takes social norms as given. Deviation from those norms, and not the norms themselves, is the focus of definitions of behavior disorders.

The other perspective suggests that abnormal behavior is behavior that interferes with the well-being of an individual or group. Coleman et al. maintain that "the best criteria for determining the normality of behavior is not whether society accepts it but rather whether it fosters the well-being of the individual and, ultimately, of the group" (p. 16). They consider "well-being" as growth and fulfillment, that is, the actualization of potentialities, as well as maintenance and survival. From this viewpoint, then, conforming behavior can be considered abnormal if it interferes with individual functioning and growth. Abnormal behavior is maladaptive, because "survival and actualization are worth striving for on both group and individual levels" and "human behavior can be evaluated in terms of its consequences for these objectives" (Coleman et al., 1984, p. 16).

This perspective values both the survival and actualization of the human species. Assessment, treatment, and prevention of abnormal behavior by mental health personnel have increasingly been concerned with the family, community, and general society, as well as with individuals: "Increasingly, therapy is defined not solely in terms of helping individuals adjust to their personal situations—no matter how frustrating or abnormal—but also in terms of alleviating group and societal conditions that may be causing or maintaining the maladaptive behavior" (p. 16).

Another important issue in understanding behavior disorders in children from the perspective of the social sciences is the broad debate about scientific and humanistic principles in research and interventions. Different theories of behavior disorders reflect quite dissimilar conceptions of people and of science. Some views are committed primarily to the basic values of logical empiricism, that is, objective science. We see this view in research in medical areas, such as biochemistry and neurology; psychological research on behavioral characteristics of children with behavior disorders; or correlates of behavior disorders such as academic performance or demographic variables. Other views are more interested in the existential nature of disturbance, and in understanding, systematically if possible, the experience of being disturbed and disturbing. We find this perspective in the more phenomenologically-oriented and humanistic perspectives such as psychoanalytic theory and "client-centered" views.

These views are not mutually exclusive, nor is one necessarily better than the other. Each has its own logic for inquiry, its own rules and rationale for developing knowledge. Depending on the assumptions we make, we may consider the problem of behavior disorders objectively as a clinical psychobiological entity to be understood and treated, or as a sociocultural problem involving conflicting values, unclear norms, or struggles with the inequitable distribution of resources. That is, some views attach the problem primarily to the person identified as behavior disordered or emotionally disturbed, while others see it more as a product of the social systems in which the person is identified. These different views have important implications for intervention strategies. Focus on the individual will lead to strategies primarily concerned with the individual's behavior, attitudes, and skills—for example, individual psychotherapy, behavior modification, and tutoring. The systems focus, on the other hand, will lead to strategies based on the nature of the environment—for example, work with families, consultation with teachers, and policy changes in schools.

CONCLUSION

The images of human difference that are embedded in a culture's values and people's viewpoints change as the culture changes. These images are reflected in and to a degree created by the cultural arts.

During the twentieth century, our views of behavioral differences have been shaped by science. Different scientific understandings of children's behavior disorders guide professional interventions. This interesting and challenging area of study is constrained by both the limits of twentieth-century science and by the rapid advances in technical areas such as data processing, neurochemistry, and psychopharmacology, and in conceptual areas such as cognition and artificial intelligence.

The study of behavior disorders has become increasingly a matter of scientific understanding, with less attention to cultural and philosophical issues. The philosophy of science on which the research is based, the ethics that guide decisions about interventions, the values that govern the quality of care, and the political ideology that determines allocation of resources all reflect the cultural regard for children with behavior disorders and their families.

How we regard the behaviorally-variant child is inseparable from how we study and understand that variance—a meeting point of culture and science. Whereas we have made great gains during the last three decades in scientific understanding of these children, we have not made equal gains in cultural awareness and sensitivity. The humanities are the primary source of wisdom in this aspect of our understanding.

Problems that prevent satisfactory understanding of children with behavior disorders include limitations inherent in research, lack of clear administrative responsibility for treating these children, communication difficulties among professionals, and the relationship between behavior disorders and social problems. Widely held views are only partial truths, working hypotheses that are subject to change. They will change, however; not just with new data, but with new ways of thinking about children and with changing values that will reflect new attitudes toward and tolerance of behavioral variance.

REFERENCES

Bettelheim, B. (1977). *The uses of enchantment: The meaning and importance of fairy tales.* New York: Vintage Books.

Coleman, J. C., Butcher, J. N., & Carson, R. C. (1984). *Abnormal psychology and modern life* (7th ed.). Glenview, IL: Scott, Foresman.

Fuller, P. (1984). Foreword. In T. Dalley (Ed.), *Art as therapy: An introduction to the use of art as a therapeutic technique.* New York: Tivstock Publications.

Hebb, D. O. (1974). What is psychology about? *American Psychologist, 29,* 71–79.

Kagan, J. (1984). *The nature of the child.* New York: Basic Books.

Kerlinger, F. N. (1979). *Behavioral research: A conceptual approach.* New York: Holt, Rinehart & Winston.

Naumberg, M. (1958). Art therapy: Its scope and function. In E. F. Hammer (Ed.), *Clinical applications of projective drawings.* Springfield, IL: Charles C Thomas.

Rappaport, J. (1977). *Community psychology: Values, research, and action.* New York: Holt, Rinehart & Winston.

Rhodes, W. C., & Head, S. (Eds.). (1974). *A study of child variance. Vol. 3. Service delivery systems.* Ann Arbor: University of Michigan.

Stone, A., & Stone, S. (1966). *The abnormal personality through literature.* Englewood Cliffs, NJ: Prentice-Hall.

Ullmann, L. P., & Krasner, L. (1975). *Psychological approach to abnormal behavior* (2nd ed.). Englewood Cliffs, NJ: Prentice-Hall.

Much Madness is divinest Sense—
To a discerning Eye—
Much Sense the Starkest Madness—
Tis the Majority
In this, as All, prevail—
Assent—and you are sane—
Demur—you're straightway dangerous—
And handled with a Chain—
POEM 435
EMILY DICKINSON

This picture was drawn by an 11-year-old boy with serious learning and behavioral problems. He has trouble with verbal expression and memory. He drew this graveyard and put his initials on a tombstone when asked to draw a picture of himself, saying "I'm the bad guy in the ground. I know I'll die soon."

CHAPTER TWO

Defining Behavioral Disorders in Children

James L. Paul
UNIVERSITY OF NORTH CAROLINA
AT CHAPEL HILL

Definitions of behavior disorders differ among child behavior specialists, reflecting different ways of understanding and labeling children's behavior problems.

Lack of a reliable and widely accepted definition has caused difficulties in identifying and estimating the prevalence of children with behavior disorders.

Barriers to developing an acceptable definition with technical and qualitative merit include: (1) the complexity of child-environment interactions; (2) the qualitative nature of the condition; (3) the transience and developmental nature of children's problems; (4) differences in viewpoints among practitioners; and (5) the inclusion of so many different kinds of problems in a single category and definition.

Conceptual issues associated with developing a definition of behavior disorders include: (1) identification with either a scientific or humanistic viewpoint to the exclusion of the other; (2) determining whether "the problem" rests in the child, the environment, or in social interactions between the child and others; and (3) the role of a developmental perspective.

An ecological perspective can be particularly useful in responding to some of the conceptual and philosophical problems in defining behavior disorders.

Both scientific and philosophical issues contribute to an understanding of the complexity of defining behavior disorders in children.

Several different labels are applied to children with behavior disorders (emotionally disturbed, emotionally handicapped, and so forth), which call into play ethical, philosophical, and political issues.

Prevalence estimates of behavior disorders in children vary widely, reflecting conceptual and measurement problems associated with definition and identification. There are philosophical issues associated with the federal government's prevalence estimate of two percent.

ONE OF THE major challenges to professionals concerned with children with behavior disorders has been development of an adequate definition. Textbooks for training psychologists and special educators consistently address this topic and just as consistently point out the reality that none of the available definitions is adequate for guiding the process of reliably identifying these children (Kauffman, 1985; Apter & Conoley, 1984; Paul & Epanchin, 1982; McDowell, Adamson, & Wood, 1982; Knoblock, 1983; Rhodes & Paul, 1978; Morse, 1985). Persistent difficulties in defining behavior disorders in children reflect important differences in points of view among professionals.

DIFFERENT DEFINITIONS AMONG SPECIALISTS

If you ask a clinical child psychologist to tell you about emotional disturbance in children, she would say that psychologists are not in complete agreement about the nature of the problem. Some psychologists consider children who are called "emotionally disturbed" as having learned patterns of ineffective behavior that get them into difficulty with their peers and with adults. Others look at the problem more in terms of the child's social and developmental history and consider it the child's failure to accomplish certain developmental tasks. The child may have certain emotional conflicts, and, perhaps, self-defeating or faulty ways of thinking about or perceiving the world. Psychologists draw on various behavioral and developmental theories to understand and treat these children.

A child psychiatrist would tell you that these children are mentally ill; the "illness" has developed during the course of the child's life in interactions with significant others. Psychiatrists will suggest possible emotional conflicts, organic problems with the child's central nervous system, and/or faulty ways of viewing or thinking about the world.

If you were to ask a special educator, he would tell you that of the many labels applied to these children, most special educators seem to prefer the label "behavior disorder." Special educators hold different views of behavior disorders. Some view these children's problems in terms of faulty learning or bad habits in social interactions; some view them in terms of conflicts in the child's inner life, or self-defeating and inappropriate ways of thinking and perceiving the world. Some special educators are eclectic and use several different perspectives or models of behavior. Generally, schools tend to be more concerned about learning and social behavior than about a child's inner life.

All of the child behavior specialists you ask would agree that the problems of children with behavior disorders vary in seriousness, with the differences manifested in terms of intensity, duration, and frequency. The specialists would agree that there are several different ways of understanding these children's needs and problems and, therefore, different ways of treating them. They will differ in their views of the roles parents, teachers, and others play either in causing or contributing to the child's difficulties and what roles these significant others can and should play in the child's treatment. The specialists will agree that the child's past and present social world is important, but will disagree on how best to understand and use that information in treatment.

Implications of Different Definitions

The existence of different definitions of behavior disorders has implications for clinical practice, research, and administration of human services and educational programs. In terms of clinical practice, there may be disagreement on the population to be served, as well as problems in communication among professionals and professional disciplines. This is especially true when one seeks an interdisciplinary perspective. For example, a mental health team composed of psychiatrist, psychologist, and social worker is typically interested in the child's social history, medical history, and the psychodynamics of his present functioning. The team obtains this information through interviews and tests, including projective tests, to put together a complete picture of the child's functioning, that is, the degree of the child's psychopathology or emotional difficulties. This interdisciplinary approach to diagnosis is based on a view of behavior disorder (this perspective prefers the general category *emotional disturbance* or *emotional disorder*) as an intrapsychic illness arising from an interaction of several factors in early childhood, including faulty nurturance, predisposing genetic factors and/or organic injury, or disease that affects the central nervous system.

A behavioral perspective, on the other hand, views behavior disorders more in terms of learned behavior that is problematic. While not necessarily denying the importance of the child's social history or the contribution of genetic and organic factors, the behavioral view focuses more on present behavior in specific settings. This view, more likely to be found in educational settings, depends less on interdisciplinary diagnosis.

In terms of research, lack of a precise quantitative definition of the population being studied and one that is widely accepted and consistently applied makes the aggregation of findings from different studies quite difficult, and replication of studies almost impossible.

In terms of administrative considerations, lack of precision in definition makes it difficult, if not impossible, to reliably identify children with behavior disorders. This difficulty is reflected in the range of prevalence estimates for this population, which varies from .5 percent to 15 percent (Kauffman, 1985). If you cannot reliably estimate the number of children with behavior disorders, then it is difficult to develop a budget for a program where funds are allocated according to the number of children to be served. This problem appears at the national, state, and local levels.

The first three chapters in this text address these philosophical and technical issues. Our general perspective is that legitimate differences among child mental health and educational specialists have emerged in the history of ideas about and scientific exploration of human behavior. Like the culture in which we live and work, our views of human behavior are rich in diversity. Although this diversity creates difficulties for professionals and social scientists involved in research, administration, or provision of clinical psychological and educational services, the philosophical pluralism that characterizes the field of behavior disorders creates a wide swath in the human sciences for the study of human behavior and personality. What is at once perplexing, for those who would understand children's behavior disorders and emotional disturbances, is also a source of creative potential in social science and in clinical practice. Our position is that the different approaches are meaningful and useful and should therefore be respected.

While erudite speculations about psychopathology date back hundreds of years (see

Kauffman [1985] for an excellent discussion of history), the professional and scientific roots of abnormal psychology reach back only into the nineteenth century. It was the late 1950s and early 1960s before special education became involved on any broad scale in teaching children labeled emotionally disturbed or behavior disordered. For special educators, it was necessary to understand these children from a perspective that informed curriculum and instruction. Definitions and theories relevant to education were conceived and developed primarily by psychologists who had the benefit of the historical, conceptual, and empirical foundations of research and treatment in the broad field of abnormal psychology. So why now is definition of children with behavior disorders so problematic?

PROBLEMS IN DEFINING BEHAVIOR DISORDERS

Complexity of the Child-Environment Interaction

The developing child is extremely complex. Physical, psychological, and social development involves interactions of factors such as the integrity of the central nervous system, cognitive functioning and emotional maturity, and factors in the child's environment such as parenting behavior and educational opportunity. Behavior is a product of these and other interactions. Behavior disorder is a state or condition that reflects a child's maladaptation to what is acceptable and expectable for his age.

If child development is complex, it is also dynamic—that is, characterized by change. The growing child is constantly in the process of maturing, and that maturation occurs in a context of social expectations that are also changing. When those expectations match the child's psychobiosocial development, a state of equilibrium exists. One way to look at successful functioning that is satisfying to both the child and the social setting is in terms of the match, or "goodness of fit," between the child and the environment. The opposite of this satisfying good match is a mismatch that is alarming or troubling. A state of mismatch, or a "bad fit," may be disturbing to the child, the setting, or both. (See Chess and Thomas, 1985, for a full discussion of the "goodness of fit" model.)

Qualitative Nature of the Condition

Behavior disordered children exhibit "disturbed" behavior in their social environment. A child who appears very sad and withdraws from interactions with other children, or one who suddenly develops a negative attitude and becomes a discipline problem at school, are examples.

There is a philosophical problem in the way we have regarded or understood experience. Poets, novelists, and musicians are among those who help us experience the qualitative verities of life. What the sciences do with understanding and the objective world, the arts do with meaning and the subjective world. Contemporary philosophy has helped reconnect the objective and the subjective, pointing out the error in distinguishing these as mutually exclusive. Whether understanding leads to feelings about the world and our experience of it, or our feelings about the world and our experience of it lead us to understand it as we do, has been a continuing debate in the history of philosophy. One can probably not answer the question from research that takes either viewpoint, but the logic and methods of inquiry have generally required us to take one view or the other.

By *qualitative experience*, we mean both the child's feelings and understanding. To understand the child's experience, one must understand both how the child feels about himself in the world and the way he thinks about his experience. While there are ways to study the child's experience systematically (for example, a clinical interview that probes the child's thoughts and feelings and projective tests that are generally unreliable), we cannot reduce experience to a number such as an intelligence quotient, social quotient, adaptive behavior index, or a developmental age.

Transience of Troubled and/or Troubling Behavior

Children are extremely sensitive to changes in their environment, and their behavior is usually a good indicator of their reactions to changes or trauma. Acute stress in the child's home, involving, for example, death, violence, or separation, has an impact that will usually be reflected in his behavior. The child's response depends on the nature of the crisis and the threat he experiences. It also depends on factors such as the child's developmental stage, the presence of reliable support systems in the time of crisis, the child's temperamental characteristics, his repertoire of psychological strategies for coping with stress, and his general state of emotional well-being.

Each child has a behavioral "track record," a social history from which we can learn how well and how consistently he has functioned. Each track record has its social context, from which we can learn about the kinds of demands with which the child has had to cope. This information helps us place the issue of transience in perspective for each child. Any clinical picture of new behavior that is of concern must take into account this kind of information. The interaction of factors like these is part of what makes children different; it also makes it difficult to develop a reliable and valid perspective. It is in this conceptual context that one may sometimes say behavior is transient or "he'll grow out of it." A child who has a behavior disorder, however, is one for whom the behavior state or condition persists. The quality or intensity of the child's behavior, the extent to which it

interferes with expected age-appropriate functioning, and its persistence over time are factors that distinguish a behavior disorder from a transient developmental disturbance.

Distinguishing between what is transient ("nothing to worry about") and a serious problem that requires treatment often involves professional evaluation and diagnosis. There are many specific behaviors or behavior patterns that indicate the seriousness of a behavior disorder.

Differences in Views Between and Among Clinicians and Special Educators

Professionals have different views of behavior disorders, and each view has its own definition and suggests a different approach to interventions. Therefore, when professionals evaluate a child's needs, the problem of definition becomes an important issue.

Professionals from different clinical disciplines who evaluate and diagnose (determine the presence or absence and nature of a behavior disorder or emotional disturbance) include but are not limited to psychiatrists, clinical psychologists, school psychologists, social workers, and special educators. The different schools of thought or perspectives within these disciplines, as well as between them, contribute to the complexity of developing a satisfactory definition.

For those who take a psychodynamic perspective, the child's social history and ways of understanding and feeling about the world—as determined, for example, by projective tests or clinical interviews—will be important. This kind of information helps us formulate a clinical picture of the child's disturbance defined primarily, although not exclusively, in terms of the child's intrapsychic conflict. This "clinical picture" provides the basis for a diagnosis and an approach to treatment and education.

For those who take a more behavioral view, there will be more interest in the child's present functioning—that is, exactly what is the child doing, when, with whom, where, and in what circumstances? This view, which defines behavior disorder in terms of learned behavior that is dysfunctional or maladaptive, leads clinicians to collect precise data about the child's behavior and its context; this information will then guide the development of a plan for intervention.

An ecological perspective leads clinicians to investigate the interactions between the child and different social systems in the school, home, and community. Since emotional disturbance or behavior disorder is defined primarily in terms of faulty connections or mismatches between the child and significant others, information about the significant others and the social systems of which they are a part is as important as the information about the child. The goal is to restore functionality and vitality to the "ecosystem" of which the child is a part; therefore the needs and strengths of both the child and those in the setting are used to develop an intervention plan that will promote harmony or equilibrium—a better "fit" between the child and the social setting.

Each perspective has a particular language; for example, *dynamics, defenses, ego* (psychodynamic); *contingencies, reinforcement, extinction* (behavioral); and *ecosystem, fit, equilibrium* (ecological). Each has assumptions about the nature of behavior and the way one changes it. The psychodynamic perspective assumes, for example, that behavior is symptomatic of underlying dynamics, and behavior is changed in a psychotherapeutic process that "gets at" the underlying dynamics or causes of the surface behavior; the behavioral view assumes that behavior is learned and maintained by reinforcers and can be changed or shaped by changing the antecedent, concurrent, and/or consequent events that extinguish maladaptive behavior and/or teach adaptive behavior; the ecological view assumes that behavior is part of the transactions between an individual and the social

setting, and it can be altered by changes in the child's needs, perceptions, and abilities to perform and/or in the understanding, needs, and resourcefulness of those in the environment. These kinds of fundamental philosophical differences contribute to the difficulties in defining and labeling the problems we refer to as behavior disorders.

Inclusiveness of Definitions

Apter and Conoley (1984) note that behavior disorder is an inclusive term associated with the categories of emotional disturbance and social maladjustment. It is generally defined as "excessive, chronic and deviant behaviors ranging from withdrawal to aggression" and "commonly described as a behavior that violates some cultural norm or others' expectations of what is considered 'appropriate' or 'normal' " (Apter & Conoley, 1984, p. 287).

Apter and Conoley suggest that the traditional category, "emotional disturbance," has been confusing partly because it has been so all-encompassing, and such an all-encompassing term is used because diagnostic categories have been so overlapping.

If a child was evaluated at the Putnam Center in Boston, he would be called atypical (Rank, 1949). Mahler (1952) introduced symbiotic psychosis in New York. In the same city, Goldfarb (1961) and Bender (1953) used childhood schizophrenia and Epstein (1954) on the West Coast referred to borderline psychosis. . . . This lack of consensus among leading professionals resulted in the use of a catch-all category—like emotionally disturbed, in which normal misbehavior was no longer distinguished from any other form. (Shopler, 1978, p. 83; Apter & Conoley, 1984, p. 20)

While it is difficult to identify mutually exclusive (or nonoverlapping) categories of behavior, Apter and Conoley suggest that the distinction between deviance and disability is important and useful because the terms represent two major perspectives in the field. "The deviance perspective defines disturbances in the violation of social rules. It serves as the basis for advocates of the behavior disorders school of thought. The disability perspective, on the other hand, views inappropriate behaviors as symptoms of underlying disturbances, the core belief of emotional disturbance advocates" (Apter & Conoley, 1984, p. 17).

The deviance perspective has the advantages of requiring investigation of the context, emphasizing the arbitrariness of the labeling process, and focusing on specific behaviors that are observable and can aid in program planning. The disadvantages are that normality may become synonymous with conformity, and the relativity of the definitional criteria may repress individual differences. The advantages of the disability perspective, on the other hand, are that it involves a culture-free classification, emphasizes early interventions, and focuses on ideology that can increase our understanding of individuals under study. The disadvantages of the disability perspective are its assumptions about internal states that cannot be verified, and the stigma associated with the label "emotionally disturbed" may sometimes outweigh the advantages of treatment.

CONCEPTUAL ISSUES IN DEFINITION

Each chapter in this book addresses specific conceptual issues related to the particular behavior disorders or topic it describes, but there are also generic conceptual issues involved in the way we think about, describe, and define behavior disorders.

Scientific vs. Humanistic Views—A Complementarity Perspective

There has been a tendency in psychology and special education to identify with either a scientific or humanistic view. Affective and cognitive interests, for example, have been dichotomized, and humanistic and behavioral concerns have at times been treated as if they were mutually exclusive. A scientific view is usually associated with a reductionistic, data-oriented, rigorous, research-based position. A humanistic view is usually more personal, more subjective, and more explicitly principle- or value-based. William James distinguished between roughly the same views as "tough minded" and "soft minded." Philosophically, this distinction generally approximates the distinction between the interests of logical empiricists or analytic philosophers, who have had so much impact on American psychology and educational research, and phenomenological or "continental" philosophers, who have had so little impact on psychology and education in the past twenty years (Phillips, 1983; Howe, 1985).

Each position is value-based, but the values are different. The nature of truth or reality and the nature of knowledge and methods for knowing are different. Both views are reflected in the literature on behavior disorders and emotional disturbance. One's approach to the study of behavior disorder and emotional disturbance, that is, whether from a scientific or humanistic perspective, will determine how one defines the problem. The criteria will be different, reflecting the differences in the world views.

While there are major differences in assumptions and in points of view, these views can be complementary. Viewing complementarity as a central feature of nature (Wheeler, 1982) seems more reasonable than a perspective that holds humanistic and scientific views as either mutually exclusive or contradictory. No single view is sufficient. A perspective of complementarity allows for an understanding of social science that fits better with research and clinical experience. A rigorous pursuit of a more credible philosophy of social science must be neither swamped in technical, epistemological (nature of knowledge and knowing) debates nor mocked by sentimental or meaningless metaphors that yield no new understanding. A complementarity perspective is likely to be most satisfactory.

Geography of Disorder/Disturbance

Another important conceptual issue in defining behavior disorder or emotional disturbance has to do with the location, or geography, of the problem—that is, is "the problem" in the child, the environment, or the interaction between the child and the environment? The third edition of the *Diagnostic and Statistical Manual of Mental Disorders* (DSM-III) distinguishes between a *mental disorder*, which involves the individual's psychological attributes, and *social deviance*, which involves conflict between the individual and the values of society. Some social theorists argue that a behavior disorder always involves the presumption of values that determine the acceptability of behavior; thus, no matter what the etiology of the disorder, it can be understood as social deviance. Others argue that neither individual nor environmental variables are sufficient to explain or even adequately describe behavior disorders. Rather, according to Rhodes (1970), both sets of variables are necessary to understand the locus of behavior disorder or disturbance as the point of encounter between the child and the community (Wood & Lakin, 1979, p. 310). Our position is that knowing about both individual and social variables is necessary to understand behavior disorders. We recognize, however, that some problems are more dependent on social/environmental variables for explanation, whereas others are more dependent on individual/organic variables. The point is that the differences in perspectives are differences in emphasis.

Role of a Developmental Perspective

Different perspectives usually include some concept of development; that is, the nature, impact, and/or consequences of a condition changes with maturation. Several theories of development, especially the stage theories of Erickson, Piaget, and Kohlberg (discussed in chapter 4), have influenced the thinking about and the definitions of emotional disturbance or behavior disorders.

Assumptions about the nature of behavior and the developmental process vary with different theories. There are differences in assumptions of the role of the environment versus child variables, such as cognition, perception, temperament, personality, and genetic predisposition; differences in views of the tractability of patterns of behavior or personality traits once a child has reached latency age; and differences of opinion regarding the long-term effects of early intervention.

Some differences among perspectives rest on empirical questions that can ultimately be answered by research. The question of the effects of early intervention, for example, has already been addressed by considerable research. Some consider the recent "Request for Proposals" by the Department of Education (1985), soliciting a proposal to conduct a longitudinal study with experimental and control groups to determine whether early intervention makes any lasting differences, to be unnecessary because collectively many smaller studies have consistently indicated positive effects.

Other issues will probably not be resolved empirically. For example, it is difficult to contrast the relevance, for treatment and education, of the view that intrapsychic conflict is acquired in the epigenetic development of the self, with a view that behavior is learned and a "surface" view of the way it is maintained is sufficient. Each of these concepts is part of a larger system of thought or theory, namely, psychodynamic and behavioral. The assumptions, logic, research methodology, and so forth reflect different philosophical perspectives, which have been and will be debated logically and empirically. Neither logic nor data is likely to resolve the differences, since proponents of each viewpoint are reasoning and observing the world with very different assumptions or, as Rappaport (1977) suggests, different values. It is this fundamental problem—the value differences among theories that are not subject to empirical resolution—that contributes to difficulties in developing a completely satisfactory definition.

There is, however, an opportunity for the continued integration of developmental theories with theories of behavior disorders and emotional disturbance. Some creative work, mostly conceptual, has already been done (Rhodes & Tracy, 1972). The relatively new area of developmental psychopathology (Rutter et al., 1976) is integrating the clinical sciences of psychopathology and child development and will have an increasing impact on professional views and treatments, and, therefore, on definitions of behavior disorders.

TYPES OF DEFINITIONS

Different types of definitions serve different professional and scientific purposes and reflect different perspectives. Cullinan and Epstein (1979) distinguish among authoritative, research, and administrative definitions, and provide several examples of authoritative definitions across perspectives:

Ecological: "In the community participation analysis of emotional disturbance, the problem is seen as . . . a reciprocal condition which exists when intense coping responses are released within a human community by a community member's atypical behavior and responses. The triggering stimulus, the rejoinder of the microcommunity, and the ensuing transactions are all involved in emotional disturbance" (Rhodes, 1970, p. 311).

Educational: "Children with behavior disorders are those who chronically and markedly respond to their environment in socially unacceptable and/or personally unsatisfying ways but who can be taught more socially acceptable and personally gratifying behavior" (Kauffman, 1979, p. 23).

Behavioral: "A psychological disorder is said to be present when a child emits behavior that deviates from a discretionary and relative social norm in that it occurs with a frequency or intensity that authoritative adults in the child's environment judge, under the circumstances, to be either too high or too low" (Ross, 1974, p. 14).

These "authoritative" definitions contrast with what Cullinan and Epstein call "research definitions," which are more precise, and "administrative definitions" such as those found in legislation or implementation documents.

Wood and Lakin (1979) analyzed definitions used in research studies to determine the extent to which the definitions are comparable, interpretable, and replicable, and concluded:

We have ended our review somewhat discouraged. For almost every study reviewed, the answers to our original questions were negative. Populations were not well defined. When definitions were similar enough verbally to encourage generalization across studies, a close look often showed that the similarity was actually quite superficial. Articles using definitions based on settings/program placement or nomination/referral were often so lacking in more detailed descriptions of subject behavior as to permit a variety of interpretations by individual readers. Where procedures for operationalizing definitions were mentioned, they were so poorly described that replication would be impossible. Continuation of such practices seems unlikely to advance our field very rapidly. (Wood & Lakin, 1979, p. 42)

Wood and Lakin go on to recommend specific technical improvements to definitions for research purposes; they suggest: "At present, we are deceived if we think we know about whom it is that most authors of research reports are writing. Whether they call their subjects 'emotionally disturbed' or 'behaviorally disordered' seems to be beside the point. More than superficial semantic changes are needed" (p. 44).

Administrative definitions, on the other hand, guide the delivery of services; they are found in the rules and regulations of agencies that provide services. An important administrative definition is that contained in the 1975 Amendments to the Equal Educational Opportunity Act and P.L. 94–142. This definition, accepted by the U.S. Department of Education and many state departments of education, describes a serious emotional disturbance* this way:

(i) The term means a condition exhibiting one or more of the following characteristics over a long period of time and to a marked degree, which adversely affects educational performance: (a) an inability to learn which cannot be explained by intellectual, sensory, or health factors; (b) an inability to build or maintain satisfactory interpersonal relationships with peers and teachers; (c) inappropriate types of behavior or feelings under normal circumstances; (d) a general pervasive mood of unhappiness or depression; or (e) a tendency to develop physical symptoms or fears associated with personal or school problems.

(ii) The term includes children who are schizophrenic. The term does not include children who are socially maladjusted, unless it is determined that they are seriously emotionally disturbed. (*Federal Register*, vol. 42, no. 163 [1977]: 42478, as amended in *Federal Register*, vol. 46 [1981]: 3866.)

AN ECOLOGICAL PERSPECTIVE

While we do not have an entirely satisfactory definition, the kind of substantive and conceptual change in thinking that Wood and Lakin believe necessary is reflected by Apter and Conoley. They suggest an ecological perspective on definition as a more comprehensive view than that provided by either a disability or a deviance perspective. In this view

Emotional disturbance . . . is not seen as residing within the person of the child or in some especially negative environmental element. Rather, it is always in the interaction between individual and

---

*There are efforts at the time of this writing to get the label changed to *behavior disorders*.

system that disorder is based. . . . each child is an inseparable part of a minisocial system comprised of parents and family, school personnel, friends, neighborhood people, perhaps social agency staff, and so on. When that little system is working harmoniously, . . . the system is balanced, no disturbance exists. . . . when the system is out of balance . . . a state of discordance exists; . . . a failure to match between the demands and expectations of the environment and the abilities of the child. It is that discordance or failure to match that defines emotional disturbance in the ecologists' perspective. (Apter & Conoley, 1984, p. 20)

The ecological perspective as an appropriate view of "emotional disturbance" was advanced by Hobbs (1966) and Rhodes (1967) and has been useful in guiding program development during the past twenty years. Hobbs's Project Re-ed has been the most dramatic and extensive program reflecting an ecological perspective. It has not, however, offered a widely accepted resolution to the problem of definition. While providing the conceptual scaffolding for different points of view—a supportive framework that permits otherwise antagonistic views to enjoy a complementary coexistence—the ecological view has not guided the development of a widely accepted theoretically-based definition with the necessary and reliable measures for identification.

PHILOSOPHY AND SCIENCE OF BEHAVIOR DISORDERS: A POINT OF VIEW

Both the philosophy and science of behavior disorders and emotional disturbance must mature beyond our present level of understanding before we can achieve an adequate definition. In the meantime, we accept definitions that limit professional practice and children's access to the services they need and, by law, have a right to. We live with serious discrepancies in prevalence estimates (from .5 percent to 15 percent) and in the number of emotionally disturbed children needing services (the conservative federal estimate is 2 percent) and the number actually served (approximately 1 percent). Given the diverse views as to these children's needs and the consequent provision of services, the question remains as to the quality and appropriateness of the service provided for those who have been identified. We continue to debate the degree to which the discrepancy between estimation and identification and provision of quality services is a problem of science or of the sociopolitical context.

It seems reasonable to conclude that our advancing sciences of behavior will give us greater understanding and effectiveness in our professional treatment and education of children with behavior disorders. The social nature of emotional disturbance and behavior disorders, however, suggests that we cannot and should not define the "condition" apart from the sociopolitical and philosophical context of values and attitudes about humankind. Preserving the social context-bound nature of the problem of human variance keeps it rightfully connected to the human condition, a connection reflected in classical literature and art (Stone & Stone, 1966). While behavior science cannot resolve the existential and ethical problems of understanding and treating children's behavior disorders, it can challenge self-limiting ideas about the malleability of human behavior and the individual's creative capacities for growth and development. It can provide new and renewing grist for the mill of social and political philosophy through more productive concepts and more effective interventions to modify the disequilibrium or mismatch between the individual labeled "disturbed" or "behavior disordered" and his setting. It can help reduce the disparity between the needs that exist (prevalence estimates) and the needs we meet (number of children served).

The interdependence of science and philosophy is perhaps nowhere more apparent than in efforts to define behavior disorders in children. Science aims to generate knowledge; philosophy concerns, among other things, the meaning, nature, value, and uses of that knowledge. The study of emotional disturbance must be kept in the realms of both science and philosophy; social science without philosophical integrity provides no warranty for defensible data, and, without the perspective of philosophy, no sure place for the individual human and ethical interests of the child or the integrity of society. Conversely, using philosophy alone leaves us with no clinical science, no empirical foundation for intervention. Philosophy helps us clarify our purpose in studying and changing behavior; it should help us understand the propriety of our decisions in our scientific study and treatment of children with behavior disorders. The unrealized hope of social science is that it provide the knowledge to fulfill our purpose in successfully identifying, treating, and educating children with behavior disorders.

LABELS

Many labels are applied to the problems of children whom we are calling "emotionally disturbed" or "behavior disordered," and the rationale for their use can be confusing. In commenting about the difficulties associated with labels such as *emotionally disturbed, emotionally handicapped,* and *behavior disordered* and the definitions attached to them, Kauffman aptly describes the confusion: "The years have brought such a blizzard of confusing labels for behavioral difficulties, often with obtuse or idiosyncratic 'diagnostic criteria' appended by their creators, that no one but a charlatan can seriously claim not to be 'snowed' " (Kauffman, 1979).

In a survey of categorical labels used by various states in 1983, the Virginia Council for Children with Behavioral Disorders found these: seriously emotionally disturbed, emotionally conflicted, seriously emotionally handicapped, emotionally handicapped, educationally handicapped, socially and emotionally maladjusted, emotional or behavioral disorder, emotionally disturbed, social or emotional maladjustment, personal and social adjustment problems, noncategorical (behavior), emotional/behavioral disorders, and severe behavior handicap, among others (Kauffman, 1985, pp. 4–5).

Wood places the issue of labeling in a balanced perspective:

While there is inevitably a negative and hostile aspect to the naming and valuing of behavior as "disturbing, disturbed, or disordered," there is frequently also something positive and well intentioned. It is this duality of valence in our definition of others as in need of special services that sparks the continuing debate about its morality. It is when the positive aspect is weak or missing that defining slips into mere labeling. We cannot fully understand the ethical dilemma we face as special educators unless we recognize the mingling in any act of definition of both positive and negative elements. (Wood, 1979, p. 4)

Acknowledging the difficulties with labeling, Morse says that "a youngster must be categorized (a harmful thing) to be a candidate for special education (a presumedly helpful thing)" (Morse, 1985, p. 47). He points out six important issues in labeling:

1. Children are often assigned labels before any diagnostic personnel get involved; that is, negative labels are assigned by peers, parents, and neighbors.

2. While the purpose of a category is to define a pattern or syndrome that suggests corrective intervention, the person is seldom exactly like the abstract description on which the label or category is based.

3. Labels can set up expectation cycles that affect what others expect of the person who is labeled and ultimately what he, based on his self-concept, expects from himself.

4. Neither labels nor specific behavioral criteria can simplify individualized interventions or prevent the negative impact of poorly trained workers.

5. Children frequently have multiple handicapping conditions. ("A child treated on the basis of the primary label with the other categories ignored is being maligned" [p. 48].)

6. A label can sometimes reduce expectations for a child to change.

Grosenick and Huntze (1979) identify issues and concerns about the definition and label used in P.L. 94–142. First, the label "seriously emotionally disturbed" focuses on psychiatrically-defined disturbances that are a relatively small percentage of school behavior problems. Second, the label "seriously emotionally disturbed" may be more stigmatizing than other labels, because it implicates or indicts parents as being in some way responsible for the problem. Third, it is not clear whether the term covers the full range of emotional problems or only the most extreme or severe problems. Fourth, the definition, based on the early definition by Bower and Lambert (1962) which identified a range of problem behaviors, is confusing now that the label for the children defined this way refers only to the "seriously" disturbed. Fifth, the law does not help much with the distinction between emotional disturbance and social maladjustment that is required in the definition.

The Executive Committee of the Council for Children with Behavior Disorders (CCBD) in November 1984 adopted a statement in support of replacing the term *seriously emotionally disturbed* with the term *behaviorally disordered*. The rationale for the proposed change was similar to that described by Grosenick and Huntze.

The committee offered seven arguments for changing the terminology in Public Law 94–142:

● The term *behavioral disorders* has greater utility for education.

● It is not associated exclusively with any particular theory of causation and, therefore, with any particular set of interventions.

- It provides a more comprehensive assessment of the population.
- It is less stigmatizing than the term *seriously emotionally disturbed.*
- It is more representative of the students who are handicapped by their behavior and currently served under P.L. 94–142.
- The professional judgment of the field appears to be moving in the direction of the term *behaviorally disordered.*
- It accurately represents a focus on educational responsibility and describes the population being served.

PREVALENCE

Prevalence estimates are problematic because of the lack of a standard definition, methodological differences in estimation, and social policy and economic factors. (Kauffman, 1985, offers a clear and useful discussion of prevalence.) Prevalence estimates have varied from 0.5 percent to more than 20 percent; the U.S. Department of Education suggests a range of 1.2 to 2.0 percent. Reviewing prevalence estimates of Achenbach and Edelbrock, 1981, Graham, 1979, Rutter, Tizard, Yule, Graham, and Whitmore, 1976, and of others, Kauffman (1985) suggests that a reasonable estimate of the prevalence of behavior disorders in children is between 6 percent and 8 percent.

There are no doubt many reasons why the federal agency has used such a low prevalence estimate and why so few children have been identified as needing special education services because of serious behavior disorders. Obviously, the problems of defining behavior disorders and identifying these children contribute substantially to the wide range of prevalence estimates. Perhaps less obvious are the political problems that may be involved. Kauffman (1984) suggests, among other things, that current political philosophy, which tends to view child behavior problems primarily in terms of discipline and behavior control, and identification of

large numbers of children as requiring costly special services has created a situation in which the government exerts pressure not to identify these children. He cites the fact that fewer than half the children conservatively believed to need special educational services (two percent) have been identified. Although the more likely prevalence is much higher, he notes that the government's response has been to suggest that the two-percent estimate was inflated.

The number of children with behavior disorders who need special services is no clearer than the definition. As long as we are unable to agree on the nature of behavior disorders and are thus unable to provide a satisfactory operational definition, we will continue to have large discrepancies in our estimates of the prevalence of behavior disorders and between the estimated prevalence and the number identified. The primary cost of failing to identify children in need of services is, of course, our failure to provide the needed services.

Kauffman (1984) suggests that part of the solution rests in professionals' being more realistic and data-based in their projections of the services they can in fact provide. Paul (1985) suggests that the political philosophy reflected in fiscal priorities that divert expenditures from human services to national defense creates a need to renew our advocacy for services for these children, even in the presence of limited knowledge.

As to identifying, defining, and providing services, Rhodes and Paul (1978) conclude:

There is no single agreed-upon boundary within which to frame a definition of special education. There is also no single standard against which to assess its efficacy. It has many different meanings, each with some basis in perceived or empirical fact. Whether it is viewed in philosophical, organizational, bureaucratic or programmatic terms, special education . . . cannot extricate itself from prevailing norms. No matter how extensive the knowledge base or how systematic the procedures by which that knowledge was formulated, special education is a manifestation of what society honors and an instrument for social policy relative to handicapped children and youth. (Rhodes & Paul, 1978, p. 6)

CONCLUSION

There are important differences in the ways specialists view behavior disorders in children. These differences in viewpoints, which have resulted in different labels and definitions of behavior disorders, have persisted despite major efforts to reduce them. Communication problems among professional disciplines, the qualitative nature and transience of the condition, and the relationship of behavior disorders to social problems are part of the problem of definition. The complexity of child-environment interactions and the inclusiveness of definitions are also sources of difficulty. The problem in definition reflects the technical and philosophical status of the science of behavior disorders.

Lack of a reliable definition has been a barrier to research and to identifying these children. Problems in definition range from technical issues of theory and measurement to public policy considerations. In the absence of a clear definition to guide reliable identification, decisions about which estimates to believe and the kind of error to make—overidentification or underidentification—are largely economic and value-based advocacy issues.

A developmental perspective that recognizes the ecological nature of behavior disorders is important. A definition must also reflect both scientific and humanistic issues.

REFERENCES

Achenbach, T. M., and Edelbrock, C. S. (1981). Behavior problems and competencies reported by parents of normal and disturbed children aged 4 through 16. *Monographs of the Society for Research in Child Development, 46* (1, Serial No. 188).

Apter, S. J., & Conoley, J. C. (1984). *Childhood behavior disorders and emotional disturbance.* Englewood Cliffs, NJ: Prentice-Hall.

Bower, E., & Lambert, N. (1962). A process for in-school screening of children with emotional handicaps. Princeton, NJ: Educational Testing Service.

Chess, S., & Thomas, A. (1985). Origins and evolution of behavior disorders. New York: Brunner/Mazel.

Cullinan, D., & Epstein, M. (1979). Administrative definitions of behavior disorders: Status and directions. In F. H. Wood & K. C. Lakin (Eds.), Disturbing, disordered or disturbed: Perspectives on the definition of problem behavior in educational settings. Minneapolis, MN: Advanced Institute for Training of Teachers for Seriously Emotionally Disturbed Children and Youth.

Graham, P. J. (1979). Epidemiological studies. In H. C. Quay & J. S. Werry (Eds.), *Psychopathological disorders of childhood* (2nd ed.). New York: John Wiley.

Grosenick, J. K., & Huntze, S. L. (1979). *National needs analysis in behavior disorders: A model for a comprehensive needs analysis in behavior disorders.* Columbia: University of Missouri, Department of Special Education.

Hobbs, N. (1966). Helping the disturbed child: Psychological and ecological strategies. *American Psychologists, 21,* 1105–1115.

Howe, K. (1985, October). Two dogmas of educational research. *Educational Researcher, 14,* 10–18.

Kauffman, J. M. (1979). An historical perspective on disordered behavior and an alternative conceptualization of exceptionality. In F. H. Wood & K. C. Lakin (Eds.), Disturbing, disordered or disturbed: Perspectives on the definition of problem behavior in educational settings. Minneapolis, MN: Advanced Institute for Training of Teachers for Seriously Emotionally Disturbed Children and Youth.

Kauffman, J. M. (1984). Saving children in the age of Big Brother: Moral and ethical issues in the identification of deviance. *Behavior Disorders, 10,* 60–70.

Kauffman, J. M. (1985). *Characteristics of children's behavior disorders* (3rd ed.). Columbus, OH: Merrill.

Knoblock, P. (1983). *Teaching emotionally disturbed children.* Boston: Houghton-Mifflin.

McDowell, R. L., Adamson, G. W., & Wood, F. H. (1982). *Teaching emotionally disturbed children.* Boston: Little, Brown.

Morse, W. C. (1985). *The education and treatment of socioemotionally impaired children and youth.* Syracuse, NY: Syracuse University Press.

Paul, J. L. (1985). Behavior disorders in the 1980s: Ethical and ideological issues. *Behavior Disorders, 11,* 67–71.

Paul, J. L., & Epanchin, B. C. (1982). *Emotional distur-bance in children*. Columbus, OH: Merrill.

Phillips, D. C. (1983, Spring). Philosophy of education: In extremis. *Educational Studies, 14*, 1–30.

Rappaport, J. (1977). *Community psychology: Values, re-search, and action*. New York: Holt, Rinehart & Win-ston.

Rhodes, W. C. (1967). The disturbing child: A problem of ecological management. *Exceptional Children, 33*, 449–455.

Rhodes, W. C. (1970). A community participation analy-sis of emotional disturbance. *Exceptional Children, 37*, 309–314.

Rhodes, W. C., & Paul, J. L. (1978). *Emotionally disturbed and deviant children: New views and approaches*. Engle-wood Cliffs, NJ: Prentice-Hall.

Rhodes, W. C., & Tracy, M. L. (Eds.). (1972). *A study of child variance: Vol. 1. Theories*. Ann Arbor: University of Michigan.

Ross, A. (1974). Psychological disorders of children. New York: McGraw-Hill.

Rutter, M., Tizard, J., Yule, W., Graham, P., & Whit-more, K. (1976). Isle of Wight studies, 1964–1974. *Psychological Medicine, 6*, 313–332.

Stone, A. & Stone, S. (1966). *The abnormal personality through literature*. Englewood Cliffs, NJ: Prentice-Hall.

Stroufe, L. A., & Rutter, M. (1984). The domain of de-velopmental psychopathology. *Child Development, 55*, 17–29.

Wheeler, J. A. (1982). Bohr, Einstein and the strange les-son of the quantum. In R. Q. Elvee (Ed.), *Mind in nature*. New York: Harper & Row.

Wood, F. H. (1979). Defining disturbing, disordered and disturbed behavior. In F. H. Wood & K. C. Lakin (Eds.), Disturbing, disordered or disturbed? Perspec-tives on the definition of problem behavior in educa-tional settings. Minneapolis, MN: Advanced Institute for Training of Teachers for Seriously Emotionally Disturbed Children and Youth.

Wood, F. H., & Lakin, K. C. (1979). Defining emotion-ally disturbed/behaviorally disordered populations for research purposes. Disturbing, disordered or dis-turbed? Perspectives on the definition of problem be-havior in educational settings. Minneapolis, MN: Advanced Institute for Training of Teachers for Seri-ously Emotionally Disturbed Children and Youth.

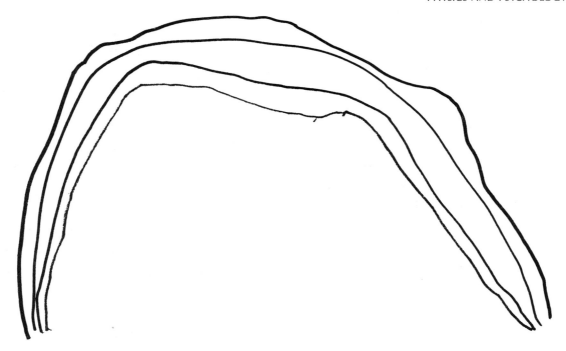

Natural science does not describe and explain nature; it is part of the interplay between nature and ourselves; it describes nature as exposed to our method of questionings.
WERNER HEISENBERG
PHYSICS AND PSYCHOLOGY

Although the 9-year-old boy who drew this picture was having trouble separating from his parents, he connected himself to his father in the drawing, saying "This is me and my Dad. We're wrestling. He hit me in the nose and I hit him here."

CHAPTER THREE

The Ideology of Social Deviance and Behavioral Disorders

James L. Paul
UNIVERSITY OF NORTH CAROLINA
AT CHAPEL HILL

Professionals need to be aware of how their personal values and the cultural context in which they work influence their understanding of and work with children with behavior disorders and their families.

Different perspectives have been important in the history of services for children with behavior disorders. These perspectives represent different research traditions and have value for practitioners.

In the history of research on behavior disorders, there has been a continuing struggle to develop research methods that satisfy the value considerations in studying human behavior without compromising their scientific credibility.

The agenda for research on behavior disorders in children cannot be understood apart from the values and sociopolitical ideology of the culture in which the research is conducted.

The value-based world views reflected in theories of behavior disorders make it essential for practitioners to be sensitive to the philosophical, political, and ethical issues involved in professional interventions.

Research on traditional mental health interventions, such as psychotherapy and special education in segregated classes, produced disappointing results. This created the necessity of a more creative and productive integration of psychology and special education in the treatment of children with behavior disorders. In 1975, Congress passed P.L. 94–142 that provided for the appropriate education of all children, including children with behavior disorders, in the least restrictive educational setting.

Paradigms, or shared ways of viewing behavior disorders, have changed radically during the past 25 years, leading us to new ways of thinking about interventions. In the history of child mental health there has been a gradual but deep shift from focusing primarily on the psychopathology of individual children to a broader concern with the interaction of children's developmental characteristics with their social environments.

The complex philosophical, clinical, and ethical issues facing researchers in the field of behavior disorders call for respect for and communication among the different research traditions.

Professionals who work with children with behavior disorders need to balance personal values and character with the technical skills. We need a corresponding emphasis on educational interventions that engage children's cognitive and affective needs and potentialities to balance technical behavioral interventions.

IN CHAPTERS 1 AND 2 we examined issues associated with defining and labeling children with behavior disorders and the relevance of the humanities and social sciences in helping us understand the nature of the problems addressed by special educators and professionals in the field of child and family mental health. This chapter will focus on the ideology of social deviance and paradigms of behavior disorders, the more formal and technical issues involved in explaining and treating children's behavior disorders.

Three fundamental assumptions guide the discussion. First, in understanding behavior disorders, social science and culture are like the two lenses of binoculars—each makes important contributions to viewing the whole. We will discuss the nature of social science and theory and examine the reciprocal influences of science and culture, including the role social scientists' values and personal philosophies play in understanding and treating children's behavior disorders.

The second major assumption is that discussing theories separately emphasizes differences that may not be significant to special educators or professionals in the field of child mental health. Paradigms, which offer a more general framework for discussing the technical and theoretical perspectives of social scientists, suggest less scientific pretense and allow us to consider ideas that transcend single perspectives.

The third assumption is that, since our understanding of behavior disorders is influenced by the sociopolitical context, and since that context changes over time, it is necessary to understand our theories and practices historically. Thus we will discuss the history of child mental health and special education with particular emphasis on values and ideology. To summarize:

- Professionals' cultural values and personal philosophies influence scientific perspectives of behavior disorders. Professionals in special education and child mental health must consider the role their own values and philosophies play in their clinical work.
- Paradigms help us emphasize ideas and themes that cut across single perspectives. These general ideas more nearly fit the orientations of practitioners, who often draw on the knowledge bases of more than one theory, than do the single theoretical perspectives that are perhaps more systematically and technically applied by researchers.
- Different perspectives collectively provide knowledge and ideas that can aid the practitioner.
- The history of ideas about and treatment of children with problems we now call behavior disorders provides us with some sense of the depth of our philosophies about and the science of behavior disorders.

SOCIAL SCIENCE AND CULTURE

The Nature of Social Science

Different theoretical perspectives have different ideological histories and sometimes different views about the nature of scientific inquiry as it applies to the study of human problems. For example, in developing psychoanalytic theory, Freud used free association and dream interpretation as primary methods for learning about individuals. Although Freud was a neurologist and well grounded in the methods of medical science, he took a phenomenological perspective when he studied human personality; that is, he understood reality to be an individual matter and primarily subjective in nature. He believed reality is what one perceives or experiences it to be and therefore emphasized the nature and meaning of individual experience and one's report of it. In contrast, Wundt and Pavlov, early pioneers in the development of behavioral theory, took a more reductionistic, logical empiricist view of science. They believed that reality is objective in nature, that it can be observed and measured. They studied behavior by observing it and finding relationships or patterns among observed events. Their emphasis, therefore, was on the validity and reliability of their observations and the order, or lawfulness, in what could be observed. While they rest on very different assumptions about the nature of reality and how we study or learn about it, both psychoanalytic theory and behavior theory have made profound contributions to our understanding of human behavior. For almost a century, social scientists have continued to find within each of these two perspectives methods for advancing our understanding of behavior.

All research rests on certain assumptions about the nature of what is being investigated and appropriate methods for the investigation. Rappaport (1977) notes that these assumptions are in fact the investigator's beliefs or values; thus, what we know or believe we know scientifically is the product of formal investigation that rests on the assumptions or values of the investigator. Polanyi (1959) argues that fact cannot be separated from value.

Whatever our philosophical predisposition, in social science we investigate parts or aspects of a larger reality (Kerlinger, 1979). We use what we learn about parts of reality to make sense of the larger picture. This leap from understanding a part of something to views about the whole of something poses another set of philosophical problems. For example, we know a good deal about the academic performance of children with behavior disorders (Pappanikou & Paul, 1977). We know a good deal about the family interaction patterns associated with aggressive and antisocial children (Patterson, 1982). We

know a good deal about the performance of children with behavior disorders on intelligence tests (Kauffman, 1985). We are much more limited, however, in defining behavior disorders to reflect the total clinical picture. Lacking the total picture makes us unable to specify discrete, measurable indicators of the condition or state of "behavior disorders," which in turn limits our ability to reliably identify these children. Further, our ability to predict with reasonable accuracy the course of a child's development once we have identified him as behavior disordered is limited.

Certainly the objective, logical empiricist orientation to social science has provided the framework—rules, procedures, and so on—that has significantly advanced our understanding and ability to treat children's behavior disorders. While the power and promise of research within this well-developed tradition cannot be overestimated, the phenomenologists would remind us that we will always have only a partial picture of the "child state" in which we are interested. Maslow (1966) recognized the limits of the reductionism of research methods borrowed from the physical sciences and argued for a methodology that better matched the subject—human behavior—of psychological research.

A View of Theory

In reviewing theories of emotional disturbance, Rhodes and Tracy (1972a) found that much that had been written about the nature of emotional disturbance as a "human state, condition, or way of behaving" (p. 14) were fragments of theories and not related to any system of ideas or concepts. He and his colleagues in the Child Variance Project at the University of Michigan (Rhodes & Tracy, 1972a) were able to discern commonalities in explanations of emotional disturbance that were logically related, so that clusters of ideas or schools of thought could be identified.

In consultation with Peay (1971), Rhodes used five rules for aggregating ideas or fragments of theories into more generic categories of theory:

1. Related theories employ similar methodologies to learn about and explain emotional disturbance; for example, psychodynamic theories have in common a clinical approach to learning about and explaining behavior, whereas behavioral theories have an experimental methodology.

2. Related theories have a common perspective in learning about and explaining human behavior; for example, sociological theories share a social basis for explaining behavior.

3. Related theories share a common view of the origin of behavior; for example, behavioral theory views behavior as learned, whereas psychodynamic theory accepts that some behavior is unconsciously motivated.

4. Related theories share a common view of approaches to treatment; for example, psychotherapy is accepted as an appropriate approach to treatment by psychodynamic theorists and behavior modification is more often associated with theories of learning.

5. Each theoretical perspective has some identity of its own, "a common ambience within its cluster group" (Rhodes & Tracy, 1972a, p. 16).

These five rules were useful in identifying "clusters of thought and action" or theory fragments that have provided the basic intellectual substructure and orienting perspectives for the field of behavior disorders during the past decade. The "theories" Rhodes and Tracy identified were biophysical, sociological, behavioral, ecological, psychodynamic, and countertheory (which we will later discuss individually). This review and classification of theory (Rhodes & Tracy, 1972a) and the work on interventions (Rhodes & Tracy, 1972b) and service delivery (Rhodes & Head, 1974) that followed provided important conceptual guidance to spe-

cial educators and psychologists in understanding the historical, philosophical, and scientific foundations on which their work rests. Whether one accepts a single theoretical orientation to behavior disorders or a more eclectic view incorporating different theoretical perspectives, researchers and textbooks writers have usually found it useful (and sometimes necessary) to identify their theoretical stance with reference to this classification of theory.

To understand theories of behavior disorders, one must understand the interactive role of culture in the development of theory and the establishment of a research agenda. Similarly, the personal values and philosophies of the social scientist affect the ideas that shape and are shaped by formal theories. Our understanding of behavior disorders thus reflects to some degree the culture in which knowledge develops and the values of the social scientists who develop it. Whether we are talking about social science shaped by culture or cultural understandings shaped by and cast in the language of social science is a value determination.

The Reciprocal Influence of Science and Culture

There is a constant interplay between the knowledge base and the value base of both science and culture. Science has its own view of reality and carefully specified methods of inquiry. Culture, on the other hand, has its own views of the nature of reality; cultural values, and the social system that mediates those values, help set the agenda for science and provide the basis for social rules governing inquiry. For example, the exploration of outer space and the commitment of necessary resources to land a person on the moon emerged from a political agenda of competition with the Russian government; however, the tremendous space and bioengineering feats that followed establishment of the outer-space agenda were made possible by the structure and rules of the physical sciences.

The ethics of inquiry provide another illustration of the interplay between culture and science. For example, the formal rules of experimentation, which make possible the development of knowledge about causes and effects, often cannot be applied to the study of human beings. It would not be acceptable to operate on a healthy person's brain for the purpose of scientific observation; it would not be acceptable to induce extreme pain or damage healthy tissue for research purposes if there were no justifiable benefit to the research participant; and it would not be acceptable to withhold treatment that might improve someone's well-being merely to facilitate research. Deception and confidentiality are also basic ethical considerations that affect the conduct of research.

Formal structures such as review committees or institutional review boards concern themselves specifically with ethical considerations in the conduct of research. Codes of ethics of professional organizations, such as the American Psychological Association, the American Medical Association, and the Council for Exceptional Children, help guide decisions in the conduct of research to assure the welfare of subjects and the quality of the research. The goals as well as the methods of research are therefore affected by sociopolitical considerations and by cultural values.

The Values and Personal Philosophies of Social Scientists

Rappaport (1977) points out that the history of the helping professions is not necessarily orderly or rational: "Some events become historical fact as a function of being remembered, recorded, written about, and interpreted. Other events are ignored and do not become facts. . . . The way events are put together is as much a function of the interpreter and the community of historians as the events themselves" (p. 26). He goes on to

say that historical fact is different from truth because it usually expresses or reflects a point of view. The viewpoint is expected to have heuristic value in describing "how the social sciences and the helping professions are influenced by faith, social forces, and values" (p. 26). Rappaport defines social forces as "political, social, cultural, and economic factors and their complex interactions extant in a society, or a segment of society, at a given moment in history" (p. 27). He suggests that scientists mediate these forces in their behavior by way of their personal values and beliefs.

As values change over time in the culture, historians reflect those values in their selective reporting. According to Holzberg, "What needs to be stressed is the intimate relationship between the philosophy of man prevailing in a given historical period and the assumptions concerning the deviant person. What is of importance is the relationship between these assumptions and the institutionalized practices for coping with deviance" (Rappaport, 1977, p. 26).

This perspective has implications for understanding the value premises of our views and interventions with children with behavior disorders. "All views of how people ought to be are by nature value statements subject to the beliefs of their advocates. When one moves from theory to application they also become action statements, again subject to the beliefs of their advocates" (Rappaport, 1977, p. 28). The point is that the sciences of behavior disorders are not independent of the values of the scientists; nor are the practices of clinicians or teachers independent of their values.

Those who would move directly to the technical aspects of clinical and educational work with children with behavior disorders without considering the philosophical issues of value-based world views reflected in theory are probably destined to come into conflict with their clients' cultural and ethnic values, albeit unwittingly. Ethically and legally, cultural differences must be understood and handled with respect and dignity. Certainly most professionals are sensitive to others' values, rights, and interests; nevertheless, those who would intervene in the lives of others with an agenda to change them must be aware of their own values and the presumptive authority for the intervention.

Besides understanding the role personal values and philosophies can play in the history and development of professional practices, it is important to consider the political nature of those practices. Rappaport describes the political dimension of professional psychological services. Referring to the work of Albee (1969), he notes that when problems are conceptualized as resulting from destructive, unequal, or inadequate social systems, then interventions leveled at those problems constitute a threat to the existing political-economic system. "All human service professionals are political, differing only in which politics they are responsive to" (Rappaport, 1977, p. 33). Reviewing Halleck's work, Rappaport argues that psychiatry has never been ethically or politically neutral. He quotes Halleck:

The person who is preoccupied with internal problems is likely to be less inclined to confront social systems . . . so long as treatment does not encourage the patient to examine or confront his environment and so long as treatment protects those who have adversely affected that patient from considering their own behavior, the net affect of treatment is to strengthen the status quo . . . there is no way in which the psychiatrist can deal with behavior that is partly generated by a social system without either strengthening or altering that system. Every encounter with a psychiatrist, therefore, has political implications . . . once this fact is appreciated the psychiatrist's search for political neutrality begins to appear illusory. (Rappaport, 1977, p. 33)

Insisting that his primary goal is preventing mental illness, the psychiatrist may not be sensitive to the extent to which his political or moral belief systems affect his decisions in a particular therapeutic approach (Halleck, 1971, p. 88; Rappaport, 1977, p. 33). (In this context it is interesting historically to note that Benjamin Rush, the father of psychiatry in the United States, was a signer of the Declaration of Independence.)

An eloquent spokesperson for the political and ethical dilemmas in psychiatry has been Thomas Szasz (1961). One of the first to speak within the ranks of psychiatry about the "medical model" and the prerogatives of psychiatrists, Szasz views mental illness as a myth. He argues that psychiatrists are basically dealing with "patients" who are having difficulty coping, and the concept of "illness," suggesting some underlying disease process, is often inappropriate.

The development of services for emotionally disturbed children has been guided by important political considerations, most of which are subtle and embedded in widely held views. The views and beliefs of the "medical model" is an example. To acknowledge the political dimension of a set of views is not to disparage it, but rather to suggest its nature and the nature of the forces that support it. We need to recognize the role of sociopolitical forces in the history of child mental health and special education services for emotionally disturbed children.

CHILD MENTAL HEALTH AND SPECIAL EDUCATION: CHANGING PROFESSIONAL ROLES AND RESPONSIBILITIES

Specific interest in the psychological treatment of children dates back to the work of Lightner Witmer, one of Wilhelm Wundt's students. In 1896, Witmer established the first psychological clinic in the U.S. at the University of Pennsylvania, to focus on research and therapy with "mentally deficient children." Like Cattell, who had also been a student of Wundt's and worked in the first experimental psychology laboratory at the

University of Leipzig, Witmer had been influenced by Wundt's experimental methods and his research on memory and sensation (Coleman, Butcher, & Carson, 1984).

Other clinics followed, including the Chicago Juvenile Psychopathic Institute (later the Institute of Juvenile Research), established by William Healy in 1909. This institute was created to help study and understand the delinquent young people who were being seen in the court system.

As the interests of clinical mental health disciplines expanded, some focused on children. The first child guidance clinic was established in the early 1920s, and the team approach to treatment became an important feature of the child guidance movement. The skills of psychiatrists, psychologists, and social workers were combined to concentrate on child-school and child-family relationships. At this early period, psychologists specialized primarily in testing, working with schools and with handicapped children (Rappaport, 1977). Much of their work involved classifying and eliminating many children from regular education.

Until the middle to late 1950s, most "professional" knowledge about and work with children with behavior disorders centered in the child mental health field. There were, of course, many children with behavior disorders in regular classrooms who had not been classified, and there were a few special schools for those who had. Many other children with severe behavior disorders had been expelled from school; some were in residential psychiatric facilities.

Professional responsibility for child mental health expanded in the 1960s, partly as the result of an insufficient number of child mental health specialists to meet the needs of emotionally disturbed children and their families. A study by the Southern Regional Education Board (Albee, 1956) indicated that basic mental health strategies and available manpower to provide services would never be sufficient. If all the child mental health specialists in the southeast were to locate in the least populated state in that region, the services would still be insufficient in that area. Further, given the time and cost of training psychiatrists, psychologists, and social workers, it would never be possible to provide a comprehensive system of mental health services for these children and their families.

Lack of trained professional personnel was only part of the problem; there was also a problem in the demonstrated efficacy of mental health interventions such as psychotherapy. While there have been many barriers to conducting well-designed studies in this area, research that has been done indicates that psychotherapy is not effective with neurotic children (Levitt, 1957). Eysenck (1952) drew a similar conclusion in his study of adults, finding that approximately two-thirds of a group of neurotic patients substantially improve in two years whether or not they get treatment.

The reality of an insufficient number of mental health personnel and the apparent inefficacy of primary mental health interventions such as psychotherapy were factors in the rethinking of services for children that occurred during the socially turbulent 1960s. Hobbs (1966), Rhodes (1967), and other psychologists began to focus on systemic issues and the child's social adaptation at home, at school, and in the community rather than on the psychopathology of the mentally ill child.

Ideas of treating "causes and not symptoms" and of "curing sick children" were reexamined, and it was proposed that symptoms alone could be treated, improving the child's social competence and his environment, without necessarily dealing with presumed causes (Hobbs, 1966). The role of insight-oriented psychotherapy was questioned and alternative concepts were developed, including reeducation and behavior modification.

A new force of child mental health workers was identified in teachers, who had knowledge of and experience with normal children. Many argued that with special training and backing from traditional child mental health specialists as consultants, teachers could work successfully with emotionally disturbed children.

A new language emerged, and concepts (such as the ecological "fit" of the child and significant others in different settings) were introduced as alternatives to the preoccupation with the child's "inner" life. The potential value of educational interventions was recognized as more than a paramedical service. New emphasis on the rights of children and families (widespread interest in families came later) came out of the social current of the civil rights movement and the human rights movement of the 1960s.

The 1960s was an exciting and challenging time for social scientists. Clinicians and educators were beginning to draw on many different disciplines for guidance in understanding and providing appropriate care and treatment for behavior-disordered children. Sociology, experimental psychology, neuropsychology, ecological psychology, social psychology, and education made important clinical and pedagogical contributions.

One of the most important events in the 1960s to affect work with children with behavior disorders was the expansion of educational responsibility. In 1963, P.L. 88–164 (the Comprehensive Community Mental Health Centers Facilities Construction Act) expanded P.L. 85–926 to include all handicapped children including the emotionally disturbed. P.L. 88–164 provided training for the new wave of special educators to work with emotionally disturbed children and established a unit within the federal government concerned with the special education of all handicapped children, which became, in 1966, the Bureau of Education for the Handicapped (BEH). The assumption of responsibility for the education of emotionally disturbed children was a major departure from the traditional view that, in the public

sector, the mental health system had more or less exclusive responsibility for treatment of these children.

In the 1960s and 1970s there was tension between the culturally deep-rooted mental health system and the educational system regarding responsibility for identifying, diagnosing, treating, and educating emotionally disturbed children. Among the issues: What is the nature of therapy? What label would best reflect the interest of education and the different clinical disciplines? How to define emotional disturbance so that it would be relevant to education? How would these children be identified? How would educators and mental health workers effectively coordinate their efforts?

Because there was no well-developed, research-based foundation for guiding work with these children in the field of education, this area of special education was necessarily based primarily on the research, clinical practices, philosophies, and nomenclature of other disciplines, primarily clinical and experimental psychology. Most of the leaders in the field were psychologists.

This situation prompted Rhodes and his colleagues to conduct the extensive and comprehensive survey of the literature on child variance mentioned earlier. While their work was progressing, new educational and psychological interventions were being developed and tested. Project Re-Education, developed by Hobbs and his colleagues at Peabody College in the early 1960s, had been fully implemented and research on the efficacy of reeducation was ongoing (Hobbs, 1968; Weinstein, 1969). Hewitt (1968) had developed the engineered classroom at the Neuropsychiatric Institute at UCLA and in the public schools in Santa Monica, California and was conducting research on the efficacy of that intervention. Morse and his colleagues had surveyed educational systems that had programs for emotionally disturbed children (Morse, Cutler, & Fink, 1964) to try to determine the effects of special classes on these students. Their findings were generally discouraging. Long, Morse, and Newman (1965) had pulled together the state of the art and science of working with these children in a single volume, *Conflict in the Classroom,* that was widely used as a textbook for training teachers of emotionally disturbed children. Morse continued to do research on interventions (Morse, 1971a,b). Haring and Phillips evaluated the efficacy of a carefully structured program that was philosophically and conceptually modeled after the work Cruickshank had done with brain-injured (later called learning disabled) children (Haring & Phillips, 1962). As in most program evaluation research, their findings, like those of Cruickshank evaluating the same educational model with brain-injured children (Cruickshank, Bentzen, Ratzeburg, & Tannhauser, 1961) were mixed and difficult to generalize. Rubin, Simson, and Betwee (1966) examined the efficacy of special classes for emotionally disturbed children and, like the research on special classes for the mentally retarded, found the results disappointing.

These were among the significant research, training, and program-development activities in the 1960s. Overall, there were modest gains in terms of carefully evaluated programs that could be shown to benefit these children, but considerable momentum developed among researchers, clinicians, and special educators to find ways to understand and provide appropriate services for emotionally disturbed children.

This momentum was maintained in the 1970s; there were considerable gains in the education and treatment of children with behavior disorders. The event that most affected the nature and quality of services for children with behavior disorders was the passage of P.L. 94–142 in 1975. By mandating free appropriate public education for all handicapped children, this law was a catalyst in aiding the development of educational and support services for these children. The legislative mandate to provide educational services, in the absence of sufficient knowledge about behavior disorders and the lack of a common view and language to describe them, established a situation in which several problems occurred. In the necessity to intervene without a clear understanding of the problems, there was a tendency to oversimplify and to accept less than adequate solutions. Narrowly conceived criteria, such as efficiency, or vague criteria, such as emotional maturity, were often accepted. Fragments of theory, brought together superficially, were used to rationalize programs in ways that did not do justice to any of the theories from which the ideas were taken. The inadequacy of program conceptions was reflected in the literature (Grosenick & Huntze, 1983). More attention has been given to intervention methodologies than to understanding the nature of the problem and the quality and ethical prerogative of interventions.

Psychology and education in the special education of children with behavior disorders have been integrated to the point that we can make several general observations:

- Different perspectives provide useful explanations of behavior disorders for educational purposes
- While each special educator cannot receive intensive training in each perspective, she needs to be aware of alternative views of the problem
- Those trained specifically in the education of behavior disordered children need to be aware of the breadth of alternative, valid perspectives on the problem of disordered or deviant behavior
- Using different perspectives, with an emphasis on pragmatism, is preferable to assuming the scientific supremacy of a single perspective
- Major issues require the continuing attention of special educators, other mental health professionals, and laypeople, including but not limited to the nature and impact

of the delivery system on the understanding and treatment of children's behavior disorders and the ethics of intervention.

PARADIGMS OF BEHAVIOR DISORDER

Debates about the relative merits of different views have been unsatisfying. The question as to which theory is best is almost nonsensical; it is more useful to ask, "Which view is most appropriate to a particular problem or situation?" Professionals disagree at all levels on which we compare theories—scientific appeal, predictive value, philosophical integrity, and utility. Thus far, there has been no significant empirically-based comparison of theories. The Southern Regional Education Board considered such a proposal in the late 1960s, but funding was not available and the research problems seemed insurmountable. In retrospect, the more central concern seems to have been using the social sciences to open up the philosophical and scientific "territory" into which the concept of emotional disturbance fell before the early 1960s—the "medical model" or the psychoanalytic view of the child. Learning, social, ecological, and organic theories have offered philosophically rich competing paradigms.

We use the concept of "paradigms" rather than "theories" of behavior disorder because the concept of *theory* has been used inconsistently and confusingly. *Theory* has a precise technical definition and serves a specific purpose in the language and conceptual system of science, whereas our focus in on *changes* in the study, understanding, and treatment of aberrant behavior.

Rappaport defined *paradigm* as "a set of shared ways of viewing a world of concern" (1977, p. 17). A paradigm brings with it certain rules for problem solving or, as he describes it, "doing normal science." It is not simply a way to interpret data on which there can be agreement, but rather "that the same data viewed through different paradigms would actually lead scientists to see different things. That is, the paradigm allows one to be open to see things that literally could not have been seen before" (p. 18). Rappaport illustrates how one sees the world differently with the adoption of a different paradigm; he points out that when medical scientists viewed deviant behavior from the perspective of illness rather than demonic possession, they began to see symptoms where previously they had seen devils. We believe that different paradigms lead to different kinds of questions about disorder, disturbance, or deviance and lead one to different conclusions about the nature and meaning of these phenomena.

Paradigm Changes

Paradigm changes occur in response to needs for a different view and understanding of a problem. Rappaport exemplifies this in his account of the beginning of community psychology. In 1965, a group of psychologists, some of whom were already working in community mental health centers, met in Boston to consider the implications of the community mental health movement for training psychologists. Some credit this meeting as the beginning of community psychology (Rappaport, 1977, p. 13). Rappaport points out that "it was the perceived need of the time, not great scientific discovery that led to the growth of the profession" (p. 12). "Community psychology as a science-profession was born in part as a consequence of the social forces operative in American society and the service professions at the beginning of the second half of this century, and in part as a consequence of dissatisfaction with existing paradigms for the application of psychology to new problem areas" (p. 25).

Paradigm changes can be unsettling because they require us to change our thinking, but these changes can also be healing. New ways of thinking can help us solve problems, including some that may have been created by the old paradigms. One example of constructive change is our shift to thinking about parent-child interactions as bilateral, rather than thinking of infants and children exclusively as the victims of parent behavior. Bell (1968) points out the reality of the child's impact on the parent, and Chess and Thomas (1984) find that children's temperamental traits are not necessarily the result of parenting but have some impact on their environment, including the parents. Before reexamination of the direction of effects in parent-child interactions, the common view was that infants and children were the recipients of parenting behavior without having any reciprocal effect on parents. Kanner's early work (1943) on the etiology of autism and his use of the concept "refrigerator mothers" illustrate this traditional view. (He has since changed his view.) Caplan (1985) says the traditional view still lingers: "Despite the gains achieved through the efforts of the women's movement during the past 15 years, the practice by many clinicians and members of the helping profession of blaming mothers for whatever goes wrong with their children continues to be a serious and pervasive problem" (p. 610).

Another source of change in our views of behavior is change in the culture's ideology and experience. Social issues can have a psychological impact on children, and they also affect the views of social scientists who study and treat children. For example, there has been some study of the impact of nuclear threat and world tension on children (Mack, 1981); while several studies have documented that nuclear war is one of children's greatest concerns, there is not agreement as to its effect on personality development and mental health (Goldberg et al., 1985). There is agreement among many social scientists, however, that this is an important research issue to pursue, and some evidence that it may be an important factor in different countries, including Russia (Chivian et al., 1985).

The questions of what children worry about and what affects their behavior are al-

ways important; the answer to both questions is *change*. Equally important are questions about what is normal and acceptable; again, the answer is *change*. Our understanding of both the nature of behavior and its acceptability is affected by the changing social environment.

Many people in that environment express views about children and their behavior—teachers, politicians, policemen, lawyers, doctors, mental health professionals, and others. They do not, however, speak with equal voices. The "weight" of one's opinion is affected by many factors, including the authority of one's position. A similar "authority of position" supports the work and views of those who provide treatment for children with behavior disorders. They mediate the value decisions of the culture about what is or is not acceptable behavior and the attitudes and standards about care. Their work reflects the prevailing paradigm of behavior that is rooted in the science of the day as well as the norms of society.

Both knowledge and social norms have changed over time, as has the view of objective science as an appropriate basis for understanding human behavior. The interaction of people's cultural views, the authority vested in caretakers, and scientific knowledge is complex, but at any period in history, it is possible to consider the orienting paradigms that direct our views and treatments of emotional and behavior disorders.

Paradigms before 1900

Prior to the 19th century, the view of behavior disorder in western civilization was predominantly metaphysical. The Priest defined the nature of deviance; either God or the devil was considered the root of behavior deviation. Man was the victim of a vengeful God rectifying sins of the past or of a malicious devil working evil; forgiveness or exorcism was the remedy. Although this period predated the scientific study of human behavior, remnants of these views continue in the culture.

Early medical paradigms of behavior deviances. The 19th century brought new paradigms of behavioral deviance in medicine. One was the paradigm of brain topography and behavior. Broca's discovery of the specific location of the speech center in the temporal cortex contributed much to the work of topographical neurology. Some believed there was a neurotopographical correlate for all behavior, and that deviant behavior (insanity) had a neurological basis that could ultimately be identified and treated (Hart, 1931). It was in this context that a Viennese neurologist, Sigmund Freud, was working. He later challenged this brain-behavior paradigm, advocating a developmental psychoanalytic paradigm. Freud's medical colleagues thought the gains in topographical neurology in the latter part of the 19th century were leading toward ultimate understanding of brain-behavior correlations which would, in turn, lead to basic organic, primarily surgical, treatments for behavior disorders (Hart, 1931). Freud argued that a theory to explain human behavior was needed as a rational basis for treatment.

Early educational paradigms. Another important paradigm to emerge in the 19th century involved the trainability of persons with deviant social behavior. Pinel (1745–1826), who developed "moral prescriptions" for the insane, was followed by Itard (1771–1838), who developed a prescription for training Victor, a young boy about 12 years old who was found roaming in the forest of Aveyron, France.

Later Seguin (1866) and Montessori (1912) developed systematic teaching methods and advanced the educational paradigm that behavior was subject to change by educational and training methods.*

---

*The educational paradigm gained considerably more force and influence later, in the mid-twentieth century. In fact, some think we have pushed the concept of educability too far (Kauffman, 1984).

It is interesting to note that the paradigm makers in the 19th century were medical doctors. That their methods were educational, their theories accounted for only part of the data, and they had only modest clinical success did not diminish the impact of their views on attitudes toward and treatment of the insane and mentally defective. Optimism about the ultimate treatability of these populations through surgical or training methods infused residential care.

The optimism of the medical and educational paradigms was supported by the spirit of broader changes in sociopolitical and religious ideologies. An emerging liberal theology toward the end of the 19th century emphasized the goodness and loving nature of God. Since "He created man in His image," man was good; the prospect of the Kingdom of Heaven's coming on earth contributed to a new sense of the value and worth of the individual. The institutional reform of asylums, "snakepits" that seared the history of human dignity, was led by Dorothea Dix (1802–1887) and other social reformers.

Paradigms since 1900

In the first quarter of the 20th century, things changed. War brought new depth to the history of man's inhumanity to man, shaking the people's faith in human goodness. Theological as well as social-philosophical perspectives changed, as reflected in social reform and changes in attitudes and public policy. The mental health movement was started with the publication, in 1908, of *A Mind That Found Itself* by Clifford Beers, describing his experience as a patient in a mental hospital. Dix's seeds of institutional reform were to grow into a major social movement committed to mental health.

Science, especially social science, also changed. There was a new and different regard for data. In the 1890s, for example, anthropology became an empirical rather than a speculative study of human and cultural differences. In the 1920s a group of philosophers known as the "Vienna Circle," writing on the nature of reality, articulated a growing dissatisfaction with the prevailing European philosophy of science. The work of the Vienna Circle and their colleagues, especially those in mathematics and philosophy, later had a profound impact on the philosophy of science that guided research in twentieth-century American psychology and education. The Circle's *logical positivism* regarded truth as observable, measurable, and thus, reportable. Subjective experience was not necessarily unreal, but since it could not be observed or measured, its reality or unreality had no meaning for purposes of science and inquiry. This view, later called *logical empiricism*, advanced the behavioral and social sciences and influenced education and views of individual differences. One important impact in terms of policies that affected treatment of children was in the concept of measurement.

The concept of quantifying human differences, predicting future behavior, and making data-based decisions about children's social and educational management received great impetus from the advent of intelligence testing. The work of Simon and Binet (1905) in France and Terman (1916) in defining and measuring intelligence and developing intelligence norms was a factor in the thinking about human deviation.

Goddard, Thorndike, Hall and other leading psychologists argued for a genetic base and thus the inheritability of intelligence. Only recently has the fragile and occasionally fraudulent empirical foundation of some of these arguments been exposed (Smith, 1985). The sociocultural factors associated with intelligence were undeniable: the largest portion of the retarded population was retarded because of cultural/familial factors. Certainly poverty was a major factor in mental retardation.

The objective quantification of difference introduced the issue of cultural bias in the administration, interpretation, and clinical application of tests. Children who were different by ethnic origin and linguistic facility from the population on which the intelligence tests were normed did not score as high. The tests became a convenient sorting device, lumping all kinds of differences under the umbrella of intelligence. Although the concept of cultural bias was recognized, it did not become a major public policy issue until the 1960s, as a facet of the larger concern for individual rights.

Paradigms of Freud and his colleagues. The importance of the work of Freud, his colleagues, and those who followed him is undeniable. Four paradigms that guided his work had consequences for the culture and for the study and practice of psychiatry and psychology:

- The importance of early experiences
- Developmental stages
- Mental illness
- The unconscious

The importance of early experience. Adult psychiatric disorders were viewed largely as products of early experience. Early psychoanalytic theories of child development were developed with a retrospective logic; that is, the child's developmental experience was logically or psychologically deduced, albeit speculatively, from the condition and memories of the adult. The adult, not the child, was the object of study. Early child development theory developed from psychoanalytic work with emotionally disturbed adults, mostly troubled women. Contemporary developmental psychologists, whose research involves direct observation of children, disagree with many early psychoanalytic views. Drive theory and the child's affective and cognitive development from birth to approximately age two are among the major challenges to the psychoanalytic theories.

Developmental stages. The paradigm of psychological stages, in contrast to linear, chronological age, as the basis for understanding development emerged from Freud's study of psychiatric patients. Psychoanalytic theory considers children's progression through a predictable and largely invariant sequence of stages as *psychosexual development.*

There have been many variations of Freud's developmental stage paradigm. Some emphasize social and cultural aspects of development (Erikson, 1950); some emphasize cognitive development (Piaget, 1965); others, moral development (Kohlberg, 1978); and, more recently, affective development (Stern, 1978). Some theorists have continued to emphasize neurological development and brain-behavior correlation (Reitan, 1959). Presently, different theories tend to emphasize one aspect of development over another, but most developmental theories recognize and even emphasize the interactive nature of development and the integrity of the developing organism.

Mental illness. Hysteria and psychosomatic illness as a paradigm was not Freud's work alone, but he made primary contributions to understanding and treating hysterical paralysis (1895). A social and political consequence of this view was to legitimize a person's going to a medical doctor for an "illness" of nonorganic origin (Trippe, 1963). If a problem is considered an illness or sickness, then the condition is considered medical; that is, symptoms with underlying psychopathology would legitimately be treated by a medical doctor. Psychiatric practice and the medically controlled mental health system have evolved with a view of emotional and behavioral disorder as mental illness. The illness or "sickness" paradigm, often referred to as the "medical model," was not seriously challenged until the 1960s (Szasz, 1961).

The unconscious. The unconscious is a central concept in the medical illness paradigm. Behavior is prompted by needs or motives associated with the person's psychosexual history, and these motives are largely outside one's conscious awareness. An iceberg metaphor has been used to suggest that only a relatively small portion of one's experience is on the surface, or conscious, and observable. A legal and social policy implication of this view is that it can relieve one of full responsibility for one's actions. Criminal lawyers and forensic psychiatrists continue to debate the issue of responsibility.

1960s: Emergence and Impact of New Paradigms

During the 1960s, people reexamined basic social values having to do with individual rights and attacked unjust social institutions. Challenges to social norms and rules for behavior caused temporary confusion and ambiguity as to traditional codes for acceptable behavior. When norms are ambiguous, it is more difficult to define deviance.

As long as the medical paradigm of illness prevailed, decisions about treatment were primarily medical decisions, but the sixties brought an attack on the "medical model" and questions about the moral premises of the mental health system. What had been considered an individual illness needing treatment by medical specialists was redefined as *coping problems* (Szasz, 1961), *maladaptive* or *dysfunctional behavior* (Skinner, 1953; Ferster, 1961), or, euphemistically, the sickness of society needing radical social reform (Bron, 1972).

The 1960s was a time for new slogans and metaphors in psychology, sociology, and education; a time of social invention as well as upheaval. Paradigms emerged to inform as well as to reflect new attitudes and institutions. Although the paradigms that came into focus in the 1960s were not necessarily new, their impact on attitudes and professional practices with behavior disordered children was.

The cultural pluralism that characterized the social struggles of the sixties helped spawn and received support from an intellectual pluralism in the social sciences. People were seeking concepts of behavior disorders consistent with the prevailing values of reform in the culture. The views of deviance and disturbance that emerged and gained support during the 1960s reflected the values and responded to needs articulated in the social ideology that was guiding and driving social change.

Three major issues emerged in the search for an appropriate view of behavior disorders in children. First, what research is available to support the theory? A strong data mentality was concerned with "facts" and accountability. The idea of managing organizations by objectives (MBO) and holding professionals accountable for clearly specified and measurable objectives became an important feature of the *Zeitgeist*. Second, what is the educational relevance of theories of psychopathology? Educators, psychologists, and other mental health professionals were concerned about the translation of theory into psychoeducational practices, since the public school systems had assumed educational responsibility for children with behavior disorders. Third, what are the value premises of the different perspectives? The concern here was with the potential ethnic, racial, or social class bias of a particular view of human difference.

Much of the debate about perspectives in the latter part of the 1960s and into the 1970s had to do with one or more of these three issues, as illustrated by the sociological, behavioral, psychoneurological, and ecological perspectives. The *sociological perspective* suggested that disturbance was in the norms and practices of social institutions rather than in the intrapsychic life of individuals. (Scheff, 1966; Goffman, 1961). This view was consistent with the emphasis on individual liberty and the attack, by civil and human rights activists, on the norms and practices of social institutions. The *behavioral perspective* emerged from the empirical tradition of learning theory and had the appeal of being data-based, with practices that were efficient

in changing behavior (Skinner, 1953). It was relatively value-free—that is, the issue of values arose in the presumption to change behavior and in the selection of the behaviors to change rather than in the nonpunitive strategies for changing behavior. Of course, punitive interventions such as electric shock and physical restraint were criticized. As a general view of learning and behavior, behavioral theory offered a way to think about behavior disorders without indicting parents or teachers for having caused the problem in the child. The *psychoneurological perspective*, rooted in research on brain functions and brain-behavior correlates (Goldstein, 1939; Luria, 1966; Reitan, 1959), and research on psychoeducational interventions, based on the clinical characteristics of persons with brain injury (Kephart, 1960; Cruickshank et al., 1961), was applied to the understanding of emotionally disturbed children (Haring & Phillips, 1962). The focus was primarily on an issue presumed to be without social bias—the integrity of the central nervous system. Current research on prenatal care, including the mother's diet and use of drugs or alcohol, and the effects of the stimulus and nurturance characteristics of the social environment during the child's early development, suggest that the child's psychoneurological development is also affected by factors that are correlated with social class. The *ecological perspective*, conceptually and empirically rooted in medical and social ecology, had the appeal of offering an integrative perspective on behavior disorders (Gump, Schoggen, & Redl, 1963; Kounin, Fuesen, & Norton, 1966; Rhodes, 1967). Without focusing solely upon parents, teachers, the social system, or the child, the ecological perspective suggested *interactions* as the locus of difficulty, requiring intervention with the child and significant others to relieve troubled interactions.

These different perspectives were useful to psychologists and special educators who were looking for scientific, efficient, and value-free or value-acceptable ways of understanding behavior disorders. The professional literature in psychology and special education from this period reflects the arguments about theory relative to these issues. The social bias in traditional mental health practices was spotlighted by the classic work correlating social class with availability of mental health services (Hollingshead & Redlich, 1958) and the revelation of ethnic and social class bias in labeling and placement (Mercer, 1973). Philosophical arguments of psychologists (Hobbs, 1966) and psychiatrists (Szasz, 1966) drew attention to serious conceptual flaws in traditional mental health philosophy and practice.

The psychodynamic perspective that directed attention primarily to the child's inner life as the source of disturbance and to the child's social history as the primary etiology has changed considerably. This view regarded academic failure and social incompetence as symptoms of the child's disturbance and thus "surface" issues. The perspective broadened to include more attention to present behavior and social competence. Behavioral and sociological views directed attention to social issues, or issues external to the child. The ecological or interactional view became a unifying perspective as opposed to the more extreme views that located emotional disturbance primarily in either the child's inner life or social context. The paradigm shift was toward consideration of the child's present psychosocial behavior, including academic and social competence, as one locus of the problem and thus an appropriate focus of interventions. Social and academic competence are now among the variables that define emotional disturbance.

The assumption of responsibility for educating these children in public schools contributed to this paradigm shift by calling for a view that was relevant to education and would lead to effective and efficient interventions in educational settings. A paradigm was necessary that (1) would fit the educational mission of public schools; (2) would fit the psychosocial role of the child as student; and (3) could be taught to teachers to guide their work with these children.

Professionals continue to differ as to which view most adequately responds to the needs of special educators in the field of children with behavior disorders. Some focus primarily on one perspective (Kauffman, 1985); others argue for an integrative (Hewett & Taylor, 1968) or an eclectic perspective (Paul & Epanchin, 1982). Most recently Morse (1985) argues that we need a new psychology to address the total child and guide our understanding of his behavior in the many situations a teacher faces. On this premise, Morse develops and elaborates the perspective of individual psychology.

RESPECT FOR DIFFERENT RESEARCH TRADITIONS AND VIEWS

Social scientists have taken different positions on the issue of how human our science can be, yet maintain the required objectivity and methodological rigor, and how scientific our approach can be and still deal with human questions. The behavioral view accepts many of the logical empiricists' assumptions reflected in Kerlinger's view—that the humanities and science deal with totally separate realities, thus there is no philosophical conflict. Behavior disorders can be understood objectively in terms of the specific, observable, and quantifiable problematic behavior that leads to a child's being labeled behavior disordered. The psychodynamic view, on the other hand, is less insistent on measurable parameters and operational definitions. Interest is in the quality of the behavior at issue and the personal story or life history of the child who comes to the attention of caregivers and acquires a label of "emotionally disturbed" or "behavior disordered."

These are philosophical differences between views. Other perspectives, such as those that focus on the sociology of behavioral variance or the psychoneurological substrate of discordant child behavior or the ecological network of interactions within which a label of "behavior disordered" or "emotionally disturbed" comes to be applied, also take positions relative to the science of behavior. A social scientist studying behavior disorders within any one of these perspectives makes assumptions or expresses values relative to what is appropriate to study and how to study it.

The philosophical differences that separate investigators cannot be reduced to "good" or "bad." All investigators are interested in data and guided by definitive rules of inquiry within their particular perspective. It is inappropriate to call legitimate philosophical differences "unscientific." This is not to suggest that the social sciences of behavior disorders are without error, faulty research designs, inappropriate analyses, unsupported conclusions, and so forth, but the legitimate philosophical differences among investigators do not devalue a particular perspective.

Behavioral research, especially research facilitated by acceptance of single-subject designs (see Tawney & Gast, 1985), has contributed to understanding and treating children with behavior disorders. This research is different from the clinical studies found in psychoanalytic literature. Clinical studies pursue personal and human questions in ways appropriate to a phenomenological perspective. Freud's theory of psychosexual development, for example, was derived from many hours of psychoanalytic case studies—listening to patients' personal stories and what the patients said about their stories. It is important to recognize that Freud was doing his work in a medical context where neurologists like himself were engaged in a reductionistic science exploring the leads of topographical neurology, hoping to establish behavioral correlates of specific areas of the brain. Resisting this reductionistic orientation, but wishing to maintain a commitment to scientific inquiry, Freud pursued the case study approach.

Freud founded the psychoanalytic institute in Vienna, where psychoanalysts were "studying the soul"* and learning new ways to investigate personal history.† While Freud's original work has undergone considerable change, much of that change has resulted from data acquired through the same kinds of investigations—clinical case studies—that Freud used. Alice Miller (1984), for example, questions infant sexuality and the Oedipal phase of child development on the basis of her twenty years of work as a psychoanalyst. She argues that what Freud treated as fantasy in his patients, and from which he extrapolated his view on early childhood development, was more probably repressed memories of parental sexual abuse. Miller considers it more likely that abused children would repress the abuse and the psychological if not physical injury because of their love for the parent. As adults, abused persons would have no memory of those childhood experiences and would unconsciously pass that violence on to their own children.

Miller uses her own clinical data to argue with Freud's view, which had been based on his clinical data. Some would call this approach "unscientific"; others would argue that some methodological compromises are necessary to study certain human questions.

---

*It has been suggested that *psyche* was substituted in the English translation for what more accurately would have been translated as *soul*, presumably to dislodge psychoanalytic study from religion and maintain its scientific character.

†In the same city during the same period, others founded the logical positivist movement. Logical positivism, later called logical empiricism, has had a significant impact on American psychology and on education. Analytic philosophers of education, rooted in logical empiricism and interested in operational definitions, measurability of variables, and so forth, are now in the majority. Twenty years ago, the "continental" or phenomenologically-oriented philosophers, who were more interested in subjective experience and personal meaning, were in the majority.

Some believe that if a study does not meet specific standards (adequate sampling, reliable measures on the variables of interest, etc.), it may be useless for scientific purposes. Others believe that since ethical considerations impose methodological constraints on studies of human subjects—for example, you cannot harm or deceive someone—researchers are forced to make compromises, which they then clearly specify in the report of their findings. These researchers generally believe that several studies, while individually limited, can be looked at together to make inferences or draw tentative conclusions. Meta-analysis is one approach to aggregating studies of similar topics.

Early childhood education is one area where it seems reasonable to look at a large number of studies of a similar topic, each with limitations from a scientific perspective, and draw conclusions. Many studies have considered the question, "does early intervention with children make a difference in their development?" Yet none has been without flaw in design, sampling, reliability of measures, or some other factor. Most professionals believe with some confidence, however, that on the basis of the number of studies that have been done and the relatively consistent direction of the findings, it is reasonable to conclude that early childhood intervention does make a difference.

CONCLUSION

The issues we face in understanding and working with children with behavior disorders range from problems in the kinds of research and the nature of the science that guides professional practices to the involvement of personal values and philosophies. Paradigms of behavior disorder, embraced by professions and supported by federal funds and policies, serve as markers of ways we have thought about and treated children with behavior disorders. We can make several observations about our dilemmas and the issues involved in the education and treatment of children with behavior disorders.

First, the rate of technological developments in psychology and education has exceeded the maturation of their philosophies. This has caused us to fail to incorporate and integrate into any meaningful and comprehensive image the development of a purposeful system of education for all children, including those with behavior disorders. Inefficient use of research and development products and ineffective collaboration of training organizations and service delivery systems are among the problems in special education and psychology.

Second, psychologists and special educators who work with emotionally disturbed children and their families must be prepared for a number of probable futures and have the skills to creatively fashion a preferred future. The focus on technical competencies must be balanced by personal affective resources and strength of character. We have begun to appreciate the need for this balance.

Third, professionals who plan to work with children with behavior disorders should be trained as decision makers; that is, they should be taught models of behavior and the logic, assumptions, and the nature of data in each. Their education should inform and facilitate their decision making about an individual child's needs. This kind of intellectual pluralism is honest and appropriately modest in view of competing or complementary points of view, guided by pragmatic considerations rather than scientific rigor. Most intervention decisions reflect compromises and a choice of one view of reality from among several legitimate alternatives.

Fourth, an educational perspective allows the opportunity to deal with cultural foundations of deviance and intervention rather than concentrate exclusively on psychological foundations. A careful study of ethics, values, and the nature of moral judgments should be part of the education of professionals—mediators of culture who are constantly engaged in making decisions about changing the behavior of children who are set apart because of their persistent violation of social norms. Rhodes (1967), for example, defined emotional disturbance as a chronic conflict between a culture bearer (the teacher) and a culture violator (the child).

Fifth, it is difficult to separate instruction from the character of the instructor. Social learning theory in general and our understanding of modeling in particular lead us to the inescapable conclusion that the teacher is part of the curriculum. What the teacher prefers, values, and believes is no less a part of what children learn than is what the teacher knows and reasons. The teacher's personal values cannot be presumed to be of lesser importance than the technical issues of learning and behavior control or the objective content of the curriculum.

Sixth, when engaged with an angry child, a frightened child, or a manipulative and disruptive child, the teacher *is* the curriculum. The teacher's ego may be the only reality that connects a situation with what would be valued and accepted in the culture. If the teacher is uncertain about his own beliefs and values and the limits of ethical propriety in changing the child's views, then the child may learn uncertainty or be exploited by the teacher's ideological preferences.

Neither philosophies of education nor theories of deviance or disturbance are sufficient to guide the education of children with behavior disorders. Who the professional is cannot be less important than what he knows or how skillful he is in teaching. A teacher or counselor who works with emotionally disturbed children must be "A decent adult; educated, well trained, able to give and receive affection, to live relaxed, and to be firm; a person with private resources for the nourishment and refreshment of his own life; not an itinerant worker but a professional through and through; a person with a sense of the significance of time, of the usefulness of today and the promise of tomorrow; a person with hope, quiet and confidence, and joy; one who has committed himself to children" (Hobbs, 1966, p. 1106).

REFERENCES

Albee, G. W. (1956). *Mental health manpower trends.* New York: Basic Books.

Albee, G. W. (1969). The relation of conceptual models of disturbed behavior to institutional and manpower requirements. In F. N. Arnhoff, E. A. Rubinstein, & J. C. Speisman (Eds.), *Manpower for mental health.* Chicago: Aldine.

Beers, C. W. (1908). *A mind that found itself: An autobiography.* New York: Longmans Green.

Bell, R. Q. (1968). A reinterpretation of the direction of effects in studies of socialization. *Psychology Review, 75,* 81–95.

Bron, A. (1972). Some strands within counterpsychology. In W. Rhodes & M. Tracy (Eds.), *A study of child variance: Conceptual project in emotional disturbance.* Ann Arbor: University of Michigan Press.

Caplan, P. J. (1985). The scapegoating of mothers: A call for change. *American Journal of Orthopsychiatry, 55*(4), 610–613.

Chess, S., & Thomas, A. (1984). *Origins of behavior disorders.* New York: Brunner/Mazel.

Chivian, E., Mack, J. E., Waletzky, J. P., Lazaroff, C., Doctor, R., & Goldenring, J. (1985). Soviet children and the threat of nuclear war: A preliminary study. *American Journal of Orthopsychiatry, 55*(4), 484–502.

Coleman, J. C., Butcher, J. N., & Carson, R. C. (1984). *Abnormal psychology and modern life* (7th ed.). Glenview, IL: Scott, Foresman.

Cruickshank, W. M., Bentzen, F. A., Ratzeburg, F. H., & Tannhauser, N. (1961). *A teaching method for brain-injured and hyperactive children.* Syracuse, NY: Syracuse University Press.

Erikson, E. H. (1950). *Childhood and society* (rev. ed., 1963). New York: W. W. Norton.

Eysenck, H. J. (1952). The effects of psychotherapy: An evaluation. *Journal of Consulting Psychology, 16,* 319–324.

Ferster, C. (1961). Positive reinforcement and behavior deficits of autistic children. *Child Development, 32,* 437–456.

Freud, S. (1963). Studies on hysteria. In J. Strachey (Ed.), *The standard edition of the complete psychological works of Sigmund Freud* (Vol. 2). London: Hogarth Press. (Original work published 1923)

Goffman, E. (1961). *Asylums.* New York: Doubleday.

Goldberg, S., LaCombe, S., Levinson, D., Parker, K., Ross, C., & Sommers, F. (1985). Thinking about the threat of nuclear war: Relevance to mental health. *American Journal of Orthopsychiatry, 55*(4), 503–513.

Goldstein, K. (1939). *The organism.* New York: American Book Company.

Grosenick, J. K., & Huntze, S. L. (1983). More questions than answers: Review and analysis of programs for behaviorally disordered children and youth. Columbia: University of Missouri, Department of Special Education.

Gump, P. V., Schoggen, P., & Redl, F. (1963). The behavior of the same child in different milieus. In R. G. Barker (Ed.), *The stream of behavior: Exploration of its structure and content.* New York: Meredith.

Halleck, S. L. (1971). *The politics of therapy.* New York: Science House.

Haring, N. G., & Phillips, E. L. (1962). *Educating emotionally disturbed children.* New York: McGraw-Hill.

Hart, B. (1931). *The psychology of insanity* (4th ed.). New York: Macmillan.

Hewett, F. M., & Taylor F. D. (1968). *The emotionally disturbed child in the classroom.* Boston: Allyn & Bacon.

Hobbs, N. (1964). Mental health's third revolution. *The American Journal of Orthopsychiatry, 34,* 822–833.

Hobbs, N. (1966). Helping the disturbed child: Psychological and ecological strategies. *American Psychologist, 21,* 1105–1115.

Hobbs, N. (1968). Re-education, reality and responsibility. In J. W. Carter (Ed.), *Research contributions from psychology to community health.* New York: Behavioral Publications.

Hobbs, N. (Ed.). (1975a). *Issues in the classification of children* (Vols. I & II). San Francisco: Jossey-Bass.

Hobbs, N. (1975b). *The futures of children.* San Francisco: Jossey-Bass.

Hollingshead, B. B., & Redlich, F. C. (1958). *Social class and mental illness: A community study.* New York: John Wiley.

Itard, J. M. G. (1932). *The wild boy of Aveyron* (G. & M. Humphrey, Trans.). New York: Appleton-Century.

Kanner, L. (1943). Autistic disturbance of affective contact. *Nervous Child, 2,* 217–250.

Kauffman, J. M. (1985). *Characteristics of children's behavior disorders* (3rd ed.). Columbus, OH: Merrill.

Kephart, N. C. (1960). *The slow learner in the classroom.* Columbus, OH: Merrill.

Kerlinger, F. N. (1979). *Behavioral research: A conceptual approach.* New York: Holt, Rinehart & Winston.

Kohlberg, L. (1978). Revisions in the theory and practice of moral development. *New Directions for Child Development, 2.*

Kounin, J. S., Fuesen, W. V., & Norton, A. E. (1966). Managing emotionally disturbed children in regular classrooms. *Journal of Educational Psychology, 57,* 1–13.

Levitt, E. E. (1957). The results of psychotherapy with children: An evaluation. *Journal of Consulting Psychology, 21*(3), 189–196.

Long, N. J., Morse, W. C., & Newman, R. G. (Eds.). (1965). *Conflict in the classroom.* Belmont, CA: Wadsworth.

Luria, A. R. (1966). *Higher cortical functions in man.* New York: Basic Books.

Mack, J. (1981). Psychosocial effects of the nuclear arms race. *Bulletin of Atomic Science, 37*(4), 18–23.

Maslow, A. H. (1966). *The psychology of science.* New York: Harper & Row.

Mercer, J. (1973). *Labelling the mentally retarded.* Riverside: University of California Press.

Miller, A. (1984). *For your own good: Hidden cruelty in child rearing and the roots of violence.* New York: Farrar, Straus & Giroux.

Montessori, M. (1912). *The Montessori method* (A. George, Trans.). New York: Stokes.

Morse, W. C., Cutler, R. L., & Fink, A. H. (1964). *Public school classes for the emotionally handicapped: A research analysis.* Washington, DC: Council for Exceptional Children.

Morse, W. C. (1971a). The crisis or helping teacher. In N. J. Long, W. C. Morse, & R. G. Newman (Eds.), *Conflict in the classroom* (2nd ed.). Belmont, CA: Wadsworth.

Morse, W. C. (1971b). Crisis intervention in school mental health and special classes for the disturbed. In N. J. Long, W. C. Morse, & R. G. Newman (Eds.), *Conflict in the classroom* (2nd ed.). Belmont, CA: Wadsworth.

Morse, W. C. (1985). *The education and treatment of socio-emotionally impaired children and youth.* Syracuse, NY: Syracuse University Press.

Pappanikou, A. J., & Paul, J. L. (1977). *Mainstreaming emotionally disturbed children.* Syracuse, NY: Syracuse University Press.

Patterson, G. R. (1982). *Coercive family process.* Eugene, OR: Castalia.

Paul, J. L., & Epanchin, B. C. (1982). *Emotional disturbance in children.* Columbus, OH: Merrill.

Peay, E. (1971). University of Michigan working paper. In W. C. Rhodes & M. L. Tracy (Eds.), *A study of child variance.* Ann Arbor: University of Michigan Press.

Piaget, J. (1965). *The moral judgment of the child.* (M. Gabain, Trans.). New York: Free Press. (Original work published 1932).

Polanyi, M. (1959). *The study of man.* Chicago: University of Chicago Press.

Rappaport, J. (1977). *Community psychology: Values, research, and action.* New York: Holt, Rinehart & Winston.

Reitan, R. M. (1959). The comparative effects of brain damage of the Halstead impairment index and the Wechsler-Bellevue Scale. *Journal of Clinical Psychology, 15,* 281–285.

Rhodes, W. C. (1967). The disturbing child: A problem of ecological management. *Exceptional Children, 33,* 449–455.

Rhodes, W. C. (1970). A community participation analysis of emotional disturbance. *Exceptional Children, 37,* 309–314.

Rhodes, W. C., & Head, S. (1974). *A study of child variance: Vol. 3. Service delivery systems.* Ann Arbor: University of Michigan Press.

Rhodes, W. C., & Tracy, M. L. (Eds.). (1972a). *A study of child variance: Vol. 1. Theories.* Ann Arbor: University of Michigan Press.

Rhodes, W. C., & Tracy, M. L. (Eds.). (1972b). *A study of child variance: Vol. 2. Interventions.* Ann Arbor: University of Michigan Press.

Rubin, E. J., Simson, C. B., & Betwee, M. C. (1966). *Emotionally handicapped children and the elementary school.* Detroit, MI: Wayne State University Press.

Scheff, T. (1966). *Being mentally ill.* Chicago: Aldine.

Seguin, E. (1866). *Idiocy and its treatment by the physiological method.* New York: Brandow.

Skinner, B. F. (1953). *Science and human behavior.* New York: Macmillan.

Smith, J. David (1985). *Minds made feeble: The myth and legacy of the Kallikaks.* Queenstown, MD: Aspen.

Stern, D. (1978). *The first relationship.* Cambridge, MA: Harvard University Press.

Szasz, T. S. (1961). *The myth of mental illness.* New York: Harper & Row.

Tawney, J. W., & Gast, D. L. (1984). *Single subject research in special education.* Columbus, OH: Merrill.

Terman, L. M. (1916). *The measurement of intelligence.* Boston: Houghton-Mifflin.

Trippe, M. (1963). Conceptual problems in research on educational provisions for disturbed children. *Exceptional Children, 29,* 400–406.

Weinstein, L. (1969). Project re-ed schools for emotionally disturbed children: Effectiveness as viewed by referring agencies, parents and teachers. *Exceptional Children, 35,* 703–711.

So when the father died the only person the boy could look to for continued affection was his mother—who hated him. . . . As a result the child doesn't eat, has lost weight, doesn't sleep, constipation and all the rest of it. And in school, whereas his marks had always been good—because he's fairly bright—after his father died they went steadily down, down and down to complete failure. . . . And then he began to steal—from his mother—because he couldn't get the love he demanded of her. . . . The child substitutes his own solution for the reality which he needs and cannot obtain. Unreality and reality become confused in him. Finally he loses track. He doesn't know one from the other and we call him insane. . . . But what gets me . . . we're checked up on all these cases; they're all gone over by a member of the staff. And when we give a history like that, they say, Oh, those are just the psychiatric findings. That gripes me. Why, it's the child's life.

WILLIAM CARLOS WILLIAMS
THE INSANE

I like gymnastics!

In the picture I drew I put a beam in because I like beam. I'm not real good but I enjoy it. I will learn more. We have a beam in our backyard I use it a lot. In the summer, I used it a lot. I take gymnastics lessons three times a week There are a lot more aporatus than beam, like; bars, rings, parallel bars, horse, floor, trampolene, (beam) and others. I like them all. Gymnastics is a lot of fun!

This drawing, by a bright and apparently well-adjusted 10-year-old girl, is realistic and optimistic. "I'm not real good but I enjoy it. I will learn more" is so unlike what we hear from conflicted, unhappy children who lack self-confidence and try to hide their self-doubt.

CHAPTER FOUR

Normal Child Development

Lynne Monson
DYNAMICS RESEARCH CORPORATION

Rune J. Simeonsson
UNIVERSITY OF NORTH CAROLINA
AT CHAPEL HILL

The developmental-interactional approach posits a continuous interplay between child development and environmental changes. It offers a comprehensive framework for understanding the relationship between normal child development and the development of behavioral and emotional problems.

Awareness of age-appropriate characteristics in conjunction with identification of the environmental demands emotionally disturbed children face should increase the sensitivity and effectiveness of professional interventions.

Such awareness builds on Piaget's theory of cognitive development, Selman's model of interpersonal negotiation strategies, and Kohlberg's moral development theory, all consonant with the developmental-interactional perspective.

Adaptation, the relationships of affect and cognition, and the developmental transitions between stages of thought and behavior are key developmental-interactional concepts in understanding psychopathology.

IN THIS CHAPTER we will discuss normal child development by looking at selected tasks, accomplishments, and behaviors that children exhibit at major stages of development. This perspective will provide a framework against which to contrast the development of children with emotional problems; give us a basis for interpreting children's behavior; and help in designing intervention strategies. This perspective is developmental-interactional.

A developmental approach posits qualitative changes over time within an individual in which differentiation and subsequent integration of increasingly refined skills occur concurrently. The interactional perspective views behavior as it occurs in interaction with the environment. Hodapp and Mueller (1982) stress the interrelatedness of the developmental and interactional viewpoints: "It is the notion of a continuous interplay between development and interactive setting, of change and evolution in both the child and his/her surroundings, which forms the basis of the developmental-interactional analysis" (p. 285).

Sroufe and Rutter (1984) stress the importance of a developmental perspective for understanding disordered behavior: "Only by understanding the nature of the developmental process—with progressive transformation and reorganization of behavior as the developing organism continually transacts with the environment—is it possible to understand the complex links between early adaptation and later disorder" (p. 20).

The "goodness of fit" model discussed by Thomas and Chess (1984) and Lerner (1982) exemplifies a developmental-interactional perspective. Adaptive functioning appears to be predicated on a good match or fit between a child's individual characteristics and the environmental demands on the child. Attitudes, values, behavioral attributes of others, and the physical characteristics of a given setting are examples of environmental demands.

We will review theoretical and empirical information on developmental characteristics and issues. Awareness of age-appropriate characteristics in conjunction with identification of the environmental demands emotionally disturbed children face should increase the sensitivity and effectiveness of professional interventions.

COGNITIVE DEVELOPMENT

Infants

Research and theory on cognitive development during infancy have been heavily influenced by Piaget's work (1952, 1954). Piaget's theory is based on several premises, one of which is that infants take an active role in their learning. The learning process begins as infants construct cognitive structures, or *schemata*, of events they experience. They then assimilate (integrate) new information into these preexisting cognitive structures. This assimilation process is in balance with an accommodation process, in which novel stimuli that do not fit into existing schemata cause changes in the infants' cognitive structures. The complementary processes of assimilation and accommodation allow infants to adapt to their environment and lead to transient states of equilibrium as well as qualitative structural changes. Furthermore, these complementary processes reflect a continuing form of adaptation throughout four qualitatively different stages in cognitive growth, which occur in an unvarying sequence. Cognitive development moves from relatively global to more differentiated and integrated states. The stage that encompasses infancy is the sensorimotor period, during which the infant's primary task is to differentiate self from the external environment. The sensorimotor period is subdivided into six stages.

Stage one. The first sensorimotor stage is the *reflexive* stage (from birth to one month), in which the infant is dominated by reflexes such as sucking and grasping. Evidence from a number of research studies shows, however, that the newborn is able to detect changes in shapes, sounds, odors, speech patterns, and hue or contour. Petersen (1982) summarizes this view by pointing out that the infant seems to prefer stimuli that offer the most information.

Additional evidence of cognitive activity on the infant's part is the refinement of reflexes (that is, the first schemata) through experience with the environment. An example of this is the increasing efficiency of newborns in searching for a nipple. They accommodate the sucking scheme to environmental influences in that they modify how they suck as they learn more about how to find the nipple (Petersen, 1982).

Stage two. The second stage (from one to four months) of the sensorimotor period reflects a heightening of perceptual cognitive abilities and enhancement of recognition memory. Social smiling begins. Infants at this stage demonstrate an initial coordination of schemata across the senses, as when they coordinate looking and grasping (Petersen, 1982).

Stage three. Between four and eight months, infants demonstrate rudimentary differentiation of self from the world. They act intentionally upon objects. An understanding of means-end relationships, object permanence, space, and time begins (Thornburg, 1984).

Stage four. Attainment of the concept of object permanence generally occurs by nine months of age (or from about eight to twelve months) and constitutes the most important cognitive task of infancy. Acquisition of this concept indicates that infants recognize the world of objects as stable and distinct from themselves. (We will discuss the significance of this achievement in stage four as it pertains to social development.)

Stage five. During stage five, from 12 to 18 months, a number of accomplishments take place, such as refinement of causality concepts and the means-end relationship (including a recognition of alternative means). Imitation skills can now be deferred.

Stage six. By 18 to 24 months, an infant has attained a strong recall memory that allows successful hidden-object retrieval across a number of visible displacements (Petersen, 1982). Imitation and the resulting possible assimilation of adult actions more than double from the first to second birthdays.

The relationship between the achievement of certain cognitive skills and language development during infancy is not clear. The beginnings of language, both receptive and expressive, are evident quite early in the newborn. Research findings indicate that newborns prefer the human voice to random sounds and that infants can discriminate phonemes (Bondy, 1980).

Early Childhood

The emergence of initial language and symbolic thinking skills as aspects of cognitive development has been researched from a number of different perspectives—learning theory, psychoanalytic theory, and the intelligence testing movement (Copple, DeLisi, & Sigel, 1981). More recent perspectives on cognitive development focus on the underlying thinking processes and derive from the theories of Piaget and Chomsky and the computer. Both Piaget and Chomsky observed behaviors in children not easily explained by traditional methodologies. For example, Chomsky was interested in children's ability to speak and understand sentences they had never heard before. He theorized a transformational grammar to explain language development, raising questions of innate versus environmental factors in cognitive development (Copple et al., 1981).

The advent of the computer highlighted the complexity of problem solving and the intricacies of human cognitive processes. The computer has also provided new, highly specific information-processing language and a methodology for testing hypotheses about specific cognitive processes (Copple et al., 1981).

Consistent with the developmental-interactional approach, we will discuss cognitive development beyond infancy primarily from Piaget's developmental perspective. Research methodologies representative of this approach have a number of disadvantages. Hogan and Quay (1984) summarize these methodological concerns in regard to cognitive differences between clinical and nonclinical groups. Problems include translating theory into tasks; ceiling and floor effects; reliability of performance; and generalization of findings from narrowly defined tasks. The advantages of the approach are its clear and specific implications for intervention and its focus on underlying thinking processes.

Between the ages of approximately 2 and 6 years, children develop internal cognitive structures or schemata to represent the objects and people in their environment, even when those objects or people are absent. This is a major achievement of the preoperational stage in Piaget's theory. During this stage, "internal imitation, which the child developed during the sensorimotor period, provides the basis for the formation of mental symbols, and meaning is attached to the symbols by their assimilation into existing schemes" (Thornburg, 1984, p. 191).

Transductive reasoning, or linking two events in all ways because they are similar in one way, is typical of children's thinking at the preoperational stage. As children begin to conceptualize objects and people, they make errors because their reasoning is intuitive rather than logical. They are as yet unable to attend to more than one dimension when classifying objects into groups. Perceptions of change in shapes, for example, can thus lead the child to believe there has also been a change in size or amount (Thornburg, 1984).

As an example of preschoolers' level of cognitive development, Copple et al. (1981) discuss mathematical thinking. Children's conceptions of number, classes, and relations have been found to be qualitatively different from those of adults. When preschoolers were asked to examine two rows of checkers, for example, they judged the number of checkers in each row to be equal as long as the end points of the rows matched. In other words, young children's conceptions of number are constrained by perceptions. More recently, researchers have documented evidence of number conservation in young children in instances when the children do not see the actual transformation. Thus, in this example, actually watching the extension of one row of checkers contributes to young children's conservation limitations.

Symbolic play is another area of cognitive development of particular interest during the preschool years. Symbolic play first emerges at about 1½ years and has importance for later learning:

Increasingly the child is not just imitating actions she has seen adults do, but is pretending to *be* the adult. Symbolic transformations of objects, situations, and roles can even be shared by several children as the development of imaginative play activity reaches a high level. In very brief form, these are the major forms of change in symbolic play during the years from 1½ to 6. (Copple et al., 1981, p. 27)

School-Age Children

Children of elementary school age have typically reached the concrete operational stage of cognitive development. They learn the symbolic use of written words and numbers, and they learn to think logically. An essential logical operation that is mastered is *decentering*, the ability to consider more than one dimension at a time. Decentering allows the child to step back from a transformation such as reshaping a ball of clay into a hot dog. The child can now recognize that although the length of the clay is greater, the width has decreased. In solving problems of this kind, the child considers both dimensions simultaneously.

Other logical operations children acquire are *conservation* and *reversibility*. Conservation is an understanding that quantity of matter (mass, weight, volume) does not change with changes in size, shape, or orientation. Reversibility is the ability to return to the origin of a logical operation and understand that it can be expressed differently; for example, one dollar equals four quarters and four quarters can be changed back into one dollar. When children can conserve, they must also have acquired reversibility.

Class inclusion and serial ordering are two other cognitive skills that develop during this stage. An example of class inclusion is the ability to recognize that an apple can be an entity by itself and at the same time be a member of the categories *fruit* and *food*.

Adolescents

Research shows a definitive change in the quality and power of thought during the 11- to 15-year age range (Neimark, 1982), the beginning of Piaget's formal operational period. It is characterized by abstract thinking, analytic thinking, systematic hypothesizing, and recursive thinking. Adolescents' "thoughts involve second-order constructs (operating on operations), abstract ideas, and understandings based on established verbal abstractions. Reality becomes secondary to possibility, and the form of the argument becomes as evident as the content" (Thornburg, 1984, p. 196).

Formal operational thought is usually measured by physical and mathematical experiments devised by Inhelder (1966). Only about 50 percent of adolescents demonstrate formal operational thought when tested with these tasks. It appears that use of these measures may result in underestimates of adolescents' actual cognitive competence, because slight changes in the tasks promptly result in improved subject performance (Neimark, 1982).

Thornburg (1984) points out two other considerations when discussing variations in demonstrations of formal operational thinking. Subject-matter content significantly affects adolescents' performance on formal operations measures. Research findings indicate that (1) task performance improves as content familiarity increases; (2) specific content area training improves performance; and (3) adolescents will offer alternative reasoning strategies rather than known wrong answers to problems in a familiar content area.

The second consideration is the level of brain growth during adolescence. There may be a biological limitation to the attainment of formal operations in early adolescence. If brain growth has reached a plateau, then instruction must be assimilated using existing thought capacities.

SOCIAL DEVELOPMENT

Infants

Hodapp and Mueller (1982) have reviewed the early social development of infants from a developmental-interactional perspective. The infant's active role in social interactions is primary. This active role is demonstrated in the development of smiling and crying behaviors, both of which progress from endogenous to external control and then to cognitive control of responses to stimuli. For example, smiling during the first week of life is spontaneous; it may occur during sleep and appears to be associated with central nervous system activity. By the third week, the infant begins to respond to the human voice with the social smile. Cognitive control of the smile manifests itself at about eight to ten weeks as the infant assimilates stimuli and then smiles upon later recognition of those stimuli.

The infant's active role is also apparent in mother-infant interactions. Researchers who have studied mother-infant interaction during the baby's third and fourth months of life (when the infant's sociability is well-established) find that control of the interaction seems to move between mother and infant. For example, the mother may make an exaggerated face to attract the baby's attention. The baby may then look at the mother and then look away, ending the interaction. Infants' imitations have been observed to be intentional, and infants have also participated actively in interpersonal interactions, thus earning the title of "skillful communicators."

An infant develops a number of cognitive skills in the second half of the first year that are important prerequisites to later social skills. Some understanding of object permanence appears to be necessary before any attachment behaviors can occur; in this vein, healthy attachment behaviors appear to be predicated on attaining an understanding of person permanence before one of object permanence. That is, infants who understand the permanence of mother before they understand the permanence of an object are likely to form a healthy attachment to the mother. Since interactions have both a social as well as a linguistic base, they appear to depend on understanding means/end and cause/effect relationships. An infant's pointing to an object so someone will hand it to him, for example, suggests an understanding of the association between means and end.

"Attachment is the idea that between approximately six and eight months the infant forms a strong affectional bond toward the mother" (Hodapp & Mueller, 1982, p. 291). Although we have, traditionally, assumed that attachment (1) is unique to the mother, (2) is associated with specific behaviors such as staying close to the mother, and (3) is unidirectional in nature (infant attached to mother), none of these statements have been supported. Hodapp and Mueller perceive attachment as a relational bond with any adult figure with whom the infant has established trust. "In this view, infants will become attached to persons from whom they have a history of positive contingent actions—that is, infants trust any person who, throughout many interactions over a sustained period of time, has responded to their needs" (p. 291).

In light of the deemphasis on the traditional concept of attachment, researchers have extended their inquiry to include father-infant interaction and peer-peer interaction. They have found that fathers may interact somewhat less than mothers with their infants, but are, in general, competent and involved, and appear to be as attentive to their infants' needs as mothers. Mothers' and fathers' interaction styles differ, however; father-infant interaction is more physically playful and exciting, while mother-infant interaction is more task-oriented and verbal.

Research on peer-peer interactions has focused primarily on dyadic interactions with familiar peers beginning in the second year of life. The interaction pattern appears to develop from (1) object-centered play to (2) behaviors demonstrated by one child contingent on behaviors of the other to (3) reciprocal interchanges. Peer-peer interactions appear to be more motoric than mother-infant exchanges.

Toddlers and Preschoolers

Chandler and Boyes (1982) describe the development of social understanding in children from an interactive approach. Social role-taking, or the ability to coordinate one's thoughts with those of another, is a skill that develops consistently with other cognitive operations (such as conservation). According to cognitive-developmental theory, children demonstrate qualitatively different abilities to comprehend what another person knows at different ages. "It follows . . . that various sorts of egocentric errors, or short-falls, in the role-taking process will necessarily arise whenever individuals are required to anticipate a kind of knowledge in others of which they are themselves not yet capable" (p. 388).

Children's modes of social understanding move from a *presymbolic stage*, in which they know about material reality, to a *symbolic stage*, in which they can symbolically express their knowledge, and finally to a *metarepresentational stage* of knowing that they know. Each of these *modes* of knowing may also be conceived as *forms* of knowing evidenced by another person. Thus, Chandler and Boyes (1982) posit that children at a particular stage in their development of social role-taking can only understand how someone else understands reality if the other person's form of knowing is at the same or a lower stage of knowing.

In this context, it may be useful to analyze the social role-taking skills of toddlers. Toddlers are considered to be in the preoperational or initial symbolic stage of cognitive development, and are, consequently, also at a presymbolic stage in their social role-taking. Research evidence of primitive forms of role-taking in infants and toddlers, such as pointing, has been explained within an interactive framework:

Preschoolers obviously appreciate that one must not only be *in* the right place to receive information but must also be *at* the right place at the right time . . . children, whose own mode of knowing the world is presymbolic in character . . . appear to possess certain real, although limited, form of role-taking competence. . . . They judge knowledge to reside in objective events which telegraph this information to any observer who gets in harm's way. Other people are consequently known to know only those bits of information they happen to be in the right place to receive.

Such knowledge, however, is assumed to be free of any orientation markers or subjective-processing considerations. (Chandler & Boyes, 1982, p. 393)

Selman (1981) discusses the functional relationship of the social understanding children exhibit and their actual interpersonal negotiation strategies. These strategies become hierarchically integrated and more differentiated as children mature. Selman's model suggests a "limited developmental range of strategies which an individual can use to relate to or negotiate with another" (p. 417).

Data-based examples of these strategies are shown in Table 4–1 for each of Selman's first four developmental levels of negotiation: use of physical force, implicit power, psychological power, and interpersonal collaboration (Selman, 1981, p. 419). The assimilative and accommodative orientations define two ways children attempt interpersonal negotiation. In the former, the child seeks to transform the *other's* thoughts, feelings, or actions during a negotiation, whereas in the latter, the child seeks to transform the *self's* wishes, to reach a balance.

Selman (1981) points out that "low level strategies are not by definition immature or pathological. For young children they are expected, for others they may at the time be adaptive" (p. 416). Thus, toddlers and preschoolers use Level 0 strategies such as grabbing or running away to negotiate interpersonal encounters.

School-Age Children

Children at Piaget's concrete operational stage begin to realize that their understanding of an object or event may not always be consistent with others' understanding. They have matured from the presymbolic stage of social understanding as outlined by Chandler and Boyes (1982) to the symbolic stage, in which they can symbolically express their knowledge.

School-age children, however, still have significant difficulty aggregating or communicating appropriately. "The role-taking abilities of concrete operational thinkers are still somewhat object centered, in that they do not yet appreciate how different patterns of attitudes, beliefs, and values exercise influence over the kinds of constructions which

persons impose upon events" (Chandler & Boyes, 1982, p. 397).

Selman's model of social role-taking contains two stages that may encompass the behaviors of elementary school-age children. The second stage of his model describes the

TABLE 4–1

Examples of Interpersonal Negotiation Strategies at Each Developmental Level

Interpersonal Orientation	
Assimilative	Accommodative
Level 0 1. Unprovoked grabbing 2. Screaming to blot out other's wishes 3. Tantrum—unprovoked 4. Actions imply intentions (projection) 5. Impulsive intrusion into others' affairs	1. Running away 2. Blank stare: stonewalls affective withdrawal 3. Fear, motoric or verbal panic 4. Robot-like obedience (no mental mediation)
Level 1 1. Interruption at will 2. Threats and verbal abuse 3. Peer power for extortion—bullying 4. Bossy style 5. No compromise 6. No forgiveness—one-way fairness 7. Power vs. power 8. Mocking of others' obvious weaknesses 9. Deflection of all blame—rejection of all responsibility (denial–distortion–lie) 10. Power and affection bribes or extortions	1. Acting victimized—powerless 2. Squealing as coping 3. Weak serve 4. Hovering behavior 5. Poor reassertion 6. Power oriented obedience
Level 2 1. Peer pitting 2. "Friendly" persuasion—slip a fast one by 3. Spontaneous expression of empathy—actively infers others' feelings 4. Ties that bind 5. Seeks alliances	1. Confronting of injustices of others 2. Following other's lead 3. Reaching out for/to help 4. Self's inadequacies as a negotiation tool 5. Use of reasoning to maneuver out of coercive situations
Level 3—Equilibrated orientation 1. Long-term relations—orientation to process 2. Anticipation of possible reactions of others to self's suggestions 3. Taking a group orientation 4. Expectation of consistency in self and other's actions 5. Use of humor and perspective as healing techniques	

Note: From "The Development of Interpersonal Competence: The Role of Understanding in Conduct" by R. L. Selman, 1981, *Developmental Review, 1,* p. 419. Copyright 1981 by Academic Press, Inc.

social-informational role-taking skills of children approximately six to eight years old, when children have a rudimentary understanding that others may have a viewpoint different from their own. It is not until the third self-reflective role-taking stage (eight to ten years of age) that children can coordinate these viewpoints. Children at this age can essentially assume the other person's point of view. What is the relationship of these levels of social understanding to actual interpersonal interactions? Selman's second stage of social understanding corresponds to his Level 1 behaviors. Negotiation behaviors at this level are generally threats, bossiness, or power-oriented obedience.

Recognition that someone else's viewpoint may differ from one's own gives rise to the need to control that other viewpoint. The alternative is to allow your own perspective to be controlled, which is an accommodative orientation behavior. In either case, the focus is on the perception of a threat of force, rather than on force itself. All negotiations are considered *you win/I lose* or *I win/you lose* situations (Selman, 1981).

Level 2 negotiation behaviors include bartering, persuasion, and bribery (Table 4–1). They reflect children's ability to coordinate perspectives and step into each other's shoes. "Decisions are viewed as successful if acceptable to each party with respect to outcomes; process is disregarded" (Selman, 1981, p. 409).

Adolescents

Adolescents' social role-taking skills are generally a reflection of the ability to think about thinking. Adolescents can appreciate that others may construe objects and events differently and that those constructions can be influenced by different attitudes, beliefs, and values. Adolescents can "recognize individual stylistic modes of knowledge construction and . . . employ fully subjectivized forms of social role-taking" (Chandler &

Boyes, 1982, p. 397). Selman describes the mutual role-taking skills of the early adolescent in his fourth stage of interpersonal understanding. The singular accomplishment at this level is the adolescent's ability to view an interaction between oneself and another as a third person—what Chandler and Boyes (1982) refer to as *thinking about thinking*.

The stage-related nature of social-cognitive development is such that, at a certain point, the adolescent realizes that mutual role-taking does not necessarily ensure complete understanding between individuals. In the final stage of social role-taking, adolescents perceive the need for social conventions to promote a general social understanding. Table 4–1 lists the negotiation behaviors consistent with a mutual understanding of perspectives. At this point in development, the secondary school student is ready to collaborate with others. The spirit of the encounter is empathic. "The goal is relevant communication and mutuality, not winning one's initial point" (Selman, 1981, p. 410). Thus, both the process and the outcome of the negotiation are important to the adolescent.

Elkind (1976) illustrates the complementarity of social-cognitive and emotional development. He discusses the relationship among egocentric structures, ego defenses, and psychopathology. Egocentric structures are assumptions about the environment that a child takes as given. The assumptions change as the child matures and moves into the next stage of cognitive development. For example, the adolescent has newly-acquired skills of conceptualizing personal thought as well as the thoughts of other people. Two specific expressions of egocentric structures in adolescence are the *personal fable* and the *imaginary audience*, which represent adolescent confusion about what thoughts are unique and what thoughts are universal.

The personal fable is the assumption that what is common to everyone is really unique to oneself. An example is the belief many adolescents hold that no one can understand their feelings of love. The imaginary audience is the assumption that other people are as interested in the adolescent as he is in himself.

Parallel to these expressions of egocentric structures are the ego defenses of *rejection* (personal fable) and *projection* (imaginary audience). Projection is the attribution to others of one's own feelings, impulses, and thoughts. Elkind (1976) suggests that such attribution cannot occur until the individual has attained the formal operational level of thought. Projection and rejection appear to reflect the cognitive assumptions of adolescence. In the extreme, the personal fable and imaginary audience could lead to megalomania and delusions of persecution, respectively. In a social-cognitive framework, a certain level of cognitive development would be necessary before such syndromes could be expressed.

Chandler (1982) explored the interactional nature of the relationship between cognitive level and ego defenses from a slightly different perspective. His findings suggest that "children's understanding of various psychological defenses is jointly dependent upon both their own levels of cognitive complexity and the structural complexities of the particular defenses" (p. 300).

MORAL DEVELOPMENT

The development of moral reasoning and moral judgment constitutes an important dimension of a child's psychological growth. The advent of symbolic reasoning combined with varied socialization experiences contribute to qualitative transitions in children's morality. Carroll and Rest (1982) define the components of a fully developed morality:

1. *Recognition and sensitivity*: translating and disambiguating a given social situation so as to be aware that a moral problem exists; to be sensitive enough to recognize that someone's welfare is at stake;

2. *Moral judgment*: determining what ideally ought to be done in the situation, what one's moral ideals call for or which moral norms apply in the given circumstances;

3. *Values and influences*: devising a plan of action with one's moral ideal in mind but also taking into account non-moral values and goals which the situation may activate, as well as the influence of situational pressures;

4. *Execution and implementation of moral action*: behaving in accordance with one's goal despite distractions, impediments, and incidental adjustments; organizing and sustaining behavior to realize one's goals. (p. 434)

The Preschool Child

Piaget's view of moral development emphasizes children's active role in the process as they move from a heteronomous morality to an autonomous morality. Children live by a heteronomous morality until about six years of age; they follow rules handed down unilaterally by a respected authority. Then, as they develop social awareness, children begin to understand the need for rules to structure cooperation. This is the beginning of an autonomous morality (Carroll & Rest, 1982).

Kohlberg and his associates expanded Piaget's perspective into a six-stage theory of moral development. Kohlberg's first stage is characterized by Piaget's heteronomous morality—a child judges something to be right or wrong according to the consequences of the action; he does not consider the actor's intentions. Choices in a moral dilemma are governed by the child's wish to have good things happen to him, and he has no need to justify these choices (Thornburg, 1984).

Some common themes in these moral development theories are:

• Emphasis on the child's interpretive, active role

• Development of schemes of social understanding as children interact with others, as opposed to mere digestion of a set of rules derived from modeling or social reinforcement

- A central concept of *justice* in moral development as children grow from a blind respect for rules to an understanding of reciprocal cooperation
- An underlying belief in qualitative transformations in the organization of cognitive structures

The development of moral reasoning occurs in gradual shifts from one structural organization to another. The more elementary-stage organizations diminish as more sophisticated levels of organization appear. Moral development is thus governed by maturation, cognitive development, and the development of social understanding (Carroll & Rest, 1982).

School-Age Children

According to Piaget's theory, the major shift in moral reasoning is from a heteronomous to an autonomous morality. This shift coincides with the transition from preoperational to concrete operational thought and is expressed in growing concepts of cooperation, mutual consent, and reciprocity. Underlying these concepts are the fundamental cognitive skills of concrete operational thought, decentration and reversibility.

Kohlberg's Stage 2 characterizes the moral behavior of children in the early elementary school years as instrumental and relativistic. Whatever action meets the child's needs and possibly the needs of others is considered the right action. Some consideration of equal sharing and reciprocity is evident; however, these elements of fairness are based on the assurance that a favor to another person will result in concrete rewards for the child (Thornburg, 1984).

Loyal behaviors toward others appear when children reach Stage 3 in Kohlberg's moral development model. Immediate consequences of actions are no longer of primary concern. Children in this stage seek to please and help others, and they want others' approval. Intentions become important for the first time. There are mutual interpersonal expectations; for example, if you are mean to me, it is right for me to be mean to you (Thornburg, 1984).

Adolescents

A "law-and-order" orientation characterizes the moral development of young adolescents in Stage 4 of Kohlberg's model. "Right behavior consists of doing one's duty, showing respect for authority, and maintaining the given social order for its own sake" (Thornburg, 1984, p. 223). The Golden Rule—act toward others as you want others to act toward you—becomes the definition of moral behavior.

The "law-and-order" orientation of Stage 4 becomes a social-contract, legalistic orientation as adolescents move into Stage 5, where individual rights, personal values, and democratic procedural rules are key concepts. These concepts are balanced in a definition of right action. Democratic consensus on actions defines what is right and is then weighed against personal values and rights (Thornburg, 1984).

Individuals functioning at Kohlberg's Stage 6 of moral development define moral behavior by abstract, universal principles. "These are universal principles of justice, of the reciprocity and equality of human rights, and of respect for the dignity of human beings as individuals" (Thornburg, 1984, p. 223). Moral behavior is defined by individual conscience in accordance with ethical principles chosen by the individual on a consistent basis.

CONCLUSION

From a developmental-interactional perspective, both the child and the environment contribute to changes in a child's development. Although the cognitive, social, and moral domains are separate, we need to emphasize the interrelationships of these areas at successive stages of development. One example of interrelationship is the infant's acquisition of object permanence as a basis for forming an affectional bond or attachment with a trusted adult. Similarly, development of decentered thought in the school-aged child contributes to comprehension of logical order in regard to physical objects as well as social relationships. In adolescence the entry into the stage of formal thought gives rise to a transitional period of self-conscious thought and behaviors.

The complexity of behavior also requires recognition of the interrelationships among developmental domains and their interaction with environmental demands. Predictions from earlier to later behavior are enhanced by knowledge of the child's temperament in responding to environmental supports or stresses. Individual differences in temperament, or the stylistic component of behavior, relate to differences in adaptive functioning. Thomas and Chess (1984) outline three temperamental constellations descriptive of most children:

- The easy child: rhythmic biological functions; adaptability; positive approach to new stimuli; pleasantness; friendliness; reasonable reaction to frustration
- The difficult child: irregular biological functions; negative withdrawal response to new stimuli; little adaptability; intense, usually negative mood expressions
- The slow-to-warm-up child: mild negative responses to new stimuli; slow adaptability; relatively regular biological functions

Although variations occur, there is predictability of temperament with development. Children characterized as difficult are most likely to develop behavior problems in early and middle childhood. Lerner (1982) reports that children whose temperament was assessed as better-matched with teacher and parent demands were rated higher by teachers in ability and adjustment, had more positive and fewer negative peer relations, and

had fewer behavior problems identified by mother.

These findings indicate that developmental outcomes are influenced by the goodness of fit of child capabilities and style of environmental demands. Thomas and Chess (1984) point out that "if demands for change and adaptation are dissonant with the particular child's capacities and therefore excessively stressful" (p. 4), behavior disorders can develop no matter what the temperament constellation. Attention to antecedent and consequent behavioral events may thus suggest appropriate intervention strategies. Lerner (1982) suggests consideration of these variables:

One would have to assess whether the child or adolescent could appropriately evaluate: (1) the demands of a particular context; (2) his or her stylistic attributes; and (3) the degree of match that exist between the two. . . . One has to determine whether the child has the ability to select and gain access to those contexts with which there is a high probability of match, and avoid those contexts where poor fit is likely. . . . One has to assess whether the child has the knowledge and skill necessary to either change himself or herself to fit the demands of the setting or, in turn, alter the context to better fit his or her attributes. . . . The common goal of all procedures would be to enhance the child's ability for self-regulation, and thereby increase the ability to actively enhance his or her own fit. (Lerner, 1982, p. 362)

The study of normal development enhances the understanding of pathology just as analysis of deviant development contributes to insight about normality. The convergence of these areas has given rise to developmental psychopathology as a field of study in its own right (Cicchetti, 1984). The developmental-interactional perspective is consistent with such an orientation, and we can derive a number of implications specific to psychopathology that are of a conceptual as well as clinical nature.

From a conceptual standpoint, a developmental-interactional perspective assumes that development, whether normal or deviant, reflects the child's adaptation to the environment. According to Piaget (1954), adaptation involves the complementary processes of assimilation and accommodation, resulting in qualitative, structural change with development. In assimilation, maintenance of existing behavior or thought is predominant; in accommodation, modification is predominant. While the ratio of these processes may vary, normal adaptation and development show a relative balance (equilibrium) between the two. Excessive or inappropriate reliance on one process to the exclusion of the other may be an expression of the distorting and maladaptive behaviors of emotionally disturbed children. Piaget considered adaptation, which is primarily based on assimilation, egocentric and autistic in nature. Based on Block's (1982) premise of the relationship of assimilation and accommodation with personality development, disturbances of these adaptive processes may reflect problems in the resolution of anxiety.

A second conceptual contribution of a developmental-interactional approach to the study of psychopathology pertains to the relationship of affect and cognition. Piaget proposed that the *structural* aspects of development are cognitive in nature, whereas the *force* of development is affective. The influence of affect on development thus comes through its role in the selection or focus on what will be learned and, subsequently, on the pace of development. In emotionally disturbed children, affective states may be intensified such that the focus and pace of adaptation are distorted. Atypical and persistent attachments or preferences for some objects or experiences and intense avoidance or fear of others are examples of disturbances in the functional relationships of cognition and affect. Evans's (1973) study on the dream conceptions of behavior-disordered, borderline, and psychotic children showed this disturbance. All the children were at an age at which the internal, subjective nature of dreams should have been comprehended, but among the border-

line and psychotic children, many responses revealed a failure to comprehend the distinction between the subjective and objective, indicating difficulties in ascertaining reality (Evans, 1973).

As Rosen (1985) summarizes, in normal development there is a surmounting of cognitive and affective realism in the mature person. Among emotionally disturbed children, there may be a disrupted relationship between affect and cognition expressed by a persistent realism with particular reference to egocentrism in the affective realm.

Disturbances in the developmental transitions of qualitative stages of thought and behavior constitute another conceptual contribution to the study of psychopathology. In normal development, the invariant sequence of transitions is usually reflected in cognitive functioning within a particular qualitative stage. A frequent characteristic of emotionally disturbed children is fluctuation of responses of different qualitative levels. Inhelder (1966) proposes that oscillations, or shifts, from one stage to another are a cognitive representation of psychopathology. Such oscillation may reflect the disturbed child's emotional need for noncontradiction in which reality is transformed or avoided so as to conform to affective demands (Schmid-Kitsikis, 1973).

The richness of the conceptual implications of the developmental-interactional approach for the study of emotional disturbance is complemented by a growing literature on interventions based on research and clinical studies. A strong clinical implication is the apparent association of psychopathology with egocentric, centered thought. The emotionally disturbed child and adolescent (as well as the adult) is likely to differ from peers in terms of greater egocentricity and lack of decentration in cognitive and social tasks. These limitations are often reflected in the expression of preoperational characteristics such as magical thinking, animism, and realism (Rosen, 1985). Research with emotionally disturbed children (Chandler, Greenspan, & Barenboim, 1974), adolescents (Lerner, Bie, & Lehrer, 1972), and adults (Suchtoliff, 1970) documents their consistent difficulty in simultaneously taking into account several dimensions or perspectives in conservation (cognitive) and role-taking (social tasks).

A primary goal of intervention is thus the promotion of decentration and perspectivism. Therapeutic interventions build on the assimilation-accommodation paradigm and involve activities and experiences that promote cognitive and affective adaptation. Interventions described by Chandler et al. (1974) and reviewed by Urbain and Kendall (1980) demonstrate the utility and potential of promoting social-cognitive growth in clinical as well as nonclinical populations. These interventions illustrate the importance of children's active role in constructing their reality. To this end it is important to design interventions to help children become self-regulators, to maximize their own potential to ensure the best fit between themselves and their environment.

REFERENCES

Adams, W. (1980). Adolescence. In S. Gabel & M. Erickson (Eds.), *Child development and developmental disabilities* (pp. 59–84). Boston: Little, Brown.

Baumrind, D. (1972). Socialization and instrumental competence in young children. In W. Hartup (Ed.), *The Young Child: Reviews of Research* (Vol. 2, pp. 202–224). Washington, DC: National Association for the Education of Young Children.

Block, J. (1982). Assimilation, accommodation, and the dynamics of personality development. *Child Development, 53*, 281–295.

Bondy, A. (1980). Infancy. In S. Gabel & M. Erickson (Eds.), *Child development and developmental disabilities* (pp. 3–20). Boston: Little, Brown.

Busch-Rossnagel, N., & Vance, A. (1982). The impact of the schools on social and emotional development. In B. Wolman (Ed.), *Handbook of Developmental Psychology* (pp. 452–467). Englewood Cliffs, NJ: Prentice-Hall.

Carroll, J., & Rest, J. (1982). Moral development. In B. Wolman (Ed.), *Handbook of developmental psychology* (pp. 434–451). Englewood Cliffs, NJ: Prentice-Hall.

Chandler, M. (1982). Social cognition and environmental structure: A critique of assimilation-side developmental psychology. *Canadian Journal of Behavioral Science, 14* (4), 290–305.

Chandler, M., & Boyes, M. (1982). Social-cognitive development. In B. Wolman (Ed.), *Handbook of developmental psychology* (pp. 387–402). Englewood Cliffs, NJ: Prentice-Hall.

Chandler, M. J., Greenspan, S., & Barenboim, C. (1974). Assessment and training of role-taking and referential communication skills in institutionalized emotionally disturbed children. *Developmental Psychology, 10*, 456–463.

Cicchetti, D. (1984). The emergence of developmental psychopathology. *Child Development, 55*, 1–7.

Copple, C., DeLisi, R. D., & Sigel, I. (1981). Cognitive development. In B. Spodek, *Handbook for theory of research in early childhood education* (pp. 3–26). New York: Free Press.

Davidson, P. (1980). The school-age child. In S. Gabel & M. Erickson (Eds.), *Child development and developmental disabilities* (pp. 43–58). Boston: Little, Brown.

Elkind, D. (1976). Cognitive development and psychopathology: Observations on egocentrism and ego defense. In E. Schopler & R. Reichler (Eds.), *Psychopathology and child development: Research and treatment* (pp. 167–184). New York: Plenum Press.

Erikson, E. (1950). *Childhood and society.* New York: W. W. Norton.

Evans, R. C. (1973). Dream conceptions and reality testing in children. *Journal of the American Academy of Child Psychiatry, 12*, 73–92.

Freud, S. (1938). *A general introduction to psychoanalysis.* Garden City, NY: Garden City Publishing.

Hartup, W. (1976). Peer interaction and the behavioral development of the individual child. In E. Schopler & R. Reichler (Eds.), *Psychopathology and child development: Research and treatment* (pp. 203–218). New York: Plenum Press.

Hodapp, R., & Mueller, E. (1982). Early social development. In B. Wolman (Ed.), *Handbook of developmental psychology* (pp. 284–300). Englewood Cliffs, NJ: Prentice-Hall.

Hogan, A., & Quay, H. (1984). Cognition in child and adolescent behavior disorders. In B. B. Lahey & A. E. Kazdin (Eds.), *Advances in clinical child psychology* (Vol. 7). New York: Plenum Press.

Honig, A. (1983). Television and young children. *Young Children, 38* (4) 63–76.

Inhelder, B. (1966). Cognitive development and its contribution to the diagnosis of some phenomena of mental deficiency. *Merrill-Palmer Quarterly, 12,* 299–321.

Lerner, R. (1982). Children and adolescents as producers of their own development. *Developmental Review, 2,* 342–370.

Lerner, S., Bie, I., & Lehrer, P. (1972). Concrete operational thinking in mentally ill adolescents. *Merrill-Palmer Quarterly, 18,* 287–291.

Neimark, E. (1982). Adolescent thought: Transition to formal operations. In B. Wolman (Ed.), *Handbook of developmental psychology* (pp. 486–502). Englewood Cliffs, NJ: Prentice-Hall.

O'Connell, J. (1983). Children of working mothers: What the research tells us. *Young Children, 38* (2), 63–70.

Petersen, G. (1982). Cognitive development in infancy. In B. Wolman (Ed.), *Handbook of developmental psychology* (pp. 323–330). Englewood Cliffs, NJ: Prentice-Hall.

Piaget, J. (1952). *The origins of intelligence in children.* New York: International University Press.

Piaget, J. (1954). *The construction of reality in the child.* New York: Basic Books.

Rice, M. (1983). The role of television in language acquisition. *Developmental Review, 3,* 211–224.

Rosen, H. (1985). *Piagetian dimensions of clinical relevance.* New York: Columbia University Press.

Routh, D. (1980). The preschool child. In S. Gabel & M. Erickson (Eds.), *Child development and developmental disabilities* (pp. 21–42). Boston: Little, Brown.

Rubenstein, E. (1983). Television and behavior: Research conclusions of the 1982 NIMH report and their policy implications. *American Psychologist, 38,* 820–825.

Schmid-Kitsikis, E. (1973). Piagetian theory and its approach to psychopathology. *American Journal of Mental Deficiency, 77,* 694–705.

Selman, R. (1981). The development of interpersonal competence: The role of understanding in conduct. *Developmental Review, 1,* 401–422.

Singer, D. (1983). A time to reexamine the role of television in our lives. *American Psychologist, 38,* 815–816.

Smilansky, S. (1968). *The effects of sociodramatic play on disadvantaged preschool children.* New York: John Wiley.

Sprigle, H. (1972). "Who wants to live on Sesame Street?" *Young Children, 28,* 91–109.

Sroufe, L., & Rutter, M. (1984). The domain of developmental psychopathology. *Child Development, 55,* 17–29.

Suchtoliff, C. C. (1970). Relation of formal thought disorder to the communicative deficits in schizophrenics. *Journal of Abnormal Psychology, 76,* 250–257.

Thomas, A., & Chess, S. (1984). Genesis and evolution of behavioral disorders: From infancy to early adult life. *The American Journal of Psychiatry, 141,* 1–9.

Thomas, A., Chess, S., & Birch, H. (1968). *Temperament and behavior disorders in children.* New York: New York University Press.

Thornburg, H. (1984). *Introduction to educational psychology.* New York: West.

Tronick, E., Als, H., Adamson, L., Wise, S., & Brazelton, T. (1978). The infant's responses to entrapment between contradictory messages in face-to-face interaction. *Journal of the American Academy of Child Psychiatry, 17,* 1–13.

Urbain, E. S., & Kendall, P. C. (1980). Review of social-cognitive problem-solving interventions with children. *Psychological Bulletin, 88,* 109–143.

Wright, J., & Huston, A. (1983). A matter of form: Potentials of television for young viewers. *American Psychologist, 38,* 835–843.

Sometimes I ain't so sho who's got 'ere a right to say when a man's crazy and when he ain't. Sometimes I think it ain't none of us pure crazy and it ain't none of us pure sane until the balance of us talks him that-a-way. It's like it ain't so much what a fellow does, but it's the way the majority of folks is looking at him when he does it.

WILLIAM FAULKNER
AS I LAY DYING

This drawing, done by an 8-year-old boy during a diagnostic interview, provided several themes to explore: the child's feelings about his relationship with his parents (who, he said, had been killed in a car wreck caused by the children); his relationship with his sister (depicted as a policewoman); and his fears about who would care for him and keep him safe ("people from the community").

CHAPTER FIVE

Assessment and Classification

Betty Cooper Epanchin
WRIGHT SCHOOL, THE NORTH CAROLINA
RE-EDUCATION CENTER AND
UNIVERSITY OF NORTH CAROLINA AT CHAPEL HILL

Assessment procedures are a shortcut to learning about an individual, but the techniques are only as good as the professional who uses them.

To obtain a representative picture of what is happening in a child's life, one must seek information from several sources: the home, the school, the child, and the peers. One must also describe the settings in which the child functions, with emphasis on defining the expectations held for the child.

When information from different sources does not correspond, it usually indicates that the child functions differently in different settings and that different people have different perceptions of and expectations for the child. It does not mean that one perspective is less valid than another.

The evaluation process in an educational setting typically differs from that in a mental health setting. The assessment questions are different, the professionals have different orientations and training, and the assessment tools are different.

When deciding which assessment device to use, the professional must consider what information is needed. Different procedures provide different types of information and require different levels of expertise from tester and consumer.

The process of classifying emotional problems is controversial, and of the several approaches to classification, all have shortcomings.

WHAT IS WRONG with Sally? Why does she behave and feel as she does? What can be done and what shall we do? These are the questions we address during the diagnostic and classification process. But because these complex questions mirror the philosophical issues within the field, they are not easily answered. Perhaps at no other juncture are the perceptions of the diagnostician and the classifier so vulnerable to personal biases as during the process of identifying the problem and prescribing an intervention. Explanations of what one sees are dependent upon what one knows, so the individual professional's training, experience, and values determine how one defines a problem and plans what to do.

Diagnostic procedures are shortcuts to understanding the problem; they allow the professional to gather a great deal of information in a relatively short time and then plan interventions. The quality of the diagnostic procedure affects the precision of the diagnostic information. If the instrument is sound, the information will be relevant and useful; if the instrument is not well constructed, the information may be inaccurate or distorted.

Unfortunately, many of the instruments used for assessing behavioral and emotional problems have questionable psychometric properties. Some have low reliability, some lack validity. *Reliability* refers to the consistency with which observers or raters report the same things. Regarding a rating scale, reliability refers to the consistency with which the rater endorses the same item; regarding an observation system, it refers to the extent to which different observers agree on the ratings. Ratings on an instrument must be consistent and records from an observation must

be reproducible by others. *Validity* refers to the degree to which an instrument measures what it is intended to measure or that an observation reflects what happened. If two children's behavioral ratings are similar (for example, off-task), but one was daydreaming and the other was tearing up the room and physically assaulting his peers, one might question the validity of the behavioral ratings. Likewise, if a well-adjusted child and an aggressive child receive similar scores on a behavior checklist, one can question the validity of the checklist.

Instruments and techniques that have poor reliability and validity are of limited use to diagnosticians, yet often these are the only instruments available. Because of the paucity of adequate measurement techniques, diagnosticians must use a number of different instruments that sample different facets of a problem or situation.

Because they must make such critical decisions during the assessment and classification process, many professionals, particularly teachers, find it an intimidating experience. They question their ability to make these decisions, especially on the basis of subjective observations; consequently, they rely heavily on assessment techniques and/or other professionals who have special training in assessment procedures. At the same time, teachers' subjective descriptions and experiences provide contextual validity to what the tests and the specialists find. The tests and the diagnosticians can hypothesize about what might be going on, but it is the teacher, the parents, and the people who are with the youngsters for large portions of time who can affirm or reject these hypotheses. Such a partnership is necessary to obtain a full and rich picture of what the child is like and what is going on in his environment to cause or perpetuate a problem.

The best and most complete evaluations are those that integrate information from different aspects of the child's life, focusing on strengths as well as weaknesses and on the level of functioning in various settings with different people. Rarely is a child just aggressive; rather, he is aggressive when faced with frustrating demands or when taunted by peers. To get a thorough picture of how a child functions in different settings, the diagnostician not only needs information from all the significant people in the child's life, he must also use instruments and techniques that have been developed from different theoretical positions.

We will review the procedures for diagnosing and classifying youngsters' problems. Although intellectual, educational, and perceptual assessment should also be part of a complete evaluation, we will not cover these techniques and procedures here. Salvia and Ysseldyke (1985) and Sattler (1982) give excellent coverage of these topics.

THE DIAGNOSTIC PROCESS

The evaluation process varies considerably from setting to setting and among different professionals so that any description of a "typical" process will not be entirely accurate. Since most troubled youngsters are evaluated in either an educational or a mental health setting, however, we will describe "typical" practices to give you an overview of what takes place. The evaluation process in these two settings often reflects different questions and concerns.

The primary focus in educational settings is on whether the child has more than the average behavioral and emotional problems and, if so, what these problems are, usually in specific behavioral terms. Normative procedures are used with comparatively little

emphasis on family dynamics. Although psychologists, social workers, and counselors who work in schools frequently have clinical training in family dynamics, most teachers and administrators do not and are therefore reluctant to presume knowledge about psychological problems. Most educational personnel are mindful of the public nature of educational institutions and tend not to explore personal family conflicts and problems because of ethical and legal constraints of confidentiality. Furthermore, educational personnel are concerned with discovering why a child has problems in school; problems outside school are not their primary concern. For these reasons, the diagnostic procedures in educational settings usually include, at a minimum, individually-administered intelligence tests, diagnostic educational tests, perceptual-motor tests, and problem-behavior checklists or adaptive-behavior ratings. The intellectual, educational, and perceptual-motor assessments are administered to rule out learning disabilities or mental retardation. Behavior checklists or adaptive-behavior ratings and observations of the child in the classroom are done to document the presence of a behavior problem. Depending upon the diagnostician's available resources and personal biases, additional data may be gathered through social histories, psychiatric interviews, projective testing, speech and hearing evaluations, and so forth. When the school's evaluation team carries out only minimal assessment procedures, it is usually left to the special teacher, after the child is placed, to learn more about the child's home, interests, feelings, and attitudes.

With the advent of P.L. 94–142, public schools now follow a more standardized approach to assessing a child. The law mandates that multiple sources of data be used and that a multidisciplinary team, including a parent or parent representative, be involved in decision making. There is evidence, however, that the evaluation process for emotionally and behaviorally disordered youngsters is problematic. In a survey of records for 60 behaviorally disordered children in Iowa, Smith, Frank, and Snider (1984) reported that 87 percent of the files were perceived by at least one rater as lacking adequate information for identification. Information about intellectual and academic functioning and health status was more available and received higher quality ratings, whereas, data on social functioning, setting analysis, and actual behavior were less available and perceived to be of lesser quality but potentially more valuable. In another study, McGinnis, Kiraly, and Smith (1984) reported that the type of behavioral information most frequently found in children's records were summaries of student behavior and family/environmental histories, neither of which were objective.

Diagnosticians in mental health settings also face problems of objectivity and usefulness of data; however, they are less concerned with labeling and placing students in services. Mental health settings are more akin to medical settings. They assume there is a problem because someone is seeking help; they do not have to decide whether a child meets a certain criterion. Their concern centers on understanding the nature of specific psychological conflicts and determining why the conflicts have developed. Mental health clinicians have the sanction to explore familial patterns as well as other relevant but confidential issues. Their records are considered medical records and therefore the content is protected; consequently, they pursue all avenues that appear relevant in answering why the individual is having problems adjusting to life circumstances.

Although both settings value the team approach, the professionals who constitute the teams and the role each performs are usually different. In educational settings, the teacher identifies a child as having problems and as having not responded to easily-instituted solutions. The teacher then discusses her perceptions with the family and requests permission to refer the child for evaluation. State regulations vary, but an evaluation usually consists of intelligence testing, achievement testing, observations in the classroom, and some sort of behavioral and/or personality assessment. After the information has been gathered, the teacher, the diagnostic tester, the parents, and a school administrator get together to discuss the results and make recommendations. This process establishes how the child performs in school in relation to measured ability, whether any specific learning disabilities exist, and how the child is behaving in relation to peers, so that it can be determined whether or not he can be labeled and thus qualify for receiving services. The school team does not usually explore underlying causes of the problem. Treatment of the problem is often pragmatic, determined by available programs and resources rather than by what is ideal. It is left to the individual teacher, counselor, or psychologist to determine clinical issues such as etiology and prognosis, if the individual considers such information important.

The team in a multidisciplinary mental health setting often follows the model developed in child guidance clinics. Parents refer their youngsters to a team of child specialists, which traditionally includes a child psychiatrist, a psychologist, and a social worker. Increasingly, however, language specialists, pediatricians, neurologists, special educators, physical and occupational therapists, nurses, and recreational therapists are members of these teams. Formerly, the child psychiatrist read the child's record and interviewed him two or three times, the psychologist administered a battery of psychological tests that included personality and ability tests, and the social worker interviewed the parents several times to obtain a developmental history and learn the parents' perceptions of the problems. Now, however, professionals tend to function in roles other than the traditional: social workers interview children; psychologists interview children and/or parents; family members may be seen together; and psychiatrists include informal psychological assessments as part of their interviews. Regardless of the roles different professionals assume, these techniques are almost always used: a diagnostic interview, projective or semiprojective testing, and a developmental history. If at any point additional problems are noted, such as awkward gait or poor motor skills, any one or a combination of specialists might be consulted. After gathering data, the team members meet to discuss their perceptions of the child and the family, agree on a psychiatric diagnosis, and formulate treatment recommendations.

Once the team decides what the problem is and what to do, they meet with the family for an interpretive conference. During this process the team conveys its opinions; this stage may require only one meeting or may be spread over several meetings, depending upon the team's perception of the family's understanding and receptiveness to the recommendations. If the team believes the child's problems are quite serious and likely to involve long, expensive, and intensive therapy, the team may feel that several sessions are needed to give the family time to understand and adjust to the recommendations; if the family entered the diagnostic study with accurate perceptions and expectations of the problem, one conference may be sufficient.

Because of the different approaches to diagnosing emotional and behavioral problems in children, some children are identified in one setting as having problems, but not in other settings. It is not uncommon for youngsters to be treated in mental health settings for anxiety and depression but require no special services in school; they may even be considered good students who present no problems. Likewise, many youngsters present behavioral and learning problems of such magnitude that they qualify for special education services but appear relatively

well-adjusted to mental health practitioners. Out of school these children seem to make a relatively good adjustment given their circumstances, but for a variety of reasons they have a great deal of difficulty in school.

Along with the differences, there are similarities in the mental health and educational settings. They use many of the same instruments and/or techniques, and both emphasize understanding the problem from a number of different perspectives: the child's, the parents', and the involved professionals'.

Although the child is the focus in both settings, in the past the two systems did not communicate easily and frequently, limiting the diagnostic processes of both by their narrow perspectives. One hopes that better cooperation and communication will develop.

ASSESSMENT INSTRUMENTS AND TECHNIQUES

There are many techniques for diagnosis, and their quality is improving. Some techniques are used directly with the child and some rely upon informants. The current emphasis is on using multiple informants and techniques during an assessment to obtain a relatively complete and valid evaluation of the problem. We no longer question which instrument or technique is most useful; now we ask what type of information we gain from various instruments and techniques. For example, most would agree that if one wants to know whether a child is depressed and unhappy, one should ask the child, directly or indirectly; if one wants to know whether the youngster engages in antisocial, acting-out behaviors, one should ask the teacher or parent. Each technique provides relevant and useful data but not necessarily the same type of data.

The Diagnostic Interview

The diagnostic interview is probably the most widely used social-emotional assessment technique, partly because it is so versatile. Regardless of the interviewer's bias and training, an interview can yield a great deal of helpful information. In a survey of 173 school psychologists, Prout (1983) found that the clinical interview was the most frequently used social-emotional assessment technique. It can be, and usually is, used by teachers and mental health professionals alike, with both parents and youngsters. As long as the professional is able to relate appropriately and empathetically with the client, this technique elicits a great deal of useful and relevant diagnostic information.

There are two types of interviews: structured and unstructured. *Unstructured interviews* have no predetermined questions or techniques. The clinician's hunches and perceptions about what is important to understanding the problems and the interviewee's concerns about the problem determine the order of content. Psychodynamic clinicians view unstructured interviews as akin to projective tests; that is, the interviews are based on the assumption that since the child may talk about or play with anything he wishes, the content he chooses represents emotionally significant data. These clinicians begin the interview by explaining who they are and what they expect of the child. At some point the child's understanding of why he is there is explored and the clinician explains his or her perception. The child is shown the room and the available toys and supplies and then given permission to do as he wishes. With older children, permission is given to talk about whatever comes to mind or to play more sophisticated games. During the interview the clinician attends to the overt content of the child's productions as well as to the unconscious messages. For example, the child's play may center on feeding and concerns of being taken care of. The clinician participates in the game or fantasy while mentally noting the concern over nurturance and dependence. At the end of the interview, the clinician explains to the child what seems to have transpired during their session and recommends future contact or work.

Behaviorists also use the interview, but for different purposes. They see it as an opportunity to clarify the problem behavior and to obtain information about the controlling antecedent and consequent stimuli. Some also see it as a time to observe and learn more about the child's personal characteristics, such as cognitive and behavioral competencies, encoding strategies, behavior-outcome and stimulus-outcome expectancies, subjective stimulus values, and self-regulatory systems and plans (Mischel, 1973).

The unstructured interview relies on subjective impressions, and has thus been criticized for being inaccurate and unquantifiable (O'Leary & Johnson, 1979). Supporters counter that the interviewer's emotional response to the interviewee is a critically important element in the process and that these emotional reactions should be examined and utilized to understand what took place.

Structured interviews follow a predetermined format and have specific, structured questions. Gross (1984) points out that the same information is obtained in both structured and unstructured interviews, but the order of content may differ. During an unstructured interview, the clinician may pursue topics that appear to be important, whereas in the structured interview, discussion focuses only on specified content. Structured interviews may also be guided by a more explicit model of behavior.

Several structured-interview formats have been developed to provide a more systematic and empirical method of gathering relevant diagnostic information. One such tool is the CAS—the Child Assessment Schedule (Hodges, Kline, Stern, Cytryn, & McKnew, 1982). The CAS consists of both interview and observation sections (see Table 5–1). The interview covers approximately 75 questions that take about 45 minutes to administer. Topics include school, friends, activities and hobbies, family, fears, worries, self-image,

TABLE 5–1
Sample Items From the Child Assessment Schedule

Part 1, Interview		False (or no)	True (or yes)
Worries and Concerns			
Many children worry about different things, what do you worry about?	Denies any worries	_____	_____
	Reports considerable worry	_____	_____
	If applicable: check all that apply to areas of concern.		
	a. Excessive worry about natural disaster (e.g., fire, flood, storms, dark) or external concerns (i.e., lose job)	_____	_____
	b. Worry about family members	_____	_____
	c. Worry about self	_____	_____
Do you worry about yourself or people in your family—like your mom and dad?	If true: check all that apply to content and target of worry.		
	a. Worries that a family member is or will become sick	_____	_____
	b. Worries that a family member will die	_____	_____
	c. Worries that parents will argue (verbal)	_____	_____
	d. Worries that parents will fight (physical)	_____	_____
	e. Worries about marital separation or divorce (i.e., that a family member will leave)	_____	_____
	f. Worries that parents' mental health (e.g., loneliness, depression, sensitivity) or says he does activities to help alleviate these problems or symptoms	_____	_____
	g. Other, specify _____	_____	_____

Part 2, Observation			
Activity level, attention span and impulsivity	Restless, fidgety, inability to sit still	_____	_____
	High activity level in terms of gross motor activity (e.g., running, climbing, crawling)	_____	_____
	Activity appears poorly organized, lacking in goal-oriented behavior	_____	_____
	Short attention span (e.g., inability to sustain attention, flits from one activity to another)	_____	_____
	Worsening of attention span in unstructured situations	_____	_____
	Impulsive (e.g., careless, sloppy, seeks immediate gratification)	_____	_____
	Low frustration tolerance (e.g., becomes distressed when wants or needs are frustrated)	_____	_____

Source: From "The Child Assessment Schedule: A Diagnostic Interview for Research and Clinical Use" by K. Hodges, J. Kline, P. Fitch, D. McKnew, and L. Cytryn, 1981, *Catalog of Selected Documents in Psychology, 11,* 56. Reprinted by permission of the authors.

mood, somatic concerns, expression of anger, and thought-disorder symptoms. The observation section has 53 items that cover topics such as insight, grooming, motor coordination, activity level (including attention span and impulsivity), spontaneous physical behaviors, estimate of cognitive ability, quality of verbal communication, quality of emotional expression, and interpersonal interaction. Clinicians rate the child on these items and combine the two sections to yield a total pathology score, content-problem scores (for example, family problems), and symptom-complex scores, which are related to the American Psychiatric Association's diagnostic system (known as the DSM–III, discussed later). Evidence shows that children give consistent answers in response to the CAS and that the information gained from this interview is important in the classification of children's emotional problems (Hodges, Kline, Stern, Cytryn, & McKnew, 1982). Rutter and Graham (1968) and Herjanic and Campbell (1977) have also developed structured diagnostic interviews for children.

A *developmental* or *social history,* usually obtained from parents through an interview, is another part of most diagnostic evaluations. The interview may be structured or unstructured, to yield information about parental perception and understanding of the presenting problems, the intensity and chronicity of the problem, a history of medical problems and illnesses, the child's current functioning, family relationships, and, sometimes, parental background.

These interviews can be illuminating with respect to parental perceptions of and attitudes toward the child; however, research suggests that data collected retrospectively, especially through unstructured interviews, may be quite inaccurate. Graham and Rutter (1968) compared the information that 268 parents reported during spontaneous open-ended interviews with the information these same parents reported in response to a series of specific questions about their children's behavior problems. Graham and Rutter concluded that "the advantages of the systematic approach in obtaining adequate information for diagnostic purposes seem overwhelming" (p. 591). One of the problems they noted with spontaneous comments during open-ended interviews is the variation in amount and type on different days. Chess, Thomas, & Birch (1966) also note problems with parent recall of developmental milestones. In a study with parents of children in the New York Longitudinal Study, these authors compared parents' recollections of events with notes taken about the children's development at the time the developmental milestones were met. They found significant distortions of parental recall in twelve of the thirty-three cases. Robins (1963) also notes distortions of parent recall.

Because of parents' apparent problems in accurately remembering specific information, it is recommended that professionals pose specific rather than general questions. For example, rather than ask parents whether a child met developmental milestones at normal ages, an interviewer might ask when the child sat, walked, used one word functionally, was toilet trained, and so on. Another technique for helping parents provide accurate and meaningful data is to let them know before the actual interview what will take place and how they can be most helpful.

Some professionals believe the most valuable data gleaned during a developmental history is information about parental attitudes, expectations, and perceptions. If the interviewer is interested in such information, questions such as "Did this seem reasonable?" or "Were you pleased with his speech?" are useful. When one needs accurate, factual information, the interviewer can request supplemental reports from the pediatrician, the hospital, or the school.

Many different professionals can use the interview technique with ease and skill to obtain the information they need. The technique is, however, easily affected by interviewers' biases, especially when the interview is unstructured. The types of questions they ask, what they remember and record, and how they understand and interpret the information are all affected by the interviewer's biases and belief systems; therefore, one must view the data obtained through the interview technique in relation to the interviewer as well as the interviewee. Evidence suggests that structured interviews yield more consistent information, but they may not tap attitudes and feelings as effectively. Gross (1984) suggests using a combination of both formats.

Problem-Behavior Checklists

Behavior checklists are another method for obtaining parental and/or teacher perceptions of children's behavior. This type of assessment has its roots in behavioral psychology, but a number of dynamically-oriented checklists have been developed in recent years. Behavior checklists are similar to adaptive-behavior scales but focus on identification of problem behaviors rather than on adaptive behaviors. The format is a list of items that describe behavior with no implication as to why the behavior might occur. The rater checks items that describe the particular child.

Table 5–2 (pp. 81–85) shows how behavior checklists vary considerably in focus, format, function, and usefulness. Some have been constructed for use with a narrow age range, such as the Preschool Behavior Questionnaire, while others may be used for larger age ranges; some are designed to sample a broad range of problem behaviors, such as the Child Behavior Checklist, while others focus on specific types of behavioral problems like hyperactivity (the Parent Symptom Questionnaire); some are intended for use as screening instruments (Children's Behavior Questionnaire), while others are comprehensive, diagnostic tools (the Personality Inventory for Children).

In many settings, behavior checklists are used as screening devices or as one of several types of confirming evidence. When a teacher or parent suspects that a child has behavior problems, these instruments are a means of determining how the child compares to others—that is, as a device for gauging the magnitude of the problem. If responses to the checklist suggest the child has more than the usual amount of problems, further study is indicated. Some of the instruments have a cutoff score, a score that indicates further study is needed. This score usually derives from comparisons of normal and clinic populations and indicates that the number of problems reported for the child are similar to clinical groups.

Behavior checklists may also be used as a guide for interviewing parents (Miller, 1977). When using checklists this way, clinicians usually ask parents to complete the checklist prior to the interview. When the interview actually starts, the clinician quickly reviews the parent responses, noting items worthy of further discussion. For example, the clinician might note that the parent checked the item "Cruel with animals or people in a shocking way (sadistic)" and then ask the parent to describe the child's sadistic behavior or to explain why she checked the item. This process can be illuminating with respect to parental expectations. For example, recently the author was talking with a parent who checked an item indicating that her child "steals." Discussing this further, however, the parent explained that the child gets food and water from the refrigerator at home without asking permission.

Some of the checklists are psychometrically sophisticated and have been used extensively for research and evaluation. Many investigators have used behavior checklists to describe or identify their sample; others have used them to obtain before and after (or pre-post) ratings in drug studies, in intervention studies, and in outcome studies evaluating treatment programs. When using the checklists for these purposes, one must take into account the limitations of the technique (which we will describe). Behavior checklists have also been used in large-scale research studies seeking epidemiological information.

Behavior checklists are constructed from reviews of the literature and from lists of problems reported by parents and/or teachers. These lists of problem behaviors are given to selected raters who rate the behavior of disturbed and normal children. The items that best discriminate disturbed children from normal children are included on the final form of the instrument. Thus, it is possible to establish a score that more often than not discriminates between groups of normal and behaviorally disordered children. Most instruments also provide factor scores or profiles and are therefore of greater diagnostic value. *Factor scores* are obtained from factor analyses of all the items; items that consistently cluster together constitute a factor, to which the test author gives a name. Most factor-analysis scales are strong in at least two factors: one containing items that describe aggressive, acting-out behavior and one containing items that describe withdrawn, anxious behaviors. Many also contain a scale with items that describe immature and incompetent behaviors. Many of these instruments have what are called broad-band and narrow-band scales. The *narrow-band* scales are subsets or factor analyses of the larger clusters, or *broad-band* scales.

When using these instruments, raters indicate whether they have observed a behavior recently, often within two months. Some believe that specifying a time period is important in test-retest reliability (Wilson & Prentice-Dunn, 1981). Several investigators find that raters tend to report fewer problems on the second administration of an instrument. Although why this occurs is still being debated, most agree that if behavior rating scales are being used for outcome research, an untreated control group is needed to determine whether decreases in problem behavior are a result of treatment or reporting.

These scales range from brief screening instruments to lengthy, detailed instruments. McMahon (1984) suggests that behavior rating scales should have a sufficient number of items to reliably assess the behavior in question but not so many items that the rater is overtaxed. More than 50 items increases the likelihood of replicable narrow-band syndromes when the scale is factor analyzed (Achenbach & Edelbrock, 1978).

Some scales allow raters to specify intensity of a behavior, while others require the rater to indicate simply whether the behavior occurs or is a problem. A number of different formats reflect rating intensity. The Child Behavior Checklist (Achenbach, 1978; Achenbach & Edelbrock, 1979), for example, requires the rater to specify whether a behavior never occurs, sometimes occurs, or frequently occurs. In contrast, the Devereux rates behavior on a seven-point scale. The Eyberg Child Behavior Inventory (Eyberg, 1980) has two scales; the Problem Scale requires the parent to determine whether the behavior is a problem, and the Intensity Scale requires parents to rate the frequency or intensity of behaviors on a seven-point scale.

Some research suggests that for clinic-referred, conduct-disordered children, maternal personal distress (anxiety and depression) is a more powerful predictor of the mother's rating of the child's behavior than is the child's actual behavior (McMahon, 1984). Because of the importance of the rater's response biases, Miller (1977) developed a means of gauging negativism in rater responses, the Normal Irritability Scale, which contains items describing normal but irritating behaviors. Raters who endorse many of these items are described as overly sensitive to deviance, and raters who endorse few of these items are considered undersensitive to pathology. Miller says this score is an index of the parent's tolerance for deviant behavior. Likewise, the Personality Inventory for Children has a Lie scale and K scale, designed to screen parental distortion.

Some scales contain both positive and negative behaviors. The Child Behavior Checklist (Achenbach, 1978; Achenbach & Edelbrock, 1979) has two pages on which the rater describes the child's prosocial behavior such as hobbies, clubs, peer relations, and friendships, and the Louisville Behavior Checklist has 13 prosocial items interspersed with problem behaviors. Many instruments contain only problem behaviors. Sandoval (1981) suggests that including items that measure social competence increases an instrument's clinical utility. Alternating problem and prosocial behaviors may also minimize measurement errors such as halo effects or allowing one's perceptions of the child to affect one's answers. If all items are negative and the rater is fond of the child, the rater may be inclined not to endorse all the observed behavior problems.

A number of studies report large discrepancies between different raters. Although personal response biases explain some of the variability, other factors are also at work. Children behave differently in different settings, for example. Teachers see children in different settings from those in which parents see them. Parents have the advantages of having known the child longer than anyone else has and of seeing the child in a variety of settings; teachers have the advantage of being able to compare the child to other children the same age.

The type of problem a child is experiencing also appears to affect correspondence between ratings. Rater agreement appears higher with children who are aggressive, hyperactive, and who act out their problems, presumably because this type of behavior is overt and observable and therefore easier to describe consistently. Most investigators and clinicians agree that one rating should not be considered more valid than another, but rather that two or more ratings should be taken as complementary information.

Several authors have developed instruments with parallel forms for use by different raters. The Louisville Behavior Checklist has a form for parents and a form for teachers; however, the dissimilarity of items on the two forms makes comparison difficult. Achenbach has a scale for parents, one for teachers, one for the child, and one for use as an observation form; the scales share a large number of common items, which enables more valid comparison of different raters' ratings of the child.

A related screening battery developed by Brown and Hammill (1978) is the Behavior Rating Profile (BRP). It has short checklists for parents and teachers, a self-report, and a peer rating. Although parent and teacher rate the child on somewhat different items, the child rates himself on items similar to those in the parent and teacher checklists, which facilitates ecological comparison. This battery is shorter than the Achenbach battery, making it less useful for diagnosis but quicker and more efficient for screening.

Bower (1969) developed the original screening instrument for identifying emotionally handicapped children. This instrument (Lambert, Hartsough, & Bower, 1979) has a battery that includes a teacher rating, a self-rating, and peer ratings, but no parent form, because it was developed for in-school screening. Since this instrument uses different techniques as well as different raters, correspondence among the measures is low. This does not mean the instrument is not worthwhile; rather, it means that teachers, peers, and the child have different perspectives.

The Taxonomy of Problem Situations (Dodge, McClaskey, & Feldman, 1985) lists situations rather than problem behaviors. The rater, usually a teacher, is instructed to endorse situations in which she has observed the child having problems and to specify the degree to which the situation is problematic. Dodge et al. group the situations into six areas: peer group entry, response to provocation, response to failure, response to success, social expectations, and teacher expectations. They propose that after identifying the social situations that cause a child to have problems, a clinician can try to determine what social skills the situation requires and then assess whether the child has the specific skills. A clinician might believe, for example, that reading nonverbal social cues is an important aspect of knowing how to join a group of children at play. He would then investigate whether a child reported to have problems entering peer groups had these skills. Deficits might indicate the need for remedial training. Although TOPS was developed for experimental purposes and is still in the experimental stages of development, it is conceptually intriguing and warrants further consideration.

As you can see from Table 5-2, there are a number of checklists from which to choose. Most are easy to use, easy to score, do not require extensive training to use and understand, and are useful in documenting the existence of problem behaviors. They enable comparison between the child in question and a norm group. Most have been standardized on groups of normal children and on children being treated in mental health clinics or residential treatment programs. Some can be useful to the researcher who is interested in detailing characteristics of a sample and/or in measuring pre- and postchanges. Behavior checklists are widely used in schools during the identification process as a means of documenting that a child displays more than the usual number of problem behaviors and therefore qualifies for special education services. Some of these instruments have been used for classification and diagnosis; however, not all are adequate for those uses. Some of the shorter instruments merely document the existence of known and observable clusters of problems.

Peer Sociometric Ratings

Peer ratings are another approach to assessing children's behavior. The recent revival of interest in this technique (Cairns, 1983) is probably the result of research that has reported a significant relationship between childhood peer ratings and adult maladjustment (Cowen, Pederson, Babigian, Izzo, & Trost, 1973). Peer ratings are conducted in several ways: the peer nomination technique, class roster ratings, or paired comparisons. Peer nominations and class roster ratings are the most common, probably because paired comparisons (in which the child is asked to choose between pairs of children) are so time-consuming to administer and score.

With the *peer nomination technique,* the examiner simply tells a group of youngsters, often a class, to choose a specified number of their peers for certain situations. For example, a class might be told to list the three classmates whom they would most like as a friend or least like to spend time with. When youngsters can read and write, they list the names of the classmates they choose; nonreaders are interviewed individually and told to point to pictures of the classmates they are choosing. Scores are the percentages of positive and negative nominations. Obviously, the type of question the interviewer asks determines the type of response; for example, youngsters may be asked to name the three people they most like to play with or the three people they most like to do science projects with. Popularity and friendship patterns probably determine how children answer the first question, whereas academic proficiency probably affects how youngsters answer the second question.

One might also ask youngsters to name a certain number of people who best fit a given description. For this format, Coie and Dodge (1983) used statements such as "Here is someone who is really good to have as part of your group because this person is agreeable and cooperates—pitches in, shares, and gives everyone a turn" and "This person has a way of upsetting everything when he or she gets into a group—doesn't share and tries to get everyone to do things their way" (p. 266).

TABLE 5-2
Behavior Checklists

Name	Purpose	Scales	Format	Unique Features
Behavior Evaluation Scale (BES) (S. B. McCarney & J. E. Leigh, 1983)	For teachers and other school personnel to identify problem behaviors. Appropriate for grades K-12	52 items contribute to 5 scales: 1) learning problems 2) interpersonal difficulties 3) inappropriate behavior 4) unhappiness/depression 5) physical symptoms/fears	All items refer to problem behaviors rated on a 7-point scale; 1 = never or not observed, 7 = continuously observed throughout the day	Scales correspond to the Bower and P.L. 94-142 definition of emotional handicaps. Facilitates translation of data into goals and objectives on IEP
Behavior Problem Checklist (H. C. Quay & D. R. Peterson, 1975)	To provide a global estimate of maladjustment and identify dimensions of deviance. Used with children 5 years-high school	55 items contribute to 3 primary scales: conduct problem personality problem inadequate-immaturity (factor analytically derived) 2 minor scales: psychotic behavior socialized delinquency	All are negative, problem behaviors. Rater checks all items that are problems for child	Extensively researched since early 1960s
Behavioral Rating Profile (L. L. Brown & D. D. Hammill, 1978)	Ecologically-based screening instrument. Grades 1-7	Teacher Scale, 30 items. Parents' Scale, 30 items. Child Scale, 60 items that yield 3 subscale scores: School, Peer, Home (20 items per scale). Also a score on sociogram	All items refer to negative behaviors. Rater responds to True/False format	Ecological emphasis. Child rates same type of problem areas as parents and teachers do; e.g., Child = "I argue a lot with my family" Parent = "Is verbally aggressive to parents"
Burks Behavior Rating Scales (H. F. Burks, 1977)	To identify *patterns* of pathological behavior. Primary-junior high	110 items yield 19 scales (factor-analytically derived examples): excessive self-blame poor ego strength excessive suffering poor anger control	All negative behaviors rated on 5-point scale; 1 = You have not noticed this behavior at all, 5 = You have noticed the behavior to a very large degree	Identifies *patterns* or profiles of children with problem behaviors

TABLE 5–2
Behavior Checklists (Continued)

Name	Purpose	Scales	Format	Unique Features
Child and Adolescent Adjustment Profile (CAAP) (R. B. Ellsworth, F. Ricks, G. Doherty, J. Derenge, & M. Pett, 1977)	Screening tool to measure adjustment for parents and teachers Children ages 3–18	20 items yield 5 adjustment factors: peer relations dependency hostility productivity withdrawal	Both prosocial and problem behaviors rated on 4-point scale from *rarely* to *almost always*; e.g.: During the last month, has s/he 4. Laughed and smiled easily? 20. Daydreamed?	Short and not offensive; even items for problem behaviors are worded neutrally Provides change norms for program evaluation
Children's Behavior Questionnaire (M. Rutter, 1967)	For teachers to screen and survey Appropriate for ages 7–13	26 items yield total disability score and two subscale scores: 1) neurotic 2) anti-social	All problem behaviors All items are negative problem behaviors Teachers respond on 3-point scale	Carefully developed, short and easy to use
Devereux Elementary School Behavior Rating Scale (G. Spivak & M. Swift, 1967)	To help teachers focus on behavioral difficulties that interfere with successful academic performance Appropriate for grades K-6	47 items form 11 behavior factors: classroom disturbance impatience disrespect-defiance external blame achievement anxiety external reliance comprehension inattentive-withdrawn irrelevant-responsiveness creative initiative need for closeness to teacher	Both proactive and problem behaviors, rated on 7-point scale; 7 = very frequently, 1 = never, e.g.: "Compared with the average child in the normal classroom, how often does the child . . . initiate classroom discussion?"	Easy to score Profile on answer sheet Less negative than many but must be considered a screening tool
Eyberg Child Behavior Inventory (S. M. Eyberg & A. W. Ross, 1978; S. M. Eyberg, 1980)	Behaviorally-specific instrument for assessing parental perceptions of problem behaviors Ages 2–16	36 items yield 2 scores: Intensity Score (refers to cumulative ratings of problem behaviors on 7-point scale) Problem Score (refers to total number of behaviors	2 types of ratings: First—rating of overt observable behaviors on 7-point scale from *never* to *always* (e.g., "whines") Second—*yes-no* response to question "Is this a problem	Response format is clever approach to differentiating parental concern about behavior from behavior occurrence

Instrument	Purpose	Scales/Scores	Format	Comments
	endorsed by parents as problematic)		for you?" All problem behaviors	Easy to score Profile on answer sheet Elementary school form also available
Hahnemann High School Behavior Rating Scale (HHSB) (G. Spivack & M. Swift, 1971, 1977)	To help teachers identify and measure classroom behaviors of junior and senior high students 12-19 years, grades 7-12	45 items yield 13 behavior factors, all relating to achievement (e.g., anxious producer, poor work habits) Each scale consists of 3 or 4 items	Some items have 5-point scale, some have 7-point scale Format and questions similar to Devereux Includes both prosocial and problem behaviors Items mostly observable; e.g., Fails to turn in assignments on time	
Jesness Inventory (C. F. Jesness, 1966)	For classification of delinquents (author reports it could be used with other youngsters) Norm sample was 8-19-year-olds, but few 8- or 19-year-olds	11 scale scores: 155 Social maladjustment Value orientation Immaturity Autism Alienation Manifest aggression Withdrawal Social anxiety Repression Denial Asocial	True/false statements; some relevant to delinquency, some standard self-perception statements 20. Most police are pretty dumb 146. I am nervous 151. Families argue too much	Shorter version also available, has both self-report and behavior checklist
Louisville Behavior Checklist (L. C. Miller, 1977)	To help parents communicate concerns about their child Two versions: E_1 for ages 4-7; E_2 for ages 7-13	164 items yield 3 broad-band and 8 narrow-band factor-analytically derived scales Total disability scale, 6 clinical scales (e.g., Psychotic Behavior), and 1 prosocial scale	Most items are problem behaviors, some prosocial items Parents answer True or False to statements, e.g.: 143. Is boisterous, rowdy	Scale for assessing tolerance of rater, which aids in understanding rater biases
Child Behavior Checklist (T. M. Achenbach, 1978; T. M. Achenbach & C. S. Edelbrock, 1979)	To provide standardized parental descriptions of wide range of problem behaviors	8-9 problem behavior scales, depending on form, grouped into 2 major factor scales: Externalizing and Internalizing Also a Social Competence Scale with questions about child's social activities at home, school, and in community	4-page instrument with open-ended questions on first 2 pages (Social Competence Scale); 3-point response format to problem behaviors	Parallel forms of almost identical items for teachers and child Also has observation form

TABLE 5–2
Behavior Checklists (Continued)

Name	Purpose	Scales	Format	Unique Features
Parent Attitudes Test (PAT) (E. L. Cowen, J. Huser, D. R. Beach, & J. Rappoport, 1970)	To sample parental attitudes toward child; Grades 1–3	4 scales of different lengths: Behavior Rating Scale, 25 items; Home Attitudes Scale, 7 items; School Attitudes Scale, 5 items	Behavior Rating Scale is all negative, observable problem behaviors; Parents rate child on 5-point scale; Home Attitudes and the School Attitudes Scales sample parents' subjective perceptions of child's adjustment on a 5-point scale; Adjective Checklist has positive and negative adjectives; parents rate how well adjectives describe child on 3-point scale	Directly samples parental attitudes and obtains information about behavior; Used as outcome measure for effectiveness of a parent training program
Parent Symptom Questionnaire (PSQ) (C. K. Conners, 1970; C. H. Goyette, C. K. Conners, & R. F. Ulrich, 1978)	Screening tool for all behavior problems; Most widely used as screening tool for hyperactivity	Short version has 48 items, factor-analyzed to yield these scales: Conduct problems; Learning disability (inattention); Psychosomatic problems; Inpulsivity-hyperactivity; Anxiety; Scores for each factor computed by summing points of all items on each factor and dividing total by number of items in factor. Score of 1.5 on factor is often used as cutoff score; Longer form (not described) has 93 items	Parents rate child on each behavioral symptom on 4-point scale; not at all = 0, very much = 3; All items are problematic behaviors	Used extensively in research; Parallel forms for teachers
Personality Inventory for Children (PIC) (R. D. Wirt, D. Lachar, J. K. Klinedinst, &	To provide comprehensive and clinically relevant personality description of child based on parental ratings	600 items contribute to 33 scales; half empirically derived, half used rational strategy of experienced judges	Gathering information about child's development ("My child had difficulty breathing at birth"); about parental	Scales measure parents' tendencies to present themselves and child in defensive way

P. D. Seat, 1977	Ages 3–16	to provide items	attitudes toward child ("My child has been difficult to manage"); about family ("The child's father dislikes his present job"); about child's behavior ("My child is sometimes cruel to animals"); about others' perceptions of child ("Others think my child is talented") Parents respond *yes* or *no*	Has been called the MMPI for children Thorough, comprehensive clinical tool for use by trained mental health professionals
The Preschool Behavior Questionnaire (L. B. Behar, & S. Stringfield, 1974)	For teachers, screening instrument for preschool children Ages 3–6	30 items yield total problem behavior score; 3 subscale scores: hostile-aggressive anxious hyperactive-distractible	All items problem behaviors Teacher rates whether item *doesn't apply, applies sometimes, certainly applies,* e.g.: 5. Not much liked by other children 12. Is disobedient	Based on Rutter's Children's Behavior Questionnaire
Taxonomy of Problem Situations (K. A. Dodge, C. L. McClaskey, & E. Feldman, 1985)	To provide taxonomy of situations and tasks likely to elicit problematic social behavior from deviant children	Six clusters of problem situations: Peer group entry Response to provocation Response to failure Response to success Social expectations Teacher expectations	Teachers rate children on 5-point scale; "this situation is *never* a problem for this child" = 1, "this situation is *almost always* a problem for this child" = 5 All the items represent potentially problematic situations but are fairly neutral, e.g., "When a peer tries to start a conversation with this child" or "When this child is teased by peers"	Focuses on problem situations Once conditions in which a child has problems are identified, social skills for that setting can be identified and assessed
Walker Problem Behavior Identification Checklist (H. Walker, 1970; 1976; 1979; 1983)	Supplement in process of identifying emotionally disturbed and behaviorally disordered Elementary-grade children	50 items contribute to total score; 5 subscale scores: acting out withdrawal distractibility disturbed peer relations immaturity Cutoff score indicating problematic behavior available	Teachers indicate whether problem behavior has been observed within past two months All items negative, e.g., 37. Has no friends 27. Has temper tantrums	Short, easy to use Clever profile aids interpretation on the 1-page instrument

According to Hops and Lewin (1984), negative nominations are used less frequently than positive ones, because many assume "that making negative nominations promotes negative concepts about, and negative interactions with, the rejectees, although there is no empirical data to support this belief" (p. 127). Cairns (1983) questions the ethics of encouraging children "to make up semipublic 'hate lists' or 'slam books' " (p. 431) and concludes that potential benefits should be weighed against potential risks. He also notes the paucity of research dealing with this question and comments

I suspect that this is one instance where psychological misconceptions (or egocentrism) about our ability to change the destiny of children's lives with brief interventions may boomerang. More generally, it seems likely that the phenomena assessed (i.e., the structure of social groups and individuals' roles in them) are considerably more enduring than are the ephemeral effects produced by their assessment. Nonetheless, it is both prudent and responsible for investigators to continue to evaluate the risk/benefit issue, and to explore procedures that are less potentially damaging but equally informative. (p. 432)

Test-retest reliability research, according to Hops and Lewin (1984), indicates that

• Stability increases with the children's ages
• Positive nominations are more stable than negative ones
• Reciprocal choices are more stable than received positive choices
• Stability decreases with increasing time between test and retest

Hymel (1983) suggests that this procedure should not be used with preschool children because of the low reliability, but as Cairns (1983) notes, the social networks in the classroom, the social structure of the class as a whole, and the child's role in the networks/structure may be obscured in other techniques.

Another common method for obtaining peer ratings is to have youngsters rate all children in a group on a Likert-type scale from *least liked* to *most liked*. Given a roster of their classmates, children are told to rate each person in relation to a question such as "Do you like to play with this person?" or "Does this person bully others?" Each child's score is the mean of all ratings received. This approach has the advantage of yielding a rating for every child. Scores tend to be less skewed than with the restricted nomination method and problems such as forgetting another child's name or not being able to spell a name are minimized. Hops and Lewin (1984) report that relatively high stability coefficients have been found for peer ratings of both preschool and elementary-age students.

Research reveals that children who do not receive many nominations in the restricted nomination format may not be rejected or neglected children, as had been assumed. Hymel and Asher (1977) found that 11 of 23 children who received no positive nominations received ratings of three or more on a five-point, Likert-type scale. They believe a rating scale provides a measure of a child's likability or acceptability whereas positive nominations represent a child's popularity as a playmate or friend. Research also shows that positive and negative nominations have different behavioral correlates and most likely are functionally and conceptually independent (Hartup, Glazer, & Charlesworth, 1967). Effects have also been reported for age and race (Coie, Dodge, & Coppotelli, 1982).

Peery (1979) devised a system for scoring sociometric techniques that extends the acceptance-rejection dimension of the straightforward scoring systems we have talked about. This system combines positive and negative nominations to yield a *social impact* score. A *social preference* score is obtained by subtracting the number of negative votes from the number of positive ones. Social preference scores are often used in the literature as an index of social status. On the basis of these two dimensions, Peery defines four classification categories: *popular* (high social impact, positive social preference), *rejected*

(high social impact, negative social preference), *isolate* (low social impact, negative social preference), and *amiable* (low social
impact, positive social preference). Coie,
Dodge, and Coppotelli (1982) add another dimension, *controversial*, for children who receive high proportions of both positive and
negative nominations.

Why children rate their peers as they do
has also been an area of interest for researchers. It was assumed that socially competent
children who understood social expectations
and rules would be more popular; however,
investigators report conflicting results in relation to this assumption (White & Blackham,
1985; Rubin, Daniels-Bierness, & Hayvren,
1983). The conflict may be a function of measurement problems, or it may indicate that
youngsters most liked by their peers are not
necessarily those with the most mature social
skills as judged by adults (Rubin & Daniels-
Beirness, 1983).

Peer ratings have many advantages; they
are easy to administer and take little time
with children who can read, require no special training, and provide valuable information about an important dimension of
children's social relations. Because they require the participation of a number of children, peer ratings are not widely used for
clinical purposes, and their primary value is
as a research tool and screening device.

Self-Report Instruments

In addition to having others rate a child, clinicians and researchers increasingly see the
value in obtaining the child's perception of
the problem. This technique has waxed and
waned in popularity over the years. In the
1950s and '60s, when ego-psychology and
phenomenology dominated the field, self-
concept measurement was quite popular, but
clinicians and investigators became disen-
chanted with the technique because respondents could so easily give socially desirable
as opposed to accurate responses. Discrepancies between observed and reported data also

led behaviorists to reject this approach. Additionally, children's ability to provide accurate
verbal and conceptual information about
themselves was questioned. But as ecological
concepts have come to influence the field, clinicians and investigators have again begun to
include this technique in assessment batteries because "to ignore a person's own perception of reality is to lose a vital data base
from which to draw treatment goals" (Finch
& Rogers, 1984).

Self-report techniques include self-concept
measures, measures of specific dimensions
of behavior such as depression and anxiety,
locus of control measures, and general personality measures. These techniques differ
conceptually, but all require the child to report self-perceptions. Table 5–3 (pp. 89–90)
describes several self-report instruments.

The usual self-concept measurement is a
paper-and-pencil task in which the youngster
indicates whether statements describe him or
her. The items are often read aloud to young
children, who circle a smiling or frowning
face. Older children who can read the items
complete the task independently. Some instruments contain different types of items
that are combined to yield a global score of
self-concept. Other instruments have factor-
analyzed items that yield cluster scores representing various aspects of self-concept.
Some instruments are intended for use with
individuals, others with groups. Some use
process statements (for example, "I can talk
about my feelings with friends"), others
sample perceptions of the self as an object
(for example, "I am more nervous than most
of my friends").

There are many self-concept instruments
available, and self-concept measurement has
been researched extensively (Wiley, 1974);
however, problems remain with respect to
measuring this construct. Studies have often
had one or more of the following problems:
inadequate or inappropriate sampling; un-
controlled independent variables (such as
age, sex, race, socioeconomic status); inadequate operational definitions of self-concept;

differences among the nature of the items used to measure self-concept from study to study; and lack of information about adequate norms and measurement statistics. As a result, many of the available instruments are not useful for clinical or research purposes.

Table 5–3 summarizes a few of the instruments that have been relatively well reviewed and that have adequate reliability and validity data. The table also includes measures of specific dimensions of behavior. Much like self-concept measures, these are paper-and-pencil tasks in which respondents agree or disagree with statements about how they feel or see themselves. Unlike self-concept measures, these instruments focus on a particular theme, such as anxiety or depression.

Locus of control instruments are similar to self-concept measures. They are usually paper-and-pencil tasks that require an individual to indicate whether a statement describes oneself. What distinguishes these instruments is their focus on the degree to which the respondent appears to feel as though she determines the outcome of events in her life or the degree to which the respondent reports feeling in charge of events in her life. Like other self-report instruments, there are measures of global locus of control and measures of specific aspects of locus of control. Table 5–3 also describes instruments intended to measure both global and specific locus of control.

All of these paper-and-pencil, self-report instruments are quick to administer and score, easy and straightforward to use, and can be valuable tools for learning how the individual perceives himself. The instruments are particularly valuable in detecting unhappy feelings, especially in withdrawn youngsters who tend to keep their feelings to themselves. Because the socially acceptable answer is usually quite apparent, youngsters who want to present themselves in a positive light can easily do so. In fact, samples show that emotionally disturbed youngsters tend to earn either low or high scores on these instruments. The high scores (no problems) may reflect an unwillingness or inability to admit to even normal problems and may therefore be another type of problem score. Enough children are straightforward and candid in reporting their self-perceptions, however, for these instruments to continue to be popular clinical and research tools.

Projective Testing

Projective testing is another method of gaining information from the youngster about himself; however, with this technique the youngster is not always aware of the nature of the information he is conveying. Projective testing is undertaken to determine the existence and nature of underlying, unconscious emotional conflicts. The technique stems from psychodynamic concepts and is based on the assumption that when given a neutral stimulus, the individual will project his unique feelings and perceptions. Clearly, it is harder to know what is an expected and socially desirable response when the stimuli are vague and do not appear to relate to "good" or "bad" behavior.

There has been a great deal of debate over the validity and appropriateness of projective techniques, especially when used in schools and nonclinical settings. Peterson and Batsche (1983) argue that recent legislation, such as Section 504 and P.L. 94–142, mandated standards that projective tests do not meet; they believe continued use of such instruments in schools could lead to litigation because of their "overreliance on high inference techniques" which increases "the likelihood of bias and misidentification" (p. 442). Knoff (1983), on the other hand, says all projective tests are not alike and equal, and that clinical interviews, which are considered acceptable techniques, are also subjective. He cites the 1982 New York State Education Department's Report of Commissioners' Decisions, which reported that few litigations even contest the use of projective testing.

TABLE 5–3
Self-Report Instruments

Name	Purpose	Scores & Number of Items	Format & Type of Items	Comments
Coopersmith Self-Esteem Inventory (S. Coopersmith, 1967)	To measure feelings of self-worth in children between ages 10–12 (has been used with a wider age range)	58 items contribute to total score	Children respond to items by checking *like me* or *unlike me* Positive and negatively-worded items; e.g., "I'm easy to like"; "I'm a failure" Items focus on parents, school, peers, personal interests	Part of a classic study on self-esteem Behavior rating form Includes questionnaire and interview format for mothers
Multidimensional Measure of Children's Perceptions of Control or Why Things Happen (J. P. Connell, 1980)	To measure children's perceptions of control Multidimensional locus of control for children 8–14 years Administered orally to children under 11	2 parallel forms, 48 items each 3 different *sources* of control: internal powerful others unknown Perceptions of *success or failure* Assesses expectations, cognitive, social, and physical competencies Assesses child's perceptions of why he succeeds or fails (personal realm of reference)	4-point response scale to items that have 4 embedded factors, e.g., "If I want to do well in school, it is up to me to do it"—*Very true/sort of true/not very true/not at all true* Internal control, cognitive domain, successful outcome, personal realm of reference	Flexible, conceptually sophisticated Used in research
Nowicki-Strickland Locus of Control Scale for Children (S. Nowicki & B. Strickland, 1973)	To measure generalized locus of control for children grades 3–12 5th-grade reading level; must be read to 3rd and 4th graders	40 items yield one general locus of control score Other investigators have identified 3–9 underlying factors	Requires yes-no response to questions, e.g., "Do you believe that whether or not people like you depends on how you act?" (yes response = internal locus of control)	2 short forms (20 and 21 items) have been developed 34-item preschool scale available Used extensively in research Only global score; many maintain locus of control has different dimensions

TABLE 5–3
Self-Report Instruments (Continued)

Name	Purpose	Scores & Number of Items	Format & Type of Items	Comments
Perceived Competence Scale for Children (S. Harter, 1982)	To measure child's perception of competencies in 4 domains: Social Physical Cognitive General For ages 8–12; also has norms for grades 3–9	28 items, 7 on each of 4 subscales: Social Physical Cognitive General	Some kids find it hard to make friends, for other kids it's pretty easy. Really true for me / Sort of true for me	Question format appears to minimize social desirability influences, but may confuse some children
Piers-Harris Children's Self-Concept Scale (E. V. Piers & D. B. Harris, 1969)	To measure set of relatively stable self-attitudes in children, ages 3–12	80 items yield global measure of self-concept Also 6 factor-analytically derived subscale scores: 1 = Behavior 2 = Intellectual and school status 3 = Physical appearance and attributes 4 = Anxiety 5 = Popularity 6 = Happiness and satisfaction	Includes items about self as object ("I am a good person"); process questions ("I cry easily") Questions about home, school, physical appearance, general self-perceptions Child responds by circling *yes* or *no*	Probably best known, well-established self-concept measure Based on phenomenological approach
The Revised Children's Manifest Anxiety Scale, or What I Think and Feel (C. R. Reynolds & B. O. Richmond, 1978)	To identify levels of chronic manifest anxiety in children grades K–12	28 anxiety items, 9 "lie" items yield total score for anxiety and a "lie" Socially desirable/defensive responses subscale score	Children respond True/False: 19. My hands feel sweaty 23. Other children are happier than I 34. I am nervous Lie items are mixed throughout: 4. I like everyone I know 28. I never get angry	Revised version of Children's Anxiety Scale (Castaneda, McCandless, & Palmermo, 1956) which was adaption of the Manifest Anxiety Scale for adults (Taylor, 1953) These instruments widely used and respected Revisions carefully conducted

Instrument	Purpose	Description	Format	Comments
Self-Concept and Ideal Self Scales (L. P. Lipsitt, 1958)	To assess actual and ideal self-concepts as well as discrepancy between the two 4th to 6th graders	44 items; 22 adjectives on each measure; self-concept, the ideal self; 3 scores: Self-concept, Ideal self, Discrepancy score	Two lists of adjectives; one prefaced with "I am . . .", one with "I would like to be . . ."; 19 socially desirable and 3 negative items each scale; Child uses 5-point rating scale ranging from *not at all to all of the time*	Conceptually interesting but relatively little work has been done with it; Has data, although somewhat limited on norms, reliability, validity
Self-Observation Scales (W. G. Katzenmeyer & A. J. Stenner, 1979)	To measure multidimensional self-perceptions for groups of children in grades K-12; 4 versions developed for different age groups: primary (K-3), intermediate (4-6), junior high (7-9), senior high (10-12)	Items and scales vary on each version; 50 items on primary form, 60 on intermediate form, 72 on the junior and senior high forms; Factor-analytically derived scales are: Self-acceptance (K-12), Self-security (K-12), Social Maturity (K-6), School Affiliation (K-12), Social Confidence (4-12), Teacher Affiliation (4-12), Peer Affiliation (4-12), Self-Assertion (7-9). (No total self-concept score)	At primary level, items read to class and children mark smiling or frowning faces; Other forms self-administered; Children respond *yes* or *no* to self-as-process and self-as-object statements, e.g., "I usually like my teachers"; "I am a happy person"	Carefully developed instrument; Large and impressive nationally representative sample; Must be machine scored, limits utility for individuals or small groups

Finally, he argues that the real issue may not be the instruments but rather the clinicians who overinterpret and misuse the techniques.

Projective instruments range from unstructured to fairly structured (sometimes called semistructured). Some instruments sample general perceptions; others focus on perceptions about specific topics, such as school and competence, feelings about self, feelings about siblings, and so on.

The Rorschach Inkblot method was developed by Hermann Rorschach in 1921. He was concerned with perception and developed the "Form Interpretation Test" not as a projective test but as a means of determining subject responses to ten inkblots. He died at the age of 37, however, only eight months after publishing his monograph, when, in his words, the method was still in its experimental stages.

Over the next 20 years, five different scoring systems were developed for the Rorschach. Samuel Beck and Marguerite Hertz, both trained in orthodox experimental psychology departments, developed empirically-oriented scoring procedures. Bruno Klopfer, who fled to the United States from Nazi Germany, began teaching a more subjective approach. Hoping to develop a vehicle to share ideas and data about the technique, he started a newsletter called the *Rorschach Research Exchange* in 1936 (which later became the *Journal of Projective Techniques* and ultimately the *Journal of Personality Assessment*). Beck (1936) strongly criticized Klopfer's more subjective technique and thus began a dispute that further separated the two. Initially, Hertz (1937, 1939) tried to mediate between the two but eventually did not agree with either; thus, three separate systems developed. Later one of Klopfer's original students, Piotrowski (1957), developed his own system, and finally, David Rapaport (Rapaport, Gill, & Schafer, 1946) and Roy Schafer (1954) developed a fifth method. As Exner and Martin (1983) point out,

By the mid 1950s, five Rorschach systems had been developed. While they all shared features drawn from Rorschach's original work, their extreme differences in administration, scoring and interpretation precluded systematic comparisons. Despite this, the clinical use of the Rorschach flourished. Unfortunately, practitioners and researchers tended to ignore the presence of the five distinct Rorschach systems; most preferred to characterize it as a single test: The Rorschach. And, many intermixed different components from different systems (e.g., a cup of Beck, a dash of Klopfer, a pinch of Rapaport) and still concluded that the product was The Rorschach. (p. 408)

Because of its ambiguous stimuli, the instrument came to be regarded as a projective technique with psychodynamic underpinnings rather than as a test of perception with acceptable psychometric properties, as it was originally intended. Exner compared the five systems and later formed the Rorschach Research Foundation; from their research, Exner and his colleagues concluded

(a) The five methods of administration did produce five relatively different kinds of records,

(b) Some scores, scoring criteria, and interpretive postulates existed within each system for which no empirical support could be generated or for which negative findings existed, and

(c) Each system included some empirically sturdy elements, yet these positive characteristics could be offset in some cases by system-specific flaws. (Exner & Martin, 1983, p. 409)

They went on to create The Comprehensive System (Exner, 1974, 1978; Exner & Weiner, 1982). These authors describe the Rorschach method as one in which the subject is required to "misperceive," which creates a problem-solving situation that provokes several psychological procedures, such as encoding data, classifying stimuli, rank ordering possible answers, and discarding responses the respondent judges to be inappropriate. All this is done within the context of the personality and in the individual's characteristic style. Exner and Martin (1983) report a number of test-retest reliability and validity studies that attest to the psychometric soundness of The Comprehensive System; however, as we mentioned, the real issue may not be the instrument but the clinician using it. What we need to ask is how consistently clinicians interpret the data to mean the same thing. Appropriately scored and interpreted, this instrument can provide valuable insights into an individual's style of problem solving, which Exner and Martin believe is strongly influenced by relatively enduring personality traits as well as current psychological states. Regarding use of the Rorschach inkblots as a projective technique, they state "projection may occur as part of the response process, but this is not always the case and it is misleading to describe the Rorschach as a 'projective test' for it is much more" (p. 412).

Instruments that use as stimuli pictures of clearly identifiable but expressionless persons, animals, or objects are a second type of projective technique. In this approach, youngsters are instructed to make up a story about the picture. The clinician gives guidelines, such as that the story should have a beginning and end and that the youngster should tell how the main character feels and thinks. Although systems for scoring content and quantity have been developed, clinicians usually focus on the qualitative aspects. Among this type of projective instrument, the Thematic Apperception Test (TAT) (Morgan & Murray, 1935) is probably the most popular. Originally designed for adults, this instrument consists of 31 ambiguous black and white drawings of adults in a variety of situations, and the clinician selects 10 to 12 of the cards to administer on the basis of which are likely to be emotionally significant to the respondent or to have the potential of eliciting projective content. The popularity of the TAT has led to development of several similar instruments specifically for children: the Roberts Apperception Test for Children (1982), the Children's Apperception Test (CAT) (Bellak & Bellak, 1949), and the School

Apperception Method (SAM) (Solomon & Starr, 1968).

The Roberts Apperception Test for Children (1982), designed for children ages 6 through 15, consists of 27 stimulus cards that show drawings of children in everyday interpersonal situations (for example, parent-child, sibling, and peer interactions). The standard administration uses only 16 cards; parallel forms for boys and girls consist of 11 cards. There are cards intended to elicit feelings about parental support and affection, sibling rivalry, school, parental conflict, dependency, fear, and aggression, enabling clinicians to ascertain how well the child can cope with standard social stressors. Children's responses are scored on eight adaptive and five clinical scales. Normative data are provided for 200 well-adjusted children ages 6 to 15.

The CAT is a series of 10 pictures of animals, again designed to elicit developmentally significant content; for example, one card shows an adult cocker spaniel and a younger cocker spaniel in the foreground and a toilet in the background. The SAM is a series of drawings of youngsters in school from which the examiner chooses cards that may be significant and may elicit projective material.

Obrzut and Cummings (1983) conclude that such instruments

May be most valid when used as a type of structured clinical interview. In this context, projective tests facilitate an understanding of the unique needs, interests, pressures, conflicts, affective and cognitive styles and coping strategies that characterize each individual adolescent or child. Given their ability to broaden our understanding of a referred child, and in the hands of an experienced user, it is likely that projective tests will continue to flourish and be improved technically over time. (p. 418)

Some techniques are often called *semiprojective*. The content they elicit is considered less "deep"; that is, they do not tap as much unconscious material as do the instruments we have already discussed. With the semi-projective technique, generally either sentence completion or drawing tasks, it is relatively easy for the respondent to give guarded, socially desirable responses, but the responses are also less variable (Hart, Kehle, & Davies, 1983). These are widely used techniques, but, again, they are in need of objective scoring systems before they can demonstrate adequate psychometric evidence for reliability and validity.

Sentence completion tasks are lists of incomplete sentences that the respondent must complete. Youngsters can complete the sentences on paper independently, or the examiner can read the sentence aloud orally and write down the youngster's responses. Three incomplete sentence lists developed for use with youngsters are the Rotter Incomplete Sentence Blank (Rotter & Rafferty, 1950), the Washington University Sentence Completion

Test (Loevinger, Wessler, & Redmore, 1970), and the Hart Sentence Completion Test for Children (Hart, 1972; 1980). The sentence completion instrument in Figure 5–1 shows some of the responses of a 12-year-old girl to 47 items. The girl had been sexually abused, and had demonstrated poor school performance and antisocial behavior. At the time of these responses, which appear candid and revealing, she was living with a specialized therapeutic family and was adjusting well.

The projective drawings also vary considerably. Children may be asked to draw a person (Machover, 1949, 1953; Koppitz, 1968), draw a house, tree, person (Buck, 1948, 1966; Buck & Hammer, 1969), draw their family (Deren, 1975), draw everyone in their family doing something (Burns, 1982) and draw a school picture that includes themselves, their teacher and a friend or two doing something (Prout and Phillips, 1974). These techniques

FIGURE 5–1
Sentence Completion

4. Someday I _will be married_

12. Homework is _fun when you know how to do it_

13. When I grow up, I want to be _a basketball player._

15. I get in trouble when _people pick on me_

25. To get along well in a group, you have to _talk about your feelings_

26. I can't learn when _a bunch of noise is around._

27. I wish my mother _could understand me more better._

28. Making friends is hard if _you don't know how to be nice._

29. What I like to do most is _keep children_

34. When I am older _I'm to go to college_

38. I get mad when _I don't get any attention_

45. If I were a parent _my kids would be in the house before it gets dark._

47. My 3 wishes are _①Mrs. Barnhill would stay here. ② I get everything I want for my birthday_
③ I want a car.

are widely used and valued as flexible tools for sampling children's attitudes but even though a number of scoring procedures exist, none are so complete that this technique meets adequate psychometric requirements of validity and reliability. As Koppitz (1983) states,

Drawings are not tests and cannot be treated as such. The value derived from children's drawings depends on the knowledge, experience, and skill of the examiner. . . . When used with caution and understanding, drawings are invaluable as part of screening or assessment batteries for elementary and secondary students. However, drawings should only be used in combination with other diagnostic instruments, observations of the student, and with developmental and background information to diagnose specific emotional problems present in children and adolescents. (p. 426)

Projective techniques are commonly used in mental health settings because they provide rich insights into an individual's unconscious and preconscious conflicts. In the hands of skilled and trained clinicians, these instruments can provide useful hypotheses to pursue in therapy; however, since schools are more concerned with here-and-now, everyday interactional problems, these tools are not especially useful and relevant in educational evaluations. Furthermore, many training programs in school psychology do not include training in projective techniques, hence educational diagnosticians have often not learned to administer these instruments. Clinicians and teachers do use semiprojective techniques as a means of informally learning what a child is thinking about and how he feels about himself. Children usually like to draw and to talk about their pictures, so the technique is useful for establishing rapport while learning about the child in a nonthreatening way.

Observation Techniques

Regardless of what other techniques are used in assessment, observation is always impor-

tant because one sees the youngster in a natural setting. Observational data give meaning and validity to the more traditional data gathered through testing and interviewing. For example, observing that a child rarely initiates interactions with peers and that peers tend to overlook the child helps the clinician plan an intervention for a child who complains of not being liked and who is described by teachers and parents as unhappy and worried about making mistakes. Not only do observations provide information about how a child is functioning in a natural setting, they also provide information about expectations for the child.

Professionals may observe a child informally and record subjective impressions; they may see an incident and describe what they saw; they may use a structured system for observation; they may devise their own observation techniques; or they may rate a child on a hierarchy of skills based on collective observations. They may even teach the youngster to observe his own behavior. When deciding how and what to do, one must consider several factors; Medley (1975) identifies four: objectivity, reliability, validity, and practicality. *Objectivity* refers to freedom from bias and clarity of definitions. An objective instrument or observation clearly conveys what happened; an objective observation system has easily defined categories that do not overlap. *Reliability* and *validity* were discussed earlier. *Practicality* refers to whether an instrument can be used within a situation's constraints; a teacher with a class of 30 children will not be able to use a complicated observation system while she is teaching.

Some common types of observation are anecdotal records, antecedent-behavior-consequent records, frequency and/or duration counts of specified behaviors, time sampling of a person's or a group's behavior, observation scales, mapping environmental variables, and rating youngsters on sequences of behavioral objectives.

Anecdotal records are prose descriptions of incidents, which vary considerably in style, format, and usefulness. The more useful records are dated, written in behavioral terms, and include specific information about antecedents and consequences of the incident being described. Inferences about thoughts and feelings provide rich information but are most useful when clearly linked to the behavior on which the inference is based. Quantitative statements based upon actual information, especially when making a comparison, are also useful. Because of the lack of structure, clinicians' biases can skew the observation, but the technique is versatile and easy to use.

Antecedent-behavior-consequent records are similar to anecdotal records in that they are prose accounts, but more structured. As Figure 5–2 illustrates, the observer records stimuli that precede a behavior, the observed behavior, and events that follow the behavior. The information helps identify which environmental factors are maintaining a behavior

FIGURE 5–2
A-B-C Observation

Time	Antecedent	Behavior	Consequence
10:45	T. Writing on board and asking class questions	G. responds to question	T. praises G.
	Activity continues— T. praises others as they answer— some raising hand, some not	G. observes interaction	
	T. asks ?	G. raises hand	T. calls on child in front of G. whose hand wasn't raised
11:00	T. asks ?	G. speaks out – gives correct answer	① T. looks at G & says "raise your hand"
	①	G. slams book shut	T. ignores G. & praises M. for raising hand
	M. gives same response G. gave	G. mumbles under breath	① T. gives warning
	②	G. shouts "unfair"	T. sends G. to Think Tank

and how to intervene to change behavior by focusing on the antecedents and consequences of problem behavior.

Frequency counts show how often the target behavior occurs within a given time. This approach is most useful when the focus of an intervention is to increase or decrease the occurrence of the target behavior. One often implements a frequency count after collecting anecdotal records to identify the target behavior. Through the prose descriptions, one can define a target behavior in precise, behavioral terms so that it is possible to count its occurrences reliably.

Children can easily do frequency counts themselves. With instruction, children can learn to count their own behavior and thereby become more aware of their behavior. Some teachers set up systems whereby teachers and children count the same behavior; when the counts agree, the child receives extra reinforcement. This system teaches children to be responsible for their own behavior and to judge their actions. Written contracts are also effective when children are monitoring their own behavior.

Recording the *duration* of an event is similar to frequency tallies. In this procedure, one keeps track of how long a specified event occurs. One might time how long Johnny stays on task during an academic period or how long it takes Johnny to settle down while in time out. Again, this is a simple but useful way to monitor behavior that children can also learn. For example, Johnny could keep track of how many pages he reads during reading period and then chart his time on a simple bar graph.

Frequency and duration counts have several advantages: they are easy to use; they provide quantified information about behavior that makes it easier to examine progress; and they can be verified with another observer, which makes them more objective. They do not, however, provide the scope of information found in anecdotal records and antecedent-behavior-consequence observations.

Time sampling is a record of behavior at predetermined time intervals. The observer can use an observation tool or system or simply record whether a target behavior is occurring. If the observer is using an observation system based on a time interval of 10 seconds, for example, every ten seconds she determines which category being used fits the child's behavior and makes a tally in that category. At the end of the observation period, a representative sample of behaviors that occurred during that time period would be available. One might find that Bobby spent 50 percent of his time off-task and 22 percent of his time out of his seat during a three-minute observation, although one could not determine the exact number of times he got out of his seat.

There is a vast array of *observation systems* from which to choose. *Mirrors of Behavior* (Simon & Boyer, 1967; 1970a; 1970b) documents 92 observational systems. Gresham's (1981) scale for observing children's social interactions is a straightforward and easy-to-use scale with six categories, two of which have subcategories: Initiating Positive Interaction (I+), subdivided into physical, verbal, and nonverbal positive interactions as well as cooperative behaviors; Receiving Positive Interaction (R+); Initiating Negative Interaction (I–), divided into physical, verbal, and nonverbal negative interactions and uncooperative behaviors; Receiving Negative Interaction (R–); and Neutral Behavior (N). Some scales are even more straightforward (Deno & Mirkin, 1977), and some are more complex and inclusive (Wood, 1973; Spaulding, 1973).

Mapping environmental variables is another approach to observation in which one carefully describes the setting in which the behavior occurs. Important variables in describing a classroom include time of observation, location of observation, specifying number of adults in the room and name of the group leader, number of children in the group, amount and nature of movement in the room, expected academic behavior (for example, reading, math, spelling), communication, and classroom behavior (Wasik & Day, 1977). Others suggest including circumstantial events such as an interaction that occurred earlier in the day that might affect later behavior—perhaps a fight between youngsters or a trip to an exciting and stimulating place. Increasingly, researchers are focusing on how manipulation of the environment can affect behavior or on comparisons of children's behavior under different environmental conditions (Wasik, 1984).

Sequences of behavioral objectives are also useful for organizing and reporting observations. Teachers can use a strategy similar to that outlined by Wood (1980):

1. Develop a comprehensive list of social and academic objectives.

2. Arrange the list in a logical hierarchy from easiest or simplest to most difficult and complex.

3. Go down the list checking off skills the child has mastered.

4. Skills that have not been mastered become the instructional objectives. The teacher should choose five or six of these skills and maintain a daily summary record of the child's performance of the skill.

Wood, Combs, Gunn, and Weller (1986) note that "this procedure has the work reducing advantages of a relatively long time interval (school day or class period) and relatively few behavior categories to be attended to at any one time while it retains the potential of an exhaustive description of desirable behavior shown by the student observed" (p. 86). Wood et al. developed extensive lists of instructional objectives for the Developmental Therapy materials for use with this approach. Braaten (1979) adapted the Developmental Therapy model for working with adolescents and other authors (Stephens, Hartman, & Lucas, 1983; Goldstein, Sprafkin, Gershaw, & Klein, 1980) have also developed lists of instructional objectives

that can be used with this approach. This kind of system requires clinical judgment on the more subjective objectives, so observers who are new to the system sometimes find it difficult to decide when a skill has been mastered or is emerging. The system may be most effective with a team of observers who can share observations and make joint decisions.

CLASSIFICATION SYSTEMS

After a team has evaluated a youngster and agreed upon the nature of the problem, the child is labeled. Labels used by educational systems have tended to be more concerned with how to group children for instruction, rather than with how to understand their behavior for treatment. It has often been left to the teacher to gather detailed diagnostic information after the child has been placed.

Because these labels are integrally tied to funding and services, and because they are vague and imprecise, political considerations and personal biases have greatly affected their usage. Local school systems allocate specific amounts of money to provide services to each classification, and face grave problems when more children are identified than there is money to serve them. School systems also have a great deal of latitude as to whom they hire to teach a class and what children they place in a class. It is not uncommon to exclude a child from classes for the emotionally and behaviorally disordered because the child does not fit in with the group or because the referring teacher or parents do not like the special teacher. Children who are having academic problems but who are not serious management problems may be served in classes for the learning disabled even though their problem is a psychiatric one. Thus, labels used in educational settings have enabled youngsters to receive or be rejected from services, but have contributed little in the way of prescribing specific treatment.

With their medical orientation, mental health systems consider classification or diagnosis important. This perspective takes three different approaches to diagnosis. The most widely used approach involves identifying and defining consensually psychiatric disorders. Knowledge about each disorder and what can be expected of someone with the disorder is compiled. This approach is said to be *atheoretical* in the sense that no assumptions are made about etiology, but the classifications are based on knowledge and beliefs about the disorder. This approach is represented in the DSM III.

A second approach to diagnosis, represented by the Group for the Advancement of Psychiatry, is based on a theory of *why* individuals become disturbed. Although behavioral symptoms are discussed, the heart of the system lies in theory, not behavioral observations or eclectic knowledge about the cluster of observed problems.

The third approach, one taken by Achenbach, is data-based. Problem behaviors are statistically analyzed through factor analyses and meaning is imposed on clusters of behaviors that occur together. Knowledge and theory about psychiatric disorders are the bases of the first two approaches; in the third approach, meaning is derived from what is observed through statistical analyses. Each approach has merit and problems.

The third edition of the Diagnostic and Statistical Manual of Mental Disorders (DSM-III), published by the American Psychiatric Association (APA), is the most widely used psychiatric classification system. It is atheoretical and descriptive as opposed to being grounded in a specific theory about etiology of mental disorders. The five axes allow for specificity in describing the nature of a disorder. For example, Axes I and II are used for classifying the presenting problem as well as other psychiatric disorders; Axis I is usually for the primary problem and Axis II for the secondary problem, although some problems, such as developmental disorders, are usually coded on Axis II even when no diagnosis is coded on Axis I. Two axes enable inclusion of both primary and underlying or secondary disorders in the diagnosis. Axis III is devoted to physical disorders or conditions that are potentially relevant to understanding the problem, such as juvenile diabetes or soft neurological signs. Axis IV is intended for rating the severity of psychosocial stressors; the manual presents a scale of zero to seven, in which 0 = *no information* and 1 = *no apparent psychosocial stressor* to 7 = *catastrophic stressors*, such as multiple family deaths. Axis V is where the highest level of adaptive functioning during the past year is rated. Again, the scale ranges from one to five. Category 1 = *superior* (a 12-year-old girl gets superior grades in school, is extremely popular among her peers, and excels in many sports, all with apparent ease and comfort); category 5 = *poor* (a 14-year-old boy is almost failing in school and has trouble getting along with peers).

The DSM-III, unlike earlier editions, has categories specifically for children and adolescents, which subsequent chapters will describe in greater detail. Creation of these categories represents a major improvement over earlier APA systems.

Because the DSM-III describes categories in detail and gives specific guidelines for distinguishing one disorder from another, many clinicians are pleased with the system. Certainly, it is more comprehensive and specific than any other psychiatric system. It is, however, atheoretical, and for that reason many clinicians criticize it for lacking prescriptive value. Its greatest utility is in classifying, but as with previous editions, clinicians do not necessarily use the categories uniformly.

The GAP, an older system published in 1966, provides a contrast to the DSM-III because it is theoretically-based and therefore intended to have prescriptive value. It was developed because existing psychiatric classification systems used the same categories for adults and children, which many thought inappropriate. The GAP is based on psycho-dynamic constructs. There are ten major categories, all of which focus upon the nature of the intrapsychic conflict and the level of psychosocial development. They are listed along a theoretical continuum from healthy to more severe and organically-based disorders. The categories and their primary characteristics are:

1. Healthy responses—age- or stage-appropriate responses, such as separation anxiety in a preschool child

2. Reactive disorders—behaviors that are in response to environmental problems, such as aggressive behavior in a child whose grandparent dies

3. Developmental deviations—deviations in development resulting from physiological or psychological factors, such as early onset of puberty accompanied by extreme moodiness and oppositional behavior

4. Psychoneurotic disorders—internalized conflicts that developed during the preschool years and stem from unresolved conflicts over aggression and/or sexual impulses; although the conflict is repressed, maladaptive behavior results

5. Personality disorders—externalized conflicts that developed during infancy and early childhood and stem from early problems with getting dependency needs met, developing autonomy, and learning how to appropriately express aggression

6. Psychotic disorders—marked and pervasive deviations in age-appropriate behavior that reflect problems in reality testing and forming attachments with others

7. Psychophysiologic disorders—disorders in which there is a significant reaction between somatic and organic components

8. Brain syndromes—behavioral disturbances that result from brain damage

9. Mental retardation—disorders that result primarily from mental retardation

10. Other—as the title implies, when previously mentioned categories do not seem appropriate

You can see from these brief descriptions that the major categories are constructed on the basis of theoretical views of disturbance; consequently, consistent use of the categories depends on consistent understanding of psychopathology. Because clinicians' knowledge and understanding of psychopathology vary, so does use of the categories. Under this system youngsters can and do receive different diagnoses depending upon who determines the diagnosis. For clinicians of the psychodynamic persuasion, however, this system has prescriptive utility.

The practice of reliably classifying children and adolescents into preexisting categories has always presented problems. Even skillful clinicians interpret the categories differently and react differently to different individuals and different materials. Several studies illustrate this phenomenon. For example, Mattison, Cantwell, Russell, and Will (1979) selected 24 case histories of child and adolescent patients. They asked twenty child psychiatrists to independently diagnose the cases using the DSM-II and the DSM-III. The average interrater agreement was 57 percent for the DSM-II and 54 percent for Axis I of the DSM-III. There was high agreement with both systems on psychotic disorders, conduct disorders, hyperactive disorders, and mental retardation, with the DSM-III showing slightly higher agreement than the DSM-II; however, there was noteworthy disagreement in both systems for disorders related primarily to anxiety and depression and that were mixed and complex. In a similar study, Freeman (1971) reported an interrater reliability of 59 percent for the major GAP categories.

These findings of relatively low overall reliability, especially with complex and internalized disorders, are not unusual. For this reason, many clinicians and researchers advocate using multivariate analyses of data on childhood and adolescent psychopathology. Lists of problems, such as those on problem behavior checklists, are reviewed, checked, and then statistically analyzed. Clusters of problems are identified through factor analyses and severity determined partly by the number of identified problem behaviors. As we discussed in relation to problem behavior checklists, adequate-to-good test-retest reliability can be demonstrated when the same rater is used; however, cross-rater reliability

is typically not as high. With respect to validity, Achenbach (1982) states

Because we lack well-validated diagnostic constructs for children's behavior disorders, we cannot assess multivariate syndromes via either face validity or correlations with diagnoses made by other means. Instead, to validate the empirically

TABLE 5–4

Approximate Relations between DSM-III and Empirically Derived Syndromes of Childhood Behavior Disorders

DSM-III		Empirically Derived Narrow-Band Syndromes
Attention deficit disorders		
314.01	With hyperactivity	Hyperactive
314.00	Without hyperactivity	——
314.80	Residual type	
Conduct disorders		
312.00	Undersocialized, aggressive	Aggressive
312.10	Undersocialized, nonaggressive	——
312.23	Socialized, aggressive	Delinquent (boys)
312.21	Socialized, nonaggressive	Delinquent (girls)
312.90	Atypical	——
Anxiety disorders of childhood or adolescence		
309.21	Separation anxiety disorder	——
313.21	Avoidant disorder	——
313.00	Overanxious disorder	Anxious
Other disorders of childhood or adolescence		
313.22	Schizoid disorder	Social withdrawal (?)
313.23	Elective mutism	Uncommunicative
313.81	Oppositional disorder	——
313.82	Identity disorder	——
Pervasive developmental disorders		
299.8	Childhood onset pervasive developmental	——
299.9	Atypical	——
302.60	Gender identity disorder of childhood	Sex problems (boys 4–5)
V62.30	Academic problem	Academic disability
Disorders not specific to childhood or adolescence		
300.30	Obsessive-compulsive disorder	Obsessive-compulsive
300.81	Somatization disorder	Somatic complaints
309.00	Adjustment disorder with depressed mood (?)	Depressed
301.22	Schizotypal personality disorder (?)	Schizoid
	——	Immature
	——	Sexual problems
	——	Sleep problems
		Cruel (girls)

Source: Achenbach, 1980, p. 410. Numbers are DSM-III statistical codes.

derived syndromes, we need to rely mainly on *bootstrapping*; that is, "lifting ourselves by our own bootstraps" by finding relations among measures that we know are imperfect. As we improve our measures and find out how well they correlate with each other, we can use the best measures as validating criteria for new measures. (p. 571)

Some studies compare results from two different instruments, but much more work is needed. Achenbach (1982) compares the DSM-III with empirically derived syndromes of childhood behavior disorders (Table 5-4).

Not only are there differences among professionals in classifying youngsters' problems, there are also differences among systems. As Forness and Cantwell note,

A child with an anxiety disorder might be seen by a psychiatrist as emotionally disturbed, although the child might present no serious problem in classroom management. A special educator, on the other hand, might term the same child behavior disordered rather than emotionally disturbed, since the former term frequently implies, in many states, a less severe problem in classroom management. Likewise, an attention-deficit disorder may be seen as primarily a learning disability by a special education teacher, while a psychiatrist may consider it under the behavior-disorder rubric. Educators in some states might still include a child with an IQ of 75 in their EMR classification, while DSM-III no longer classifies borderline intellectual functioning (IQ 70 to 85) as a disorder but rather lists it under "conditions not attributable to a mental disorder." (Forness & Cantwell, 1982, p. 52)

Despite the numerous problems with diagnosis and classification, the practice remains politically and professionally necessary. For example, organizations that are responsible for providing care need a means of classification so they can allocate financial aid, tally the extent of services, and plan systems of service delivery. Professionals need efficient means of communicating with each other about the perceived nature of a problem and the perceived type of necessary treatment. It is easier to say that a child is conduct disordered and in need of consistent, predictable, structured, intensive treatment than to give a lengthy history of the child's problems. Because of the importance such labels can assume in a child's life, professionals must carefully consider the implications of the labels they affix.

CONCLUSION

Assessment is the first step in treatment. If an assessment is cursory, inaccurate, or poorly managed, consequent treatment may be inadequate. This critical process unfortunately often remains an art rather than a science despite the impressive improvements in instruments. A professional's skill in relating to a client, observing subtle cues, following up on intuitions, and collaborating with others determines the quality of an assessment.

Personal biases influence the questions professionals ask, the instruments they use, how they conceptualize the problem, and what interventions they recommend. Because of the many ways bias enters into the process, the use of several different methods of assessment and participation of several different professionals along with parents and other significant people are now legally mandated in educational settings and clinically advised in mental health settings.

REFERENCES

Achenbach, T. M. (1978). The child behavior profile: I. Boys aged 6–11. *Journal of Consulting and Clinical Psychology, 46,* 478–488.

Achenbach, T. M. (1982). *Developmental psychopathology* (2nd ed.). New York: John Wiley.

Achenbach, T. M. (1980). DSM-III in light of empirical research on the classification of child psychopathology. *Journal of the American Academy of Child Psychiatry, 19,* 395–412.

Achenbach, T. M., & Edelbrock, C. S. (1978). The classification of child psychopathology: A review and analysis of empirical efforts. *Psychological Bulletin, 85,* 1275–1301.

Achenbach, T. M., & Edelbrock, C. S. (1979). The child behavior profile. II. Boys aged 12–16 and girls aged 6–12 and 12–16. *Journal of Consulting and Clinical Psychology, 47,* 223–233.

American Psychiatric Association (1980). Diagnostic and statistical manual of mental disorders (3rd ed.). Washington, DC: American Psychiatric Association.

Beck, S. J. (1936). Autism in Rorschach scoring. *American Journal of Orthopsychiatry, 6,* 83–85.

Behar, L. B., & Stringfield, S. (1974). A behavior rating scale for the preschool child. *Developmental Psychology, 10,* 601–610.

Bellak, L., & Bellak, S. S. (1949). The Children's Apperception Test. New York: CPS Company.

Braaten, S. (1979). The Madison school program: Programming for secondary level severely emotionally disturbed youth. *Behavioral Disorders, 4,* 153–162.

Bower, E. M. (1969). *Early identification of emotionally handicapped children in school* (2nd ed.). Springfield, IL: Charles C Thomas.

Brown, L. L., & Hammill, D. D. (1978). Behavior Rating Profile: An Ecological Approach to Behavioral Assessment. Austin, TX: PRO-ED.

Buck, J. N. (1966). The House-Tree-Person technique (Revised Manual). Beverly Hills, CA: Western Psychological Services.

Buck, J. N. (1948). The H-T-P technique: A qualitative and quantitative scoring manual. *Journal of Clinical Psychology, 4,* 317–396.

Buck, J. N., & Hammer, E. F. (Eds.) (1969). *Advances in House-Tree-Person Technique: Variations and applications.* Beverly Hills, CA: Western Psychological Services.

Burks, H. F. (1977). Burks' Behavior Rating Scales (BBRS). Los Angeles: Western Psychological Services.

Burns, R. C. (1982). *Self-growth in families: Kinetic Family Drawings (K-F-D) research and application.* New York: Brunner/Mazel.

Cairns, R. B. (1983). Sociometry, psychometry, and social structure: A commentary on six recent studies of popular, rejected, and neglected children. *Merrill-Palmer Quarterly, 29,* 429–438.

Chess, S., Thomas, A., & Birch, H. G. (1966). Distortions in developmental reporting made by parents of behaviorally disturbed children. *Journal of the American Academy of Child Psychiatry, 5,* 226–234.

Coie, J. D., & Dodge, K. A. (1983). Continuities and changes in children's social status: A five-year longitudinal study. *Merrill-Palmer Quarterly, 29,* 261–282.

Coie, J. D., Dodge, K. A., & Coppotelli, H. (1982). Dimensions and types of social status: A cross-age perspective. *Developmental Psychology, 18,* 557–570.

Connell, J. P. (1980). A new measure of children's perceptions of control: Individual differences, situational determinants and developmental change. Unpublished manuscript, University of Rochester.

Conners, C. K. (1970). Symptom patterns in hyperkinetic, neurotic, and normal children. *Child Development, 41,* 667–682.

Coopersmith, S. (1967). Coopersmith Self-Esteem Inventory. In *The antecedents of self-esteem.* San Francisco: W. H. Freeman.

Cowen, E. L., Huser, J., Beach, D. R., & Rappoport, J. (1970). Parental perceptions of young children and their relation to indexes of adjustment. *Journal of Consulting and Clinical Psychology, 34,* 97–103.

Cowen, E. L., Pederson, A., Babigian, H., Izzo, L. D., & Trost, M. A. (1973). Long-term follow-up of early detected vulnerable children. *Journal of Consulting and Clinical Psychology, 41,* 438–446.

Deno, S. L., & Mirkin, P. K. (1977). *Data based program modification: An intervention program for serving handicapped students.* Minneapolis: Leadership Training Institute/Special Education, University of Minnesota. (Available from the Council for Exceptional Children, Reston, Virginia)

Deren, S. (1975). An empirical evaluation of the validity of the Draw-A-Family Test. *Journal of Clinical Psychology, 31,* 47–52.

Dodge, K. A., McClaskey, C. L., & Feldman, E. (1985). Situational approach to the assessment of social competence in children. *Journal of Consulting and Clinical Psychology, 53,* 344–353.

Ellsworth, R. B., Ricks, F., Doherty, G., Derenge, J., & Pett, M. (1977). Child and Adolescent Adjustment Profile (CAAP). Roanoke, VA: Institute for Program Evaluation.

Exner, J. E. (1974). *The Rorschach: A comprehensive system* (Vol. I). New York: John Wiley.

Exner, J. E. (1978). *The Rorschach: A comprehensive system* (Vol. II). New York: John Wiley.

Exner, J. E., & Martin, L. S. (1983). The Rorschach: A history and description of the comprehensive system. *School Psychology Review, 12,* 407–413.

Exner, J. E., & Weiner, I. B. (1982). *The Rorschach: A comprehensive system* (Vol. III). New York: John Wiley.

Eyberg, S. M. (1980). Eyberg Child Behavior Inventory. *Journal of Clinical Child Psychology, 9,* 29.

Eyberg, S. M., & Ross, A. W. (1978). Assessment of child behavior problems: The validation of a new inventory. *Journal of Clinical Child Psychology, 7,* 113–116.

Finch, A. J., & Rogers, T. R. (1984). Self-report instruments. In T. H. Ollendick and M. Hersen, *Child behavioral assessment: Principles and procedures.* New York: Pergamon Press.

Freeman, M. (1971). A reliability study of psychiatric diagnosis in childhood and adolescence. *Journal of Child Psychology and Psychiatry, 12,* 43–54.

Forness, S. R., & Cantwell, D. P. (1982). DSM-III psychiatric diagnoses and special education categories. *The Journal of Special Education, 16,* 49–63.

Goldstein, A. P., Sprafkin, R. P., Gershaw, M. J., & Klein, P. (1980). Skill-streaming the adolescent: A structured learning approach to teaching prosocial skills. Champaign, IL: Publisher.

Goyette, C. H., Conners, C. K., & Ulrich, R. G. (1978). Normative data on Revised Conners Parent and Teacher Rating Scales. *Journal of Abnormal Child Psychology, 6,* 221–236.

Graham, P., & Rutter, M. (1968). The reliability and validity of the psychiatric assessment of the child. II: Interview with the parent. *British Journal of Psychiatry, 114,* 581–592.

Gresham, F. M. (1981). Validity of social skills measures in assessing the social competence of low-status children: A multivariate investigation. *Developmental Psychology, 17,* 390–398.

Gross, A. M. (1984). Behavioral interviewing. In T. H. Ollendick and M. Hersen, *Child behavioral assessment: Principles and procedures.* New York: Pergamon Press.

Group for the Advancement of Psychiatry (GAP) (1966). *Psychopathological disorders in childhood: Theoretical considerations and a proposed classification* (Vol. VI, Report No. 62). New York: GAP.

Hart, D. H. (1972). The Hart Sentence Completion Test for Children. Unpublished manuscript, Salt Lake City, Utah, Educational Support Systems.

Hart, D. H. (1980). A quantitative scoring system for the Hart Sentence Completion Test for Children. Unpublished manuscript, Salt Lake City, Utah, Educational Support Systems.

Hart, D. H., Kehle, T. H., & Davies, M. V. (1983). Effectiveness of sentence completion techniques: A review of the Hart Sentence Completion Test for Children. *School Psychology Review, 12,* 428–434.

Harter, S. (1982). The perceived competence scale for children. *Child Development, 53,* 87–97.

Hartup, W. W., Glazer, J. A., & Charlesworth, R. (1967). Peer reinforcement and sociometric status. *Child Development, 38,* 1017–1024.

Herjanic, B., & Campbell, W. (1977). Differentiating psychiatrically disturbed children on the basis of a structured interview. *Journal of Abnormal Child Psychology, 5,* 127–133.

Hertz, M. R. (1937). Discussion on "Some recent Rorschach problems." *Rorschach Research Exchange, 2,* 53–65.

Hertz, M. R. (1939). On the standardization of the Rorschach method. *Rorschach Research Exchange, 3,* 120–133.

Hodges, K., Kline, J., Fitch, P., McKnew, D., & Cytryn, L. (1982). The child assessment schedule: A diagnostic interview for research and clinical use. *Catalog of Selected Documents in Psychology, 11,* 56.

Hodges, K., Kline, J., Stern, L., Cytryn, L., & McKnew, D. (1982). The development of a child assessment schedule for research and clinical use. *Journal of Abnormal Child Psychology, 10,* 173–189.

Hodges, K., McKnew, D., Cytryn, L., Stern, L., & Kline, J. (1982). The child assessment schedule (CAS) diagnostic interview: A report on reliability and validity. *Journal of the American Academy of Child Psychiatry, 21,* 468–473.

Hops, H., & Lewin, L. (1984). Peer sociometric forms. In T. H. Ollendick and M. Hersen (Eds.), *Child behavioral assessment: Principles and procedures.* New York: Pergamon Press.

Hymel, S. (1983). Preschool children's peer relations: Issues in sociometric status. *Merrill-Palmer Quarterly, 29,* 283–307.

Hymel, S., & Asher, S. R. (1977). Assessment and training of isolated children's social skills. Paper presented at the biennial meeting of the Society for Research in Child Development, New Orleans, March 1977. ERIC Document Reproduction Service No. ED 136 930.

Jesness, C. F. (1966). Jesness Inventory. Palo Alto, CA: Consulting Psychologists Press.

Katzenmeyer, W. G., & Stenner, A. J. (1979). Self-Observation Scales. Durham, NC: NTS Research Corporation.

Knoff, H. M. (1983). Justifying projective/personality assessment in school psychology: A response to Batsche and Peterson. *School Psychology Review, 12,* 446–451.

Koppitz, E. M. (1968). *Psychological evaluation of children's human figure drawings.* New York: Grune & Stratton.

Koppitz, E. M. (1983). Projective drawings with children and adolescents. *School Psychology Review, 12,* 421–427.

Lambert, N. M., Hartsough, C. S., & Bower, E. M. (1979). A process for early identification of emotionally disturbed children. Monterey, CA: Publishers Test Service.

Lipsitt, L. P. (1958). A self-concept scale for children and its relationship to the children's form of the Manifest Anxiety Scale. *Child Development, 29,* 463–471.

Loevinger, J., Wessler, R., & Redmore, C. (1970). *Measuring ego development: Vol. 1. Construction and use of a sentence completion test; Vol. 2. Scoring manual for women and girls.* San Francisco: Jossey-Bass.

Machover, K. (1949). *Personality projection in the drawings of a human figure.* Springfield, IL: Charles C Thomas.

Machover, K. (1953). Human figure drawings of children. *Journal of Projective Techniques, 17,* 85–91.

Mattison, R., Cantwell, D. P., Russell, A. T., & Will, L. (1979). A comparison of DMS-II and DSM-III in the diagnosis of childhood psychiatric disorders. *Archives of General Psychiatry, 36,* 1217–1222.

McCarney, S. B., & Leigh, J. E. (1983). Behavior Evaluation Scale (BES). Austin, TX: PRO-ED.

McGinnis, E., Kiraly, J., & Smith, C. R. (1984). The types of data used in identifying public school students as behaviorally disordered. *Behavioral Disorders, 9,* 239–246.

McMahon, R. J. (1984). Behavioral checklists and rating scales. In T. H. Ollendick and M. Hersen (Eds.), *Child behavioral assessment: Principles and procedures.* New York: Pergamon Press.

Medley, D. M. (1975). Systematic observation schedules as measuring instruments. In R. A. Weinberg and F. H. Wood, *Observation of pupils and teachers in mainstream and special education settings: Alternative strategies.* Minneapolis, MN: Leadership Training Institute, Special Education, University of Minnesota. (Copies available from the Council for Exceptional Children).

Miller, L. C. (1977). Louisville Behavior Checklist manual. Los Angeles: Western Psychological Services.

Mischel, W. (1973). Toward a cognitive social learning reconceptualization of personality. *Psychological Review, 80,* 252–283.

Morgan, C. D., & Murray, H. A. (1935). A method of investigating phantasies: The Thematic Apperception Test. *Archives of Neurology and Psychiatry, 34,* 289–306.

Nowicki, S., & Strickland, B. (1973). A locus of control scale for children. *Journal of Consulting and Clinical Psychology, 40,* 148–154.

Obrzut, J. E., & Cummings, J. A. (1983). The projective approach to personality assessment: An analysis of thematic picture techniques. *School Psychology Review, 12,* 414–420.

O'Leary, K. D., & Johnson, B. J. (1979). Psychological assessment. In H. C. Quay & J. S. Werry (Eds.), *Psychopathological disorders of childhood* (2nd ed.). New York: John Wiley.

Peery, J. C. (1979). Popular, amiable, isolated, rejected: A reconceptualization of sociometric status in preschool children. *Child Development, 50,* 1231–1234.

Peterson, D. W., & Batsche, G. M. (1983). School psychology and projective assessment: A growing incompatibility. *School Psychology Review, 12,* 440–445.

Piers, E. V., & Harris, D. B. (1969). Children's Self-Concept Scale (The Way I Feel About Myself). Nashville, TN: Counselor Recordings and Tests.

Piotrowski, Z. (1957). *Perceptanalysis.* New York: Macmillan.

Prout, H. T. (1983). School psychologists and social-emotional assessment techniques: Patterns in training and use. *School Psychology Review, 12,* 377–383.

Prout, H. T., & Phillips, P. D. (1974). A clinical note: The Kinetic School Drawing. *Psychology in the Schools, 11,* 303–306.

Quay, H. C., & Peterson, D. R. (1975). Behavior Problem Checklist. Manual available from D. R. Peterson, Graduate School of Applied and Professional Psychology, Busch Campus, P. O. Box 88199, Piscataway, N. J. 08854.

Rapaport, D., Gill, M., & Schafer, R. (1946). *Diagnostic psychological testing* (2 vols.). Chicago: Yearbook.

Reynolds, C. R., & Richmond, B. O. (1978). What I Think and Feel: A revised measure of children's manifest anxiety. *Journal of Abnormal Child Psychology, 6,* 271–280.

Roberts, G. (1982). Roberts Apperception Test for Children. Los Angeles: Western Psychological Corp.

Robins, L. (1963). The accuracy of parental recall of aspects of child development and of child rearing practices. *Journal of Abnormal and Social Psychology, 66,* 261.

Rotter, J. B., & Rafferty, J. E. (1950). Manual: The Rotter Incomplete Sentences Blank. New York: Psychological Corporation.

Rubin, K. H., & Daniels-Beirness, T. (1983). Concurrent and predictive correlates of sociometric status in kindergarten and grade 1 children. *Merrill-Palmer Quarterly, 29,* 337–351.

Rubin, K. H., Daniels-Beirness, T., & Hayvren, M. (1983). Social and social-cognitive correlates of sociometric status in preschool and kindergarten children. *Canadian Journal of Behavioral Science, 14,* 338–349.

Rutter, M. (1967). Children's Behavior Questionnaire. *Journal of Child Psychology and Psychiatry, 8,* 1–11.

Rutter, M., & Graham, P. (1968). The reliability and validity of the psychiatric assessment of the child. *British Journal of Psychiatry, 114,* 563–579.

Salvia, J., & Ysseldyke, J. E. (1985). *Assessment in special education* (3rd ed.). Boston: Houghton Mifflin.

Sandoval, J. (1981). Format effects in two teacher rating scales of hyperactivity. *Journal of Abnormal Child Psychology, 9,* 203–218.

Sattler, J. M. (1982). *Assessment of children's intelligence and special abilities* (2nd ed.). Boston: Allyn & Bacon.

Schafer, R. (1954). *Psychoanalytic interpretation in Rorschach testing.* New York: Grune & Stratton.

Scheiderer, E. G. (1977). Effects of instructions and modeling in producing self-disclosure in the initial clinical interview. *Journal of Consulting and Clinical Psychology, 45,* 378–384.

Simon, A., & Boyer, G. (Eds.) (1967). *Mirrors for behavior: An anthology of classroom observation instruments* (Vols. 1–6). Philadelphia: Research for Better Schools, ED 029 833.

Simon, A., & Boyer, E. G. (Eds.) (1970a). *Mirrors for behavior: An anthology of classroom observation instruments*

(Vols. 7–14 and Summary). Philadelphia: Research for Better Schools, ED 031 613.

Simon, A., & Boyer, E. G. (Eds.) (1970b). *Mirrors for behavior: An anthology of classroom observation instruments* (Supplementary Vols. A & B). Philadelphia: Research for Better Schools, ED 042 93.

Smith, C. R., Frank, A. R., & Snider, B. C. (1984). School psychologists' and teachers' perceptions of data used in the identification of behaviorally disordered students. *Behavioral Disorders, 10,* 27–32.

Solomon, I. L., & Starr, B. D. (1968). School Apperception Method (SAM). New York: Springer.

Spaulding, R. L. (1973). The coping analysis schedule for educational settings (CASES). Paper presented at the annual meeting of the American Educational Research Association, New Orleans, LA. (ERIC Document Reproduction Service No. ED 166 246).

Spivak, G., & Swift, M. (1967). Devereux Elementary School Behavior Rating Scale (DESB). Devon, PA: Devereux Foundation.

Spivak, G., & Swift, M. (1971). Hahnemann High School Behavior Rating Scale (HHSB). Philadelphia: Hahnemann Medical College and Hospital, Department of Mental Health Sciences.

Spivak, G., & Swift, M. (1977). The Hahnemann High School Behavior (HHSB) Rating Scale. *Journal of Abnormal Child Psychology, 5,* 299–307.

Stephens, T., Hartman, C., & Lucas, V. (1983). *Teaching children basic skills: A curriculum handbook* (2nd ed.). Columbus, OH: Merrill.

Walker, H. M. (1983). Walker Problem Behavior Identification Checklist (WPBIC)–Revised. Los Angeles: Western Psychological Services.

Wasik, B. H. (1984). Clinical applications of direct behavioral observation: A look at the past and the future. In B. B. Lahey & A. E. Kazdin (Eds.), *Advances in Clinical Child Psychology* (vol. 7). New York: Plenum Press.

Wasik, B. H., & Day, B. (1977). Measuring open and traditional learning environments and children's classroom behavior. *Forum on Education, 5,* 27–38.

White, P. E., & Blackham, G. J. (1985). Interpersonal problem-solving ability and sociometric status in elementary school children. *Journal of School Psychology, 23,* 255–260.

Wiley, R. (1974). *The self-concept: A review of methodological considerations and measuring instruments* (rev. ed.). Lincoln: University of Nebraska Press.

Wilson, D. R., & Prentice-Dunn, S. (1981). Rating scales in the assessment of child behavior. *Journal of Clinical Child Psychology, 10,* 121–126.

Wirt, R. D., Lachar, D., Klinedinst, J. K., & Seat, P. D. (1977). Personality Inventory for Children. Los Angeles: Western Psychological Services.

Wood, F. H. (1973). Pupil observation schedule. Minneapolis MN: Special Education Programs, University of Minnesota. (Unpublished copy available from the author)

Wood, F. H. (1980). Observing skills for teachers. In M. C. Reynolds (Ed.), *Social environment of the schools: What research and experience say to the teacher of exceptional children.* Reston, VA: Council for Exceptional Children.

Wood, M. M., Combs, C., Gunn, A., & Weller, D. (1986). *Developmental therapy in the classroom* (2nd ed.). Austin, TX: PRO-ED.

SECTION TWO

Undercontrolled Behavior

This section presents current research and clinical understanding of two major behavior disorders in children, hyperactivity and hyperaggressiveness. These problems have traditionally been viewed from many different perspectives, some of which emphasize internal variables such as brain injury and others that emphasize social-environmental variables.

Our point of view is that behavior is a function of a child's social interactions, with contributions from organic and temperamental factors and from factors in the child's social environment, especially the family. The nature and quality of these interactions define the child's behavior disorder in terms of the relative "goodness of fit" between the child and the environments. Hyperactivity and hyperaggressiveness in children are examples of problematic "fits." Often called *undercontrolled behavior,* these problems result when a child does not have sufficient control to meet environmental expectations effectively.

A 12-year-old aggressive boy drew this picture
in bright red ink. He said he was turning red
from anger at not having been able to play foos-
ball longer the day before, but the diagnostician
felt his anger was caused by being asked to do
something he couldn't do very well—"Draw a
picture of yourself doing something." Had the
child known the diagnostician better, he would
probably have refused to comply and avoided
the task by becoming aggressive.

CHAPTER SIX

Aggressive Behavior in Children and Adolescents

Betty Cooper Epanchin
WRIGHT SCHOOL, THE NORTH CAROLINA
RE-EDUCATION CENTER AND
UNIVERSITY OF NORTH CAROLINA AT CHAPEL HILL

Aggressive behavior is probably the most common presenting problem among youngsters classified as emotionally and behaviorally disturbed, and data suggest that the incidence of antisocial, aggressive behavior is rising.

Decidedly more boys than girls are referred for aggressive behavior, although the reasons for this are not clear.

Hyperaggressiveness tends to be quite stable over time, in contrast to other personality dimensions that change as the individual grows and changes.

All humans behave aggressively at different times in their lives. As they age, their aggressiveness usually changes from physical to verbal.

Youngsters behave aggressively for many reasons: internal conflict, learning from models and reward systems, organic factors, cognitive distortions, and a "lack of fit" between child and environment.

Numerous interventions have been effective with these youngsters: therapy, residential treatment, medication, behavioral interventions, and programs that help the child acquire more adaptive social skills and knowledge.

Children who are referred for help because of hyperaggressive, antisocial behavior as children have a disproportionate number of mental health and legal/social problems as adults.

Buddy is 14 years old. For the past six years, a social service agency has had custody of Buddy because his mother cannot control him and his father's whereabouts is unknown. Since the agency obtained custody, Buddy has lived in several foster homes, two residential treatment centers for children, and a training school. He visits his mother intermittently. He has attended a different school almost every year, and, since third grade, has been classified as behaviorally disordered.

Buddy has no real friends. Children often allow him to do as he wishes and rarely disagree with him, but not because they like him. He intimidates them, and through intimidation, controls them. Teachers also acquiesce to him. When faced with school work that he thinks is too hard, he has been known to destroy his book and throw his desk across the room while cursing at the teacher for giving him the work. His threats and outbursts disrupt the class and interfere with other children's concentration, so many teachers elect to ignore his oppositional behavior rather than confront him and provoke a major disruption.

When he was nine years old, it was discovered during a routine school dental checkup that he needed extensive dental work. After the social service agency agreed to pay for Buddy's dental work, a well-intentioned teacher volunteered to take him to a dentist who specialized in working with children. Buddy went reluctantly; once there, he refused to cooperate. After almost an hour of cajoling, describing the procedure, encouraging, and generally trying to provide psychological support, the dentist, his assistant, the hygienist, and the teacher decided that the only way to proceed was to hold him in the chair. It took all four adults to do this. Buddy was frightened, and he dealt with his fear the only way he knew how: he fought. Even though he was only nine, he demonstrated a great deal of strength.

Apparently situations that require him to trust and depend on others are particularly frightening to him. When he begins to care about a teacher or child care worker, he seems especially belligerent and uses every opportunity to engage in power struggles. He once verbalized how hard it was to get to like someone and then have to leave them.

Buddy's behavior is not always inappropriate. When he is offered concrete and desirable rewards, he can, and usually does, behave appropriately. Once he obtains the reward, however, he returns to his recalcitrant ways, which makes teachers and child care workers feel used.

His WISC-R Full-scale IQ at age 14 was 76; his Performance Scale was higher by 10 points than his Verbal Scale Score. Previous test results had been higher, reflecting a decline in scores over the years. He was first tested when he was 7. At that time he earned a Full-scale IQ on the WISC-R of 94, with the Performance Scale 14 points higher than the Verbal Scale. Academically, he has always had difficulty. He should now be in the ninth grade, but functions at a third-grade level in both reading and math skills.

Buddy's problems are obvious: he is an aggressive child. His characteristic way of dealing with the world is through aggression. When frightened, he fights—and since he frequently fears that others will discover how inadequate and needy he is, he is frequently frightened. He does not appear to know other ways to solve problems or deal with his emotions. His aggressiveness is so consistent, so frequent, and at such a high level that most people would agree he has a serious problem. This is not always the case, however, when dealing with children who behave aggressively. Some youngsters who appear unhappy and withdrawn sometimes quite unexpectedly behave quite aggressively. For example, Darrell, age 11, was a quiet, constricted boy who tried to do well and be successful in school. One day in the bathroom he appeared to lose control of himself and threw the paint jars he was cleaning against the wall, creating a horrible mess of paint and broken jars all over the room. Investigation showed that Darrell had some minor learning problems, but had always been able to cope with them through hard work, until the year of his outburst. This year much more was demanded of him in school, and he was having a great deal of difficulty meeting those demands successfully. His outburst was a momentary loss of control brought on by his inability to meet his high self-expectations.

Linda, age 14, is another example of a youngster who exhibited excessive verbal aggressiveness. At school she was a model student, and when with her father, she was fairly easy to deal with. But when she was with her mother or with both parents together, she appeared to deliberately provoke her mother, who in turn reacted with hostility. The two argued constantly, and Linda was often vicious toward her mother. Linda's problems started as a normal developmental crisis, but because her mother was unable to adapt to the changes in her daughter, Linda's behavior became more and more problematic. Linda loved her mother and felt guilty about her anger toward her, but her need to become independent and to establish her female identity were in direct conflict with her mother's wish for her daughter to remain little and asexual.

Aggressive behavior is observable from a very early age in normal individuals. Infants bite their mothers, and they scream when not fed as quickly as they want. Young children hit their playmates when angry; they grab toys from their friends; they yell angry wishes at their parents, such as "I wish you were dead." As they grow and develop, society and their parents expect this kind of behavior to be replaced by more socially acceptable ways of expressing frustration and disappointment.

Many emotionally handicapped children appear not to have learned socially desirable behaviors or are unable to function on a more mature level. Most children labeled emotionally disturbed have at one time or another been described as aggressive. Aggressiveness appears to be the most problematic behavior for schools, and classes for the emotionally and behaviorally disturbed usually have a majority of youngsters who have trouble with aggressive feelings and impulses.

AGGRESSION DEFINED

Aggressive behavior is defined as behavior that inflicts physical or psychological injury on another person. It includes *physical assaults*, such as hitting, kicking, biting, and shoving, and *verbal assaults*, such as making threats, hurling insults, and name-calling. It also includes destruction of property and disruptive behavior that interferes with another person's pleasure or achievements.

But for a behavior to be considered aggressive, it must also be hostile in intent. Accidental hurtful behavior is usually not considered aggressive. If after hitting a ball a child slings down a baseball bat and accidentally hits another child, he may inflict injury, but since it is unintentional, the behavior would probably not be considered aggressive.

Personal beliefs and social norms also determine whether an act is aggressive. Some observers might consider young boys' rough-housing to be aggressive, while others (and probably the boys themselves) would see it as just having fun. Conversely, some forms of behavior are considered aggressive even though no personal injury or property damage occurs. Someone who attempts to hurt another by firing a gun or by striking with a lethal object but who fails in his attempt is still seen as behaving aggressively. Even subversive, underhanded behavior meant only to annoy or pester is sometimes labeled aggressive or passive aggressive, depending on the observer's bias. Obviously, harmful effects alone cannot serve as the discriminating element in a definition of aggression.

Some psychologists differentiate hostile aggression from instrumental aggression or defensive aggression. *Hostile aggression* is person-directed; the goal of such behavior is to hurt. *Instrumental aggression* serves the purpose of acquiring or retrieving an object, territory, or privilege. This kind of aggression often occurs when a goal is blocked and is far more common in young children. *Defensive aggression* is hostile and assertive responses to perceived threats or intentional frustration. The distinction among these types of aggression, however, is not always easy to make. A child who fights with a classmate may want both to hurt the classmate and obtain the attention and admiration of other classmates. Likewise, a child who hits a provoker with an unusually hard blow may be both protecting himself and evoking approval from classmates.

In dealing with the topic of aggression, therefore, one must consider motivation so as to discriminate among the multiple types and causes of aggression. Unfortunately this is often not easy to do, especially in young children, because of their developing and changing natures.

CLASSIFICATION

Since there are multiple types and causes of aggression, there are also multiple ways an aggressive child may be diagnosed. In fact, children classified as psychotic, as organic, as anxious, and as having a number of other disorders often have histories of aggressive outbursts. These children's aggressive behavior is a symptom of other problems, such as depression, psychosis, anxiety, and so forth; accordingly, their diagnosis reflects their major problem, not necessarily the aggressive symptoms. When primary problems are chronic aggressive and antisocial behavior, however, children are usually classified as

having a conduct disorder in the DSM-III system.

The DSM-III classifies four types of conduct disorders: the *undersocialized* aggressive and nonaggressive and the *socialized* aggressive and nonaggressive. A conduct disorder is characterized by behavior that violates the basic rights of others. Children with conduct disorders externalize tension and guilt; they blame others and see others as angry and hostile. Associated problems include poor frustration tolerance, irritability, and oppositional and provocative behavior. Youngsters diagnosed as having a *socialized conduct disorder* behave in an antisocial way but have social attachments to others; youngsters with an *undersocialized conduct disorder* are more callous, isolated, and egocentric in their antisocial behavior. These various categories further illustrate how complex the process of classification can be, because it is often hard to determine whether a child who is behaving antisocially "feels guilt" or "shows concern" and what the quality of a social relationship is like. Most children feel bad when they behave aggressively or antisocially, so these judgments are less often straightforward than they are matters of degree. Furthermore, it is often difficult to determine whether the antisocial behavior in a socialized, nonaggressive conduct disorder is secondary to depression, feelings of self-depreciation, and so on. Professional biases also influence decisions.

We see the same type of classification problems in the GAP. This system classifies such children as personality disorders with specific subcategories of Oppositional Personality, Tension-Discharge Disorders, and Sociosyntonic Personality Disorder. Children who have been emotionally neglected, who have grown up in undersocialized families, who have histories of antisocial behavior, and who project their hostility onto others are diagnosed as having personality disorders. Children who appear to be conflicted about their hostility and unhappy with themselves for having such feelings tend to be classified as neurotic.

As we saw in chapter 5, multivariate classification systems approach the problem of diagnosis quite differently from the DSM and the GAP. Rather than relying upon an individual's theoretical beliefs about what causes aggressiveness or what type of symptoms appear to occur together, classification systems empirically determine which problem behaviors cluster together in factor analyses. Using this approach, researchers consistently find that one of the strongest factors is composed of items describing aggressive, antisocial, undercontrolled behavior. Table 6–1 shows samples of the scales by Achenbach, Walker, Quay and Peterson, and Miller. All the scales have different items, but a common theme of hostility toward others, de-

struction of property, poor impulse control, and socialization problems is apparent.

Many of these children have difficulty in school (Walker, 1979). Probably the majority of youngsters classified as eligible for special education services could be described as aggressive and undercontrolled. Their disruptive, disturbing behavior interferes with their academic progress, causing schools to seek help for them. Many of these children have attention deficits and a wide variety of learning problems that include specific learning disabilities along with major motivational problems, but they are referred for their problematic behavior rather than their learning problems. It is only when they get into specialized settings that the learning problems are noticed. A number of these youngsters are also reported to have slightly lower

TABLE 6–1
Selected Items from Four Behavior Checklists That Sample the Aggressive, Acting-out Dimension of Problem Behavior

Scale	Sample Items
Behavior Problem Checklist (Quay & Peterson, 1975)	3. Disruptiveness, tendency to annoy others. 7. Fighting. 8. Temper tantrums. 10. Disobedience, difficulty in disciplinary control. 13. Destructiveness in regard to own or others' property.
Child Behavior Checklist (Achenbach, 1978)	3. Argues a lot. 22. Disobedient at home. 86. Stubborn, sullen, or irritable. 95. Temper tantrums or hot temper. 104. Unusually loud.
Louisville Behavior Checklist (Miller, 1977)	4. Constantly fighting or beating up others. 6. Has temper tantrums; yells, screams, cries, kicks feet over the least thing. 13. Bullies or frightens others. 29. Is disruptive; tendency to annoy and bother others. 36. Defies parents, is unmanageable.
Walker Problem Behavior Identification Checklist (Walker, 1983)	5. Argues and must have the last word in verbal exchanges. 7. Has temper tantrums. 11. Openly strikes back with angry behavior to teasing of other children. 13. Displays physical aggression toward objects or persons. 14. Reacts with defiance to instructions or commands.

than average verbal skills and intellectual ability, although the findings are not consistent (Hogan & Quay, 1984). Again, because they act out their frustrations in antisocial ways, they are often described as behaviorally disordered or conduct problems. Conduct disorders are consistently seen as more ominous when they occur in conjunction with low intelligence and academic achievement (Kauffman, 1985).

Some evidence suggests that when aggressive children become adolescents and are physically bigger, their aggressive behavior may bias clinicians, causing them to classify the youngsters as conduct disorders regardless of other symptoms. Lewis, Lewis, Unger, and Goldman (1984) studied 114 adolescents who had been hospitalized in psychiatric units. Youngsters who had been diagnosed as conduct disorders were compared to children who had never been so diagnosed. There were no significant symptomatic differences. Violent behavior, regardless of other symptoms, appeared to be the major distinguishing factor. Lewis et al. concluded that "with its focus on manifest behaviors and its lack of clear exclusionary criteria, the conduct disorder diagnosis obfuscates other potentially treatable neuropsychiatric disorders" (p. 514).

Incidence/Prevalence

Studies of pathological conditions during childhood and adolescence suggest that conduct disorders are the most common and most stable of all childhood psychiatric problems (Rutter, 1970). Recent evidence also suggests that conduct disorders are increasing. Robins (1986) conducted a cross-sectional study of 3007 adults residing in households in the St. Louis metropolitan area as part of a larger study on incidence and prevalence of DSM-III diagnoses in the adult population. These individuals came from three different mental health catchment areas: an inner city, a suburban area, and a mix of small towns and rural areas. Robins described her sample as closely resembling the U.S. population with respect to age and sex distribution, as somewhat more urban, and as having a somewhat higher proportion of black adults than the overall population. She conducted interviews with 80 percent of the selected households using the Diagnostic Interview Schedule (DIS) (Robins, Helzer, Croughan, & Ratcliff, 1981).

Persons reporting three symptoms of a conduct disorder before the age of 15 were classified as having had a conduct disorder as a child. Drawn from the DSM-III, symptoms of a conduct disorder were: stealing, sexual intercourse, fighting, discipline problems in school, chronic lying, truancy, expulsion or suspension from school, getting drunk or using illicit drugs, vandalism, doing poorly in school despite adequate intelligence (underachieving), getting arrested or sent to juvenile court, or running away

FIGURE 6–1
**Male vs. Female Rates of
Conduct Disorder in 5 Age Cohorts**

Reprinted by permission.

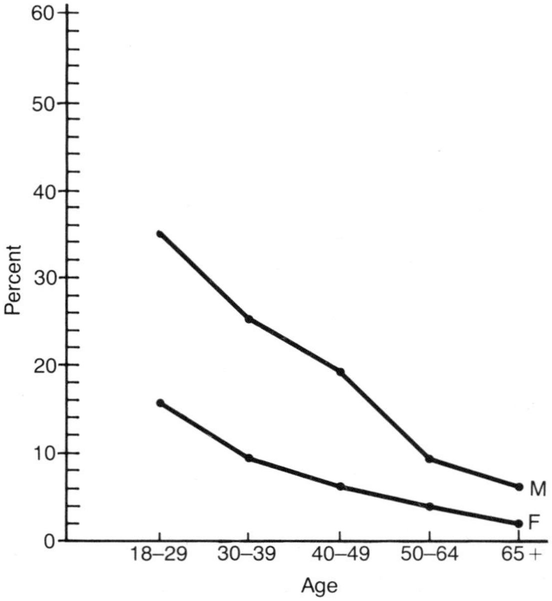

overnight. Subjects were grouped in age cohorts and interview data were compared across cohorts.

Results suggested that the rates of conduct disorder were greater in each successive birth cohort and that this pattern held for males and females. As you can see in Figure 6-1, in the cohort of 65+, 6 percent of the men and .5 percent of the women were classified as having been conduct disordered; whereas in the cohort age 19–29, 36 percent of the men and 13 percent of the women were classified as having been conduct disordered. Early death or lapses in memory were not taken as possible explanations for these rather alarming results. Robins postulates that one possible explanation for this dramatic rise in the rate of conduct disorders is increasing urbanization, which may have provided the younger cohorts with more anonymous opportunities for antisocial behavior. This hypothesis is under investigation. Another explanation Robins offers is the progressive secularization of values that may reduce internal barriers against antisocial behavior; however, these data do not permit that kind of analysis. Robins also notes that since the consequences of antisocial behavior remain grave, the rapid rise in the rate of conduct disorders is disturbing.

STABILITY OF AGGRESSION

One of the liveliest issues debated in the psychological literature is whether an individual's personality determines behavior or whether a situation and its demands and rewards determine behavior. Called the *consistency issue*, this debate covers a variety of complex issues, such as the degree of stability of certain aspects of behavior over time and across situations. Mischel (1968) concluded that noncognitive personality dimensions are generally not consistent. Aggressiveness, however, appears to be surprisingly stable (Lochman, 1984). Olweus (1979) reported that marked individual differences in habitual aggression level were manifested early, certainly by the age of three, and that this pattern of aggressiveness remained almost as stable over time as did intelligence measures. Compared to other behavioral patterns, it is perhaps the most stable pattern (Gersten, Langner, Eisenberg, Simcha-Fagan, & McCarthy, 1976).

Developmental Aspects

Aggressive behavior is a common and persistent problem among children of all ages, but how children behave aggressively does appear to change with age. Many years ago, Florence Goodenough (1931) noted, "With advancing age, the forms of behavior displayed during anger become more definitely directed toward a given end, while the primitive bodily responses of the infant and young child are gradually replaced by substitute reactions commonly of a somewhat less violent and more symbolic character" (p. 69). Many other authors have also observed that between the ages of two and six, children begin to rely on speech rather than on physical attack when angry.

Another age change Goodenough noted was the nature of "after reactions." Young children's expressions of anger tended to be transient and fairly short-lived, whereas after the age of four, children tended to sulk, whine, brood, and pout after an outburst. She also reported that infants' angry outbursts were most often caused by physical discomforts and need for attention, whereas toddlers tended to become angry in response to efforts to "habit train." Around the age of three, social difficulties with peers precipitated anger, and this remained so for several years.

Likewise, Patterson (1975) found that two- and three-year-olds displayed the highest rates of whining, crying, yelling, and other high intensity, coercive behaviors. Children's parents became less tolerant of such behaviors with age, and consequently intervened more frequently. By the age of four, a substantial reduction in the number of negative commands, destructive behavior, and attempts to humiliate was reported. Five-year-olds were noted to use less noncompliance, negativism, and negative physical actions than did younger children.

Hartup (1974) found other age differences. He hypothesized that (1) when compared to preschool children, grade school children would display a greater proportion of hostile, "person-directed" aggression than "object-oriented" instrumental aggression; (2) threats to self-esteem would lead to person-oriented hostility rather than object-oriented aggression, especially in older children; and (3) when goals were blocked, instrumental aggression would be more likely to result, especially among younger children. Since children under the age of six have limited capacities for understanding others' motives and intentions and for evaluating themselves, these hypotheses clearly have a developmental component. Results suggested that, overall, older children were not as aggressive as younger children, that older black children were more aggressive than older white children, and that the age and race differences were accounted for mostly by instrumental aggression. Among the older subjects, a significantly higher percentage of aggressive interactions were hostile, as predicted. Also as predicted, blocking of goals produced a significantly higher percentage of instrumental aggression among younger children.

When considering developmental changes, however, situational factors are relevant in addition to cognitive factors. Social learning theorists maintain that age changes in aggressive behavior are largely the result of an ongoing process of children's learning to discriminate under what circumstances and in what situations certain behaviors will or will not be rewarded (Bandura & Walters, 1963). Shantz and Pentz (1972) list examples of discrimination learning: "it is more appropriate to respond aggressively to arbitrary than nonarbitrary frustration; that aggression toward siblings and peers is more appropriate than aggression directed toward authority figures; and that aggression toward people unable to control their provocative behavior is unacceptable."

Sex Differences

Studies report that boys are more aggressive than girls. Eme (1979) describes "the decisive male preponderance in aggressive behavior" as "the most unequivocal sex difference in the literature" (p. 583). The reason for this difference has been debated for several decades. A common explanation is *differential socialization*. Dramatic support came from Mead's (1949) observations that among the Tchambuli, women were the more aggressive, dominant personalities. Brown (1965) points out, however, that when the Tchambuli went to war, it was the men who fought.

Although the differential socialization hypothesis has wide support, few consider male aggressiveness a socialization issue alone. Maccoby and Jacklin (1974) reviewed 94 studies on sex differences in aggression that covered data on humans from two years of age through adulthood. Fifty-two studies reported males to be more aggressive than females, five found the reverse, and 37 found no sex differences in aggression, prompting Maccoby and Jacklin to contend that males' greater aggressiveness has a biological component. A number of other researchers note biological differences between males and females. Sheldon found positive correlations between mesomorphy (a physique that is strong, tough, resistant to injury, and generally equipped for strenuous and exacting physical demands) and aggressiveness and delinquency (Hall & Lindzey, 1957). Animal research demonstrates that, although the male of a species is generally more aggressive in both laboratory and naturalistic settings, injecting the female pre- or postnatally with the male hormone *androgen* causes her to become equally aggressive (Eme, 1979). Similarly, Willerman (1979) found that boys were more likely to have a higher activity level than girls.

These studies have been criticized, however, for several serious methodological defects. For example, Tieger (1980) reviewed the work of Maccoby and Jacklin, as well as other more recent work, and rejected the "biological predisposition" hypothesis. Tieger notes that the form of androgen used in the studies was much more potent than naturally-circulating androgens. He also observes that the introduction of androgen into the body causes weight gain and masculinized appearance, changes that could affect interactions but which the researchers did not take into account. Tieger also observes that males are not reliably more aggressive than females before the age of six, a finding he believes refutes a biological hypothesis. He poses instead a dynamic person-environment interactive model to account for the sex-typing for aggression. Despite Tieger's compelling arguments, however, questions remain as to the reasons for these differences, although their existence seems generally accepted.

ETIOLOGICAL HYPOTHESES

As to why some youngsters become hyperaggressive, we find evidence for both external (social and environmental) factors and internal (organismic and personality) factors. While no one can answer the question of etiology simply and conclusively, accumulating evidence indicates that the etiology is complex, rooted in a variety of causes.

Psychodynamic Hypotheses

From this perspective aggression is seen as an innate force or drive that must be channeled and civilized. Freud (1930) viewed aggression as a drive equal in importance to the sex drive. He stated, "the inclination to aggression is an original, self-subsisting instinctual disposition in man, and . . . it constitutes the greatest impediment to civili-

zation . . . Man's natural aggressive instinct, the hostility of each against all and of all against each, opposes this programme of civilization."

Since Freud's day psychodynamic clinicians have continued to integrate research and clinical observations into their dynamic formulations of why children become aggressive. Common to most formulations is a *dysfunctional ego* that is unable, for a variety of reasons, to cope adequately with environmental demands. Berman (1984) explains:

The psychic apparatus, a coherent organization of psychic functions, is made up of three agencies, referred to as the id, ego, and superego. The psychic functions of these agencies seek to establish a homeostasis between the internal needs of the human and the external environment that provides these needs. The psychic apparatus has its organic basis in the brain, the most complex of all human organs. . . . Unlike other animal species, man's aggression is not controlled by primitive instincts in order to supply the essential needs to survive. Instead, a long period of time and arduous training are required to integrate aggressive impulses into a harmonious relationship with other psychic functions. This creates a serious dilemma for man—a ghost in the machine, so to speak—for aggression has to be modulated psychologically by the ego, not by the built-in mechanisms that control the instincts of other species. This ego is highly vulnerable to both internal influences of a physical or psychological nature and external influences from maternal nurturance to social expectations. Therefore, many children are unable to develop and maintain sufficient control over this drive. (p. 4)

Thus, from this perspective, defective egos are the basis of hyperaggressiveness, coming as a momentary loss of control because of the excessive demands of a situation or resulting from chronic failures in development. Early experiences are believed to significantly affect the developing personality. When children experience excessive neglect, abuse, or personal stress from external or internal factors, the developing personality, specifically the ego, expends its psychic energy merely coping with the stressors. Other more fortunate youngsters are free to spend their psychic energy in gaining greater understanding of and control over themselves and their world, whereas the less fortunate youngsters do not develop age appropriate skills in self-control and in social relations. Therefore, they perceive and react differently from well-adjusted youngsters. Children who encounter problems in development experience a cumulative deficit that significantly affects the evolving personality.

A wide variety of problems manifest themselves in aggressive behavior. Clinicians who subscribe to this perspective often note that anger is a secondary emotion; primary emotions are sadness and fear. Many youngsters who behave aggressively do so to protect themselves from their own fears and pain. Some of the aggressive reactions are transitory and followed by remorse and guilt, while others are chronic and so ingrained in the personality that the children feel little or no remorse for their behavior.

Especially when aggressive reactions are common, vicious cycles develop in these youngsters' lives (Long, 1966). Conflicts cause their faulty egos to react defensively in an effort to ward off or protect themselves from unpleasant feelings. Their defensive behavior, however, is problematic, because of their inadequate coping strategies; they become active, assaultive, impulsive, and generally disruptive and antisocial. Rather than allay their anxieties, this behavior gets them deeper in trouble by antagonizing others and thus supporting their original fears and self-doubts. Through their defective superegos, or consciences, they are able to delude themselves into believing that their actions are justified and reasonable rather than antisocial and hurtful to others.

Most of the etiological hypotheses from this perspective are grounded in observations gathered from clinical practice, and the supporting data derive largely from clinical case studies. Because little of the literature is based upon systematically-collected, large-

group empirical data, some criticize the validity of this position. One need only read the observations of researchers and clinicians such as Fritz Redl to understand why support for psychodynamic notions is widespread, especially in mental health settings (Redl, 1966; Redl & Wineman, 1957).

Organic Hypotheses

Biological factors have been related to aggressive behavior in both adult human populations and in animals; however, much less work has been done with children. Brown and Goodwin (1984) attribute this partly to the difficulty in defining aggression as precisely as necessary for scientific or experimental work. One solution to this definitional problem has been to use samples of delinquents, but as we will see in Chapter 11, not all delinquents are hyperaggressive.

Another problem in conducting this type of research is the ever-changing nature of the developing human organism. An individual's biological factors change with age, making controlled research difficult. Despite the problems, organic hypotheses that have been explored can be grouped under one of three general etiological factors: genetic, biochemical, and central nervous system disorders.

Research on *genetic influences* has gained impetus from studies reporting that the risk for becoming delinquent substantially increases if one or more of the family members has a criminal record (Farrington, Gundry, & West, 1975). It is necessary in this kind of research to eliminate the confounding variable of environmental influences, which has been done through two different approaches: the twin method and adoption studies. The twin method compares genetically identical twins (monozygotic) to same-sex fraternal twins (dizygotic). Since both members of each pair share the same home environment, the assumption is that differences in concordance rates result from a genetic contribution. Although many of the investigations have been plagued with small samples, results consistently yield a higher concordance rate for identical twins than for fraternal twins (Rosenthal, 1975). For example, Mednick and Hutchings (1978) compared the criminality concordance rates in monozygotic and dizygotic twins and found a much higher rate in the monozygotic twins (36 percent as compared to 12.5 percent). In adoption studies, investigators track adopted children and compare their adjustment as adults to both their biological and adopted families. Two major studies report that adoptees whose biological parents were criminals are significantly more likely to become criminals than those whose biological parents have no record (Dorfman, 1984).

With respect to *biochemical bases* of aggression, investigators have pursued several hypotheses. One of the more promising approaches has to do with neurotransmitters. Adequate brain functioning depends upon transmission of messages across synapses from neuron to neuron along established pathways. Special chemicals, called *neurotransmitters*, help the neurons "fire." Much research is underway to clarify the nature of the relationship between neurotransmitter anomalies and pathological behavior, especially aggression (Dorfman, 1984; Brown & Goodwin, 1984).

Evidence for central nervous system disorders rests largely in studies comparing neurological and psychological indicators of brain dysfunction in groups of aggressive, delinquent youngsters with groups of other youngsters. Various electroencephalogram (EEG) abnormalities have also been associated with aggressive and assaultive behavior in both adults and children (Mikkelsen, Brown, Minichiello, Millican, & Rapoport, 1982). Lewis (1976) studied 285 children referred by the juvenile court. Eighteen manifested symptoms suggestive of psychomotor seizures, and all had experienced episodes of apparent loss of fully conscious contact with

reality. Fourteen of the 18 had physically assaulted others, which the authors interpreted as suggestive of an association between psychomotor epileptic symptoms and aggressiveness. Pincus and Tucker (1978) reviewed studies that found various forms of neurological damage in individuals who were repeatedly violent under minimally provocative situations. In a later study, Lewis, Pincus, Shanok, and Glaser (1982) studied 97 adjudicated delinquents in a Connecticut correctional facility. They obtained histories of violent behavior as well as thorough neuropsychiatric evaluations. Clinical features classified as psychomotor symptoms included:

Observed episodes of periodic loss of fully conscious contact with reality; loss of memory for particular acts . . . followed by confusion, headache, sleep, or fatigue; episodes of inability to understand spoken words or conversations despite the awareness that people were speaking; frequent dizzy spells, falling episodes, or blackouts unrelated . . . to alcohol or drug use, illness, or hypotension; spontaneous episodes of emotion such as anxiety, fear, or rage, with no identifiable psychodynamic provocations; multiple episodes of déjà vu; olfactory or gustatory hallucinations; episodes of macropsia, micropsia, or other kinds of metamorphopsias; dreamlike states; and automatic behaviors and/or forced thinking. (p. 883)

EEG abnormalities and/or a history of generalized seizures were counted if coupled with other psychomotor symptoms. Seventy-eight percent of the boys studied had one or more signs or symptoms of psychomotor epilepsy and a significant positive correlation was found between number of psychomotor signs and symptoms and degree of violence ($r = .384$, $p < .001$). The clinicians judged that 11 of the 97 definitely had psychomotor seizures and 7 probably had them. They then studied the timing and nature of violent acts. Five violent acts had been committed during a seizure and six probably were, although the authors note the figures were likely underestimated. They conclude that psychomotor epilepsy was far more prevalent in delinquent populations than in the general population (18 percent in their sample as compared to .5 percent in the general population).

Wolff, Waber, Bauermeister, Cohen, and Ferber (1982) also found more minor pathology or "soft" signs in a delinquent sample than in two control groups, one a lower-middle class area, drawn from the same geographic area as the detention facility, and one drawn from a nearby community with distinctly upper-middle class demographic characteristics. Neuropsychological measures were also obtained. In the delinquent sample, neurological functioning predicted language performance, but this was not the case with the controls. Wolff et al. point out, however, that minor neurological signs have been related to poor obstetrical or pediatric care and infantile undernutrition, and, indeed, these signs were more frequent in their lower-middle class controls.

Krynicki (1978) compared three groups: behavior disordered individuals who had histories of multiple assaultive incidents, behavior disordered individuals who had histories of two or fewer assaultive episodes, and individuals with diagnosed organic brain syndromes. The behavior disordered group with histories of two or fewer assaultive episodes differed from the other two groups with respect to EEG abnormalities, degree of established hand dominance, perseveration errors in a visuomotor task, and verbal short-term memory. The assaultive individuals and the organic brain syndrome individuals were indistinguishable on the measures used in the study.

Most clinicians acknowledge the importance of this perspective, but feel it has little direct relevance to practice. Knowing that a child lost control and behaved aggressively may help clinicians be more tolerant of the youngster, realizing that the aggression was not personally directed at them; however, the behavior must still be controlled. Even when medication is used, other approaches are still needed.

Social Learning Hypotheses

Social learning theorists see the origin and maintenance of aggressive behavior as learned, through such processes as imitation and reinforcement. According to Kauffman (1985),

Social learning theory asserts that aversive experiences (which may include frustration or unpleasant stimuli of any kind) produce a state of emotional arousal and that the anticipated consequences of a given behavior (which may have been gained through direct experience, observational learning, or cognitive processes) generate motivation. The outcome of arousal and motivation may vary greatly from individual to individual depending upon a variety of factors, such as reinforcement history, physiological status, and the social situation. Therefore, the same aversive experience may cause some persons to exhibit dependent behavior, others to strive to achieve, some to withdraw resignedly from the situation, still others to aggress, and so on. (p. 221)

Kauffman (1985) summarizes findings from social learning theorists, primarily Bandura and Goldstein, that pose hypotheses about how children become aggressive:

- Children learn many aggressive responses through observation of models. Family members, peers, and other persons known to the child or characters in fiction or the mass media may serve as models.
- Children are more likely to imitate high status individuals and/or individuals who are either rewarded or not punished for aggressive behavior.
- Children learn aggressive behavior when they behave aggressively and either receive no aversive consequences or successfully obtain rewards by harming or overcoming their victims.
- Children are more likely to be aggressive when they are aversively stimulated by

behaviors such as physical assault, verbal threats, taunts, or insults; when their goal-directed behavior is thwarted; or when positive reinforcement decreases or ends. Through observation and/or practice, some children learn that they can obtain what they want by engaging in aggressive behavior. This is especially true when alternative means of obtaining reinforcement are not readily available or have not been learned, and when aggression is sanctioned by social authorities.

- Children's aggressive behavior is maintained by external reinforcement, such as tangible and social rewards; by vicarious reinforcement, such as observing others gain rewards through aggression; and by self-reinforcement.

- Cognitive processes that justify hostile action, such as "I didn't start it" or "He made me do it," or that dehumanize the victim, such as "he's trash" or a "retard," also perpetuate aggression.

- Punishment may heighten or maintain aggression when there are no positive alternatives to the punished response or when punishment is delayed or inconsistent.

- In males and in children who have a history of aggressiveness, viewing televised aggression increases aggressive behavior.

- Families of aggressive children are characterized by high rates of aggressiveness in all family members and by parental use of inconsistent and punitive control techniques.

- Aggressive behavior exerts a coercive influence on others. When a person acts aggressively toward another, it is likely that the other will respond with aggressiveness.

Hence, social learning theorists stress the importance of learning through direct or observed experiences while also acknowledging the importance of individual human differences. We find widespread support for this position. Social learning hypotheses for explaining aggressiveness are based upon research, much of which has been carefully controlled and executed. Behavioral therapists have been effective in changing aggressive behavior (as we will see when we discuss intervention), and this approach can be implemented efficiently and effectively. The approach has had particular relevance for educators and other school personnel because it is easy to use in group settings. In addition, many of the tenets of social learning theory fit easily with other popular theories, such as the interactionist.

Social Cognition

Increasingly, researchers are paying attention to social cognition and how it relates to aggressive behavior (Camp, 1977; Mullis & Hanson, 1983; Asarnow & Callan, 1985; Milich & Dodge, 1984; Anolik, 1981; Santostefano & Rieder, 1984; Dodge & Frame, 1982). They hypothesize that a developmental lag or deficit in social cognition causes much of the behavior classified as deviant. From this perspective, one might argue that it is not the behavior that is deviant, but how children see and understand behavior, which can be attributed to a developmental delay or lag. For example, Dodge and his colleagues (Dodge, 1980; Dodge & Frame, 1982; Richard & Dodge, 1982; Dodge, Murphy, & Buchsbaum, 1984) consider cognition an important factor in inhibiting defensive aggression. When someone believes a peer intentionally caused a negative outcome, the typical response is aggression against the peer; when one perceives that a peer caused a negative outcome accidentally, the typical response is inhibition of aggression.

Since a child's abilities to differentiate others' intentions and integrate that information into his own behavior are thought to be developmentally acquired milestones, Dodge (1980) hypothesizes that variations in children's defensive aggressive behavior may relate to variations in cognitive development.

In other words, the 10-year-old who is persistently aggressive in unintentionally negative interactions may be so because of a *cue-utilization* deficiency related to a lag in development or because of a *cue-distortion* related to his expectation of others. In a series of studies, Dodge and Frame (1982) found that these distortions ·or biases exist under different situations.

This intention-cue detection skill has also been related to social competence. Using carefully developed videotapes, Dodge, Murphy, and Buchsbaum (1984) found that older children were more able than younger children to use social cues in identifying prosocial and accidental intentions. This skill was independent of verbal skills and general perceptual discrimination. Even kindergartners were able to accurately label a hostile cue 91 percent of the time. The researchers also found that both socially rejected and socially neglected groups of children were less accurate than popular children in detecting prosocial and accidental behavior; when they were inaccurate, they were biased toward making hostile attributions. Other studies (Coie, Dodge, & Coppotelli, 1982) show that socially neglected children tend to be withdrawn, thus raising the question as to why some children·respond to a hostile attribution with aggression while others withdraw.

Camp (1977) studied the verbal self-regulatory behavior of aggressive and normal 6½- to 8½-year-old boys. She observes that an absence of verbal mediation or ineffective verbal mediation, as well as fast reaction time, led to poorer performances by the aggressive boys on a number of cognitive tasks. Since these differences could not be attributed to differences in intellectual or verbal ability, she poses a *production deficiency*—that is, failure to exercise linguistic control over one's behavior.

Investigators have examined the perspective-taking ability of disturbed and delinquent youngsters. This skill involves the ability to understand how things appear to another individual, how they look from another's perspective. Rotenberg (1974) distinguishes between affective and cognitive role-taking. Affective role-taking is more similar to sympathy, whereas cognitive role-taking is more similar to empathy. Waterman, Sobesky, Sivlern, Aoki, and McCaulay (1981) compared heterogeneous emotionally disturbed and normal fifth and sixth graders and found significant differences on cognitive perspective-taking. An unexpected finding was that teacher ratings on an antisocial behavior scale related positively to affective perspective-taking skills.

Investigating problem-solving skills, Richard and Dodge (1982) examined the relationship between social adjustment and the cognitive skills of solving interpersonal problems. Samples of popular, aggressive, and isolated boys at two age levels were given six hypothetical situations and asked to generate solutions to the problems. They were then asked to generate solutions to problems the experimenter presented. The popular subgroup generated more solutions than either of the other two groups, which did not differ. All groups initially generated "appropriate" solutions to the problems, but only the popular group could generate a number of appropriate solutions. All groups could evaluate the effectiveness of solutions when they were presented.

The Social Problem-Solving Test–Revised (Rubin, 1983) is an example of the type of instrument used to assess children's problem solving abilities. Figure 6–2 illustrates the types of social dilemmas children are asked about. When shown this card, the child is told, "This girl's name is Tammy and this is Colleen. Tammy is five years old and Colleen is three years old. Tammy is older than Colleen. Colleen has been playing with the balloon for a long, long time. Tammy would really like to play with the balloon. What do you think Tammy could say or do so that she could play with the balloon?" After the child responds, the examiner asks, "If that didn't work, what else could Tammy do or say so that she could have the balloon?" The examiner then asks, "What would you do or say if you wanted to play with the balloon?"

These are the responses of four aggressive, acting-out youngsters who were students in a residential treatment program for emotionally disturbed children:

Child #1's responses to the three questions:

Question #1: That's a nice balloon. Can I hold it?

Question #2: Say "Your balloon might pop" or be sneaky and say "There's a red place on your arm. I'll hold your balloon while you get it off." Then take the scissors and cut the string.

Question #3: Pop it or cut the string, grab it and say "Forget you!"

Child #2's responses to the three questions:

Question #1: Can I play with my balloon now? If you don't, I'll pop your balloon.

Question #2: Shoot him down with the shotgun.

Question #3: It's my balloon.

FIGURE 6–2
Sample Card from the Social Problem-Solving Test–Revised

Reprinted by permission of the author.

Child #3's responses to the three questions:

Question #1: Go up and grab it.
Question #2: Ask first, then grab; go buy her own balloon; throw it away so wouldn't fight.
Question #3: Pop it so then both of us couldn't play with it.

Child #4's responses to the three questions:

Question #1: I'll let you play with my racetrack.
Question #2: I'll get one bigger and prettier; you won't be my friend.
Question #3: Could I please hold the balloon?

It appears that the children understood, at least superficially, that polite requests were appropriate, but these children did not utilize polite responses consistently; rather, they quickly reverted to threatening, hostile responses.

Critics of social cognition approaches maintain that human behavior is determined by more complex factors than cognition and development alone; nonetheless, research is providing useful insights into how youngsters perceive and understand their environments.

Interactional Hypotheses

In their "goodness of fit" model, Chess and Thomas (1984) pose an integrative approach to understanding the development of psychological problems in children and adolescents. Their work has grown out of their involvement with the New York Longitudinal Study, one of the few prospective longitudinal studies of childhood behavior disorders. This study followed 133 children and their families from birth to early adulthood, with particular emphasis on the development of behavior problems over time. This interactive model posits:

When the organism's capacities, motivations and style of behaving and the demands and expectations of the environment are in accord, then goodness of fit results. Such consonance between organism and environment potentiates optimal positive development. Should there be dissonance between the capacities and characteristics of the organism on the one hand and the environmental opportunities and demands on the other hand, there is poorness of fit, which leads to maladaptive functioning and distorted development. Goodness of fit and consonance, poorness of fit and dissonance are never abstractions. They have meaning only in terms of the values and demands of a given socioeconomic group or culture. (Chess & Thomas, 1984, p. 21)

One of the important child characteristics that has been investigated is temperament, which was defined as the "how" of the child's behavior. Nine categories of temperament were scored on a 3-point scale (see Chapter 4), and temperamental constellations were identified. The first type, called the "easy child," described children who were positive in their approaches to new stimuli, adapted quickly and easily to changes in their environment, and quickly developed regular sleeping and eating schedules. "Easy children" constituted 40 percent of their sample. At the opposite end of the behavioral spectrum was the "difficult child." Children so classified included babies who exhibited irregular patterns of eating, sleeping, bowel movements; who tended to cry a great deal, to be irritable, and to have difficulty with change. These children constituted 10 percent of the sample. A third type was the "slow-to-warm-up child." Children in this category were between the other two types; with time, they adapted, and their responses were less intense or negative than those of the "difficult child," but they were notably less flexible than the "easy children." Slow-to-warm-up children constituted about 15 percent of the sample.

Chess and Thomas hypothesize that when the expectations and demands of the environment are in accord with the child's ability to respond, "consonance" results, making optimal development possible. "Dissonance" occurs when the environment's demands and the child's capacities do not match. Chess and Thomas believe that because difficult children are more demanding and less flexible, they are at greater risk for developmental problems; indeed, more of them had problems in childhood that were severe enough to warrant diagnosis. The few children who developed severe problems, however, were not necessarily those classified as "at risk." Idiosyncratic environmental factors were seen as determinants of some of the serious problems. For example, "Bernice" was classified at age three as having an easy temperament and her parents as having low parental conflict. Throughout her early and middle childhood years, she had a high activity level and intense reactions in selected situations, but her parents' firm, consistent, and supportive limits helped her behavior problems to quickly disappear. At age 13, with the onset of puberty, she again began having behavioral problems; shortly thereafter, her father died unexpectedly. Her mother, bereft of her husband and his stabilizing influence and under stress from her full-time work and the needs of three other youngsters, was unable to deal effectively with Bernice's problems. Bernice's problems escalated, and she developed a "severe sociopathic behavior disorder," with symptoms that included truancy, sexual promiscuity, stealing, and lying. Her relationship with her family became so destructive to all members that when she reached 18, her mother told Bernice that she was on her own and that she (the mother) would no longer be legally responsible for Bernice. Bernice worked in a bar for two years, then applied for professional training at a top art institute. Initially she was turned down because of poor high school grades, so she went to a less demanding school, made good grades, and reapplied. She was admitted and successfully completed her training. Through fortuitous connections, she obtained a job on a low rung of the career ladder, but with her talent and persistence, she was promoted and became successful. At age 22, Chess and Thomas (1984) saw her as

. . . psychologically prepared to take advantage and prosper if she is fortunate in her career opportunities and in the positive attributes of her next heterosexual relationship. If, however, she meets with serious difficulties in her work or with the next man to whom she becomes attached, it appears a toss-up as to whether she could cope successfully and productively with such a stressful situation. (p. 125)

Although Chess and Thomas's data leave many questions as to what causes a conduct disorder to develop, one may infer from these data that complex factors contribute to development of conduct disorders. The causes are complex, not always predictable, and influenced by environmental as well as individual factors.

INTERVENTIONS

Effective interventions for managing aggressive behaviors include individual, family, and group psychotherapy; various behavioral interventions; medication; and variations of cognitive interventions. A number of factors are relevant in deciding which approach to use: appropriateness of the intervention in a given setting (long-term, insight-oriented psychotherapy is not appropriate for short-term crisis treatment settings); the professional's type and level of skill (teachers do not administer medicine or engage in regressive, dynamic psychotherapy); and the responsible professional's biases and beliefs (a behaviorally-oriented clinician is likely to be more effective when using strategies he believes to be effective than when using an approach he doubts). Several interventions have apparently been effective with some types of problems, so professional preferences can be honored; other types of problems have been more resistant to lasting change. Thus, whatever approach is used, the most important consideration is whether the youngster is responding positively.

Psychodynamically-based Approaches

The psychodynamic perspective has an extensive body of clinical literature on how to understand and deal with aggressive youngsters. Over the years, there have been several changes in how psychodynamic clinicians treat aggressive youngsters. Historically, a permissive, cathartic, "get-it-off-your-chest" and "get-it-out-of-your-system" approach was the intervention of choice. The assumption was that aggressive youngsters behaved as they did because of their unconscious, hostile feelings, and that if they were given the opportunity to vent their feelings with a trusted, caring person, they would come to understand their problems and no longer need to act out aggressively. For some, this method still seems to work. Especially for verbal, fairly bright youngsters who are suffering conflict and guilt, expressive, fairly permissive psychotherapy can be beneficial, as Amanda's case illustrates:

Amanda's parents divorced when she was 13 years old. Her father had an affair and ultimately chose to leave the family. Amanda's mother and two brothers were furious and cut off all contact with the father. Amanda felt she should do the same, but she had mixed feelings. She wanted contact with him, and she knew and liked the woman with whom he was involved, but she was also furious with him for causing so much pain in the family. These intense and conflicting feelings were difficult for her to handle; consequently, she became more and more belligerent and hostile. Her acting out was cyclical; each time she saw her father, talked to him, or in any way made a gesture toward him, such as buying him a birthday present, she became sarcastic and oppositional at home. She was uncooperative and had major temper tantrums, calling her mother and brothers hateful names. After each major outburst, she was

punished, which seemed to make her feel better. She would become repentant and apologize for the angry and hurtful things she had said. Her behavior would remain reasonable until her next wave of guilt, which usually occurred when she had contact with her father.

Amanda felt guilty about her feelings and acted out this guilt in a verbally aggressive manner. She was a bright, verbal youngster who had had reasonably good relationships with her family before the parents' divorce. Guilt over her anger caused her to feel conflicted and "bad." When she was 14 she began therapy with a male therapist who encouraged her to express her feelings about the "terrible mess" in her life. As she began to dredge past events up from her memory, old hurts surfaced and were reexamined. It was beneficial for her to discover that others were not horrified by her thoughts and feelings and that there were understandable reasons for her feeling so angry and guilty. Her aggressiveness subsided; she later commented to her therapist, "How could you stand me? I was awful!" She had not wanted to be so angry and hostile, but her feelings and the guilt over these feelings overwhelmed her. Therapy helped her sort out these issues, become more accepting of her feelings, and learn how to handle her feelings appropriately, instead of self-destructively.

But many aggressive youngsters have difficulty forming trusting, dependent relationships with adults. They are not comfortable dealing with their problems verbally, and tend to have an outburst, then forget what upset them. For some children, expressing aggression seems to beget more aggression rather than abate it, and when therapists bring up conflictual topics, these youngsters act out rather than work to resolve the issues. There has been a move away from treating these children with permissive, individual psychotherapy. Interventions based in ego psychology that are designed to help the child develop inner controls and better means of discharging tension are often more appropriate. We will mention only a few examples of psychodynamically-based psychotherapeutic interventions; for additional reading in this area, Fritz Redl's *When We Deal With Children* offers illuminating descriptions of this approach.

Psychodynamically-based family therapy has been tried with families characterized by "dissociated relationships" (Rabinowitz, 1969); that is, the parents did not see themselves as in charge and as the caregivers of the family. The acting-out child was often running the family, and family members derived no pleasure from being a family. Therapy focused on helping the parents learn how to guide and discipline their children while also helping the youngsters accept more personal responsibility.

Family therapy can be particularly appropriate when the aggressive youngster has become the scapegoat of the family and a way for family members to resist dealing with their own problems. Therapists encourage the expression of family members' individual feelings, to highlight the diversity of opinion within the family that is typically avoided. The identified child has usually become the misdirected target of the other members' feelings, and the child is in turn acting out the conflicts. It can be difficult to help people face feelings they fear and then to see how the consequences of these feelings affect their actions. Families are resistant to change, and therapists need a great deal of skill to see the conflictual issues and help families begin to deal with their problems.

As a consequence of the difficulties of working with aggressive youngsters and their parents on an outpatient basis, many therapists opt for separating the aggressive child from the family, to make the therapeutic work more manageable and understandable. In well-staffed residential programs, an around-the-clock treatment program enables youngsters to function in a therapeutic milieu. Therapy, remedial school, recreation, and other remedial and therapeutic activities are scheduled throughout the day. Professionals work closely as a team to implement the therapeutic goals. In this kind of setting, professionals can observe the youngster in different activities and with different people, which helps them understand when and why the child behaves as he does. It also contributes to therapeutic communication, because the therapist knows what is going on with the child rather than relying on the child or the parents to convey the difficulties. When the child knows the teacher will tell the therapist about an outburst, the child is often more willing to bring it up himself, giving his version of the problem.

Because many children explode and then forget their problems, the Life Space Interview technique has been developed to deal therapeutically with here-and-now problems as they arise. It is fruitless to wait until the therapy hour to explore these children's feelings; the problem is gone by then, and the therapist is merely bringing up a new problem. Furthermore, the 50-minute hour is in itself hard for some of these youngsters, who have trouble talking about their feelings for any length of time.

Introduced by Fritz Redl, this technique utilizes clinical concepts of interviewing in naturalistic settings. Adults in the child's life are trained to deal with problems as they arise and for no longer than the child can tolerate. During the course of the day, the child may participate in several short Life Space Interviews.

Fritz Redl (1966) explained how and why the Life Space Interview and the therapeutic milieu were used at Pioneer House, one of the early and excellent residential treatment programs for "children who hate."

Among the kinds of therapeutic help the children on our ward are badly in need of is that of at least partial "superego repair." No matter what else ails them, something went wrong in the building and development of the type of value sensitivity or conscience children normally develop over the years. It is our impression that the more serious cases of superego damage can never be tackled by any kind of individual therapy alone; it must also be accompanied by an all-out total life-space engulfing approach, well attuned to this job, with plenty of "clinical resilience" built in, in order to guarantee a long-range focus on this major task. Beyond what the individual therapist can do for such a child, it is our impression that we must provide living space for that child in which he can afford to let go of distorted defenses and allow himself the necessary emotional ties that have to precede any primary value identification whatever. It also seems clear to us that all experiences of daily life have to be geared to avoid guilt-flooding panic and more paranoid interpretations of daily life events than are compatible with an already heightened sibling rivalry. (p. 78)

The Life Space Interview is the tool through which adults in the child's life help the child let go of distorted defenses and avoid guilt-flooding panic. The interview can be conducted with an individual child or with groups of children; it can be conducted in the classroom, on the playground, or just about anywhere. This flexible, psychotherapeutic technique has great clinical effectiveness for people who are trained to use it.

Morse (1980) describes a seven-step process for conducting a Life Space Interview. The primary goal is "a degree of behavioral compliance accompanied by life space relief" (p. 267), which he sees as fostering adjustment. These steps are:

1. Find out how the child (or group) perceived the event that precipitated the LSI.

2. Determine whether the child sees the event as isolated; if so, it hardly merits a great deal of attention. If the adult sees it as a central issue but the child does not, focus with the child on other similar episodes so that eventually the child will understand its significance.

3. After learning how the child perceived the event, clarify what really happened. As the event is reconstructed, recognize concomitant feelings and impulses.

4. Throughout the LSI, but particularly as the child's distortions are challenged, strive to convey a sense of acceptance. Try to convey to the child the right to be heard without condoning the problem behavior. Respond to the feelings behind the defense rather than attack the defenses.

5. As a strategy for helping the child learn better ways of dealing with similar situations, explore the implications or logical consequences of behavior in a nonpunitive, nonjudgmental way.

6. Look for sources of motivation to change in the child. The constant question is, "What can I do to help the child change?"

7. After examining motivation to change, the interview may be concluded. If the child has not arrived at a resolution, explain reality limits in a neutral, unmoralistic way. If a plan can be worked out for resolving the problem or for preventing similar problems in the future, take steps in that direction. Before agreeing to the plan, feel confident that the plan will be successful.

To maximize the potential of an LSI, Redl and Wineman (1957) suggest the need for certain conditions.

● *Sufficient time.* Starting a serious discussion five minutes before the school bus comes ensures that the discussion will be rushed and probably unproductive.

● *The child should be in the right frame of mind.* The child must be psychologically ready to enter into a discussion. A child who is acutely upset is not in a condition to consider a situation calmly. Likewise, if the child has settled down and put the problem out of her mind, bringing it up again may reactivate her fury.

● *The adult should be in the right frame of mind.* While an adult is still recovering from fury triggered by a child's outburst, it is clearly not a good time to initiate an LSI. The adult's own feelings would interfere.

● *Appropriate setting.* Airing private issues in public can make the child uncomfortable and interfere with the interview and the adult-child relationship. Conducting an interview in a highly stimulating environment may prove too distracting.

- *The issue should be closely related to other issues the child is presently working on.* To bombard children with all their problems at once is likely to overwhelm them and accomplish nothing. Problems should be raised one at a time and in a careful sequence.

- *The child should be psychologically ready to understand.* Focusing on issues a child is firmly defending against risks either antagonizing the child or being dismissed as incompetent. The problem must be "close to consciousness." Underlying this issue is the belief that people understand and remember selectively; hence, issues should be raised when children are ready to understand.

Much of the literature on these techniques is based on clinical case studies. Although clinically affirmed as effective, group efficacy data are relatively scarce, probably because evaluation of these approaches is so complex. For example, if one questions the effectiveness of psychotherapy, one must ensure that the intervention one is evaluating was standardly administered, which is difficult to do. Most evidence implies that psychotherapy is an interactive process; the client's and therapist's interactions affect each other's actions. Thus, it is probably impossible to hold the treatment constant. Research now tends to focus on specific aspects of therapy, such as "What type of youngster tends to persist in outpatient therapy?" or "Which therapist behaviors are related to positive outcome?" Consequently, there is a growing body of literature that illuminates psychodynamically-based psychotherapeutic interventions, but little data to allow the practitioner to compare the effectiveness of this approach to others.

For practitioners interested in using psychodynamically-based interventions, some guidelines will help determine whom to refer for what services and how to determine whether the intervention is effective.

- Individual psychotherapy on an outpatient basis may not be the most efficacious intervention for nonverbal youngsters from unstable environments who have a tendency to blame others for their problems.

- Conflicted, angry youngsters who are verbal and have relatively supportive families are good candidates for individual psychotherapy.

- Teachers who feel they need more effective techniques for solving problems with children and for communicating therapeutically with them should familiarize themselves with Life Space Interviewing and perhaps seek consultation with someone trained in the technique.

- Residential treatment is often the treatment of choice for youngsters who do not take responsibility for their actions, because constant therapeutic interactions help them face their part in problems and feel safe and secure in trying new, less self-destructive ways of dealing with problems.

One of the major strengths of this perspective is the light it casts on the motivation behind behavior. Understanding "why" often helps practitioners respond appropriately. For example, many aggressive youngsters unconsciously act on the belief that it is better to be on the offensive and attack first, rather than be attacked. If an adult understands that fear of emotional hurt motivates the aggressive behavior, the adult is more likely to be able to resist countering aggression with aggression, and instead provide security and safety for the aggressive but fearful youngster.

Medication

A few psychoactive drugs have been used with aggressive children, but according to Leventhal (1984), the number of neurochemical mechanisms that may mediate aggressive and violent behavior theoretically far exceeds the number of drugs that have been developed. After reviewing the data supporting the use of drugs in treatment of aggression, Leventhal concluded:

1. Lithium carbonate and Propranolol both have promise in treating aggressive adolescents.

2. Neuroleptics, or antipsychotic drugs, such as Mellaril (thioridazine), Serentil (mesoridazine), Thorazine (chloropromazine), Haldol (haloperidol), and Stelazine (trifluoperazine) have been used successfully to reduce aggressive and violent behavior, but the side effect of tardive dyskinesia negates their usefulness except on a short-term basis.

3. Antidepressants such as Elavil (amitriptyline) may be effective in controlling aggression when it occurs in conjunction with depression, but in the absence of depression, antidepressants may actually facilitate the expression of aggression.

4. Psychostimulant medications used in treatment of children with *attention deficit disorders* (see Chapter 7) are limited in efficacy to youngsters who exhibit antisocial behavior in conjunction with attentional problems and hyperactivity.

5. Minor tranquilizers such as Librium (chlordiazepoxide) and Valium (diazepam) have been reported to induce "paradoxical rage reactions" and increased hostility in some patients, and thus have limited potential for managing aggressive behavior. "The exceptions are the cases of individuals who demonstrate a clear anxiety syndrome or—possibly—as an adjunct to the treatment of LSD or PCP intoxication" (Leventhal, 1984, p. 334).

Behavioral Approaches

The educational and psychological literature show a large array of behavioral interventions that focus on aggressive behavior. We will merely highlight examples of use of this perspective. The interested reader is referred to Walker (1979), Kerr and Nelson (1987), Morris and Kratochwill (1983), and Alberto and Troutman (1986) for discussions of how to use this approach with aggressive behavior.

Our examples illustrate approaches designed to decrease aggressive behavior; increase socially appropriate behavior that is incompatible with aggressive behavior; model appropriate behavior for expressing frustrations and anger; and teach parents better parenting skills so that aggressive behavior can be better managed ecologically.

Techniques for decreasing aggressive behavior. Most techniques that have successfully diminished aggressive behavior have relied on punishment, such as time-out and response-cost programs. *Time out* refers to the practice of removing the child from a rewarding situation contingent upon his behavior. The two types of time out are nonseclusionary and seclusionary.

Nonseclusionary time out involves removal from some forms of reinforcers but not physically from the room. For example, Foxx and Shapiro (1978) had children wear a ribbon-tie while they behaved appropriately; when they misbehaved, the tie was removed for three minutes and the child was denied access to edible reinforcers and participation in activities during that time. Sibley, Abbott, and Cooper (1969) provide another example of nonseclusionary time out. In this study, a kindergarten boy was placed in a cubicle in the classroom when he behaved aggressively. A significant decrease in aggressive behavior was noted when the time out procedures were instituted.

Seclusionary time out involves removing the child from the classroom and placing him in a secluded area, such as a time-out room, when he exhibits an aggressive behavior. Now considered an aversive technique in many school districts and mental health programs, this procedure can be effective in reducing aggression, but it must be monitored carefully and administratively sanctioned.

Use of operant conditioning to *increase prosocial behaviors* that are incompatible with aggressive behavior is generally considered a more acceptable and successful practice than punishment alone. Positive reinforcement, token economies, and behavioral contracts have all been used to teach social behavior.

Grieger, Kauffman, and Grieger (1976) used peer praise to increase friendly, cooperative behavior in a kindergarten class. After collecting baseline data, a treatment condition was instituted in which children were encouraged to talk publicly about the friendly actions of their classmates. Friendly children also received a happy-face badge. During reversal, children were asked to talk about unfriendly acts. No other punishment was instituted. In the final phase of the experiment, friendly acts were again reported. The results appear in Figure 6–3.

Token economies and behavioral contracting are also widely used to teach prosocial behaviors. In a token economy, children receive tokens for desired behavior and backup reinforcers for the tokens. Depending upon what seems more appropriate for the children, they may cash in tokens shortly after receiving them, or save them for long periods. Children usually exchange tokens for either treats or privileges. Behavioral contracts may be used in conjunction with token economies. The behavioral contract describes

in language the child can easily understand what behavior the adult wants to see from the child and what the adult will do if the child does or does not meet expectations. Bristol (1976) decreased an eight-year-old boy's fighting behavior with a behavioral contract among the boy, the teacher, and the parents, and through use of a token economy. Each morning the child received a card that the teacher signed during the morning, at lunch, and at the end of the day if the child did not engage in fighting. The teacher's signatures served as points the child could cash in for privileges, such as being student helper or extending his bedtime by 15 minutes. While the program was in effect, the boy's fighting decreased substantially, but, during a brief reversal period, it rose to above baseline levels. When the program was reinstated, fighting again decreased. A seven-month follow-up indicated that the boy was doing well without a special program.

Modeling is demonstrating behavior (Alberto & Troutman, 1986). Observational learning techniques are used to teach alternative behaviors. Many years ago, Chittenden

FIGURE 6–3
Number of Aggressive Acts of Children in Class

Source: "Effects of Peer Reporting on Cooperative Play and Aggression of Kindergarten Children" by T. Grieger, J. M. Kauffman, & R. M. Greiger, *Journal of School Psychology*, 1976, 14. Reprinted with permission.

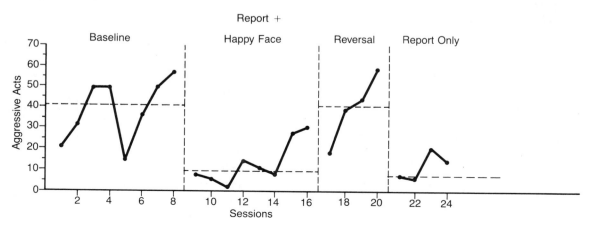

(1942) demonstrated that aggressive behavior in preschoolers decreased after they observed role-plays in which doll models responded aggressively and unaggressively to irritating stimuli. Positive consequences resulted when the dolls behaved prosocially, but negative consequences occurred when the dolls behaved aggressively. Following observation of these plays, Chittenden noted a decrease in aggression. Modeling can easily be combined with other behavioral and cognitive techniques, as we will see later.

Teaching parents more effective behavior management skills has been effective in reducing children's aggressive behavior. Some of the best examples of this approach appear in the work of Gerald Patterson and his colleagues at the Oregon Research Institute. Their program grew out of many years of observing parent-child interactions in families of conduct-disordered youngsters. Based on these observations, they hypothesized that inadequate parenting skills were the basis of conduct disorders, and they developed a treatment package for training parents to manage their children more appropriately (Patterson, Reid, Jones, & Conger, 1975). The program required parents to read and be tested on behavioral principles and then apply them in their homes with their children. Parents were taught to pinpoint problem areas, to collect appropriate data on the problems, and to implement change techniques in the context of a parent training group. The investigators made home visits when necessary.

The original program lasted an average of three to four months and took an average of 31.5 hours of professional time. Improvement in the youngsters' behavior was reported on a number of measures both at termination and at follow-up, and the model has been successfully replicated by other clinicians (Fleischman, 1981; Eyberg & Johnson, 1974).

The improved behavior, however, did not generalize to school; consequently, a parallel program was developed for use in the schools (Patterson, Cobb, & Ray, 1972). It was also noted that parents needed more than child-management skill training to implement the program effectively; hence, help to parents in dealing with social problems, negotiation skills, depression, and marital conflict was added to the treatment when it was deemed appropriate (Patterson, 1975; Patterson & Reid, 1973).

These modifications by Patterson et al. illustrate some of the problems professionals encounter when using this approach. Behaviors learned in one setting do not necessarily generalize to other settings without specific training, and sometimes behavioral gains are not maintained over time without constant application of the treatment. This perspective has been demonstrated to be a powerful tool for managing aggressive behavior, and useful techniques for observing and recording behavioral change have resulted from this work. Recently, investigators show promising results by combining behavioral interventions with cognitive interventions in an effort to deal with aggressive behavior.

Cognitively-based Approaches

Since distorted and inadequate social cognition is considered the cause of aggressive behavior, programs have been directed at helping the child learn new ways of problem solving, of behaving in social situations, and of coping more effectively with anger-arousing situations.

The *Think Aloud* program (Camp & Bash, 1978) was designed to help young aggressive boys increase their social and cognitive problem-solving skills so as to have better control over their impulsive and self-defeating aggressive behaviors. The program is based on research that found aggressive boys often fail to use their verbal skills to think through complex problems; instead, they act impulsively and aggressively. The researchers hypothesized that if they could teach the boys to slow down and use good verbal skills in problem solving, their problem behavior might decrease; more importantly, their poor problem-solving skills might increase. Methods for increasing these skills were based on research that suggested self-guiding speech was effective in helping special-needs children improve cognitive and behavioral performance (Meichenbaum & Goodman, 1971); that modeling was a critically important part of the process of transferring self-guiding speech into self-discipline (Hetherington & McIntyre, 1975); and that learning to think of alternative solutions to problems is important in improving social behavior (Spivak & Shure, 1974). As work on the program proceeded, the authors realized that aggressive youngsters were not the only children for whom such training might be beneficial, so they expanded the basic program for use in regular classrooms. There are now programs for individuals as well as for classrooms, and programs for grades one through six.

The initial phase of the program develops an organized approach to problem solving. At first working with cognitive problems, students are taught to ask themselves four questions: (1) What is my problem? or What am I supposed to do? (2) How can I do it? or What is my plan? (3) Am I using my plan? and (4) How did I do? They should answer the first two questions before they begin work. The first question focuses the child on the task; the second question helps the child think of alternative strategies, so that if the first strategy is not successful, he has remaining alternatives that may lead to success; and the third question increases self-control while the child implements plans. The fourth question, asked after the task is completed, helps children develop self-evaluation skills. This question also precedes the teacher assessment, and helps reduce the teacher-student conflict that sometimes occurs during evaluation procedures.

After children master this procedure, interpersonal problems are introduced. Much of this phase of the program draws from Spivak and Shure's work (1974). The nine interpersonal lessons deal with identifying and sharing emotions, recognizing physical causality, recognizing emotional causality, anticipating what might happen next, and problem solving that uses the four-step process. As children generate alternatives or solutions to the problems, they learn to question whether it is safe and fair; how it makes them and others feel; and whether it solves the problem. This instruction in interpersonal language and consequential thinking helps prepare children for the next phase, practicing verbal situations and role playing, to learn to apply the skills to real-life conflict resolution.

Most of the evaluation studies have employed the basic individual program. Results suggest that treated children have surpassed controls on a number of cognitive tests (Camp, Blom, Hebert, & van Doorninck, 1977). Prosocial behavior increased among Think Aloud graduates more than among controls, and aggressive behavior decreased in treated youngsters, but also in the controls.

Another program for teaching skill-deficit youngsters (especially aggressive ones) how to interact more appropriately is Structured Learning. This program, now available for elementary ages as well, uses a developmental sequence of social skills as an initial assessment tool and as a curriculum guide (Goldstein, Sprafkin, Gershaw, & Klein, 1980; McGinnis, Goldstein, Sprafkin, & Gershaw, 1984). Teachers or trainers rate whether the youngster is *never, seldom, sometimes, often,* or *always* good at using the skill. Skills targeted for training are grouped into six areas: beginning social skills, advanced social skills, skills for dealing with feelings, skill alternatives to aggression, skills for dealing with stress, and planning skills. Skills range from basic to more complicated in each area; for example, in the group of skills for dealing with stress, the first item is "making a complaint" and the last is "dealing with group pressure."

There are four steps for teaching each skill—modeling, role playing, feedback, and transfer training. Each has been established in the literature as an effective method for changing behavior. During the modeling phase, small groups of youngsters observe others using a specified social skill in various settings. Videotapes, audiotapes, films, or live role playing between the teachers make the lesson interesting. Next, the group analyzes the skill and discusses its applications. Group members then role play the skill with their trainers and other group members. In the third phase, the trainer gives the youngster corrective feedback about his performance. As the child becomes more proficient in the skill, rewards are sometimes used. The final phase is transfer of training, during which youngsters practice the skill outside the training session.

In their books, *Skillstreaming the Adolescent: A Structured Learning Approach to Teaching Prosocial Skills* and *Skillstreaming the Elementary School Child*, the authors provide an annotated bibliography of research on the effectiveness of this program (Goldstein et al., 1980; McGinnis et al., 1984). Although much of the research is unpublished, the emphasis on utilizing empirical data for evaluating and modifying the program is impressive, and the research largely supports the program's effectiveness.

The Anger Control Program (Lochman, Nelson, & Sims, 1981) was designed to help elementary school children gain control over their aggressive behaviors. It integrates cognitive, behavioral, and social problem-solving strategies and is based on a systematic model of anger arousal. In this model, the problem is not the stimulus event that provokes the child's anger, but how the child processes or understands the event; for example, if someone calls a child a "punk," the child may perceive the label as affectionate teasing or as a hostile rebuke. In this program children were taught to inhibit their

initial aggressive reactions, to cognitively relabel stimuli they perceived as threatening, and to generate alternative coping responses as resolutions to the problems. The program was designed for children to meet twice-weekly in small groups for 40-minute sessions. Each session included group discussion before and after structured experimental, modeling, and behavioral rehearsal activities. Table 6–2 lists goals and activities for the twelve sessions. Posttreatment testing showed improvements in on-task and aggressive behaviors, and subsequent studies comparing the efficacy of Anger Control with other interventions have found Anger Control to be more effective (Lochman, Burch, Curry, & Lampron, 1984).

OUTCOME

What happens to aggressive children with and without treatment is a question that can be addressed only through an elaborate and expensive research design. Not surprisingly, few such studies have been conducted. The carefully controlled studies have for the most part reported fairly consistent findings.

Lee Robins (1966) conducted one of the most thorough studies of what happens to these youngsters when they grow up. She located 524 persons who had been seen 30 years earlier in a child guidance clinic and compared them to 100 controls who graduated from elementary school during the same time frame. Structured interviews were conducted with 82 percent of the initial sample and adult records were obtained for 98 percent. Based on the data from the interviews and records, two psychiatrists were able to agree 88 percent of the time as to whether the individual was psychiatrically ill, and in 71 percent of the cases, they agreed upon a relatively specific diagnosis. Robins (1980) concluded:

Children referred for antisocial behavior differed much more from the control subjects in their adult adjustment than did children referred for temper

TABLE 6-2
Goals for Anger Control Program

Session	Goals	Activities
1	Introduce group rules Promote self-awareness by noting differences and similarities between group members physically, behaviorally, emotionally, attitudinally	Taking pictures of each group member with instant camera Body tracings of members on large pieces of paper Perception of Gestalt Vase/Face design
2	Explore children's reactions to cooperating with, being controlled by, being distracted by peers	Acting like pairs of robots Building domino towers while being verbally distracted by peers
3	Problem identification—learn which specific aspects of a situation create problem and lead to anger arousal	
4	Generate alternative solutions to problems	Cartoon sequences of interpersonal problem (e.g., children fighting over a bicycle) Role-playing
5, 6	Evaluate alternative solution by identifying positive and negative consequences and deciding relative value of alternatives	Cartoon sequences Role-playing
7	Increase physiological awareness of anger arousal with increased awareness acting as cue for problem solving Use positive self-statements when provoked	Viewing a modeling videotape, depicting young boy telling offscreen narrator how he felt about being reprimanded by mother for not doing homework; child also described internal negative self-statements he made when angry (e.g., "I want to get back at my mother and teacher for making me miss a television show"), and positive self-statements he could use to decrease his anger arousal (e.g., "If I stick to the homework rules, I can watch TV sooner")
8	Integrate techniques of physiological awareness, self-talk, and social problem solving Self-talk techniques include positive self-statements and covert inhibiting speech (e.g., "Stop! Think! What Should I Do?")	Viewing three modeling videotapes of children experiencing reactive anger to being punished by a teacher for something they did not do, to peer teasing, and to being ignored by peers After each problem situation, children were encouraged to identify problem and generate alternative solutions Typed alternate solutions were presented for each problem, prefaced by use of covert inhibiting speech to disrupt the reflexive aggressive response Children evaluated various alternatives
9	Integrate and practice techniques modeled in Session 8	Role-playing Beginning development of two anger arousal "scenes" which group videotaped in same format as modeling tape
10, 11, 12	Integrate and practice techniques modeled in Session 8	Role-plays Completion of group's videotape Discussion of anger-control efforts at school and home

Reprinted by permission of *The Journal of Clinical Child Psychology.*

tantrums, learning problems, sleep and eating disturbance, speech difficulties and all problems other than antisocial behavior. The more severe the antisocial behavior, whether measured by numbers of symptoms, by number of episodes, or by arrestability of the behavior, the more disturbed was the adult adjustment. Children referred to the clinic without numerous symptoms had no worse an outcome than had the control subjects.

Several trends were noted among the adults diagnosed as sociopathic personalities. This disorder occurred almost exclusively in boys referred for antisocial behavior, particularly theft. Most had histories of juvenile theft, incorrigibility, running away from home, truancy, associating with bad companions, sexual activities, and staying out late. Most had been discipline problems at school, had been retained at least one grade by the time they were referred, and most never graduated from elementary school. Their average age of referral to the clinic was 14, but they had histories of difficulties dating back an average of 7 years.

One must consider a number of issues when interpreting outcome data. First, in predicting outcome, it makes a great deal of difference what type of aggressive child one is talking about. Research suggests that the "garden variety" aggressive child is not that different from other children (Harris, 1979; Griffin, in press). Hyperaggressive, antisocial children, however, differ from other children on a number of important dimensions. Unfortunately, many studies do not adequately specify the type of child being treated. A common practice has been to have others rate the most aggressive youngsters in a group. This process identifies youngsters who are aggressive relative to their classmates; it does not necessarily identify only the chronically aggressive youngsters for whom the prognosis is so poor. In fact, it is likely that many of the identified youngsters are the "garden variety" types.

Second, in evaluating outcome, it matters what outcome criterion is used. Recidivism is often used, yet sometimes this criterion reflects success rather than failure—clients, having become more aware of and more uncomfortable with their problems, seek additional help. Independent adult functioning is sometimes used as a criterion of successful living, but this can also be inappropriate when it does not represent progress in treatment; for example, some youngsters enter treatment at a much higher level than others, and independent living may not have been a goal because it was assumed.

A related problem has to do with generalizability. Programs have been successful in devising interventions that help children decrease aggressive behavior; however, whether the improvements generalize to other settings is often not addressed or does not occur. Nelson and Kauffman (1977) concluded that many studies on outcome report change during treatment, but neither the type nor amount of change during treatment was predictive of adjustment at follow-up.

Third, when considering progress in relation to treatment, it is essential to define treatment so that comparable treatments may be compared. Unfortunately, few programs provide this documentation. Without information on the treatment that contributes to the process of change, little can be said about what affects outcome.

CONCLUSION

Hyperaggressive, antisocial behavior is a serious, albeit common, problem of childhood and adolescence. It causes children to be rejected by their peers and to have difficulty in school. Although we can identify no single cause to explain why this behavior develops, a variety of factors seem relevant. Research supports the contention that many aggressive children tend to be more active, more intense, and more emotive than others from birth onward, but that alone does not explain why conduct disorders develop. Many come from homes in which problems are solved through antisocial means, thus providing models for learning aggression. Many experience unusual amounts of stress and chaos while growing up, which interferes with normal growth and development. Many appear to have mild neurological and/or physiological problems that may exacerbate their social development. Aggression is often the means of coping with unmanageable environmental demands. Evidence also supports the notion that some of these youngsters' social, emotional, and learning skills are developmentally delayed compared to their "normal" counterparts. Given the long-standing nature of these problems and the hostility and unpleasantness many of the youngsters display, it is not surprising that the behavior pattern is hard to change.

Most aggressive youngsters receive help in the schools. Self-contained classrooms, resource rooms, counseling services, and consultation to teachers in mainstream classrooms are widely used models for providing help. Extensive behavioral technology has been developed that is effective for help-

ing these youngsters bring their behavior under control, and several curricula are available to help teachers teach appropriate social behavior. Most states and communities have developed a variety of care giving components to provide additional help when it is needed.

Common to almost all the interventions and programs is the goal of helping the child gain control, or better control, over his hyperaggressive behavior. Many of these children curse, hit, or destroy before thinking, then feel bad about their outburst—but only for a short while. Then they find an excuse to absolve them of guilt or distort the problem so they need not feel guilty or responsible any longer. Many interventions consequently focus not only on improving the problematic behavior, but also on helping the child see the situation differently. These goals are usually best accomplished through a number of complementary approaches that focus on both the identified aggressive youngster and the environment.

REFERENCES

Achenbach, T. M. (1978). The Child Behavior Profile: I. Boys aged 6–11. *Journal of Consulting and Clinical Psychology, 46,* 478–488.

Alberto, P. A., & Troutman, A. C. (1986). Applied behavior analysis for teachers, 2nd. ed. Columbus, OH: Merrill.

American Psychiatric Association. (1980). *Diagnostic and statistical manual of mental disorders,* 3rd ed. Washington, DC: APA.

Anolik, S. A. (1981). Imaginary audience behavior and perceptions of parents among delinquent and nondelinquent adolescents. *Journal of Youth and Adolescence, 10,* 443–454.

Asarnow, J. R., & Callan, J. W. (1985). Boys with peer adjustment problems: Social cognitive processes. *Journal of Consulting and Clinical Psychology, 53,* 880–887.

Bandura, A., & Walters, R. H. (1963). *Social learning and personality development.* New York: Holt, Rinehart & Winston.

Berman, S. (1984). The relationship of aggressive behavior and violence to psychic reorganization in adolescence. In C. R. Keith (Ed.) *The aggressive adolescent: Clinical perspectives.* New York: Free Press.

Bristol, M. M. (1976). Control of physical aggression through school- and home-based reinforcement. In J. D. Krumboltz & C. E. Thoresen (Eds.), *Counseling methods.* New York: Holt, Rinehart & Winston.

Brown, G. L., & Goodwin, F. K. (1984). Aggression, adolescence, and psychobiology. In C. R. Keith (Ed.), *The aggressive adolescent: Clinical perspectives.* New York: Free Press.

Brown, R. (1965). *Social psychology.* New York: Free Press.

Camp, B. (1977). Verbal mediation in young aggressive boys. *Journal of Abnormal Psychology, 86,* 145–156.

Camp, B. W., & Bash, M. A. (1978). *Think Aloud: Group Manual.* Denver, CO: University of Colorado Medical School. (Also available from Research Press, Champaign, IL.)

Camp, B. W., Blom, G. E., Hebert, F., & van Doorninck, W. J. (1977). "Think Aloud": A program for developing self-control in young aggressive boys. *Journal of Abnormal Child Psychology, 5,* 157–169.

Chess, S., & Thomas, A. (1984). *Origins and evolution of behavior disorders: From infancy to early adult life.* New York: Brunner/Mazel.

Chittenden, G. E. (1942). An experimental study in

measuring and modifying assertive behavior in young children. *Monographs of the Society for Research in Child Development, 7* (whole #31).

Coie, J. D., Dodge, K. A., & Coppotelli, H. (1982). Dimensions and types of social status: A cross-age perspective. *Developmental Psychology, 18,* 261–282.

Dodge, K. A. (1980) Social cognition and children's aggressive behavior. *Child Development, 51,* 162–170.

Dodge, K. A., & Frame, C. L. (1982). Social cognitive biases and deficits in aggressive boys. *Child Development, 53,* 620–635.

Dodge, K. A., Murphy, R. R., & Buchsbaum, K. (1984). The assessment of intention-cue detection skills in children: Implications for developmental psychopathology. *Child Development, 55,* 163–173.

Dorfman, A. (1984). The criminal mind. *Science Digest, 92* (10), 44–47.

Eme, R. F. (1979). Sex differences in childhood psychopathology: A review. *Psychological Bulletin, 86,* 574–595.

Eyberg, S. M., & Johnson, S. M. (1974). Multiple assessment of behavior modification with families: Effects of contingency contracting and order of treated problems. *Journal of Consulting and Clinical Psychology, 42,* 594–606.

Farrington, S. P., Gundry, G., & West, D. J. (1975). The familial transmission of criminality. *Medicine, Science and the Law, 15,* 177–186.

Feshbach, S. (1970). Aggression. In P. Mussen (Ed.), *Carmichael's manual of child psychology* (Vol. 2). New York: John Wiley.

Fleischman, M. J. (1981). A replication of Patterson's "intervention for boys with conduct problems." *Journal of Consulting and Clinical Psychology, 49,* 342–351.

Foxx, R. M., & Shapiro, S. T. (1978). The time-out ribbon: A nonexclusionary time-out procedure. *Journal of Applied Behavior Analysis, 11,* 125–136.

Freud, S. (1961). Civilization and its discontents. In J. Strachey (Ed. and Trans.), *The standard edition of the complete psychological works of Sigmund Freud* (Vol. 21). London: Hogarth Press. (Original work published 1930)

Gersten, J. C., Langner, T. S., Eisenberg, J. G., Simcha-Fagan, D., & McCarthy, E. D. (1976). Stability and change in types of behavioral disturbance of children and adolescents. *Journal of Abnormal Child Psychology, 4,* 111–127.

Goldstein, A. P., Sprafkin, R. P., Gershaw, N. J., & Klein, P. (1980). *Skill-streaming the adolescent: A structured learning approach to teaching prosocial skills.* Champaign, IL: Research Press.

Goodenough, F. L. (1931). *Anger in young children.* Minneapolis: University of Minnesota Press.

Grieger, T., Kauffman, J. M., & Grieger, R. M. (1976). Effects of peer reporting on cooperative play and aggression of kindergarten children. *Journal of School Psychology, 14,* 307–313.

Griffin, G. (in press). Predictive characteristics of violent adolescents. *Exceptional Children.*

Guthrie, K., & Finger, B. (1983). "Willie M." treatment for disturbed youngsters: Ambitious community-based service system lurches forward. *North Carolina Insight, 6* (2,3), 56–68.

Hall, C. S., & Lindzey, G. (1957). *Theories of personality.* New York: John Wiley.

Harris, A. (1979). An empirical test of the situation specificity/consistency of aggressive behavior. *Child Behavior Therapy, 1,* 257–270.

Hartup, W. W. (1974). Aggression in childhood: Developmental perspectives. *American Psychologist, 29,* 336–341.

Hetherington, E. M., & McIntyre, C. W. (1975). Developmental psychology. *Annual Review of Psychology, 26,* 97–136.

Hogan, A., & Quay, H. (1984). Cognition in child and adolescent behavior disorders. In B. B. Lahey & A. E. Kazdin (Eds.), *Advances in clinical child psychology* (Vol. 7). New York: Plenum Press.

Kauffman, J. M. (1985). *Characteristics of children's behavior disorders* (3rd ed.). Columbus, OH: Merrill.

Kerr, M. M., & Nelson, C. M. (1987). *Strategies for managing behavior problems in the classroom* (2nd ed.). Columbus, OH: Merrill.

Krynicki, V. E. (1978). Cerebral dysfunction in repetitively assaultive adolescents. *Journal of Nervous and Mental Disease, 166,* 59–67.

Leventhal, B. L. (1984). The neuropharmacology of violent and aggressive behavior in children and adolescents. In C. R. Keith (Ed.), *The aggressive adolescent: Clinical perspectives.* New York: Free Press.

Lewis, D. O. (1976). Delinquency, psychomotor epileptic symptoms, and paranoid ideation: A triad. *American Journal of Psychiatry, 133,* 1395–1398.

Lewis, D. O., Lewis, M., Unger, L., & Goldman, C. (1984). Conduct disorder and its synonyms: Diagnoses of dubious validity and usefulness. *American Journal of Psychiatry, 141,* 514–519.

Lewis, D. O., Pincus, J. H., Shanok, S., & Glaser, G. H. (1982). Psychomotor epilepsy and violence in a group of incarcerated adolescent boys. *American Journal of Psychiatry, 139,* 882–887.

Lochman, J. E. (1984). Psychological characteristics and assessment of aggressive adolescents. In C. Keith (Ed.), *Aggression in adolescence.* New York: Free Press.

Lochman, J. E., Burch, P. R., Curry, J. F., & Lampron, L. B. (1984). Treatment and generalization effects of cognitive-behavioral and goal-setting interventions with aggressive boys. *Journal of Consulting and Clinical Psychology, 52,* 915–916.

Lochman, J. E., Nelson, W. M., & Sims, J. P. (1981). A cognitive behavioral program for use with aggressive children. *Journal of Clinical Child Psychology, 10,* 146–148.

Long, N. J. (1966). *Direct help to the classroom teacher.*

Washington, DC: School Research Program, the Washington School of Psychiatry.

Maccoby, E., & Jacklin, C. (1974). *The psychology of sex differences.* Stanford, CA: Stanford University Press.

McGinnis, E., & Goldstein, A. P., with Sprafkin, R. P., & Gershaw, N. J. (1984). *Skill-streaming the elementary school child: A guide for teaching prosocial skills.* Champaign, IL: Research Press.

Mead, M. (1949). *Male and female.* New York: Morrow.

Mednick, S. A., & Hutchings, B. (1978). Genetic and psychophysiological factors in asocial behavior. *Journal of the American Academy of Child Psychiatry, 17,* 209–223.

Meichenbaum, D. H., & Goodman, J. (1971). Training impulsive children to talk to themselves: A means of developing self-control. *Journal of Abnormal Psychology, 77,* 115–126.

Mikkelsen, E. J., Brown, G. L., Minichiello, M. D., Millican, F. K., & Rapoport, J. L. (1982). Neurologic status in hyperactive, enuretic, encopretic, and normal boys. *Journal of the American Academy of Child Psychiatry, 21,* 75–81.

Milich, R., & Dodge, K. A. (1984). Social information processing in child psychiatric populations. *Journal of Abnormal Child Psychology, 12,* 471–490.

Miller, L. C. (1977). Louisville Behavior Checklist. Los Angeles: Western Psychological Services.

Mischel, W. (1968). *Personality and assessment.* New York: John Wiley.

Morris, R., & Kratochwill, T. R. (1983). *The practice of child therapy.* New York: Pergamon Press.

Morse, W. C. (1980). Worksheet on Life Space Interviewing for teachers. In N. J. Long, W. C. Morse, & R. G. Newman (Eds.), *Conflict in the classroom: The education of emotionally disturbed children* (4th ed.). Belmont, CA: Wadsworth.

Mullis, R. L., & Hanson, R. A. (1983). Perspective-taking among offender and nonoffender youth. *Adolescence, 18,* 831–836.

Nelson, C. M., & Kauffman, J. M. (1977). Educational programming for secondary school age delinquent and maladjusted pupils. *Behavioral Disorders, 2,* 102–113.

Olweus, D. (1979). Familial and temperamental determinants of aggressive behavior in adolescent boys: A causal analysis. *Developmental Psychology, 16,* 644–660.

Patterson, G. R. (1975). *Families.* Champaign, IL: Research Press.

Patterson, G. R., Cobb, J. A., & Ray, R. S. (1972). A social engineering technology for retraining the families of aggressive boys. In H. E. Adams & I. P. Unikel, *Issues and trends in behavior therapy.* Springfield, IL: Charles C Thomas.

Patterson, G. R., & Reid, J. B. (1973). Intervention for families of aggressive boys: A replication study. *Behaviour Research and Therapy, 11,* 383–394.

Patterson, G. R., Reid, J. B., Jones, R. R., & Conger, R. E. (1975). *A social learning approach to family intervention* (Vol. I). Eugene, OR: Castalia.

Pincus, J. H., & Tucker, G. J. (1978). Violence in children and adults: A neurological view. *American Academy of Child Psychiatry, 17,* 277–288.

Quay, H. C., & Peterson, D. R. (1975). Manual for the Behavior Problem Checklist. Available from D. R. Peterson, Graduate School of Applied and Professional Psychology, Busch Campus, P.O. Box 88199, Piscataway, NJ 08854.

Rabinowitz, C. (1969). Therapy for underprivileged delinquent families. In O. Pollock & A. Friedman (Eds.), *Family dynamics and female sexual delinquency.* Palo Alto, CA: Science and Behavior Books.

Redl, F. (1966). *When we deal with children.* New York: Free Press.

Redl, F., & Wineman, D. (1957). *The aggressive child.* New York: Free Press.

Richard, B. A., & Dodge, K. A. (1982). Social maladjustment and problem solving in school-aged children. *Journal of Consulting and Clinical Psychology, 50,* 226–233.

Robins, L. N. (1966). Deviant children grown up: A sociological and psychiatric study of sociopathic personality. Baltimore: Williams & Wilkins.

Robins, L. N. (1980). Deviant children grown up: A sociological and psychiatric study of sociopathic personality. In N. J. Long, W. C. Morse, & R. G. Newman (Eds.), *Conflict in the classroom: The education of emotionally disturbed children* (4th ed.). Belmont, CA: Wadsworth.

Robins, L. N. (1986). Changes in conduct disorders over time. In D. Farran & J. D. McKinney (Eds.), *Risk in intellectual and psychosocial development.* Orlando, FL: Academic Press.

Robins, L. N., Helzer, J. E., Croughan, J., & Ratcliff, K. S. (1981). The NIMH Diagnostic Interview Schedule: Its history, characteristics, and validity. *Archives of General Psychiatry, 38,* 381–389.

Rosenthal, D. (1975). Heredity in criminality. *Criminal Justice and Behavior, 2,* 3–21.

Rotenberg, M. (1974). Conceptual and methodological notes on affective and cognitive role-taking: An illustrative experiment with delinquent and nondelinquent boys. *Journal of Genetic Psychology, 125,* 177–185.

Rubin, K. H. (1983). The Social Problem-Solving Test–Revised. (Available from the author, University of Waterloo, Canada)

Rutter, M. L. (1970). Psycho-social disorders in childhood and their outcome in adult life. *Journal of the Royal College of Physicians London, 4,* 211–218.

Santostefano, S., & Rieder, C. (1984). Cognitive controls and aggression in children: The concept of cognitive-affective balance. *Journal of Consulting and Clinical Psychology, 52,* 46–56.

Shantz, D. W., & Pentz, T. (1972). Situational effects on justifiableness of aggression at three age levels. *Child Development, 43,* 274–281.

Sibley, S., Abbott, M. S., & Cooper, B. C. (1969). Modification of the classroom behavior of a disadvantaged kindergarten boy by social reinforcement and isolation. *Journal of Experimental Child Psychology, 7,* 203–219.

Sindelar, K. (1982). Willie M: Treatment for troubled children. *School Law Bulletin, 13* (1), 1–9.

Spivak, G., & Shure, M. B. (1974). *Social adjustment of young children: A cognitive approach to solving real-life problems.* San Francisco: Jossey-Bass.

Thomas, A., & Chess, S. (1984). Genesis and evolution of behavioral disorders: From infancy to early adult life. *The American Journal of Psychiatry, 141* (1), 1–9.

Tieger, T. (1980). On the biological basis of sex differences in aggression. *Child Development, 51,* 943–963.

Walker, H. M. (1979). *The acting-out child: Coping with classroom disruption.* Boston: Allyn & Bacon.

Walker, H. M. (1983). Walker Problem Behavior Identification Checklist. Los Angeles: Western Psychological Corporation.

Waterman, J. M., Sobesky, W. E., Silvern, P., Aoki, B., & McCaulay, M. (1981). Social perspective-taking and adjustment in emotionally disturbed, learning-disabled, and normal children. *Journal of Abnormal Child Psychology, 9,* 133–148.

Willerman, L. (1979). *The psychology of individual and group differences.* San Francisco: Freeman.

Wolff, P. H., Waber, D., Bauermeister, M., Cohen, C., & Ferber, R. (1982). The neuropsychological status of adolescent delinquent boys. *Journal of Child Psychiatry and Psychology, 23,* 267–279.

He had been a child of action, always doing things, running around, getting into trouble; he could remember that part of his life clearly. And yet it seemed to belong to another boy . . . Sometimes he felt a flurry of panic, to think that he was nothing at all.

JOYCE CAROL OATES
WONDERLAND

These drawings are by a 7-year-old (left) and an 11-year-old (right) who had been diagnosed as having attention-deficit disorders. The drawings are immature and poorly executed, with little attention to detail.

CHAPTER SEVEN

Childhood Hyperactivity

Randall W. Evans

C. Thomas Gualtieri

Paula K. Shear
BIOLOGICAL SCIENCES RESEARCH CENTER
UNIVERSITY OF NORTH CAROLINA AT CHAPEL HILL
SCHOOL OF MEDICINE

Childhood hyperactivity is a serious disorder that can negatively affect the child's academic and social progress for many years.

The emphasis on hyperactivity as the major characteristic of hyperactive children has shifted to an emphasis on cognitive impairment. This is, in part, reflected in the relabeling of hyperactivity as "Attention Deficit Disorder with Hyperactivity" (DSM-III, 1980).

Prevalence estimates range from 5 percent to 15 percent. Research in this area is confounded by many variables such as socioeconomic status, gender, and place of birth. Also, definitions vary widely, and measurement problems contribute to problems of reliability in identification.

While there is no single known cause of hyperactivity in children, several etiological perspectives have research and clinical support. These perspectives include those that look at hyperactivity as a "dysmaturational" disorder, as a disturbance of specific brain systems, as genetically transmitted, as a severe psychological disturbance, or as a disorder arising from "external" agents such as diet, environmental pollutants, crowding, lack of stimulation, and so forth.

Because of diagnostic heterogeneity, there is no single effective treatment mode or method for dealing with hyperactive children. Two methods of treatment have been shown to be efficacious for a large segment of this population—pharmacotherapy and behavior therapy. Research and clinical experience suggest that a combination of these two methods is best in the short term. There is little information on long-term effects.

DEFINITION

Childhood hyperactivity is a serious disorder, with long-term consequences for about 50 percent of children who are diagnosed during the primary school years. What may first appear to the child's parents, teachers, or even peers as an inability to "sit still," pay attention, or control impulses may actually be the initial signs of a behavior disturbance that may plague the child's academic and social progress for many years. The potential severity of the disorder, and of its possible extension into adult life, is documented by well-controlled research by clinician/scientists, many of whom have focused their professional careers on this complex syndrome.

Hyperactivity as a recognizable diagnostic entity is both an old and a new concept. Early descriptions of the disorder emphasize not only the excessive overactivity these children exhibit, but a panoply of other symptoms as well, including impulsivity, aggressiveness, impaired academic achievement, clumsiness, "soft" neurological signs, low frustration tolerance, and interpersonal difficulties. Aman (1976) and others (Werry, Weiss, & Douglas, 1964; Barkley, 1978) emphasize that these early descriptions of the syndrome recognized behavioral overactivity as the core manifestation of the disorder.

This symptom of hyperactivity as the most common characteristic of the hyperactive child, however, is currently under challenge by researchers and practitioners. While this may first appear to be a somewhat contradictory hypothesis, professionals are finding that hyperactive children as a group also have considerable difficulty on cognitive tasks, particularly on measures that require the child to maintain a relatively lengthy attentional set. This shift, or at least alternative emphasis, to cognitive impairments found in the hyperactive child has contributed to a redefinition of the syndrome.

Before describing the specific current diagnostic criteria for children with excessive overactivity, we should briefly review previous diagnostic descriptions. Barkley (1981) emphasizes that as early as the turn of the century, behavioral and cognitive difficulties of retarded and brain damaged children appeared in the scientific literature. The symptoms of these afflicted individuals included concentration problems, impulsiveness, restlessness, and heightened activity, and, because these patients had either known or strongly-suspected central nervous system disorders, their problems were directly attributed to "organic" pathology. This assumption persisted for decades and still permeates the literature. Contemporary scientist/clinicians have attempted to disprove this long-held notion of a brain-based disorder of hyperactivity by showing that most children exposed to brain trauma do *not* develop hyperactivity and that *fewer* than one in twenty hyperactive children have demonstrable brain pathology (Rutter, 1977). Because of this persistent belief of a biologically-rooted etiology of hyperactivity, terms such as "minimal brain damage," "neurologically-based learning disability," and "minimal brain dysfunction" were employed as the medically-accepted diagnoses for children who exhibited a primary symptom of overactivity.

Within the last decade, classification systems have emerged that attempt to describe the hyperactive child with greater precision and reliability. The most recent advance was developed by the American Psychiatric Association in its third edition of the Diagnostic and Statistical Manual (DSM-III, 1980). Based in part on recent, controlled investigations concerning the cognitive impairments of the hyperactive child, the DSM-III has relabeled hyperactivity as "Attention Deficit Disorder with Hyperactivity" (ADD-HA). This emphasis on the attentional problems of the hyperactive child helps explain why hyperactive children as a group respond positively to stimulant medicines, and also why they often show impaired learning skills. In this chapter, we will use the terms *hyperactivity* and *ADD-HA* interchangeably. These are the DSM-III criteria for ADD-HA:

The child displays, for his or her mental and chronological age, signs of developmentally inappropriate inattention, impulsivity, and hyperactivity. The signs must be reported by adults in the child's environment, such as parents and teachers. Because the symptoms are typically variable, they may not be observed directly by the clinician. When the reports of teachers and parents conflict, primary consideration should be given to the teacher reports because of greater familiarity with age-appropriate norms. Symptoms typically worsen in situations that require self-application, as in the classroom. Signs of the disorder may be absent when the child is in a new or a one-to-one situation.

The number of symptoms specified is for children between the ages of eight and ten, the peak age range for referral. In younger children, more severe forms of the symptoms and a greater number of symptoms are usually present. The opposite is true of older children.

A. Inattention. At least three of the following:
   1. often fails to finish things he or she starts
   2. often doesn't seem to listen
   3. easily distracted
   4. has difficulty concentrating on schoolwork or other tasks requiring sustained attention
   5. has difficulty sticking to a play activity
B. Impulsivity. At least three of the following:
   1. often acts before thinking
   2. shifts excessively from one activity to another

   3. has difficulty organizing work (this not being due to cognitive impairment)
   4. needs a lot of supervision
   5. frequently calls out in class
   6. has difficulty awaiting turn in games or group situations
C. Hyperactivity. At least two of the following:
   1. runs about or climbs on things excessively
   2. has difficulty sitting still or fidgets excessively
   3. has difficulty staying seated
   4. moves about excessively during sleep
   5. is always "on the go" or acts as if "driven by a motor"
D. Onset before the age of seven.
E. Duration of at least six months.
F. Not due to Schizophrenia, Affective Disorder, or Severe or Profound Mental Retardation.*

INCIDENCE AND PREVALENCE

The recent reclassification of the disorder in DSM-III has made discussion of the incidence and prevalence rates of the ADD-HA child more difficult. A number of consistent findings, however, suggest that at least 5 percent of the overall child population and an upward limit of 15 percent of this population at one time or another meet DSM-III criteria for ADD-HA. Unfortunately, these statistics are confounded by many variables, including the child's socioeconomic status (SES), gender, and even place of birth (Trites, 1979). For example, both the incidence and severity of hyperactivity correlate negatively with descending SES status. Some researchers theorize that individuals with lower SES come from environments where pre- and postnatal medical care is substandard, resulting in an "at-risk" status for the child. Others emphasize that lower SES correlates positively with a greater likelihood for family instability and

*From the Diagnostic and Statistical Manual of Mental Disorders (3rd Ed.) Washington DC: American Psychiatric Association, 1980. Copyright 1980 by the American Psychiatric Association. Reprinted by permission.

also with parental psychiatric disorders. All these factors may help explain the greater prevalence of hyperactivity in lower SES families. It is also possible that low SES children are inadequately prepared for the increasingly rigorous demands of primary school or less motivated to perform well in the classroom.

Without question, hyperactivity is more prevalent among boys than girls. DSM-III reports this ratio to be as high as 10:1; more conservative figures usually reflect a 6:1 ratio. Several hypotheses have been advanced for this gender disparity. One emphasizes that males generally show a greater preponderance of neurodevelopmental problems than females. Genetic studies support this claim, suggesting that hyperactivity is a sex-linked disorder. Males also show learning problems approximately three times more often than females, and, as mentioned, an increasing incidence of learning problems is found among ADD-HA children. Geschwind and Galaburda (1985) suggest that this male predominance pattern may reflect a selective deficiency in the males' immune system as a potential underlying etiology.

Another tentative hypothesis as to why males greatly exceed females within the diagnostic category is that boys are "allowed" to be more active than girls. This assumption, however, has never been proven scientifically valid. One other theory is that males are biologically predisposed not only to pre-, peri-, and postnatal complications, but that they also experience psychiatric and neurological disorders at a significantly greater rate than their female peers (Gualtieri & Hicks, 1985b). Termed an "immunoreactive theory of selective male affliction," this hypothesis draws on findings from a wide variety of childhood disorders including hyperactivity.

Finally, regarding the prevalence of hyperactivity in the United States versus other countries (Trites, 1979), it appears at first glance that many European countries rarely report hyperactivity, whereas in Canada the statistic is much higher. Close inspection of these findings, however, reveals that definitions of the disorder vary from country to country, and in some, the ADD-HA child is referred to as a "conduct disordered" child. Review of current medical literature in the U.S. reports an incidence rate of approximately 6 percent for childhood hyperactivity.

One can see that even the description or diagnostic classification of the hyperactive is not simple. Development of the DSM-III strategy will probably diminish some of the debate over the diagnosis and will also likely result in clarification of the nature of the disorder—that is, as a primary attentional deficit accompanied by a serious behavior disturbance of overactivity.

A reasonable and valid diagnostic alternative to the DSM-III classification of ADD-HA is to employ psychological test scores and behavior rating systems. This approach has several advantages: (1) predetermined test "cutoff" points reduce the reliability error of examiners' subjective bias; (2) diagnostic criteria can be defined to include only those children who are truly deviant (for example, two or more standard deviations from the mean "average" score); (3) standardized assessment procedures can be used in a variety of settings and locations, thereby reducing the potential contaminant of "situational" influences; and (4) parametric test data are more amenable to complex statistical analysis than are nonparametric data.

A number of reliable psychological tests and behavior rating scales have been developed to help characterize the ADD-HA child in relation to his or her peers. The most popular behavior rating measure to date, the Conners Parent Rating Scale (a teacher version is also available), allows parents and teachers to rate the child's cognitive, emotional, and behavioral status on a number of dimensions, including conduct problems, learning problems, psychosomatic problems, impulsivity-hyperactivity, and anxiety. This scale has been found to be sensitive to the effects of prescribed medicine for hyperactiv-

FIGURE 7–1

Parent's Questionnaire (Goyette, Conners, & Ulrich, 1978)

Name of Child _____ Date _____

Please answer all questions. Beside each item below, indicate the degree of the problem by a check mark (✔)

	Not at all	Just a little	Pretty much	Very much
1. Picks at things (nails, fingers, hair, clothing).	___	___	___	___
2. Sassy to grown-ups.	___	___	___	___
3. Problems with making or keeping friends.	___	___	___	___
4. Excitable, impulsive.	___	___	___	___
5. Wants to run things.	___	___	___	___
6. Sucks or chews (thumb; clothing; blankets).	___	___	___	___
7. Cries easily or often.	___	___	___	___
8. Carries a chip on his shoulder.	___	___	___	___
9. Daydreams.	___	___	___	___
10. Difficulty in learning.	___	___	___	___
11. Restless in the "squirmy" sense.	___	___	___	___
12. Fearful (of new situations; new people or places; going to school).	___	___	___	___
13. Restless, always up and on the go.	___	___	___	___
14. Destructive.	___	___	___	___
15. Tells lies or stories that aren't true.	___	___	___	___
16. Shy.	___	___	___	___
17. Gets into more trouble than others same age.	___	___	___	___
18. Speaks differently from others same age (baby talk; stuttering; hard to understand).	___	___	___	___
19. Denies mistakes or blames others.	___	___	___	___
20. Quarrelsome.	___	___	___	___
21. Pouts and sulks.	___	___	___	___
22. Steals.	___	___	___	___
23. Disobedient or obeys but resentfully.	___	___	___	___
24. Worries more than others (about being alone; illness or death).	___	___	___	___
25. Fails to finish things.	___	___	___	___
26. Feelings easily hurt.	___	___	___	___
27. Bullies others.	___	___	___	___
28. Unable to stop a repetitive activity.	___	___	___	___
29. Cruel.	___	___	___	___
30. Childish or immature (wants help he shouldn't need; clings; needs constant reassurance).	___	___	___	___
31. Distractibility or attention span a problem.	___	___	___	___
32. Headaches.	___	___	___	___
33. Mood changes quickly and drastically.	___	___	___	___
34. Doesn't like or doesn't follow rules or restrictions.	___	___	___	___
35. Fights constantly.	___	___	___	___
36. Doesn't get along well with brothers and sisters.	___	___	___	___
37. Easily frustrated in efforts.	___	___	___	___
38. Disturbs other children.	___	___	___	___
39. Basically an unhappy child.	___	___	___	___
40. Problems with eating (poor appetite; up between bites).	___	___	___	___
41. Stomach aches.	___	___	___	___
42. Problems with sleep (can't fall asleep; up too early; up in the night).	___	___	___	___
43. Other aches and pains.	___	___	___	___
44. Vomiting or nausea.	___	___	___	___
45. Feels cheated in family circle.	___	___	___	___
46. Boasts and brags.	___	___	___	___
47. Lets self be pushed around.	___	___	___	___
48. Bowel problems (frequently loose; irregular habits; constipation).	___	___	___	___

ity, and it also has adequate norms (Goyette, Conners, & Ulrich, 1978). The measure is frequently used in pharmacologic research studies where a criterion score is set for inclusion as deviant. For example, by establishing a cutoff point of at least two standard deviations above the mean on a particular dimension, one statistically limits inclusion to approximately two percent of the population. This rather rigorous inclusion criterion assures homogeneity of the sample, an issue of considerable importance when one considers the historically diagnostic ambiguity of the disorder.

Reliable psychological test measures can also be employed as a discriminating classification variable. For example, tests of attentional status can be used similarly to the behavior rating scales for inclusion/exclusion decisions. The frequently used Continuous Performance Task (CPT) (Rosvold, Mirsky, Sarason, Bransome, & Beck, 1956) has been shown to discriminate reliably between hyperactive and nonhyperactive children (Barkley, 1977; Sykes, Douglas, Weiss, & Minde, 1971), although it may not discriminate between ADD-HA children and children with conduct disorders. The test is also a reliable index of drug response.

Thus, classifying a child as "hyperactive" is a complex and multifaceted process. DSM-III has removed some of the ambiguity by including criteria that encompass age determinants, duration of symptoms, and behavioral and cognitive manifestations as critical variables. Research demonstrates the utility of employing psychological assessment procedures and behavior rating scales as additional discriminating characteristics. Without doubt, using both strategies enhances the reliability of the diagnostic process.

ETIOLOGICAL PERSPECTIVES

Discovering the cause of childhood hyperactivity appears to be as difficult as diagnosis.

No single etiological perspective accounts for all hyperactive children. Overactivity and poor attention span, the cardinal features of this disorder, can result from a variety of biological and psychological circumstances, leading many scientists to believe we will never find a single cause for hyperactivity. A number of etiological perspectives for the disorder, however, have gained substantial credibility within research and clinical forums. Theories with particular prominence emphasize hyperactivity as an underlying "dysmaturational" disorder (Kinsbourne, 1973); as a disturbance of specific brain systems, including biochemical imbalances (Gualtieri & Hicks, 1985b); as genetically transmitted; as a severe psychological disturbance; or as a disorder arising from "external" variables, such as diet, environmental pollutants, crowding, lack of stimulation, and so on.

Hyperactivity as a Neurological Disorder

Several theories relate hyperactivity to biological aberrations. These models view hyperactivity as a result of extreme variations along the "normal curve" of development (a "dysmaturational" disorder), as genetically transmitted, or as the result of specific maldevelopment or insult to specific brain structures.

The dysmaturational syndrome espoused by Kinsbourne (1973) views hyperactivity as representing a statistically-related biological observation. That is, if one assumes the theoretical viewpoint that all dimensions of normal human behavior follow a normal bell-curve distribution, then a specific statistical percentage of that behavior (for example, attention span or activity level) will fall at the extreme of the distribution at some point during development. When two or more of these dimensions occur in a particular individual, as in the hyperactive child, for example, a significant deviation has occurred. An example of a developmental aspect of the dysmaturational hypothesis comes from the observation of the child's activity level. Hyperactivity is often first noted during kindergarten and early school years, yet often diminishes with maturity. The theory implies that these individuals show no gross evidence of a biological disorder; rather, they represent extreme deviations of normality. Certain "soft signs" of neurological disorder symptomatology may be present—asymmetrical reflexes, delayed or slow learning, minor physical anomalies—and by most definitions, these soft signs in an otherwise physically healthy child should dissipate in the normal course of maturation.

Children with these "deviant" characteristics who were seen by physicians, psychologists, and other health professionals were often labeled as having minimal brain dysfunction (MBD). The MBD terminology first emerged in the early 1960s, but has undergone considerable criticism within the last decade. Many scientists and clinicians believe the MBD concept is confusing and, in most circumstances, misleading. The diagnosis is confusing in that qualitative differences between normal children and children diagnosed with MBD were small and, consequently, "normal" children were occasionally misdiagnosed as MBD. Assigning a label of "brain damage" to anyone, child or adult, has many negative social connotations. For one thing, laypeople often perceive it as a serious, debilitating, permanent condition. The potential misuse of the term is not offset by an advantage of communicating specific information about an individual.

Kinsbourne's view stresses that clinicians should view neurological "soft signs" from a developmental perspective; he adds that "soft signs" differ from "hard signs" in that the child's age is the determining factor as to whether the sign represents an abnormality. The theory implies that eventually the child will "catch up" following a normal progression of neurological development. The model also implies the importance of the interaction between early experience and learning skills.

Another theory of the etiology of hyperactivity that is gaining scientific validity regards hyperactivity as a disorder arising from a biochemical imbalance within specific regions of the brain. The biochemical compounds are composed of a certain class of neurotransmitter substances called *monoamines*. The monoamines are found in increasing proportion within particular brain regions, specifically the neostriatum. One of the monoamines, *dopamine*, has been found to exist in diminished proportions among groups of hyperactive children. It is from this observation that certain drugs, such as Ritalin and Cylert, which facilitate the transmission of monoamines, are said to improve the overactivity levels of the hyperactive child.

The theory represents a combined neuropsychological-psychopharmacologic approach for testing a specific brain-related hypothesis of hyperactivity. The hypothesis originates in a more general theory that conceptualizes severe attentional impairments and hyperkinesis as a disorder of neural systems concerned with the regulation of "cerebral homeostasis." The particular neural systems involved strongly implicate the frontal and prefrontal areas of the brain. These areas regulate attention, maintain cognitive set, and control the impact of competing stimuli. Considerable scientific literature supports the frontal cortex as the "executor" of these complex functions (Pribam, 1977).

The argument in support of the frontal hypothesis of ADD is based on the following evidence: (1) many performance and behavioral problems are common to ADD children and patients with known damage to frontal cortex; (2) frontal-striatal surgical and chemical lesions have been successful animal models of ADD-HA; (3) drugs that are effective in ADD-HA are usually effective in the animal models; (4) these drugs seem to exert their (syndrome-specific) effects dopaminergically; and (5) frontal systems are rich in dopamine-containing neurons.

Children with attentional impairments and heightened activity are characterized by many of the same problems as patients with damage to the frontal lobes: distractibility, impulsivity, and emotional instability. The earliest descriptions of these symptoms and the "frontal syndrome" stressed problems in distractibility and impulse control. Modern descriptions of hyperkinesis and the frontal syndrome are strikingly similar. Wender (1971), for example, describes the distractibility of hyperactive children:

With the MBD child, as with an infant, striking external stimuli will interrupt a mental set. When he is told to perform a task he may start willingly enough and then forget to complete it; he abandons tasks in the middle. An irrelevant stimulus, a bright toy, an interesting noise, fixes his attention until another stimulus seizes it. These arresting stimuli may also come from within. The child's mental set, his internal "plan ahead," may also be interrupted by "ideas," "wishes," or drives which well up suddenly disrupting the smooth performance and completion of extended tasks or behavior patterns. (Wender, 1971, p. 142)

This description could also serve as a clinical analogy to frontal syndrome patients. Others have also interpreted frontal syndrome performance difficulties in terms of their sensitivity to distraction. There is general agreement that one of the functions of the frontal lobes is to inhibit interference among brain events, and that the reduced inhibition witnessed among frontal syndrome patients leads to distractibility and short attention span.

The frontal syndrome hypothesis of ADD-HA may also be supported by our affirmation in clinical studies that stimulant effects on a wide range of dependent measures are uncorrelated and that stimulant effects are rate-dependent. These findings suggest that stimulant drug treatment of ADD children corrects a fundamental dysfunction of neuroregulatory, or homeostatic, mecha-

nisms, and that the neural substrate for this activity is probably found in dopaminergic projections to frontal cortex. Investigations are presently under way to test this neural substrate theory of hyperactivity. Considerable research supports the impression that hyperactivity is in large part a disorder associated with a neurochemical imbalance, specifically in the frontal lobe.

Genetic Factors

A potential genetic basis for any disorder arises when evidence shows a clustering of some or similar symptoms of the disorder in question among the close relatives of an afflicted individual. With this assumption in mind, a number of observations suggest a hereditary pattern in the clinical syndrome of hyperactivity; for example:

- Families of hyperactive children show a higher incidence of other emotional and behavioral disturbances, including sociopathy, alcoholism, and depression (Cadoret & Gath, 1980). In addition, hyperactive children are at greater risk for developing these disorders as adults, compared to nonhyperactive, "normal" children (Cantwell, 1972). These difficulties are observed with significantly less frequency in the adopted family members of hyperactive children.

- Controlled studies investigating the cognitive pattern of hyperactive children suggest that their parents show a disproportionally higher incidence of inattentiveness and impulsivity (Morrison & Stewart, 1971).

- Data are available from twin studies indicating that hyperactive symptoms occur with much higher prevalence among monozygotic versus dyzygotic twins (Cadoret & Gath, 1980).

Environmental Factors: Toxins

Since the publication of Feingold's *Why Your Child is Hyperactive* in 1975, considerable controversy has arisen regarding the relationship of diet to childhood hyperactivity. The model espoused by Feingold suggests that hyperactive children show an abnormal, elevated sensitivity to synthetic food colors, synthetic flavors, and certain "natural constituents." Theoretically, removal of these substances from the child's diet is strongly associated with a reduction of activity level. These natural compounds are particularly present in some fruits (apples, oranges, grapes) and vegetables (cucumbers, tomatoes). Artificial "toxins," including preservatives, and antioxidants are also implicated. Feingold also emphasizes that other disturbances of behavior, including sociopathy, learning disabilities, and autism, may be treated primarily through diet.

The more convincing arguments for the Feingold diet arise from single case reports wherein a particular child's behavior has greatly improved following implementation of the diet; however, the majority of these case studies are not well-controlled experimentally and do not meet strict scientific research criteria (for example, placebo-controlled, or "crossover" design). Studies that have used these research criteria do not yield the significant claims made by Feingold. Perhaps a small, isolated sample of hyperactive children are supersensitive to these substances, but this possible subgroup by no means represents the majority of the hyperactive population. Some scientists have even implied that children who are Feingold diet "responders" are actually allergic to the compounds, and not truly hyperactive.

Barkley (1981) concludes that future studies relating diet to activity level should emphasize (1) *clinically* significant behavior change as indicative of therapeutic efficacy; (2) potential contraindications to the Feingold diet regime; (3) hypotheses regarding the underlying mechanism of the effects of food additives on behavior, with emphasis on specificity of one additive's effects versus another's. Scientific validation cannot be advanced until these criteria are met.

Other suggestions for "external" sources for hyperactivity include excessive amounts of sugar in the child's diet (Prinze, Roberts, & Hartman, 1980), allergic responses (Taylor, 1980), and vitamin deficiencies (Smith, 1976). These hypotheses also suffer from a lack of scientific validation.

Social Factors

Many etiological studies of childhood hyperactivity focus on its relationship to biological variables. When biological associations are not found to account for all the variance within a given study, the remaining variance is often attributed to psychological and/or psychosocial factors. While it is important to weed out all the potential contributions to the phenomenon of hyperactivity, there has clearly been less emphasis on social variables versus biological factors. In other words, psychosocial factors are often used as a catchall category for the unknown etiological concomitants to the disorder.

The Kauai study (Werner, Berman, & French, 1971), which followed more than 1000 pregnancies from birth to age 18, illustrates the complexity and difficulty of performing longitudinal, multidimensional research. Besides obtaining an extensive medical history from each subject, the Werner group also accumulated records on school behavior and home support systems. The investigators found that when perinatal stress was examined in relation to school achievement or hyperactivity at age ten, no significant relationships emerged, with the exception of mental retardation and demonstrable physical handicaps. When social variables were included in the analysis, however, significant relationships emerged between severity of perinatal stress and behavioral measures for those subjects with lower socioeconomic status. Subjects who had below-average emotional home support were also shown to be at significant risk.

Some say the Kauai study was not able to predict hyperactivity from any of the social factors; however, school achievement and nonhyperactive-related "emotional problems" were predicted at age ten when social factors were included in the analysis. The conclusion is that a group of at-risk children exist whose environment may not make up for insults during the prenatal period.

In another epidemiological study, Nichols and Chen (1981) examined the behavioral, cognitive, emotional, and neurological status of 30,000 children from birth to age seven. Nichols found several associations between behavioral and neurological scores, one of which was a surprisingly weak association between the cognitive and neurological measures. One must be cautious, however, in overinterpreting the data, since we must consider the severity of one factor versus another before delineating its overall contribution to the problem. In severely deprived backgrounds where emotional and educational levels are grossly deviant, for example, these "social" factors contribute much more to etiology than do milder perinatal factors, such as mild bleeding during pregnancy or maternal smoking.

Another popular, although entirely unproven and scientifically unfounded, psychosocial argument for childhood hyperactivity is the "bad parenting" hypothesis. That is, hyperactivity (and other significant behavior problems) arise when parents have poor behavior-management and child-rearing skills. While no one will argue that parental inconsistency and/or inappropriate use of reinforcements and punishments can lead to troublesome behaviors, evidence relating "bad parenting" to the cause of hyperactivity is extremely weak. This model does not explain the often-noted early onset and cross-situational nature of the disorder (Barkley, 1981). Nor does it explain the preponderance of evidence that these children exhibit, to a larger degree, neurological and physical signs and learning disabilities. In addition, drug studies have shown that parenting styles "normalize" following a successful

medication trial. Finally, considerable evidence shows that hyperactive children often have "normal" siblings in the family (with the same environmental setting).

Thus, there is little evidence that psychological or psychosocial factors explain the etiology of childhood hyperactivity. Extreme psychosocial variables explain a considerable degree of the variance in some studies; however, the argument for a single cause for the disorder, particularly a psychosocial factor, is weak.

TREATMENT INTERVENTION

Treatment of the hyperactive child should follow a thorough evaluation of the child's emotional, behavioral, and biological states. We can no longer automatically assign a child to a particular treatment program because he is "hyper." Because there are varying degrees of the hyperactive syndrome, one must consider all the behavioral, emotional, and cognitive concomitants of the problem to tailor treatment for a hyperactive child. Because of the diagnostic heterogeneity, no one treatment mode has emerged for dealing with hyperactive children, although two methods appear to be quite efficacious for a large segment of this population—pharmacotherapy and behavior therapy.

Pharmacotherapy of Hyperactivity

Hyperactivity is probably the most frequent diagnosis in pediatric psychiatry. It is estimated that over 500,000 American children are receiving stimulant drug treatment for hyperkinesis. Added to other medications used for behavioral management of the hyperactive child, the total in treatment approaches 700,000 children. The majority are six to ten, and most discontinue the drug after two or three years of treatment. Several investigations document the efficacy of the stimulant drugs, particularly Ritalin, and to a lesser extent, Cylert and Dexedrine. Table 7–1 summarizes the application of these drugs to hyperactivity.

To examine the effects of a particular drug on a specific aspect of behavior, one should follow these methodological guidelines:

1. The investigation should be placebo-controlled; that is, at some point in the investigation, the subject (patient) or group of subjects takes an inert substance, and the same measurement on behavior is recorded.

2. The study should be "double-blind," meaning that neither the investigator nor the subject is aware of the experimental condition (that is, whether the subject is receiving a drug or placebo).

3. The design should have a "crossover" component; that is, each subject participates in each aspect of the experiment. In the case of a stimulant trial, the subject should undergo a drugged state and be evaluated, then experience the placebo phase at another time.

4. The subject selection should be random; each client should be placed into a particular experimental condition without bias.

In addition to these important design criteria, studies with hyperactive children would, ideally, assess all aspects of possible behavior change. This would include an evaluation of the child's emotional, cognitive, and behavioral status within each condition. Optimally, the child would also be evaluated, at least behaviorally, by both the parents and teachers.

We have mentioned the psychostimulant drug Ritalin (the generic name is *methylphenidate*) as the most frequently prescribed drug for management of childhood hyperactivity. Parents and teachers are often puzzled as to how a "stimulating" compound could decrease the activity level of an "excited" individual. What used to be called the "paradoxical" action of stimulant medicines within this population is actually not paradoxical at all. Briefly, most popular biochemical theories of childhood hyperactivity view the hyperactive syndrome as arising from an imbalance of a certain class of neurotransmitter substances. Behavioral symptoms resulting from this imbalance are poorly directed, poorly controlled, and poorly focused activity (symptoms characteristic of the hyperactive child). From a pharmacological point of view, stimulant drugs facilitate the availability of these substances, which results in a "normalizing" effect on the child's behavior. In other words, these drugs "stimulate" the

TABLE 7–1
Pharmacokinetic Profiles

	Dextroamphetamine (Dexedrine)	Methylphenidate (Ritalin)	Pemoline (Cylert)
How supplied (mg)	5, 10	5, 10, 20	18.75, 37.5, 75
Single dose range (mg/kg/dose)	.15–.5	.3–.7	.5–2.5
Daily dose range (mg/kg/day)	.3–1.25	.6–1.7	.5–3.0
(mg/day)	5–40	10–60	37.5–112.5
Usual starting dose (mg)	2.5 daily or BID	5 daily or BID	18.75 daily
Onset of behavioral effect	1 hour	1 hour	Variable
Duration of behavioral effect (hours)	4	3–4	Not available

child to become more attentive in both thought and action, by increasing arousal in the central nervous system.

Few studies have employed the necessary design criteria to answer the question of the effectiveness of medication in hyperactive children. The work of John Werry, Robert Sprague, Virginia Douglas, and Keith Conners and their associates, represents the best research to date regarding stimulant drug effects with hyperactive children. They discuss recommended doses of common psychotropic drugs prescribed for children and suggest guidelines regarding medical management of children on psychotropic drugs.

Behavioral Effects

Conners (1971) has done extensive research on hyperactive children on methylphenidate, with particular attention to how parents and teachers perceive changes in the child's behavior on and off drugs. For the most part, these studies demonstrate considerable evidence that methylphenidate improves behavior on a number of dimensions, including reduction in aggressive behavior, impulsivity, noisiness, and acting out. The drug has also consistently improved the child's ability to persevere on assigned cognitive tasks (particularly tasks of sustained attention).

Whalen and her associates (1978) have also shown that methylphenidate improves the classroom interaction between hyperactive children and their classmates. Whalen emphasizes that "structured" activity settings were particularly drug responsive, as opposed to more informal ("free play") settings. Werry and Aman (1975) compared the effects of methylphenidate and haloperidol (a major tranquilizer) on an activity-level measure. They found that methylphenidate was superior to haloperidol in reducing activity level, although both drugs were more efficacious than a placebo (except in extremely high doses).

In addition to group investigations, clinicians have employed single-case studies to demonstrate the utility of stimulant compounds for hyperactivity. Case studies have a number of advantages over group studies:

- One can more thoroughly describe the child's environmental variables that may influence behavior
- A crossover design is more feasible when N = 1
- A better understanding of the drug's action is possible because one can thoroughly assess several dimensions of behavior
- "Group effects" among heterogeneous populations are often difficult to obtain

When Conners and Wells (1979) and Taylor (1979) used a single-case study approach, their research suggested that stimulant drugs do not reverse any specific pathology per se, but rather that the drugs have multiple effects on several behaviors. For example, a reduction in activity level can be accompanied by decreases in the child's self-esteem and diminished frustration tolerance. In other words, positive responses are often accompanied by negative reactions. This research emphasizes that when conflicting outcomes appear, the clinician, parent, and teacher must carefully assess the total picture underlying the drug response.

Case studies and group investigations often show discrepancies in drug responsiveness as reported by clinicians and teachers. Many authors report a positive drug response to relatively low doses of stimulant drugs. (Drug responsiveness is assessed by laboratory measures of attention, learning, and activity level.) But in a classroom situation, which is usually less structured than the laboratory, no significant improvements in behavior or performance are observed. On the other hand, when the dosage is increased, teachers often report that the child's classroom behavior improves, while on the same laboratory measures, the child's performance is likely to be relatively impaired. The challenge is to prescribe an optimal dosage range that will not inhibit learning but will provide the behavioral control needed in the classroom. The differential effects of stimulant drugs on cognition and behavior illustrate the importance of consistent interaction among the parents, teachers, and physicians of the hyperactive child.

Effects on Cognition

Within the last ten years, investigations have demonstrated that stimulant drugs not only have a desired action on behavior, but that they also alter the individual's "thinking" skills. We have mentioned that low doses of stimulants generally have a favorable effect on a hyperactive child's ability to perform on laboratory measures of attention and learning. There are even preliminary indications that low doses of stimulant drugs enhance *normal* children's performance on these tasks. Less information is available, however, on two related issues concerning the effects of stimulant drugs on thinking skills. First, do the drugs affect different aspects of cognition? For example, do they also improve memory, IQ, language, or perceptual motor skills? If so, to what degree? Second, what are the long-term effects of the medicines on cognitive performance? For example, if a child's attention improves with a particular stimulant, will this improvement eventually be translated into better grades at school?

Differential effects. Stimulant drug effects on attention and activity level are well documented, so we will not discuss them here. Roughly 75 percent of all hyperactive children who receive stimulants show improvements in attentional skills and reduced activity levels. Solanto (1984) and Barkley (1977) provide excellent reviews of these issues.

Hyperactive children and normal children perform differently on a number of cognitive tests; usually, the normal child outperforms the hyperactive child. One task, the paired-associate learning paradigm, reliably discriminates hyperactive from nonhyperactive children. Methylphenidate treatment generally enhances performance on this mea-

sure for both groups, although the hyperactive children typically show a more dramatic response. On other measures of memory, hyperactive children often show better response to stimulant drugs compared to their nonhyperactive peers. These other tests may involve recall or recognition of previously learned material.

Stimulant drugs, as well as amphetamines, may facilitate memory functions in several ways:

● These drugs appear to enhance acquisition of information, with lesser effects on retrieval. "Effortful" learning seems particularly drug sensitive as opposed to learning that is less demanding (Evans, Gualtieri, & Amara, 1986).

● Not all hyperactive children show beneficial cognitive effects of drug therapy (Evans, Gualtieri, & Hicks, 1986). The documented heterogeneity of symptoms of hyperactive children suggests that there are probably subgroups within the diagnosis; that is, some children are more prone to show a positive behavioral response to drugs, whereas others may show a positive cognitive response without significant changes in their behavior.

● Sufficient data suggest that it is difficult to predict how a child will respond to drug treatment (Hicks & Gualtieri, 1983). Studies have attempted to show "state-dependent" versus "rate-dependent" learning; thus far, the findings are equivocal. Studies on the cognitive functioning of the hyperactive child suggest that a medication trial is often indicated, but that it is difficult to predict what dimension of behavior (whether activity level, attention span, learning, or memory) will be most affected by the drug.

Stimulant drugs have no immediate demonstrable effects on a child's overall intellectual functioning or achievement level in school. Studies that have attempted to demonstrate differences on these measures have suffered from inadequate design, lack of appropriate controls, and excessive "external" variables beyond the examiner's control—such as frequent school changes, different teachers, and so on.

The literature on potential differential pharmacological effects on the cognitive performance of hyperactive children has raised more questions than it has answered. Most children do show a favorable drug response when attentional status is assessed. Other studies report favorable indices of improved performance on memory and learning tasks. But most studies investigate a child's overall cognitive status, rather than focus on specific aspects of thinking. One cannot assume, for example, that a child's memory is specifically enhanced following pharmacotherapy if one has not assessed other functions involved in memory functioning, such as attentional status, perceptual skills, and IQ. Only after careful investigation of the many aspects of cognition with a given subject can one make a reliable statement concerning functional dissociability of drug response. Researchers at the University of North Carolina and at Children's Hospital in Washington, D.C. are currently dealing with this difficult problem.

Long-term effects. If a hyperactive child's attentional and/or behavioral status improves following drug therapy, it makes sense that improvement in academic or social behavior will follow. Recent research, however, does not support this idea. Studies by Gadow (1983), Quinn and Rapoport (1975), and Kavole (1982) have failed to demonstrate drug treatment response on traditional measures of academic achievement. Barkley and Cunningham (1979) reported that in 17 studies investigating stimulant effects on achievement test performance, approximately 83 percent showed no effect at all.

Gadow emphasizes that these negative findings probably result from several sources, including heterogeneity of research groups, insensitivity of traditional achievement tests to any type of drug treatment, and lack of adequate controls. These findings do not suggest that stimulant drugs should not be used to control activity level and to improve a child's cognitive skills in the short term, but they do imply that long-term results are more difficult to predict.

Behavioral Intervention

In many instances, behavior modification techniques and other systematic behaviorally-oriented therapies have been successful in treating childhood hyperactivity. In addition to the cognitive difficulties some hyperactive children encounter, many of these children experience a panoply of behavioral disturbances, including aggressiveness, low frustration tolerance, impulsivity, and noncompliance. Poor social interaction is also quite common among hyperactive children. It is with these behaviors, which involve social skills, that the effects of stimulant medication are less predictable. Behaviorally-oriented therapies, used alone or in conjunction with pharmacotherapy, show promise with the hyperactive population when addressing these behaviors.

Hinshaw, Henker, and Whalen (1984) mention two reasonable behaviorally-oriented treatment alternatives for hyperactive children—behavioral and cognitive-behavioral strategies. The former typically encompasses traditional, classical models of operant conditioning to effect behavior change. The latter strategy usually involves problem-solving and verbal-mediation techniques to change behavior. One must be aware of fundamental principles of behavioral and cognitive-behavioral theory before initiating or evaluating treatment effectiveness. (Barkley [1981] provides an excellent discussion of these critical theoretical assumptions.)

Investigation of behavior therapy approaches in the treatment of childhood hyperactivity reveals an extensive diversity of techniques. Approaches include positive reinforcement, punishment, token economies, behavioral contracts, and modeling. From among the various labels and treatment alternatives, some basic principles emerge within most behavioral programs:

1. An empirical basis for evaluation therapy

2. Antecedents and consequences of a given behavior

3. Ongoing empirical assessment of treatment intervention

As Mash and Dalby (1979) emphasize, most behavior therapies do not make assumptions about the etiology of a given disorder with regard to predicting treatment success. Rather, an empirical and pragmatic approach is the current guiding rule for intervention. Most behavior therapists argue that, regardless of etiology, environmental events strongly influence the emergence, coordination, or extinction of a given behavior.

One may ask why one would need a behavioral strategy to manage hyperactivity when the stimulant medications have shown reliable efficacy. The answer is based on several clinical observations indicating that pharmacological intervention for hyperactivity has some limitations, including:

1. Stimulant drugs are not without side effects, including insomnia, irritability, and anorexia.

2. The long-term consequences of taking these drugs are not completely understood; for example, there does *not* seem to be a substantial, positive response to the medicines in terms of improved academic performance.

3. Approximately 25 percent of hyperactive children show no response to medication.

4. Our research and that of others (Campbell, Endman, & Bernfeld, 1977) suggest that some children experience diminished self-esteem and reduced social interactions while on stimulant drugs.

5. Many parents refuse to put their children on medicines if for no other reason than denying the severity of the problem, refusing to admit that the child is sick or deviant.

These and other reasons may indicate the need for a behaviorally-oriented management approach. Behavioral models that have met with at least partial success use these strategies:

● Reinforcement/punishment paradigms (Firestone & Douglas, 1975; O'Leary, Pelham, Rosenbaum, & Price, 1976)

● Classroom intervention (O'Leary et al., 1976)

● Behavior contracting

Mash and Dalby (1979) mention that in the laboratory setting, hyperactive children may respond to reinforcement procedures in a "unique" way as compared to their nonhyperactive peers. That is, hyperactive children are more likely to become "overinvolved" in the reinforcers and display diminished performance under random or partial reinforcement schedules (Parry & Douglas, 1973). It also appears that hyperactive children quickly return to baseline behavior following termination of the reinforcers. These children also appear especially sensitive to changes in the reinforcement schedules as compared to normal children.

In our clinical practice and medication trials, we have witnessed the hyperactive child's vulnerabilities within traditional reinforcement paradigms; from this experience, we offer these guidelines:

1. When a child is first started on a reinforcement program, the schedules should allow for consistent, continuous, and behavior-contingent reinforcement. Any changes from this pattern should be instituted slowly and gradually.

2. Self-reinforcement programs have been successful with hyperactive children (Barkley & Cunningham, 1979). Therefore, if possible, the child should be taught to administer his own rewards.

3. Hyperactive children are more likely to show initial "resistance" to a reinforcement schedule; that is, they are quite likely to show a deterioration in behavior before they exhibit a favorable response to the program. The importance of persistence on the part of the administrator of the program cannot be overemphasized.

4. One should always use "individualized" reinforcers. One must choose the child's specific reinforcer carefully, since experience shows that one person's pleasure can be another's poison.

Following these simple guidelines enhances the probability of success for a reinforcement program. Wolraich (1979) gives a more thorough discussion of behavioral programs for managing childhood hyperactivity.

Cognitive-behavior modification emphasizes the individual's active involvement in the program of behavior change. Typical strategies in a cognitive-behavior framework include self-regulation, self-observation, self-monitoring, and self-reinforcement. The rationale for employing self-control strategies with hyperactive children is that if a child can be taught self-control in specific circumstances, then "response generalization" can occur—that is, the behavior change will generalize across many different situations and across time, thereby reducing the necessity for reinforcers (Mash & Dalby, 1979). This theory also assumes that greater self-control results in greater self-esteem.

Unfortunately, few well-controlled investigations of cognitive behavior strategies have been performed. In an earlier study, Meichenbaum and Goodman (1971) taught five children verbal self-control strategies (for example, to talk to themselves to increase self-directed control) and found that, after four half-hours of training, their performance improved on several cognitive tests; however, no tests of school achievement were administered, and it did not appear that the improvement generalized to the classroom. Douglas, Parry, Marton, and Garson (1976) did a follow-up of the Meichenbaum strategy that included achievement test scores within the dependent measures. After three months of

training, a six-month follow-up visit yielded only one isolated improvement (listening comprehension).

The use of behavior modifying techniques in the *classroom* has been reviewed elsewhere (Howlin, 1985). The effectiveness of behavior techniques in modifying "disruptive" behavior (talking out, aggressiveness, out-of-seat behavior) depends to a large degree on the teacher's experience in dealing with HAC; the availability of appropriate reinforcement and "punishment" (for example, time out and withholding reinforcers); focusing on successful academic achievement as the primary goal rather than emphasizing a decrease in disruptive behavior; and emphasizing the relationship between classroom and home programs (by using similar reinforcement strategies for generalization effects). Trites (1979) reminds us that behavioral interventions will receive more use in the classroom in light of the failure of drug interventions alone to show a significant effect on academic performance.

The cognitive-behavior strategy as a sole intervention with hyperactive children is not without its critics. Friedling and O'Leary (1979) were unable to find any significant effects with cognitive training, but were able to show significance when similar behaviors were managed with a token economy program. They concluded that the most efficacious approach to employing cognitive-behavior tasks with the hyperactive child is to include other strategies in conjunction with the cognitive-behavior approach. There is also little evidence to suggest that teaching self-control strategies results in generalization to nontargeted behavior.

Douglas et al. (1976) concluded that we need more large-scale investigations to evaluate the relative effectiveness of cognitive training and contingency management of the hyperactive syndrome. This research would need to emphasize comparisons to traditional behavioral programs as well as to pharmacologic interventions. Douglas also adds that research designs should allow a reasonable time to pass to measure long-term effectiveness of the program.

A COMBINED APPROACH

Hinshaw, Henker, and Whalen (1984), in reviewing the literature and conducting studies of their own in the area of individual and combined effects of behavioral and pharmacologic interventions for hyperactivity, acknowledge the limitations of using each approach independently. They conclude that the combination method yields greater benefits for hyperactive children than either approach used separately. This assumption was tested this way: a group of carefully selected hyperactive boys ($N = 24$) with a primary diagnosis of hyperactivity and a history of positive response to stimulant treatment were chosen as subjects. These children did not display significant learning problems and showed no symptoms of organicity, psychosis, or family turmoil. All subjects scored in the hyperactive range on a standardized psychometric behavior-rating instrument. The subject group was relatively homogeneous, and there was no doubt that these children were clinically hyperactive. A control group was established for comparison. The environment for the study was naturalistic—classroom, playground, small-group settings. The boys received daily training in cognitive-behavioral strategies, including self-instructional procedures for academic tasks, anger control in peer provocation situations, and instruction in self-evaluation skills. The medication intervention (methylphenidate) was placebo-controlled and double-blind. The dependent measures included assessments of appropriate and negative social behavior, nonsocial behavior, adult rating of behavior, and the child's self-evaluation ratings.

Results of the investigation indicated that both the drug and reinforced self-evaluation procedures were superior. Rank order of treatment effectiveness revealed that the best combination was a medication plus cognitive-behavioral self-evaluation. Placebo plus reinforcement alone proved the least effective method of intervention. The study also found that medication enhanced the accuracy of the participants' self-evaluation.

The results of the Hinshaw et al. study are encouraging. The design and methodology were sound. Our clinical and research experience in inpatient settings supports the impression that a combination of medication and behavioral management is the best treatment of childhood hyperactivity in the short term. Unfortunately, we still lack information about the potentially positive long-term effects of such strategies, but so far, the evidence suggests that stimulants alone have little effect in social, vocational, or educational outcomes.

Alternative Treatments

Pharmacological and behavioral therapies make up the majority of successful treatment strategies for childhood hyperactivity. Other approaches, including diet restrictions (such as the Feingold diet), adding amounts of certain vitamins or minerals (usually zinc), cutting back on the child's sugar intake, or treating the child as one might treat certain allergies, have all been proposed as either unitary or conjunctive treatment approaches. Scientific opinion is unanimous that the chances of significantly arresting a child's hyperactivity using one of these strategies as the sole treatment are extremely rare. These treatments may, in rare cases, even attenuate or directly interfere with the positive effects of a successful medication or behavioral therapy.

CONCLUSION

Several misconceptions continue to flourish regarding the description, prevalence, incidence, etiology, and treatment for childhood hyperactivity. The notion that bad parents "condition" bad kids has no place in the scientific literature. Parents have been blamed for decades for "allowing" their children to become hyperactive. One cannot support this assumption within the rigors of scientific methodology. We do find that hyperactivity exists in even the best family situations and is absent in the most impoverished situations. The point is to redirect or at least distribute treatment emphasis to proven strategies—pharmacotherapy and/or continuous behavioral methods—to reduce hyperactive behavior.

Thorough evaluation of the child's cognitive, behavioral, and emotional states should precede treatment for hyperactivity. Recent research shows that both medications and behavioral strategies have differential effects. Positive behavioral changes are not always accompanied by desirable changes in cognitive and emotional states and vice versa. Clinical studies also demonstrate that it is difficult to predict which children will respond to a particular treatment. It therefore becomes necessary for clinicians, parents, and teachers to assess children systematically in a pretreatment condition and again following treatment. Several strategies may also have to be tried before deciding which treatment is best for the child.

REFERENCES

Aman, M. (1976). Stimulant drug effects in developmental disorders and hyperactivity: Toward a resolution of disparate findings. *Journal of Abnormal Child Psychology, 4* (4), 389–410.

American Psychiatric Association. (1980). *Diagnostic and Statistical Manual of Mental Disorders* (3rd ed.). Washington, DC.

Barkley, R. (1977). A review of stimulant drug research with hyperactive children. *Journal of Child Psychology and Psychiatry, 18,* 137–165.

Barkley, R. A. (1978). Recent developments in research on hyperactive children. *Journal of Pediatric Psychology, 3* (4), 158–163.

Barkley, R. A. (1981). Hyperactivity. In E. Mash & L. Teudal (Eds.), *Behavioral assessment of childhood disorders* (pp. 127–184). New York: Guilford Press.

Barkley, R. A., & Cunningham, C. E. (1979). The effects of methylphenidate on the mother-child interactions of hyperactive children. *Archives of General Psychiatry, 36,* 201–208.

Cadoret, R. J., & Gath, A. (1980). Biological correlates of hyperactivity: Evidence for a genetic factor. In S. Sells, M. Roff, & J. Strauss (Eds.), *Human functioning and longitudinal perspectives.* Baltimore, MD: Williams & Wilkins.

Campbell, S. B., Endman, M. W., & Bernfeld, G. (1977). A three-year follow-up of hyperactive preschoolers in elementary school. *Journal of Child Psychology and Psychiatry, 18,* 239–249.

Cantwell, O. P. (1972). Psychiatric illness in the families of hyperactive children. *Archives of General Psychiatry, 27,* 414–417.

Conners, C. K. (1971). Recent drug studies with hyperkinetic children. *Journal of Learning Disabilities, 4,* 476–483.

Conners, C. K., & Wells, K. (1979). Method and theory for psychopharmacology with children. In R. L. Trites (Ed.), *Hyperactivity in children.* Baltimore, MD: University Park Press.

Douglas, V. I., Parry, P., Marton, P., & Garson, C. (1976). Assessment of a cognitive training program for hyperactive children. *Journal of Abnormal Child Psychology, 4* (4), 389–410.

Evans, R. W., Gualtieri, C. T., & Amara, I. (1986). Methylphenidate and memory: Dissociated effects in hyperactive children. *Psychopharmacology, 90,* 211–216.

Evans, R. W., Gualtieri, C. T., & Hicks, R. E. (1986). A neuropathic substrate for stimulant drug effects in hyperactive children. *Clinical Neuropharmacology, 9,* 264–281.

Feingold, B. F. (1975). *Why your child is hyperactive.* New York: Random House.

Firestone, P., & Douglas, V. I. (1975). The effects of reward and punishment on reaction times and autonomic activity in hyperactive and normal children. *Journal of Abnormal Child Psychology, 3,* 210–216.

Friedling, C., & O'Leary, S. G. (1979). Effects of self-instructional training on second and third grade hyperactive children: A failure to replicate. *Journal of Applied Behavior Analysis, 12,* 211–219.

Gadow, K. (1983). Effects of stimulant drugs on academic performance in hyperactive and learning disabled children. *Journal of Learning Disabilities, 16* (5), 290–299.

Geschwind, N., & Galaburda, A. M. (1985). Cerebral lateralization. Biological mechanisms, associations, and pathology: A hypothesis and a program for research. *Archives of Neurology, 42,* 521–552.

Goyette, C. H., Conners, C. K., & Ulrich, R. F. (1978). Normative data of revised Conners Parent and Teacher Rating Scales. *Journal of Abnormal Child Psychology, 6,* 221–223.

Gualtieri, C. T., & Hicks, R. E. (1985a). An immunoreactive theory of selective male affliction. *Neuroscience and Biobehavioral Review.*

Gualtieri, C. T., & Hicks, R. E. (1985b). A neural substrate of childhood hyperactivity. *Pediatric Clinics of North America.*

Hicks, R. E., & Gualtieri, C. T. (1983). Stimulant effects and hyperactive children: Noncorrelated effects and systematic relationships. In L. Bloomingdale (Ed.), *Attention deficit disorder II.* New York: Spectrum.

Hinshaw, S., Henker, B., & Whalen, C. (1984). Cognitive-behavioral and pharmacologic interventions for hyperactive boys: Comparative and combined effects. *Journal of Consulting and Clinical Psychology, 52* (5), 739–749.

Howlin, P. (1985). Special education treatment. In M. Rutter & L. Hersov, *Child and adolescent psychiatry.* Oxford: Oxford University Press.

Kavole, K. (1982). The efficacy of stimulant drug treatment for hyperactivity: A meta-analysis. *Journal of Learning Disabilities, 15,* 280–289.

Kinsbourne, M. (1973). Minimal brain dysfunction as a neuro-developmental lag. *Annals of the New York Academy of Science, 205,* 263–273.

Mash, E. J., & Dalby, J. T. (1979). Behavioral interventions for hyperactivity. In R. L. Trites (Ed.), *Hyperactivity in children.* Baltimore, MD: University Park Press.

Meichenbaum, D. H., & Goodman, J. (1971). Training impulsive children to talk to themselves: A means of developing self-control. *Journal of Abnormal Psychology, 77,* 115–126.

Morrison, J. R., & Stewart, M. A. (1971). A family study of the hyperactive child. *Biological Psychiatry, 3,* 189–195.

Nichols, P., & Chen, W. (1981). *Minimal brain dysfunction: A prospective study.* Hillsdale, NJ: Erlbaum.

O'Leary, K. D., Pelham, W. E., Rosenbaum, S., & Price, G. H. (1976). Behavioral treatment of hyperkinetic children: An experimental evaluation of its usefulness. *Clinical Pediatrics, 15,* 510–515.

Parry, C., & Douglas, V. I. (1973). The effect of reward on the performance of hyperactive children. *Dissertation Abstracts International, 34:*6220B.

Pribam, K. H. (1977). The primate frontal cortex-executive of the brain. In K. H. Pribam & A. R. Luria (Eds.), *Psychophysiology of the frontal lobes.* New York: Academic Press.

Prinze, R. J., Roberts, W. A., & Hartman, E. (1980). Dietary correlates of hyperactive behavior in children.

Journal of Consulting and Clinical Psychology, 48, 760–769.

Quinn, P., & Rapoport, J. (1975). One-year follow-up of hyperactive boys treated with imipramine and methylphenidate. *American Journal of Psychiatry, 132,* 241–245.

Rosvold, E., Mirsky, A., Sarason, I., Bransome, E., & Beck, L. (1956). A continuous performance test of brain damage. *Journal of Counseling Psychology, 20,* 343–350.

Rutter, M. (1977). Brain damage syndromes in childhood: Concepts and findings. *Journal of Child Psychology and Psychiatry, 18,* 1–21.

Smith, L. (1976). *Your child's behavior chemistry.* New York: Random House.

Solanto, M. V. (1984). Neuropharmacological basis of stimulant drug action in attention deficit disorder with hyperactivity: A review and synthesis. *Psychological Bulletin, 95* (3), 387–409.

Sprague, R. L., & Sleator, E. K. (1977). Methylphenidate in hyperkinetic children: Differences in dose effects on learning and social behavior. *Science, 198,* 1274–1276.

Sykes, D., Douglas, V., Weiss, G., & Minde, K. (1971). Attention in hyperactive children and the effect of methylphenidate (Ritalin). *Journal of Child Psychology and Psychiatry, 12,* 129–139.

Taylor, E. (1979). The use of drugs in hyperkinetic states: Clinical issues. *Neuropharmacology, 18,* 951–958.

Taylor, J. F. (1980). *The hyperactive child and the family.* New York: Everest House.

Trites, R. L. (1979). *Hyperactivity in children.* Baltimore, MD: University Park Press.

Wender, P. H. (1971). *Minimal brain dysfunction in children.* New York: Wiley Interscience.

Werry, J. S., & Aman, M. G. (1975). Methylphenidate and haloperidol in children. *Archives of General Psychiatry, 32,* 790–795.

Werry, J. S., Weiss, G., & Douglas, V. (1964). Studies on the hyperactive child: I. Some preliminary findings. *Canadian Psychiatric Association Journal, 9,* 120–130.

Werner, E., Berman, J., & French, F. (1971). *The children of Kauai: A longitudinal study from the prenatal period to age ten.* Honolulu: University of Hawaii Press.

Whalen, C. K., Collins, B. E., Henker, B., Alkus, S. R., Adams, A., & Stapp, J. (1978). Behavior observations of hyperactive children and methylphenidate effects in systematically structured classroom environments: Now you see them, now you don't. *Journal of Pediatric Psychology, 3* (4), 177–187.

Wolraich, M. L. (1979). Behavior modification therapy in hyperactive children. *Clinical Pediatrics, 18,* 563–569.

SECTION THREE

Overcontrolled Behavior

Behavior disorders in children are usually associated with negative or undesirable psychological states, such as unhappiness and distress. Previously, most behavior disorders were considered symptoms of psychological conflict in the child, an internalized response pattern to problems in the environment. We now characterize them as interactional problems involving the child's "fit" with his environment. Predisposing factors, such as temperament, often make it difficult to manage the child. We also often find troubled circumstances in the family, school, or neighborhood. Anxiety, depression, and psychosis are the complex products of these as well as individual psychological characteristics. We will discuss these behavior disorders in terms of research into individual psychological variables and the impinging social context. Prevention and treatment require recognition of the ecological nature of the disorders.

If he stayed in bed they would come up and tap his chest and put a ther-
mometer in his mouth and look at his tongue, and they would discover that
he was malingering. It was true that he felt ill, a sick empty sensation in his
stomach and a rapidly beating heart, but he knew that the cause was only
fear, fear of the party, fear of being made to hide by himself in the dark,
uncompanioned by Peter and with no nightlight to make a blessed breach.

GRAHAM GREENE
THE END OF THE PARTY

The 10-year-old boy who drew this picture appeared anxious to his diagnostician and his
teacher. He meticulously reproduced the shorts
he was wearing, then drew "a funny monster
who is going to eat me for breakfast." The monster may be a concrete representation of his fears
and worries.

CHAPTER EIGHT

Anxiety and Stress-Related Disorders

Betty Cooper Epanchin
WRIGHT SCHOOL, THE RE-EDUCATION CENTER
OF NORTH CAROLINA AND
UNIVERSITY OF NORTH CAROLINA AT CHAPEL HILL

Anxiety and stress are part of everyday life and, in manageable doses, can motivate individuals to improve and grow. Too much stress, however, can cause an individual to become overwhelmed with anxiety.

Anxiety disorders are manifested in different ways: phobias, school refusal, obsessive-compulsive disorders, physiological disorders that are psychologically based, and eating disturbances, to mention a few.

A number of different theories have been posited to explain why these disorders develop. Intrapsychic conflict, learning, organic and physiological factors, and socioanthropological and environmental stress have all been implicated.

Research suggests that children with anxiety disorders are often the most responsive to treatment.

Several interventions have been successful with these youngsters: expressive therapies, medication, and behavioral programs.

Although most professionals believe the prognosis for anxiety disorders is generally good, outcome studies consistently report that the personality styles reflected in these disorders remain fairly stable, even though the intensity of the problems may diminish.

TODAY'S CHILDREN GROW up in a world unlike that of past generations. They grow up knowing their world could end in a moment if there were an atomic explosion. They hear and see daily accounts of horror: families are murdered, children are kidnapped, heroes die in space, presidents are shot. On a more personal level, their social and familial networks are often limited. Cousins barely know cousins, neighbors may not speak to neighbors. Grandparents live in distant places, and parents often live apart. Coupled with the lack of secure social supports is the push to grow up fast and to achieve. As Elkind (1981) notes, we expect our children to be miniature adults, and we groom them from birth to achieve. We dress them in designer fashions; we teach them to read during their preschool years; and we send them to computer camp during their summer vacations. Given this fast-paced, complex, uncertain society in which we live, it is not surprising that stress and anxiety are common emotions for children and adults alike.

Everyone has moments of feeling insecure, of being incapable of meeting the demands of a situation, of anticipating a negative outcome to one's efforts, of not being able to accomplish what one expects of oneself, and of feeling torn between conflicting demands. When present for only short periods, moderate amounts of stress and anxiety are not unduly harmful. In fact, it can be argued that they actually promote growth and development; because they are unpleasant, individuals work to resolve the conflict or master the fear to rid themselves of the unpleasantness. Stress becomes problematic when the environment contains excessive stressors or when the demands of the environment exceed the individual's ability to respond successfully.

When children become overwhelmed by anxiety, regardless of the cause, stress-related and anxiety-based disorders may develop. Behaviors associated with these disorders include preoccupation, irritability, fearfulness, overdependence on others, sleep problems, stomachaches, lethargy, shyness, unhappiness, lack of motivation, frequent crying spells, headaches, nausea, loss of appetite, poor school work, and carelessness in carrying out responsibilities.

Traditionally clinicians have differentiated reactions that are reality-based and triggered by environmental stressors from reactions that are caused by one's internal, mental distortions. Reactions to the environment are *reactive disorders*; reactions to internal factors are *neurotic disorders*. *Neuroses* are irrational worries and conflicts that are not responsive to commonsense interventions.

If a child has been abused and neglected, it is rational and "normal" for the child to feel anxious when an unknown adult raises a hand or looks threatening. If a problem child responds to simple, commonsense interventions, such as more time and attention or more consistent discipline, the child is probably a "normal" child going through a stressful time. If the child's reactions are out of proportion to the situation and distorted, however, the child might be described as neurotic.

Kessler (1966) describes a neurosis as a problem to which the child reacts in the present as though imagined or real events of the past were still part of reality. She observes that neurotic children utilize "magical thinking," meaning that they operate as if their thoughts were the equivalent of deeds; that is, they equate a hostile thought with a hostile deed. Consequently, neurotic youngsters distort and misperceive situations and overreact to their own thoughts and feelings, but they never lose touch with reality. One difference between a neurotic and a psychotic, then, is that the neurotic recognizes these thoughts as harmless in and of themselves, once they are discussed.

In theory the distinction between a reactive disorder and a neurotic disorder appears clear-cut, but in reality it can be difficult to make. Most of the children who suffer these disorders come from relatively normal, socially responsible families, who have often had major stressors to adjust to, such as divorce, death, job failures, a major illness, and so forth. Determining when a child's problem is no longer a reactive disorder or when it is serious enough to warrant intervention can be quite difficult.

Some characteristics of when and how these feelings appear are important when determining whether a child's or adolescent's problems are serious enough, perhaps *pathological*, to warrant intervention. First, the concepts of intensity, duration, and frequency are of utmost importance. If an adolescent occasionally complains of a stomachache and has trouble sleeping before difficult exams, we empathize with her distress, but do not consider the behavior problematic, especially when she is able to maintain her poise during the exam by doing her best, then comes home to catch up on her sleep. Second, the age and stage appropriateness of developmental functioning is a factor in evaluating the severity of a youngster's anxiety level. A five-year-old who has trouble leaving her mother at the beginning of kindergarten is much less alarming than a twelve-year-old who reacts that way. Finally, and perhaps most obviously, current living circumstances are particularly relevant when evaluating the child's emotional status. When parents separate and a child becomes listless, daydreams

a great deal, and does poorly in school, we do not see the behavior as abnormal. If, however, this behavior lasts a long time, with no relief and no evidence of the child's adjusting, we become concerned that the behavior may be pathological.

The anxiety-based and stress-related disorders of childhood and adolescence are usually considered fairly benign; nonetheless, they can be disturbing to behold. With some of these disorders, the youngster is in acute distress—a state that is hard to witness and even harder to help. Reasoning and reassurance are not effective in abating the distress, because the child's behavior is beyond the control of reason. These youngsters feel upset or fearful; they know the feelings are unfounded, but they do not know what to do to make the feelings go away.

These disorders can also be baffling. Most of these children appear to be "normal." School people often question why a neurotic child is in therapy because, from their view, the child appears to be doing well. What they are not always able to see is the child's internal anguish. And, when they do witness the anguish, school personnel often find it hard to understand why "commonsense" reasoning does not help. It can be confusing to witness irrational reactions from an otherwise seemingly "normal" youngster.

A related factor that makes some of these disorders so difficult to understand is that the children sometimes present misleading, paradoxical behavior. They will appear angry when they are fearful, or indifferent when they are feeling guilty and "bad." They will focus on and talk about little details, apparently calmly, when they are actually quite upset, and the content of their talk may have little to do with their concerns. It is hard to empathize when the child's affect is so disguised.

These problems are often compounded by "significant others"—parents and teachers—feeling that they have somehow "caused" the child's reactions. They wonder what they have said or failed to say to upset the child so, and their self-absorption makes it difficult for them to remain supportive and helpful. What starts as a simple psychological conflict can become a complex ecological issue as youngsters ensnare others in their problems.

Because the word *neurosis* has been closely tied to psychodynamic theory, the DSM-III dropped the term from its nomenclature and instead uses descriptive terms for the specific disorders that are not so philosophically determined. Since the term is so widely used, however, it is often retained as a secondary descriptor for some of the disorders; for example, a major classification is *Phobic Disorders*, with *Phobic Neuroses* as a secondary title.

There are several disorders in the DSM-III in which stress and anxiety have a mediating or significant role; that is, they are manifested in response to stress and are experienced as anxiety. Some of the more familiar are the Adjustment Reaction categories, the Obsessive and Compulsive Disorders, the Somatoform Disorders, Separation Anxiety Disorder, and Phobic Disorders.

TYPES OF ANXIETY-BASED DISORDERS IN CHILDREN AND ADOLESCENTS

Adjustment Disorders

Claire, age 5, is the elder of two children born to a middle-class family. Her father is an architect and her mother a kindergarten teacher. When Claire was 4, her maternal grandmother died of cancer after a long and painful illness. During the prolonged illness, Claire's mother had made many trips to see her mother. Because the ethic of "keep a stiff upper lip" and "be strong for your family's sake" was so ingrained in Claire's mother, she never cried in front of the children nor shared her sadness and pain with them. The children sensed their mother's despair and, being "normal," egocentric preschoolers, presumed they had caused her unhappiness. Claire became irritable, grouchy, oppositional, and generally uncooperative at home. At school, her teacher saw no change in behavior.

Claire's problem behavior would most likely be described as an *adjustment disorder*. Probably the most common diagnosis for children and adolescents, an adjustment disorder may include virtually any symptom or group of symptoms that appear to be precipitated by situational stress. The diagnosis can apply to one of any age—child, adolescent, or adult. It can refer to any number of problem behaviors, all of which are reactions to an identifiable psychosocial stressor. For example, a diagnosis for a youngster with this disorder might be Adjustment Disorder with Anxious Mood (or with Depressed Mood or with Academic Inhibition). The GAP system calls these Reactive Disorders and describes them as arising from a variety of events or situations such as illness, accident, or hospitalization; loss of a parent; attitudes and behaviors of others; school pressures; or premature or inadequate stimulation.

Although many factors affect the outcome of adjustment disorders, they generally do not continue into adulthood. Studies of treated and untreated children diagnosed as having an adjustment reaction indicate that it is more prevalent among males than females, but the difference in prevalence does not manifest itself until children enter school (Richman, Stevenson, & Graham, 1975). Investigators attribute this disparity to the greater stress male children experience as a result of their biological immaturity, their temperament, expectations for their behavior, and the feminine environment in which they live (Gove & Herb, 1974).

Behaviorally, youngsters diagnosed as having an adjustment disorder display many different symptoms. The basis of this category is problem behavior in reaction to situational stress that is fairly transitory and not serious. It often happens that children are first diagnosed as having an adjustment disorder, and if they do not respond to treatment, the diagnosis is changed to a more specific, encapsulated diagnosis.

Phobias

Phobias are persistent, irrational, and disproportionate fears that are beyond the individual's control and, in the case of children, are excessive for the child's age and stage. Table 8–1 lists common fears among children at various ages. Phobias are more intense and longer-lasting than common fears. For example, someone with an *ailurophobia* (fear of cats) may know a particular cat is gentle and will not hurt, yet still panic when the cat comes close. No amount of logical reasoning helps the person control the fear.

Some phobias can be debilitating. Individuals with *aquaphobia* (fear of water) may drive many extra miles each day to avoid having to cross a river or may be unwilling to travel because of their fear of having to cross bodies of water.

Melita, age 7, witnessed an automobile accident when she was 5½ in which a mother was killed and a child severely injured. Thereafter, she was terrified of riding in a car. Even now, a year and a half later, she feels nauseous, dizzy, and ex-tremely anxious when forced to get in a car. Reasoning does not help to calm her. Furthermore, she thinks about car wrecks constantly, and when she begins worrying about a wreck, cannot get her mind off it.

Melita's fears can be classified as phobic because they are out of proportion to the situation; cannot be controlled by reason and are beyond her control; cause her to avoid cars; have persisted over a period of time; are maladaptive; and are not age or stage specific. Like many phobic youngsters, she also ruminates and obsesses about her fears, but these obsessions are not seen as primary.

Classification. Table 8–2 lists selected phobias of children. These phobias may occur alone, as part of another symptom complex, or may occur in individuals who otherwise appear normal. When they occur along with other problems, usually excessive anxiety, the clinician must determine which is the primary problem.

Phobias are sometimes difficult to diagnose in children because normally developing youngsters have fears of specific stimuli such as animals, machines, the dark, loud noises, and so on. Consequently, when diag-

TABLE 8–1
Common Fears Among Children

Age Range	Fears
0–12 months	Loud noises, strangers, unexpected events
1 year	Strangers, toilets, separation from parents
2 years	Vacuum cleaners, sirens, thunder, animals, dark rooms, separation from parents
3–4 years	Separation from parents, animals (large dogs), darkness, masks
5 years	Bodily harm, nightmares (plus fears of 3–4-year-olds)
6 years	Bodily injury, supernatural beings (ghosts, monsters, etc.), sleeping or staying alone, separation from parents
7–8 years	Same as 6-year-olds, plus fears based upon media events
9–12 years	Tests, making mistakes, their physical appearance, bodily injury, death
12–adulthood	Making mistakes, looking foolish, loss of friends or peer approval, physical attractiveness, sexual adequacy

Source: Clarizio & McCoy, 1983; Morris & Kratochwill, 1983.

nosing a phobia in a child, one must give particular attention to the severity, persistence, and maladaptiveness of the child's fearful reactions.

Prevalence. Data on the rate of occurrence of phobias in children and adolescents vary, but Morris and Kratochwill (1983) observe that when considering children who need treatment, the estimates are consistently under eight percent.

School Refusal

School refusal is one of the more frequent anxiety-based problems of childhood. Fear of or refusal to go to school is a disorder that appears to include a range of problems from a mild, easily treated fear to a serious, com-

TABLE 8–2
Selected Phobias Which Children Experience

Technical Name	Phobia
Acrophobia	height
Agoraphobia	open spaces
Aichmophobia	sharp and pointed objects
Ailurophobia	cats
Arachnophobia	spiders
Anthophobia	flowers
Anthropophobia	people
Aquaphobia	water
Astraphobia	lightning
Brontophobia	thunder
Claustrophobia	closed spaces
Cynophobia	dogs
Equinophobia	horses
Menophobia	being alone
Mikrophobia	germs
Murophobia	mice
Numerophobia	number
Nyctophobia	darkness
Ophidiophobia	snakes
Pyrophobia	fire
Thanatophobia	death
Trichophobia	hair
Xenophobia	stranger
Zoophobia	animal

From *Treating Children's Fears and Phobias* by R.J. Morris and T.R. Kratochwill, 1983, New York: Pergamon Press. Reprinted by permission.

plicated set of problems. The typical picture of a child with school refusal is one who most of the time seems well-adjusted and reasonably happy, but who, in the mornings before school, feels horrible, has a stomachache, and even runs a fever. Children with school refusal also appear frightened and, when forced away from their parents, can appear acutely distraught. These periods of upset tend to pass as soon as the threat of having to go to school or of separation from the parents passes. Some children also settle down as soon as the crisis of separation is over. If they are forced to separate, they cry and appear extremely upset, but after the parent has left, they settle down and seem quite unconcerned. More persistent children, when forced to separate, have been known to run away from school at the first opportunity.

Many authors note how controlling these outbursts can be. "It is astonishing how a child can 'one-up' adults, including school personnel and mental health professionals, especially if he appears frightened, 'disturbed,' or 'helpless' " (Leventhal, Weinberger, Stander, & Stearns, 1967, p. 69).

This disorder was formerly called *school phobia*, but many objected on the grounds that the problem is not necessarily a fear of school, but rather other fears, such as separation from the parents. Since many instances of school refusal are not classic phobias, the DSM-III makes provisions for the clinician to choose from several classifications depending on what the primary problem appears to be. Even so, the disorder is still widely debated with respect to definition and etiology. One definition of school refusal includes five conditions: "(1) severe difficulty in attending school; (2) severe emotional upset; (3) staying home with the knowledge of the parents; (4) absence of significant antisocial disorders; [and] (5) school absence lasts for several consecutive days, weeks, or even months" (Atkinson, Quarrington, & Cyr, 1985, p. 84).

This disorder may occur in the preschool years, if a child really panics about separation, but more typically it begins around 11 or 12 years of age and may persist, with periods of remission and exacerbation, for several years. Atkinson et al. (1985) suggest that age is a crucial distinction when considering severity. Cases of early onset in primary school children present quite different clinical conditions from those occurring at puberty or in early adolescence.

Classification. Several authors propose subcategories of school refusers (Hersov, 1960; Coolidge, Hahn, & Peck, 1957; Kennedy, 1965). Each proposal is different, but there are common assumptions: that there are mild and more serious forms of the disorder and that school refusal often occurs in complex family systems that contribute to the child's inability to separate emotionally from the family.

The DSM-III classifies school refusal as a "Separation Anxiety Disorder" that is differentiated from the classification of school phobia. The Separation Anxiety Disorder refers to a youngster who fears to the point of panic the prospect of separation, usually from the primary attachment figures. Diagnostic criteria in the DSM-III for this disorder include several factors, of which at least three must be present:

- Unrealistic worry that some type of harm will befall the child's major attachment figure
- Unrealistic concern that something will happen to separate the child from the attachment figure
- Persistent reluctance or refusal to go to school in order to stay with the major attachment figure
- Persistent reluctance or refusal to sleep away from the major attachment figure
- Fear of being left at home alone and becoming upset if not allowed to follow the major attachment figure around the house
- Repeated nightmares about separation

- Complaints of physical symptoms on school days, such as stomachaches, headaches, nausea, etc.
- Signs of excessive distress when separated from, or anticipating separation from, the major attachment figure
- Social withdrawal, apathy, sadness, or difficulty concentrating on work or play when not with a major attachment figure

According to the DSM-III, children with this disorder often have a number of other fears that range from monsters and animals to going to sleep.

While researchers describe pathological relationships between family members of school refusers, the DSM-III notes merely that the disorder usually occurs in close-knit, caring families and tends to occur more frequently within family groups than in the general population.

Prevalence. The DSM-III describes this disorder as "apparently not uncommon" and as occurring in both sexes with equal frequency. Leton (1962) found "school phobia" to occur at a rate of three per 1000 pupils; seven out of 1000 pupils were found to exhibit the symptoms but in a milder form.

Outcome. Several researchers have investigated what happens to these youngsters over time. Rodriguez, Rodriguez, and Eisenberg (1959) followed up 41 children who were school refusers fifteen months to three years after treatment. Regular school attendance was the criterion for success, and 29 (71 percent) were successful. Younger children appeared to have better outcomes than did older ones, and most of the youngsters (23 of 29) attending school were making satisfactory academic and social progress.

Investigators at the Judge Baker Guidance Center conducted 10- and 21-year follow-up studies on 66 youngsters who had been treated during childhood for school phobia. At the ten-year follow-up, 49 were reevaluated. On the basis of interviews and testing,

47 were grouped according to current adjustment (for two youngsters there was insufficient information). Thirteen (3 boys, 10 girls) were judged to be "progressing satisfactorily" and to be normal adolescents or young adults; 20 (7 boys, 13 girls) were described as showing a "definite limitation in the growth process"; and 14 (9 boys, 5 girls) were at a "serious impasse in all areas of life" or had apparently "given up realistic attempts to move into psychological adulthood" (Coolidge, Brodie, & Feeney, 1964, p. 681).

At the 21-year follow-up, only 44 subjects were located, and 27 agreed to be interviewed. Information was available regarding the 12 who refused to be interviewed. All but two of the 39 completed high school, 22 completed college or junior college, and 8 completed a graduate degree. Of the 13 who were doing well at the 10-year follow-up, 10 were located, and 8 were interviewed. Only 3 of the 8 still seemed well-adjusted; the remaining 5 exhibited "frank neurotic problems." Of the 20 youngsters in the middle group at the 10-year follow-up, 14 were found and 11 interviewed. Three were essentially normal young adults; 5 showed definite symptomatology; and 3 were severely handicapped or unable to function independently. Of the 14 in the lowest functioning group at the 10-year follow-up, 10 were located and 8 were interviewed. Only one of these individuals was progressing satisfactorily at the 21-year follow-up; one fit into the middle category; and the remaining six continued to have serious problems, ranging from being completely housebound to living a constricted, acutely uncomfortable existence. Coolidge and Brodie (1976) conclude that "school phobia is an expression of powerful internal pathology and frequently is symptomatic of severe pathology in the family framework; in which cases, it clearly indicates the family's disturbed view of the outside world. We realize again that the child and its family must be treated with all the vigor available" (pp. 23–24). Although the 21-year follow-up study had a few design limitations, no control group, and refusal to participate by a number of subjects, it still offers clinical insights into the adult adjustment of youngsters who were school refusers.

In another follow-up study, Waldron (1976) compared the mental health of 42 young adults who had been diagnosed as neurotic during their childhood to 20 control subjects. Twenty-four of the former neurotics had been school phobic. These subjects were compared to former patients who had been diagnosed as neurotic, and few differences emerged. Compared to the neurotics, the phobic subjects were somewhat more dependent, had a greater tendency to somatize, and had had more difficulty completing their secondary school education. Otherwise, they were not distinguishable from the neurotics. When the entire sample was considered, Waldron also found that most of the neurotics had impaired mental health as adults, whereas the controls did not, leading him to conclude that children with neurotic difficulties serious enough for them to receive professional help have a less optimistic prognosis for adult mental health than do normal control subjects.

Obsessive-Compulsive Disorders

Charlotte is a quiet, shy, fourteen-year-old girl who looks somewhat unhappy most of the time. She is bright and does well in school, but her classmates do not particularly like her because she is "the teacher's pet" and "Miss Goody Two Shoes." Her father is an alcoholic, and her parents fight a great deal. Charlotte usually avoids open conflict with her parents, although when things become unbearable for her, she has temper tantrums that resemble those of very young children. Her sister, Anne, thinks she is a bit "weird" because she has rituals she must follow: she fixes her toiletries in a certain way and becomes enraged if anyone changes them. She eats her food in a pattern—meat, vegetable, then starch, and she never mixes one with the other. She will not eat casseroles that have vegetables, starches, and meat mixed together. She has a ritual before going to bed; if disturbed, she cannot seem to get to sleep.

Charlotte has an obsessive-compulsive disorder (also called a Psychoneurotic Disorder, Obsessive-Compulsive Type in the GAP). The essential features of this disorder are recurrent obsessions and compulsions. *Obsessions* are defined as persistent ideas, thoughts, images, or impulses that are objectionable to the individual; the individual therefore attempts to ignore or suppress them, but cannot. *Compulsions* are similar to obsessions; they are defined as repetitive, stereotypic behaviors performed in an effort to ward off feared but senseless dangers. Compulsions serve the immediate purpose of reducing anxiety, but as they are akin to magical thinking, they are not effective for long periods. The child who is afraid of a monster under his bed, for example, may have a magical formula he must follow to feel protected from the monster—such as touching the headboard and counting to ten. The ritual may allow him to get to sleep at night, but it does not remove the fear from night to night. Rationally, he knows the ritual will not really prevent the feared event, but the impulse to carry out the ritual is so strong that if he resists the impulse, anxiety mounts.

Prevalence. This disorder rarely occurs during childhood, but is more common in adolescence. According to the DSM-III, it is equally common in males and females. Judd (1965) surveyed 405 cases under the age of 12 who were consecutively admitted to a psychiatric service. He also surveyed patients who were 16 and older. In both, he found a prevalence rate of 1.2 percent for obsessive-compulsive disorders. Adams (1972) reported a prevalence rate of between .1 percent and 3 percent in children from child psychiatry services, with males outnumbering females. Berman (1942) reviewed 3,050 cases admitted to the Children's Services at Bellevue be-

tween 1935 and 1939. Sixty-two were diagnosed as obsessive-compulsive, but upon careful scrutiny, only six met the stringent guidelines. More recently, Hollingsworth, Tanguay, Grossman, and Pabst (1980) reviewed the medical records of 8,367 child and adolescent patients treated at the UCLA-NPI from 1959 to 1975. Fifty had been diagnosed as obsessive-compulsives, but again after careful scrutiny, only 17 actually met the criteria; thirteen were male and four were female.

Probably because this disorder is so rare, the question arises as to whether it even occurs in children (Judd, 1965), but a number of authors describe treating children with such problems. Freud (1913) himself reported the development of the first symptoms of an adult obsessional neurosis between the ages of six and eight.

Obsessive-compulsive behaviors are common, and it is often difficult to determine whether the observed behaviors are the compulsive rituals of normal children, the result of an obsessive-compulsive neurosis, or the individual's efforts to maintain control over psychotic thoughts. Some obsessive-compulsive children have developed childhood schizophrenia (Judd, 1965), and some psychotic or borderline psychotic youngsters rely heavily on obsessive-compulsive behaviors to maintain control.

Carr (1974) observes that obsessive-compulsive individuals are unusually pessimistic in their outlook and much more cautious than others, so that potentially harmful situations create unusually high levels of anxiety that they reduce and control through compulsive behaviors. Carr maintains that people with obsessive-compulsive disorders need help in acquiring a more positive outlook. (Some of the cognitive restructuring techniques described in Chapter 9 seem to fit his recommendations.)

Adams (1972) studied 30 children with obsessional neuroses and concluded that the children tended to be of superior intelligence, came from "all-American" families, lived in intact monogamous families with both parents, and generally presented a WASP-ish picture. Parents of these children tended as a group to be highly verbal, to value etiquette and conventional correctness, to place a premium on social isolation or withdrawal (they were not members of social clubs and had few close friendships), to emphasize the importance of cleanliness, and to adhere to an instrumental morality (goodness is a means of obtaining goals rather than an end in itself). Adams describes the families and children as

People who are cut off from genuine awareness of their true selves, floundering in semicommitment and distrust of all values, estranged from their natures both as human animals and as human persons. As befitted their social perspective and social position, they could not be described as happy and productive people—in their marriages, their self-concepts, or their parenting roles. The fullness of life was a concept and a condition quite beyond their reach. The neurosis of their offspring appeared to be only one of many indices of the maladaptive or malfunctional state of their otherwise cozy but rather hollow existence as families. As fraught with the danger of absurdity as such a notion is, "the pathology of normalcy" comes to mind as a comment upon their life-style. (Adams, 1972, p. 1417)

Outcome. In the Hollingsworth et al. (1980) study, 15 of the 17 youngsters who met the stringent diagnosis for obsessive-compulsive disorder were located for follow-up, and 10 of the 15 agreed to participate in a structured follow-up interview. Among the youngsters who agreed to participate, the mean age at follow-up was 19.9; an average of 6.5 years had elapsed between the time of initial evaluation and follow-up. Seven of the 10 still had some obsessive-compulsive behaviors, but less than at their pretreatment level. One had decompensated in an acute schizophrenic reaction but had recovered, and one had been hospitalized for suicidal ideation and depression. None had chronic social/legal problems. None had married, and all reported

problems with their social life and peer relationships. Only 3 of the 10 were dating. All 10 were doing well in school; one had graduated from a major university, and all of college age were in college.

Somatoform Disorders

The somatoform group of disorders refers to physical problems for which there is no organic basis and for which there is strong evidence of psychological factors or conflicts. The best known is Conversion Disorder, also called Hysterical Neurosis, Conversion Type, which is a loss or alteration of functioning that appears physiologically-based but is apparently an expression of psychological conflict or need. The DSM-III reports that hysteria rarely occurs now, but was relatively common several decades ago. Rae (1977) reports incidence figures ranging from 5 percent to 24 percent of referrals to medical settings. He maintains that disagreement over the definition of hysterical conversion reactions accounts for the variation in reported incidence.

Children and adolescents diagnosed as having a conversion disorder or hysterical neurosis exhibit many physical symptoms, the most common of which are abdominal pain and vomiting, heart palpitations, breathing difficulty, dizziness, fatigue, and feelings of weakness. Onset before age nine is considered unusual, and before age five, extremely rare. Occasionally these disorders occur in children, but most often appear during adolescence and persist into adulthood. They are, as a group, more common in females.

Although hysteria appears to occur infrequently, it is an important phenomenon to study because the terminology and concepts have been so important in the history of understanding psychological problems. Also, some authors think such disorders occur more frequently than most studies report (Rock, 1971). Rock suggests that the disorders go undetected because most children with these disorders are referred to pediatricians or general practitioners instead of psychiatrists. On the other hand, others (Goodyer, 1981; Dubowitz & Hersov, 1976) report instances in which organic problems were overlooked and diagnoses of hysteria were made. Polly's case illustrates what can happen when professionals dismiss a youngster's complaints as hysterical without a thorough physical evaluation and thorough psychological/psychiatric evaluations and environmental assessments.

Polly was the younger daughter in a family of four. Neither parent was employed; her father was unable to work and received worker's compensation. Her mother felt she had too many family responsibilities to work. Both parents grew up away from their biological parents, the father in an orphanage and the mother in a foster home. Both appeared overwhelmed and depressed. Polly's older sister was the joy of their lives. They saw her as bright, attractive, popular, and successful, whereas Polly was a constant problem for them. In the parents' words, "we love her, but the sun comes out when Polly leaves the room." Polly was making poor grades in school, was listless and unhappy, and often complained of aches and pains. Her parents dismissed her complaints as a bid for attention, and her pediatrician concurred.

Polly was referred to the school-based committee for evaluation. Her teacher noted how unhealthy and unhappy Polly appeared and requested a physical exam in addition to a psychological evaluation to determine how best to meet Polly's needs. The evaluation revealed that Polly had leukemia!

To guess that her complaints were hypochondriacal was somewhat reasonable; she came from a strained and impoverished environment that had little to offer a needy child. To diagnose such a problem without supportive data, however, was irresponsible.

Outcome. Follow-up studies of children diagnosed as hysterical or as having a conversion reaction generally reveal that problems persist into adulthood, although the hysterical symptoms themselves sometimes disappear. Robins and O'Neal (1953) conducted a nine-year follow-up study of 41 children hospitalized with hysterical symptomatology; they located 37 and interviewed 23. Five were still diagnosed as hysteric; of the 19 remaining clients, only two were "completely well." The others had a variety of anxiety-based disorders or physical, organically-based problems. No male with hysteric symptoms was found at follow-up.

Anorexia Nervosa

Julie is a pretty, intelligent 15-year-old who has been hospitalized twice for anorexia nervosa. She is the youngest of three children in an intact family. Her father is a professor at a prominent university and her mother is an artist with her studio in the home. The two older children are also bright and successful. The oldest, a son, has graduated from one of the Ivy League schools and is now in medical school. The older sister is currently attending a small, private, liberal arts school and earning almost straight As. She, too, expects to do graduate work. Julie has always been a good student and, according to her parents, after numerous food allergies as a baby, was the easiest to raise. Julie, however, thinks she is ugly, fat, not well-liked by her peers, and not as competent as her siblings. She also thinks her parents think the two older siblings are brighter and more productive. When she was 13, Julie started overeating and then gagging herself afterwards. This quickly led to strict dieting and strenuous exercise. Julie had a boyfriend, Nick, but shortly before the second hospitalization, they quit dating. There had been much conflict between them: Nick wanted more sexual intimacy than Julie. She finally acquiesced, but felt much ambivalence and guilt afterward. She feels Nick broke up with her because he thought she was promiscuous.

The term *anorexia nervosa* means "nervous loss of appetite." In 1873 Charles Laseque published an article on hysterical anorexia that described many of the features of a modern anorexic; the term was then coined by Sir William Gull in 1874. He described his patients as between the ages of 16 and 23, usually female, and with the following symptoms: amenorrhea, constipation, loss of appetite, slow pulse, slow respiration, and emaciation. He attributed their loss of appetite to a "morbid mental state" (Kessler, 1966). Those symptoms continue to be characteristic of anorexia nervosa.

Common criteria for diagnosing anorexia are: (1) severe weight loss from failure to eat (20 to 25 percent of body weight and/or weight loss to 20 percent or more below expected weight for height for age); (2) amenorrhea; and (3) body-image distortion. Children with anorexia usually insist they are overweight when in fact they are grotesquely emaciated (Rollins & Piazza, 1978). Although there are various descriptions of youngsters with anorexia nervosa, the typical profile is of a bright, well-behaved, somewhat anxious achiever who may have had feeding problems as a young child (Bemis, 1978).

Prevalence. Investigators report a growing incidence of anorexia nervosa over the past twenty years, but precise statistics are hard to find because of difficulty in defining the disorder. For example, Swift (1982) reports that 20 years ago, one anorexic per year was admitted to the University of Wisconsin Hospital; now there are over 70 admissions per year. Crisp, Palmer, and Kalucy (1976) found that the prevalence rate among female adolescents in Greater London was one in 100 in private schools and one in 330 in public schools. Among cases of anorexia nervosa, mortality rates range from a low of 2 percent to a high of 18 percent (Silber, 1984).
One reason given for the increase in prevalence rates is the greater awareness of anorexia by physicians and the general public. The death of a celebrity like the singer Karen Carpenter from anorexia heightens public awareness of the disorder and its dangers.

HYPOTHESES ABOUT THE ETIOLOGY OF ANXIETY-BASED DISORDERS

Anxiety and stress-related disorders are among the oldest documented psychological problems. Hippocrates applied the Greek word *hustera*, meaning uterus, to a convulsive condition he observed in widows and spinsters, presumably because of migration of the uterus (Kessler, 1966). Hippocrates, among others, thought sexual abstention would cause symptoms such as seizures and shortness of breath. From Hippocrates's day to the present, we have attributed deviant behavior to witchcraft, to neurology, to learning, and to sociocultural factors. But the two traditions of psychoanalysis and behaviorism have probably given us the richest literature on anxiety-mediated disorders, although these ideas are currently challenged by ecological, sociocultural concepts.

Psychoanalytic Assumptions

In the late 19th century, Jean Martin Charcot began to write about hysteria. He equated *hysteria* and *hypnosis* in two ways: both represent a special kind of consciousness that allows people not to feel painful stimuli at certain times, and people experiencing either one are susceptible to external influences (suggestion). Accordingly, the idea evolved that hysteria was not a disease, but rather "a dysfunctional use of a naturally high level of suggestibility" (Jones, 1980, p. 429).

Sigmund Freud, one of Charcot's students, became interested in the phenomenon of hysteria and with his friend, Josef Breuer, developed a theory of *conservation of psychic energy*. This theory proposed that an emotional drive that found no outlet was converted to a physical symptom. People with *hysteria* were believed not to have adequately resolved the Oedipal complex; their sexual drives thus had a taint that was abhorrent to them and consequently caused anxiety. They dissociated themselves from conscious awareness of their sexual impulses through *repression*. Since their sexual feelings and impulses had no acceptable channel for expression, they were released through physical symptoms. The physical symptoms then became the focus of their anxiety. In this way the symptom reduced their anxiety, and was thus considered a primary gain.

Hysteria and conversion reactions, like many other aberrant conditions, were classified as neuroses. *Neuroses* were defined as a class of behaviors that developed from "unconscious conflicts over the handling of sexual and aggressive impulses which, though removed from awareness by the mechanism of repression, remain active and unresolved" (GAP, 1966, p. 229). Freud thought unresolved Oedipal conflicts caused the child to experience guilt, which in turn created anxiety. Since anxiety was an unpleasant affect, one defended against it by means of various symptoms, such as conversion reactions, phobias, compulsions, and so forth.

Phobias were also believed to result from unresolved Oedipal conflicts. In one of his more famous cases, Freud (1909; 1953) reported the analysis of Little Hans, a young boy who had loving, possessive wishes for his mother that caused him to have hostile, jealous feelings toward his father (normal Oedipal wishes). These noxious wishes were first repressed, then projected onto his father (instead of his wanting to attack his father, he imagined that his father wanted to attack him), but being fearful of his father was also noxious, so the wish was displaced onto horses (it was not the beloved father who was dangerous but the horse). Fearing horses instead of his father then released him from ambivalent feelings toward his father and distanced him from his own unconscious wishes toward his mother.

Obsessive-compulsive neuroses were believed to arise from conflicts during toilet training. Theoretically, a child with an obsessive-compulsive neurosis regressed "to the anal-sadistic level of libidinal organization" when faced with psychological struggles dealing with aggression and cleanliness (Kessler, 1966). Neurotic conflicts caused the child to have recurring, disturbing ideas. As a means of "undoing" those thoughts, the child developed a compul-

sion to act. Common compulsions were hand washing, checking a door to see if it were locked, following a certain order when carrying out a task, and touching objects a certain number of times. These compulsions supposedly had the power to undo the tension created by the obsessive ideations.

The classic psychoanalytic interpretation of anorexia equated eating behavior with sexual instinct:

The physical and psychological symptoms of anorexia nervosa are explained as products of oral ambivalence, with the refusal of nourishment representing a defense against oral impregnation fantasies, bulimia conceptualized as a breakthrough of unconscious desires for gratification and amenorrhea both as a symbol of pregnancy and a denial of femininity. (Bemis, 1978, p. 600)

Psychodynamic hypotheses have also been developed for anxiety-mediated, stress-related disorders. All see dynamic intrapsychic conflict as the cause of the behavioral disturbance, but specifics regarding the nature of this conflict vary considerably. Examples from the literature on school refusal illustrate the diversity of psychodynamic ideas.

School refusal is conceptualized as a fear of separation from primary love objects. Most writers attach much significance to a mutually dependent, mutually hostile relationship often observed between mother and child. It is hypothesized that mothers of children with separation anxiety or school refusal tend to be overprotective for a variety of reasons: they may feel incompetent in their role as mother; they may never have resolved their dependency on their own mothers; they may have turned to their children as substitutes for a poor and ungratifying marriage; or they may lack outside interests and therefore depend on their children for gratification. The children, likewise, because of their own poorly resolved dependency, have tended to regress to wanting the more nourishing and protective relationship of infancy. Yet this mutual dependence breeds resentment and hostility. When the mothers felt too drained by their children's demands, they became angered. The children reacted to their mothers' ambivalence with anger, and thus a conflicted relationship developed (Waldfogel, Coolidge, & Hahn, 1957).

Some psychodynamic writers (Leventhal & Sills, 1964; Rubenstein & Hastings, 1980), however, maintain that separation anxiety is not the critical factor for children who had attended school successfully for several years before the onset of problems. Leventhal and Sills postulate a "parsimonious power" theory in which the relevant dynamic in school refusal behavior is that "these children commonly overvalue themselves and their achievements and then try to hold onto their unrealistic self-image. When this is threatened in the school situation, they suffer anxiety and retreat to another situation where they can maintain their narcissistic self-image" (1964, p. 686).

Radin (1967) believes refusal results from overly permissive, submissive, and indulgent parents who heap unwarranted praise on their children. These child-rearing practices seemed to cause the child's infantile fantasies of omnipotence to persist unchecked until the child entered school. The reality of school or other sources of realistic evaluations exposed the vulnerable child and threatened his omnipotent self-image, which in turn forced the child to want to return home and reestablish the magical position of earlier days.

Behavioral Hypotheses

Behaviorists disagree with the basic assumptions proffered by the psychoanalytic and psychodynamic positions. They focus on learning paradigms to explain why behavioral disturbances develop. Watson and Raynor (1920) conducted one of the early classic studies. They investigated the question of why phobias develop and postulated a classi-

cal conditioning paradigm in which the youngster associated a neutral stimulus with a frightening or noxious stimulus; in the process, the neutral stimulus assumed the negative associations of the frightening or noxious stimulus. A familiar example of this was "Little Albert" (Watson & Raynor, 1920). Albert was an especially calm infant who was unafraid of stimuli such as rabbits, dogs, white rats, and cotton. When he was 11 months old, Watson started sounding a loud noise each time Albert reached for a white rat. Albert reacted by jumping and falling forward when he first heard the loud noise. After several such pairings, each time the rat was presented without the loud noise, Albert still withdrew his hand, whimpered, fell, and crawled away. Thereafter, similar but milder reactions were also elicited when rabbits, dogs, fur coats, cotton, a Santa Claus mask, and Watson's hair were presented. In the language of behaviorism, the emotional response, fear, was conditioned to the stimulus, the white rat, and the fear was generalized to similar stimuli.

Since the days of Little Albert, several behavioral hypotheses have emerged to explain "neurotic" or anxiety-mediated behavior problems. Mowrer (1960) postulates a two-factor learning theory as a cause of obsessive-compulsive disorders, described by Milby, Wendorf, and Meredith:

This theory states that obsessive thought produces anxiety because in experience it has been associated with unconditioned, anxiety-arousing stimuli. Obsessions then elicit conditioned anxiety, the reduction of which is reinforcing. Compulsions become established and maintained as they follow and serve to reduce anxiety. They become elaborated via response chaining. Thus, factor one is classical conditioning of the anxiety response, and factor two is instrumental conditioning of compulsive behavior reinforced by reduction of anxiety, i.e., negative reinforcement. (Milby et al., 1983, p. 8)

As is typical of this perspective, more attention is given to changing behavior than to dealing with underlying motivations.

Kauffman's (1985) statements illustrate this position.

It has been more useful to analyze anorexia as a fear of getting fat by eating too much than as a fear of sexual maturity, pregnancy, aggression, and the like. Anorexics often express a fear of becoming overweight, and so working with the fear of getting fat does not require obtuse reference to hidden drives or impulses. Furthermore, proper eating is the behavior that will change an anorexic into a nonanorexic person, and eating or the resulting weight gain can be reinforced directly without reference to "underlying" emotional problems. (Kauffman, 1985, pp. 288–89)

We find the same attitude in relation to behavioral literature on hysteria.

Biological Hypotheses

Biological factors have been implicated in anxiety disorders to a lesser extent and usually only on an interactive basis. Eysenck (1976) hypothesizes that constitutional factors are important in the acquisition of phobias and fearfulness. From his perspective, maladaptive and unreasonable fears are innate or learned through modeling. He believes introverted and anxious people are more sensitized to being conditioned or to learning to be frightened. They "incubate" anxiety in response to conditioned fear stimuli even without painful consequences.

Especially with anorexia nervosa, researchers have considered physiological factors. Rollins and Piazza (1978) maintain that anorexia is a developmental deviation of the normal adolescent process that often occurs in combination with physiological deviations. For example, over half the girls they studied developed amenorrhea before malnutrition alone could account for it. Other physiological abnormalities have also been implicated, and no doubt these problems are part of the picture, but the question under scrutiny is whether they are primary or secondary. Animals with lesions of the hypothalamus behave similarly to anorexics, leading to the hypothesis that anorexia (or starvation) may damage the hypothalamus and, conversely, that psychic stress might somehow interfere with hypothalamic functioning.

Bemis (1978) concludes that "although there is still no consensus as to whether organic factors in anorexia nervosa are primary or secondary to the disorder, it is clear that they form part of a vicious circle in which abnormal physiology further affects emotional state. At the present stage of understanding, it is impossible to classify anorexia nervosa definitely as a functional or organic disorder, and continued investigation in both areas is clearly imperative" (p. 611).

Socioanthropologic Explanations

Anxiety-mediated disorders have also been related to socioanthropological hypotheses. Comparisons of incidence rates for conversion reactions show higher rates in subcultures where "psychological sophistication is low and cultural repression is high" than in urban subcultures (Rae, 1977, p. 71). For example, Proctor (1958) found an incidence figure for childhood hysteria of 13 percent (25 children) in a sample drawn from North Carolina's "Bible Belt." This figure was larger than expected, so he investigated the circumstances, and proposed that all behavior is culturally determined, including the form by which psychic conflicts are managed. Proctor says "historically there is no shift in the type of neurosis seen without a concurrent change in the milieu. For example, we no longer see the devil neurosis or St. Vitus dance of a few hundred years ago, presumably because of changes in the morals, manners and mores" (p. 400).

In North Carolina's Bible Belt, he observed that the area was largely rural, of low educational level, and generally of a low economic status. The Southern Missionary Baptist faith dominated, with a "dour, pleasure-inhibiting fundamentalist rural religion which frowns on smoking, drinking and sex . . . it is not uncommon for sex to be taboo, yet to find repeated exposures to the primal scene, the son sleeping with the mother to an advanced age, or the daughter with the father. This results in great stimulation with denial of even verbal discharge, and we are reminded at this point of Freud's ideas about accumulated tension and its relation to hysteria" (p. 309).

Later, Jones (1980) found a higher-than-expected frequency of conversion reactions in a Santa Fe Indian hospital. She, too, concludes that the expression of intrapsychic conflicts took this form because of cultural patterns within the group. She further speculates that the availability of public health services reinforced this mode of expression and provided secondary as well as primary gains. Most recently, Hensley (1985) found a higher-than-expected frequency of hysteric reactions in a small Australian sample (nine children). These children were also from lower socioeconomic families who were educationally disadvantaged, and many were geographically isolated. The families were, for the most part, large, and the parents' financial and adaptive resources inadequate. Hensley describes the language as restricted and similar to Minuchin's description of urban slum families in the United States:

Rarely do members talk about their feelings or comment on the feelings of others. When the therapist requests verbal expression of feelings the response is usually a global positive or negative stereotype: sad or happy, angry or well, and bad or okay are the major descriptions of feeling. (Minuchin, 1967, p. 206)

One child in Hensley's sample presented with symptoms that fit a psychoanalytic explanation; all the others seemed to have learned the "sick role." These youngsters presented "a pantomime of illness" that in Hensley's opinion was likely to be the only kind of communication that would allow them to be singled out from their siblings for notice, special care, or privilege.

Some have also considered cultural factors as possible explanations for the increased incidence of anorexia nervosa. Harper (1984) notes that today's culture places great value in being thin, and that anorexic behavior is common for some groups. He also notes that "the current epidemic [of anorexia] appeared at first nearly exclusively in the white upper middle classes, but is now seen in girls of working class backgrounds as well, while the disorder is still rare among those of Asian background; among blacks it is seen seldom, and then only in those assimilated to white culture" (p. 822).

Environmental Stress as a Precipitating Factor

Stressors in the environment also precipitate anxiety-based disorders. In his sample of 10 children drawn from different backgrounds, races, and countries, Rock (1971) reports that hysterical symptoms were precipitated by stressful, traumatic events. Likewise, in an extensive study at UCLA-NPI, two striking characteristics were noted in a sample of 17 obsessive-compulsive youngsters (Hollingsworth et al., 1980). Eighty-two percent of the parents had serious medical illnesses and/or severe psychopathology, and some of the youngsters had serious medical illnesses. The authors speculate as to why these symptoms develop:

Many of the obsessions did, in fact, relate to realistic fears and worries which the child may have had based upon his experiences in a rather chaotic home environment. It may be that when stress reaches a level at which it can no longer be handled by primitive defenses such as denial, it begins to haunt the individual as an obsession. The compulsive symptomatology might best be understood as a primitive defense. It is primitive in that the magical solutions inherent in the compulsions are relatively similar to the type of cognitive processing seen in the 4–7 year old child. Normally, as an individual grows up, he learns to handle such anxiety with more advanced defenses. Seven of the 10 children were rated in the original records as "overtalkative." We speculate that the cognitive style of these children was such that they handled anxiety over family stress by obsessive-compulsive defenses. After learning this verbal intellectual cognitive style by mid-latency, they continued to apply this emotional and behavioral pattern even when not under stress, and they appear in follow-up to have been unable to extricate themselves from this manner of dealing with the world around them. (Hollingsworth et al., 1980, p. 143)

An Integrative Model

The "goodness of fit" model discussed in Chapter 6 (Chess & Thomas, 1984) allows us to integrate many of the hypotheses we have mentioned into a well-grounded, carefully-researched framework. This model grew out of the New York Longitudinal Study begun in 1956. This study followed 133 subjects from infancy into early adult life for the purpose of exploring the function of children's individual temperament in the course of normal and deviant psychological development. The study explored how individual temperamental differences might predispose a youngster to maladjustment, hypothesizing that consonance between individual temperament and skills and environmental expectations and responses determines outcome. When there is a "good fit"—the child can please the environment and environment can please the child—healthy development proceeds. When there is dissonance, in this case dissatisfaction between child and family, problems result.

Few of the subjects developed anxiety-mediated disorders, although at different points during the study, many were described as having an adjustment reaction or as being depressed. Nonetheless, because of the research design, it was possible to study the youngsters' intrapsychic and psychological development and to observe, specifically, the relationship between anxiety and symptom formation. These data provide insight

into "neurotic" conflicts: they support the efficacy of the concept of defense mechanisms, but do not support the view that anxiety is the primary influence in the ontogenesis of behavior disorders. Chess and Thomas note:

Where anxiety has evolved in the course of the development of the behavior disorder, it has been a secondary phenomenon, a consequence rather than a cause of symptom formation and expression. In addition, the removal of symptoms by a successful parent guidance procedure has had positive consequences for the child's functioning and has not resulted in the appearance of overt anxiety or new substitute symptoms. (p. 283)

They also observe that once anxiety developed, it affected the child's subsequent development and elaboration of symptoms. They note that to accept the existence and utility of defense does not automatically mean that one must also accept "the psychoanalytic theoretical assumptions regarding the conflict between primitive asocial instinctual impulses and the repressing forces of socialization, which then require one or another defensive strategy for the resolution of the conflict" (p. 283).

This model has appeal from a logical viewpoint as well as from a research base. Most theories for understanding anxiety-mediated disorders arose from retrospective reconstructions of disturbed individuals' lives. Such data are undoubtedly affected by lapses in individuals' memories as well as by a number of sociocultural and political factors, many of which remain unknown to the theories' architects. Furthermore, "theories based on such retrospective data almost inevitably tend to become reductionistic, selectively emphasizing certain factors at the expense of other still unknown or unrecognized ones" (p. ix). While Chess and Thomas's work is limited by what they chose to study (a fact they acknowledge), the longitudinal design of their study enables investigators to observe emerging and changing personalities from a less biased position than recall alone provides.

This approach has practical appeal as well, for it suggests that spontaneous interventions of caring individuals in the children's environment were instrumental in fostering good development and in remediating problematic development. Parents, teachers, and other school personnel who ascribe to this approach should adopt a flexible, practical, eclectic approach to intervention. Highly active children may suffer if forced to sit still for long periods, so personnel should plan for their activity needs. Distractible children cannot attend for long periods of time, so teachers should structure short, varied activities. Anxious children may have trouble with vague, unclear directions on assignments, so teachers need to be specific and clear about what they want. In essence, parents and professionals need to observe carefully to see how children respond, then do what works to effect a better fit.

INTERVENTIONS FOR ANXIETY-MEDIATED DISORDERS

There has always been debate between the behavioral and the psychodynamic therapists about whether focusing merely on symptoms without addressing underlying psychological issues is effective on a long-term basis. The behaviorists argue that long-term therapy is inappropriate because symptoms can be removed in a short time. Psychodynamic clinicians argue that symptoms will reappear if underlying problems are not addressed. Blanchard and Hersen (1976) offer something of a resolution to this debate with their observation that psychodynamic writers base their observations primarily on cases of hysterical neuroses, whereas behaviorists base their position primarily on treatment of phobias. Blanchard and Hersen's viewpoint is that these two types of behavior are maintained by different environmental circumstances; consequently, they require different types of interventions.

When neurotic children are referred to mental health professionals, today's treatment is usually a compromise approach. For most neurotic children, long-term, intensive psychotherapy is not available nor appropriate. Likewise, conditioning the child without also intervening in the environment is rarely sufficient. Consequently, clinicians, regardless of their philosophical bias, direct the treatment plan at the child as well as at others in the ecology. The goals of most treatment plans for neurotic youngsters are to help clients feel more competent, more contented with themselves, and less guilty or self-accusatory. It is likely, however, that most mildly neurotic youngsters are dealt with at school and in their communities without being identified or classified. Caring, empathetic teachers, counselors, neighbors, and clergy all provide help intuitively; in doing so, they circumvent the need for additional professional help.

Expressive Therapies

The three common types of interventions in schools or in mental health centers are expressive therapies, behavioral programs, and medical interventions.

There are different therapeutic techniques through which individuals can be encouraged to express their feelings and, in the process, learn about and become more comfortable with their feelings. Therapies include art, music, drama, and dance therapy, bibliotherapy, and different types of psychotherapy. All are based on the belief that it is therapeutic to be able to express one's conflicted feelings and to have others accept and understand those feelings. For someone who is conflicted and guilty, it is soothing to learn that one's feelings are neither "strange" nor "bad."

Psychotherapy. The medium of expression in psychotherapy is usually talk, although young children may use puppets, dolls, and toys to help them express themselves. Of the many different psychotherapeutic techniques, Frank (1975) maintains that all have some common conditions: all emphasize establishing a trusting, tolerant, caring relationship between client and therapist; creating a special setting in which to work, a sanctuary "presided over by a tolerant protector" (p. 124); and providing the client with a conceptual framework for understanding problems and a predictable way of working with their problems.

There has been a great deal of research as to the effectiveness of therapy. The debate now appears to be moot—for some clients it is useful and productive. Questions now center on what elements contribute to the effectiveness of therapy, what can and cannot be accomplished in therapy, and who can do what under various circumstances (Strupp, 1986). Research shows clear differences as to therapists' effectiveness (Luborsky et al., 1986) and some suggest that the most important factor in determining success is the nonspecific quality of the client-therapist relationship. Parloff (1986) says the nature of this relationship may be more important at the beginning of therapy, but as work proceeds, other factors become more important. "The therapist provides the patient with the opportunity to learn that the feared consequences of the patient's carefully avoided thoughts and behavior may not in fact occur; or if they do occur they are not accompanied or followed by the anticipated disaster. The therapist encourages the patient, in the context of a relatively safe setting, to test out new ways of behaving. The patient is thus helped to recognize that a wider range of behavior is safely available" (p. 527). During the course of therapy, the client also learns new ways of understanding problems and more appropriate and adaptive responses to problematic situations, which results in the client's developing greater self-esteem. "In effect, treatment may begin by artificially instilling in patients a sense of confidence in the therapist, and it ends with the patients developing a realistic sense of mastery and confidence in themselves" (p. 528). Thus, Parloff sees the

relationship between client and therapist and the techniques used to teach the client independence and confidence as "reciprocally interactive"; neither the relationship nor the techniques can be understood without considering the other. Here is an example of how this happens:

Hope was an eight-year-old girl whose parents divorced, and her father remarried. He had a child with his second wife, and the birth of this child created much anguish for his daughter. She developed intense school refusal symptoms that eventually caused her mother to seek professional help. Therapy was recommended. In therapy, she vented her feelings by acting out scenes with the dolls in the dollhouse, by drawing pictures, by talking about what was happening at home, and by writing her father letters, many of which were never mailed. Her therapist used these products as a springboard to help Hope learn more about why she felt as she did. Hope initially refused to talk about her feelings calmly, and if her therapist asked questions or encouraged her to think about troublesome topics, she would change the subject, become silly, and use various deviant behaviors to avoid discussing problems. She also tested her therapist, calling her names and challenging observations and interpretations. Gradually, as she grew to trust her therapist and the process of therapy, Hope began to focus on her conflicts. She realized that she still loved her father despite the pain he had caused her family and that it was sadness and guilt that caused her anger. It took some time for her to believe that it was not "bad" to feel so angry and hurt. After many discussions about her feelings, what caused them, how she dealt with them, and the less self-destructive alternatives she had available to her, she began to be more tolerant of herself. She talked about how sad she felt that the new baby, and not she, was with her father; how she regretted that she never got to see him; and how she was afraid he would love the baby more than her. Her therapist responded with empathetic observations and reassurance that it was perfectly "normal" to want to be loved, valued, and special to her parents, that her feelings were "quite normal." As Hope began to feel that her feelings were acceptable and understandable, she began sharing them with both of her parents. Talking with her parents helped her to realize that even though her parents were still angry with each other, they were not angry with her, that they understood her feelings, and that they both still loved her.

Therapy did not make the painful realities in Hope's life disappear, nor did it change her personality, but to all who knew her well, it seemed to help her become more accepting of herself and to learn to talk to others about her feelings rather than keep them to herself and feel miserable. These changes were still evident fourteen years later.

Art therapy. Art is another means for encouraging children to express their feelings and communicate with others. It is also a socially acceptable means of releasing pent-up feelings. Uhlin and De Chiara (1984) note that art education and art therapy are similar in that both are directed at helping the individual master techniques that are bound to the inner psyche, and both support the power of art as an expressive and integrative experience; the difference is that art education is product-focused, and art therapy is process-focused. This is not to say that the art therapist does not value the finished product, but rather realizes that the process of working in the artistic medium has value in and of itself.

Angela was an eight-year-old girl who often used art as a means of expressing her wish for power and control over others. Her mother had died unexpectedly from complications in a routine operation, and her father was a business executive who was often away on trips. She was a short, small child who had difficulty dealing with her agemates. She tended to shrink from them rather than play with them or stand up to them when they were unkind to her. Her pictures frequently conveyed stories of one animal's overpowering another. The overpowered animal usually disappeared or was destroyed.

She entered therapy because of her extreme withdrawal and difficulty getting along with her peers. For over a year she communicated with her therapist about her feelings primarily through art. At home, at school, and in therapy, when she was upset or angry, she drew pictures and cartoons as

a means of expressing her feelings. Gradually, as she became more confident of herself and more trusting of others, she began drawing people instead of animals and began to talk directly to people instead of through her drawings.

Art, music, drama, and creative movement are all wonderful mediums for self-expression. Teachers can use them as a standard part of the curriculum for all children; counselors can use them with small groups of troubled children. They are excellent ways for adults to learn about children's feelings and thoughts, and they are excellent ways to communicate indirectly and safely with a troubled and frightened child. A comprehensive book, *Art for Exceptional Children* (Uhlin & De Chiara, 1984), provides many practical ideas as to which activities are likely to be successful with disturbed youngsters and how to go about setting up the activities. Wood (1981a, 1981b) has also developed two sourcebooks for teachers interested in using music, movement, physical skills, fantasy, and make-believe as means of helping youngsters become less constricted, more confident, and more communicative.

Most of these therapeutic modalities have been severely criticized for lack of empirical data to support their efficacy; however, too many clinicians and clients attest to the efficacy of these techniques to dismiss them as unfounded. Nonetheless, we do need more data about what works and how to best implement these therapies.

Behavioral Therapies

There are at least five categories of behavioral therapies: systematic desensitization, flooding therapies, contingency management, modeling, and self-control strategies (Morris & Kratochwill, 1983).

Systematic desensitization. Developed by Joseph Wolpe in the early 1950s, systematic desensitization is the most widely used technique for dealing with children's fears and phobias, and can be used with other neuroses as well. The basic assumption is that a fear response can be inhibited by substituting an activity that is antagonistic to the fear response. Typically, the response that is inhibited is *anxiety* and the activity that is substituted is *relaxation*. Ordinarily, the process begins with the therapist explaining the procedure to the child and the parents, developing with them a *fear hierarchy* (a list of the child's fears in order of intensity), then teaching the child to relax. After the child knows how to relax, he is gradually exposed in small and graduated steps to the source of the fear. This exposure may be "in vivo," in fantasy, or through pictures. The child's ability to tolerate the exposure determines how quickly or slowly the procedure progresses. Garvey and Hegrenes (1966) used this procedure with a 10-year-old school-phobic boy: (1) the therapist and the child sat in a car in front of the school; (2) they got out of the car and started walking toward the curb; (3) they walked to the sidewalk; (4) they went to the bottom of the steps of the school; (5) they went to the top of the steps at the entry of the school; (6) they went to the door of the school; (7) they entered the school; (8) they approached the classroom; (9) they entered the classroom; (10) they stayed in the classroom with the teacher but without other children; (11) they were in the classroom with the teacher and a few children; (12) they were in the classroom with the entire class. The process ranged over 20 consecutive days (including Saturdays and Sundays) and involved about 20 to 40 minutes per day. A two-year follow-up revealed that no further school phobia manifested itself.

Flooding therapies. Flooding therapies make use of anxiety-provoking stimuli, but not in the gradual manner of systematic desensitization. Instead, the child is exposed to the anxiety-provoking stimuli for a long period and without any relaxation training. The purpose of the exposure is to produce a frightening imaginal experience of such magnitude that it will actually make the child less fearful. *Implosive therapy* is a variant of the flooding therapies based on the assumption that repeated exposure to a threatening stimulus in a safe environment will cause it to lose its power to elicit anxiety and the fear response will gradually extinguish. Boyd (1980) points out that implosive therapy has the advantage that peers do not witness it, thus protecting the youngster from negative peer feedback.

Smith and Sharpe (1970) used implosive therapy with a 13-year-old school-phobic boy. The youngster was seen for six consecutive daily sessions. In the first and all subsequent sessions, he was asked to imagine, as vividly as possible, anxiety-arousing scenes and discuss his feelings in relation to the visual imagery. This was one of the scenes:

After walking through the halls of the school, which are deserted and strangely silent, Billy finds himself at the stage door of the auditorium. The door opens and the patient is confronted by the leering school principal, who says in a sadistic tone of voice, "We have all been waiting for you." He can hear many voices from inside the auditorium chanting, "We want Billy." Billy looks to his mother for assistance, but she coldly says, "I'm through taking care of you. You're on your own from now on." She turns and leaves. (Smith & Sharpe, 1970, p. 241)

A thirteen-week follow-up revealed that Billy had continued to attend school regularly and that his grades had improved. Although implosive therapy has been demonstrated to be effective, many clinicians are reluctant to use the intensely anxiety-producing procedures when there are effective alternatives. In addition, a therapist who elects to use such procedures takes the risk that the technique will be so aversive that the client will refuse to return.

Contingency management procedures. Among contingency management procedures are positive reinforcement, shaping, extinction, and stimulus fading. Patterson (1965) describes a rather novel variation of positive reinforcement that illustrates this type of approach. He used doll play, tangible reinforcers, and social reinforcement to reduce the school-refusal behavior of a seven-year-old boy. The treatment took place for four days per week, 15 minutes per session for 23 sessions. In the play sessions, situations involving separation from the mother were enacted, and the boy was reinforced for making fearless statements. As follow-up to the therapy sessions, the mother reinforced the boy at home for being away from her. By the ninth session, a visiting teacher began tutoring him and, within a few sessions, accompanied him to school.

Gradually the boy was left alone at school. At a three-month follow-up, the school reported "dramatic improvement" in his adjustment and "no further evidence of fearfulness." Patterson concludes that this approach is an effective therapy package for reducing children's fears, but that in this case there is little doubt that the parents and the teacher enhanced the generalizability of the child's behavior from the therapy room to the natural environment. He also points out that to maximize effectiveness, it was important that the therapist become a "secondary reinforcer."

Modeling. Modeling—learning by observing others—can be carried out in several different ways. *Symbolic modeling* refers to the use of models on videotapes or film; and *live* or *"vicarious" modeling* refers to the use of live children as models. For example, fearful children can observe other children participating in an activity with the feared object. *Participant modeling* involves first having children watch a model interact with the feared object and then having them gradually interact with the feared object themselves (Graziano, DeGiovanni, & Garcia, 1979). Researchers report these approaches to be effective when the model experiences a positive and/or safe outcome. For example, Melamed and Siegel (1975) used symbolic modeling with 60 youngsters admitted to a pediatric ward for

surgery. The children were divided into experimental and control groups. The experimental group was shown a film of a seven-year-old who underwent the same surgical procedure the children were to have; the control group was shown a film about a boy on a nature outing. The experimental group displayed significantly less sweat-gland activity, self-reported medical fears, and anxiety-related behavior than did the controls. Ritter (1968) compared participant modeling to live modeling in a study with 44 children who were fearful of snakes. The children were randomly assigned to one of the two treatment groups or to the control group. In the participant-modeling treatment condition, children observed five children and one adult handle snakes, then the fearful children held the snake with assistance. In the live-modeling treatment, the fearful children observed five children and one adult handling and holding the snakes. Post-treatment assessment indicated that the participant-modeling group performed considerably better than the live-modeling group on measures of avoidance and fearfulness, but that both treatment groups evinced less fearfulness than the controls.

The model's characteristics are also important. Models are apparently more effective when the model is someone with whom the child can identify. Meichenbaum (1971) compared the effectiveness of a *coping model*—one that initially displays apprehension of the object but learns to "cope" with it—to a *mastery model*—one who was fearless and confident from the start. He found that coping models were more effective than mastery models, but both were more effective than no treatment. Not all research supports Meichenbaum's findings, however (Kornhaber & Schroeder, 1975).

When considering this research, one must remember several issues. Most research used nonclinically-referred populations; it remains to be seen how extremely anxious youngsters would perform. Also, how well this treatment generalizes and how well gains are maintained are still under investigation, although present data suggest the approach is a reasonable alternative for treating children's fears.

Self-control therapy. Self-control interventions help the child become aware of specific aspects of his negative thinking; learn to generate, with the help of the therapist, more appropriate self-statements; and learn how to apply these new self-statements in the process of learning new social and cognitive skills. Common to the interventions used with this approach is an emphasis on cognition and its role in behavior change, along with the view that individuals can monitor their own behavior. The therapist serves as the motivator or instigator who teaches the client how, when, and where to use learned cognitions to acquire more personally satisfying behavior patterns (Kanfer, 1980).

A study conducted by Kanfer, Karoly, and Newman (1975) illustrates this approach. Forty-five kindergarten children who were afraid of staying in a dark room by themselves were assigned to one of two treatment groups or to a control group. Children in the treatment groups were taught (1) competence-related sentences, such as "I am a brave boy/girl" or "I can take care of myself in the dark"; and (2) stimulus-related statements, such as "The dark is a fun place to be" or "There are many good things in the dark." Children in the control group were taught neutral statements (for example, "Mary had a little lamb"). Following mastery of the sentences, the children were put in a well-lighted room by themselves and instructed to listen to a tape that elaborated on the meaning of the sentences the children had learned. Posttesting indicated that both treatment groups did better than the controls on dark-tolerance measures and that the competence treatment subjects were somewhat better than the stimulus-sentences treatment group. A few other investigators

have experimented with this approach with conflicting results; given the paucity of information, it is not yet possible to say how and with whom this approach works best, although it appears to be promising.

Medication

Using medication in the early phases of treatment helps reduce anxiety in all the disorders we've discussed. Conceptually, it is a crutch to help the child respond positively, and usually, the use is short-term. In the Gittelman-Klein and Klein study (1975), subjects were selected after intense efforts to force the children to return to school. The investigators found imipramine (Tofranil) clearly superior to a placebo in helping children to go to school because it freed the children from panicky responses and morbid fears when separated from their parents. The average dose of Tofranil as used for this disorder is 75 to 100 mg/day with a maximum upper limit of 200 mg/day (Gadow, 1979).

Most of the drugs commonly used for anxiety disorders are also used for depression. Chapter 9 includes an outline of the drugs that have been used, their effectiveness, and their side effects.

Regardless of the intervention, most authors stress that it be initiated early. It seems that the longer the problem festers, the more intense the reaction. With early intervention, whether out of school or in school, these disorders generally have a positive outcome.

CONCLUSION

This chapter is not a comprehensive coverage of all anxiety and stress-related disorders. We have not, for example, discussed important disorders such as elective mutism and a number of psychophysiological problems, but rather have described several well-known disorders to illustrate the detrimental effects excessive anxiety and stress can have on the developing human. Although it is generally believed that this group of disorders is less debilitating than psychotic or antisocial disorders, we must nonetheless take them seriously, because growing evidence suggests that youngsters who experience childhood problems are likely to have problems as adults, albeit sometimes different problems. The ability to cope with stress and anxiety is an essential skill in our modern society.

It is clear that diagnosing and treating anxiety disorders is a complex and controversial process, but there is consensus on several issues:

1. Sociocultural factors influence how one experiences, expresses, and understands stress and anxiety.

2. Lack of competence is basic to children's emotional problems. Regardless of the reason for the deficit, these children need to acquire more adaptive coping skills. Phobics need to learn to manage panic reactions; hys-

terics need to learn to express their needs more effectively; anorexics need to learn other ways to deal with their fears and anxieties about weight, appearance, growing up, and heterosexual relationships.

3. Effective interventions are multifaceted, with attention to environmental interventions, personal interventions, and skill-building interventions.

4. Effective interventions are usually integrative and eclectic. Time and again we find that problems recur if the intervention does not focus on all aspects of the problem.

5. Organic factors warrant additional investigation. Accumulating evidence supports the importance and relevance of physiological factors in anxiety disorders.

6. We need more carefully controlled research that delves into specific aspects of effective interventions and carefully defines the group under study.

REFERENCES

Adams, P. L. (1972). Family characteristics of obsessive children. *American Journal of Psychiatry, 128,* 98–101.

Atkinson, L., Quarrington, B., & Cyr, J. J. (1985). School refusal: The heterogeneity of a concept. *American Journal of Orthopsychiatry, 55,* 83–101.

Bemis, K. M. (1978). Current approaches to the etiology and treatment of anorexia nervosa. *Psychological Bulletin, 85,* 593–617.

Berman, L. (1942). Obsessive, compulsive neurosis in children. *Journal of Nervous Mental Diseases, 95,* 26–39.

Blanchard, E. B., & Hersen, M. (1976). Behavioral treatment of hysterical neurosis: Symptom substitution and symptom return reconsidered. *Psychiatry, 39,* 118–129.

Boyd, L. T. (1980). Emotive imagery in the behavioral management of adolescent school phobia: A case approach. *School Psychology Digest, 9,* 186–189.

Carr, A. T. (1974). Compulsive neurosis: A review of the literature. *Psychological Bulletin, 81,* 311–318.

Chess, S., & Thomas, A. (1984). *Origins and evolution of behavior disorders: From infancy to early adult life.* New York: Brunner/Mazel.

Clarizio, H. F., & McCoy, G. F. (1983). *Behavior disorders in children* (3rd ed.). New York: Harper & Row.

Coolidge, J. C., & Brodie, R. D. (1976). A 21-year follow-up study of 66 school-phobic children. Unpublished

manuscript, available from J. C. Coolidge, Judge Baker Guidance Center, Boston.

Coolidge, J. C., Brodie, R. D., & Feeney, B. (1964). A ten-year follow-up study of sixty-six school-phobic children. *American Journal of Orthopsychiatry, 34,* 675–684.

Coolidge, J. C., Hahn, P. B., & Peck, A. L. (1957). School phobia: Neurotic crisis or way of life. *American Journal of Orthopsychiatry, 27,* 296–306.

Crisp, A. H., Palmer, J. L., & Kalucy, R. S. (1976). How common is anorexia nervosa? A prevalence study. *British Journal of Psychiatry, 128,* 549–554.

Dubowitz, V., & Hersov, L. (1976). Management of children with non-organic (hysterical) disorders of motor function. *Developmental Medicine and Child Neurology, 18,* 358–386.

Elkind, D. (1981). *The hurried child: Growing up too fast too soon.* Reading, MA: Addison-Wesley.

Eysenck, H. J. (1976). The learning theory model of neurosis—A new approach. *Behaviour Research and Therapy, 14,* 251–267.

Frank, J. (1975). General psychotherapy: The restoration of morale. In D. Freedman & J. Dyrud (Eds.), *American Handbook of Psychiatry,* 2nd ed. (Vol. 5). New York: Basic Books.

Freud, S. (1913). Predisposition to obsessional neurosis.

school personnel. Reston, VA: Council for Exceptional Children.

Garvey, W., & Hegrenes, J. (1966). Desensitization technique in the treatment of school phobia. *American Journal of Orthopsychiatry, 36,* 147–152.

Gittelman-Klein, R., & Klein, D. (1975). School phobia: Diagnostic considerations in the light of imipramine effects. *The Journal of Nervous and Mental Disease, 156,* 199–215.

Goodyer, I. (1981). Hysterical conversion reactions in childhood. *Child Psychology and Psychiatry, 22,* 179–188.

Gove, W. R., & Herb, T. R. (1974). Stress and mental illness among the young: A comparison of the sexes. *Social Forces, 53,* 256–265.

Graziano, A. M., DeGiovanni, I., & Garcia, K. (1979). Behavioral treatments of children's fears: A review. *Psychological Bulletin, 86,* 804–830.

Group for the Advancement of Psychiatry (GAP). (1966). *Psychopathological disorders in childhood: Theoretical considerations and a proposed classification.* New York: GAP.

Harper, G. (1984). Anorexia nervosa: What kind of disorder? The "consensus" model, myths, and clinical implications. *Pediatric Annals, 13,* 812–828.

Hensley, V. R. (1985). Hysteria in childhood: A note on Proctor's incidence figures 27 years later. *American Journal of Orthopsychiatry, 55,* 140–142.

Hersov, L. A. (1960). Refusal to go to school. *Child Psychology and Psychiatry, 1,* 137–145.

Herzog, D. B. (1984). Pharmacotherapy of anorexia nervosa and bulimia. *Pediatric Annals, 13,* 915–923.

Hollingsworth, C. E., Tanguay, P. E., Grossman, L., & Pabst, P. (1980). Long-term outcome of obsessive-compulsive disorder in childhood. *Journal of the American Academy of Child Psychiatry, 19,* 134–144.

Jones, M. (1980). Conversion reaction: Anachronism or evolutionary form? A review of the neurologic, behavioral, and psychoanalytic literature. *Psychological Bulletin, 87,* 427–441.

Judd, L. L. (1965). Obsessive compulsive neurosis in children. *Archives of General Psychiatry, 12,* 136–143.

Kanfer, F. H., (1980). Self-management methods. In R. H. Kanfer and A. P. Goldstein (Eds.), *Helping people change* (2nd ed.). Elmsford, NY: Pergamon Press.

Kanfer, F. H., Karoly, P., & Newman, A. (1975). Reduction of children's fear of the dark by competence-related and situation threat-related verbal cues. *Journal of Consulting and Clinical Psychology, 43,* 251–258.

Kauffman, J. M. (1985). *Characteristics of children's behavior disorders* (3rd ed.). Columbus, OH: Merrill.

Kennedy, W. A. (1965). School phobia: Rapid treatment of fifty cases. *Journal of Abnormal Psychology, 70,* 285–289.

Kessler, J. W. (1966). *Psychopathology of childhood.* Englewood Cliffs, NJ: Prentice-Hall.

Kornhaber, R. C., & Schroeder, H. E. (1975). Importance of model similarity on the extinction of avoidance behavior in children. *Journal of Consulting and Clinical Psychology, 43,* 601–607.

Leton, D. A. (1962). Assessment of school phobia. *Mental Hygiene, 46,* 256–264.

Leventhal, T., & Sills, M. (1964). Self-image in school phobia. *American Journal of Orthopsychiatry, 34,* 685–695.

Leventhal, T., Weinberger, G., Stander, R. J., & Stearns, R. P. (1967). Therapeutic strategies with school phobics. *American Journal of Orthopsychiatry, 37,* 64–70.

Luborsky, L., Crits-Christoph, P., McLellan, A. T., Woody, G., Piper, W., Liberman, B., Imber, S., & Pilkonis, A. (1986). Do therapists vary much in their success? Findings from four outcome studies. *American Journal of Orthopsychiatry, 56,* 501–512.

Meichenbaum, D. (1971). Examination of model characteristics in reducing avoidance behavior. *Journal of Personality and Social Psychology, 17,* 298–307.

Melamed, B. G., & Siegel, L. J. (1975). Reduction of anxiety in children facing hospitalization and surgery by use of filmed modeling. *Journal of Consulting and Clinical Psychology, 43,* 511–521.

Milby, J. B., Wendorf, D., & Meredith, R. L. (1983). Obsessive-compulsive disorders. In R. J. Morris & T. R. Kratochwill (Eds.), *The Practice of Child Therapy.* New York: Pergamon Press.

Minuchin, S. (1967). *Families of the slums: An exploration of their structure and treatment.* New York: Basic Books.

Morris, R. J., & Kratochwill, T. R. (1983). *Treating children's fears and phobias: A behavioral approach.* New York: Pergamon Press.

Mowrer, O. H. (1960). *Learning theory and behavior.* New York: John Wiley.

Parloff, M. B. (1986). Frank's "common elements" in psychotherapy: Nonspecific factors and placebos. *American Journal of Orthopsychiatry, 56,* 521–530.

Patterson, G. (1965). A learning theory approach to the treatment of the school phobic child. In L. P. Ullmann & L. Krasner (Eds.), *Case studies in behavior modification.* New York: Holt, Rinehart & Winston.

Proctor, J. (1958). Hysteria in childhood. *American Journal of Orthopsychiatry, 28,* 394–407.

Radin, S. S. (1967). Psychodynamic aspects of school phobia. *Comprehensive Psychiatry, 8,* 119–128.

Rae, W. A. (1977). Childhood conversion reactions: A review of incidence in pediatric settings. *Journal of Clinical Child Psychology, 6,* 69–72.

Richman, N., Stevenson, J. E., & Graham, P. J. (1975). Prevalence of behaviour problems in 3-year-old children: An epidemiological study in a London borough. *Journal of Child Psychology and Psychiatry, 16,* 277–287.

Ritter, B. (1968). The group desensitization of children's snake phobias using vicarious and contact desensitization procedures. *Behaviour Research and Therapy, 6,* 1–6.

Robins, E., & O'Neal, P. (1953). Clinical features of hysteria in children, with a note on prognosis. A two- to seventeen-year follow-up study of 41 patients. *Nervous Child, 10,* 246–271.

Rock, N. L. (1971). Conversion reactions in childhood: A clinical study on childhood neuroses. *Journal of American Academy of Child Psychology, 10,* 65–93.

Rodriguez, A., Rodriguez, M., & Eisenberg, L. (1959). The outcome of school phobia: A follow-up study based on 41 cases. *American Journal of Orthopsychiatry, 29,* 321–332.

Rollins, N., & Piazza, E. (1978). Diagnosis of anorexia nervosa: A critical reappraisal. *Journal of the American Academy of Child Psychiatry, 17,* 126–137.

Rubenstein, J., & Hastings, E. (1980). School refusal in adolescence. *Adolescence, 15,* 775–782.

Silber, T. (1984). Anorexia nervosa: Morbidity and mortality. *Pediatric Annals, 13,* 851–859.

Smith, S. L., & Sharpe, T. M., (1970). Treatment of a school phobia with implosive therapy. *Journal of Consulting and Clinical Psychology, 35,* 239–243.

Strupp, H. H. (1986). The nonspecific hypothesis of therapeutic effectiveness: A current assessment. *American Journal of Orthopsychiatry, 56,* 513–520.

Swift, W. J. (1982). The long-term outcome of early onset anorexia nervosa: A critical review. *Journal of the American Academy of Child Psychiatry, 21,* 38–46.

Uhlin, D. M., & De Chiara, E. (1984). *Art for exceptional children* (3rd. ed.). Dubuque, IA: Wm. C. Brown.

Waldfogel, S., Coolidge, J. C., & Hahn, P. B. (1957). The development, meaning and management of school phobia. *American Journal of Orthopsychiatry, 27,* 754–780.

Waldron, S. (1976). The significance of childhood neurosis for adult mental health: A follow-up study. *American Journal of Psychiatry, 133,* 532–538.

Watson, J. B., & Raynor, R. (1920). Conditioned emotional reactions. *Journal of Experimental Psychology, 3,* 1–14.

Wolpe, J. (1969). *The practice of behavior therapy.* Elmsford, NY: Pergamon Press.

Wood, M. M. (1981a). *Developmental therapy sourcebook: Vol. 1. Music, movement, and physical skills.* Baltimore, MD: University Park Press.

Wood, M. M. (1981b). *Developmental therapy sourcebook: Vol. 2. Fantasy and make-believe.* Baltimore, MD: University Park Press.

The doctor says there are such boys springing up amongst us—boys of a sort unknown in the last generation—the outcome of new visions of life. They seem to see all its terrors before they are old enough to have staying power to resist them. He says it is the beginning of the coming universal wish not to live.

THOMAS HARDY
JUDE THE OBSCURE

Although Victor is 12 years old and of above-average intelligence, his drawing of himself is clearly immature. The second outline of his body is his "armor," which he may wish he had to protect himself from the pain in his life. Or, it may be like the appearance he presents—pleasant, happy, and apparently well-adjusted.

CHAPTER NINE

Childhood and Adolescent Depression

Betty Cooper Epanchin
WRIGHT SCHOOL, THE RE-EDUCATION CENTER
OF NORTH CAROLINA AND
UNIVERSITY OF NORTH CAROLINA AT CHAPEL HILL

Children express unhappy, depressed feelings in different ways as they grow and mature. Babies cry, withdraw, and become listless; young children become irritable and restless; older children tend to look unhappy and lethargic.

Depression in children is difficult to detect. It often coexists with other disorders, and frequently the other disorder is diagnosed.

There are several systems for diagnosing depression, but all have shortcomings. The DSM-III presents probably the most commonly used criteria for diagnosing depression.

Until recently, depression was rarely diagnosed in children; however, recent surveys suggest that this disorder is fairly common in youthful populations, especially among female adolescents.

Biological, psychodynamic, cognitive, and learning hypotheses have been proposed to explain why depression develops. The notion of "learned helplessness" is intriguing and particularly relevant to professionals who are working with depressed youngsters in school settings.

Social skills training, cognitive retraining, self-monitoring strategies, medication, and traditional psychotherapy have all been successful with depressed youngsters.

It is not clear whether depressed children grow up to be depressed adults. Well-designed, carefully controlled studies should address this issue. Data suggest that the outcome of treatment depends on the nature of the child's available support system.

Clyde is a moody, irritable, and lethargic eleven-year-old boy. He is receiving services in a self-contained classroom for behavior disordered youngsters because of his behavioral and academic problems. Despite average intelligence, he is achieving two years below his age mates. In the special setting he does well behaviorally, but each time his teacher has tried to mainstream him, he has gotten into fights with other children or has been rude and oppositional with the teacher; consequently, he has been returned to the special class. His classmates describe him as likable, but he has no close friends. He often looks unhappy, but rarely acknowledges feeling unhappy.

His mother died in an automobile accident when he was 22 months old, and his older sister died from a drug overdose when he was six. His father remarried when Clyde was four, but has never talked with Clyde or his brothers and sisters about his first wife and her death. Although Clyde's father seems relatively happy in his second marriage, his wife feels that the first wife's presence is still very much felt, though not acknowledged. Clyde and his stepmother argue a great deal. She feels he has never given her a chance to be a loving mother. He doesn't talk about his feelings to her and seems aloof and distant. The only person with whom he appears to have a fairly good relationship is his older brother, to whom he once confessed feeling as if he were bad luck to others—that when he loved people, they always got hurt.

Clyde is depressed, and we see his depression in his sullen, angry, distancing behavior. To people who do not know him well, he appears oppositional, angry, and somewhat detached, but to those who know him well, he is clearly an unhappy boy who expresses his misery in a hostile manner that makes others angry at him.

Sarah is a 15-year-old girl who has few friends. She sits by herself in school, talks in a quiet voice, rarely smiles or shows emotion, and rarely interacts with others unless they initiate the interaction. She doesn't appear to be interested in schoolwork, and her appearance is sloppy. Although she is attractive, it is often difficult to see her good features because she wears an oversized, shapeless coat almost all the time. Her classmates tease her, saying she stinks, which is sometimes the case. Sarah is one of twelve children who live crowded together in substandard housing from which her father is absent, and school officials do not know where he is or how long he has been gone. The family lacks financial resources, and apparently lacks a happy and caring emotional life as well. In fact, Sarah is quite similar to her mother and older siblings. Interestingly, her younger siblings (ages three and five) appear happy and energetic.

Sarah is also a depressed youngster, but in contrast to Clyde, she looks depressed to all who come in contact with her. When teachers and counselors first meet her, they want to help and try very hard to "reach her" and to "get her out of her shell," but after repeated failures, they give up and allow her just to sit in the classroom. She has been absent from school frequently, but the school social worker has given up trying to do anything about it because the mother is so passive. Now school personnel tend to overlook Sarah. They do not know what else to do, and they do not understand how to help.

Victor is a short, pudgy 12-year-old who smiles a lot and tries very hard to please people. His teachers say he looks and acts like the Pillsbury Dough Boy. Although his classmates seem to like him, he has few close friends. On individually-administered intelligence tests, he has earned IQ scores in the range of 115 to 125, yet he has failed two grades. Both times he was tested, his scores on the Performance section of the intelligence test were higher than his scores on the Verbal section

(20 points' difference on the last administration), and both times the examiners raised the question of language problems, but no clear support has been found for them. The second examiner noted Victor's lack of motivation and unwillingness to try on items he did not know, which depressed his scores on the Verbal subtests. Although he appears to be a happy, cheerful youngster, he has little energy, gives up easily, and on self-report measures, he reports feeling unhappy about himself. His score on the Children's Depression Inventory was elevated, indicating many depressive symptoms.

His parents are divorced, and his mother has remarried. His stepfather drinks excessively, and when drunk, is abusive to the mother. Both his mother and stepfather accuse Victor of being a "sissy," and both express concern that he will become a homosexual. They continuously compare him to his same-aged stepbrother, whom they consider the "ideal" son. Victor has apparently tried to choke himself on several occasions, but no one in his family is particularly concerned, since "obviously he can't do it."

Victor, too, is a depressed youngster, and perhaps even suicidal. He desperately needs affection and approval from people, but they do not realize how desperate he is because they are so involved in their own problems and because he is so guarded and hard to get to know.

As we see in these examples, depression in children manifests itself in different ways. Some depressed children appear depressed, some appear angry, and some seem "normal." Children's moods and behavior do not always match, which can make it difficult to identify depressed children. It should not be surprising, therefore, that this topic has spawned much debate among professionals.

Adult depression occurs on at least three different levels: as a *symptom*, as a *syndrome*, and as a *disorder*. Everyone shows symptoms of depression at one time or another, usually, although not necessarily, in response to situational stressors and traumas. This type of reaction can be called a *depressed mood*; someone in a depressed mood is likely to report feeling "down" and sad. The individual is likely to have crying spells, to lack energy, and to have insomnia, but these are temporary symptoms that do not interfere with functioning for prolonged periods. Depression as a *syndrome* occurs when these feelings and behavior are not fleeting and when they occur along with other symptoms such as decline in motivation, decrease in energy level, and feelings of self-depreciation. The depression may occur as a primary problem or secondary to other disorders, such as a drug or alcohol problem. Depression as a *disorder* connotes a characteristic clinical picture that has an expected course of onset, response to treatment, and expected outcome, much like other illnesses. It is considered a fully-developed psychiatric problem.

It can be difficult to differentiate among the three types of depression. For example, how does one determine when a grief reaction is no longer "normal"? Is depression precipitated by a serious illness a psychiatric condition? Is the condition depression if it is common in the general population? (Surveys in London report that among working-class women, 22 percent were definitely depressed and among women in general, another 19 percent were borderline depressed.) Although there is no clear definition for determining what type of depression a person may have, there is an emotional state described as a "black cloud," during which people report feeling empty, "flat," and indifferent to their surroundings; others exhibit a hostile withdrawal and rebuff efforts to comfort them. People who have had this type of depression describe it as very different from the unhappiness and depression that all people feel occasionally.

The professional debate about depression has been most intense with respect to depression as a clinical disorder in children. Debate ranges from what constitutes depression in children to whether depressed children become depressed adults. Researchers also question whether children have endogenous or organically-based depression as adults do and in youngsters who appear to have more than one disorder, such as depression and conduct disorder, which is the predominant problem. Although it is generally accepted that even very young children may be depressed, there is still debate as to what symptoms are indicative of depression. The literature shows several different criteria for identifying depressed youngsters, and which set is used appears to make a great deal of difference; for example, youngsters classified as depressed by the Weinberg criteria are not necessarily depressed according to the DSM-III. What factors cause depression are also widely debated.

AGE DIFFERENCES IN THE EXPRESSION OF DEPRESSION

Symptoms of depression vary in relation to the child's age. Infants (around six to nine months) who are suddenly separated from the care of a constant and caring adult become lethargic and pale. They lose interest in people, food, and the environment in general. Spitz (1946) described this as an "anaclitic depression," from the Greek word *anaklinein,* meaning "to lean upon," because it arises from the loss of the primary dependency figure or the person on whom the child leans.

Anaclitic depression was usually reversed in the infants Spitz (1946) studied if the mother returned to the infant within three to five months; if the mother returned after longer periods of separation, the infants did not respond. Furthermore, infants who were separated from their primary caretaker for long periods manifested inadequate development and higher susceptibility to physical disorders and sickness. Although Spitz's research has been criticized methodologically (Pinneau, 1955), his general conclusions that separating a child unwillingly from an attachment figure early in life has long-lasting effects and often results in depression during later childhood or adulthood have

been corroborated by other investigators (Bowlby, 1958).

Bowlby's (1973) research elaborates on depression in the infant. He posits a three-stage process in the development of depression in infants who are unwillingly separated from their primary caregiver: *protest, despair,* and *detachment.* During the protest stage, infants scream loudly at bedtime, lose their appetites, and demonstrate behaviors that were previously successful in bringing forth their mothers. The despair stage is characterized by withdrawal and obvious sadness and unhappiness. The baby no longer actively tries to get the mother back; rather, he despairs. In the detachment stage the child appears to have forgotten his mother's face. He is somewhat cheerful and responsive to others, but is withdrawn when reunited with the mother. Bowlby reports that although adequate care during the separation and healthy attachment before and after the separation help mitigate the harmful effects of unwilling separation, it is nonetheless detrimental to the child's development of trust and confidence.

This protest-despair-detachment sequence appears most frequently between the ages of six months and four years. Rutter (1986) postulates that children under six months have not established enduring selective bonds, and children four and over can understand that separation does not mean abandonment. Unfortunately, not much research has been done on depression in young, preschool children, so the literature is mostly speculative. Mahler (1966) hypothesized that when attachment figures did not understand and therefore respond appropriately to young children, the children reacted with anger and attempts to coerce the caregiver. If communication did not improve, the child's anger and frustration were directed at herself ("I'm stupid or bad because they aren't happy with me"). Such feelings cause a sense of helplessness, resignation, and depression. In Mahler's view, preschool youngsters manifested depression in much the same way that older children did. Rosenthal and Rosenthal (1984), studying 16 suicidally depressed children between the ages of two-and-a-half and five, found that all of them had disturbed attachment behavior and 13 of the 16 had histories of abuse and neglect. Their results are consistent with Mahler's notion that when young children do not have a warm and supportive relationship with their primary caregivers, some of them may blame themselves for this void and feel depressed and inadequate.

Some authorities (Lesse, 1974) maintain that depression in school-age children is "masked"; that is, the children present a multitude of symptoms that hide or mask their underlying depression. Symptoms range from psychosomatic complaints to disobedience, truancy, aggressiveness, refusal to go to school, and temper tantrums. These behaviors are "defensive" in nature, that is, the intent is to "ward off the unbearable feelings of despair" (Lesse, 1974). Cantwell (1982) notes that "there are a number of problems with this concept, the most striking being that the behaviors variously cited as masking depression cover the gamut of psychopathology in childhood. How these diverse behaviors are linked to underlying, unexpressed depressive affect is not made clear" (p. 43). He maintains that the concepts of "masked depression" and "depressive equivalent" have lost credibility. Although the concept of masked depression may no longer be popular, a number of authors note that depression occurs frequently with conduct disorders.

If we use stringent criteria, we find relatively few depressed elementary school-age children. With stringent criteria, children are diagnosed as depressed only when they act unhappy, lethargic, ineffective, or report feeling depressed. But when we do use such stringent, operational criteria for diagnosing depression, depression during childhood is predictive of depression as an adult. These findings raise questions about whether, at least for some people, depression is a coping style, a means of dealing with stress, which may be acquired as early as the elementary school years.

The available data suggest that many adolescents are depressed. They report feelings of wanting to leave home, of not being understood, of being alienated and rejected, and of restlessness. Withdrawal from family and other social activities, indifference to personal appearance, and other symptoms typical of adult depression are common. Especially among males, depression is also manifested by negativistic, antisocial, irritable behavior. Determining whether these symptoms indicate a serious depression can be especially difficult for the diagnostician because "normal adolescence" is also a time of moodiness and, occasionally, social withdrawal.

We know little about the reasons for these age differences. Perhaps the problems that appear to be depression in young children are not the same as the depression we know in adults. Or perhaps the experience of feeling miserable and depressed is common across ages, but familial, cognitive, cultural, social, and biological influences that affect the developing child give us an ever-changing clinical picture of depression. This area obviously requires more research.

ASSESSMENT OF DEPRESSION IN CHILDREN AND ADOLESCENTS

In school, where so many emotional and behavioral problems of childhood and adolescence are first noticed, depression can easily be overlooked by teachers and evaluators alike because the behaviors associated with it do not constantly demand attention. Depressed children often "fade into the woodwork" rather than act out their pain. Consequently, it is especially important that teachers and counselors be attuned to youngsters who are withdrawn and appear to have few friends, as well as to all youngsters' comments about feelings of inadequacy and of being mistreated, blamed, criticized, and abandoned. Likewise, most traditional evaluation tools do not specifically focus on depression. Unless evaluators routinely screen for depression, it can easily be overlooked, and other overt symptoms, such as antisocial behavior or learning problems, may be taken as the sole problem.

Self-expression activities such as art and creative writing provide excellent opportunities for teachers to hear about and see youngsters' feelings. For example, when one depressed youngster was asked to draw a picture of himself, he drew a picture of a house, colored it with bright, cheerful colors, and added a shining sun in the corner of the paper. Looking carefully, the evaluator could see a small face smiling out of part of one of the windows. The child who drew this picture was initially described by the psychologist who tested him as guarded and unwilling to talk about his feelings, but as a relationship developed between them, he poured out feelings of being alone and unloved.

A drawing done by Victor, whom we described at the beginning of the chapter, is shown on page 192. He is 12 years old and of above average intelligence, but the drawing is clearly immature. The second outline of his body is his "armor." Perhaps Victor wished he had an armor to protect him from all the pain in his life, or perhaps the armor is like the appearance he presents of himself—happy, pleasant, and apparently well-adjusted.

Sometimes a youngster's artwork requires very little interpretation. An evaluator looked at one child's drawing and felt that it clearly conveyed feelings of depression and despair. Meeting the child, he found that the 14-year-old also looked and acted depressed. He was withdrawn and isolated from others. He had little energy and no joie de vivre.

Self-expression activities that are part of the classroom or of an evaluation can be illuminating, but because of their subjective nature, teachers and evaluators need more evidence before considering a youngster depressed. When teachers note depressive themes in students' work, they should begin to look more closely to determine whether the depressive symptoms are more than a passing mood. Likewise, evaluators should use other assessment devices to substantiate their observations.

Children's self-report instruments are another excellent source for detecting unhappiness and depression. Several inventories have been developed to screen devices for youthful depression. The most widely used self-report inventory is the Children's Depression Inventory (CDI), patterned after the Beck Depression Inventory for adults. It can be administered to children between the ages of 7 and 17, is quick and easy to use, and demonstrates reasonable internal consistency. It is a 27-item, symptom-oriented scale, sampling symptoms of unhappy feelings and moods, the capacity to have fun and enjoy oneself, energy levels, feelings of competence, and interpersonal behaviors. Each item consists of three choices scored from zero to two, with zero less indicative of depression. The item format varies; some items begin with the most serious symptoms, while others begin with the least serious. Kazdin, French, Unis, Esveldt-Dawson, and Sherick (1983) developed the Hopelessness Scale for Children, another instrument that screens feelings of despair and depression. Children respond to 17 items, indicating whether a statement is or is not true of them. As with most self-report instruments, desirable responses are readily recognizable on both of these instruments, so children who wish to hide their unhappiness may not accurately report their feelings of depression. Research shows, however, that many youngsters willingly share their feelings, and for this reason, some evaluators include a self-report depression inventory in their assessment battery because it helps them focus on youngsters' feelings of depression and self-depreciation quickly and easily.

Other self-report measures correlate significantly with depression. For example, Mullins, Siegel, and Hodges (1985) find that the level of self-reported depressive symptoms is significantly related to an external locus of control and negative life events. They believe their results show that "identifiable stressors predate and perhaps precipitate depressive symptoms in children" and that "a child's mood may in large part be determined by problems in the environment as opposed to a specific deficit in cognitive coping ability. Such problems may well lead to or reinforce children's perceptions that outcomes are independent of responses" (p. 312).

The interview format is also frequently used to determine whether a child is depressed. This technique is highly dependent on the interviewer's knowledge of how depression is manifested in children, as well as of what developmental changes occur in critical areas such as cognition and language. Perspective-taking skills and self-reflective skills greatly affect how a child can respond to questions during an interview.

Semistructured interviews, developed primarily for research, also give clinicians examples of the types of questions one might ask to explore an individual's feelings of depression. The Bellevue Index of Depression (BID) (Petti, 1978; 1983), the Schedule for Affective Disorders and Schizophrenia, kiddie version (K-SADS) (Puig-Antich & Chambers, 1978), the Interview Schedule for Children (ICD) (Kovacs, 1978), and the Diagnostic Interview Schedule for Children and Adolescents (DICA) (Herjanic, 1976) are all semistructured interview formats for children and youth. They are series of standard questions about how the child feels and perceives the world, focusing on issues related to depression. Appropriate language and phrasing are important in the interview format to ensure that one collects the same type of data from all the children, that the questions are age appropriate, and that the data can be evaluated or quantified similarly. While maintaining the flexibility of the interview format, the semistructured technique reduces the error of information variance, which occurs when different children are asked different questions; the researcher thus gathers different information but interprets the experience rather than the interview as having been different. Sometimes the parent is interviewed first to obtain more factual information about the child's history and the onset and duration of symptoms, to gather background for the child's phenomenological view of his life and feelings.

Depressed youngsters are often identified in school settings because they begin having learning problems that precipitate a referral. A common symptom of depression in children is a drop in academic performance, so observant teachers should pay particular attention to good students who suddenly show a marked change in performance.

When teachers, counselors, or school psychologists suspect that a youngster is depressed, either on the basis of these instruments or through observations of the child's behavior, they should not hesitate to refer the child to a trained and licensed professional who has experience in evaluating depressed children. As we have mentioned throughout this chapter, depression is a complex disorder that is difficult to assess with respect to severity, but failure to identify it can have dire consequences. To ensure that a child receives the best possible evaluation, school personnel should always send along specific observations and comments about why they are concerned and what they hope to obtain from the evaluation. When information from the school is not part of the referral information, mental health professionals may overlook or underestimate the seriousness of the depression.

DIAGNOSIS OF DEPRESSION

Many depressed youngsters are not classified as emotionally disturbed or behavior disordered in school settings because the symptoms of depression are unobtrusive. Simple depression rarely presents behavior problems, so it is uncommon for obviously depressed, unhappy children to be placed in self-contained classrooms. These youngsters are more often served by the school counselor or in programs for children with learning problems. Since depression appears to affect performance, some children who are first identified because of academic problems may even be labeled learning disabled.

Mental health settings have a number of categories for diagnosing depressed youngsters. Infants who show the classic symptoms of "failure to thrive" may be classified as having a "reactive attachment disorder of infancy" in the DSM-III. With older children, a clearly identifiable stressor in the environment and an apparently transitory reaction may lead to a label of "adjustment reaction." When the reaction is acute and pronounced and of at least two weeks' duration, it may be called a Major Depressive Episode. When it is more long-standing and characterized only by the unhappy mood, however, it is called a Dysthymic Disorder.

Children diagnosed as having a Dysthymic Disorder (or a depressive neurosis) must appear chronically unhappy or disinterested. The feelings of unhappiness must have persisted at least intermittently for a minimum of one year. If the depressed periods have been intermittent, the normal periods should not have lasted more than a few months for the child to be so diagnosed. During the depressed periods, at least three of these symptoms must be present:

- Insomnia or hypersomnia
- Low energy or chronic tiredness
- Feelings of inadequacy, loss of self-esteem, or self-deprecation
- Decreased effectiveness or productivity at school, work, or home
- Decreased attention, concentration, or ability to think clearly

- Social withdrawal
- Loss of interest in or enjoyment of pleasurable activities
- Irritability or excessive anger (in children, expressed toward parents or caretakers)
- Inability to respond with apparent pleasure to praise or rewards
- Less active or talkative than usual, or feels slowed down or restless
- Pessimistic attitude toward the future, brooding about past events, or feeling sorry for self
- Tearfulness or crying
- Recurrent thoughts of death or suicide

Children diagnosed as having a major depressive disorder display the same symptomatology, but it is more serious and of a longer duration.

The DSM-III also has a category called a Bipolar Affective Disorder, also called a *manic depressive disorder*, characterized by rapid and pronounced mood swings from manic states to depressed and angry states. During the manic states, the individual is hyperactive, easily distracted, has an inflated self-perception, a decreased need for sleep, and "excessive involvement in activities that have a high potential for painful consequences" (APA, 1980, p. 206). The depressed states are similar to the depression we have described. This disorder is generally believed to have a strong biological, perhaps genetic, component, and adults with bipolar illness have been successfully treated with drug therapy. The psychiatric literature increasingly reports the onset of manic depressive illness or bipolar disorder as beginning around puberty and possibly even earlier.

PREVALENCE

Depression has been called "the common cold" of adult psychiatry. Studies confirm the high prevalence of depression in adults, especially among white women living in urban areas. Depressive disorders tend to cluster in families as well.

In contrast, relatively few studies have looked at youthful depression. Earls (1984) found prevalence rates of 9 percent to 10 percent for "failure to thrive" among a rural infant population and 4 percent to 8 percent among preschool children, with girls having nearly twice the rate of depressed mood as boys. Fully-developed depressive disorders appear to be rare in school-age children, although depressive feelings are more common. Earls reviewed prevalence studies that used nonpatient populations and found low but somewhat discrepant rates of depression in school-age youngsters. Rates varied from two boys in a sample of 103 children to no cases. In the Isle of Wight study, Rutter, Izard, and Whitmore (1970/1981) found a prevalence rate for affective disorders of 1.4/ 1000, but among 10- to 11-year-olds, 13 percent showed a depressed mood during an interview, 9 percent appeared preoccupied with depressing topics, 17 percent failed to smile, and 15 percent were not emotionally responsive. Among clinical school-age populations, rates of depression are generally much higher: 16 percent among outpatients and 36 percent among inpatients of a psychiatric service (Earls, 1984).

There is a marked and significant increase in depressive symptoms from school age to adolescence, especially among girls. Earls cites one study that used a self-report measure in a junior high school and found that one-third of the youngsters reported moderate to severe depressive symptoms! Alienation from peers and parents seemed significant in explaining the high rate of reported depression. Studies using other methods to identify depression in nonpatient adolescent populations report rates in the range of 2 to 3 percent.

The definition of depression and the methods used to identify depressed youngsters have a great deal to do with the prevalence figures; however, it appears that girls are more likely to experience depressive disorders than boys, that depressive disorders increase with age during childhood and adolescence, and that depression in youthful populations is not as common as it is among adult populations.

ETIOLOGICAL HYPOTHESES OF DEPRESSION

There are at least four major sets of hypotheses as to why children become depressed. Grouped according to their emphasis, the perspectives are biological, psychodynamic, cognitive, and learning experiences.

Biological Factors

Probably because of the major advances with respect to the diagnosis and treatment of depression in adults, attention is focusing on biological factors. Subtypes of adult depression have now been identified with clinical, laboratory tests. These efforts are being pursued with children, and, according to Cantwell (1982) and Cytryn, McKnew, Zahn-Waxler, and Gershon (1986), the preliminary data suggest that many of the biological parameters seen in depressed adults also appear in some depressed children. These biological parameters include, but are not limited to, hypersecretion of cortisol, positive dexamethasone suppression test, hypersecretion of growth hormone in sleep, diminished growth hormone response to an insulin tolerance test, and diminished excretion of urinary metabolites. Cytryn et al. (1986) note that children with major depressive disorders respond to the same medications as do adults with major depressive disorders.

Studies have also looked at genetic factors. The tendency for depression to occur in family members has been noted repeatedly in adults and children alike; however, the results are questionable because the studies have, for the most part, been plagued by methodological problems, such as small samples, retrospective data gathering, failure to use control groups, and/or failure to have raters rate subjects blindly. Nonetheless, at least two adoption studies (Cadoret, 1978; Mendlewicz & Rainer, 1977) report increased prevalence rates for depression among adoptees whose biological parents had a major affective disorder.

Another example of the type of research that supports a genetic hypothesis is Cantwell's (1982) report of an overall monozygotic twin concordance rate of 76 percent as opposed to an overall dizygotic twin concordance rate of 19 percent and of monozygotic twins reared apart of 67 percent. Studying children of depressed adults, several investigators have found that the children had higher incidences of disturbance of all kinds but McKnew, Cytryn, Efron, Gershon, and Bunney (1979) found that children of depressed adults not only had higher rates of psychopathology in general but also higher rates of diagnosable depression. Gershon, Hamovit, and Guroff (1983) report that having one parent with a depressive disorder was associated with a 27 percent risk of the offspring's having a depressive disorder, and having two parents with depressive disorders increased the risk to 74 percent, a familial association greater than most psychiatric disorders.

Genetic studies continue to have the problem of determining what is environmentally determined versus what is genetically determined, and if genetically determined, in what way. To illustrate the type of research that confounds the problem, Weissman, Paykel, and Klerman (1972) found that depressed women were less involved with their children, had impaired communication, greater guilt, more resentment, lack of affection, and increased friction when they were depressed. The effect of this kind of childrearing remains unclear.

It is unlikely that childhood depression is caused solely by biological factors. Rather, biological makeup and inherited predisposition, as well as precipitating stressors in the environment, all contribute to the development of childhood depression.

Psychodynamic Theories

From a psychodynamic perspective, depression is the result of hostility turned against the self. This perspective distinguishes between grief and melancholia. Grief results from the loss of a love object. There are few ambivalent or guilty feelings; self-regard remains intact; and, after a period of withdrawal (which Freud referred to as the "work of mourning"), the person's interest in life returns. Melancholia, however, includes ambivalent feelings of anger and hostility toward the love object, which cause the individual to feel guilty. The superego defends against these guilty feelings by unconsciously chastising the self instead of feeling angry toward the love object. The inward-turned anger leads to depression. Since children's superegos are not fully developed, some analytic authors argue that depression as a superego conflict cannot exist in children (Beres, 1966).

From this perspective, loss of a loved object during childhood has great potential for producing depression that is likely to carry over into adulthood. Children in the process of separating psychologically from their parents have ambivalent feelings, and this ambivalence greatly complicates their ability to grieve. Furthermore, young children lack the conceptual ability to understand that death is forever, so they are unable to deal maturely with the death of a significant person.

Wolfenstein (1966) proposed an interesting explanation of why such loss can have such devastating effects. She hypothesized that children must pass through the traumas and mourning of adolescence before they have the ability to mourn and recover maturely. The postadolescent youth knows he can survive a loss because he has survived other losses and traumas during adolescence, but the young child has no such perspective. Children cannot attain the psychological detachment that older people can; therefore, they deny the finality of the loss. The painful process of "decathexis," or detaching from the loved object, is delayed by the denial of the permanence of death. The child expects the loved object to return. When depressed moods emerge, especially during adolescence, they are isolated from the thoughts of the dead loved object. Wolfenstein illustrates this process in her case study of a boy whose mother died from cancer when he was ten years old. He did not cry after her death, he wanted to return to school at once and carry on as if nothing had happened, he continued his usual activities; but he became diffusely irritable and quick to anger. After an altercation with his grandmother, who was taking care of him, he finally agreed with her that he was feeling bad about his mother's death. He then confessed that he felt he had caused her death because she fixed breakfast for him and did other things for him when she was sick and weak. "Their discussion went on far into the night, and at the end the boy, greatly relieved, and with the intolerance for prolonged distress characteristic of his age, exclaimed, 'I feel great!' " (p. 119). Three years after his mother's death and in response to the end of a series of books he had read, he wept profusely. Wolfenstein describes this as a breakthrough of his inhibited grief and as "mourning at a distance." She saw the child's difficulty in mourning as a developmental unreadiness to do the work of mourning. In her opinion, only after adolescence is one developmentally capable of mourning, and unless the child works through these feelings, the conflict remains unresolved and for the most part unconscious.

Not all psychodynamic writers, however, ascribe to the superego conflict explanation of depression, although many argue that depression does not really occur in children. For example, Rie (1966) argued that depression results from a discrepancy between the real self and the ideal self, but since stable self-representation does not develop until adolescence, depression was not believed to exist in children. In contrast, Bibring (1953), an ego-psychologist, saw depression as an affect related to the ego's awareness of its helplessness. Helplessness led to the collapse of self-esteem, which resulted in depression. From this perspective it was quite possible for children to develop depression. The debate as to whether children can really be depressed has dominated the psychodynamic literature and is probably the primary reason that until recently the term *depression* has been omitted from the lexicon of child psychopathology.

Cognitive Theories

Cognitive theorists consider depression a thought disorder that causes the individual to distort perceptions of self, the environment, and the future. For example, an attractive individual may see himself as unattractive because of some mild physical defect that he blows out of proportion. One may expect defeat and failure. One may believe the environment makes insurmountable demands, or is excessively critical, or constantly disparaging. One may see the future as full of problems, hardships, and frustration. These cognitive distortions develop during childhood in response to trauma and loss and are reactivated by later events. In effect, the individual does not learn more mature cognitive means of understanding loss and disappointment.

Becker (1977) describes these childish distortions as: (1) *arbitrary inference,* or drawing conclusions without adequate evidence; (2) *selective abstraction,* or ignoring the context of a situation and focusing only on one aspect of it; (3) *overgeneralization,* or making sweeping generalizations from inadequate knowledge; (4) *magnification* and *minimization,* or over- or underestimating the significance of information; and (5) *personalization,* or attaching excessive subjective significance to impersonal events. An example of a cognitive distortion is the child who does not study for a test, fails it, and concludes that she failed because she is dumb rather than because she did not study.

Behavioral Theories

Behaviorists emphasize the loss of positive reinforcement to explain why depression develops, and the underlying principles are the same for adults and children alike. Ferster (1974) posits that the occurrence of a significant stress or change in a person's life can cause the reduction of positive reinforcers that maintain behaviors such as socializing. With the loss, the behaviors are, in effect, put on an extinction schedule. As the behavior diminishes, it is reinforced less often, which further reduces its frequency and establishes a cyclical pattern. Ferster also notes how behaviors such as complaining, inactivity, and withdrawal can be positively reinforced by the attention of others. Lewinsohn (1974) says depression develops from reduced positive reinforcement in an individual who has a deficit in the social skills needed to elicit positive reinforcement.

The *model of "learned helplessness"* is related to the behavioral and cognitive theories. It grew out of research originally done with dogs, in which the dogs received unavoidable shocks (Seligman & Maier, 1967). They were later exposed to a shuttle box in which avoidance of shock required jumping over a hurdle after an onset warning signal. The experimental dogs did not learn to escape the shock by jumping over the hurdle after the warning signal, whereas the control dogs who had not been shocked earlier learned quickly to escape the shock. Not only were the experimental dogs unable to learn how to avoid the shock, they also showed no motivation to try to escape and demonstrated little overt emotionality while being shocked; instead they sat and endured the shock without whimpering.

Noting similarities between the dogs'

behavior and the behavior of depressed individuals, Seligman and his colleagues conducted studies with depressed and nondepressed subjects. Depressed subjects perceived themselves as having less control over the reinforcement than did nondepressed subjects working on the same task. The similarities between the animal studies and the studies with depressed individuals led Seligman to develop a model for learned helplessness in relation to depression. Fundamental to this model is the assumption that when outcomes are not contingent upon behavior, the individual learns that he has no control over his environment or that he is helpless to influence his environment. This leads to depression.

The initial model elicited much criticism because "it failed to do justice to the complexities of people" (Seligman & Peterson, 1986, p. 226). It did not address the question of why individuals respond differently to uncontrollable conditions; it did not adequately clarify how helplessness is generalized across time and situations; and it did not explain the loss of self-esteem common among depressed individuals. These issues led to a reformulation that focused on how an individual learns to feel helpless (Abramson, Seligman, & Teasdale, 1978). There are four important aspects to the reformulated model:

1. Depression consists of four classes of deficits: motivational, cognitive, self-esteem, and affective.
2. When highly desired outcomes are believed improbable or highly aversive outcomes are believed probable, and the individual expects that no response in his repertoire will change their likelihood, (helplessness) depression results.
3. The generality of the depressive deficits will depend on the globality of the attribution for helplessness, the chronicity of the depression deficits will depend on the stability of the attribution for helplessness, and whether self-esteem is lowered will depend on the internality of the attribution for helplessness.
4. The intensity of the deficits depends on the strength, or certainty, of the expectation of uncontrollability and, in the case of the affective and

self-esteem deficits, on the importance of the outcome. (Abramson, Seligman, & Teasdale, 1978, p. 68)

Most work using this model has been done with adults, but many of the principles appear to apply also to children, although the supporting data are preliminary. For example, Seligman and Peterson (1986) demonstrate that depression as measured by the CDI was negatively related to good problem solving as measured by the Block Design subtest of the WISC-R and an anagrams measure. The relationship between CDI scores and latency measures was particularly strong: the more depressed the child, the slower the response. Depressed children also tended to make comments such as "How many more problems are there?" and "I never do well when I get timed." More competent youngsters responded with statements such as "I am really smart" and "I like the anagrams because they are more challenging" (Seligman & Peterson, 1986, p. 232). These parallel findings with adult samples.

In a subsequent study, Seligman and Peterson (1986) empirically related depressive symptoms to a negative attributional style. In this study of 96 third-, fourth-, fifth-, and sixth-graders, scores on the CDI were correlated with the scores on the Children's Attributional Style Questionnaire (CASQ) at two different times. The CASQ's 48 items describe an event and identify two possible causes. Respondents are instructed to choose the better explanation for the event. Three attributional dimensions are measured: *internal-external* (internal = characteristics possessed by the individual attributor); *stable-unstable* (stable = persist over time); and *global-specific* (global = causes present in a variety of situations).

This study reliably measured self-report of depressive symptoms and attributional styles of 9- to 13-year-olds, and the scores were stable over six months. Girls reported more depressive symptoms than boys, but perhaps most importantly, attributional style correlated highly with depression in

children, even more strongly than among college students or adult inpatients. Compared to nondepressed children, children with depressive symptoms made more internal, stable, and global attributions for bad events and more external, unstable, and specific attributions for good events. Note that these studies were conducted with children who reported having depressive symptoms, not with youngsters who had been clinically diagnosed as depressed, and the findings might not generalize to such a group.

In yet another study, Seligman and Peterson (1986) found that in a sample of 47 mothers and 36 fathers of children who had participated in the previously described study, there were positive correlations between the mothers' and children's attributional styles for bad events and between their depressive symptoms, but the fathers' attributional styles and depressive symptoms did not relate to either their mates' or their children's. The researchers interpreted these results as suggestive of an "interpersonal vicious cycle" in which "the child may learn attributional style (or depressive symptoms) from its mother, and then the depressions of mother and child may maintain each other, particularly when each possesses the insidious attributional style" (p. 244).

Seligman and Peterson believe depression based on learned helplessness is only one type of depression and acknowledge the importance of physiological states that can cause an individual to be depressed. Nonetheless, the implications of this research are particularly intriguing to persons working with children in school settings. If attributions are learned, as evidence suggests, then perhaps children can be taught productive, enhancing attributions instead of destructive, maladaptive attributions.

TREATMENT

Some interventions have been found useful for treating depression, but few have been carefully researched and supported by extensive empirical data. Cantwell (1982) notes that "it is an unfortunate truth in child psychiatry that treatment is more often based on the theoretical orientation of the clinician than on the evidence for the efficacy of the treatment modality" (p. 79). This certainly appears to be the case with respect to depression in children and adolescents.

The most traditional approach to treating depressed youngsters is individual psychotherapy for both the child and the family. This type of intervention has been demonstrated to be effective with adults (Weissman, 1979), and Cantwell maintains that "since children are very intimately involved both in families and in school and are developing organisms, it is likely that psychosocial intervention will play at least as important a role in depressive disorders in childhood as it does with adults" (p. 86).

The usual goals of psychotherapy are to increase the child's feelings of self-worth through improved relationships with significant others and through increased skills in dealing with problems. Recent interventions have grown out of the behavioral and cognitive models for understanding depression: social skills training, activity increase programs, attribution retraining, cognitive therapy, and self-control therapy (Kaslow & Rehm, 1983). Some are conducted during individual therapy sessions and others in group sessions.

Social skills training as an intervention for depression has mostly involved teaching adults appropriate assertive social skills to use in problematic situations. This approach is based on the belief that depressed individuals do not have the necessary social skills to obtain reinforcement from their social environment, which results in their receiving low rates of response-contingent positive reinforcement. The skills have included specific behaviors, such as tone and quality of voice, as well as more complicated skills, such as interpersonal negotiation strategies.

Methods include modeling, instruction, role play, feedback, homework practice, and situation logs.

We find an example of this approach in a study by Schloss, Schloss, and Harris (1984), who used modeling, behavior rehearsal, feedback, and contingent reinforcement to increase social interaction skills in three severely depressed adolescents. A multiple-baseline analysis revealed that change in behavior was associated with introduction of the treatment. At a nine-month follow-up, some of the gains had been maintained. A few other studies have used this approach (Calpin & Cincirpini, 1978; Calpin & Kornblith, 1977; and Petti, Bornstein, Delamater, & Conners, 1980), and their results provide support for the fruitfulness of the approach and its potential usefulness in a variety of settings by a variety of professionals.

The intent of *activity increase programs* is to increase the number of pleasant and rewarding activities in an individual's life. This is based on the assumption that lack of response-contingent positive reinforcements may stem from reinforcement-poor environments. Techniques in this approach include obtaining a baseline of mood and activity level, identifying activities associated with positive and negative moods, increasing those activities associated with positive mood, decreasing activities associated with negative mood, and setting up environmental contingencies to support increased participation in activities associated with positive moods and decreased participation in activities associated with negative moods. Again, more of this work has been done with adults, but changes in activity level have been associated with changes in depression. This approach has a commonsense appeal and, again, is one that could be utilized in naturally-occurring settings such as schools.

Attribution retraining focuses on the insidious attributional style that "filters failure in such a way as to produce the affective, motivational, and self-esteem deficits associated with depression" (Kaslow & Rehm, 1983). Typically psychotherapy is the modality used for changing these destructive attributions. A model developed by Abramson, Seligman, and Teasdale (1978) illustrates this approach. These authors believe depression results from overgeneralizations and from attributing results to global, stable, and internal factors; therefore, therapy focused on four goals:

• Reducing the likelihood that aversive outcomes would occur

• Reducing the desirability of the highly preferred outcomes that are causing failure and loss of self-esteem (for example, helping a child readjust goals from being miserable if she's not the very best student to being in the top 25 percent and having more time to play)

• Changing the individual's expectation of not being able to control events to being able to control them by (1) teaching necessary social skills and/or (2) using role plays of successful response-outcome sequences to modify distorted expectations that efforts will fail

• Changing unrealistic attributions for failure toward external, unstable, specific factors while also changing unrealistic attributions for success to internal, stable, and global factors (for example, helping a youngster see that he failed an exam because the material was taken exclusively from class notes and he had spent most of his time studying the texts)

There is some empirical evidence for the success of this approach, and it has logical and practical appeal. Teachers can give youngsters feedback that teaches and models adaptive attributions. Dweck (1975) compared two experimental interventions with a group of children who had extreme reactions to failure. Half the group was given only successful experiences, while the other half was given attribution retraining. Children in the attribution retraining were taught to take responsibility for their failure and to attribute

it to lack of effort—that is, to make internal, unstable, specific attributions for their failure. After training, the children in the success-only treatment group continued to deteriorate when confronted with failure, whereas the youngsters in the attribution-retraining group maintained and improved their performance. Dweck used a slightly different attribution training model than did Seligman, but nonetheless found positive results, and the approach obviously merits further attention and research.

Cognitive therapy entails working with clients to explore their distorted conceptualizations and dysfunctional attitudes and beliefs in an effort to modify their negative thinking biases. The client's assumptions about why events occur are treated as hypotheses that need validation and careful examination. In exploring these attitudes, beliefs, and assumptions, the client and therapist identify, monitor, and evaluate destructive distortions, and consider alternative interpretations and beliefs. Beck and his colleagues evaluated this approach with depressed adults (Kaslow & Rehm, 1983), and there is supporting data, but much less work has been done with children. We know, however, that modifications will be needed with children; for example, children are not capable of abstract thought until they reach the stage of formal operations in early adolescence, raising the question of whether they can despair about the future if they cannot project themselves into the future.

Nonetheless, a few interventions have been directed at modifying children's self-perceptions as a means of modifying their depressive cognitive styles. Positive self-statement training has met with some success (Craighead, Wilcoxin-Craighead, & Meyers, 1978), and more integrated, school-based approaches for modifying self-perceptions have been successful. Butler, Miezitis, Friedman, and Cole (1980), for example, recommend that teachers use frequent and regular contacts, expressions of affection and approval, and many success experiences with depressed children. Whole-class interventions include having all the children write about their best characteristics and the characteristics they would like to change to help the depressed child see that everyone has things about themselves they are not particularly happy about.

Self-control strategies teach components of self-control. This approach assumes that depressed individuals have deficits in self-monitoring, self-evaluation, or self-reinforcement. As evidence of these deficits, one might find (1) selective attention to negative events to the exclusion of positive events; (2) selective monitoring of immediate as opposed to delayed consequences of one's behavior; (3) overly-stringent criteria for self-evaluation; (4) failure to accurately attribute responsibility for one's behavior; (5) inadequate self-reinforcement; (6) excessive self-punishment. Research with depressed children demonstrates that various self-control skills are lacking (Kaslow, 1981). Self-control strategies are receiving a great deal of attention in the cognitive-behavior therapy literature and are applicable in classrooms and other settings as both a preventive technique and a remedial intervention.

To make sequential decisions about which treatments to use in which order, Kaslow and Rehm (1983) developed a decision-making matrix (see Figure 9–1). This flowchart is based on the assumptions that certain skills are prerequisites to other skills, and some deficits are more fundamental than others. If depression is secondary to another behavior disorder such as an attention deficit disorder, for example, then focusing first on the primary problem seems appropriate. Likewise, improving a social skill deficit may be necessary before one can help an individual increase his or her activity level or become more involved socially. Another assumption underlying this decision-making matrix is that overt behavioral change should precede attempts to change distorted thinking.

An alternative approach to dealing with depression has been simultaneous use of different interventions. Petti, Bornstein, Delamater, and Conners (1980) illustrate this kind of treatment program with a ten-and-a-half-year-old girl who was depressed, had school problems, and problems with her foster family. While the child was hospitalized, she participated in individual psychotherapy. Goals of the therapy were to help her develop a better understanding of her conflicts, especially with her natural and foster families, and to help her develop more positive feelings about herself. The school simultaneously began a psychoeducational intervention to help her develop better academic skills and more appropriate school behavior, both of which would ultimately improve her feelings about herself and her skills. Social skills training was instituted to help her improve her ability to get along with her classmates and foster family. Family therapy was instituted with both the foster and natural family to help them see more of the girl's positive qualities and help them develop better childrearing skills to deal with her problem behavior. After five weeks of hospitalization she received imipramine (at a dose of 5 mg. per kg.) to enhance her ability to respond to the therapeutic program. Positive results were reported for the hospital treatment; 3- and 6-week posttreatment follow-up data suggested that most of the gains were maintained.

Hospitalization or treatment in a residential facility is also often recommended when professionals are uncertain about a child's potential for suicide. These settings enable careful observation and assessment of the suicidal potential, and medication trials can be carefully monitored and supervised.

Medication is an area of growing interest in the treatment of children's depression. Medication has been an accepted, effective intervention with adults for some time, but much less work has been done with children. Rancurello (1985) notes that, although a broad spectrum of childhood symptoms have been

FIGURE 9–1
Flowchart for Ordering Intervention Targets in Treating Depression in Children

Note: From "Childhood Depression" by N. J. Kaslow and L. P. Rehm, 1983, in R. J. Morris and T. R. Kratochwill (Eds.), *The Practice of Child Therapy.* New York: Pergamon Press. Reprinted by permission of Pergamon Press.

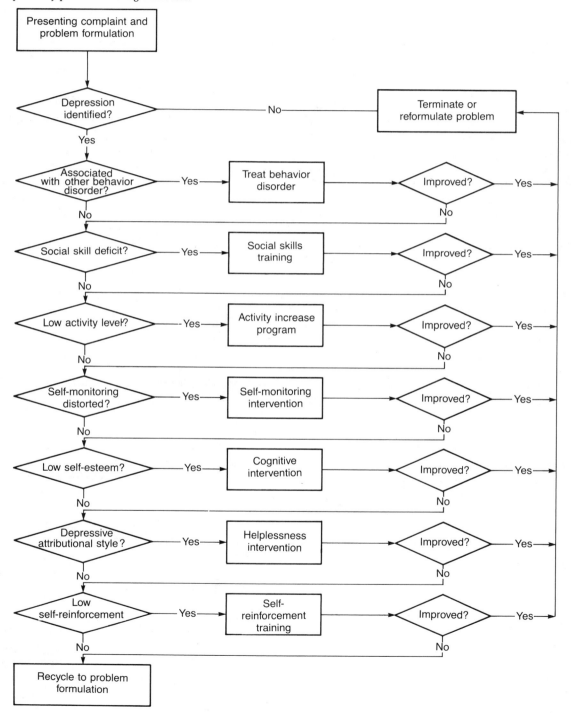

treated with antidepressants, most research has been plagued by methodological problems. Werry (1982) says stimulants were overused and nonpharmacological interventions underused with hyperactive youngsters in the 1970s, and speculates that in the 1980s, antidepressant agents are overused while the concept of depression in youngsters is ignored. Rancurello comments that "compared to the stimulant drugs, the risks associated with prescribing antidepressants are greater and their effects on cognition, growth/metabolism, and development are largely untested" (p. 88).

Imipramine, or Tofranil, is probably the most frequently used antidepressant with children. The few good clinical studies on the effectiveness of this drug show mixed results. It does, however, have some serious side effects, which include dry mouth, drowsiness, dizziness, lethargy, tremors, sweating, insomnia, nausea, constipation, appetite disturbance, and cardiac conduction changes. Withdrawal symptoms have also been reported: gastrointestinal complaints, drowsiness, decreased appetite, tearfulness, apathy or withdrawal, headaches, agitation, irritability or moodiness, and insomnia. Because of the potentially negative side effects of this medication, it requires extremely cautious use and careful monitoring.

Some antidepressant drugs commonly used with adults (cyclic antidepressants such as desipramine, amitriptyline, and nortriptyline, and monoamine oxidase inhibitors and lithium) have been tried with children, but none have extensive, carefully-controlled research to support their use. Rancurello (1985) notes:

Children tend to exhibit developmentally dependent differences in how they distribute, metabolize, and excrete drugs. These mechanisms are distinct from those seen in either neonates or adults. Children are able to tolerate higher mg/kg doses of pharmacologic agents than adults, and often require adult-like maintenance doses despite a lower absolute body weight. (p. 88)

Given that the long-term effects of these drugs are unknown and that they may have rather serious side effects, the need for prudent use is obvious. Rancurello reports that none of the cyclic antidepressants have FDA approval for use with depressed children, and a clinician who uses these drugs with youngsters may be liable if serious, unexpected cardiovascular side effects occur.

With respect to the MAO inhibitors, Rancurello (1985) states that "there appear to be no legitimate uses for the MAO inhibitors in the treatment of children at this time" (p. 97). Lithium also requires cautious use with children. Adults who exhibit manic-depressive symptoms (bipolar disorder) have been successfully treated with lithium for some time, and Rancurello reports the practice is also generally acceptable for adolescents who present with symptoms of bipolar illness, but diagnosis of these symptoms is very rare in children; therefore, caution must be exercised with this drug.

OUTCOME

There have been few solid outcome studies dealing with depression in children and adolescents. Poznanski, Krahenbuhl, and Zrull (1976) conducted one of the most widely cited studies. They conducted a follow-up study six and a half years after treatment of ten children who had been affectively depressed during childhood. Of these ten, five were clinically depressed at the time of the study and the remaining five had a number of psychiatric problems. One tended to be sarcastic and blame others for his problems; one was in treatment with a private psychiatrist (the reason for referral was depression); one held his head down throughout the interview, but his verbalizations neither confirmed nor refuted a diagnosis of depression; one was guarded and anxious during the interview but no depression was noted; and one was on heroin, so it was impossible to determine whether he was depressed. While clinically interesting, this study was limited by its small sample size and the fact that the interviews were not blind-rated.

Herjanic (1976) conducted a similar study of 20 children from St. Louis Children's Hospital who had been diagnosed as depressed at the time of discharge. At the time of the follow-up interviews, only one clearly had a depressive disorder; one had a schizoaffective disorder, and one had an undiagnosed illness that might develop into a depressive disorder; ten had no psychiatric diagnosis; two were antisocial; and five were undiagnosed. Cantwell (1982) cites other studies that followed children treated in psychiatric hospitals and outpatient clinics. No evidence emerged of a specific "predepressive" childhood disorder that predicts depression in adulthood.

One problem in studying the outcome of depression in children has been how best to identify a sample of depressed youngsters. If the criteria for determining whether a child is depressed are based strictly upon overt, behavioral symptomatology and direct self-report, there is a fairly high correspondence between childhood and adult depression. When the diagnosis is based upon *assumptions* that depression must be the underlying problem, however, the correspondence between depression in childhood and later life is not as close. Data on the long-term effectiveness of interventions with depressed youngsters are unavailable, although there is ample evidence to suggest that long-term outcome is related to the individual's available support system.

CONCLUSION

Depression in children and adolescents can be manifested in many different ways. They may look and act depressed and unhappy, or they may be irritable, lethargic, hyperactive, enuretic, and aloof. Depression may be the only observed problem, or it may occur along with other psychological disorders, such as conduct or phobic disorders. Depression can apparently result from a variety of factors: painful losses and situations, biogenetic factors, and/or interactions that result in distorted, self-punishing attitudes and perceptions.

Some of the interventions used to treat depression are psychotherapy, cognitive restructuring, medication, teaching social skills, and self-reinforcement training. All demonstrate limited to good short-term success. It is likely that how well a youngster responds to an intervention is related, at least in part, to how well the caregivers understand the depression and how well they implement the intervention. Understanding the nature of the conflict and implementing an intervention based on a meaningful relationship can be difficult, because the children are typically aloof, hard to engage, and can be irritating. James (1984) describes some of the difficulties a caregiving individual may encounter. They may have *listening difficulties*— "How can I listen to this drivel when I have problems of my own?" They may feel *resentment* of the client—"This client is making me mad. I can't handle all this misery and I'm bored listening to it. I ought to be ashamed of myself . . . I should be feeling differently." The caregiver may also find dealing with depressed individuals threatening—feelings of *professional inadequacy* may surface; the caregiver may not feel he knows enough, or may fear the responsibility of dealing with someone who is perhaps potentially suicidal, or the caregiver may face tough decisions as to whether to respect confidential material the client has shared versus informing others of potentially suicidal behavior. Depression is such an interactive phenomenon that professionals must pay careful attention to their own feelings about the depressed child, because these feelings are likely to affect how one reacts to the youngster and how one is able to collaborate and cooperate with fellow professionals.

The caregiver must also consider what function the depression or the self-destructive behavior serves. Depression may serve as an excuse from feared responsibility, or a defense against anger at someone else—mother, father, sibling, and so on. The point

is that caregivers need to see the world through the client's eyes to understand the nature of the depression, the types of intervention that appear to fit the client's needs, and the individual's potential for suicide, which we will examine in chapter 13.

REFERENCES

Abramson, L. Y., Seligman, M. E. P., & Teasdale, J. D. (1978). Learned helplessness in humans: Critique and reformulation. *Journal of Abnormal Psychology, 87,* 49–74.

American Psychiatric Association. (1980). *Diagnostic and statistical manual of mental disorders* (3rd ed.). Washington, DC: APA.

Becker, J. (1977). *Affective disorders.* Morristown, NY: General Learning Press.

Beres, D. (1966). Superego and depression. In R. M. Lowenstein, L. M. Newman, M. Schen, & A. J. Solnit (Eds.), *Psychoanalysis: A general psychology.* New York: International Universities Press.

Bibring, E. (1953). The mechanism of depression. In P. Greenacre (Ed.), *Affective disorders.* New York: International Universities Press.

Bowlby, J. (1958). The nature of the child's tie to his mother. *International Journal of Psychoanalysis, 39,* 350–373.

Bowlby, J. (1973). *Attachment and loss* (Vol. 2). New York: Basic Books.

Butler, L. F., Miezitis, S., Friedman, R. J., & Cole, E. (1980). The effect of two school-based intervention programs on depressive symptoms in pre-adolescent children. *American Educational Research Journal, 17,* 111–119.

Cadoret, R. J. (1978). Evidence for genetic inheritance of primary affective disorder in adoptees. *American Journal of Psychiatry, 135,* 463–466.

Calpin, J. P., & Cincirpini, P. M. (1978). A multiple baseline analysis of social skills training in children. Paper presented at Midwestern Association for Behavior Analysis, Chicago.

Calpin, J. P., & Kornblith, S. J. (1977). Training of aggressive children in conflict resolution skills. Paper presented at the meeting of the Association for the Advancement of Behavior Therapy, Chicago.

Cantwell, D. P. (1982). Childhood depression: A review of current research. In B. B. Lahey, & A. E. Kazdin, (Eds.), *Advances in clinical child psychology* (Vol. 5). New York: Plenum Press.

Carlson, G. A., & Cantwell, D. P. (1980). Unmasking masked depression in children and adolescents. *American Journal of Psychiatry, 137,* 445–449.

Craighead, W. E., Wilcoxin-Craighead, L. W., & Meyers, A. W. (1978). New directions in behavior modification with children. In M. Hersen, R. M. Eisler, &

P. M. Miller (Eds.), *Progress in behavior modification* (Vol. 6). New York: Academic Press.

Cytryn, L., McKnew, J. H., Zahn-Waxler, C., & Gershon, E. S. (1986). Developmental issues in risk research: The offspring of affectively ill parents. In M. Rutter, C. E. Izard, & P. B. Read, *Depression in young people: Developmental and clinical perspectives.* New York: Guilford Press.

Dweck, C. S. (1975). The role of expectations and attributions in the alleviation of learned helplessness. *Journal of Personality and Social Psychology, 31,* 674–685.

Earls, F. (1984). The epidemiology of depression in children and adolescents. *Pediatric Annals, 13,* 23–31.

Ferster, C. B. (1974). Behavioral approaches to depression. In R. J. Friedman & M. M. Katz (Eds.), *The psychology of depression: Contemporary theory and research.* New York: Holt, Rinehart & Winston.

Gershon, E. S., Hamovit, J., & Guroff, J. J. (1983). A family study of schizoaffective, bipolar I, bipolar II, unipolar, and normal control probands. *Archives of General Psychiatry, 39,* 1157–1167.

Herjanic, B. (1976). Diagnostic interview for children and adolescents (Ages 9–17) (DICA). Unpublished manuscript. (Available from B. Herjanic, Washington University School of Medicine, St. Louis, MO)

Herjanic, B., & Campbell, W. (1977). Differentiating psychiatrically disturbed children on the basis of a structured interview. *Journal of Abnormal Child Psychology, 5,* 127–134.

Jacobson, E. (1971). *Depression: Comparative studies of normal, neurotic and psychotic conditions.* New York: International Universities Press.

James, N. (1984). Psychology of suicide. In C. L. Halton & S. M. Valente, *Suicide: Assessment and intervention* (2nd ed.). Norwalk, CT: Appleton-Century-Crofts.

Kaslow, N. J. (1981). Social and cognitive correlates of depression in children from a developmental perspective. Paper presented in L. P. Rehm (Chair), Empirical studies in childhood depression. Symposium presented at the annual meeting of the American Psychological Association, Los Angeles.

Kaslow, N. J., & Rehm, L. P. (1983). Childhood depression. In R. J. Morris & T. R. Kratochwill (Eds.), *The practice of child therapy* (pp. 27–52). New York: Pergamon Press.

Kazdin, A. E., French, N. H., Unis, A. S., Esveldt-Dawson, K., & Sherick, R. B. (1983). Hopelessness, depression, and suicidal intent among psychiatrically disturbed inpatient children. *Journal of Consulting and Clinical Psychology, 51,* 504–510.

Kovacs, M. (1978). The interview schedule for children (ISC) Form C. Unpublished manuscript. (Available from M. Kovacs, Western Psychiatric Institute and Clinic, Pittsburgh, PA)

Kovacs, M. (1986). A developmental perspective on methods and measures in the assessment of depressive disorders: The clinical interview. In M. Rutter, C. E. Izard, & P. B. Read (Eds.), *Depression in young people: Developmental and clinical perspectives.* New York: Guilford Press.

Lesse, S. (1974). *Masked depression.* New York: Aronson.

Lewinsohn, P. H. (1974). A behavioral approach to depression. In R. J. Friedman and M. M. Katz (Eds.), *The psychology of depression: Contemporary theory and research.* New York: Holt, Rinehart & Winston.

Mahler, M. (1966). Notes on the development of basic moods: The depressive affect. In R. M. Lowenstein, L. M. Newman, M. Schur, & A. J. Solnit (Eds.), *Psychoanalysis—A general psychology.* New York: International Universities Press.

McKnew, D. H., Cytryn, L., Efron, A. M., Gershon, E. S., & Bunney, W. E. (1979). Offspring of patients with affective disorders. *British Journal of Psychiatry, 134,* 148–152.

Mendlewicz, J., & Rainer, J. D. (1977). Adoption study supporting genetic transmission in manic-depressive illness. *Nature, 268,* 327–329.

Mullins, L. L., Siegel, L. J., & Hodges, K. (1985). Cognitive problem-solving and life event correlates of depressive symptoms in children. *Journal of Abnormal Child Psychology, 13,* 305–314.

Petti, T. A. (1978). Depression in hospitalized child psychiatry patients: Approaches to measuring depression. *Journal of the American Academy of Child Psychiatry, 17,* 49–59.

Petti, T. A. (1983). Depression and withdrawal in children. In T. H. Ollendick & M. Hersen (Eds.), *Handbook of child psychopathology.* New York: Plenum Press.

Petti, T. A., Bornstein, M., Delamater, A., & Conners, C. K. (1980). Evaluation and multimodality treatment of a depressed prepubertal girl. *Journal of the American Academy of Child Psychiatry, 19,* 690–702.

Pinneau, S. R. (1955). The infantile disorders of hospitalism and anaclitic-depression. *Psychological Bulletin, 52,* 429–452.

Poznanski, E. O., Krahenbuhl, V., & Zrull, J. P. (1976). Childhood depression: A longitudinal perspective. *Journal of the American Academy of Child Psychiatry, 15,* 491–501.

Puig-Antich, J., & Chambers, W. (1978). Schedule for affective disorders and schizophrenia for school-age children (6–16 years). Kiddie-SADS (K-SADS). Unpublished manuscript. (Available from J. Puig-Antich, Department of Child and Adolescent Psychiatry, New York State Psychiatric Institute, New York, NY).

Rancurello, M. (1985). Clinical applications of antidepressant drugs in childhood behavioral and emotional disorders. *Psychiatric Annals, 15,* 88–100.

Rie, M. E. (1966). Depression in childhood: A survey of some pertinent contributions. *Journal of the American Academy of Child Psychiatry, 5,* 653–685.

Rosenthal, P. A., & Rosenthal, S. (1984). Suicidal behavior in preschool children. *American Journal of Psychiatry, 141,* 520–525.

Rutter, M. (1986). The developmental psychopathology of depression: Issues and perspectives. In M. Rutter, C. E. Izard, & P. B. Read (Eds.), *Depression in young people: Clinical and developmental perspectives.* New York: Guilford Press.

Rutter, M., Izard, J., & Whitmore, K. (1970/1981). *Education, health and behaviour.* Huntington, NY: Krieger. (Original work published 1970, London: Longmans.)

Schloss, P. J., Schloss, C. N., & Harris, L. (1984). A multiple baseline analysis of an interpersonal skills training program for depressed youth. *Behavioral Disorders, 9,* 182–188.

Seligman, M. E. P., & Maier, S. F. (1967). Failure to escape traumatic shock. *Journal of Experimental Psychology, 74,* 1–9.

Seligman, M. E. P., & Peterson, C. (1986). A learned helplessness perspective on childhood depression: Theory and research. In M. Rutter, C. E. Izard, & P. B. Read (Eds.), *Depression in young people: Developmental and clinical perspectives.* New York: Guilford Press.

Spitz, R. (1946). Anaclitic depression. *The psychoanalytic study of the child.* New York: International Universities Press, 2, 313–342.

Weissman, M. M. (1979). The psychological treatment of depression. *Archives of General Psychiatry, 36,* 1261–1269.

Weissman, M. M., Paykel, E. S., & Klerman, G. L. (1972). The depressed woman as a mother. *Social Psychiatry, 7,* 98–108.

Weller, E. B., & Weller, R. A. (1985). Clinical aspects of childhood depression. *Psychiatric Annals, 15,* 368–374.

Werry, J. S. (1982). Pharmacotherapy. In B. Lahey & A. Kazdin (Eds.), *Advances in clinical child psychology* (Vol. 5). New York: Plenum Press.

Wolfenstein, M. (1966). How is mourning possible? *Psychoanalytic Study of the Child, 21,* 93–126.

Zeitlin, H. (1972). A study of patients who attended the children's department and later the adults' department of the same psychiatric hospital. M. Phil. dissertation, University of London. Cited in Rutter, Izard, & Reed (1986).

Zeitlin, H. (1985). The natural history of psychiatric disorder in children. Institute of Psychiatry Maudsley Monograph. London: Oxford University Press (in press). Cited in Rutter, Izard & Reed (1986).

The 7-year-old boy who drew this picture "of
someone you like" had been diagnosed as having pervasive developmental disorder. He identified his drawing as the teacher's aide in his
classroom who had missed a great deal of school
because of stomach problems.

CHAPTER TEN

Pervasive Developmental Disorders

Charles R. Keith
DUKE UNIVERSITY MEDICAL CENTER

Pervasive developmental disorder is a rare but potentially devastating disturbance that can damage any or all major areas of a child's emotional and cognitive development.

No specific etiological factor has been proven.

Although biological factors probably cause pervasive development disorders, the quality of care the child receives and the point at which intervention begins appear to be important in determining outcome.

A wide array of interventions have been used effectively with pervasive developmental disorders.

Outcome studies are providing evidence that early intervention brings the most favorable results with pervasive developmental disorder.

THE CLASSIFICATION OF pervasive developmental disorder (PDD) includes children with notable developmental distortions, as opposed to delays, in several psychological functions such as attention, perception, reality testing, and motor movement. These children were formerly described as *symbiotic psychotic, atypical,* and *childhood schizophrenics.* The DSM-III dropped the term *psychosis* because it is generally felt that this disorder is unrelated to adult psychoses. Pervasive developmental disorder is an umbrella term that includes two subcategories: *infantile autism* and *childhood onset, pervasive developmental disorder.* Despite its rarity, this disorder has attracted the interest and efforts of numerous investigators, clinicians, and educators, resulting in voluminous scientific literature over the past several decades (Wing, 1985; Goldfarb, 1980; Churchill et al., 1971; Rutter, 1978; Campbell & Green, 1985; Ward, 1970; Achenbach, 1982). Even though much research has been done, however, many questions remain regarding classification, etiology, and treatment.

Pervasive developmental disorder typically becomes detectable in the first few days, weeks, or months of life. By 12 months of age, when a normal infant is rapidly developing communicative and cognitive skills, and social smiling is firmly entrenched, the infant with a pervasive developmental disorder is failing these most crucial avenues of human relatedness. Over these early months, the parents of these infants gradually become aware that their child is not as responsive as other children of similar age. Then they often remember the infant's first days of life and recall that the child was different from the siblings—perhaps did not mold to their bodies when picked up, or light up with ex-

citement when stimulated with social games. The child is often thought to be deaf (Koegel & Schreibman, 1976).

Most children with pervasive developmental disorder have been diagnosed by age three, because the signs and symptoms are so striking and devastating for the child and the parents. Though different investigators emphasize one or another aspect of the syndrome, all generally agree that these are regular features:

• Relative or complete failure to develop interactive human relatedness
• Relative or complete failure to develop normal social language, usually in the context of widespread or variable cognitive deficits
• Stereotyped, repetitive, persistent mannerisms and behaviors, which the child strongly resists changing or stopping, such as twirling objects, hand-flapping, and toe-walking

Laurie, a four-year-old girl, illustrates the typical presenting picture.

The only activities Laurie engaged in spontaneously were destructive. She ripped buttons off her clothes, tore her sheets, ripped wallpaper off the walls. If she got hold of a piece of ribbon, she shredded it to a mass of fine fuzzy matter until it looked like a ball of absorbent cotton. Similarly she tore shag rugs to shreds, or her blankets. . . .

When spoken to, Laurie turned her face away. When annoyed or scolded, she simply stared at her hand or into empty space. As time passed, she withdrew more and more. . . .

Her pediatrician convinced the mother to have her examined by a competent team of psychiatrist and psychologist. On this first examination Laurie was described as a lovely child with long blond hair who sat quietly and made no response to the examiner's questions. When he stretched out his arms to her, she came to him immediately, her own arms outstretched, but with no facial expression of pleasure to go with the gesture. She let him carry her to his office, without any concern about leaving her mother, and during the hour with him showed no signs of anxiety at the separation.

Laurie's contact with the examiner was bland; she treated him as an object. At times she grinned a little, but not in response to any obvious outer stimuli. She proceeded to build with blocks in a perfectionist manner. Any effort on the part of the examiner to alter her arrangements upset her. With crayons she drew mostly squares, with some scribbling or "windows." If handed a half-finished square by the examiner, she finished it hastily, as if she could not tolerate open or incomplete figures. She never talked, never responded to any verbal request of any kind. She laughed in an odd manner at times, and now and then there was evidence of deep-seated agitation. When returning to the mother she seemed completely indifferent. (Bettelheim, 1967, p. 97)

As with most other severe childhood problems, pervasive developmental disorder is more frequent in males (3:1), though when girls develop the syndrome, it may be more severe than in males (Tsai, Stewart, & August, 1981; Lord, Schopler, & Revicki, 1982). The prevalence of autism is two to four per 10,000 (Treffert, 1970; Lotter, 1966; Wing, 1978). All social classes are probably equally affected, and it occurs in all races (Gillberg & Schaumann, 1982; Tsai et al., 1982). Some investigators suggest the possibility that the "pure" form of infantile autism (that is, without accompanying signs of neurological damage or organic brain damage) may occur more frequently in families of high social class (Rimland, 1971; Green et al., 1984; Brown, 1978; Cantwell, Baker, & Rutter, 1978).

When the features of pervasive developmental disorder appear after age three (called *childhood onset* in the DSM-III), the clinical picture may be less severe, as there is usually more evidence of normal development such as some language and social relatedness. Close examination usually reveals, however, that features of the disorder can be traced back to the first and second years of life. According to the DSM-III, this is an extremely rare disorder.

CLASSIFICATION

In the American Psychiatric Association's *Diagnostic and Statistical Manual* (1980), the rubric of pervasive developmental disorder was adopted to emphasize the widespread developmental lags and distortions that are central to understanding the disorder. The terms *psychosis* and *childhood schizophrenia* were dropped because of the uncertainty as to whether this disorder is related to the psychoses and schizophrenic reactions found in later childhood and adolescence. For example, delusions and hallucinations are rare in pervasive developmental disorders, yet central to the diagnosis of later-onset schizophrenia. A family history of schizophrenia is unusual in pervasive developmental disorders and common in schizophrenia (Goldfarb, Spitzer, & Endicott, 1976). Data such as these lead some to believe that schizophrenia is a basically different process or syndrome with a different etiology, family history, and natural disease course (Kolvin, 1971; Kolvin, Garside, & Kidd, 1971; Kolvin, Humphrey, & McNay, 1971; Kolvin, Ounsted, Humphrey, & McNay, 1971; Kolvin, Ounsted, Richardson, & Garside, 1971; Kolvin, Ounsted, & Roth, 1971; Green et al., 1984). Others maintain, however, that the differences between pervasive developmental disorders and schizophrenia are primarily the result of the early onset of pervasive developmental disorder, which causes widespread damage to a child's nascent development. Later-onset schizophrenia may be the same basic process, arising later in life; it may appear different because of the considerable development in language and social areas that has occurred (DeMyer, Churchill, Pontius, & Gilkey, 1971; Anthony, 1962; Fish, 1979; Petty, Ornitz, Michelman, & Zimmerman, 1984).

The DSM-III diagnostic criteria for infantile autism are

- Onset before 30 months of age
- Pervasive lack of responsiveness to other people (autism)
- Gross deficits in language development
- Peculiar speech patterns (if speech is present), such as immediate and delayed echolalia (that is, repeating another person's words over and over), metaphorical language, pronominal reversal (that is, saying "you" hit the dog when the child is describing himself hitting the dog)
- Bizarre responses to the environment, such as resistance to change, peculiar interests, or attachment to animate or inanimate objects (usually the latter)
- Absence of delusions, hallucinations, or loosening of associations and incoherence (as found in schizophrenia)

The DSM-III diagnostic criteria for childhood onset pervasive developmental disorder include at least three of the following:

- Sudden, excessive anxiety, manifested by such symptoms as free-floating anxiety, catastrophic reactions to everyday occurrences, inability to be consoled when upset, unexplained panic attacks
- Constricted or inappropriate affect, including lack of appropriate fear reactions, unexplained rage reactions, and extreme mood lability
- Resistance to change in the environment (for example, becoming upset if dinnertime is changed) or insistence on doing something the same way every time (for example, always putting on clothes in the same order)
- Oddities of motor movement, such as peculiar posturing, peculiar hand or finger movements, or walking on tiptoe

- Abnormalities of speech, such as questionlike melody, monotonous voice
- Hyper- or hyposensitivity to sensory stimuli (for example, *hyperacusis*)
- Self-mutilation (for example, biting or hitting oneself, head banging)

Onset of the full syndrome occurs after 30 months of age and before 12 years of age, and delusions, hallucinations, incoherence, or marked loosening of associations are absent.

If a clinician says a child was diagnosed as having "infantile autism" by DSM-III criteria, for example, she means only that, in her judgment (which may, of course, be biased), the above criteria were met. The criteria represent a consensus of a group of clinicians that these signs and symptoms cluster together and are common in a group of children who are given the diagnostic label "infantile autism." One must keep these conceptual limitations in mind, and not take the criteria as a definition of a disease. (It may be discovered some day that they do define a specific disease with a specific etiology, but there is as yet no evidence for this.) One or more of these criteria is associated with a wide range of human conditions, such as congenital blindness, mental retardation, and toxic, metabolic, and viral diseases involving the central nervous system, and even sometimes in more normal children under severe stress (Markowitz, 1983; Chess, 1971; Gillberg & Forsell, 1984; Stubbs, Ash, & Williams, 1984; Ciaranello, Vandenberg, & Anders, 1982; Coleman, 1978). Another complication arises if a child meets only three or four of the criteria. Does he then not have "infantile autism," implying that infantile autism is a specific unitary disease state that one either has or doesn't have? In the clinical and educational world, young children may show a wide spectrum of autistic signs, from the mildest to the most severe, and only a minority will meet all six DSM-III criteria, and thus receive the diagnosis of infantile autism.

To complicate matters further, some severely disturbed children (a group probably far more numerous than those who meet the six criteria of infantile autism) also do not meet the DSM-III criteria of schizophrenia, which requires children to have hallucinations and delusions, both of which are rather rare before the age of nine. Fish and Ritvo (1979) discuss the limitations of these DSM-III diagnostic categories and the need for future revisions.

Why, then, have researchers recently tried to more clearly define the psychopathological syndromes of infantile autism and childhood onset pervasive developmental disorder, using ever more rigorous criteria, even if it means omitting groups of affected children, as Fish and Ritvo (1979) note? The answer is that it is an attempt to clear up some of the confusion in the field. One clinical investigator's autistic or schizophrenic child patients may be quite different from another's, so that group comparisons of etiology, treatment, and outcomes become confusing and often meaningless. Rigorously defining subject populations is thus essential for research.

Diagnostic groupings can, however, serve different purposes in different settings (Schopler, 1983). In the public educational setting, the educator knows that a diagnostic label is necessary for administrative funding and programming. An autistic child in the school setting might fall under the label of "mental retardation," "learning disability," or "communication disorder" to receive special services. In service settings such as schools, diagnostic classifications tend to be broad to implement services for a heterogeneous population. In research settings, diagnostic classifications tend to be rigorous, narrower, and more focused so as to separate homogeneous subsets from a heterogeneous population and thus facilitate investigations and group comparisons. In the political arena, diagnostic classifications can be used to mobilize special interest groups and to influence the legislative process. A recent example is the change in Public Law 94–142,

which now subsumes infantile autism under "other health impaired" instead of "emotional disorders." The parents and professionals who advocated this change felt it would remove some of the pejorative connotations of "emotional disorder," thus facilitating the mobilization of political support and further funding of special programs for autistic children. Thus, diagnostic terminology and classification schemes change depending upon their context. Understanding and accepting these contextual shifts enable the clinician, researcher, and educator to maintain a broad perspective and to understand one another's position. As we will see, planning treatment for the individual child requires still another diagnostic shift in thinking, as the diagnosis of infantile autism must be transformed into a detailed developmental assessment of the child's progress or lack of progress along multiple lines of development.

The classification *childhood onset pervasive developmental disorder* is a controversial diagnosis arising from case descriptions of children who became seriously disturbed after age three. There have been no recent studies. This category may be a milder form of infantile autism. There is doubt as to whether an autistic process can truly arise after age three. If it should, one would strongly suspect the onset of a toxic, metabolic, or degenerative central nervous system disease process. We will use both terms in this chapter. When studies specify autistic children, we use the term *autism;* otherwise, we use the phrase *pervasive developmental disorder,* as it is more inclusive.

ETIOLOGICAL HYPOTHESES

Historical View

The medical literature of the 1800s contains anecdotes concerning psychotic children, but no systematic studies (Kanner, 1971). Around 1900, when the great systematizers in psychiatry (like Kraeplin) were conceptualizing the modern clinical syndromes, childhood schizophrenia (then called *dementia praecoccissima* or *dementia infantilis*) was regularly included as a category. The causes of these dementias were thought to be incurable toxic and degenerative processes in the brain (Gianascol, 1963). One of the first accounts of treatment of an autistic child was published in the *Ladies' Home Journal* in 1919, and is still worthwhile reading today (Witmer, 1973).

The more systematic, detailed descriptions of schizophrenic children in the early 1930s heralded the modern era. Potter (1933) emphasized the child's developmental immaturity, and how it affects symptomatology and makes the syndrome appear different from adult schizophrenia.

Lauretta Bender, in the late 1930s, began reporting on an extensive series of schizophrenic children whom she treated in an inpatient unit at Bellevue Hospital (Bender, 1964, 1970). Her conceptualizations of the disorder bridged the biological and the psychodynamic perspectives in a manner still quite germane today. She emphasized a biologically determined *maturational lag*, which in turn damaged ego functioning and defense formation. The vulnerable individual then experienced overwhelming anxiety when faced with life stresses, resulting in the breakdown of defenses and emergence of schizophrenic symptoms.

Bender believed that *early childhood schizophrenia*, later to be called *infantile autism*, was on a spectrum with adolescent and adult schizophrenia and different in symptomatology primarily because the breakdown occurred early in life. As we have noted, most now concur with the position that autism and schizophrenia are two separate entities; however, cases continue to be reported showing that some children with clear-cut infantile autism later develop the classical signs and symptoms of schizophrenia (Petty et al., 1984).

In 1943, Leo Kanner at Johns Hopkins

published case vignettes of 11 children in an article entitled "Autistic Disturbances of Affective Contact." These case vignettes became the foundation for the eventual syndrome of infantile autism. He felt this new syndrome was distinct from the schizophrenias of childhood and was characterized by onset in the early months of life and by a striking paucity of human interaction. Kanner felt that many of the parents in his series were obsessive and aloof, which may have played some part in the onset of the disorder, but he later retracted this statement. These case vignettes are still considered classic descriptions of the infantile autism syndrome.

Also during the 1940s, several psychoanalysts who had left Europe at the outbreak of World War II began to report on their work with psychotic and "atypical" young children. This work is best epitomized by Rank (1949), Putnam (1948), and Mahler and Furer (1968). They reported that their child patients had many of the features of Kanner's patients (as did Bender's young schizophrenics). These psychoanalytic investigators emphasized the inborn vulnerabilities and unusual sensitivities of these children and how these constitutional proclivities interacted with the personalities of the caretakers, particularly the mother, to produce a cycle of frustration, despair, mutual withdrawal, and early severe developmental handicaps in the child (Coleman, Frankel, Ritvo, & Freeman, 1976; Bergman & Escalona, 1949). That these mother-child interactions are crucial for the formation of early defensive and adaptive patterns in the first days of life is exemplified by Massie's (1978a, 1978b) studies of home movies of infants who were later diagnosed as autistic. Another example is a study by Tronick and his co-workers (1978) that illustrated how even two-week-old normal infants become withdrawn when the mother holds her face motionless for three minutes. As a result of these constitutional and interactional difficulties, the young child does not actually separate from the mother and become an autonomous person with a clear sense of self.

As one reads the case studies of Kanner, Mahler, and Rank from the '40s and '50s, it becomes clear that two perspectives, the neuropsychiatric and the psychodynamic, were emerging. In those early days, the neuropsychiatrist Kanner referred congenially to the analytic literature, and Lauretta Bender could move back and forth between neuropsychiatric and psychoanalytic perspectives. Sadly for the field, this early respect for different perspectives gave way over the ensuing years. Psychodynamic authors often ignored the neuropsychiatric and organic viewpoints, whereas neuropsychiatrists and neuropsychologists often labeled the psychoanalytic or psychodynamic viewpoint as "parent blaming," a "myth," "harmful," or simply ignored it (Wing & Wing, 1971; Schopler et al., 1971; Schopler & Reichler, 1972).

This chapter demonstrates that both points of view have merit for understanding pervasive developmental disorders (and for that matter, the other psychological problems of childhood as well). Table 10–1 highlights the differences of the two viewpoints to emphasize the tenets of each and how they complement each other.

Current Hypotheses

Recent work has focused on the importance of language and cognitive deficits in understanding children with pervasive developmental disorders. In England, Rutter, Wing, and others expanded the neuropsychiatric perspective concerning infantile autism. Wing conducted epidemiological studies to ascertain the frequency and types of autistic symptomatology in all severely handicapped children in an entire district, whereas most group studies had depended on selective populations from clinical settings. Wing found a triad of symptomatology in the language, social, and cognitive spheres, in

varying proportions, in a wide variety of handicapped children such as the mentally retarded and organically brain damaged (Wing, 1981).

Rutter (1972, 1978) summarized his and others' studies showing that the onset of language by age five is the most crucial prognosticator for improvement, either spontaneously or by way of treatment (Brown, 1963). The children who do not develop spoken language tend to show more evidence of organic brain damage and severely delayed cognitive function, as indicated, for instance, by low IQ scores. The majority of autistic children have IQs below 70. Kanner's original observations had led to the belief that most autistic children were intelligent, as evidenced by islands of splinter skills such as rote mathematical ability or excessive interest in certain types of music (Rimland, 1978). The remainder of their intelligence was thought to be "hidden" behind their remoteness and avoidance of human interaction. Many now believe, however, that most autistic children are truly retarded as a result of some type of inborn central nervous system disorder and the cumulative effects of their isolation on the development of cognitive skills. One-third of autistic children, particularly those with lower IQs and definite evidence of organic brain damage, develop epileptic seizures, usually of the grand mal type, during adolescence (Bartak & Rutter, 1976). The greater incidence of pregnancy and birth complications with autistic children may explain some of the organic findings (Funderburk et al., 1983; Gillberg & Gillberg, 1983; Tsai & Stewart, 1983). Rutter and other neuropsychiatrists describe widespread perceptual and cognitive processing disorders in many autistic children (Masterton & Biederman, 1983; Kootz, Marinelli, & Cohen, 1982), including vestibular processing abnormalities (Ornitz & Ritvo, 1968; Ornitz, 1970; Ornitz, Guthrie, & Farley, 1978), a heightened sensory rejection (Kootz & Cohen, 1981; Kootz, Marinelli, & Cohen, 1981; Kootz et al., 1982) and delayed galvanic skin response (Palkovitz & Wiesenfeld, 1980) and cortical-evoked responsiveness (James & Barry, 1983). All major areas of the brain have been implicated as underlying these perceptual anomalies, including the left hemisphere, right parietal lobe, frontal lobe, and the reticular-activating system of the brain stem (Hutt, Hutt, Lee, & Ounsted, 1964; Rimland, 1964; Arnold & Schwartz, 1983; Dawson, 1983; Hetcler & Griffin, 1981; McCann, 1981; Tanguay & Edwards, 1982; Blackstock, 1978).

Rutter is the leading proponent of considering autism a symptom in a wide-ranging variety of childhood disorders, including the organic syndromes, moving the focus away from the "pure," more nonorganic autistic child Kanner originally described. Fish and Ritvo (1979) point out that "pure" autistic children may have more features of the schizophrenic and may thus be a somewhat distinct subgroup that can be lost when lumped with children with multiple organic brain etiologies (also see Prior & Chen, 1976).

TABLE 10–1
Neuropsychiatric and Psychodynamic Views of Infantile Autism

Neuropsychiatric Viewpoint	Psychodynamic (Psychoanalytic) Viewpoint
Methods of Study	
Rigorously defined groups, often including controls	Individual case study
Standardized measurements of cognitive, language, physical, and metabolic parameters	Detailed descriptions of lines of development of individual child
Concern with diagnostic clarity and precision, such as development of diagnostic checklists (for compilation of checklists, see DeMyer et al., 1971; Krug, Arick, & Almond, 1980)	Loosely defined categories covering broad range of children
Etiology	
Central nervous system damage or dysfunction	Constitutional vulnerability interacting with primary caretakers
Data of Interest	
Objective and descriptive data: test scores serum levels of metabolites results of neurological examinations electroencephalograms parent checklists, etc.	Descriptive and inferred data involving individual child's activity, thoughts, and affects, and meaning of the event to the child (how child perceives the world)
Role of Parent	
Secondary frustration at child's unresponsiveness (frustration may interfere with parenting)	Usual range of caretaking (play vital role, as any other parent, in whatever personality emerges)
Treatment	
Educational, behavioral methodologies Parent training and management Continuing search for specific pharmacologic and other biological treatment approaches Specific treatment strategy usually involves highly structured tasks presented to child by adults	Psychotherapeutic interaction with child and parent Concomitant emphasis on therapeutic milieu, including education Use of child's spontaneous activity (verbal or motoric) as guide to adult's therapeutic interventions
Treatment Goals	
Increased social adaptation and advances in cognitive language and independent living skills	To relate more meaningfully with others which in turn leads to greater social skills and language use

You are probably aware by now that after decades of classification studies, much uncertainty remains. Rutter reminds us that this is to be expected and accepted in an area of study in which no definitive etiologies of the autistic state have been discovered. (That rubella and other known causes of organic brain damage are often associated with autism does not yet prove causality; the majority of children with organic brain damage do not develop autism.) Tanguay (1984) suggests that attempts to further define and classify the autistic syndrome based on symptom complexes (as in DSM-III) may no longer be fruitful, and that we should instead focus on clarifying the disturbances in the autistic child's developmental lines, such as cognition (Schopler, Rutter, & Chess, 1979). This might make possible diagnostic schemes based on patterns of developmental lines, such as how far the child has advanced on each line and how integrated the lines are with one another. (Anna Freud [1965] in the early 1960s also recommended basing diagnoses on a developmental line approach.)

Others besides neuropsychiatrists and psychoanalysts have been active in the field as well. Behaviorists report that the autistic child's repertoire of behavior is responsive to conditioning (Murphy, 1982; Lovaas, 1971). Lovaas set up extensive training programs to modify autistic children's behavior, such as aggressive, destructive outbursts, mutism, and difficulties relating to others, which we will discuss with treatment.

Applying their observational skills to autistic children, ethologists and ecologists found them to be quite interactive with the environment, challenging some of the stereotypes, such as "they are unresponsive to the environment" (Schroeder, Mulick, & Rojahn, 1980; Donnellan, Anderson, & Mesaros, 1984). Provocative reports by the Tinbergens, well-known animal ethologists (1972, 1983), challenge therapeutic nihilism and provide a dynamic perspective.

The neurobiological sciences mushroomed in the 1970s and '80s, bringing to the investigative scene a wide array of neurochemical assays, CAT scans, chromosomal mapping techniques, and other increasingly sensitive measures of genetic, neuroendocrine, neurotransmitter, and neuronal functioning (Brown et al., 1982; Goldfine et al., 1985). Autisticlike symptoms were described in mother-separated infant monkeys (Harlow & McKinney, 1971). Hopes have been raised that the biological side of the developmental equation concerning autism will be illuminated (Hanson & Gottesman, 1976). In terms of genetic studies, early observers noted a concordance rate for monozygotic autistic twins of 40 to 50 percent (Folstein & Rutter, 1977), but a recent study shows a surprisingly high concordance rate of 90 percent (Ritvo, Freeman, Mason-Brothers, Mo, & Ritvo, 1985). The authors made the diagnoses of the twins, raising the spectre of possible bias. Concordance rates of monozygotic twins in the field of adult schizophrenia were once reported to be in the 70 to 90 percent range, but more recent studies place the rate at around 40 to 50 percent. It was also thought that autism did not "run" in families, but recent genealogical studies indicate that certain families do have higher than expected rates of autism (Ritvo, Ritvo, & Mason-Brothers, 1982; Ritvo et al., 1985). Siblings of an autistic child have a ten times greater chance of developing the syndrome than do members of the general population (Verhees, 1976). Whatever genetic diathesis there is for autism, it tends to be self-limiting, as few autistic adults sire children. Only one child has been reported definitely to have been born of an autistic parent (Kanner & Eisenberg, 1955).

Although earlier biochemical studies of autistic children presented conflicting findings, groups of autistic children have been studied in the past five to ten years with the newer assay techniques (Young, Kavanaugh, Anderson, Shaywitz, & Cohen, 1982; Young, Kyprie, Ross, & Cohen, 1980; Gillberg, Trygstad, & Foss, 1982; Goldberg, Hattab, Meir, Ebstein, & Belmaker, 1984; Cohen, Caparulo, & Shaywitz, 1978). A subgroup of autistic children showed abnormalities in the CAT scan, such as enlarged ventricles (Gillberg & Svendsen, 1983; Caparulo et al., 1981; Campbell et al., 1982). Another subgroup had abnormalities in the spinal fluid levels of the neurotransmitter *serotonin*, and others showed immature, poorly organized EEGs (Tanguay, Ornitz, Forsythe, & Ritvo, 1976). Even hemodialysis was attempted without success (Varley, Kolff, Trupin, & Reichler, 1981). So far, no clear-cut abnormality in central nervous system architecture or functioning has been found to occur in a majority of autistic subjects, illustrating again that autistic children are heterogeneous and bring a wide array of neurodevelopmental disorders into their developmental process (Coleman & Gillberg, 1985).

INTERVENTIONS

Educational Intervention

Defining education broadly as the systematic teaching of adaptive skills appropriate to a child's developmental level, education becomes a vital component of all treatment modalities for children with pervasive developmental disorders. It takes place in public schools (Stiver & Dobbins, 1980), hospitals, milieu treatment settings, day facilities, and home-based programs using parents as teachers, and combines with all psychotherapeutic approaches. Three issues underlie educational efforts with these children.

Educational diagnosis. Precise educational diagnosis involves detailed descriptions of how far the child has developed in the social, adaptive, cognitive, motoric, language, and other lines of development. All educators agree that the teacher's efforts must begin where the child is, no matter how delayed

the development or how elementary and simple the educational tasks (Rutter, 1970; Tiegerman & Primavera, 1981). Presenting tasks that are too complicated may quickly overwhelm the child, leading to frustration and stimulus overload, which in turn may result in withdrawal and resumption of stereotypic behaviors whose purpose is to control excessive stimulation and environmental uncertainty. Sometimes even the simplest task, such as buttoning a coat, must be broken down into substeps; the child must master each step before moving to the next, and master all of them before attempting the entire sequence of buttoning. These techniques are similar to those for teaching the mentally retarded and are not unique for children with pervasive developmental disorders.

The teacher-pupil relationship. Children with a pervasive developmental disorder often appear not to need or wish to please the teacher. They often given an impression of self-sufficient aloneness and avoid the teacher's efforts to engage in mutual tasks. But without a working relationship, it is often difficult to obtain an accurate educational diagnosis. To develop this working relationship, the teacher must usually work alone with a child over an extended period. This one-to-one encounter, whether in the context of a classroom or an individual tutorial, allows teacher and child to maintain absolute focus on each other and makes it possible for the teacher to gain the child's attention and respond immediately when the child withdraws. The one-to-one relationship also allows the teacher to carefully follow and tune in with the child's spontaneous behaviors, for example, gaze aversion (Tiegerman & Primavera, 1984) and use them as bridges to engage in mutual activity that gradually evolves into the more usual teacher-pupil relationship (Hurtig, Ensrud, & Tomblin, 1982; Clark & Rutter, 1977). Group instruction, with its greater stimulation and reduced teacher attention, can usually only be instituted if the child makes gains in the one-to-one relationship. Creative intuition, boundless patience, gentle firmness, and empathic observation are among the necessary educational tools for the teacher. The educator must be able to verbalize the inevitable frustrations and talk about the evolving process with a colleague or supervisor. Otherwise, teachers become discouraged by the children's slow and often erratic progress. Some educational programs for severely handicapped, communicationally disordered, and children with pervasive developmental disorders emphasize full-day intensive didactic instruction upon the child's entry into the program. These programs emphasize the child's cognitive disorders rather than the interpersonal and emotional disturbances. These programs must also individualize each child's curriculum, however, and teach to each child's level.

The educational setting. Familiar, structured, simple settings, free of clutter, distractions, and interruptions, are usually the most comfortable and productive for both teacher and child (Clark & Rutter, 1981; Ferrara & Hill, 1980; Bartak, 1978). This kind of setting can be arranged in the home, outpatient clinic, hospital, or even in the public school. Educational equipment should be simple, with only a few items available to the child at any one time. The duration of task work depends on the child's level of development, age, ability to sustain interest, and the teacher's stamina. Education in a formal sense begins as soon as the diagnosis is made, which is usually in the second or third year of life. The educational milieu centers around the concept of providing assistance and buffering for the child's uncertain abilities to manage stimuli, frustration, and the relationship with the teacher. As the child gains perceptual and performance stability, reduces avoidance patterns, and can tolerate lengthier interactions with the teacher, then the milieu itself

can take on more complexity; for example, the child can have different teachers for different tasks, move toward a longer school day, become involved in small group activities, and begin to try more complex educational tasks. For most children with pervasive developmental disorders, especially those with low IQs and concomitant organic brain disorders, the educational pace is quite slow. Adolescents with this disorder are often still struggling with basic social and language skills, and sometimes show an increase in destructive behavior with the onset of puberty that presents a therapeutic challenge (Favell, 1983). Hence, the educational process usually extends over an indefinite period. Most programs for children with pervasive developmental disorder are now entering their second and third decades, so the issues of treating and educating the adolescent and adult clients are beginning to appear in the literature (Schopler & Mesibov, 1983).

Professionals such as speech, occupational, and physical therapists have become integrated components of the educational team for children with pervasive developmental disorder. Occupational and physical therapists concentrate in the perceptual-motor and physical activity areas. Some studies show that vigorous exercise while holding a teacher's hand reduces subsequent self-stimulation and improves academic performance (Kern, Koegel, & Dunlap, 1984). The roles of the speech therapist and special educator in the area of language development are a major focus of most educational programming for autistic children (Rutter, 1980). The autistic child's language deficits appear central to the child's continuing social withdrawal and emerging cognitive deficits (Howlin, 1980; Curtis, 1981; Menyuk & Wilbur, 1981). The language deficits and oddities are numerous. A persistent absence of spoken language, particularly past age five, is most ominous; when spoken language does appear, it often lacks the normal affective intonation and has a mechanical or singsong rhythm (Needleman, Ritvo, & Freeman, 1980). Words may remain sparse, sentence structure incomplete, and pronouns reversed; word content may appear loose and have private idiosyncratic meanings (Park [1983] describes a classic example). Though the DSM-III says the thoughts of autistic children should not be "loose and disorganized" (otherwise one would have to consider a diagnosis of schizophrenia), in actuality much autistic language is loose, fragmented, and guided by private autistic fantasies and thinking processes. Some say a more normal, affectively appropriate language can develop only in the context of a meaningful, interpersonal relationship. Just teaching or training the child to parrot words such as "I am hungry" gives the child a repertoire of mechanical phrases that often falls far short of a viable social language. Some clinical investigators (Lancioni, 1983; Bonvillian, Nelson, & Rhyne, 1981; Konstantareas, 1984) have been training autistic children to use sign or pictorial language to bypass a verbal, expressive handicap. Another method involves giving the autistic child control over auditory feedback, enabling him to control and screen out unwanted sounds, leading to improved verbalization (Smith, Olson, Barger, & McConnell, 1981). (For recent reviews of educational issues and programs, see Fredericks, Buckley, Baldwin, Moore, and Stremel-Campbell [1983]; Rutter [1970]; Olley [1983]; and Gallagher and Wiegerink [1976].)

A program well-known for its educational emphasis is Treatment and Education of Autistic and Related Communication Handicapped Children (TEACCH), based at the University of North Carolina. This is a statewide program for working with infantile autism and other types of severe disturbances in special classrooms, often in public school settings, under the supervision of TEACCH staff. Children undergo thorough psychological and educational evaluation before placement. When possible, parents attend weekly parent training conferences at the TEACCH centers where they observe TEACCH staff working with their children. The parents then carry out the educational tasks in the home setting (Mesibov, Schopler, & Sloan, 1983; Lansing & Schopler, 1978; Callias, 1983; Schopler et al., 1971).

Knoblock (1982, 1983) has been a leader in developing programs for autistic children in normal peer and public school settings. Using the developmental curriculum created by Wood (1975) at the Rutland Center, Knoblock placed five autistic children, each with his or her own curriculum, with a normal peer group of 15 children, under the aegis of four teachers. The encouraging results led to establishment of several similar groups in the Syracuse, New York, public schools.

Behavioral Therapy

Basic behavioral conditioning processes underlie all educational and treatment modalities. Rewarding and fostering or discouraging and punishing the behaviors of others with whom we relate educationally and therapeutically occurs continuously via myriad conscious and designed responses and unconscious, spontaneous responses. Behavior therapy gathers up and makes explicit these environmental interactive responses so they can be used in a controlled, measurable, organized way to facilitate agreed-upon positive, adaptive behaviors and extinguish the undesirable and maladaptive. *Behavior* in this broad sense includes such areas as speech and language, social responsiveness, and attentional focusing, as well as motoric behavior such as hand-flapping.

Formal behavioral therapy has been useful in modifying many autistic behaviors, including socially unacceptable motor behaviors, repeated destructive behavior toward self and others, and avoidant defenses, and in fostering language acquisition and its use in speech (Lovaas, 1977). In this particular area, most studies report gains in language skills, with the gains usually proportional to the initial level of language development.

Many autistic children reach ceilings of language development and valiant efforts to proceed further can be of no avail (Lord & O'Neill, 1983; Howlin, 1980). It is possible that they reach some central nervous system limitation that behavior therapy cannot transcend, so that the autistic child or adolescent learns a repertoire of phrases and responses but not a truly functional social, conversational language. Problems of generalization also occur.

Some provocative and controversial behavioral techniques have been used for persistent self-destructive behavior and marked withdrawal and mutism. These include electric shocks, food deprivation, and social isolation to force the child to relate to the therapist, who is the only source of food (Lichstein & Schreibman, 1976; Parents Speak Section, 1976; Schechter, Shurley, Toussieng, & Maier, 1969). Behavioral therapists defend these techniques by saying that they are usually applied only when all other treatment modalities have failed and when the child's life may be endangered by the symptom.

Lovaas (1978) maintains that the often poor results of treatment reflect its insufficiency and faulty delivery, such as using parents who cannot be expected to maintain exhausting behavioral treatment programs in the home. He describes a team of behavioral therapists who enter the child's home to conduct a 30- to 40-hour per week behavioral program for lengthy periods (Lovaas, 1980, 1981).

Milieu Therapy

Milieu therapy is the planned therapeutic use of all aspects of the child's living environment (Bettelheim & Sanders, 1979; Redl & Wineman, 1957). The concept was first systematically developed for adult psychiatric patients at the psychoanalytically-oriented Menninger Hospital in the 1930s, where all members of the staff took on a therapeutic role with the patient. Also, use of the inanimate environment was carefully spelled out

as to how it could be used for therapeutic gain, including use of the daily activity schedule, making objects, bedtime routines, cleaning and toileting activities, and so on. These activities have always been considered important, but in milieu therapy, the staff and patient thought and talked about the meaning of the activities for a particular person at a particular time. Clinical and programming decisions were then based on these meanings. Considerable staff effort is expended in meeting and talking about impressions and feelings concerning the patient (Stanton & Schwartz, 1954). Bettelheim describes in detail the meaning of the most minute, seemingly insignificant daily activities to a psychotic child in the classic *Love is Not Enough* (1950).

Milieu therapy can to some extent be applied to treatment settings other than long-term inpatient units, but its most intensive impact occurs in 24-hour, around-the-clock settings. Removing the child from the home often brings criticism, since another current philosophy is *normalization*—trying to keep the child in the home and the public school. Unfortunately, principles such as normalization can become dicta; one reads statements such as "the best treatment occurs in the home using parents as teachers," which can mislead one into thinking this is the best treatment for all children (Bristol & Schopler, 1983). This is not so. Children with pervasive developmental disorders have a wide range of social and cognitive skills and levels of psychopathology, including a variety of parental and family strengths and weaknesses, and some are not adequately treated in the community or in the home (Lettick, 1983). Well-staffed, inpatient milieu therapy programs are still needed for some children, and their demise has left a gap in the treatment modality spectrum (Wenar & Ruttenberg, 1976).

Psychotherapy

Over the past two decades, the neuropsychiatric literature has severely criticized psychotherapy for children with pervasive developmental disorders. Statements about the purported harmful effects of psychotherapy could lead to the conclusion that its effects have been proven and that psychotherapy is a dead issue, but that is not the case (Ney, Palvesky, & Markely, 1971; Bartak & Rutter, 1973). Some studies purport to show the ineffectiveness of psychotherapy for children with pervasive developmental disorders, but many clinicians contend that this intervention is helpful in understanding the child's inner life, his feelings and emotions. Therapy with these children almost always takes place within the context of a general treatment program involving parent support, parent therapy, education, and so forth (Weil, 1973).

Dynamic psychotherapy is a structured, slowly evolving interaction between child and therapist (Tustin, 1972; Resch, Grand, & Meyerson, 1981; Call, 1963; Lowry, 1985). The therapist attaches meaning to the child's activities by means of the therapist's intuitive responses to the child's material; an example is holding the child to prevent running away, then inferring that the child wants to be held but is running away because of fear of being held (Schopler, 1962). Another example is soothing the distressed child and responding systematically to whatever spontaneous verbalizations there might be so that the child connects specific words with human affective responses. Thus, therapy usually involves years of patient, steady work. Signs of progress are the child's missing the therapist during inevitable absences, the therapist's increasing involvement in symbolic play with the child, and eventual use of words to express affect (such as anger toward the therapist). Dynamic psychotherapy works best with children who have less organic brain damage, higher IQs, and some use of language—as is the case with all the other modalities.

Parent therapy is a crucial component of the child's therapy. Regular supportive and expressive sessions with the parents help them verbalize and master their discouragement and sense of failure in parenting, and address whatever personal problems they may bring to the parenting role that interferes with their relationship with their child. When the parent (usually the mother) has sufficient personal strength, she can become engaged in the therapy with the child's therapist. Mahler and Furer (1968) call this the *triadic model*. The triadic work weaves between educational and psychotherapeutic issues and extends over a lengthy period (Bergman, 1971).

DesLauriers (1978) has developed a treatment model called *theraplay*, based on a supposed neurophysiological disorder of the central nervous system involving conflict between two arousal systems, which he believes is fundamental to the etiology of pervasive developmental disorder. Though it is unclear how the hypothesized central nervous system arousal disorder has any connection with the theraplay treatment, it is clear that the treatment bears considerable similarity to psychoanalytic psychotherapy. In theraplay, the therapist empathically participates in the child's spontaneous activity no matter how meager and stereotypic. Through the bodily and emotional stimulation provided by the therapist, the child with a pervasive developmental disorder gradually learns to relate more appropriately and to relinquish stereotypes for the pleasure of the therapeutic relationship.

Medication

Over the decades, stimulants, sedatives, tranquilizers, antianxiety drugs, and megavitamins have been given to children with pervasive developmental disorders in attempts to find pharmacological means to ameliorate the severe, sometimes deteriorating psychopathology (Campbell et al., 1972). Since little is known about the neurochemical factors in autism, most medication trials have been empirical. No medication has been consistently helpful, which is not surprising when one considers the heterogeneity of the population.

The most widely used class of drugs are the phenothiazines (major tranquilizers) such as Thorazine, Mellaril, Stelazine, and a butyrophenone compound, Haldol (Campbell et al., 1982). Most clinicians use the phenothiazines when a child with a pervasive developmental disorder is going through an agitated and/or destructive period which does not respond sufficiently to psychological and environmental modalities. When the child is more tranquil, the drugs are usually withdrawn gradually to smaller doses or ended. Since a pervasive developmental disorder runs over a lengthy course of years or a lifetime, drugs with potentially damaging side effects, such as the phenothiazines, are usually given only intermittently as needed for acute episodes. Some children respond positively to phenothiazines even if they are not in acute episodes, and thus may be left indefinitely on the lowest possible dosage to obtain the maximum clinical effects and minimize the potential for side effects. This class of drugs has many distressing side effects. One of the most fearful is *tardive dyskinesia*, which usually appears as twisting, writhing movements of the tongue, face, and upper torso. The possibility of adding this difficulty to an already socially handicapped child militates against the extensive use of phenothiazines. In addition, tranquilizers can improve one set of symptoms but leave the child less responsive to the environment, an often unfavorable tradeoff. Extensive use of tranquilizers for controlling the behavior of retarded and psychotic children in large, understaffed state institutions has long been of concern (Zimmerman & Heistad, 1982).

An appetite suppressant, *fenfluramine*, is currently under investigation at several research centers for its possible efficacy with children with a pervasive developmental dis-

order (Ritvo, Freeman, Geller, & Yuwiler, 1983; Ritvo et al., 1984; August, Raz, & Baird, 1985). Some studies (Campbell & Green, 1985) show that a subgroup of children with a pervasive developmental disorder have elevated serotonin blood levels, which fenfluramine tends to reduce. Preliminary results indicate that some children are helped, but many are not (Leventhal, 1984). Investigators are trying to learn how to identify which children will be helped, as the positive drug effects do not seem to correlate with the hypothesis regarding blood serotonin levels. Like the phenothiazines, fenfluramine has many worrisome side effects. These findings reinforce the decades-old discoveries that some treatments help some children but not others, often unpredictably.

The use of "megadoses" of vitamins for various conditions has become popular in recent years, though the scientific community usually greets these claims with skepticism. Large doses of *pyridoxine* (vitamin B_6) have been used with suggestively positive results (Rimland, Calloway, & Dreyfus, 1978; Lelord, Muh, Barthelemy, Martineau, & Garreau, 1981). The rationale for megavitamin therapy is that children with pervasive developmental disorder may have a genetically-linked metabolic disturbance that alters central nervous system physiology. Large doses of vitamins may override or swamp the deficiency or metabolic error and thereby normalize cellular metabolism. This theory remains speculative, and there is presently little interest in pursuing further megavitamin clinical trials.

The range of treatment methodologies we have described is essentially the same as for other severe psychopathologies of childhood, though each must adapt to the unique needs of the child with a pervasive developmental disorder. All have their place, none are mutually exclusive, and none should be dismissed as inappropriate or ineffective in light of current clinical experience. In recent years, the field of adult schizophrenia has become more integrated in its thinking about multiple treatment perspectives than has the field of childhood autism. As research in the field of infantile autism continues to mature, there should be renewed interest in integrating perspectives and treatment methodologies (Helm, 1976).

OUTCOME

Follow-up studies of children with pervasive developmental disorders into adolescence and adulthood indicate that only 5 to 17 percent have a good outcome—that is, satisfactory adjustment in school and work. Over 50 percent are eventually institutionalized, with 51 to 74 percent of those having a poor outcome—defined as persisting severe handicaps with little or no independent social life (DeMyer et al., 1973). Though the various treatments bring about improvement, it is not clear yet whether it is possible to significantly increase the number of children who gain eventual normalcy in social relationships and in their ability to work. Clinicians feel that any gains are important to the individual child and the parents, however, even if the overall results continue to appear poor. Most outcome studies involve groups of children, which may obscure some individual patterns of change. There are individual children who do surprisingly well in overcoming the symptomatology of pervasive developmental disorders (Bemporad, 1979). Adolescence appears to be a crucial period when some of the children lose symptoms, develop other syndromes (Komoto, Usui, & Hirata, 1984), or become more verbal and socially adept (Campbell, Hardesty, Breuer, & Polevy, 1978). There have been reports of children who have been mute until age nine or later who begin to talk, but, unfortunately, these spontaneous forward moves in development (Hobson, 1984) are offset by other children who suddenly deteriorate in latency or adolescence. Deterioration sometimes correlates with external events and stresses, but at other times there seems no obvious explana-

tion, and one is left to wonder if some central nervous system degenerative process is at work (Gillberg & Schaumann, 1981).

Bettelheim (1967) reports one of the better outcomes in a follow-up of 40 autistic and psychotic children treated at the Orthogenic School. He reports that almost 80 percent had good to fair results in late adolescence and young adulthood, with only 20 percent showing poor results. Bettelheim's positive outcomes, compared to the bleak figures for the remainder of the field, have prompted critics to dismiss his findings. Bettelheim did not provide sufficient details of all 40 cases to enable comparisons to other studies (although he provides the most intensive case studies in the field); hence, skeptics wonder if many of his cases were less-impaired children with a better prognosis, which inflated his good-to-fair outcome totals. Schopler (1976) says that even if Bettelheim's results were valid, his treatment methodology is unreproducible, since there will never be another Bettelheim with his unique charisma. Bettelheim and Sanders (1979), on the other hand, describe their model as reproducible and, in fact, less expensive than some other models in the field. Whatever the merits of the criticisms, they should not lead us to overlook Bettelheim's central message, namely, that the best treatment results may well come from the most intensive treatment, and that continued poor treatment results should make the field question its treatment efforts and methodologies. Szurek and Berlin (1973) report favorable treatment results, though not as favorable as Bettelheim's. Using a psychodynamic milieu model somewhat similar to Bettelheim's, they treated psychotic and autistic children for one to three years in an inpatient setting with follow-up psychotherapy and parent work. All concede that the more organic brain dysfunction and the lower the IQ, the poorer the outcome.

Three recent outcome studies emphasize the issue of intensive early intervention (Simeonsson, Olley, & Rosenthal, in press). Lovaas (1982) reports that instituting intensive 40-hour-per-week behavioral therapy with children with a pervasive developmental disorder before the age of three brought about normalization after two years of therapy for 50 percent. A control group of same-age children with pervasive developmental disorders received only 10 hours per week of intensive therapy, and none achieved normalization. Some of the normalized children with pervasive developmental disorders have now been followed up for 10 years, and many have held their gains.

Even more startling is a recent report by Strain, Jamieson, & Hoyson (1985) that describes six children with pervasive developmental disorders, ages three to four, all with IQs in the retarded range, who were treated with intensive, individualized behavioral programs within a normal peer group. The treatment was conducted three hours per day, five days per week, for 12 months of the year, and lasted over two years. Using several social and learning scales, all six children became indistinguishable from the normal children. Further emphasizing the beneficial impact of early intervention, Fenske, Zalenski, Krantz, and McClannahan (in press) found that an intensive treatment program instituted with children under five brought about substantial gains in two-thirds, whereas if the same program were not started until after the child's fifth birthday, only one in nine showed

substantial improvement.

These recent findings may usher in a phase of renewed optimism in the field of pervasive developmental disorder. We can hope that the quality and intensity of the treatment relationship in the context of the autistic child's development may again become paramount, and issues of immutability as a result of organic deficiencies will be reexamined.

CONCLUSION

This chapter has presented a multifaceted perspective of the child with pervasive developmental disorder. Though much remains to be learned about this disorder, it is now abundantly clear that many, if not most, of these children can be helped by early, intensive treatment. Treatment must always begin with a thorough understanding of the child's developmental level of social, cognitive, language, and other skills necessary for adaptation. Only through this diagnostic understanding can treatment begin at the child's level. Treatment itself consists of two reciprocally interactive processes: (1) the educator's relationship with the child, which fosters trust and acceptance; and (2) a dynamic curriculum geared to the child's evolving abilities and emphasizing the areas of the child's functioning, which is crucial for adaptation and social relatedness.

REFERENCES

Achenbach, T. M. (1982). Psychotic and other pervasive developmental disorders. In *Developmental Psychopathology* (pp. 414–464). New York: John Wiley.

American Psychiatric Association. (1980). *Diagnostic and Statistical Manual of Mental Disorders*, 3rd ed. New York: APA.

Anthony, E. J. (1962). Low grade psychosis in childhood. In B. W. Richards (Ed.), *Proceedings of London Conference in scientific study of mental deficiency*, 2 (p. 398). London: Dagenham, May & Baker.

Arnold, G., & Schwartz, S. (1983). Hemispheric lateralization of language in autistic and aphasic children. *Journal of Autism and Developmental Disorders, 13,* 129–139.

August, G., Raz, N., & Baird, T. D. (1985). Brief Report: Effects of fenfluramine in behavioral, cognitive, and affective disturbances in children. *Journal of Autism and Developmental Disorders, 15,* 97–107.

August, G., Stewart, M. A., & Tsai, L. (1981). The incidence of cognitive disabilities in the siblings of autistic children. *British Journal of Psychiatry, 138,* 416–422.

Bartak, L. (1978). Educational approaches. In M. Rutter & E. Schopler (Eds.), *Autism—A reappraisal of concepts and treatment* (pp. 428–438). New York: Plenum Press.

Bartak, L., & Rutter, M. (1973). Special educational treatment of autistic children: A comparative study. I. Design of study and characteristics of units. *Journal of Child Psychology and Psychiatry, 14*, 161–179.

Bartak, L., & Rutter, M. (1976). Differences between mentally retarded and normally intelligent autistic children. *Journal of Autism and Childhood Schizophrenia, 6*, 109–120.

Bemporad, J. R. (1979). Adult recollections of a formerly autistic child. *Journal of Autism and Developmental Disorders, 9*, 179–197.

Bender, L. (1964). A twenty-five year view of therapeutic results. In P. H. Hoch & J. Zubin (Eds.), *The evaluation of psychiatric treatment* (pp. 129–142). New York: Grune & Stratton.

Bender, L. (1970). The life course of schizophrenic children. *Biological Psychiatry, 2*, 167–172.

Bergman, A. (1971). "I and you": The separation-individuation process in the treatment of a symbiotic child. In J. B. McDevitt & C. F. Settlage (Eds.), *Separation-Individuation Essays in honor of Margaret S. Mahler* (pp. 325–355). New York: International Universities Press.

Bergman, P., & Escalona, S. (1949). Unusual sensitivities in very young children. *Psychoanalytic Study of the Child, 3 & 4* (pp. 333–352). New York: International Universities Press.

Berlin, I. N. (1978). Psychotherapeutic work with parents of psychotic children. In M. Rutter & E. Schopler (Eds.), *Autism—A reappraisal of concepts and treatment* (pp. 303–311). New York: Plenum Press.

Berlin, I. N., & Szurek, S. A. (1973). Parental blame: An obstacle in psychotherapeutic work with schizophrenic children and their families. In S. A. Szurek & I. N. Berlin (Eds.), *Clinical studies in childhood psychosis* (pp. 115–126). New York: Brunner/Mazel.

Bettelheim, B. (1950). *Love is not enough—The treatment of emotionally disturbed children.* New York: Free Press.

Bettelheim, B. (1967). *The empty fortress.* New York: Free Press.

Bettelheim, B., & Sanders, J. (1979). Milieu therapy: The Orthogenic School model. In J. Noshpitz (Ed.-in-chief) & S. Harrison (Ed.), *Basic handbook of child psychiatry* (Vol. III, pp. 216–230). New York: Basic Books.

Blackstock, E. G. (1978). Cerebral asymmetry and the development of infantile autism. *Journal of Autism and Childhood Schizophrenia, 8*, 339–353.

Blank, H. R., Smith, O. C., & Bruch, H. (1944). Schizophrenia in a four-year-old boy. *American Journal of Psychiatry, 100*, 805–810.

Bonvillian, J. D., Nelson, K. E., & Rhyne, J. M. (1981). Sign language and autism. *Journal of Autism and Developmental Disabilities, 11*, 125–137.

Bristol, M. M., & Schopler, E. (1983). Stress and coping in families of autistic adolescents. In E. Schopler & G. B. Mesibov (Eds.), *Autism in adolescents and adults* (pp. 251–278). New York: Plenum Press.

Brown, J. L. (1963). Follow-up of children with atypical development (Infantile Psychosis). *American Journal of Orthopsychiatry, 33*, 855–861.

Brown, J. L. (1978). Long-term follow-up of 100 "atypical" children. In M. Rutter & E. Schopler (Eds.), *Autism—A reappraisal of concepts and treatment* (pp. 463–474). New York: Plenum Press.

Brown, W. T., Jenkins, E. C., Friedman, E., Brooks, J., Wisniewski, K., Raguthu, S., & French, J. (1982). Autism is associated with Fragile-X syndrome. *Journal of Autism and Developmental Disorders, 12*, 303–308.

Call, J. (1963) Interlocking affective freeze between an autistic child and his "as-if" mother. *Journal of the American Academy of Child Psychiatry, 2*, 319–344.

Callias, M. (1983). Educational aims and methods. In M. Rutter & E. Schopler (Eds.), *Autism—A reappraisal of concepts and treatment* (pp. 453–461). New York: Plenum Press.

Campbell, M., Anderson, L. T., Small, A. M., Perry, R., Green, W. H., & Caplan, R. (1982). Effects of haloperidol on learning and behavior in autistic children. *Journal of Autism and Developmental Disorders, 12*, 167–175.

Campbell, M., Fish, B., David, R., Shapiro, T., Collins, P., & Koh, C. (1972). Response to triiodo-thyronine & dextroamphetamine: A study of preschool schizophrenic children. *Journal of Autism and Childhood Schizophrenia, 2*, 343–358.

Campbell, M., & Green, W. H. (1985). Pervasive developmental disorders of childhood. In H. I. Kaplan & B. J. Sadock (Eds.), *Comprehensive textbook of psychiatry,* 2nd ed. (Vol. 4, pp. 1672–1683). Baltimore, MD: Williams & Wilkins.

Campbell, M., Hardesty, A. S., Breuer, H., & Polevy, N. (1978). Childhood psychosis in perspective—A followup of ten children. *Journal of the American Academy of Child Psychiatry, 17*, 14–28.

Campbell, M., & Hersh, S. P. (1971). Observations on the vicissitudes of aggression in two siblings. *Journal of Autism and Childhood Schizophrenia, 1*, 398–410.

Campbell, M., Rosenbloom, S., Perry, R., George, A. E., Kricheff, I. I., Anderson, L., Small, A. M., & Jennings, S. J. (1982). Computerized axial tomography in young autistic children. *American Journal of Psychiatry, 139*, 510–512.

Cantwell, D. P., Baker, L., & Rutter, M. (1978). Family factors. In M. Rutter & E. Schopler (Eds.), *Autism—A reappraisal of concepts and treatment* (pp. 269–296). New York: Plenum Press.

Caparulo, B. K., Cohen, D. J., Rothman, S. L., Young, J. G., Katz, J. D., Shaywitz, S. E., & Shaywitz, B. A. (1981). Computed tomographic brain scanning in children with developmental neuropsychiatric disorders. *Journal of the American Academy of Child Psychiatry, 20*, 338–357.

Chess, S. (1971). Autism in children with congenital rubella. *Journal of Autism and Schizophrenia, 1*, 33–47.

Churchill, D. W., Alpern, G. D., & DeMyer, M. K. (1971). *Infantile Autism*. Springfield, IL: Charles C Thomas.

Ciaranello, R. D., Vandenberg, S. R., & Anders, T. F. (1982). Intrinsic and extrinsic determinants of neuronal development: Relation to infantile autism. *Journal of Autism and Developmental Disorders, 12*, 115–145.

Clark, P., & Rutter, M. (1977). Compliance and resistance in autistic children. *Journal of Autism and Childhood Schizophrenia, 7*, 33–48.

Clark, P., & Rutter, M. (1981). Autistic children's responses to structure and to interpersonal demands. *Journal of Autism and Developmental Disorders, 11*, 201–217.

Cohen, D. J., Caparulo, B. K., & Shaywitz, B. A. (1978). Neurochemical and developmental models of childhood autism. In G. Serban (Ed.), *Cognitive defects in the development of mental illness* (pp. 66–100). New York: Brunner/Mazel.

Coleman, M. (1978). Cognitive defects of infantile autism. In G. Serban (Ed.), *Cognitive defects in the development of mental illness* (pp. 1–23). New York: Brunner/Mazel.

Coleman, R. S., Frankel, F., Ritvo, E., & Freeman, B. J. (1976). The effects of fluorescent and incandescent illumination upon repetitive behaviors in autistic children. *Journal of Autism and Childhood Schizophrenia, 6*, 157–162.

Coleman, M., & Gillberg, C. (1985). *The biology of the autistic syndrome*. New York: Praeger.

Curtis, S. (1981). Dissociations between language and cognition, cases and implications. *Journal of Autism and Developmental Disorders, 11*, 15–30.

Dawson, G. (1983). Lateralized brain dysfunction in autism: Evidence from the Halstead-Reitan neuropsychological battery. *Journal of Autism and Developmental Disorders, 13*, 269.

DeMyer, M. K., Barton, S., DeMyer, W. E., Norton, J. A., Allen, J., & Steele, R. (1973). Prognosis in autism: A follow-up study. *Journal of Autism and Childhood Schizophrenia, 3*, 199–246.

DeMyer, M. K., Churchill, D. W., Pontius, W., & Gilkey, K. M. (1971). A comparison of five diagnostic systems for childhood schizophrenia and infantile autism. *Journal of Autism and Childhood Schizophrenia, 1*, 175–189.

DeMyer, M. K., Pontius, W., Norton, J. A., Barton, S., Allen, J., & Steele, R. (1972). Parental practices and innate activity in normal, autistic and brain-damaged infants. *Journal of Autism and Childhood Schizophrenia, 2*, 49–66.

DesLauriers, A. M. (1978). Play, symbols and the development of language. In M. Rutter & E. Schopler (Eds.), *Autism—A reappraisal of concepts and treatment* (pp. 313–326). New York: Plenum Press.

Donnellan, A. M., Anderson, J. L., & Mesaros, R. A. (1984). An observational study of stereotypic behavior and proximity related to the occurrence of autistic child-family member interactions. *Journal of Autism and Developmental Disorders, 14*, 205–210.

Donovan, W. L., & Leavitt, L. A. (1985). Physiologic assessment of mother-infant attachment. *Journal of the American Academy of Child Psychiatry, 24*, 65–70.

Favell, J. E. (1983). Management of aggressive behavior. In E. Schopler & G. B. Mesibov (Eds.), *Autism in adolescents and adults* (pp. 187–222). New York: Plenum Press.

Fenske, E. C., Zalenski, S., Krantz, P. J., & McClannahan, L. E. (in press). Age at intervention and treatment outcome for autistic children in a comprehensive intervention program. *Analysis and Intervention in Developmental Disabilities*.

Ferrara, C., & Hill, S. D. (1980). Responsiveness of autistic children to the predictability of social and nonsocial toys. *Journal of Autism and Developmental Disorders, 10*, 51–57.

Fish, B. (1979). The recognition of infantile psychosis. In J. G. Howells (Ed.), *Modern perspectives in the psychiatry of infancy* (pp. 450–474). New York: Brunner/Mazel.

Fish, B., & Ritvo, E. R. (1979). Psychoses of childhood. In J. Noshpitz (Ed.), *Basic handbook of child psychiatry* (Vol. II, pp. 249–304). New York: Basic Books.

Folstein, S., & Rutter, M. (1977). Infantile autism: The genetic study of 21 twin pairs. *Journal of Child Psychology and Psychiatry, 18*, 297–321.

Fredericks, H. D., Buckley, J., Baldwin, V. L., Moore, W., & Stremel-Campbell, K. (1983). The educational needs of the autistic adolescent. In E. Schopler & G. B. Mesibov (Eds.), *Autism in adolescents and adults* (pp. 79–109). New York: Plenum Press.

Freedman, D. A., Fox-Kolenda, B. J., & Brown, S. L. (1970). A multi-handicapped Rubella baby: The first 18 months. *Journal of the American Academy of Child Psychiatry, 9*, 298–317.

Freud, A. (1965). *Normality and pathology in childhood*. New York: International Universities Press.

Funderburk, S. J., Carter, J., Tanguay, P., Freeman, B. J., & Westlake, J. R. (1983). Parental and reproductive problems and gestational hormonal exposure in autistic and schizophrenic children. *Journal of Autism and Developmental Disorders, 13*, 325–333.

Gallagher, J. J., & Wiegerink, R. (1976). Educational strategies for the autistic child. *Journal of Autism and Childhood Schizophrenia, 6*, 15–26.

Gianascol, A. J. (1963). Psychodynamic approaches to childhood schizophrenia: A review. *Journal of Nervous and Mental Disease, 137*, 336–340.

Gillberg, C., & Forsell, C. (1984). Childhood psychosis and neurofibromatosis—More than a coincidence? *Journal of Autism and Developmental Disorders, 14*, 1–8.

Gillberg, C., & Gillberg, I. D. (1983). Infantile autism: A total population study of reduced optimality in the pre-, peri-, and neonatal period. *Journal of Autism and Developmental Disorders, 13,* 153–166.

Gillberg, C., & Schaumann, H. (1981). Infantile autism and puberty. *Journal of Autism and Developmental Disorders, 11,* 365–371.

Gillberg, C., & Schaumann, H. (1982). Social class and infantile autism. *Journal of Autism and Developmental Disorders, 12,* 223–228.

Gillberg, C., & Svendsen, P. (1983). Childhood psychosis and computed tomographic brain scan findings. *Journal of Autism and Developmental Disorders, 13,* 19–32.

Gillberg, C., Trygstad, O., & Foss, I. (1982). Childhood psychosis and urinary excretion of peptides and protein associated peptide complexes. *Journal of Autism and Developmental Disorders, 12,* 229.

Goldberg, M., Hattab, J., Meir, D., Ebstein, R. P., & Belmaker, R. H. (1984). Plasma cyclic AMP and cyclic GMP in childhood—Onset psychoses. *Journal of Autism and Developmental Disorders, 14,* 159–164.

Goldfarb, W. (1980). Pervasive developmental disorders of childhood. In H. I. Kaplan, A. M. Freedman, & B. J. Sadock (Eds.), *Comprehensive textbook of psychiatry,* 3rd ed. (Vol. 3, pp. 2517–2537). Baltimore, MD: Williams & Wilkins.

Goldfarb, W., Spitzer, R. L., & Endicott, J. (1976). A study of psychopathology of parents of psychotic children by structured interview. *Journal of Autism and Developmental Disorders, 6,* 327–338.

Goldfine, P. E., McPherson, P. M., Heath, G. A., Hardesty, V. A., Beauregard, L. J., & Gordon, B. (1985). Association of Fragile-X syndrome with autism. *American Journal of Psychiatry, 141,* 108–110.

Grandin, T. (1983). Coping strategies: Letter to the editor. *Journal of Autism and Developmental Disorders, 13,* 217–222.

Green, W. H., Campbell, M., Hardesty, A. S., Grega, D. M., Padron-Gayol, M., Shell, J., & Erlenmeyer-Kimling, L. (1984). A comparison of schizophrenic and autistic children. *Journal of the American Academy of Child Psychiatry, 23,* 399–409.

Hanson, D. R., & Gottesman, I. I. (1976). The genetics, if any, of infantile autism and childhood schizophrenia. *Journal of Autism and Developmental Disabilities, 13,* 217–222.

Harlow, H. F., & McKinney, W. T., Jr. (1971). Nonhuman primates and psychoses. *Journal of Autism and Childhood Schizophrenia, 1,* 368–375.

Helm, D. (1976). Psychodynamic and behavior modification approaches to the treatment of infantile autism. *Journal of Autism and Childhood Schizophrenia, 6,* 27–41.

Hetcler, B. E., & Griffin, J. L. (1981). Infantile autism and the temporal lobe of the brain. *Journal of Autism and Developmental Disorders, 11,* 317–330.

Hobson, R. P. (1984). Early childhood autism and the question of egocentrism. *Journal of Autism and Developmental Disorders, 14,* 85–104.

Holmes, N., Hemsley, R., Rickett, J., & Likierman, H. (1982). Parents as co-therapists: Their perceptions of a home-based behavioral treatment for autistic children. *Journal of Autism and Developmental Disorders, 12,* 331–342.

Holter, F. R., & Ruttenberg, B. A. (1971). Psychotherapeutic treatment of autistic children. *Journal of Autism and Childhood Schizophrenia, 1,* 206–214.

Howlin, P. (1980). The home treatment of autistic children. In L. A. Hersov & M. Berger (Eds.), *Language and language disorders in childhood—A book supplement to the Journal of Child Psychology and Psychiatry, No. 2* (pp. 115–145). Oxford: Pergamon Press.

Howlin, P. (1984). The acquisition of grammatical morphemes in autistic children: A critique and replication of the findings of Bartolucci, Pierce, and Streiner, 1980. *Journal of Autism and Developmental Disorders, 14,* 127–136.

Hurtig, R., Ensrud, S., & Tomblin, J. B. (1982). The communicative function of question production in autistic children. *Journal of Autism and Developmental Disorders, 12,* 57–69.

Hutt, S. J., Hutt, C., Lee, D., & Ounsted, C. (1964). Arousal and childhood autism. *Nature, 204,* 908–909.

James, A. L., & Barry, R. J. (1983). Developmental effects on the cerebral lateralization of autistic, retarded and normal children. *Journal of Autism and Developmental Disorders, 13,* 43–56.

Kanner, L. (1943). Autistic disturbances of affective contact. *Nervous Child, 2,* 217–250.

Kanner, L. (1971a). Childhood psychosis: A historical review. *Journal of Autism and Childhood Schizophrenia, 1,* 14–19.

Kanner, L. (1971b). Follow-up study of 11 autistic children originally reported in 1943. *Journal of Autism & Childhood Schizophrenia, 1,* 119–145.

Kanner, L., & Eisenberg, L. (1955). Notes on the follow-up studies of autistic children. *Proceedings of the American Psychopathological Association, 44,* 227–239.

Kern, L., Koegel, R. L., & Dunlap, G. (1984). The influence of vigorous vs. mild exercise on autistic stereotyped behaviors. *Journal of Autism and Developmental Disorders, 14,* 57–67.

Klein, M. (1930). The importance of symbol formation in the development of the ego. *International Journal of Psychoanalysis, 11,* 24–39.

Knoblock, P. (1982). *Teaching and mainstreaming autistic children.* Denver, CO: Love.

Knoblock, P. (1983). *Teaching emotionally disturbed children.* Boston: Houghton Mifflin.

Koegel, R. L., & Schreibman, L. (1976). Identification of consistent responding to auditory stimuli by a functionally "deaf" autistic child. *Journal of Autism and Childhood Schizophrenia, 6,* 147–156.

Kolvin, I. (1971). Studies in childhood psychoses: I. Diagnostic criteria and classification. *British Journal of Psychiatry, 118,* 381–384.

Kolvin, I., Garside, R. F., & Kidd, J. S. H. (1971). Studies in childhood psychoses: IV. Parental personality and attitude and childhood psychoses. *British Journal of Psychiatry, 118,* 403–406.

Kolvin, I., Humphrey, M., & McNay, A. (1971). Studies in childhood psychoses: VI. Cognitive factors in childhood psychoses. *British Journal of Psychiatry, 118,* 415–419.

Kolvin, I., Ounsted, C., Humphrey, M., & McNay, A. (1971). Studies in childhood psychoses: II. The phenomenology of childhood psychoses. *British Journal of Psychiatry, 118,* 385–395.

Kolvin, I., Ounsted, C., Richardson, L. M., & Garside, R. F. (1971). Studies in childhood psychoses: III. The family and social background in childhood psychoses. *British Journal of Psychiatry, 118,* 396–402.

Kolvin, I., Ounsted, C., & Roth, M. (1971). Studies in childhood psychoses: V. Cerebral dysfunction and childhood psychoses. *British Journal of Psychiatry, 118,* 407–414.

Komoto, J., Usui, S., & Hirata, J. (1984). Infantile autism and affective disorder. *Journal of Autism and Developmental Disorders, 14,* 81–84.

Konstantareas, M. M. (1984). Sign language as a communication prosthesis with language-impaired children. *Journal of Autism and Developmental Disorders, 14,* 9–25.

Kootz, J. P., & Cohen, D. J. (1981). Modulation of sensory intake in autistic children. *Journal of the American Academy of Child Psychiatry, 20,* 692–701.

Kootz, J. P., Marinelli, B., & Cohen, D. J. (1981). Sensory receptor sensitivity in autistic children. *Archives of General Psychiatry, 38,* 271–273.

Kootz, J. P., Marinelli, B., & Cohen, D. J. (1982). Modulation of response to environmental stimulation in autistic children. *Journal of Autism and Developmental Disorders, 12,* 185–193.

Kotsopoulos, S. (1976). Infantile autism in dizygotic twins. *Journal of Autism and Childhood Schizophrenia, 6,* 133–138.

Krug, D. A., Arick, J., & Almond, P. (1980). Behavior checklist for identifying severely handicapped individuals with high levels of autistic behavior. *Journal of Child Psychology and Psychiatry, 21,* 221–229.

Lancioni, G. E. (1983). Using pictorial representations as communication means with low-functioning children. *Journal of Autism and Developmental Disorders, 13,* 87–105.

Lansing, M. D., & Schopler, E. (1978). Individualized education: A public school model. In M. Rutter & E. Schopler (Eds.), *Autism—A reappraisal of concepts and treatment* (pp. 439–452). New York: Plenum Press.

Lelord, G., Muh, J. P., Barthelemy, C., Martineau, J., & Garreau, B. (1981). Effects of Pyridoxine and Magnesium on autistic symptoms—Initial observations. *Journal of Autism and Developmental Disorders, 11,* 219–230.

Lettick, A. L. (1983). Benhaven. In E. Schopler and G. B. Mesibov (Eds.), *Autism in adolescents and adults* (pp. 355–379). New York: Plenum Press.

Leventhal, B. (1984). The American Academy of Child Psychiatry Newsletter, 3615 Wisconsin Ave., N.W., Washington, D.C., 20016.

Lichstein, K. L., & Schreibman, L. (1976). Employing electric shock with autistic children. *Journal of Autism and Childhood Schizophrenia, 6,* 163–173.

Lord, C., & O'Neill, P. J. (1983). Language and communication needs of adolescents with autism. In E. Schopler & G. B. Mesibov (Eds.), *Autism in adolescents and adults* (pp. 57–77). New York: Plenum Press.

Lord, C., Schopler, E., & Revicki, D. (1982). Sex differences in autism. *Journal of Autism and Developmental Disorders, 12,* 317–330.

Lotter, V. (1966). Services for a group of autistic children in Middlesex. In J. K. Wing (Ed.), *Early childhood autism.* Oxford: Pergamon Press.

Lovaas, I. O. (1971). Considerations in the development of a behavioral treatment program for psychotic children. In D. W. Churchill, G. D. Alpern, & M. K. DeMyer (Eds.), *Infantile autism* (pp. 124–144). Springfield, IL: Charles C Thomas.

Lovaas, I. O. (1977). *The autistic child: Language development.* New York: John Wiley.

Lovaas, I. O. (1978). Parents as therapists. In M. Rutter & E. Schopler (Eds.), *Autism—A reappraisal of concepts and treatment* (pp. 369–378). New York: Plenum Press.

Lovaas, I. O. (1980). Behavioral teaching with young autistic children. In B. Wilcox & A. Thompson (Eds.), *Critical issues in educating autistic children and youth* (pp. 220–233). Washington, DC: U. S. Dept. of Education, Office of Special Education.

Lovaas, I. O. (1981). *Teaching developmentally disabled children: The ME book.* Baltimore, MD: University Park Press.

Lovaas, I. O. (1982, August). *An overview of the Young Autism Project.* Paper presented at the meeting of the American Psychological Association, Washington, DC.

Lowry, E. F. (1985). Autistic aloofness reconsidered: Case reports of two children. *Bulletin of the Menninger Clinic, 49,* 135–150.

Mahler, M. S., & Furer, M. (1968). On human symbiosis and the vicissitudes of individuation. *Infantile psychosis* (Vol. 1). New York: International Universities Press.

Markowitz, P. I. (1983). Autism in child with congenital cytomegalovirus infection. *Journal of Autism and Developmental Disorders, 13.*

Massie, H. N. (1978a). Blind ratings of mother-infant interaction in home movies of prepsychotic and normal infants. *American Journal of Psychiatry, 135,* 1371–1374.

Massie, H. N. (1978b). The early natural history of childhood psychosis: Ten cases studied by analysis of home movies of the infancies of the children. *Journal of the American Academy of Child Psychiatry, 17,* 29–45.

Masterton, B. A., & Biederman, G. B. (1983). Proprioceptive vs. visual control in autistic children. *Journal of Autism and Developmental Disorders, 13,* 141.

McCann, B. S. (1981). Hemispheric asymmetries and early autism. *Journal of Autism and Developmental Disorders, 11,* 401–411.

Menyuk, P., & Wilbur, R. (1981). (Guest Eds.) Preface to special issue on language disorders. *Journal of Autism and Developmental Disorders, 11,* 1–13.

Mesibov, G. B., Schopler, E., & Sloan, J. L. (1983). Service development for adolescents and adults in North Carolina's TEACCH program. In E. Schopler & G. B. Mesibov (Eds.), *Autism in adolescents and adults.* New York: Plenum Press.

Murphy, G. (1982). Sensory reinforcement in the mentally handicapped and autistic child: A review. *Journal of Autism and Developmental Disorders, 12,* 265–278.

Needleman, R., Ritvo, E. R., & Freeman, B. J. (1980). Objectively defined linguistic parameters in children with autism and other developmental disabilities. *Journal of Autism and Developmental Disorders, 10,* 389–398.

Ney, P. G., Palvesky, A. E., & Markely, J. (1971). Relative effectiveness of operant conditioning and play therapy on childhood schizophrenia. *Journal of Autism and Childhood Schizophrenia, 1,* 337–349.

Olley, J. G. (Ed.) (1983). Book Reviews. *Journal of Autism and Developmental Disorders, 13,* 435–446.

Ornitz, E. M. (1970). Vestibular dysfunction in schizophrenia and childhood autism. *Comprehensive Psychiatry, 11,* 159–173.

Ornitz, E. M., Guthrie, D., & Farley, A. J. (1978). The early symptoms of childhood autism. In G. Serban (Ed.), *The development of mental illness* (pp. 24–42). New York: Brunner/Mazel.

Ornitz, E. M., & Ritvo, E. R. (1968). Neurophysiological mechanisms underlying perceptual inconstancy in autistic and schizophrenic children. *Archives of General Psychiatry, 18,* 76–98.

Palkovitz, R. J., & Wiesenfeld, A. R. (1980). Differential autonomic responses of autistic and normal children. *Journal of Autism and Developmental Disorders, 10,* 347–360.

Parents Speak Section. (1976). Reactions to "Employing electric shock with autistic children." *Journal of Autism and Childhood Schizophrenia, 6,* 289–294.

Park, C. C. (1983). Growing out of autism. In E. Schopler & G. B. Mesibov (Eds.), *Autism in adolescents and adults* (pp. 279–295). New York: Plenum Press.

Petty, L., Ornitz, E. M., Michelman, J. D., & Zimmerman, E. G. (1984). Autistic children who become schizophrenic. *Archives of General Psychiatry, 41,* 129–135.

Potter, H. W. (1933). Schizophrenia in children. *American Journal of Psychiatry, 12,* 1253.

Prior, M. R., & Chen, C. S. (1976). Short-term and serial memory in autistic, retarded and normal children. *Journal of Autism and Childhood Schizophrenia, 6,* 121–131.

Putnam, M. (1948). Case study of an atypical two-and-a-half-year-old, Round table. *American Journal of Orthopsychiatry, 18,* 1–30.

Rank, B. (1949). Adaptation of the psychoanalytic technique for the treatment of young children with atypical development. *American Journal of Orthopsychiatry, 19,* 130–139.

Redl, F., & Wineman, D. (1957). *The aggressive child.* New York: Free Press.

Reichard, S., & Tillman, C. (1950). Patterns of parent-child relationships in schizophrenia. *Psychiatry, 13,* 247–257.

Reichler, R. J., & Schopler, E. (1971). Observations on the nature of human relatedness. *Journal of Autism and Childhood Schizophrenia, 1,* 283–296.

Resch, R. C., Grand, S., & Meyerson, K. (1981). From the object to the person—The treatment of a two-year-old girl with infantile autism. *Bulletin of the Menninger Clinic,* 281–306.

Rimland, B. (1964). *Infantile autism.* New York: Appleton-Century-Crofts.

Rimland, B. (1971). The differentiation of childhood psychoses: An analysis of checklists for 2,218 psychotic children. *Journal of Autism and Childhood Schizophrenia, 1,* 161–174.

Rimland, B. (1978). Savant capabilities of autistic children and their cognitive implications. In G. Serban (Ed.), *Cognitive defects in the development of mental illness* (pp. 43–63). New York: Brunner/Mazel.

Rimland, B., Calloway, E., & Dreyfus, P. (1978). Effects of high doses of vitamin B_6 in autistic children: A double-blind crossover study. *American Journal of Psychiatry, 135,* 472–475.

Ritvo, E. R., Freeman, B. J., Geller, E., & Yuwiler, A. (1983). Effects of fenfluramine on 14 outpatients with the syndrome of autism. *Journal of the American Academy of Child Psychiatry, 22,* 549–558.

Ritvo, E. R., Freeman, B. J., Mason-Brothers, A., Mo, A., & Ritvo, A. M. (1985). Concordance for the syndrome of autism in forty pairs of afflicted twins. *American Journal of Psychiatry, 142,* 74–77.

Ritvo, E. R., Freeman, B. J., Yuwiler, A., Geller, E., Yokota, A., Schroth, P., & Novak, P. (1984). Study of fenfluramine in outpatients with the syndrome of autism. *Journal of Pediatrics, 105,* 823–828.

Ritvo, E. R., Ritvo, E. C., & Mason-Brothers, A. (1982). Genetic and immunohematologic factors in autism. *Journal of Autism and Developmental Disorders, 12,* 109–114.

Ritvo, E. R., Spence, M. A., Freeman, B. J., Mason-Brothers, A., Mo, A., & Marazita, M. L. (1985). Evidence for autosomal recessive inheritance in 46 families with multiple incidences of autism. *American Journal of Psychiatry, 142,* 187–192.

Rosenthal, J., Massie, H., & Wulff, K. (1980). A comparison of cognitive development in normal and psychotic children in the first two years of life from home movies. *Journal of Autism and Developmental Disorders, 10,* 433–444.

Rutter, M. (1970). Autism: Educational issues. *Special Education, 59,* 6–10.

Rutter, M. (1972). Childhood schizophrenia reconsidered. *Journal of Autism and Childhood Schizophrenia, 2,* 313–337.

Rutter, M. (1978a). Developmental issues and prognosis. In M. Rutter & E. Schopler (Eds.), *Autism—A reappraisal of concepts and treatment* (pp. 497–505). New York: Plenum Press.

Rutter, M. (1978b). Diagnosis and definition. In M. Rutter & E. Schopler (Eds.), *Autism—A reappraisal of concepts and treatment* (pp. 1–25). New York: Plenum Press.

Rutter, M. (1980). Language training with autistic children: How does it work and what does it achieve? In L. A. Hersov & M. Berger (Eds.), *Language and language disorders in childhood—A book supplement to the Journal of Child Psychology and Psychiatry, No. 2* (pp. 147–172). Oxford: Pergamon Press.

Rutter, M., & Bartak, L. (1971). Causes of infantile autism: Some considerations from recent research. *Journal of Autism and Childhood Schizophrenia, 1,* 20–32.

Rutter, M., & Schopler, E. (Eds.) (1978). *Autism—A reappraisal of concepts and treatment.* New York: Plenum Press.

Schechter, M. D., Shurley, J. T., Toussieng, P. W., & Maier, W. J. (1969). Sensory isolation therapy of autistic children: A preliminary report. *Journal of Pediatrics, 74,* 564–569.

Schopler, E. (1962). The development of body image and symbol formation through bodily contact with an autistic child. *Journal of Child Psychology and Psychiatry, 3,* 191–202.

Schopler, E. (1976a). The art and science of Bruno Bettelheim [Review of *A home for the heart*]. *Journal of Autism and Childhood Schizophrenia, 6,* 193–202.

Schopler, E. (1976b). Toward reducing behavior problems in autistic children. *Journal of Autism and Childhood Schizophrenia, 6,* 1–13.

Schopler, E. (1983). New developments in the definition and diagnosis of autism. In B. B. Lahey & A. E. Kazdin (Eds.), *Advances in clinical child psychology.* New York: Plenum Press.

Schopler, E., Brehm, S. S., Kinsbourne, M., & Reichler, R. J. (1971). Effect of treatment structure on development in autistic children. *Archives of General Psychiatry, 24,* 415–421.

Schopler, E., & Loftin, J. (1969). Thought disorders in parents of psychotic children: A function of test anxiety. *Archives of General Psychiatry, 20,* 174–181.

Schopler, E., & Mesibov, G. B. (Eds.). (1983). *Autism in adolescents and adults.* New York: Plenum Press.

Schopler, E., & Reichler, R. J. (1971). Parents as cotherapists in the treatment of psychotic children. *Journal of Autism and Childhood Schizophrenia, 1,* 87–102.

Schopler, E., & Reichler, R. J. (1972). How well do parents understand their own psychotic child? *Journal of Autism and Childhood Schizophrenia, 2,* 387–400.

Schopler, E., Rutter, M., & Chess, S. (1979). Editorial: Change of journal scope and title. *Journal of Autism and Developmental Disorders, 91,* 1–10.

Schroeder, S. R., Mulick, J. A., & Rojahn, J. (1980). The definition, taxonomy, epidemiology, and ecology of self-injurious behavior. *Journal of Autism and Developmental Disorders, 10,* 417–432.

Simeonsson, R. J., Olley, J. G., & Rosenthal, S. L. (in press). Early intervention for children with autism. In M. J. Guralnick & F. C. Bennett (Eds.), *The effectiveness of early intervention for at-risk children.* New York: Academic Press.

Smith, D. E. P., Olson, M., Barger, F., & McConnell, J. U. (1981). The effects of improved auditory feedback on the verbalizations of an autistic child. *Journal of Autism and Developmental Disorders, 11,* 449–454.

Stanton, A. H., & Schwartz, M. S. (Eds.). (1954). *The mental hospital.* New York: Basic Books.

Stiver, R. L., & Dobbins, J. P. (1980). Treatment of atypical anorexia nervosa in public school: An autistic child. *Journal of Autism and Developmental Disorders, 10,* 67–83.

Stoufe, L. A., Stuecher, H. U., & Stutzer, W. (1973). The functional significance of autistic behaviors for the psychotic child. *Journal of Abnormal Child Psychology, 1,* 225–240.

Strain, P. S., Jamieson, B. J., & Hoyson, M. H. (1985). Learning experiences . . . An alternative program for preschoolers and parents: A comprehensive service system for the mainstreaming of autisticlike preschoolers. In C. J. Meisel (Ed.), *Mainstreaming handicapped children: Outcomes, controversies and new directions* (pp. 251–269). Hillsdale, NJ: Erlbaum.

Stubbs, E. G., Ash, E., & Williams, C. P. S. (1984). Autism and congenital cytomegalovirus. *Journal of Autism and Developmental Disorders, 14,* 183–189.

Szurek, S. A., & Berlin, I. N. (Eds.). (1973a). *Clinical studies in childhood psychosis.* New York: Brunner/Mazel.

Szurek, S. A., & Berlin, I. N. (1973b). The problem of blame in therapy with parents and their children. In S. A. Szurek & I. N. Berlin (Eds.), *Clinical studies in childhood psychosis* (pp. 87–114). New York: Brunner/Mazel.

Tanguay, P. E. (1984). Toward a new classification of serious psychopathology in children. *Journal of the American Academy of Child Psychiatry, 23,* 373–384.

Tanguay, P. E., & Edwards, R. M. (1982). Electrophysiological studies of autism: The whisper of a bang. *Journal of Autism and Developmental Disorders, 12*, 177–184.

Tanguay, P. E., Ornitz, E. M., Forsythe, A. B., & Ritvo, E. R. (1976). Rapid eye movement (REM) activity in normal and autistic children during REM sleep. *Journal of Autism and Childhood Schizophrenia, 6*, 275–288.

Tiegerman, E., & Primavera, L. (1981). Object manipulation: An interactional strategy with autistic children. *Journal of Autism and Developmental Disorders, 11*, 427–438.

Tiegerman, E., & Primavera, L. H. (1984). Imitating the autistic child: Facilitating communicative gaze behavior. *Journal of Autism and Developmental Disorders, 14*, 27–38.

Tinbergen, N., & Tinbergen, E. H. (1983). *'Autistic Children': New hope for a cure*. London: George Allen and Unwin.

Tinbergen, E. H., & Tinbergen, N. (1972). Early childhood autism—An ethological approach. *Advances in ethology* (pp. 8–53). Berlin: P. Parey.

Treffert, D. A. (1970). Epidemiology of infantile autism. *Archives of General Psychiatry, 22*, 431–438.

Tronick, E., Als, H., Adamson, L., Wise, S., & Brazelton, T. B. (1978). The infant's response to entrapment between contradictory messages in face-to-face interaction. *Journal of the American Academy of Child Psychiatry, 17*, 1–13.

Tsai, L. Y., & Stewart, M. A. (1983). Etiological implication of maternal age and birth order in infantile autism. *Journal of Autism and Developmental Disorders, 13*.

Tsai, L., Stewart, M. A., & August, G. (1981). Implication of sex differences on the familial transmission of infantile autism. *Journal of Autism and Developmental Disorders, 11*, 165–173.

Tsai, L., Stewart, M. A., Faust, M., & Shook, S. (1982). Social class distribution of fathers of children enrolled in the Iowa Autism program. *Journal of Autism and Developmental Disorders, 12*, 211–221.

Tustin, F. (1972). *Autism and childhood psychosis*. New York: Science House.

Varley, C., Kolff, C., Trupin, E., & Reichler, R. J. (1981). Hemodialysis as a treatment for infantile autism. *Journal of Autism and Developmental Disorders, 10*, 399–404.

Verhees, B. (1976). A pair of classically early infantile autistic siblings. *Journal of Autism and Childhood Schizophrenia, 6*, 53–59.

Ward, A. J. (1970). Early infantile autism—diagnosis, etiology and treatment. *Psychological Bulletin, 73*, 350–362.

Weil, A. P. (1973). Ego strengthening prior to analysis. *Psychoanalytic Study of the Child, 28*, 287–301.

Wenar, C., & Ruttenberg, B. A. (1976). The use of BRIAC for evaluating therapeutic effectiveness. *Journal of Autism and Childhood Schizophrenia, 6*, 175–191.

Wing, L. (1978). Social, behavioral, and cognitive characteristics: An epidemiological approach. In M. Rutter & E. Schopler (Eds.), *Autism—A reappraisal of concepts and treatment* (pp. 27–45). New York: Plenum Press.

Wing, L. (1981). Language, social and cognitive impairment in autism and severe mental retardation. *Journal of Autism and Developmental Disorders, 11*, 31–44.

Wing, L. (1985). *Autistic children*. New York: Brunner/Mazel.

Wing, L., & Wing, J. K. (1971). Multiple improvements in early childhood autism. *Journal of Autism and Childhood Schizophrenia, 1*, 256–266.

Witmer, L. (1973). What I did with Don. *Ladies' Home Journal, 36*, 41, 122, 123. Also reprinted in S. A. Szurek & I. N. Berlin (Eds.), *Clinical studies in childhood psychosis* (pp. 48–64). New York: Brunner/Mazel.

Wolchik, S. A. (1983). Language patterns of young autistic and normal children. *Journal of Autism and Developmental Disorders, 13*, 167–180.

Wolf, E. G., Wenar, C., & Ruttenberg, B. A. (1972). A comparison of personality variables in autistic and mentally retarded children. *Journal of Autism and Childhood Schizophrenia, 2*, 92–108.

Wood, M. M. (1975). *Developmental therapy: A textbook for teachers as therapists of emotionally disturbed young children*. Baltimore, MD: University Park Press.

Young, J. G., Kavanaugh, M. E., Anderson, G. M., Shaywitz, B. A., & Cohen, D. J. (1982). Clinical neurochemistry of autism and associated disorders. *Journal of Autism and Developmental Disorders, 12*, 147–165.

Young, J. G., Kyprie, R. M., Ross, N. T., & Cohen, D. J. (1980). Serum dopamine-beta-hydroxylase activity: Clinical applications in child psychiatry. *Journal of Autism and Developmental Disorders, 10*, 1–14.

Zimmerman, R. L., & Heistad, G. T. (1982). Studies of the long-term efficacy of antipsychotic drugs in controlling the behavior of institutionalized retardates. *Journal of the American Academy of Child Psychiatry, 21*, 136–143.

Very early in the morning, before sunrise, some workmen came into the house. Ivan Dmitritch knew perfectly well that they had come to mend the stove in the kitchen, but terror told him that they were police officers disguised as workmen. He slipped stealthily out of the flat, and, overcome by terror, ran along the street without his cap and coat. Dogs raced after him barking, a peasant shouted somewhere behind him, the wind whistled in his ears, and it seemed to Ivan Dmitritch that the force and violence of the whole world was massed together behind his back and was chasing after him.

ANTON CHEKHOV
WARD NO. 6

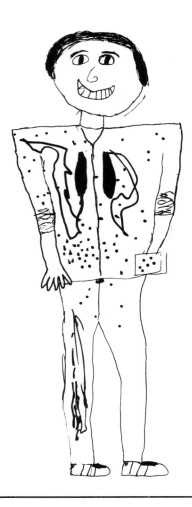

This self-portrait is by a 10-year-old boy diagnosed as borderline psychotic. Probably the most striking feature of the drawing is the way the boy blended internal and external body features. The dark areas on the chest are "lungs which are attached to ribs"; the dots are the pattern on his shirt.

CHAPTER ELEVEN

Psychoses of Childhood and Adolescence: Schizophrenic Reactions and Borderline States

Charles R. Keith
DUKE UNIVERSITY MEDICAL CENTER

Although pervasive developmental disorders and childhood schizophrenia have overlapping features, there are some distinct differences between the two. Debate continues as to whether the two are separate and different syndromes or two points in a spectrum.

Perceptual and cognitive processing disorders appear central to the schizophrenic syndrome. Although the specific role of genetic and neurobiochemical factors remains unclear, it is likely that they, too, are important in determining how such disorders develop.

Developmental and familial background factors are also likely contributors to the schizophrenic syndrome.

Schools can provide structured and supportive environments to schizophrenic children and adolescents, thus enabling them to remain in their communities.

Many children and their families benefit from establishing and maintaining long-term involvement with therapists and/or local mental health clinics.

Carefully monitored tranquilizer therapy is an important part of many schizophrenic youths' total treatment programs.

WE WILL ADDRESS schizophrenic reactions and borderline states in separate sections of this chapter so we can focus on the unique properties of each. We will first talk about schizophrenic reactions, as they overlap the topic of Chapter 10, pervasive developmental disorders.

SCHIZOPHRENIC REACTIONS OF LATER CHILDHOOD AND ADOLESCENCE

The early school years bring a respite from the onset of childhood psychosis, but by the age of 10 or 11, the incidence begins to increase again. Though early autism predominantly strikes boys, the schizophrenic reactions of later childhood affect boys only a little more than girls (1.5:1) (Campbell & Green, 1985). With the later onset of schizophrenic reactions, however, the symptoms become more similar to adult schizophrenia. Use of the term *schizophrenic* for these later onset psychoses reflects the belief that the illness is similar to, and often continuous with, adolescent and adult schizophrenia (Bender, 1967).

Before the onset of overt schizophrenic reactions, a child has usually had a history of acting "odd," has had trouble with schoolwork and peer relations, and has sometimes had a conduct disturbance. No specific or unique premonitory personality characteristics have been found in the premorbid history of the schizophrenic child (Watt, 1984; Neale, Winters, & Weintraub, 1984). Green et al. (1984) found that only 20 percent of their series of schizophrenic children had shown somewhat normal development before eruption of the symptoms in the late elementary school years.

Disturbances in the thought and cognitive processes are central to the disorder. The child may complain of *delusions* (false beliefs) that something is wrong with his body—such as having cancer, or that insects are crawling on him, or that someone is controlling his thoughts. *Hallucinations* (false sensations) are more common in the auditory sphere; for example, a child may hear accusatory voices calling her a bad person. Visual hallucinations are less common, and when present by themselves, raise the possibility of an organic, toxic brain process. The hallucinations and delusions are usually refractory to persuasion by others. If others try too hard to persuade the child of the unreality of these experiences, the child may become silent about them.

As the disorder progresses, the normal connectedness of thoughts may dissolve, so that thought content becomes "loose," idiosyncratic, and loses its usual social-conversational interactive meanings. The child may become preoccupied with repetitive, privately meaningful phrases, which at first glance appear nonsensical to the normal listener. By empathic, reflective listening, however, the teacher can discern meaningful patterns and sense how the seemingly disorganized phrases and words convey anxiety and the child's attempt to master it.

An eight-year-old boy became panicky after a small fight at school. He believed someone in his household would kill him, thought his body was invaded by devils, and heard God's voice talking to him. He paced back and forth crying out, "Who am I, who am I?" (Green et al., 1984, p. 405)

Emotional (affect) expression often appears inappropriate to the activity or interpersonal situation at hand. The schizophrenic child may smile when a situation calls for sadness or seriousness, or become serious and angry when those around him are jocular. The inappropriate affect is a major factor in the child's appearing odd and withdrawn, and may be partly the result of the child's preoccupation with inner fantasies and anxieties that are stirring up the affects.

Though the onset of schizophrenia is still rare before puberty, in adolescence, particularly later adolescence, it becomes more frequent, leading to a lifetime prevalence rate of one percent (Babigian, 1985). Most adult schizophrenics had their first psychotic break in adolescence. (The old term for schizophrenia, *dementia praecox,* meant "onset in adolescence" [De Sanctis, 1973].)

All these cascading signs and symptoms usually lead to some degree of social withdrawal, as the child becomes increasingly preoccupied with her inner world. The withdrawal can be punctuated with intense outbursts of fear, anxiety, and out-of-control behavior. In contrast to the autistic child, who often has an IQ below 70, the schizophrenic child usually has an IQ above 70.

The IQ may fall during acute episodes because the psychosis can interfere with reality testing and hence with performance on psychological tests. Nor do schizophrenic children as a group have as high levels of organicity and organic brain damage as do autistics, although there may be a positive relationship between temporal lobe seizures and schizophrenic reactions (Koella & Trimble, 1982). It was once believed, however, that grand mal seizures protected a person from schizophrenia or caused remission of symptoms, which led to the use of "shock" treatments through the utilization of insulin, metrazol, and ECT.

Stress is often a factor in the eruption of overt symptoms that may have been latent for years. The advent of puberty is a major stress, bringing a need for the adolescent to move toward independence from parents and into intimacy with others, particularly the opposite sex. A fragile sense of separation from the parents may have gone unnoticed because of the child's buffering by the parents and the family. When the youth goes off to college, for instance, the unstable ego boundaries may collapse, resulting in an acute schizophrenic reaction.

Familial and parental psychopathology is much more obvious in relation to schizophrenic youth than in the autistic syndrome (Bender & Grugett, 1956). Twenty to 40 percent of the parents may themselves suffer from a schizophrenic disorder. The lower social classes are also overrepresented in schizophrenia (Weiner, 1985). Studies suggest that this is not because of recent downward mobility—that is, mentally ill individuals entering the lower socioeconomic class as a result of difficulties working and relating—but that the *weltanschauung* of the lower class individual, which often involves helplessness and a sense of being at the mercy of powerful forces, may predispose to schizophrenic mental sets (Kohn, 1976).

Classification

Currently the most widely used classification system for the schizophrenic reactions is the *Diagnostic and Statistical Manual* of the American Psychiatric Association, DSM-III (1980). Criteria for childhood schizophrenia are the same as for adult schizophrenia, which some consider appropriate since studies show the syndromes are essentially similar (Kolvin, 1971; Kolvin, Garside, & Kidd, 1971; Kolvin, Ounsted, Humphrey, & McNay, 1971; Kolvin, Richardson, & Garside, 1971; Kolvin & Roth, 1971; Green et al., 1984). Critics such as Fish and Ritvo (1979) and Cantor, Evans, Pearce, and Pizcot-Pearce (1982) say that many severely disturbed children are left out of this classification because it does not sufficiently consider developmental factors such as hallucinations and delusions that do not usually appear before age nine.

These are the DSM-III criteria for schizophrenia:

• At least one of the following—delusions, hallucinations, and loosening of thought processes

• Deterioration from a previous level of functioning such as schoolwork, social relations, and self-care

• A duration of at least six months at some time during a person's life

• Depressive and manic symptoms must be secondary and occur after the onset of psychotic symptoms

• Onset before age 45

• Not caused by organic mental disorders or mental retardation

These exacting criteria mean that children and adolescents with some but not all the criteria will not receive the diagnosis of schizophrenic reaction (as we discussed in the previous chapter regarding infantile autism). For instance, children may have acute episodes of delusions and hallucinations during severe stress (Rothstein, 1981; Burke, DelBeccaro, McCauley, & Clark, 1985). These symptoms are alarming, often resulting in emergency room visits, but they may remit suddenly when the stress is over.

By adolescence, schizophrenic symptoms can usually be subdivided into these descriptive types:

• *Disorganized*—a mixture of rapidly changing affects, delusions, hallucinations, and behavioral states, such as agitation alternating with lethargy; the patient often appears "silly" and childish (this was formerly called the "hebephrenic" type)

• *Catatonic*—mutism, muscular rigidity, and inactivity are the key features; the individual may adopt postures and poses for lengthy periods, suddenly interrupting this state with acute excitement and agitation, which, when untreated, can lead to exhaustion and death

• *Paranoid*—persecutory, grandiose delusions are prominent, such as the individual's imagining himself a king or Christ and that others are trying to destroy him; acting on these delusional fears can be extremely dangerous, as the person may kill those he suspects of persecuting him

• *Residual type*—the individual has had episodes of schizophrenia in the past, but symptoms have become muted; overt delusions, hallucinations, and other florid symptoms are not prominent, yet the patient may appear withdrawn, odd, and display loose thinking when engaging in conversation; a form of chronic schizophrenia frequently found in formerly hospitalized patients who have been discharged into the community; by late adolescence, some individuals may show signs of this chronic state (Lehman & Cancro, 1985)

Children and adolescents may have psychotic episodes related to severe depression (Freeman, Poznanski, Grossman, Buchsbaum, & Baregas, 1985), stress, sensitivity to alcohol, and use of street drugs such as angel dust (PCP) (*Clinical Psychiatry News*, 1984), or speed (amphetamine), and physical illness or injury involving the central nervous system (Burke, DelBeccaro, McCauley, & Clark, 1985). Differentiating these acute psychoses from schizophrenia can be difficult, but is usually possible because of the different premorbid history, brevity of the psychosis, lack of typical family pathology, and a return to the usual, more normal functioning when the offending agent is removed.

Etiology

Late childhood and adolescent schizophrenia merges with the larger field of adult schizophrenia; hence, our discussion of etiology will embrace the entire field of schizophrenia, albeit briefly. (For a more complete discussion, see Cancro, 1985.)

Genetic factors. Monozygotic twins show a higher concordance rate (40 to 60 percent) for schizophrenia than do dizygotic twins (10 to 15 percent), indicating that an as yet undefined genetic factor is at work.

Adoption-away studies have been carried out in Scandinavia, where careful demographic, psychiatric, and census records are kept on the entire population. There it has been possible to find out the fate of children of biological schizophrenic parents when the children have been given up for adoption in the first few months of life and raised in families where the adoptive parents were not schizophrenic. This information enables investigators to tease apart genetic, biological factors from the influence of being raised by a mentally ill, schizophrenic parent. Studies found that adopted-away children of schizophrenic parents who were followed into early adulthood developed schizophrenia at a higher rate than did a control group of adopted-away children from nonschizophrenic biological parents, suggesting again a genetic diathesis carried within the adopted child as he enters his nonschizophrenic family setting (Weiner, 1985; Kety, Rowland, Sidman, & Matthysee, 1982).

Critics of these adopted-away studies point out that the children were not placed in the adoptive families until the age of four to five months on the average. The quality of care before adoption is not known. Also, studies show that schizophrenic women who give up their children for adoption tend to be more severely ill, have a longer duration of illness, and to have had poor prenatal care as a result of more stressful social and economic conditions. Adoption-away studies have also been criticized on methodological and statistical grounds (Lidz, Blatt, & Cook, 1981). It has been pointed out that adopting away actually results in a lower rate of schizophrenia in the children than the 10 percent usually found when one parent is schizophrenic (Rosenthal, 1970). Thus, whatever genetic diathesis is demonstrated by the adoption studies, it is outweighed by social, developmental, and other factors.

Biological factors. Some chronic schizophrenic individuals show enlarged ventricles in the brain; most do not. Subtle EEG abnormalities are found in some patients but not others. New imaging techniques, such as positron emission tomography (PET), using radioactively-labeled metabolites, show a decrease in the metabolic rates in the frontal lobes and increase in left hemisphere blood flow of the brains of some schizophrenics as compared to normals (Weiner, 1985; Delisi et al., 1985; Andreasen, Dennert, Olson, & Damasio, 1982; Gur, 1984). These studies have been confounded by problems such as not sufficiently defining patient variables, dietary and physical exercise abnormalities, difficulties in replicating findings from one laboratory to the next, and uncertainty as to whether the abnormal finding is secondary to a schizophrenic illness or is primarily causative (Baron, Levitt, Gruen, Kane, & Asnis, 1984). An example of these research complexities was the discovery that a phenothiazine drug (Thorazine) brought relief for some of the more disturbing schizophrenic symptoms, such as delusions and hallucinations. Soon after this discovery, phenothiazines became (and remain) the predominant pharmacological agent used in this condition. The drug acts by blocking the neurotransmitter *dopamine*; the discovery immediately raised hopes that dopamine abnormalities might be crucial to understanding schizophrenia, but initial hopes of finding "the cause" of schizophrenia in a neurotransmitter abnormality have proven fruitless. In fact, the dopamine-blocking action of phenothiazines may be only secondary and even peripheral to basic understanding of the schizophrenic disease process (Snyder, 1976). The research direction was analogous to treating a high fever with aspirin and bringing great relief to the patient, which could conceivably raise hopes that a deficiency in the blood aspirin level had led to the fever. Of course, this is fallacious reasoning, but in areas of obscurity and uncertainty such as the etiology of schizophrenia, it is easy for investigators and clinicians to seize onto such hope (Rosenberg, 1983).

Clearly, the day is past when an investigator can reasonably hope to find one abnormality that will "explain" the diverse heterogeneous condition of schizophrenia. (A recent biological hypothesis attempts to explain the diversity of the syndrome as the product of a "slow virus" that stealthily invades and damages the central nervous system functioning in various areas of the brain over a period of decades.)

Perceptual processing disorders. Many investigators now feel it might be more fruitful to address the widespread perceptual processing disorders in the schizophrenic syndrome rather than to look for single unitary etiologic agents. Neuropsychological testing reveals widespread intersensory integration defects in many, if not most, schizophrenics (Braff & Saccuzzo, 1985; Gottschalk, 1978; Taylor & Abrams, 1984; Kwentus, Hart, Peck, & Kornstein, 1985; Wexler & Heninger, 1979). Abnormal tracking movements of the eyes have been found in many schizophrenics (Siever, Coursey, Alterman, Buchsbaum, & Murphy, 1984; Holzman, 1978). These abnormalities appear to be present between acute psychotic episodes and, hence, may be trait markers (Chapman, Chapman, Raulin, & Edell, 1978). These perceptual processing difficulties show up in parents, siblings, and relatives of schizophrenics in higher-than-expected rates. The difficulties in processing sensory data may be one of the vulnerabilities that leads to the more obvious perceptual distortions such as hallucinations during acute phases of the illness.

Family dysfunction. Goldfarb (1980) was one of the first investigators in the field of childhood schizophrenia to systematically study parent and family characteristics. He showed that parents of schizophrenic children with major signs of organic brain damage did not show the high levels of psychopathology as did parents of schizophrenic children without organic handicaps. He suggested that parent-child conflicts were more etiologically significant in the latter group. Though a later study failed to replicate these earlier findings, Goldfarb still demonstrated that 18 to 25 percent of parents of schizophrenic children were schizophrenic themselves.

Recent studies of young children of schizophrenic parents show them to have little more pathology than other children at the same socioeconomic level (Sameroff, Barocas, & Seifer, 1984), though they underwent more difficult birth processes (McNeill & Kaij, 1984). The eventually high level of schizophrenia in these children (around 10 percent) results from adolescent and adult onset of the syndrome. Children of schizophrenic parents may do better in their early years than do children of depressed parents (McNeill & Kaij, 1984). This finding suggests that parental depression is more sweeping and damaging than parental schizophrenia in its effects on parental attention and caretaking efforts.

Clinicians and researchers describe the faulty communications and double binding that enmeshes the schizophrenic adolescent in the disordered family unit (Reichard & Tillman, 1950; Wynne & Singer, 1963; Lidz & Fleck, 1985). They do not claim that the disturbed communication is "the only cause" of schizophrenia, but that it may trigger and facilitate the overt syndrome in susceptible individuals (Reiss, 1976). Some say, however, that these findings of communication disorders in schizophrenic families do not hold up well under tightly controlled experimental conditions (Hirsch & Leff, 1971).

Developmental perspective. Whether developmental vulnerabilities are based in genetic, biological, biochemical, perceptual, or familial factors, their effect is seen in the child and adolescent's development of maladaptive and adaptive defenses, identifications, and unique coping styles (Kernberg, 1980). Studies of these vulnerabilities seek commonalities among schizophrenic individuals. The developmental perspective complements group studies by emphasizing unique, idiosyncratic, individual differences; nonetheless, there are some commonalities among developmental factors in schizophrenic youths (Bullard, 1984).

There tends to be regression to earlier levels of functioning in many areas of the personality during schizophrenic episodes. There is loss of reality testing and a return to the more magical, omnipotent modes of cognition of the young child. The child of two or three years of age believes that thoughts are equivalent to actions and that others can know his thoughts. Hence, the schizophrenic can be afraid that others are reading or controlling his mind. The overly strict and punitive conscience that is normal in the young child reappears in the delusions and hallucinations of the schizophrenic; for instance, auditory hallucinations in the form of voices demanding the death of the patient contain primitive, punitive moral demands. Separation-individuation issues reemerge during the psychotic regressions as the patient may believe he is attached to others and that bodily boundaries are distorted and fragmented. Fear of engulfment by others, a normal passing fear of the young child, can be a major factor in the schizoid withdrawal of some schizophrenic patients.

Interventions

The same basic array of interventions described for infantile autism are applicable for the child and adolescent schizophrenic; however, the schizophrenic youth's better development in language, cognition, and social relationship skills means that treatment can often start at more advanced levels of verbal interaction, group activities, and academic programming. Most schizophrenic youth live in the community and attend public schools. The advent of tranquilizers (phenothiazines) and the loss of long-term milieu treatment facilities mean that most schizophrenic children and adolescents are treated within the family and the regular school system while receiving some type of supportive or intensive outpatient psychotherapy and drug management from a nearby mental health facility.

Educational interventions. Many schizophrenic youth, particularly those with adolescent onset, have functioned in regular classrooms prior to their overt illness. If sufficient remission is achieved through treatment, the youth may be able to return to the regular school setting and function without specific school intervention. Others may require supportive counseling from guidance personnel. Liaison between school personnel and the psychiatric treatment team is crucial to work out these individualized programs.

The perceptual processing disorders mentioned earlier may be subtle and not grossly evident in school performance. It is necessary to manage outbursts of psychotic thinking or socially bizarre behavior in the school setting, because they can jeopardize the patient's remaining in the community. School personnel sometimes become anxious at such outbursts and ask that the child be rehospitalized or removed from the school. Often, team conferences, emergency psychotherapeutic intervention, change in antipsychotic medication, or working out a family crisis will allow the youth to continue in regular school. School personnel can collaborate with the child's therapist in encouraging, educating, and, occasionally, insisting that the youth take his "upset" or "crazy" thoughts to the therapist and not allow them to intrude in the normal school setting. Patients need to learn to wall off the schizophrenic symptomatology to function in a normal setting.

For other schizophrenic children, particularly those with onset during the elementary school years or earlier, there may be such extensive personality dysfunction that special programming in the schools is necessary. Just as with infantile autism, the general programming principle is to ascertain where the child is socially and educationally and match the program to the level of the child's abilities.

Milieu therapy and hospital treatment. As described in the previous chapter, inpatient treatment for schizophrenic youth is primarily short-term (30 days to 3 months), with the goal of returning the child to the family and community as soon as possible. This is the treatment of choice in many situations; at other times, the child and family can be helped further by a longer stay (Szurek & Berlin, 1973). Thus, some children may be forced back into the community before they are able to function adequately in the family and school setting.

Some communities have day programs and other types of partial care as "step-down" intermediate programs to provide educational and other services for children leaving inpatient settings. Most communities do not offer intermediate care, however, and the child must reenter his family and the public school directly. A well-known example of a day facility for schizophrenic youth is the League School in New York City. Young children can be admitted to an intermediate program and treated for years without necessarily requiring inpatient treatment (Fenichel, Freedman, & Klapper, 1960; Fenichel, 1976).

Unfortunately, by the late teens or early twenties, some schizophrenic youth have failed to respond to treatment—either because it is insufficient or because of factors within the patient and the milieu. These youths may join the ranks of the chronic schizophrenics and require some type of continuous supportive care, often for years or decades. This situation has reached crisis proportions in some larger urban communities as the deinstitutionalization movement has begun to turn out large numbers of chronically mentally ill individuals into the streets without providing for sufficient community follow-up care.

Behavior therapy. Target symptoms such as inappropriate social gestures or bizarre verbalizations can be treated with behavioral therapy, as described in the previous chapter in relation to autism.

Medication and other organic therapies. The major tranquilizers are the drugs of first choice in treating acute schizophrenic symptomatology. Improvement can often be dramatic; an agitated, destructive, bizarre, delusional adolescent in the emergency room can become calm and conversational within minutes after injection of phenothiazine antipsychotic medication such as Thorazine or the butyrophenone Haldol. The tranquilizers are usually given in sufficiently high doses to bring about remission or reduction of the symptoms, then gradually tapered to lower doses and eventually discontinued. It was once thought that all schizophrenic individuals should be maintained on long-term drug therapy, but it now appears that only about 50 percent are helped by long-term medication regimes. Tranquilizers primarily reduce symptoms and anxiety but do not "cure" the basic structural fault that gave rise to the schizophrenic process (Simpson & May, 1985). Electroshock therapy is occasionally used when tranquilizers fail to calm an agitated, deteriorating patient.

As noted in Chapter 10, the long-term side effects of the phenothiazines and butyrophenones, such as tardive dyskinesia, can be alarming and cause as much or more distress than the schizophrenic process itself. The longer the duration of tranquilizer therapy and, hence, the greater total dosage of ingested drug, the greater the frequency of tardive dyskinesia. Other side effects, such as lethargy, hypotension (a fall in blood pressure), and muscle tightness can be problematic. Some male adolescents are intolerant of the sense of being "manacled" or "tied down" by tranquilizers and may panic when given medication. Cumulative experience over decades indicates that judicious use of tranquilizers to control active schizophrenic symptoms (for example, delusions and hallucinations) combined with long-term psychosocial treatment programs (individual, group, family, and institutional therapy) to support and enhance adaptive living skills results in the best treatment outcomes (Liberman, 1985).

Psychotherapy. In the early 1900s, Freud said schizophrenics could not be treated by psychoanalytic psychotherapeutic methods because they could not invest the therapist with "transference"—an emotional investment that had once been directed toward other important people in the patient's life. Hence, Freud believed the schizophrenic remained too involved with the self (was too autistic) to be reached by therapeutic treatment relationships. Freud actually, however, had little direct experience with schizophrenics. When early psychoanalysts tried to treat schizophrenics, they discovered to their surprise that instead of a lack of transference, there was too much of it! The patients invested and sometimes engulfed their therapists with primitive fantasies, casting the therapist in the role of lover, parent, magical savior, or persecutor. By the late 1930s, several intuitively gifted psychodynamic clinicians such as Freida Fromm-Reichmann (1948, 1954) were beginning to treat schizophrenics intensively, usually in hospital settings. Through long effort, they found that a reality-oriented treatment relationship can be established with many but not all schizophrenics. By providing support for the beleagured ego functions, such as poor reality testing, therapists could help patients verbalize their primitive fantasies and annihilation fears and learn that these thoughts and feelings will not destroy the patient or the therapist. The patients often perceived their caretakers, such as the mother, as malignant and destructive and came to fear that the therapist was also. Repeatedly verbalizing and experiencing these projections and distortions within the consistency and safety of the therapeutic relationship allowed the

growth of greater reality testing and improvement of ego functioning (Elkisch, 1971).

Ekstein and his co-workers became the leading spokesmen in the 1950s for intensive psychoanalytic treatment of schizophrenic children, best carried out within the supportive milieu of a long-term hospital facility. The ability to work with the child's metaphors and to actually enter the child's fantasy world was crucial for eventual success. The child's psychotic fantasies were viewed as communicative metaphors conveying the child's perception of the world to the therapist. If the metaphor, often in the form of a psychotic fantasy, was viewed as "nonsense" and maladaptive, the child would not share it and instead would become more distant from the therapist (Ekstein & Wallerstein, 1954, 1956; Ekstein, 1980; Browning, 1984; Rosenfeld & Sprince, 1965).

Researchers now believe that a combination of supportive and insight psychotherapy in combination with appropriate phenothiazines provides the best long-term treatment for patients with schizophrenic reactions. The therapy may last for years, varying in frequency from several sessions per week to once a month, depending on the patient's needs and the therapist's orientation, skills, and availability. It is usually essential to work therapeutically with parents and other family members who form the vital support system (Schulz, 1985; Liberman, 1985).

When the family is too disturbed to provide a sufficiently supportive milieu, other arrangements must be found for the child or adolescent schizophrenic. Besides hospital and day care settings, foster care may be necessary to allow the patient to continue in outpatient therapy and school. For patients with sufficient social skills, group homes and halfway houses may provide a supportive environment during temporary crises or disruptions of their home life or as halfway points in the patient's move toward eventual adult independence.

Outcome

The best prognosis occurs in childhood and adolescent schizophrenics who have had the better premorbid development and family history. The worst prognosis occurs in those who have had more damaged development (such as severe schizoid behavior and neuropsychological delays), and more pathological family structure before the overt schizophrenic illness (Kydd & Werry, 1972). After a definitive schizophrenic process has set in, it is difficult to talk of "cure" or complete attainment of normalcy. The patient gets better or worse depending on the efficacy of treatment, integrity of the social support system, and the patient's own life skills and how well he can maintain them during and between acute episodes. As with infantile autism, there appear to be unknown factors that tip the balance for ill or for good; some patients may improve almost spontaneously and function surprisingly well, whereas others, despite intensive treatment efforts, undergo a malignant, regressive process. Decades of research do show, however, that the majority of schizophrenics can be significantly helped by appropriate treatment.

BORDERLINE PERSONALITY DISORDER

The concept of "borderline" arose to describe a group of children, adolescents, and adults who did not fit the usual picture of psychosis and schizophrenia, yet at the same time did not fall under the rubric of the higher-level functioning neuroses. Neither did they show the stability of character pathology found in conduct disorders. Instead, they showed features of all three syndromes, yet never crossed the "border" into one of these well-known general classifications. That such an awkward word as *borderline* should achieve the status of a major diagnosis should not beguile us into underestimating the importance and frequency of this group of individuals for the clinician and the educator (Robson, 1983).

Description

This description of a borderline child also covers the basic features found in the borderline adolescent and adult.

The child may appear normal when the environment is providing sufficient structure, that is, "things are going just right." When the child encounters a disappointment, embarrassment, or criticism, or when a situation becomes unstructured, the borderline child may experience acute regression as manifested by a wide variety of behaviors and symptoms. These include angry outbursts, sudden impulsive behaviors out of proportion to the situational context, such as running away and attacking others, destroying objects, or hurting herself. If the child cannot muster sufficient inner resources to halt the regression or if significant others cannot respond sufficiently to soothe and contain the child, the regression may deepen until there is a loss of contact with reality and the child may appear psychotic. These psychoticlike episodes can terrify both the child and those around him, such as teachers and peers. Once the borderline child regains inner and external control, there can be a surprisingly sudden cessation of the psychoticlike behavior and resumption of the almost normal functioning of before the upset. Herein lies some of the puzzle of this syndrome. These children do not have the ongoing, often aloof, withdrawn, pervasive disorder of the schizophrenic child. The borderline child's functioning is variable and often responds quickly to interpersonal contact with others. In fact, the borderline person is frightened of aloneness and quite dependent upon and needful of others.

In developmental terms, borderline persons are not adequately psychologically separated from their primary caretakers, usually the mother, so that they remain desperate for contact with others. When alone, they appear unable to recall sufficiently the emotional presence of a caretaker, which exacerbates the anxiety and disruptive behaviors that are in part maladaptive attempts to regain contact with the need-supplying person. Yet, at the same time, the close contact stirs up intense longings and anxiety over merging with the maternal representation in the mind. These merger fears result in feelings that one's body boundaries are dissolving, leading to the increasing levels of panic called *annihilation* or *separation anxiety* (Rinsley, 1980).

The borderline person's responses to psychological testing dramatically illustrate these issues (Arnow & Cooper, 1984; Leichtman & Nathan, 1983). Clinical psychologists usually begin testing sessions with the more structured Wechsler IQ test. The modal borderline patient usually functions appropriately during the IQ test and attains an IQ within the normal range. No neuropsychological deficits, sometimes found among schizophrenic children, are specifically related to the borderline syndrome.

As the testing moves to more unstructured tests, such as the Thematic Apperception Test (TAT), the borderline vulnerabilities begin to emerge. There is less structure in these test stimuli for the child to use to control inner anxieties. The more personal human responses required in the TAT tap into the borderline's intense concerns, needs, and fears of others. Instead of using higher-level neurotic defenses (such as intellectualization) to deal with the emerging anxiety, there is instead a breakdown or failure of defenses. More primitive fantasies and dangers, such as fear of death or loss of ego boundaries, emerge in the TAT stories. When testing moves to the least-structured tests, such as the Rorschach, the borderline patient's thinking processes may become loose and disorganized, and he may be unable to maintain

perceptual control and distance over the inkblot stimuli. At this point, the borderline child may definitely appear psychotic and is sometimes unable to continue with the test. Children may flee the testing room or attempt to destroy the "dangerous" testing materials. Yet, when the testing is terminated and the child walks out of the office, he may suddenly appear reconstituted, having regained his usual mode of pretest functioning. What happens in testing is a microcosm of what happens day in and day out in the child's family, school, and peer life.

This variability of functioning gives the borderline youth a reputation of being difficult, stormy, and impetuous. As with all the syndromes, however, there are degrees of psychopathology. Some borderline individuals have greater capacity to ward off anxieties and can function well in major areas of life. Some can perform at high levels in the work arena, achieving status in the scientific and business worlds, yet suffer in their intimate personal relationships because of their anxieties and needs. Some cope by giving up close relations with others, having learned that pain and terror will result. Chronic depression can accompany and result from their despair and failures.

Epidemiological studies are virtually nonexistent because of recent recognition of the syndrome in its variable, confusing appearance in everyday life. Studies so far have dealt only with hospitalized and outpatient psychiatric populations, and contain all the biases of selection resulting from the study of clinic populations. The syndrome is apparently much more common than schizophrenia and may have a prevalence of four to five percent in the general population. Sex differences are unclear, though the borderline state may be more common in girls.

Emotional problems and borderline features are quite common in the parents of borderline youth. Constitutional factors that could compound the difficulties with separa-

tion of the child from the parents are still unclear. No specific neurological abnormalities
have been found in borderline children (Marcus, Ousiew, & Hans, 1983).

Classification

The only classification in general use today
appeared for the first time in the most recent
edition of the *Diagnostic and Statistical Manual*
of the American Psychiatric Association
(1980). There was considerable debate as to
whether to include the "borderline" category. Many felt it had not been sufficiently
defined and clarified; others felt the process
of clarification could be facilitated by including the borderline state in DSM-III, which
would then allow for necessary revisions in
the diagnostic criteria in the forthcoming
DSM-IV.

A diagnosis of Borderline Personality Disorder must meet at least five of these criteria:

- Impulsivity or unpredictability
- Pattern of unstable, intense interpersonal relationships characterized by idealiza-
tion, devaluation, and manipulation
- Inappropriate, intensely angry outbursts
- Identity disturbances, such as uncertainties of self boundaries, gender and sexual
identity, and work goals
- Emotional instability and rapidly fluctuating moods
- Intolerance of being alone
- Physically self-damaging acts, such as
suicidal gestures, fights, and recurrent accidents
- Chronic feelings of emptiness and
boredom

The borderline diagnosis was placed under the general category of *personality disorder*
rather than *psychosis*. While psychotic episodes are common (even though psychotic
episodes did not become one of the final diagnostic criteria), most clinicians believe that
psychosis is not the crucial feature of the
syndrome. Instead, the central feature is a
disturbance in characterological structure
and functioning; psychoses are only secondary to a temporary breakdown of the usual
characterological modes of adapting (Gunderson & Kolb, 1978; Sheehy, Goldsmith, &
Charles, 1980). Some believe the borderline
mode of character functioning is quite stable
over time and is not a way station to another
syndrome such as schizophrenic reaction,
conduct disturbance, depression, and so
forth (Gunderson & Elliott, 1985). The jury is
still out on this question, however, as others
continue to report cases of borderline youths
crossing the "border" and becoming clearly
schizophrenic (Kestenbaum, 1983).

Others believe the borderline personality
structure is a common mode of functioning
intertwined with other syndromes, such as
depression, schizophrenia, conduct disturbances, and antisocial personality disorders
and hence does not merit a discrete diagnostic category of its own. For instance, a high
percentage of borderline adolescents and
adults also suffer from major depressions
(Carroll, Greden, & Feinberg, 1981; McNamara et al., 1984; Pope et al., 1983; Stone,
1980). Chronically delinquent and antisocial
groups also have high numbers of borderline
individuals (Alessi, McManus, Brickman, &
Grapentine, 1984).

To further complicate matters, the borderline concept began primarily as a clinical, in-
ferential, dynamic formulation of a particular
type of personality functioning that clinicians
used in variable contexts (Berg, 1982; A.
Freud, 1969). The DSM-III attempts to define
syndromes by observable manifestations,
such as symptoms and behaviors, that will
lead to acceptable levels of interrater reliability. Recent studies indicate that the two views
of borderline—the broad psychodynamic
clinical formulation and the DSM-III's more
focused descriptive criteria—may have some
congruence (Kernberg et al., 1981). Others
continue to be skeptical (Nuetzel, 1985).

Cohen and his co-workers (1983) believe
the DSM-III criteria are unsuitable for chil-

dren and so have devised their own criteria that take into account the child's developmental level. Their classification scheme emphasizes neuromaturational and attentional difficulties which tie the borderline syndrome into the Attentional Deficit Disorder. This, in turn, opens up many neurobiological research possibilities.

One of the more clinically helpful classification schemes (Pine, 1974, 1980, 1983) stresses that the overt borderline syndrome can arise from several psychodynamic states. Hence, Pine emphasizes that there is not *a* borderline child but *several types* of borderline children. Some children regress suddenly, changing from normal to odd-appearing, without exhibiting massive anxiety. Here the sudden regressions relieve anxiety even though the outside world is anxious about what has happened. Other children become disorganized and borderline because of external stress. We often find this in patients from highly stressed, socially disorganized families. These children can appear almost normal when placed in a benign environment. Other children maintain a chronically high level of internalized ego deviance despite changes in the external environment. These children may appear worse in a benign environment because of the revelation of their inner pathology. Sometimes a child adopts and partially internalizes a parent's psychosis to maintain a tie with the need-supplying object (*folie à deux*). Separating the child from the parent and placement in a benign environment often bring about dramatic changes toward normality (Simonds & Glenn, 1976). Another group of children adopt massive, developmentally damaging defenses such as mutism or pseudoimbecility at an early age. These defenses result in severe failures in learning and ego limitations and deviance. This type of child may appear odd, brittle, and have many features of the borderline syndrome. Schizoid, aloof children can be quite withdrawn and preoccupied with a vivid inner fantasy life, yet not be overtly psychotic. The DSM-III placed this type of schizoid child in a separate diagnostic group, but Pine believes it can be fruitful to include this child in his broad perspective of borderline. Some children use a primitive, massive defense of splitting, resulting in an appearance of normality on the surface while they are plagued with a murderous, vengeful fantasy life. These are the "good" children who may go beserk and kill.

Pine's broad conceptual scheme is clinically valuable, though quite distinct from the DSM-III diagnosis of borderline, which is more rigorous and symptom-based.

Etiology

The principal etiology is thought to be a developmental failure in the psychological separation of the borderline child from the mother. Evidence for this conclusion comes from clinical and psychological test data indicating that the borderline child's primary concerns are dyadic; that is, there is almost exclusive emphasis on the relationship of the child vis-à-vis the caretaker and whether the caretaker will supply vital needs (Rosenfeld & Sprince, 1963; Anthony & Gilpin, 1981). High-level concerns with sexual possessiveness and competitiveness (Oedipal-level issues) are not prominent in the borderline child's thoughts and fantasies. The developmental fixation at the level of separation-individuation is accompanied by a fragile sense of self and autonomy, difficulties being alone, and a wide range of ego limitations in the control of emotions, conscience functioning, and ability to relate to others (Adler & Buie, 1979). IQ and cognitive abilities may be affected, but this factor is much less prominent than in the schizophrenic and autistic syndromes (Cohen, Shaywitz, Young, & Shaywitz, 1983). The difficulties of the mother as primary caretaker in providing a sufficiently appropriate emotional climate for adequate separation of the child are usually obvious. Excessive struggles, failures in timing, and unpredictable availability are common features of the maternal side of the separation-individuation equation. (As we emphasized in Chapter 10, this is not "blaming" the parent, but only indicating the crucial role the parent plays in the child's navigation through the shoals of the separation-individuation phase.)

Though constitutional factors are still unclear, each borderline child brings her own strengths, style, and vulnerabilities into the separation-individuation phase. Chance factors, such as a severe physical illness of the child or a parent or the death of a parent, may critically tip the balance of developmental factors toward pathology. Socioeconomic stresses, sibling configurations, and presence or absence of the father all play their role, though none specifically cause the borderline syndrome. All these factors feed into and cause stresses in the final common pathway, the separation-individuation process between parent and child. One must keep in mind that this process takes place inside the mind of the child in terms of mental representations of himself as separate from the mother, as well as in the observable external world of daily interactions between mother and child.

Borderline conditions in children are usually clearly traceable to the second and third years of life (Rinsley, 1984). This is not an intermittent condition, nor does it arise anew in the school years. It is a chronic, characterological condition that has its onset in the early years of character formation.

The finding that many borderline individuals also have major depression, conduct disturbance, and other syndromes does not mean that one causes the other. Some believe that failure in successful mastery of the separation from the mother leaves the borderline individual suffering from a core of abandonment depression—feelings of hopelessness and impotent rage at the failure to become an autonomous person. This core depression usually emerges in the course of intensive therapy, perhaps most easily observed in an inpatient setting that provides sufficient

therapeutic controls over impulsive, self-destructive behavior. Emergence of this depression and its eventual mastery are thought to herald a spurt in ego development and a successful outcome of treatment. Investigators have not yet linked this depressive core with the overt major depressions found in many borderline individuals.

Interventions

The principal treatment for borderline children and adolescents is intensive psychotherapy with concomitant parent and family therapy (Lewis & Brown, 1979). If there are sufficient family strengths, therapy can be carried out productively on an outpatient basis. Often a period of inpatient treatment is necessary to contain out-of-control destructive behavior and to allow the youth the opportunity to experience and verbalize the intense rage and depression that has fueled the use of maladaptive defenses (Hanson, Bemporad, & Smith, 1983). Masterson (1980) says his series of borderline adolescents required a minimum of nine months of structured inpatient care to bring about sufficient change to enable the youths to enter productive outpatient treatment.

The school plays a crucial role in outpatient and inpatient therapeutic programs (Schimmer, 1983). The structure provided by the teacher and classroom organization shores up the borderline child's fragile ego structure and helps contain turbulent feelings and fantasies. The borderline youth is generally in touch with reality and relates readily with others, and is thus often amenable to educational clarification and confrontation of his problematic and disruptive behaviors. For instance, borderline individuals tend to "split" those around them into "all good" and "all bad" people, which can cause dissension among the school staff as they start to blame each other rather than firmly confronting and helping the child to tone down the splitting (Adler, 1973; Akhtar & Byrne, 1983; Grala, 1980). A confident teacher and firm school structure can provide a foundation for the child's general functioning, a counterbalance for a disturbed family environment, and hold the boat steady while therapy is taking hold. Sometimes the school's firmness in insisting on treatment is the only thing that will make it possible for some families to get into therapy and stay in. Psychotherapy for the borderline child and parents is lengthy and often fraught with crises, requiring patience and cooperation between the school and clinic.

Environmental issues and accompanying syndromes that inflame and exacerbate the borderline symptoms may require additional specific treatment. A chaotic, destructive social situation may require school, social service, and legal intervention. Severe depression may be helped by antidepressant medications. Borderline children who are prone to acute psychotic episodes can be helped by phenothiazines such as Thorazine to alleviate the psychotic upheaval (Cole, Solomon, Gunderson, Sunderland, & Simmonds, 1984; Petti, 1983).

Outcome

Systematic outcome studies have not been done because of difficulties in obtaining consensus on the diagnosis and the recent interest in the borderline conditions. Clinicians generally report that if the patient and family remain in treatment long enough, there is usually improvement, though the characterologic vulnerability to borderline regressions usually remains. Masterson (1980) reported that 75 percent of his adolescent borderline patients achieved moderate to significant long-term gains, whereas only 25 percent did not, although some question his broad use of the borderline diagnosis to cover many conditions such as anorexia.

Fortunate life circumstances and the patient's ability to use social supports improve prognosis. Borderline children have been reported to become schizophrenic in adolescence. The appearance of antisocial symptoms and use of drugs and alcohol as a borderline child enters adolescence make treatment more difficult and prognosis poorer.

CONCLUSION

Of all the problems of children and adolescents, childhood and adolescent schizophrenia and borderline personality disorder are among the most puzzling and frightening. Children with these problems often have the capacity to appear almost normal—then, with little or no warning, regress to primitive levels of functioning. These sudden fluctuations of mood and level of functioning have caused many professionals to avoid working with them. Historically, these youngsters have been viewed as among the most severely handicapped, and indeed, some of them are; however, with the advent of modern psychotropic drugs, sensitive and varied therapies, and appropriate educational services, the majority of these children are being helped to cope and function more effectively.

Like other disorders, these conditions require multimodal interventions. The children usually require outpatient or inpatient psychiatric treatment, often including medication trials, special education services, family counseling, and vocational and recreational interventions. Because of the children's tendencies to see people as either good or bad with no in-between, and because of their propensity to transfer their internalized perceptions of authority or nurturing figures onto other figures, they can be extremely difficult to work with. They frequently pit worker against worker and often project a sense of helplessness and despair so believable that it can be difficult to see how much they are distorting the world. It is thus especially important for professionals who work with these children to collaborate on shared goals.

REFERENCES

Adler, G. (1973). Hospital treatment of borderline patients. *American Journal of Psychiatry, 130,* 32–35.

Adler, G., & Buie, D. H. (1979). Aloneness and borderline psychopathology: The possible relevance of child development issues. *International Journal of Psychoanalysis, 60,* 83–96.

Akhtar, S., & Byrne, J. P. (1983). The concept of splitting and its clinical relevance. *American Journal of Psychiatry, 140,* 1013–1016.

Alessi, N. E., McManus, M., Brickman, A., & Grapentine, L. (1984). Suicidal behavior among serious juvenile offenders. *American Journal of Psychiatry, 141,* 286–287.

American Psychiatric Association. (1980). *Diagnostic and Statistical Manual of Mental Disorders,* 3rd ed. New York: APA.

Andreasen, N. C., Dennert, J. W., Olsen, S. A., & Damasio, A. R. (1982). *American Journal of Psychiatry, 139,* 427–430.

Anthony, E. J., & Gilpin, D. C. (Eds.). (1981). *The borderline child: Part III. Three further clinical faces of childhood.* Jamaica, NY: Spectrum.

Arnow, D., & Cooper, S. H. (1984). The borderline patient's regression on the Rorschach Test. *Bulletin of the Menninger Clinic, 48,* 25–36.

Babigian, H. M. (1985). Schizophrenia: Epidemiology. In H. I. Kaplan & B. J. Sadock (Eds.), *Comprehensive textbook of psychiatry,* 4th ed. (Vol. 1, pp. 643–649). Baltimore, MD: Williams & Wilkins.

Baron, M., Levitt, M., Gruen, R., Kane, J., & Asnis, L. (1984). Platelet monoamine oxidase activity and genetic vulnerability to schizophrenia. *American Journal of Psychiatry, 141,* 836–842.

Bender, L. (1967). Theory and treatment of childhood schizophrenia. *Acta Paedopsychiatrica, 34,* 298–307.

Bender, L., & Grugett, A. E. (1956). A study of certain epidemiological problems in a group of children with childhood schizophrenia. *American Journal of Orthopsychiatry, 26,* 131–145.

Berg, M. (1982). Borderline psychopathology—on the frontiers of psychiatry. *Bulletin of the Menninger Clinic, 46,* 113–129.

Braff, D. L., & Saccuzzo, D. P. (1985). The time course of information-processing deficits in schizophrenia. *American Journal of Psychiatry, 142,* 170–174.

Browning, D. L. (1984). Control and transitional reality in the treatment of a psychotic child. *Bulletin of the Menninger Clinic, 48,* 141–154.

Bullard, D. (1984). Researchers identify subgroups of schizophrenic patients based on developmental characteristics. *Psychiatric News,* Oct. 5.

Burke, P., DelBeccaro, M., McCauley, E., & Clark, C. (1985). Hallucinations in children. *Journal of the American Academy of Child Psychiatry, 24,* 71–75.

Campbell, M., & Green, W. H. (1985). Pervasive developmental disorders of childhood. In H. I. Kaplan & B. J. Sadock (Eds.), *Comprehensive textbook of psychiatry,* 4th ed. (Vol. 2). Baltimore, MD: Williams & Wilkins.

Cancro, R. (1985). History and overview of schizophrenia. In H. I. Kaplan & B. J. Sadock (Eds.), *Comprehensive textbook of psychiatry,* 4th ed. (Vol. 1). Baltimore, MD: Williams & Wilkins.

Cantor, S., Evans, J., Pearce, J., & Pizcot-Pearce, T. (1982). Childhood schizophrenia: Present but not accounted for. *American Journal of Psychiatry, 139,* 758–762.

Carroll, B. J., Greden, J. F., & Feinberg, M. (1981). Neuroendocrine evaluation of depression in borderline patients. *Psychiatric Clinics of North America, 4,* 89–99.

Chapman, L. J., Chapman, J. P., Raulin, M. L., & Edell, W. S. (1978). Schizotypy and thought disorder as a high risk approach to schizophrenia. In G. Serban (Ed.), *Cognitive defects in the development of mental illness* (pp. 351–360). New York: Brunner/Mazel.

Cohen, D. J., Shaywitz, S. E., Young, J. G., & Shaywitz, B. A. (1983). Borderline syndromes and attention deficit disorders in childhood: Clinical and neurochemical perspectives. In K. S. Robson (Ed.), *The borderline child* (pp. 197–222) New York: McGraw-Hill.

Cole, J. O., Solomon, M., Gunderson, J., Sunderland, P., III, & Simmonds, P. (1984). Drug therapy in borderline patients. *Comprehensive Psychiatry, 25* (3), 249–254.

Delisi, L. E., Buchsbaum, M. S., Holcomb, H. H., Dowling-Zimmerman, S., van Kammen, D. P., Carpenter, W., Kessler, R., & Cohen, R. M. (1985). Clinical correlates of decreased anteroposterior metabolic gradients in positron emission tomography (PET) of schizophrenic patients. *American Journal of Psychiatry, 142,* 78–81.

DeSanctis, S. (1973). On some varieties of Dementia Praecox. In S. A. Szurek & I. N. Berlin (Eds.), *Clinical studies in childhood psychosis* (pp. 31–47) New York: Brunner/Mazel. Also in Howells, J. G. (Ed.). *Modern perspectives in international child psychiatry* (pp. 590–609). New York: Brunner/Mazel.

Ekstein, R. (1980). Concerning the psychology and psychotherapeutic treatment of borderline and psychotic conditions of childhood. In S. I. Greenspan & G. H. Pollock (Eds.), *The course of life: Psychoanalytic contributions toward understanding personality development. Vol. II. Latency, adolescence and youth.* Washington, DC: National Institute of Mental Health.

Ekstein, R., Mandelbaum, A., & Wallerstein, J. (1959). Countertransference in the residential treatment of children: Treatment failures. In *Psychoanalytic Study of the Child*. New York: International Universities Press.

Ekstein, R., & Wallerstein, J. (1954). Observations on the psychology of borderline and psychotic children. *Psychoanalytic Study of the Child, 9*, 344–369.

Ekstein, R., & Wallerstein, J. (1956). Observations on the psychotherapy of borderline and psychotic children. *Psychoanalytic Study of the Child, 11*, 303–311.

Elkisch, P. (1971). Initiating separation-individuation in the simultaneous treatment of a child and his mother. In J. B. McDevitt & C. G. Settlage (Eds.), *Separation-individuation: Essays in honor of Margaret S. Mahler* (pp. 356–376). New York: International Universities Press.

Fenichel, C. (1976). Psychoeducational approaches for seriously disturbed children in the classroom. In W. J. Long, W. C. Morse, & R. G. Newman (Eds.), *Conflict in the classroom*, 3rd ed. (pp. 223–229). Belmont, CA: Wadsworth.

Fenichel, C., Freedman, A., & Klapper, Z. (1960). A day school for schizophrenic children. *American Journal of Orthopsychiatry, 30*, 130–148.

Fish, B., & Ritvo, E. R. (1979). Psychoses of childhood. In J. Noshpitz (Ed.), *Basic handbook of child psychiatry* (Vol. 2). New York: Basic Books.

Freeman, L. N., Poznanski, E. O., Grossman, J. A., Buchsbaum, Y. Y., & Baregas, M. E. (1985). Psychotic and depressed children: A new entity. *Journal of the American Academy of Child Psychiatry, 24*, 95–102.

Freud, A. (1969). The assessment of borderline cases. In *The Writings of Anna Freud* (Vol. 5). New York: International Universities Press.

Fromm-Reichmann, F. (1948). Notes on the development of treatment of schizophrenics by psychoanalytic psychotherapy. *Psychiatry, 11*, 263–272.

Fromm-Reichmann, F. (1954). Psychotherapy of schizophrenia. *American Journal of Psychiatry, 111*, 410–419.

Goldfarb, W. (1980). Pervasive developmental disorders of childhood. In H. I. Kaplan, A. M. Freedman, & B. J. Sadock (Eds.), *Comprehensive textbook of psychiatry*, 3rd ed. (Vol. 3), pp. 2527–2537). Baltimore, MD: Williams & Wilkins.

Gottschalk, L. H. (1978). Cognitive defect in the schizophrenic syndrome as assessed by speech patterns. In G. Serban (Ed.), *Cognitive defects in the development of mental illness* (pp. 314–350). New York: Brunner/Mazel.

Grala, C. (1980). The concept of splitting and its manifestations on the Rorschach Test. *Bulletin of the Menninger Clinic, 44*, 253–271.

Green, W. H., Campbell, M., Hardesty, A. S., Grega, D. M., Padron-Gayol, M., Shell, J., & Erlenmeyer-Kimling, L. (1984). A comparison of schizophrenic and autistic children. *Journal of the American Academy of Child Psychiatry, 23*, 399–409.

Gunderson, J. G., & Elliott, G. R. (1985). The interface between borderline personality disorder and affective disorder. *American Journal of Psychiatry, 142*, 277–288.

Gunderson, J. G., & Kolb, J. E. (1978). Discriminating features of borderline patients. *American Journal of Psychiatry, 135*, 792–796.

Gur, R. E. (1984). Left hemisphere overactivity in schizophrenics. *Clinical Psychiatry News, 12* (5), 16.

Hanson, G., Bemporad, J. R., & Smith, H. F. (1983). The day and residential treatment of the borderline child. In K. S. Robson (Ed.), *The borderline child*. New York: McGraw-Hill.

Hirsch, S. R., & Leff, J. P. (1971). Parental abnormalities of verbal communication in the transmission of schizophrenia. *Psychological Medicine, 1*, 118–127.

Holzman, P. S. (1978). Cognitive improvement and cognitive stability: Towards a theory of thought disorders. In G. Serban (Ed.), *Cognitive defects in the development of mental illness* (pp. 361–376). New York: Brunner/Mazel.

Kernberg, O. F., Goldstein, E. G., Carr, C. A., Hunt, H. F., Bauer, S. F., & Blumenthal, R. (1981). Diagnosing borderline personality. *Journal of Nervous & Mental Disease, 169*, 225–281.

Kernberg, P. F. (1980). Childhood psychosis: A psychoanalytic perspective. In S. I. Greenspan & G. H. Pollock (Eds.), *The course of life: Psychoanalytic contributions toward understanding personality development. Vol. 1. Infancy and early childhood*. Washington, DC: National Institute of Mental Health.

Kestenbaum, C. J. (1983). The borderline child at risk for major psychiatric disorder in adult life. In K. S. Robson (Ed.), *The borderline child*. New York: McGraw-Hill.

Kety, S., Rowland, L. P., Sidman, R. L., & Matthysee, S. W. (1982). *Genetics of neurological and psychiatric disorders*. New York: Raven Press.

Koella, W. P., & Trimble, M. R. (1982). *Temporal lobe epilepsy, mania, and schizophrenia and the Limbic system*. Basel, Switzerland: S. Karger.

Kohn, M. L. (1976). The interaction of social class and other factors in the etiology of schizophrenia. *American Journal of Psychiatry, 133*, 177–180.

Kolvin, I. (1971). Studies in the childhood psychoses: I. Diagnostic criteria and classification. *British Journal of Psychiatry, 118*, 381–384.

Kolvin, I., Garside, R. F., & Kidd, J. S. H. (1971). Studies in the childhood psychoses: IV. Parental personality and attitude and childhood psychoses. *British Journal of Psychiatry, 118*, 403–406.

Kolvin, I., Ounsted, C., Humphrey, M., & McNay, A. (1971). Studies in the childhood psychoses: II. The phenomenology of childhood psychoses. *British Journal of Psychiatry, 118*, 385–395.

Kolvin, I., Richardson, L. M., & Garside, R. F. (1971). Studies in the childhood psychoses: III. The family and social background in childhood. *British Journal of Psychiatry, 118*, 396–402.

Kolvin, I., & Roth, M. (1971). Studies in the childhood psychoses: V. Cerebral dysfunction and childhood psychoses. *British Journal of Psychiatry, 118*, 407–414.

Kwentus, J. A., Hart, R. P., Peck, E. T., & Kornstein, S. (1985). Psychiatric complications of closed head injuries. *Psychosomatics, 26*, 8–17.

Kydd, R. R., & Werry, J. S. (1972). Schizophrenia in children under 16 years. *Journal of Autism & Developmental Disorders, 12*, 343–357.

Lehman, H. E., & Cancro, R. (1985). Schizophrenia: Clinical features. In H. I. Kaplan & B. J. Sadock (Eds.), *Comprehensive textbook of psychiatry*, 4th ed. (Vol. 1, pp. 680–712). Baltimore, MD: Williams & Wilkins.

Leichtman, M., & Nathan, S. (1983). A clinical approach to the psychological testing of borderline children. In K. S. Robson (Ed.), *The borderline child*. New York: McGraw-Hill.

Lewis, M., & Brown, T. E. (1979). Psychotherapy in the residential treatment of the borderline child. *Child Psychiatry & Human Development, 9*, 181–188.

Liberman, R. P. (1985). Schizophrenia: Psychosocial treatment. In H. I. Kaplan & B. J. Sadock (Eds.), *Comprehensive textbook of psychiatry*, 4th ed. (Vol. 1, pp. 724–735). Baltimore, MD: Williams & Wilkins.

Lidz, T., Blatt, S., & Cook, B. (1981). Critique of the Danish-American studies of the adopted-away offspring of schizophrenic parents. *American Journal of Psychiatry, 138*, 1063–1068.

Lidz, T., & Fleck, S. (1985). Schizophrenia and the family. New York: International Universities Press.

Marcus, J., Ousiew, F., & Hans, S. (1983). Neurological dysfunction in borderline children. In K. S. Robson (Ed.), *The borderline child* (pp. 171–196). New York: McGraw-Hill.

Masterson, J. (1980). *From borderline adolescent to functioning adult: The test of time*. New York: Brunner/Mazel.

McNamara, E., Reynolds, C. F., Soloff, P. H., Mathias, R., Rossi, A., Spiker, D., Coble, P. A., & Kupfer, D. J. (1984). EEG sleep evaluation of depression in borderline patients. *American Journal of Psychiatry, 141*, 182–186.

McNeill, T. F., & Kaij, L. (1984). Offspring of women with nonorganic psychoses. In N. F. Watt, E. J. Anthony, L. C. Wynne, & J. E. Rolf (Eds.), *Children at risk for schizophrenia* (pp. 465–481). New York: Cambridge University Press.

Neale, J. M., Winters, K. C., & Weintraub, S. (1984). Information processing deficits in children at high risk for schizophrenia. In N. F. Watt, E. J. Anthony, L. C. Wynne, & J. E. Rolf (Eds.), *Children at risk for schizophrenia* (pp. 264–278). New York: Cambridge University Press.

Nuetzel, E. J. (1985). DSM-III and the use of the term borderline. *Bulletin of the Menninger Clinic, 49*, 124–134.

Petti, T. A. (1983). Psychopharmacologic treatment of borderline children. In K. S. Robson (Ed.), *The borderline child* (pp. 235–256). New York: McGraw-Hill.

Pine, F. (1974). On the concept "borderline": A clinical essay. In *The Psychoanalytic Study of the Child* (pp. 341–368). New Haven, CN: Yale University Press.

Pine, F. (1980). On phase-characteristic pathology of the school aged child: Disturbances of personality development and organization (borderline conditions) of learning and of behavior. In S. I. Greenspan & G. H. Pollock (Eds.), *The course of life: Psychoanalytic contributions toward understanding personality development: Vol. II. Latency, adolescence, and youth* (pp. 165–203). Washington, DC: National Institute of Mental Health.

Pine, F. (1983). A working nosology of borderline syndromes in children. In K. S. Robson (Ed.), *The borderline child* (pp. 83–100). New York: McGraw-Hill.

Pope, H. G., Jr., Jonas, J. M., & Hudson, J. I. (1983). The validity of DSM-III borderline personality disorder. *Archives of General Psychiatry, 40*, 23–30.

Reichard, S., & Tillman, C. (1950). Patterns of parent-child relationships in schizophrenia. *Psychiatry, 13*, 247–257.

Reiss, D. (1976). The family and schizophrenia. *American Journal of Psychiatry, 133*, 181–185.

Rinsley, D. B. (1980). Diagnosis and treatment of borderline and narcissistic children and adolescents. *Bulletin of the Menninger Clinic, 44*, 147–170.

Rinsley, D. B. (1984). A comparison of borderline and narcissistic personality disorders. *Bulletin of the Menninger Clinic, 48*, 1–9.

Robson, K. S. (Ed.). (1983). *The borderline child*. New York: McGraw-Hill.

Rosenberg, S. (1983). "Schizophrenia": The science and politics of psychiatry. *Contemporary Psychiatry, 2*, 10–13.

Rosenfeld, S. K., & Sprince, M. P. (1963). An attempt to formulate the meaning of the concept "borderline." In *Psychoanalytic Study of the Child* (pp. 603–635). New York: International Universities Press.

Rosenfeld, S. K., & Sprince, M. P. (1965). Some thoughts on the technical handling of borderline children. In *Psychoanalytic Study of the Child* (pp. 495–516). New York: International Universities Press.

Rosenthal, D. (1970). *Genetic theory and abnormal behavior*. New York: McGraw-Hill.

Rothstein, A. (1981). Hallucinatory phenomena in childhood. *Journal of the American Academy of Child Psychiatry, 20*, 623–635.

Sameroff, A. J., Barocas, R., & Seifer, R. (1984). The early development of children born to mentally ill women. In N. F. Watt, E. J. Anthony, L. C. Wynne, & J. E. Rolf (Eds.), *Children at risk for schizophrenia* (pp. 482–514). New York: Cambridge University Press.

Schimmer, R. (1983). The borderline personality organization in elementary school: Conflict and treatment. In K. S. Robson (Ed.), *The borderline child* (pp. 277–293). New York: McGraw-Hill.

Schulz, C. G. (1985). Schizophrenia: Individual therapy. In H. I. Kaplan & B. J. Sadock (Eds.), *Comprehensive textbook of psychiatry*, 4th ed. (Vol. 1, pp. 734–746). Baltimore, MD: Williams & Wilkins.

Sheehy, M., Goldsmith, L., & Charles, E. (1980). A comparative study of borderline parents in a psychiatric outpatient clinic. *American Journal of Psychiatry, 137,* 1374–1379.

Siever, L. J., Coursey, R. D., Alterman, I. S., Buchsbaum, M. S., & Murphy, D. L. (1984). Impaired smooth pursuit eye movement: Vulnerability marker for schizotypal personality disorder in a normal volunteer population. *American Journal of Psychiatry, 141,* 1560–1566.

Simonds, J. F., & Glenn, T. (1976). Folie à deux in a child. *Journal of Autism and Childhood Schizophrenia, 6,* 61–73.

Simpson, G. M., & May, P. R. A. (1985). Schizophrenia: Somatic treatment. In H. I. Kaplan & B. J. Sadock (Eds.), *Comprehensive textbook of psychiatry*, 4th ed. (Vol. 1). Baltimore, MD: Williams & Wilkins.

Snyder, S. H. (1976). The dopamine hypothesis of schizophrenia: Focus on the dopamine receptor. *American Journal of Psychiatry, 133,* 197–202.

Stone, M. H. (1980). *The borderline syndromes.* New York: McGraw-Hill.

Szurek, S. A., & Berlin, I. N. (1973). *Clinical studies in childhood psychosis.* New York: Brunner/Mazel.

Taylor, M. A., & Abrams, R. (1984). Cognitive impairment in schizophrenia. *American Journal of Psychiatry, 141,* 196–201.

Watt, N. F. (1984). In a nutshell: The first two decades of high risk research in schizophrenia. In N. F. Watt, E. J. Anthony, L. C. Wynne, & J. E. Rolf (Eds.), *Children at risk for schizophrenia* (pp. 572–595). New York: Cambridge University Press.

Watt, N. F., Anthony, E. J., Wynne, L. C., & Rolf, J. E. (Eds.). (1984). *Children at risk for schizophrenia.* New York: Cambridge University Press.

Weiner, H. (1985). Schizophrenia: Etiology. In H. I. Kaplan & B. J. Sadock (Eds.), *Comprehensive textbook of psychiatry*, 4th ed. (Vol. 1). Baltimore, MD: Williams & Wilkins.

Wexler, B. E., & Heninger, G. R. (1979). Alterations in cerebral laterality during acute psychotic illness. *Archives of General Psychiatry, 36,* 278–284.

Wynne, L. C., & Singer, M. T. (1963). Thought disorder and family relations of schizophrenics: I. A research strategy. *Archives of General Psychiatry, 9,* 191–198.

Young psychotics in emergency room should be tested for PCP. *Clinical Psychiatry News,* 1984.

SECTION FOUR

Social and Educational Problems

The social issues that have an impact on families and schools in turn affect children's psychological well-being. Single, working parents, economic stress, and consciousness of nuclear threat are some of these larger social issues. These and many other economic, social, political, and physiological realities create stress and affect children's views of life and the views of those who care for and teach them.

Delinquency, suicidal feelings, and drug and alcohol abuse are major social problems that indicate a child is in trouble. They reflect the child's and society's failure to mutually accommodate needs. These problems of "fit" between individual children and society are often accompanied by problems in learning. Learning ability is impaired by excessive stress, and impairments may contribute to the child's adjustment difficulties through faulty social reasoning and defeating social behavior.

This section presents research on these major behavior disorders. Predisposing factors in the child and the family contribute to the problems of fit between child and society. We will also discuss the larger social issues that exacerbate the problems of fit, such as the phenomenon of childhood drug abuse, along with issues such as values conflicts and problems in schooling and public institutional policies.

Tyranny is a habit; it grows upon us and, in the long run, turns into a disease. I say that the most decent man in the world can, through habit, become as brutish and coarse as a wild beast. Blood and power intoxicate, callousness and vice develop; the most abnormal things become first acceptable, then sweet to the mind and heart.

FYODOR DOSTOEVSKY
THE HOUSE OF THE DEAD

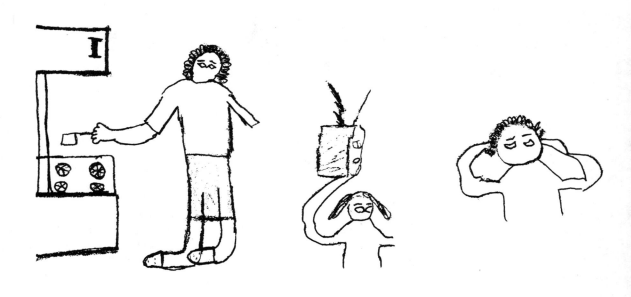

The 13-year-old boy who drew this picture had been charged with theft and assault with a deadly weapon. He did not know his biological father; his siblings' father was in prison, but when at home, he favored his own children and was often insensitive to this boy. Asked to draw a picture of his family, he included his mother, sister, and brother, but "didn't feel like putting me in it."

CHAPTER TWELVE

Delinquency

Betty Cooper Epanchin
WRIGHT SCHOOL, THE NORTH CAROLINA
RE-EDUCATION CENTER AND
UNIVERSITY OF NORTH CAROLINA AT CHAPEL HILL

Delinquency is a legal, not a psychological or psychiatric term. Accordingly, within groups of delinquents we see a variety of psychiatric/psychological and educational problems.

Although it is difficult to accurately determine how widespread delinquency is, there is no doubt that it is a serious social problem worldwide.

Research indicates that delinquents are a heterogeneous group, and that to understand the problem of delinquency, we must study social as well as psychological factors.

Youngsters who are at greatest risk for becoming adult criminals are those who commit violent crimes, have neurological disorders, and come from families in which the parents have histories of antisocial behavior. At-risk youngsters can usually be detected from an early age.

Over the years, interventions for delinquents have reflected fluctuating philosophies. Punitive, rehabilitative, and therapeutic goals have predominated. There is a push toward early identification so that delinquency can be averted, but once the youngsters are in the court system, a model of social justice prevails.

Historically, delinquents have been a recalcitrant group to treat. Many programs have been successful in changing the delinquent's behavior while the delinquent was involved in the program, but after the delinquent was back in the home environment, problems returned. Current programs emphasize work on social, ecological, educational, and psychological problems concomitantly.

Rico, age 14, hates school. He is a poor student who complains that the work is boring; consequently, he skips school often. A number of his friends are also frequently truant, so Rico has company when he is not in school.

Johnny, age 12, has a bad temper. When a woman in a department store accused him of stealing a shirt, he appeared to lose control. He called her lewd names and struck her.

Derrell, age 17, habitually shoplifts; he has vandalized public property, and he frequently uses illicit drugs. He has few friends and is alienated from his family.

Gloria, age 14, has run away from home on four occasions. Each time she disappeared for several days without contacting her parents. Her parents describe her as unmanageable and promiscuous. They feel helpless in dealing with her and are fearful that she will drop out of school and/or get pregnant.

All four of these youngsters *could* be classified as delinquent. All four have violated a law; if they were apprehended and convicted in a court of law, they would be classified as delinquents. If they escape conviction, however, they technically would not be delinquents, despite their delinquent behavior.

Delinquency is a legal term, not an educational or psychological/psychiatric one. The term *juvenile delinquent* refers to a youngster, usually between the ages of eight and eighteen, who has been convicted of committing an illegal act. For juveniles, an illegal act is defined as a violation of either the adult criminal code or the status provisions, that is, violations that apply only to juveniles. Usually called *status offenses*, these violations include behaviors such as truancy, running away from home, being unmanageable or incorrigible, and using alcohol. The range of specific behaviors included in status provisions varies from country to country and

state to state. There is even variation from court to court, not necessarily because of the law, but rather because of individual juvenile court judges' biases and practices. Status offenses are an important factor to consider when defining delinquency, because approximately half of the two million young people who go through the juvenile courts each year are there for offenses that would not be considered crimes if the individual were an adult (Coleman, Butcher, & Carson, 1984).

Although *juvenile* usually refers to ages eight to eighteen, this also varies in different states and countries. Children under eight who commit crimes are not usually considered delinquent because it is assumed that they are too immature to understand the significance and consequences of their actions. We see more variation in the upper-age range as to what constitutes being a juvenile. Some states consider 16-year-old youngsters legally of age, and in some states, although a youngster may still be classified as a juvenile, the case may be heard in adult court because the crime was particularly heinous.

INCIDENCE

In 1984, 1,537,688 youngsters under eighteen were arrested and brought before U.S. juvenile courts for a variety of offenses, excluding traffic violations. As Table 12–1 shows, this figure represents 17 percent of all arrests made during 1984. Thefts and burglaries were the most frequent crimes, but many violent crimes were also committed.

These figures are particularly bothersome when one considers that many more youngsters came into contact with law enforcement officers, but were not, for a variety of reasons, officially processed and are therefore not included in the statistics. In fact, official statistics are likely to reflect just the tip of the iceberg because of the variations in how they are collected; not only is there variation in convicted behaviors, there is also considerable variation in compiling data.

Another factor that leads professionals to question the statistics is the issue of how much delinquent behavior is even apprehended, let alone prosecuted and convicted. Based on anonymous self-report surveys of delinquent behavior, many more youngsters commit delinquent acts than are ever apprehended. These findings are consistent, suggesting that many youngsters commit crimes that are never detected; however, it is also likely that this research technique has its flaws.

To conduct self-report surveys of delinquent activity, researchers ask youngsters to indicate whether or not they have ever committed specified delinquent behaviors. Many self-report measures have a disproportionate number of less serious offenses, and some have had overlap among items, resulting in spuriously high delinquency scores; for example, both skipping class and skipping school may be listed on an instrument, and if a child had skipped school one day, he might endorse the item about skipping class. Some instruments use response categories of "never," "once or twice," and "more than three times;" collapsing frequency categories this way might group a youngster who had shoplifted three times in one year with one who had shoplifted fifty times. This method severely truncates the distribution among youngsters who engage in considerable delinquency. Additionally, many self-report studies have used small or unrepresentative samples, raising questions about the generalizability of their results.

In short, there is no precise way to determine the extent of delinquency; however, reports consistently agree that official statistics are probably underestimates. Most reports

TABLE 12–1
Total Arrests, Distributions by Age, During 1984 (estimated population for 1984 = 179,871,000)

Offense Charged	Total all Ages	Ages 18 and Over	Ages 15–17	Ages 14 and Under
Total	8,921,708	7,384,020	1,012,928	524,760
Percent distribution	100.0%	82.8%	11.3%	5.9%
Murder/nonnegligent manslaughter	13,676	12,672	866	138
Forcible rape	28,336	23,939	2,916	1,481
Robbery	108,614	80,819	20,589	7,206
Aggravated assault	231,620	200,472	21,182	9,966
Burglary	334,399	206,691	78,004	49,704
Larceny-theft	1,009,743	670,958	182,190	156,595
Motor vehicle theft	93,285	59,447	25,334	8,504
Arson	14,675	8,431	2,153	4,091
Violent crime	382,246	317,902	45,553	18,791
Property crime	1,452,102	945,527	287,681	218,894
Curfew and loitering law violations	67,243	0	48,338	18,905
Runaways	114,275	0	64,263	50,012

Data gathered from Uniform Crime Reports, Department of Justice, Bureau of Investigation, July 28, 1985 also agree that delinquency is an increasingly serious national social problem.

CLASSIFICATION

As pointed out, delinquency is a legal term; therefore, educational and psychiatric diagnostic categories do not necessarily apply to all these youngsters, although the labels do fit many of them. Of those classified with a psychiatric diagnosis, the DSM-III conduct disorder and the GAP Tension-Discharge Disorder are probably the most commonly used categories for delinquents, although other classifications can also be appropriate.

Some authors (Coleman et al., 1984) observe that the legal term *delinquent* generally calls for some punishment or corrective action, whereas a mental health diagnosis calls for help and remediation. Since there are no widely accepted, clear-cut criteria for determining who should go where, individual biases of the recommending professionals are significant determinants. Shanok, Malani, Ninan, Guggenheim, Weinstein, and Lewis (1983) provide fascinating data to illustrate this point. They compared the psychiatric, neurological, and experiential characteristics of a sample of delinquent and nondelinquent adolescent psychiatric inpatients; the groups were similar on almost all dimensions, with the exception of the number of inpatient hospitalizations and the extent of aggressive, violent behavior. Only on these two variables was the delinquent group more impaired. The authors note that the aggressive behavior did not start when the youngsters were adolescents; it had occurred for many years, but "adolescents are larger than little children, and the same behaviors that in small children are easily controlled by caretaking adults are harder to manage in adolescents. Thus, behaviors that in childhood are regarded as pathological are often considered dangerous and bad in adolescence" (p. 585).

In a similar study, Lewis, Pincus, Shanok, and Glaser (1982) compare the neuropsychiatric, intellectual, and educational status of extremely violent, incarcerated boys to less violent incarcerated boys. Again, more psychotic symptomatology and major and minor neurological abnormalities were found in the violent delinquents. The violent delinquents were also more likely to have experienced and witnessed extreme physical abuse.

Faretra (1981) also found that many children who were described as disturbed during their childhood came to be involved with the courts rather than mental health settings as adults. In an eighteen-year follow-up of 66 disturbed and violent adolescents who had been admitted to a large mental health hospital in 1960, she reported that of the 42 subjects originally diagnosed as schizophrenic, only eight had been consistently involved with mental health services. One-third had been involved with the correctional system, and one-third had mixed histories of both court and psychiatric involvement. Shanok et al. (1983) conclude:

It is ironic that as more and more research reveals the existence of severe psychopathology in delinquent adolescents, the sociopolitical climate in the United States is moving toward holding younger and younger children responsible as adults for their delinquent acts. Many hospitalized delinquent children are eventually returned to the custody of the court. It is extremely hard to negotiate therapeutic dispositions for psychiatrically disturbed adolescents who have a delinquent record. Our findings clarify the need for society to decide whether the psychiatric system or the correctional system will take responsibility for providing appropriate care for these multiply handicapped, often extremely aggressive youngsters. (p. 585)

The educational system has also had to struggle with how to classify and treat these youngsters. The definition of emotional handicaps used in P.L. 94–142 was originally proposed by Eli Bower in 1957, after an extensive research project to identify the characteristics of emotionally handicapped youngsters. The original definition avoided presumptions about the child's inner life or psychiatric condition and focused on behavior that could be observed in a school setting and that teachers, administrators, and pupil personnel workers could understand conceptually. Children identified by this definition were undoubtedly disturbing to others, and it was expected that their behavior would vary in quality and degree from setting to setting. In fact, according to the original definition, the emotionally disturbed child "had to be socially maladjusted in school" (Bower, 1982, p. 58). The current definition of an emotionally handicapped youngster, however, specifically excludes the socially maladjusted "unless they are also seriously emotionally disturbed" (Federal Register, Section 121a.5, 1977). Bower calls this exclusion "a codicil to reassure traditional psychopathologists and budget personnel that . . . just plain bad boys and girls, predelinquents, and sociopaths will not skyrocket the costs" (p. 56). He also notes that emotional problems cut across all other disabilities:

Feelings and social competence chase each other around like particles in a cyclotron at ever-increasing speeds. In some cases, the end result can be aggressive withdrawal or aggressive striking out at others. While some may argue that delinquent behavior is learned and normal for some subgroups in our society, there is no psychological mechanism that deprives such children of feelings. True, many of them act tough and uncaring about self and others. Such shells are difficult to penetrate; striking back at discomfort may indeed be healthier than caving in. Nevertheless, most clinicians have found the same cognitive-emotional structures and difficulties in the so-called socially maladjusted as in the emotionally disturbed. Similarly, prisons may house as many emotionally disturbed individuals as do mental hospitals. (Bower, 1982, p. 56)

Factor analytic approaches may offer more objective information about the nature of delinquents' psychological problems. Using case histories of 115 institutionalized male delinquents, Quay (1964) obtained ratings on a total of 24 behavioral traits. He then factor-analyzed these data and found four relatively independent factors that he labeled *socialized-subcultural delinquency, unsocialized-psychopathic delinquency, disturbed-neurotic delinquency,* and *inadequate-immature delinquency.* Earlier, Hewitt and Jenkins (1946) had found similar results using visual inspection of correlations. (These clusters mirror types of aggressiveness discussed in Chapter 6.)

The *socialized-subcultural delinquents* were youngsters who scored high on items such as "has bad companions," "stays out late at night," "is accepted by a delinquent subgroup," and "has strong allegiance to selected peers." These individuals were rated low on items such as "is shy and seclusive." These are relatively normal youngsters who tend to be of lower socioeconomic status and who relate to a delinquent subculture. Theoretically, they are socially maladjusted but not emotionally disturbed.

The *unsocialized-psychopathic delinquents* were solitary individuals who were defiant of authority, assaultive, quarrelsome, irritable, impudent, verbally aggressive, felt persecuted, were distrustful of others, had inadequate guilt feelings, were unable to profit from praise or punishment, and sought out rather than tried to avoid trouble. They are much like the conduct disordered or psychopathic youngsters we talked about earlier. Jurkovic and Prentice (1977) found that this group differed significantly from nondelinquents in moral development, while neurotic and subcultural delinquents did not.

The *disturbed-neurotic delinquents* appeared to be unhappy, timid, shy, withdrawn, and prone to worrying and feeling guilty. Physical complaints were often part of their picture. These individuals were less aggressive, more accepting of authority, more amenable to change, and less likely to repeat their delinquent behavior. Their delinquent behavior may be secondary to their emotional problems.

The *inadequate-immature delinquents,* a less prominent dimension, were individuals who were easily frustrated, picked on by others, passive and preoccupied, and usually not accepted by their delinquent peers. Rather than major psychological problems, these youngsters appeared to have a poorly developed behavioral repertoire, to be relatively inadequate in their functioning, and to be unable to cope with the demands of their environment (Quay, 1979). These children are likely to be hyperactive and/or inattentive, have significant problems in learning and achieving, and function intellectually on a lower, less verbal level. Quay (1979) suggests that the unsocialized-psychopathic and the immature types have a greater likelihood of serious problems than do the disturbed-neurotic and the socialized-subcultural types.

We can see, therefore, that there are different types of delinquents with different types of needs. Although our traditional educational and psychological diagnoses do not correspond exactly to the types of identified delinquents, many obviously have serious learning and psychiatric problems. As one frequently finds when examining classification systems, there is evidence that social and political factors as well as clinicians' personal and professional biases influence the labels we assign. Children who are culturally different and behaviorally threatening to those responsible for classifying them are apparently more likely to receive the more punitive classification of *delinquent.*

FACTORS CORRELATING WITH DELINQUENCY

Given the variation in defining a delinquent and in specifying how a delinquent should be classified, one must address the question of whether the classification *delinquent* distinguishes a group of youngsters from others consistently. Who are the "real delinquents"? A number of factors correlate with delinquency—for example, being male, being black, being from the lower socioeconomic groups, and having trouble in school correlate positively with delinquency. Few believe these factors *cause* delinquency, yet the combination clearly puts these youngsters at risk.

Gender

Statistics in all countries consistently show that more males than females appear before the courts for delinquent behavior (Rutter & Giller, 1983). Regardless of how the data are gathered and on what basis, sex differences consistently appear in delinquent and antisocial behavior. Statistics in the popular press indicate a dramatic increase in female delinquency, but as Bowker (1978) points out, the figures are misleading. The base rate of female delinquency in 1960 was so low that expressing an increase in percentages makes the figures appear quite dramatic. In absolute terms, however, violent crimes committed by males increased significantly more than those committed by females.

Besides quantitative sex differences, we also find qualitative differences in the types of crimes committed and in disposition of cases. Girls are more likely than boys to be taken to court for conduct problems such as running away, incorrigibility, and fornication, and when girls are involved in violent crime, the victims are more likely to be family members or intimates (Erskine, 1984). Evidence also suggests that courts are more likely to refer girls for clinical assessment in a psychiatric, psychological, social work setting (Caplan, Awad, Wilks, & White, 1980).

Why these differences occur, however, is still a controversial issue. As we discussed in Chapter 6, differential socialization and biological differences have been identified as causative factors in why boys are more aggressive than girls. Also, a number of studies show that marital discord between parents correlates with antisocial behavior in boys but not in girls (Block, Block, & Morrison, 1981; Emery & O'Leary, 1982; Whitehead,

1979), leading investigators to question whether boys are more vulnerable to family discord or whether girls and boys show their psychological scars in different ways.

Social Class

Historically, an inverse relationship between social class and delinquency has been assumed, and, indeed, some studies using official police records and court data have supported this assumption; however, a number of self-report studies have not found such differences. Attempts to reconcile these discrepancies have centered on two positions. Some investigators argue that there are really no significant social class differences and that the reported discrepancies stem from biases that cause youngsters from different social classes to be processed differently in the juvenile courts (Knopf, 1984). Others maintain that there are significant social class differences, but that they do not show up because of methodological shortcomings in the self-report research (Elliott & Ageton, 1980).

The National Youth Survey (Elliott & Huizinga, 1983) was undertaken in an effort to rectify some of the methodological shortcomings of earlier research. This survey was based on a probability sample of 1,725 youngsters between the ages of 11 and 17 and used a carefully constructed self-report instrument. Results indicated that middle-class youngsters were less likely to be involved in serious offenses than were working- or lower-class youth, and that middle-class youngsters committed fewer offenses overall than did working- and lower-class youngsters. With respect to less serious offenses, however, few significant class differences were found, especially among females. The authors also concluded that the differences could not be explained by racial differences or by an interaction of race and class effects.

Poverty and poor living conditions may well "predispose to delinquency, not through any direct effects on the child, but rather because serious socioeconomic disadvantage has an adverse effect on the parents, such that parental disorders and difficulties are more likely to develop and that good parenting is impeded" (Rutter & Giller, 1983, p. 185). After reviewing many studies of social class differences in delinquent populations, Rutter and Giller also conclude that the close association between low social status and delinquency applies mainly at the extremes of the social scale; that it is partly the result of differences in how youngsters from different social classes are detected and prosecuted; and that, insofar as it applies to real differences in delinquent activities, the association is largely confined to the more serious delinquent acts.

Race

Studies that use official U.S. crime statistics consistently find that crime rates among blacks are well above those for whites. In sharp contrast to the official statistics, self-report studies tend to show negligible differences between the delinquency rates of black and white youths (Elliott & Ageton, 1980). The issues under investigation are essentially the same as those regarding social class, and again, results from the National Youth Survey (Elliott & Ageton, 1980) show significant race differences for total scores on the self-report of delinquency survey, with blacks reporting higher frequencies than whites (mean score of 79 vs. 47). The authors maintain that the extended frequency range used in their study contributes to the findings that differentiate black and white youth. Specifically, they found that black youth reported three times as much vandalism and evasion-of-payment offenses as white youth, and these two relatively minor offenses caused the race differences for predatory crimes. When items were weighted so that no one item contributed disproportionately to the total score, there were no significant differences between blacks and whites on predatory crimes against property, but significant differences with respect to crimes against persons, with blacks reporting substantially greater frequencies than whites on most of the items. Thus, in this carefully executed study, race differences were more extreme at the high end of the frequency continuum, where self-report and official correlates of delinquent behavior are relatively similar.

In the United Kingdom, the delinquency rate for Asians has been equal to or lower than that for the white population every time it has been studied. In contrast to the 1950s and 1960s, the arrest rate for blacks is now substantially above that for whites, especially for violent crimes. These racial differences transcend social class differences and are not clearly understood (Rutter & Giller, 1983).

Intelligence

It was long believed that humans were free moral agents capable of behaving as they rationally chose to behave, regardless of past experience and present circumstances. Failure to behave within legal expectations was believed to be the result of a defect in rational abilities that prevented distinguishing right from wrong. While intelligence is no longer causally related to delinquency, it is still regarded as an important factor.

Heterogeneous or unselected samples of delinquents have not earned significantly lower IQ scores on intelligence measures (Hogan & Quay, 1984), but some evidence suggests that a lower IQ may predispose a youngster to earlier and more serious delinquent behavior (Gibson & West, 1970; Hirschi & Hindelang, 1977). This relationship appears in self-report data (but with less magnitude than in official data), in teacher ratings of disruptive behavior, in studies of convictions, and in clinical assessments of conduct disturbance, and has been consistently reported in both British and American studies (Rutter & Giller, 1983). There is

also evidence that a large number of delinquents' verbal skills are lower than their performance skills (Hogan & Quay, 1984).

Many hypotheses have been formulated to explain this relationship. One suggestion is that lowered IQ leads to educational failure, which leads to low self-esteem and antagonism toward school, which in turn contributes to conduct problems and delinquency. After studying 76 white prisoners in the Georgia penal system, Heilbrun (1979) found that intelligence in combination with unsocialized personality qualities differentiated violent and impulsive criminals from others. He suggests that intelligence may exert an important mediating role in delinquency behavior. Delinquency or conduct problems have also been implicated as a cause of poor intellectual and educational performance; however, low intelligence has been demonstrated to predate the delinquency (Rutter & Giller, 1983).

It has also been suggested that bright delinquents commit just as many delinquent acts, but are able to avoid detection and prosecution. Self-report studies indicate, however, that children with lower IQs actually commit more delinquent acts, thus helping to refute this hypothesis.

Educational Achievement

Related to the issue of intelligence is that of educational achievement. Delinquents as a group are consistently academically deficient. In a sample of 73 delinquents, Offord, Poushinsky, and Sullivan (1978) report that half had failed the first grade and all but four had failed by the end of third grade. By the end of elementary school, low achievement, low vocabulary, and poor verbal reasoning are strongly associated with delinquency (Loeber & Dishion, 1983). The reason for these differences is again unclear.

Many question whether delinquent youngsters have undetected learning disabilities (Lane, 1980; Zinkus & Gottlieb, 1979). Prevalence estimates of learning disabilities among juvenile delinquents are higher and more varied than in the general population, ranging from 26 to 73 percent (Keilitz, Zaremba, & Broder, 1979).

An area repeatedly identified as problematic for delinquents is that of verbal functioning. When comparing delinquents to a control group of nondelinquents from similar socioeconomic background, Wolff, Waber, Bauermeister, Cohen, and Ferber (1982) found language deficits that could not be attributed to nonspecific social-environmental influences in the delinquent group. King (1975) also found language an important factor in distinguishing homocidal youngsters from their more adaptive peers. He describes all the youth in his sample as educationally deprived, but with particular deficits in reading and language arts. He also notes that a most disabling deficit was their "inability or disinclination to master the prevailing language" (p. 138). King suggests that, because they are unable to fathom the language cues of the prevailing society, these youngsters respond to what he describes as "inner cues," leading to an unproductive, isolated, defensive, omnipotent position of "I know it all." To protect their psychological position:

They strove to reduce the symbols of communication between these two worlds to the primitive expedients of terse speech, and, ultimately, action. Terseness and action warded off talk and the cognitive challenge of reason, so difficult for them to deal with. They attempted to make action the language of communication. By limiting the responses of others to reactions to their behavior, the youths also reduced the potential of possible interchange concerning the act to a comfortable and comprehensible level. When there was a language, it was not only terse but action loaded, assaultive, or provocative. Make me! Fuck you! Who, me! I didn't do it! Get off me! Motherfucker! All are compelling phrases which cut off discourse. (King, 1975, p. 138)

King also observes that some people, intending to help these youngsters, adapt their own language so the children can easily understand them; in doing so, they lose the opportunity to help the children learn to communicate more effectively and inadvertently encourage them to maintain their dysfunctional communication system.

When these youngsters got to school, King (1975) notes that their behavior and language immediately clashed with expectations. "School was experienced as a stress-filled arena, often for battle. Violent eruptions, chronic truancy, poor motivation, short attention spans were more than symptoms of maladjustment; they represented the clash of two alien systems of communication" (p. 139). Violence was the way these youngsters coped and would continue to cope until their communication and social deficiencies were addressed.

As with intelligence, some believe that youngsters' learning disabilities lead to classroom failure, which in turn leads to the development of conduct problems and delinquency. Others suggest that learning disabled youngsters have socially troublesome personality characteristics that make them susceptible to delinquency. Both hypotheses are too simplistic. Contrary to expectations, Keilitz et al. (1979) found that both learning disabled and normal youngsters reported engaging in the same types and number of delinquent activities. These authors speculate that a "different treatment" rationale may explain the link between learning disability and juvenile delinquency; that is, the juvenile justice system processes children who are failing in school differently than it does children who are succeeding academically.

Social and Moral Reasoning

Since delinquents, by definition, are social rule breakers, a logical area of investigation has been the delinquents' understanding of social and moral conventions. Results are mixed and complex, although, overall, delinquents generally demonstrate less mature social and moral judgment (Blasi, 1980; Hogan

& Quay, 1984). Chandler (1973) found delinquents to be more egocentric than controls; Rotenberg (1974) found them to be less competent in affective role-taking; Ellis (1982) found them to score lower on an empathy measure; and Jurkovic and Prentice (1977) found psychopathic delinquents to be consistently more immature than other groups of delinquents and controls in their level of moral reasoning, their perspective-taking skills, and their abstract thinking on cognitive tasks. Bear and Richards (1981) found deficits in moral reasoning to be associated with conduct disorders; likewise, Campagna and Harter (1975), Hudgins and Prentice (1973), Emler, Heather, and Winton (1978), and Hains and Miller (1980) found higher mean moral judgment scores for controls relative to delinquents. After extensive review of the literature, however, Jurkovic (1980) concluded that immature moral reasoning does not necessarily lead to delinquency, nor does more mature moral reasoning inoculate against it.

Another line of related investigation is delinquents' self-perception. Ryall (1974) studied 150 boys ages 13 to 14 who had committed a large number of offenses. Results indicated that delinquency produced excitement, peer group status, and material rewards. Being delinquent gave these boys a sense of prestige, of status in the eyes of their peers. Delinquency was an area of personal achievement and central to their self-perception.

Family and Home Atmosphere Differences

Investigators have identified family and home atmosphere variables associated with juvenile delinquents: parental criminality, inadequate parental supervision, insensitive and hostile attitudes toward family members, marital conflict, harsh and inconsistent discipline, and large family size. Also, substantially more delinquent than nondelinquent

children come from broken homes in which one parent is absent through death, separation, divorce, or desertion (Anderson, 1969; Glueck & Glueck, 1968; Cortes & Gatti, 1972). The association between these variables and delinquency and conduct disorders appears consistently in different social and ethnic groups and in different countries with relatively different cultures and systems of social control (Friday, 1980).

Investigations reveal specific, problematic family interactions associated with the development of conduct disorders and delinquency. For example, parents of aggressive, delinquent children differ from parents of normal children in a number of ways. They tend to be more punitive than parents of "normal" children (Patterson, 1982); they issue more commands (Forehand, King, Peed, & Yoder, 1975); they are more likely to give attention to and provide positive consequences for deviant behavior (Snyder, 1977); they are less effective in stopping deviant behavior (Patterson, 1982); they give less specific behavioral feedback to their children (Forehand et al., 1975); and they engage in prolonged negative interchanges with their children (Patterson, 1982).

Why do these differences exist? Does the child, because of genetic or organic factors, cause the negative parental reactions? Or do the parental problems cause the child's aberrant reactions? Detailed analyses of interactional sequences have resulted in what Patterson (1982) calls a "performance theory of coercive family processes." In this research, molecular analyses of parental discipline have been linked with molar family functioning (see Figure 12–1), and it appears that parents of problem children do not provide the conditions for children to learn prosocial behaviors or, conversely, to avoid antisocial behaviors because there are no clearly articulated household rules for behaving; children's behavior is not carefully monitored; specific feedback about appropriate and inappropriate behavior is not clearly

FIGURE 12–1
Child-Family Interactions

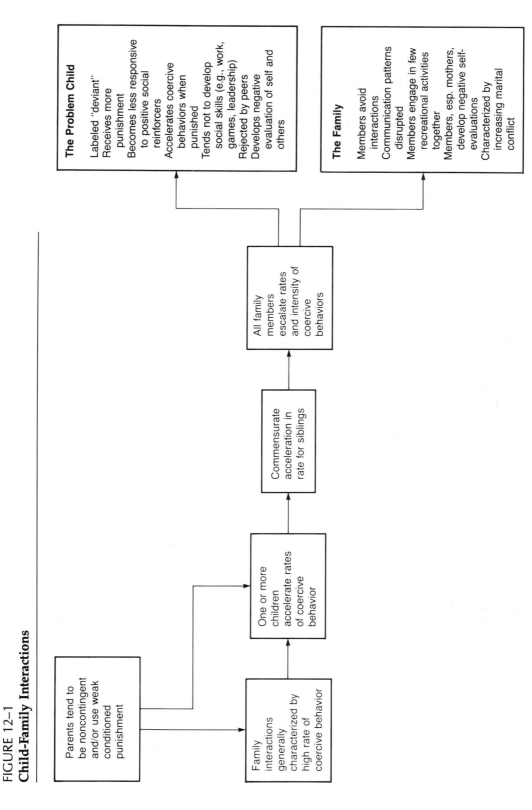

273

given; and effective contingencies for appropriate and inappropriate behavior are not used. The result of these types of parent-child interactions is a chaotic and confusing environment that gives children ambiguous and confusing messages about how to behave. This confusion is coupled with an atmosphere lacking in warmth and encouragement. Patterson and his colleagues observe that these parents rarely engage in interested, "how-was-your-day" conversations with their children, nor did they share leisure activities with them. This void of pleasurable activities and interactions further reduces the family influences; that is, because the interactions are so frequently negative and rarely countered by warm and positive interactions, parental influence is very limited. Although the parents told the youngsters not to engage in certain antisocial behaviors, they were not effective because they had such weak positive ties. Furthermore, because the youngsters had experienced such confusing family interactions, they had often failed to learn how to solve interpersonal problems effectively.

Environment

Researchers consistently report substantially higher delinquency rates in cities than in small towns and rural areas. These findings hold in both Europe and the United States and from both victim and self-report data. It has been suggested that perhaps people with psychosocial problems drift into the cities, settling in poor, slummy areas, but data show that delinquency rates fell in boys who moved out of an urban area into a rural area (Osborn, 1980). There is also evidence that parents experience more stress and adversity in urban areas, and this stress may actually account for the reported urban/rural differences (Rutter, Yule, Quinton, Rowlands, Yule, & Berger, 1975). Even if parental stress is the significant factor for higher delin-

quency rates in urban areas, the question remains as to why urban parents experience more stress.

Urban areas with high delinquency rates are usually those with a high proportion of low-social status individuals, a low proportion of owner-occupiers, a high proportion of overcrowded homes, and various features such as shared accommodations. Although these observations are consistently reported, we still don't know what they mean. Perhaps individuals living in such environments feel they have little control over their social environment, that they are not safe, that they have little privacy, and that their environment is so unattractive it is not worth taking care of.

Related research on the effects of physical environment on behavior suggests that physical design may either predispose towards or protect against crime. Vandalism is particularly high in semipublic areas that are out of general sight; in blocks with impersonal entrances used as throughways to other locations; in blocks with large semipublic spaces that residents cannot easily supervise; and in neighborhoods with little or no landscaping. High vandalism occurs in schools that face railroad tracks, motorways, or vacant land (Rutter & Giller, 1983).

In summary, research consistently indicates that many adolescents of all social classes and races and both genders engage in minor delinquent behavior, but of those who engage in serious delinquent behavior, a disproportionate number are from poor, minority, inner-city families, and many more are male than female. A large proportion have learning problems, frequently related to language, and many have lower-than-average scores on intelligence tests. While intelligence does not differentiate delinquents from nondelinquents, lower IQ scores place a child at greater risk for becoming delinquent. Many, if not most, of these youngsters also come from multiproblem families in which the predominant communication is critical rather than supportive.

HYPOTHESES FOR EXPLAINING DELINQUENCY

Some hypotheses as to why youngsters become delinquents are based on individual differences, while others maintain that social forces are the determinants. The individually-focused, psychological theories assume that each delinquent has qualities that made him or her vulnerable to antisocial behavior. We discussed some of the psychological hypotheses as to why youngsters become delinquent in Chapter 6, when we considered causes of hyperaggressiveness, so we will only mention them here. The ego's inability to deal with stress, social learning, temperament, cognitive distortions of social events, and deficiencies in psychoneurological functioning are all important individual factors in explaining why delinquency develops.

In contrast, the sociocultural hypotheses are based on the assumption that the delinquent youngster is not intrinsically different from other youngsters; he is a delinquent because of social, cultural, and political forces rather than because of individual psychological or physiological factors.

Subcultural Phenomenon

Investigators have examined delinquency in underprivileged areas of large cities and found that minor delinquent behaviors were part of a pattern of acceptable behavior among lower-class, underdisciplined boys (Downes, 1966; Mays, 1954). Petty thefts and "lifting" from their work were part of the subcultural ethos for that social group.

While this conclusion may be partly the case in minor offenses, it does not appear to be so in major offenses. Ample evidence shows that the victims of most crime in high-delinquency areas are other poor people. As Kornhauser (1978) points out, "the belief that powerless people will endorse in their subcultures actions by which they are grievously injured is unreasonable. . . . No group of people will construct a culture or a subculture that makes their own lives impossible. . . . That is why the search for subcultures that differ markedly in their orientation to crime is doomed to failure" (p. 218).

Labeling Theory

From the perspective of labeling theorists, one's view of self is influenced by others' reactions. A stigmatizing label of "delinquent" is provided by legal processing, which adversely affects the labeled person's self-concept; as a consequence, the labeled person then becomes more likely to engage in delinquent activities. Farrington (1977) tested the hypothesis that individuals who are convicted and hence labeled will increase their delinquent behavior as a result. He compared youth from the Cambridge Study in Development who were convicted in court between the ages of 14 and 18 to a matched sample of youth with similar scores on a self-report delinquency questionnaire administered when both groups were 14 years of age. The scores were compared again at ages 16 and 18. The average score of the convicted boys increased from 59.5 and 69.3 over the four years, whereas the average score of those who did not appear in court fell from 59.5 to 51.3. Because the difference could not be accounted for in terms of differences in family background of the two groups, Farrington interpreted the results as supportive of the hypothesis that public labeling increases deviant behavior.

These youth were again compared at age 21 (Farrington, Osborn, & West, 1978). In this study, 215 working-class boys completed self-report delinquency questionnaires, which differed from the previous questionnaires. Those who had first been convicted between the ages of 18 and 21 reported an increase in delinquent behavior, which was accompanied by an increase in aggressive attitudes. The self-reported delinquency of those first convicted before age 14, however, decreased significantly by age 21 whether or not the youth had additional convictions or had served an institutional sentence. Interestingly, aggressive attitudes remained high in the group that reported a decrease in delinquent behavior. Farrington, Osborn, and West concluded that "the deviance amplifying effects of first convictions wears off after a number of years, and that labeling theory requires revision to explain this" (1978, p. 283).

These findings can be explained by factors other than labeling, however. It could be that increased interaction with other delinquents increases delinquency, or it could be that the court experience was so trivial that the youngsters learned that crime pays—that is, they can get away with it.

Cultural Transmission Theory

The early work of Clifford Shaw and Henry McKay (1942) led to the development of the cultural transmission theory. They noted that, regardless of changes in a community's ethnic or racial makeup, the relative distributional pattern of delinquency throughout the city of Chicago remained fairly stable over time. Shaw and McKay saw the spatial distribution of delinquency as a product of "larger economic and social processes characterizing the history and growth of the city and of the local communities which comprise it" (1942, p. 14). Their work was an extension of the ecological studies of the effects of growing urbanization on patterns of social organization. A community's growth and development were seen as giving it a "character" that distinguished it from other communities

and that was embodied in its institutions and groupings. This character was believed to persist regardless of what group was currently dominant in the community. The basic evidence to support this hypothesis was the stability of the citywide delinquency pattern despite the shifting of population groups from one area to another (Bursik & Webb, 1982).

Since computers were not available when the original analyses were conducted, the data were analyzed by visual inspection of the mapped distributions. Later, through elaborate computer analyses, Bursik and Webb (1982) reexamined Shaw and McKay's data and added data up to 1970. Their analyses supported the Shaw and McKay findings through 1950, that delinquency rates remained stable in communities regardless of group occupancy. From that point onward, however, neighborhoods that underwent rapid compositional changes tended to reflect changes in delinquency rates. The rapid changes were associated with black migration during the 1950s, when race-restrictive covenants were banned. The delinquency rate in stable, nonwhite neighborhoods, however, did not change. Bursik and Webb maintain that the *nature* of change rather than the dominant group in a community is related to its delinquency rate. They argue that "when the existing community changes almost completely within a very short period of time, the social institution and social networks may disappear altogether, or existing institutions may persevere in the changed neighborhood but be very resistant to the inclusion of new residents. . . . Thus, it appears that, during the time it takes to stabilize and establish a community, delinquency is more likely" (Bursik & Webb, 1982, pp. 39–40).

Anomie

Durkheim's concept of *anomie* referred to the strain caused by the gap between cultural goals and the means available for achieving goals. Merton (1938, 1957) extended Durkheim's concepts by hypothesizing that delinquency is the result of this type of socially-induced pressure, or *anomie dysjuncture;* young people become delinquents because they are frustrated by their lack of opportunity to obtain economic success or by their inability to obtain social status and prestige through legal means. This, too, is a class-based theory that assumes most delinquency occurs among lower-class youth. Cloward and Ohlin (1960) elaborated upon Merton's ideas in their "opportunity structure theory." They attempted to explain why strain results in one form of deviance rather than another by suggesting that the particular adaptation depends on the availability of illegitimate means and the opportunities for learning deviant roles. There is some empirical support for this notion (Elliott & Voss, 1974).

Social Control

The perspective of social control assumes that everyone has a predisposition to commit delinquent acts; the question is how people learn *not* to offend (Hirschi, 1969). Why do people violate the rules in which they believe? Nye (1958) argues that, although there are direct social controls, indirect and internalized controls based on affectional identification with parents are the most crucial. Hirschi maintains that delinquent acts result when an individual's bond to society is weak or broken. The key elements in that bond are provided by attachments to other people, commitment to an organized society, involvement in conventional activities, and belief in a common value system. Both Hirschi (1969) and Hindelang (1973) report support for this theory, and other authors note the importance of a sense of alienation and the growing schism between the "haves" and the "have-nots" when searching for underlying causes of delinquency.

FOLLOW-UP STUDIES

What happens to juvenile delinquents when they become adults? Do most of them end up in prison? Researchers using somewhat different research designs find relatively similar results. The Gluecks (1968) conducted a follow-up study of 438 (out of 500) former delinquents and 442 (out of 500) controls who had participated in their original 1950 study. In 1950, the boys had ranged in age from 9 to 17 years old ($X = 14.5$). At follow-up, these young men ranged in age from 25 to 31. On all dimensions, the former delinquents showed a less favorable outcome than the controls. The delinquents had more psychological problems and were more often characterized as psychopathic. They also showed higher rates of marital instability, were more likely to be on welfare, had more friends who were criminals or disreputable, and were less likely to have learned a trade. Although the number of serious crimes had declined with age, drunkenness, vagrancy, simple assault, and family-related offenses such as desertion had increased. Within the previous six years, 84.4 percent of the former delinquents had been convicted of a crime, whereas the vast majority of the controls were law-abiding.

Robins (1966) also noted the malignancy of antisocial behavior, but found an interesting age variable. In this sample, conduct disordered, psychopathic individuals tended to "age out" of their antisocial behavior by the time they became 40 years of age. Antisocial behavior of the father was the *only* childhood variable that predicted that sociopathic individuals would not decrease their antisocial behavior as they grew older. Quoting A.E. Housman's lines, "When shall I be dead and rid/Of the wrong my father did?" Robins notes that the mechanism that related the father's behavior to his offspring's antisocial behavior was not at all clear. Many of the fathers were out of the youngsters' homes as they were growing up, so direct contact and modeling alone were not sufficient explanations. It was also interesting that a few variables tended to predict improvement: maintaining contact with wives and other relatives; short incarcerations followed by prolonged supervision by parole officers; holding jobs in which they had little direct supervision; and having payments to make on desired objects such as a car.

Pincus and Tucker (1978) reported that 20 percent of criminally aggressive youngsters are psychotic by the time they are eighteen; 40 percent continue their antisocial behavior into adulthood; and only 20 percent are well-adjusted adults. They also reported that youngsters who commit crimes against property are more likely to "reform" than are youngsters who commit violent crimes, particularly if those who commit the violent crimes have histories of alcoholism and seizure disorders or other neurological disorders.

INTERVENTIONS

Before the twentieth century, children who disobeyed the law were dealt with as adults. They received adult penalties, and no efforts were made to rehabilitate them. They were considered criminals needing punishment, not children in need of help with their emotional, cognitive, and social development. But with the greater concern for social justice that emerged at the end of the nineteenth century, some efforts at social reform began. Attention focused on the large number of young people from vastly different cultures who posed problems for the existing social order. People began to recognize that these youngsters needed rehabilitation rather than the harsh, punitive treatment of the judicial system. The assumption was that deviant youngsters needed moral development so they could be "properly" socialized for the emerging industrial society (Sarri, 1980).

Accordingly, the juvenile court system was established in an effort to provide antisocial youngsters with an "enlightened" approach

to rehabilitation. Illinois was the first state to establish a statewide juvenile court system in 1899. By 1912, all but two states had juvenile court systems.

Several facets of the juvenile courts were different from the regular judicial system. The courtroom was closed to the public, and the records were confidential. Hearings were, by design, informal and nonadversarial. Judges were allowed enormous latitude in dealing with cases; their actions were to be guided by what they perceived as "the best interests of the child." The goals of the juvenile court were "to investigate, diagnose, and prescribe treatment, not to adjudicate guilt or fix blame. The individual's background was more important than the facts of a given incident," and "delinquency was thought of almost as a disease, to be diagnosed by specialists and the patient kindly but firmly dosed" (President's Commission, 1967, p. 3). It was widely accepted that to meet these goals, the juvenile court had the authority to terminate parental rights, to institutionalize, to place offenders on probation, or to dismiss the case, while few rights were guaranteed to the children. The concept of *parens patriae*—the right of the state to assume the power of guardianship—prevailed. Delinquency was broadly defined to include everything from serious felonies to smoking and idling one's time. In the decades following the inception of the juvenile court system, however, limited resources, social changes, and public pressure gradually caused the system to deviate from its rehabilitative stance and become more concerned with social control. The juvenile courts were inconsistent in processing cases and in interacting with other child care institutions and agencies.

In 1967 the U.S. Supreme Court heard the case of Gerald Gault, a 15-year-old boy from Arizona, who had received the maximum seven-year sentence in the state's correctional facility for children for placing obscene phone calls. The same offense committed by an adult and heard in an adult court carried a maximum sentence of a 50-dollar fine or two months in jail. The Supreme Court recognized the variability within the juvenile courts and ordered the instatement of procedural safeguards: the right to counsel, the right to written notice of charges, and the right to confront witnesses and secure sworn testimony (Burlingame, 1984). The Gault case was significant in the transition of juvenile justice from a rehabilitation model to a social justice model.

Shortly after the Gault case, several laws were enacted to improve the treatment of juvenile delinquents. The Juvenile Justice and Delinquency Prevention Act (P.L. 93–415), passed in 1974, mandated that the Department of Justice carry out these responsibilities: coordinating all federal efforts on juvenile delinquency; developing community programs for the prevention of delinquency; establishing programs for diversion from the juvenile justice system through community-based alternatives; eliminating the detention of juveniles with adults; and implementing programs that would keep status offenders out of detention or correctional centers. Also in 1974, the Runaway and Homeless Act was passed to assist youthful runaways by providing shelter, social assistance, medical care, and counseling, in an effort to divert them from prostitution, drug activity, and other illegal and self-destructive activities. This legislation marked a shift in the population served by juvenile correction centers. Status offenders were no longer sent to training schools, which meant that other agencies had to assume more responsibility for them. It also meant that training schools were left with a large percentage of the hard-core, antisocial youngsters.

This brief survey of the history of the juvenile justice system shows how it has been influenced by conflicting ideologies. On the one hand, the court has been expected to maintain social control and order, and on the other, it has been mandated to rehabilitate

youths who range from social nuisances to serious offenders. The courts have also been expected to promote social justice by means of local resources. Sarri (1980) defines a social justice model as one that strives to protect the well-being of youth and society, based ideologically on principles of equal justice, due process, and procedural fairness. Sarri says this model defines the problem in terms of behavioral allegations and definitions of criminal behavior instead of focusing on a youth's threat to the community or considering him as handicapped. In the social justice model, the court is concerned with determining guilt or innocence and processing cases quickly and fairly, rather than providing treatment or imposing retributive justice. There is dispositional equality and low rates of detention.

Parallel shifts in dealing with delinquent youngsters have also occurred in mental health and education. Over the years, educational and psychological professionals tried a number of different interventions that included vocational and remedial education in alternative schools, training schools, halfway houses, group homes, parole, probation, incarceration, treatment in residential centers, psychotherapy, and group therapy. Many programs initially seemed promising, but follow-up data revealed no cures. Table 12–2 summarizes some of the better programs. As we see from the table, good programs were able to change youngsters' behavior while they were in the program; however, the gains often did not last once the child was back in the community. When professionals' good-faith efforts were not successful, the children gradually became those "no one wanted" (Redl & Wineman, 1957) or "throwaway children." They made the professionals feel inadequate, and when forced to decide whom to help, professionals often chose those they could more easily help and called the delinquent youngsters "untreatable."

It is undoubtedly difficult to work with delinquents, but our failures are not the result

TABLE 12–2
Programs for Treating Delinquency

Program Name	Description	Outcome	Significance
Cambridge-Somerville Youth Study McCord (1978) Teuber & Powers (1966) Powers & Witmer (1951)	Begun in 1935, project compared control and treatment groups of boys from high-risk urban area Each boy's family assigned a counselor as "big brother" counselor and advocate Families received counseling, remedial education, medical and psychiatric care, and various camp and club activities	Initially positive gains 30-year follow-up showed experimental group had significantly more problems	Research exhaustive and sophisticated for its day Extensive data made it possible to identify factors associated with success When counselor and subject *both* saw relationship as positive, outcome was more positive
Highfields (Weeks, 1958) McCorkle, Elias, & Bixby (1958) Vorrath & Brendtro (1974, 1985) Whittaker (1979) Empey & Lubeck (1972)	Treatment in permissive group therapy program compared to treatment in conventional disciplinary reformatory Group therapy technique called "guided group interaction," also "positive peer culture"	Recidivism rate initially lower for Highfields boys Over time, no differences between the two groups	Technique of positive-peer culture still useful for harnessing power of group's influence
Achievement Place: Phillips (1968) Phillips, Phillips, Fixsen & Wolf (1971) Bailey, Wolf & Phillips (1970) Bailey, Timbers, Phillips & Wolf (1971) Fixsen, Phillips & Wolf, (1973) Liberman, Ferris, Salgado & Salgado (1975)	Community-based group homes Used behavioral principles to teach adjustment to community	Immediate behavioral gains Follow-up showed recidivism rate lower, school adjustment better, in Achievement Place boys than in comparison groups	Carefully described, techniques thoroughly documented Replicated many times Initially, token economy system was "work horse" of program Later research suggested social aspects of interactions between youngster and teaching parent were "heart of the program"
Contingencies Applicable to Special Education (CASE) Cohen & Filipczak (1971)	Behaviorally-engineered educational program Focused on developing academic skills as means of increasing employability Compared subjects to institutionalized youth	Recidivism rate lower at 2 years No differences in rate at 5 years	Highlighted importance of developing academic skills Showed importance of establishing supportive after-care environment
Kentfields: Davidson & Robinson (1975)	Community program based on behavior modification and community psychology principles Developed as alternative to institutionalization	Costs reduced Arrest rates reduced significantly No comparison group, so effects could have resulted from subjects' maturity	Demonstrated that community-based project could effectively change people's attitudes toward delinquents Provided cost-effective alternative to incarceration

TABLE 12–2
Programs for Treating Delinquency (Continued)

Program Name	Description	Outcome	Significance
The Buddy System: O'Donnell, Lydgate & Fo (1979) Fo & O'Donnell (1975)	Nonprofessionals (under supervision of trained professional) were change agents in community-based program Delinquents and predelinquents Behavioral principles used	Immediate, positive gains in both treatment and control groups At two-year follow-up, treated *predelinquents* had higher arrest records Arrest rate lower for treated delinquents	Raised doubts about wisdom of treating youngsters convicted of serious crimes with at-risk youngsters or those convicted only of status offenses
Cascadia Juvenile Reception-Diagnostic Center: Sarason (1968, 1978) Sarason & Ganzer (1973)	Delinquents in treatment groups taught how to behave in socially acceptable and effective way in everyday life situations Delinquents in control group participated in "high-quality" institutional program	Recidivism rate at 3 years and 5 years significantly lower for treatment groups	Highlighted effectiveness and importance of teaching delinquents concrete ways to deal with realistic social problems
California Community Treatment Project: Palmer (1974) Warren (1969, 1977)	Based on premise that not all offenders are alike Classification system developed Attempt made to match type of problem with type of treatment	Identified 3 main types of delinquents and treatment recommendations for each: 1) For conflicted youth, individual or group psychotherapy with well-matched therapist; positive outcome 2) For passive-conformist youth, participation in activity groups that focused on here-and-now interpersonal problems in community-based settings Outcome mixed 3) For "psychopathic" youth, treatment was "concerned control" Outcome mixed	Impressive efforts to match treatment, treater, client, and setting
Youth Center Research Project: Jesness (1975)	1,130 boys randomly assigned to treatment group based on behavioral principles or treatment group based on transactional analysis 929 participants in programs, released on	Both programs showed positive attitudinal and behavioral changes initially, but differential effects found "Least mature" benefited more from behavioral program; "manipulator"	Underscores differential effects of treatment for various types of youngsters

TABLE 12–2
Programs for Treating Delinquency (Continued)

Program Name	Description	Outcome	Significance
	parole, followed for 2 years	subjects responded better to transactional analysis program Subjects in transactional analysis program reported more positive regard for staff After 2 years, only 215 (23%) of 929 boys had kept parole records clear	
Comprehensive Vocationally-Oriented Psychotherapy: Massimo & Shore (1967) Shore & Massimo (1979)	Therapists contacted youths immediately upon their dropping out of school or being suspended from school Therapists worked with youths in communities Focused on appropriate action for solving practical, reality issues Used whatever arose as opportunity to teach necessary skills and dealing with problems therapeutically	10 in experimental group, 10 in control group 80% of experimental group improved; 80% of control group deteriorated At 15-year follow-up, experimental group had maintained improved status	Although number in treated and untreated groups was small, provocative ideas generated as to what constitutes relevant treatment and how one person can and should function as therapist, teacher, case manager, and advocate

of an inability to help individuals. Rather, the failure appears to have been minimizing the severity and magnitude of the delinquency problem, and therefore assuming that if we help the youngster, we solve the problem. For the most part, we have not adequately linked service components to other service components; we have not collaborated and communicated with other professionals and agencies to the extent necessary; and we have not systematically dealt with social, economic, educational, and psychological issues simultaneously. In short, we have too often naively focused on the delinquent child rather than on the child in the context of the family and community. We believed that good people's good intentions would solve problems; experience has taught us otherwise.

Gibbs (1984) predicts that if we do not find more effective interventions, "the riots of the 1960s and 1970s will seem pale by comparison to the potential widespread violence that may be triggered by an inevitable confrontation between the 'haves' and the 'have-nots' over shrinking natural and material resources." She sees this danger as "increasingly exacerbated by those conservative politicians and spokesmen who foster a growing public perception of black youth as welfare cheaters and antisocial parasites, as threats to the 'American Way of Life' " (p. 12). She details ways the coordinated efforts of professionals and community leaders could provide effective programs for the needs of black youth, and her suggestions are appropriate for all youngsters who are either at risk for becoming delinquents or have been adjudicated as delinquent. Her suggested programs include alternative secondary education programs, employment opportunities, sex education and family planning programs, comprehensive services for teenage parents, community-based recreational activities, and drug counseling.

Basic to Gibbs's (1984) recommendations is the assumption that no one technique or program is sufficient for meeting the multitude of needs in delinquent, antisocial youngsters. They need interventions that address not only their individual psychological needs, but also their physical, social, educational, and economic needs, and these interventions need to be flexible enough so that when an individual progresses or regresses, there is an efficient means of meeting the changing needs. Furthermore, these interventions need to be coordinated so that the client benefits from rather than becomes overwhelmed by them. It is usually the responsibility of mental health departments to ensure that this range of services is available for children of different ages and that there is easy access to these services. It is the responsibility of both mental health and public instruction to ensure that multiple services are coordinated so that they help the client rather than confuse or overwhelm him.

Knitzer (1982) concludes that "overall, states are failing to meet these responsibilities. Children's needs are unmet, and families unserved" (p. 43). She describes the task of creating "systems of care for children" as the "unmet challenge" and notes that at the time of her survey, only seven states had taken explicit steps to develop a range of services and reduce the fragmentation of services.

One of the states she cites as having a continuum of care is North Carolina, whose system developed partly as a result of a class-action lawsuit that was settled in September 1980. The *Willie M.* lawsuit on behalf of four plaintiffs alleged that the defendants (the governor, the superintendent of public instruction, and the secretary of human resources) were violating the plaintiffs' federal constitutional rights to due process and

equal protection and the constitutional prohibition against cruel and unusual punishment by confining them without providing appropriate treatment. The suit also alleged that the defendants were abridging two federal statutes—P.L. 94–142, by denying them appropriate educational treatment, and Section 504 of the Rehabilitation Act of 1973, by excluding them from treatment programs because of their handicaps. Three state statutory claims were also raised—the right of handicapped children to an appropriate education, the right of minor patients in a treatment facility to appropriate treatment, and the right of children in youth centers to appropriate treatment. The plaintiffs represented all North Carolina youths under the age of eighteen years who "now or someday will suffer from serious emotional, mental, or neurological handicaps; who are violent or assaultive; and who are or someday will be institutionalized or put in residential programs that do not provide appropriate treatment and education." The defendants conceded liability, and the suit was settled without a trial (Sindelar, 1982).

The delivery system that emerged as a result of this suit is a community-based continuum of services with a variety of different types of programs. The state has been divided into zones with a continuum of services in each. Each zone received state funding in a lump grant to use to develop services where there was the greatest need.

At the heart of the North Carolina service delivery system is the case manager, a professional role that historically has served chronic populations. Case managers are professionally trained individuals responsible for seeing that their clients receive the best possible services so as to maximize the clients' growth, autonomy, and social functioning. They function as a "facilitator, linker, supporter, broker, monitor, bridger, catalyst, and advocate" (Sanborn, 1983, p. 181). A case manager's success depends partly on his or her ability to determine the client's potential growth, current functioning, and level of stressors. One needs clinical skills for this, and administrative and advocacy skills as well. Case managers must know what services are available and how to access them, and for a case manager to function effectively, there must be appropriate services and a continuum of care available.

A continuum of care offers a range of service components varying in intensity from least restrictive to most restrictive. The services need to be located within or close to the client's community so that children and youth can be served in the least restrictive setting. Each service component should provide a dynamic and active treatment process so that children can be moved into different settings as their needs change. The continuum of care includes residential treatment centers, in-home specialized treatment, day treatment programs, therapeutic camping, a variety of educational services, and after school care.

Although few states have moved to implement the role of the case manager, many states have adopted the concept of a continuum of care. Many states have gaps in the continuum, which often omits the "throwaway" children. The following paragraphs describe three programs for serving unwanted, delinquent, and antisocial children.

Homebuilders (Haapala, 1984; Knitzer, 1982) is an emergency service program that focuses on families who are on the verge of disintegrating because of multiple problems, including intense family conflicts, alcohol or drug abuse, suspected spouse or child abuse, threatened separation of husband and wife, the child's commitment of a status offense, or failure to meet the child's serious emotional, behavioral, or developmental needs in the home. Located in Tacoma, Washington, this program started in the early 1970s to serve only children in the juvenile justice or child welfare systems. Because of its successes with families, in 1979 the program received a contract from the Division of Mental Health to serve 25 children under the age of 18 who

were severely emotionally disturbed and likely to be placed in a psychiatric hospital.

The primary goal of the program is to keep youngsters with their families while also providing the most effective type of intervention as well as controlling costs. A more specific goal is to help the families become more skillful in relating to each other, in problem solving, in managing feelings (especially anger) appropriately, and in altering self-defeating behavior patterns. Staff accomplish these goals by providing support to families through a crisis as well as by functioning as participant observers, advocates, case managers, and teachers of psychoeducational life skills.

Homebuilders staff work with the families in their homes and respond rapidly to crises. Face-to-face interviews with each family member take place within 24 hours of the referral, and referrals are accepted seven days a week, 24 hours a day. Therapists, who work with only two or three families at a time, are on call around the clock and can be at a family's home within a few hours. Staff make a point of being available to families when the families need them and for as long as they are needed. The families typically stay in the program from one to five months. After discharge, there are also regular contacts to see where the child is living and how the family is faring.

Staff report that by working with families in their homes, they are able to increase the number of family members who are willing to participate in the counseling. Many of the clients served by Homebuilders have had unsuccessful experiences with social service and mental health and are therefore reluctant to try again. Clients tend to be impulsive and act out their conflicts at the moment trouble arises. They have trouble saving an issue to deal with in an office two or three days later, and, in short, they often do not respond well to the traditional service delivery model. In-home, immediate help may appear more relevant and is clearly more accessible.

In their advocacy role, Homebuilders staff

try to get children involved in appropriate school and/or work programs. They also help unravel the chain of responsibility in complex cases so that coordinated treatment can be provided. Homebuilders has dealt with families who have had as many as 15 different case managers from various agencies. "Homebuilders also spends time deprogramming psychiatric 'labels' with staff and families. Even so, the noise these labels make and the ways in which everyone reacts to them are terribly difficult to overcome" (Knitzer, 1982, p. 31).

Despite the difficult clientele and the challenges of working with other systems, Homebuilders has established an impressive record. At a three-month follow-up of 792 children treated from 1975 to 1981, Haapala (1984) reported that 94 percent were averted from foster, group, or institutional care.

Pressley Ridge Youth Development Extension (PRYDE) is an example of an in-home, specialized treatment program. It illustrates how youngsters can be treated individually within the context of a normal family instead of in an institution. This "foster family-based treatment" program is an extension of Pressley Ridge School, a 150-year-old, private childcare and treatment agency in Pittsburgh, Pennsylvania. The program's mission is to "provide troubled and troubling children and adolescents with a noninstitutional treatment alternative in the private homes of treatment parents and to return these youths to their communities or families better adjusted: that is, more skilled, more effective, more confident, more adequately equipped to deal with their natural ecology in the present and future" (Hawkins, Meadowcroft, Trout, & Luster, 1985, p. 221).

This program serves children who are usually referred through child welfare and the juvenile courts. Many have histories of multiple institutional placements. Aggressiveness, attention-getting behavior, hyperactivity, and "unethical" behavior are the most prevalent behavior problems noted at admission. Children range in age from 4 to 18; the average age is 13.5 years. Slightly more are black (58 percent), and 50 percent are females.

The "agent of treatment" in this model is the "professional parent," a highly qualified, well-educated parent who has received preservice and inservice training and is paid a salary comparable to a beginning child care worker in an institution. The professional parents are responsible for all aspects of the child's treatment, which includes using a point system, much like that developed in the Achievement Place model, as well as driving the child to Little League or dance class.

During preservice training, parents receive 10 two-and-a-half-hour training sessions in social reinforcement, analyzing interactions and their probable effects, active listening, I-messages, negotiation, time out, reinforcement of incompatible behaviors, extinction, relationship building, task analysis, point systems, helping youth make friends, advocating for a youth, keeping daily records, stress management, emergency medical procedures, and parent evaluation. A monthly two-hour inservice workshop is held during which relevant topics are discussed. Parents are evaluated at six month, 12 month, and then at yearly intervals. Evaluation includes direct observations of the parents' interacting with their child-client, a satisfaction questionnaire completed by the youth, and data gathered from inservice and daily records. Raises are contingent upon these evaluations.

Since its inception in 1981, 82 percent of the youngsters enrolled in the program have been returned to their communities, either to independent living situations or to their families. Since 1982, at six months after discharge, only one child had reentered the child welfare-juvenile court system. Furthermore, the costs of the program compare favorably with other comparable services; for example, the

PRYDE per diem cost is $48, versus the average Pennsylvania group home cost of $64.

City Lights is a comprehensive day treatment model in Washington, D.C. The children in this program have

been written off by the schools as unteachable, by the juvenile justice system as intractable, and by the mental health system as untreatable. These are youth so successful at failure that they exhaust and discourage even the most idealistic among us who reach out to them with hope and one more chance. Because they fail consistently at home, at school and at work, such youths are rapidly moving to permanently disadvantaged status in our society. (Tolmach, 1985, p. 214)

The overriding concept of this program is to create "an environment that guarantees the novelty of success to experts at failure" (p. 214). The program is an eclectic, therapeutic milieu that incorporates the best of many interventions and focuses on social, psychological, educational, vocational, and economic deficits by utilizing a multidisciplinary staff to plan individualized interventions in these areas.

Critical elements of the program are remedial and vocational education, group and individual therapy for the youngster, and family therapy with his or her family system, all of which are carefully articulated in a therapeutic milieu. All aspects of the program emphasize establishing trusting relationships between staff and clients (youngster and family). "Therapy on demand" in the form of Life Space Interviews is available to youngsters when the need arises. By dealing with small problems as they arise to disturb the child, staff demonstrate sensitivity to the youngsters' needs and ability to help with problems.

Besides the on-the-spot therapeutic interviews, telephone therapy is another means of reaching out into the youngsters' lives and introducing positives where there have been negatives. Because many of the children are mistrustful, the intimacy of individual psychotherapy is often threatening. The anxiety generated by fears of intimacy is often acted out in antisocial, explosive behavior. To avoid such encounters, the staff do not force intimacy until the child is ready; instead, they use overtures such as calling the youngster at home at night to give praise for even the smallest of the day's accomplishments. These contacts help the youngster become more trusting, and also appear to soften parents' mistrust. Mothers who are accustomed to complaints and criticism respond positively to "I want to talk with Andy about the good day he had at school." This psychological support fosters the development of trusting relationships between youngster and staff and the family systems and staff. After rapport and trust develop, staff are able to offer individual and group therapy and family counselling to the clients.

Novel and relevant school activities, in addition to the positive relationship between student and teacher, help motivate the youngster to try in spite of repeated past failures. Self-paced, computer-assisted instruction helps students evaluate their performance, control their rate of progress, and receive frequent reinforcement for successes. The basic curriculum of the program is the Comprehensive Competencies Program (CCP), an integrated curriculum of paper-and-pencil lessons, software, cassettes, and filmstrips compiled from the most effective materials developed for CETA and Job Corps. Materials are available for instructing students, from the nonreader level to the college level, in life skills (comparison shopping, application for food stamps, job interview skills), along with the basic academic content of math, social studies, and reading. Ongoing, objective evaluation of progress and immediate positive reinforcement for success are used throughout. Education is considered therapeutic, and therapy is considered a form of education, thus deliberately blurring professional roles. For example, class meetings, a form of group therapy, are a daily part of the academic schedule, and tutorials in the computer language LOGO allow students and teachers to work and talk privately over a period of months. These tutorial sessions in many ways resemble individual therapy.

The milieu offers a variety of activities to promote the clients' growth as well as help the youngsters become positively integrated into their communities. A gospel singer who is also an accomplished musician meets with the youngsters weekly to teach vocal skills, lead a choral group that performs in the community, and enhance awareness of the black culture. A staff social worker who is also a professional ice skater teaches ice skating to help youngsters develop social and motor skills. Children go horseback riding and, in the process, learn skills of controlling themselves and anticipating consequences of their behavior. Students who progress behaviorally and academically are offered part-time employment and thus access to legitimate means of earning much-needed money. Other community activities, such as spiritual programs offered by the city's black churches, Tae kwon do, physical fitness activities, tennis instruction, chess tournaments, and visits to museums and theatres are also an important part of the milieu, with the goal of helping youngsters learn how to spend their leisure time productively.

Physical well-being is also stressed; children learn biofeedback and meditation and relaxation techniques as means of controlling the anxiety that triggers their impulsive, antisocial behavior. Since the long-term side effects of many psychotropic medications are known to be detrimental, the staff work with psychiatrists to reduce medication whenever possible. Students are also encouraged to use the adolescent pregnancy programs and medical and dental services at community centers.

As we have emphasized, this program recognizes the importance of a supportive community network. Staff work hard to enlist help from families, churches, and service organizations so that no youngster leaves the program without support. To mobilize families' latent strengths, therapeutic interventions are used in addition to group and family therapy. Disorganized families, including foster families, learn to interact more constructively, using the Family Education Program model developed by Salvador Minuchin. Mothers' Groups, which are supportive social groups, help lessen single parents' isolation and frustration. Multiple family groups help families learn from each other, and Kinship groups are an effort to offer positive support systems for clients in the community.

This program incorporates a number of elements that are important in dealing with delinquents and an administrative structure that supports its staff in providing for this difficult population. So as to monitor client progress carefully and to protect good staff relations, daily 30-minute staff meetings are held to review work with clients. Another biweekly process group with an outside consultant helps the staff deal with feelings and conflicts that might otherwise inhibit the professional team's cohesion.

City Lights is still a new program; its start-up grant was funded in May, 1981, so the efficacy data are limited. Based on the limited data, however, academic gains of 1.5 grade levels per school year have been achieved (notable when one considers that these youngsters made virtually no progress during many of their years in school); greater stability within natural and foster families has reduced the need for institutional placement; only 10 percent of the students have been returned to institutions or to jail and only 7 percent have dropped out of the program of their own accord. After acknowledging the limitations of these data, Tolmach (1985) nonetheless concludes that "we have demonstrated in our first 3 years at City

Lights that troubled black adolescents who have learned to be distrustful, fearful, mean, and sullen can learn to change, to trust, and to believe in their ability to succeed" (p. 218).

All three of these programs demonstrate effectiveness in helping recalcitrant youths and their families change their behavior. Short-term follow-up indicates that the gains are maintained after discharge; the important question is whether they can be maintained over time. Most research reports that youths regress when they return to their problematic environments, but few programs have emphasized the importance of changing ecological and social factors while also working with the child. Since the so-far successful programs have focused on not only the child but also the complex system in which he lives, one hopes the gains will be more stable.

CONCLUSION

Delinquents are not a homogeneous group. Complex factors appear to be important in explaining why an individual child becomes a delinquent. Many children may have neurological abnormalities that predispose them to violent behavior. Many come from chaotic, disorganized families in which they have few opportunities to learn socially acceptable ways of dealing with feelings and getting their psychological needs met. Social forces also appear to influence the development of delinquency. While all of the findings so far contribute to our understanding of delinquency, none are sufficient in themselves to explain the phenomenon. Likewise, few interventions have had unequivocal success with this group. Perhaps this inadequacy results from the focus of most theories and programs on a particular aspect of these youngsters and their lives, whereas it has become abundantly clear that juvenile delinquency is a problem not easily solved by good intentions or simple solutions. It is a complex problem that requires different

viewpoints and several different simultaneously administered, carefully coordinated interventions and service components.

We have at least, however, learned some principles about effective treatment.

● Children who display violent or antisocial behavior need thorough and careful evaluations as soon as the behaviors appear. The growing evidence that many of these youngsters have neurological, psychiatric, and social problems calls for early intervention.

● Community-based interventions provide youngsters with emotional support from significant people in their lives while also exposing them to the social realities with which they must learn to cope more effectively.

● Practical, job-related skill development is important. Training children to be successful in a program without focusing on the world beyond does not appear to be beneficial. Many of these youngsters, with long histories of school failure and disinterest, do not respond to programs that do not demonstrate relevance.

● Attention should focus on with whom the youthful offender interacts. Most states have now diverted status offenders from the correctional system to prevent placement of children and youth in adult facilities, because vulnerable youngsters who come into contact with hardened offenders are more likely to become offenders themselves.

● Programs need to build in evaluation systems. Evaluation demonstrates a program's effectiveness and contributes to the ongoing refinement of knowledge about how to understand and deal with this difficult problem.

● Perhaps most importantly, services need to be coordinated to meet more of the child's and family's needs so that agencies and individuals are not working at cross-purposes. Coordination not only improves the quality of service delivery, but also reduces costs by eliminating duplication.

REFERENCES

Anderson, L. M. (1969). Personality characteristics of parents of neurotic, aggressive, and normal preadolescent boys. *Journal of Consulting and Clinical Psychology, 33*, 574–582.

Bailey, J. S., Timbers, G. D., Phillips, E. L., & Wolf, M. M. (1971). Modification of articulation errors of pre-delinquents by their peers. *Journal of Applied Behavior Analysis, 4*, 265–281.

Bailey, J. S., Wolf, M. M., & Phillips, E. L. (1970). Home-based reinforcement and the modification of pre-delinquent classroom behavior. *Journal of Applied Behavior Analysis, 3*, 323–333.

Bandura, A. (1969). Social-learning theory of identificatory processes. In D. A. Goslin (Ed.), *Handbook of socialization theory and research*. New York: Rand McNally.

Bear, G. C., & Richards, H. C. (1981). Moral reasoning and conduct problems in the classroom. *Journal of Educational Psychology, 73*, 644–670.

Blasi, A. (1980). Bridging moral cognition and moral action: A critical review of the literature. *Psychological Bulletin, 88*, 1–45.

Block, J. H., Block, J., & Morrison, A. (1981). Parental agreement-disagreement on child rearing orientations and gender-related personality correlates in children. *Child Development, 52*, 965–974.

Bower, E. M. (1982). Defining emotional disturbance: Public policy and research. *Psychology in the Schools, 19*, 55–60.

Bowker, L. H. (1978). Incidence of female crime and delinquency: A comparison of official and self-report studies. *International Journal of Women's Studies, 1*, 178–192.

Bowlby, J. (1969). *Attachment and loss: I. Attachment*. London: Hogarth Press.

Brown, G. L., & Goodwin, F. K. (1984). Aggression, adolescence and psychobiology. In C. R. Keith (Ed.), *The aggressive adolescent: Clinical perspectives*. New York: Free Press.

Burlingame, W. V. (1984). Political and legal issues involving the aggressive adolescent. In C. R. Keith (Ed.), *The aggressive adolescent: Clinical perspectives*. New York: Free Press.

Bursik, R. J., & Webb, J. (1982). Community change and patterns of delinquency. *American Journal of Sociology, 88*, 24–42.

Campagna, A. F., & Harter, S. (1975). Moral judgment in sociopathic and normal children. *Journal of Personality and Social Psychology, 31*, 199–205.

Caplan, P. J., Awad, G. A., Wilks, C., & White, G. (1980). Sex differences in a delinquent clinic population. *British Journal of Criminology, 29*, 311–328.

Chandler, M. J. (1973). Egocentrism and anti-social behavior: The assessment and training of social perspective-taking skills. *Developmental Psychology, 9*, 326–332.

Cloward, R. A., & Ohlin, L. E. (1960). *Delinquency and opportunity*. Glencoe, IL: Free Press.

Cohen, H. J., & Filipczak, J. (1971). *A new learning environment*. San Francisco: Jossey-Bass.

Coleman, J. C., Butcher, J. N., & Carson, R. C. (1984). *Abnormal psychology and modern life* (7th ed.). Glenview, IL: Scott, Foresman.

Cortes, J. B., & Gatti, F. M. (1972). *Delinquency and crime: A biopsychosocial approach*. New York: Seminar Press.

Davidson, W. S., & Robinson, M. J. (1975). Community psychology and behavior modification: A community based program for the prevention of delinquency. *Corrective and Social Psychiatry, 21*, 1–12.

Dorfman, A. (1984). The criminal mind. *Science Digest, 92*, 44–47.

Downes, D. (1966). *The delinquent solution: A study of subcultural theory*. London: Routledge & Kegan Paul.

Elliott, D. S., & Ageton, S. S. (1980). Reconciling race and class differences in self-reported and official estimates of delinquency. *American Sociological Review, 45*, 95–110.

Elliott, D. S., & Huizinga, D. (1983). Social class and delinquent behavior in a national youth panel. *Criminology, 21*, 149–177.

Elliott, D. S., & Voss, H. L. (1974). *Delinquency and dropout*. Toronto: Lexington Books.

Ellis, P. L. (1982). Empathy: A factor in anti-social behavior. *Journal of Abnormal Child Psychology, 10*, 123–134.

Emery, R. E., & O'Leary, K. D. (1982). Children's perceptions of marital discord and behavior problems of boys and girls. *Journal of Abnormal Child Psychology, 10*, 11–24.

Emler, N. P., Heather, N., & Winton, M. (1978). Delinquency and the development of moral reasoning. *British Journal of Social and Clinical Psychology, 17*, 325–331.

Empey, L. T., & Lubeck, S. G. (1972). *The Silverlake experiment: Testing delinquency theory and community intervention*. Chicago: Aldine.

Erskine, C. (1984). Female delinquency, feminism, and psychoanalysis. In C. R. Keith (Ed.), *The aggressive adolescent: Clinical perspectives*. New York: Free Press.

Faretra, G. (1981). A profile of aggression from adolescence to adulthood: An 18-year follow-up of psychiatrically disturbed and violent adolescents. *American Journal of Orthopsychiatry, 51*, 439–453.

Farrington, D. P. (1977). The effects of public labelling. *British Journal of Criminology, 17*, 112–125.

Farrington, D. P. (1979). Longitudinal research on crime and delinquency. In N. Morris & M. Tonry (Eds.), *Criminal justice: An annual review of research* (Vol. 1), pp. 289–348. Chicago & London: University of Chicago Press.

Farrington, D. P., Gundry, G., & West, D. J. (1975). The familial transmission of criminality. *Medicine, Science and the Law, 15,* 177–186.

Farrington, D. P., Osborn, S., & West, D. J. (1978). The persistence of labelling effects. *British Journal of Criminology, 18,* 277–284.

Fixsen, D. L., Phillips, E. L., & Wolf, M. M. (1973). Achievement Place: Experiments in self-government with predelinquents. *Journal of Applied Behavior Analysis, 6,* 31–49.

Fo, W. S., & O'Donnell, C. R. (1974). The buddy system: Relationships and contingency conditions in a community intervention program for youth with nonprofessionals as behavior change agents. *Journal of Consulting and Clinical Psychology, 42,* 163–169.

Fo, W. S., & O'Donnell, C. R. (1975). The buddy system: Effect of community intervention on delinquent offenses. *Behavior Therapy, 6,* 525–534.

Forehand, R., King, H., Peed, S., & Yoder, P. (1975). Mother-child interaction: Comparison of a noncompliant clinic group and a non-clinic group. *Behavior Research and Therapy, 13,* 79–84.

Friday, P. (1980). International review of youth crime and delinquency. In G. Newman (Ed.), *Deviance and crime: International perspectives.* London: Sage.

Gibbs, J. T. (1984). Black adolescents and youth: An endangered species. *American Journal of Orthopsychiatry, 54,* 6–21.

Gibson, H. B., & West, D. J. (1970). Social and intellectual handicaps as precursors of early delinquency. *British Journal of Criminology, 10,* 21–32.

Glueck, S., & Glueck, E. (1968). *Delinquents and nondelinquents in perspective.* Cambridge, MA: Harvard University Press.

Haapala, D. A. (1984). A discrimination of successful treatment outcomes for in-home family therapy: Homebuilders Model. Unpublished paper available from author at Behavioral Sciences Institute, 1717 South 341st Place, Suite B, Federal Way, WA 98003.

Hains, A. A., & Miller, D. J. (1980). Moral and cognitive development in delinquent and nondelinquent children and adolescents. *Journal of Genetic Psychology, 137,* 21–35.

Hawkins, R. P., Meadowcroft, P., Trout, B. A., & Luster, W. C. (1985). Foster family-based treatment. *Journal of Clinical Child Psychology, 14,* 220–228.

Heilbrun, A. B. (1979). Psychopathy and violent crime. *Journal of Consulting and Clinical Psychology, 47,* 509–516.

Hewitt, L. C., & Jenkins, R. L. (1946). *Fundamental patterns of maladjustment: The dynamics of their origin.* Springfield, IL: State of Illinois.

Hindelang, M. (1973). Causes of delinquency: A partial replication and extension. *Social Problems, 20,* 471–487.

Hirschi, T. (1969). *Causes of delinquency.* Berkeley: University of California Press.

Hirschi, T., & Hindelang, M. J. (1977). Intelligence and delinquency: A revisionist review. *American Sociological Review, 42,* 571–587.

Hoeffler, S. A., & Bornstein, P. H. (1975). Achievement Place: An evaluative review. *Criminal Justice and Behavior, 2,* 146–168.

Hogan, A., & Quay, H. (1984). Cognition in child and adolescent behavior disorders. In B. B. Lahey & A. E. Kazdin (Eds.), *Advances in clinical child psychology* (Vol. 7). New York: Plenum Press.

Hudgins, W., & Prentice, N. M. (1973). Moral judgments in delinquent and nondelinquent adolescents and their mothers. *Journal of Abnormal Psychology, 82,* 145–152.

Jesness, C. F. (1975). Comparative effectiveness of behavior modification and transactional analysis programs for delinquents. *Journal of Consulting Clinical Psychology, 43,* 758–779.

Jurkovic, G. J. (1980). The juvenile delinquent as a moral philosopher: A structural developmental perspective. *Psychological Bulletin, 88,* 709–727.

Jurkovic, G. J., & Prentice, N. M. (1977). Relation of moral and cognitive development to dimensions of juvenile delinquency. *Journal of Abnormal Psychology, 86,* 414–420.

Keilitz, E., Zaremba, B. A., & Broder, P. K. (1979). The link between learning disabilities and juvenile delinquency: Some issues and answers. *Learning Disability Quarterly, 2,* 2–11.

Keith, C. R. (1984). Individual psychotherapy and psychoanalysis with the aggressive adolescent: A historical review. In C. R. Keith (Ed.), *The aggressive adolescent: Clinical perspectives.* New York: Free Press.

King, C. H. (1975). The ego and the integration of violence in homicidal youth. *American Journal of Orthopsychiatry, 45,* 134–145.

Knight, B. J., & West, D. J. (1975). Temporary and continuing delinquency. *British Journal of Criminology, 17,* 43–50.

Knitzer, J. (1982). *Unclaimed children: The failure of public responsibility to children and adolescents in need of mental health services.* Washington, DC: Children's Defense Fund.

Knopf, I. J. (1984). *Childhood psychopathology: A developmental approach* (2nd ed.). Englewood Cliffs, NJ: Prentice-Hall.

Kornhauser, R. R. (1978). *Social sources of delinquency: An appraisal of analytic models.* Chicago: University of Chicago Press.

Krynicki, V. (1978). Cerebral dysfunction in repetitively assaultive adolescents. *The Journal of Nervous and Mental Disease, 166,* 59–67.

Lane, B. A. (1980). The relationship of learning disabilities to juvenile delinquency: Current status. *Journal of*

Learning Disabilities, 13, 20–29.

Lewis, D. O. (1976). Delinquency, psychomotor epileptic symptoms, and paranoid ideation: A triad. *American Journal of Psychiatry, 133,* 1395–1398.

Lewis, D. O., Pincus, J. H., Shanok, S. S., & Glaser, G. H. (1982). Psychosomotor epilepsy and violence in a group of incarcerated adolescent boys. *American Journal of Psychiatry, 139,* 882–887.

Lewis, D. O., Shanok, S. S., Pincus, J. H., & Glaser, G. H. (1979). Violent juvenile delinquents: Psychiatric, neurological, psychological and abuse factors. *Journal of the American Academy of Child Psychiatry, 18,* 307–319.

Liberman, R. P., Ferris, C., Salgado, P., & Salgado, J. (1975). Replication of the Achievement Place model in California. *Journal of Applied Behavior Analysis, 18,* 287–299.

Loeber, R., & Dishion, T. (1983). Early predictors of male delinquency: A review. *Psychological Bulletin, 94,* 68–99.

Massimo, J. L., & Shore, M. F. (1967). Comprehensive vocationally oriented psychotherapy: A new treatment technique for lower-class adolescent delinquent boys. *Psychiatry, 30,* 229–236.

Mays, J. B. (1954). *Growing up in the city.* Liverpool, England: University Press.

McCord, J. (1978). A thirty-year follow-up of treatment effects. *American Psychologist, 33,* 284–289.

McCord, J. (1979). Some child-rearing antecedents of criminal behavior in adult men. *Journal of Personality and Social Psychology, 37,* 1477–1488.

McCorkle, L., Elias, A., & Bixby, F. (1958). *The Highfields story: A unique experiment in the treatment of juvenile delinquency.* New York: Holt, Rinehart & Winston.

Mednick, S. A., & Hutchings, B. (1978). Genetic and psychophysiological factors in asocial behavior. *Journal of the American Academy of Child Psychiatry, 17,* 209–223.

Merton, R. K. (1938). Social structure and anomie. *American Sociological Review, 3,* 672–682.

Merton, R. K. (1957). *Social theory and social structure.* New York: Free Press.

Mikkelsen, E. J., Brown, G. L., Minichiello, M. D., Millican, E. K., & Rappaport, J. L. (1982). Neurologic status in hyperactive, enuretic, encopretic, and normal boys. *Journal of the American Academy of Child Psychiatry, 21,* 75–81.

Nye, F. I. (1958). *Family relationships and delinquent behavior.* New York: John Wiley.

O'Donnell, C. R., Lydgate, T., & Fo, W. S. (1979). The buddy system: Review and follow-up. *Child Behavior Therapy, 1,* 161–169.

Offord, D. R., Poushinsky, M. F., & Sullivan, K. (1978). School performance, IQ and delinquency. *British Journal of Criminology, 18,* 110–127.

Osborn, S. G. (1980). Moving home, leaving London and delinquent trends. *British Journal of Criminology, 20,* 54–61.

Osborn, S. G., & West, D. J. (1979). Conviction records of fathers and sons compared. *British Journal of Criminology, 19,* 120–133.

Palmer, T. B. (1974). The youth authority's community treatment project. *Federal Probation, 38,* 3–14.

Patterson, G. R. (1976). Aggressive child: Victim and architect of a coercive system. In L. A. Hamerlynck, L. C. Handy, & E. J. Mash (Eds.), *Behavior modification in families.* New York: Brunner/Mazel.

Patterson, G. R. (1977). Accelerating stimuli for two classes of coercive behaviors. *Journal of Abnormal Child Psychology, 5,* 335–350.

Patterson, G. R. (1982). *Coercive family processes.* Eugene, OR: Castalia.

Phillips, E. L. (1968). Achievement Place: Token reinforcement procedures in a home-style rehabilitation setting for "pre-delinquent" boys. *Journal of Applied Behavior Analysis, 1,* 213–223.

Phillips, E. L., Phillips, E. A., Fixsen, D. L., & Wolf, M. M. (1971). Achievement Place: Modification of the behaviors of pre-delinquent boys within a token economy. *Journal of Applied Behavior Analysis, 4,* 45–49.

Pincus, J. H., & Tucker, G. J. (1978). Violence in children and adults. *Journal of the American Academy of Child Psychiatry, 17,* 277–288.

Powers, E., & Witmer, H. (1951). *An experiment in the prevention of delinquency: The Cambridge-Somerville Youth Study.* New York: Columbia University Press.

President's Commission on Law Enforcement and Administration of Justice. (1969). Task force report on juvenile delinquency and youth crime. Washington, DC.

Quay, H. C. (1964). Dimensions of personality in delinquent boys as inferred from factor analysis of case history data. *Child Development, 35,* 479–484.

Quay, H. C. (1979). Classification. In H. C. Quay & J. S. Werry (Eds.), *Psychopathological disorders of childhood* (2nd ed.). New York: John Wiley.

Redl, F., & Wineman, D. (1957). *The aggressive child.* New York: Free Press.

Robins, L. N. (1966). *Deviant children grown up.* Baltimore, MD: Williams & Wilkins.

Robins, L. N., & Lewis, R. G. (1966). The role of the anti-social family in school completion and delinquency: A three-generation study. *Sociological Quarterly, 7,* 500–514.

Robins, L., West, P. A., & Herjanic, B. L. (1975). Arrests and delinquency in two generations: A study of black urban families and their children. *Journal of Child Psychology and Psychiatry, 16,* 125–140.

Rosenthal, A. (1975). Heredity in criminality. *Criminal Justice and Behavior, 2,* 3–21.

Rotenberg, M. (1974). Conceptual and methodological notes on affective and cognitive role-taking: An illus-

trative experiment with delinquent and nondelinquent boys. *Journal of Genetic Psychology, 125,*
177–185.

Rutter, M., & Giller, H. (1983). *Juvenile delinquency:
Trends and perspectives.* New York: Guilford Press.

Rutter, M., Yule, B., Quinton, D., Rowlands, O., Yule,
W., & Berger, M. (1975). Attainment and adjustment
in two geographical areas: III. Some factors account-
ing for area differences. *British Journal of Psychiatry,
126,* 520–533.

Ryall, R. (1974). Delinquency: The problem for treatment. *Social Work Today, 15,* 98–104.

Sanborn, C. J. (1983). Case management: A summary.
In C. J. Sanborn (Ed.), *Case management in mental
health services.* New York: Haworth Press.

Sarason, I. G. (1968). Verbal learning, modeling, and
juvenile delinquency. *American Psychologist, 23,*
254–266.

Sarason, I. G. (1978). A cognitive social learning approach to juvenile delinquency. In R. Hare & D.
Schalling (Eds.), *Psychopathic behavior: Approach to research* (pp. 299–317). New York: John Wiley.

Sarason, I. G., & Ganzer, V. J. (1973). Modeling and
group discussion in the rehabilitation of juvenile
delinquents. *Journal of Counseling Psychology, 20,*
442–449.

Sarri, R. C. (1980). Juvenile justice: Where we have been
and are today. In J. B. Jordan, D. A. Sabatino, &
R. C. Sarri (Eds.), *Disruptive youth in school.* Reston,
VA: Council for Exceptional Children.

Shanok, S. S., Malani, S. C., Ninan, O. P., Guggenheim, P., Weinstein, H., & Lewis, D. O. (1983). A
comparison of delinquent and nondelinquent adolescent psychiatric inpatients. *American Journal of Psychiatry, 140,* 582–585.

Shaw, C., & McKay, H. (1942). *Juvenile delinquency and
urban areas.* Chicago: University of Chicago Press.

Shore, M. F. (1984). Juvenile delinquency in the United
States: National issues and new directions for intervention. *Juvenile delinquency: An international perspective.* Boscoville Foundation.

Shore, M. F., & Massimo, J. L. (1979). Fifteen years after
treatment: A follow-up study of comprehensive
vocationally-oriented psychotherapy. *American Journal of Orthopsychiatry, 49,* 240–245.

Sindelar, K. A. (1982). Willie M: Treatment for troubled
children. *School Law Bulletin, 13*(1), 1–9.

Skrzypek, G. J. (1969). Effects of perceptual isolation
and arousal on anxiety, complexity preference, and

novelty preference in psychopathic and neurotic delinquents. *Journal of Abnormal Psychology, 74,* 321–329.

Snyder, J. J. (1977). A reinforcement analysis of interaction in problem and non-problem children. *Journal of
Abnormal Psychology, 86,* 528–535.

Teuber, H., & Powers, E. (1966). Evaluating therapy in a
delinquency prevention program. In G. E. Stollak,
B. G. Guerney, & M. Rothberg (Eds.), *Psychotherapy
research: Selected readings.* Chicago: Rand McNally.

Tolmach, J. (1985). "There ain't nobody on my side": A
new day treatment program for black urban youth.
Journal of Clinical Child Psychology, 14, 214–219.

Unger, K. V. (1978). Learning disabilities and juvenile
delinquency. *Journal of Juvenile and Family Courts, 29,*
25–30.

Vorrath, H. H., & Brendtro, L. K. (1974). *Positive peer culture.* Chicago: DeGruyther/Aldine. (Second edition
published 1985)

Wadsworth, M. (1979). *Roots of delinquency: Infancy, adolescence and crime.* Oxford, England: Margin Robert-
son.

Warren, M. Q. (1969). The case for differential treatment
of delinquents. *Annals of the American Academy of Political and Social Science, 381,* 47–60.

Warren, M. Q. (1977). Correctional treatment and coer-
cion: The differential effectiveness perspective.
Criminal Justice and Behavior, 4, 355–376.

Weeks, H. A. (1958). *Youthful offenders at Highfields: An
evaluation of the effects of the short-term treatment of delinquent boys.* Ann Arbor: University of Michigan
Press.

Whitehead, L. (1979). Sex differences in children's responses to family stress: A re-evaluation. *Journal of
Child Psychology and Psychiatry, 20,* 247–254.

Whittaker, J. K. (1979). *Caring for troubled children.* San
Francisco: Jossey-Bass.

Wilson, H. (1974). Parenting in poverty. *British Journal of
Social Work, 4,* 241–254.

Wilson, H. (1980). Parental supervision: A neglected aspect of delinquency. *British Journal of Criminology, 20,*
203–235.

Wolff, P. H., Waber, D., Bauermeister, M., Cohen, C., &
Ferber, R. (1982). The neurophysiological status of
adolescent delinquent boys. *Journal of Child Psychology and Psychiatry, 23,* 267–279.

Zinkus, P. W., & Gottlieb, M. G. (1979). Patterns of perceptual deficits in academically deficient juvenile delinquents. *Psychology in the Schools, 16,* 19–27.

He pictured himself lying sick unto death and his aunt bending over him beseeching one little forgiving word, but he would turn his face to the wall, and die with that word unsaid. Ah, how would she feel then? And he pictured himself brought home from the river, dead, with his curls all wet, how her tears would fall like rain, and her lips pray God to give her back her boy and she would never, never abuse him anymore! But he would lie there cold and white and make no sign—a poor little sufferer, whose griefs were at an end.

MARK TWAIN
THE ADVENTURES OF TOM SAWYER

A new teacher asked her class of eight emotionally disturbed and behaviorally disordered children to draw pictures of things that were special to them, so she could get to know them better. The depressed and angry child who drew this picture said, "I love tornadoes. They make big messes!"

CHAPTER THIRTEEN

Suicide in Young People

Betty Cooper Epanchin
WRIGHT SCHOOL, THE RE-EDUCATION CENTER
OF NORTH CAROLINA AND
UNIVERSITY OF NORTH CAROLINA AT CHAPEL HILL

Suicide among adolescents between the ages of 14 and 24 has apparently increased significantly in recent years.

Since the beginning of modern civilization, philosophers, theologians, historians, and scientists have been interested in and concerned about the topic of suicide; thus, to adequately study this multidimensional problem, a multidisciplinary view is needed.

Suicidal young people constitute a heterogeneous group. Research identifies factors that place youngsters at risk for suicide; few of these factors have to do with traditional psychological classifications.

Professionals who work with young people need to know what factors place a child at risk for committing suicide and what action to take if a youngster appears to be potentially suicidal. Professionals must identify and work with community resources.

Schools and other institutions can play a strategic role in preventing youthful suicides.

Different approaches to prevention are being used, and most systematic efforts appear promising.

IN JUNE, 1982, the *New York Times* reported "Two teenagers attempting to prove their love for each other leaped from a sixth-floor fire escape!" In April, 1985, Ann Landers's column featured the story of a 13-year-old girl's suicide under the headline, "Show of affection might have saved suicide victim." In October, 1984, the CBS Tuesday Night Movies series featured a drama about a 17-year-old boy who committed suicide in "Silence of the Heart." In February, 1986, all the major television news broadcasts carried the story of three teenage suicides that occurred during one week in Omaha, Nebraska. Legislation directed at preventing suicide among the young has been passed in California and Florida, and many school systems have instigated suicide prevention programs using local, state, and federal money. The topic of youthful suicide is of national and international concern.

How frequently does youthful suicide occur, and is it really on the rise? What leads a young person to kill himself? What are these youngsters like? Can we do anything to stop this tragic loss of life? Is anything being done to lower the suicide rate among young people?

PREVALENCE OF SUICIDE AMONG THE YOUNG

Although suicide among our young is still considered a rare occurrence, statistics indicate that suicide in the age group of 14 to 24 has increased rather dramatically in recent years. In the United States, 5.9 per 100,000 youths between the ages of 15 and 19 committed suicide in 1970, and 8.0 per 100,000 committed suicide in 1978. This represents a 35.6 percent increase between 1970 and 1978. Among females in this age range, the suicide rate in 1970 was 2.9 per 100,000; in 1978, it was 3.1 per 100,000, a 6.9 percent increase. But among males, the rate was 8.8 percent per 100,000 in 1970 and 12.8 percent in 1978—a 45.5 percent increase in 8 years (Hatton & Valente, 1984). Table 13–1 illustrates the increase in suicide rates by age and gender from 1950 to 1979.

For youngsters under 14, the prevalence rates are very low (1 in 100,000 for ages 10 to 14), but among teenagers and young adults, suicide is the second or third leading cause of death. As Table 13–1 illustrates, there is a strong male preponderance. Hawton and Osborn (1984) report a ratio of roughly 1.4 to 1 and 3.6 to 1 between males to females, although even higher ratios have been reported (Sheras, 1983).

Studies dealing with attempted suicide, or *parasuicide*, report much higher rates. Jacobziner (1965) found that for every completed suicide, there were 100 attempted suicides; Otto (1972) found three or four attempts for every completed suicide among males, whereas among females, 25 or 30 parasuicides occur for every one suicide. Hawton and Osborn (1984) report one study that found a ratio of 160 to 1, parasuicide to suicide. The rate of parasuicides is also increasing, perhaps as much as 250 percent (Kreitman & Schreiber, 1979), with girls outnumbering boys in suicide attempts. In the early 1960s the suicide rate among teenagers in the U.S. was higher for whites than for nonwhites; however, the pattern has recently reversed. By 1972, the suicide rate for nonwhites exceeded that for whites.

Methods for committing suicide vary with age and gender. Table 13–2 shows methods of suicide by sex and age in percentages. Firearms and explosives are the most common methods for adolescents; males appear to choose more violent methods than females, who more often use poison; and younger children more often use hanging or strangulation. Other authors (Husain & Vandiver, 1984) note that deliberate self-poisoning is the most frequently used method among suicide attempters.

Prevalence data on youthful suicide are generally believed to be underestimates. It is often difficult to determine whether a death was intentional or accidental. For example, a youngster who drives his car into a bridge abutment at a high speed and leaves no skid marks could have done so deliberately or could have fallen asleep at the wheel. Likewise, a youngster who uses drugs and alcohol together may do so in ignorance or deliberately. The accidental death rate is extraordinarily high among school age children, which causes some to question whether some of the deaths may be unreported suicides. When there is doubt as to whether a child's death is suicide or accident, it is frequently recorded as accidental, probably in an effort to protect the family:

Suicidal deaths may go unreported because of the stigma, guilt feelings of the survivors, or the extremely sensitive feelings associated with the taking of one's life. External forces influencing suppression of the statistics originate in the attitudes of family, church and insurance companies. The taboo also affects coroners, medical examiners and physicians, who may at times be inclined to list a more socially acceptable mode of death on the death certificate. (Hatton & Valente, 1984, p. 17)

Hatton and Valente also note that many coroners believe their primary obligation is to rule out homicide, and once they do this, further examination is minimal, often leaving suicides undetected.

Detection of suicide often requires a "psychological autopsy." This entails inquiry into the youngster's environment in an effort to identify signs of self-destruction, such as empty prescription bottles, guns, or a suicide note. The investigation is usually conducted by a suicide-prevention team, which interviews significant persons in the youngster's life and pays particular attention to the youngster's lifestyle in the period immediately preceding the suicide. As Weissman (1974) points out, however, "the material comes from secondary sources, people who knew the victim, not, of course, from the victim himself. This leaves a gap between what others say about a person after a tragic act, and what the person might have said about himself" (p. 27). Furthermore, probing into the circumstances surrounding a youngster's death can be so painful for the grief-stricken

TABLE 13–1
Suicide Rates per 100,000

| Year | Females | | | Males | | |
	10–14 yrs	15–19 yrs	20–24 yrs	10–14 yrs	15–19 yrs	20–24 yrs
1950	0.1	1.8	3.3	0.5	3.5	9.3
1960	0.2	1.6	2.9	0.9	5.6	11.5
1970	0.3	2.9	5.7	0.9	8.8	19.3
1975	0.4	2.9	6.7	1.2	12.0	25.9
1977	0.3	3.3	7.1	1.6	14.0	29.2
1978	0.4	3.0	6.3	1.2	12.6	26.8
1979	0.5	3.2	6.3	1.1	13.4	26.5

Source: From "The Epidemiology of Suicide in Adolescents" by L. Eisenberg, 1984, *Pediatric Annals, 13*, pp. 47–54. Adapted by permission.

and guilty survivors that the investigative team may feel it inappropriate and unethical to pursue the matter. Reviewing records from institutions with which the child was affiliated is also problematic because records rarely contain the type of detailed information needed.

In all probability, the statistics that describe parasuicides are also underestimates for all the same reasons. An additional problem in these statistics has to do with how cases of attempted suicide are identified. The statistics frequently reflect only cases admitted to general hospitals, but Whitehead, Johnson, and Ferrence (1973) found that when they also surveyed psychiatric hospitals, jails, and social and health agencies that dealt with outpatients, the number of identified overdoses and self-injuries increased more than 100 percent over the number based only on general hospital referrals!

Defining a suicide attempt is also problematic because such a wide range of behavior can fit into this category. Most teenagers, at one point in their lives, think about suicide. Many talk idly about it; some make threats; fewer make faint gestures, such as taking a few pills or superficially cutting themselves; even fewer make serious attempts. Studies vary with respect to which of these factors they include in definitions of parasuicide. Also, as with completed suicides, it is sometimes difficult to determine whether an event

was consciously or unconsciously motivated by self-destructive forces or was simply an accident. Some might claim that a nine-year-old child who runs in front of a school bus as it begins to move is suicidal; others would call the same event an accident. If the boy had been depressed, or had expressed the wish that he were dead, it might be easier to classify the behavior as suicidal.

HISTORICAL ATTITUDES TOWARD SUICIDE

The problem of suicide has always been part of civilization. Valente maintains:

A history of suicide is a history of man's eternal quest for the meaning of life, death, and the hereafter. The vital issues of life and death as well as the existence or nonexistence of the soul have been for millennia the almost exclusive province of theologians and philosophers. . . . Advances in modern medicine, the urbanization of society, the population explosion, and the use of science rather than religion to explain the unknown leads to the secularization of death and suicide. Finally, in our own century, the study of suicide becomes a scientific discipline and is referred to as suicidology. The individual is no longer castigated for committing or attempting to commit suicide but rather is excused because of forces beyond his or her control. (Valente, 1984, p. 1)

The evolution of attitudes toward suicide is interesting and relevant to current under-

TABLE 13–2
Methods of Suicide by Sex for Three Age Groups (1975)

Method	Age 10–14		Age 15–19		Age 20–24	
	Males	Females	Males	Females	Males	Females
Poisoning	0	19%	5%	24%	9%	29%
Gases	1%	0	7%	3%	8%	8%
Hanging/Strangulation/ Suffocation	47%	22%	22%	12%	17%	8%
Firearms/Explosives	51%	52%	62%	54%	60%	44%
Other Methods	1%	7%	4%	7%	6%	11%
	100%	100%	100%	100%	100%	100%

Data from the Mortality Statistics Branch, National Center for Health Statistics, U.S. Department of Health, Education, and Welfare.

standing and attitudes. During Roman times, suicide was considered an acceptable and honorable alternative to a life of shame and misery, as illustrated by the poet Seneca's statement, "Against all the injuries of life, I have the refuge of death" (McAnarney, 1979, p. 765), and at another time, "Do you like to live? Live. Do you not like to live? It is in your power to return from whence you came" (Valente, 1984, p. 3). Seneca, who lived during Nero's time, chose to commit suicide. It was his right as a Roman citizen; however, it was against Roman law for slaves, soldiers, and criminals to commit suicide. Soldiers and slaves were considered property of the state and therefore were not independent agents; suicide was considered an admission of guilt on the part of criminals and resulted in confiscation of their property.

Among the early Christians, suicide was a way to achieve martyrdom, eternal glory in heaven, and, in a few instances, sainthood. Eusebius, Bishop of Caesarea (ca. 260–340 A.D.), relates in his *Ecclesiastical History* that virgins committed suicide rather than be raped and Christians committed suicide rather than be tortured. He speaks of "the magnificent martyrs of Christ . . . regarding death as a prize snatched from the wickedness of evil men" (p. 3).

We know of at least two instances of mass suicide in antiquity. One occurred in Greece when maidens began hanging themselves for unknown reasons; the other occurred in 73 A.D. when 960 Jewish defenders of Masada committed a mass suicide. In response to both events, the leaders set forth more stringent laws regarding the legality of suicide and changes appeared in church law. Not long after Eusebius, St. Augustine (354–430) stated in *City of God* that the virgins had committed suicide in vain, for it is the mind and not the body that sins.

At the Council of Braga in 563 it was written into Canon Law that funeral rites should be denied to persons committing suicide. In 693, at the Council of Toledo, laws were extended even to those who attempted suicide,

and in 1284, persons who committed suicide had to be buried outside the city walls in open fields. St. Thomas Aquinas justified the church's position against suicide on the basis of three reasons: it was against nature and therefore a mortal sin; it was an injury to the community in which the person lived and participated; and it was a crime against God. It was reasoned that since God gave life, only He should take it away.

Suicide has been forbidden in the Western world and in other cultures. Islam forbids it as an act against God; several Indian tribes believed the soul of a person who committed suicide was not allowed into the land of the souls but must wander aimlessly forever. In Dahomey in Africa, the body of a person who committed suicide was thrown in the fields to be devoured by wild beasts instead of given a burial. The practices of not allowing someone to be buried among others or even to be buried at all stemmed from the belief that the suicide's damned soul would haunt the living and bring about disasters such as floods, famine, and disease.

As life took on greater value in the present and came to be considered more than a transition to the hereafter, thoughts about death and suicide began to change. The leading scientists of the seventeenth century—Galileo, Newton, Descartes—were also philosophers. They scrutinized the nature of human beings both scientifically and philosophically. By the eighteenth century, many were beginning to see human problems as environmentally based. Montesquieu wrote in *Persian Letters* that "when I am overwhelmed by pain, poverty, and scorn, why does one want to prevent me from putting an end to my troubles, and to deprive me cruelly of a remedy which is in my hands? . . . Life has been given to me as a gift. I can therefore return it when it is no longer" (Valente, 1984, p. 8).

By the nineteenth century, people began to study suicide with scientific methodologies. They gathered statistics on frequency and questioned cause and etiology. Valente (1984) says modern suicidology began with

Emile Durkheim's *Le Suicide* in 1897, in which Durkheim advocated looking at suicide on a societal rather than an individual basis. He describes four types of suicides: the "egoists," the "altruists," the "anomics," and the "fatalistics." He defined the egoists as persons who committed suicide because of their alienation from or lack of integration into society. Durkheim believed Catholics were more integrated into society and therefore less prone to suicide. The altruists were those who lived in societies with strict laws that allowed or expected suicide under certain circumstances. People who commit hara-kiri and the captain who goes down with his ship are examples of altruists. The anomics were persons who committed suicide in response to sudden changes in their places or roles in society, like those who lost their jobs or fortunes and then committed suicide during the Great Depression. Durkheim thought there were few fatalistics in modern society— people who felt their futures were blocked and their passions choked by oppressive discipline. Durkheim's examples were slaves and childless married women; although these examples are rare in today's culture, that probable sense of despair and fatalism is also felt by many of the young people who commit suicide today. The high rise in suicide among minorities, for example, may well reflect a hopelessness about ever achieving economic success.

Not long after Durkheim, Freud's theories began to influence thought. He focused on the individual and attributed suicide to aggression the individual turned inward or against the self:

Probably no one finds the mental energy required to kill himself unless, in the first place, in doing so he is at the same time killing an object with whom he has identified himself and, in the second place, is turning against himself a death-wish which had been directed against someone else. (Freud, 1955, p. 162)

As Valente points out, Freud's theory explains *how* but not *why*. Furthermore, since many people turn aggression inward, it does not explain why some actually commit suicide while others remain depressed or find other outlets for their anger.

Much more disciplined investigation has been conducted since the days of Freud and Durkheim. Many factors associated with suicide have been identified, but understanding why some people commit suicide is still not possible. Laws against suicide have been eliminated, but a stigma remains, and survivors typically feel a great deal of guilt, which makes objective study difficult. Valente (1984) maintains that "we need to repair the schism that occurred in the eighteenth century between science and philosophy. A revival of the 'marriage' might help us define more clearly the issues . . . the study of suicide is a multidimensional problem requiring a multidisciplinary approach. This is in essence what the history of suicide teaches us" (p. 11).

CHARACTERISTICS OF SUICIDAL YOUNG PEOPLE

Reading about youngsters who have committed suicide, one is immediately struck by their diversity. This is *not* a category of people who can easily be grouped on specific behavioral dimensions. This is a heterogeneous group of individuals characterized by an action that apparently has very personal meaning and motivation. We can use several dimensions to describe the characteristics of suicidal youngsters.

Psychiatric Diagnosis

The most frequent diagnosis for suicidal youngsters is depression (Carlson & Cantwell, 1982), although many who attempt and/or commit suicide are not clinically depressed. Shaffer (1974) found that 22 youngsters in his sample of 30 had antisocial symptoms, typically associated with conduct disorders. Greuling and DeBlassie (1980) report that the largest single group of suicidal youngsters are impulsive character disorders who, when angry, make homicidal as well as suicidal gestures. Pfeffer (1984) reports that the most frequent diagnosis for youngsters with both suicidal and assaultive tendencies was borderline personality. Psychosis has consistently been associated with a relatively small percentage of suicidal youngsters: Greuling and DeBlassie report that roughly 16 percent of all adolescent suicide attempts were diagnosed as psychotic.

Recent studies such as that of Cohen-Sandler, Berman, and King (1982) suggest that it is not depression per se but rather the *aspects* of depression—excessive life stress and a sense of hopelessness in dealing with one's life circumstances—that lead most youngsters to attempt or commit suicide. This study used 76 children between the ages of 5 and 14 who were consecutively discharged from an inpatient psychiatric unit. Extensive clinical data gathered at admission were used to assign the youngsters to one of three groups: suicidal, depressed but non-suicidal, and psychiatric controls. By reviewing their medical records, the researchers compared the children on measures of life stress and symptomatology. The suicidal children appeared to have had greater amounts of stress as they matured, with the stress increasing over time. They also had had more chaotic and disruptive family events that had resulted in losses and separations from important people. Sixty-five percent of the suicidal youngsters were also diagnosed as depressed; however, only 38 percent of the depressed children had engaged in suicidal behavior. Cohen-Sandler et al. conclude that the "suicide attempts of children in this study, when understood in the context of their dynamic biographies, represent active coping efforts to counteract the sense of helplessness they felt in being unable to effect changes in the stressful, chaotic conditions of their families" (p. 184).

Other recent studies show hopelessness to be significantly related to suicidal intent. Kazdin, French, Unis, Esveldt-Dawson, and Sherick (1983) studied 66 youngsters between the ages of 8 and 13 who had been hospitalized on a psychiatric ward. Kazdin et al. devised a Hopelessness Scale for Children; the children in their study responded *true* or *false* to items such as "All I can see ahead of me are bad things, not good things" and "There's no use in really trying to get something I want, because I probably won't get it." Children who had attempted suicide showed significantly greater hopelessness than did nonsuicidal children, and, when hopelessness was controlled, measures of depression did not correlate significantly with suicidal intent. Based on their findings, it appears that suicidal intent more clearly relates to hopelessness than to depression; perhaps the critical factor in explaining the overlapping relationship between depression and suicide is a sense of hopelessness.

One must remember that, under the best circumstances, it is difficult to diagnose internal moods. Alfred Alvarez (1971) described suicidal individuals' motives as "devious, contradictory, labyrinthine, and mostly out of sight" (p. 89). Furthermore, until recently, children's depression was rarely diagnosed; overt behaviors were more often the basis for diagnoses. As we discussed in Chapter 9, depressive feelings are often acted out through aggressive behavior; hence, many of the youngsters described as suicidal and antisocial may be primarily depressed but use antisocial means of expressing their feelings. Finally, many, if not most, youngsters who commit suicide are not in treatment at the time of their suicide. The diagnoses are often determined posthumously, a practice that raises questions about their validity. Nonetheless, psychiatric diagnoses are more descriptive and precise than some other organizers that are used.

Suicidal Motivation

Events and feelings preceding the suicidal gesture or suicide attempt have been studied in an attempt to determine motivation.

Again, there are problems with using this organizer. The information comes from informants, after the suicide, and the real meaning of the event or the individual's feeling is, as Camus observed, "within the silence of the heart" (Camus, 1955, p. 4).

Loss of a loved one. A frequently identified precipitating factor is loss of a loved one. Lawler, Nakielny, and Wright (1963) found that several of the suicidal youngsters they studied had lost a parent through death or separation, a few had lost teachers, one had lost a family pet, and several had lost prestige through failure in school. Mattsson, Seese, and Hawkins (1969) conducted a retrospective and follow-up study of 75 youngsters who had made suicidal gestures, and they too found that loss of a love object (17, or 23 percent) was one of the most frequently mentioned precipitating factors.

Vivienne Loomis, whose story is told in *Vivienne* (Mack & Hickler, 1981), committed suicide when she was 14 years old. A number of factors appeared to contribute to her suicide, among which was her love for her sixth-grade teacher, John May, a young man who had given her much encouragement and support.

John May, a Vietnam draft objector and a Quaker from California, came East to do his alternate service; he was working in the private school Vivienne attended. He saw Vivienne as an unusually sensitive and creative young girl, and set about trying to help her feel better about herself and her abilities. (Vivienne had been an outcast in school the previous year.) Vivienne in turn idolized him, and when she learned of his plans to return to California when his service was over, she became increasingly distraught. Her journal entry shortly after she learned about his plans contained the first hint of her suicidal thoughts.

During the next two years of Vivienne's life, a number of other changes occurred, all

of which represented emotional losses to her. Her family made plans to move from her childhood home; she changed schools, leaving behind friends and security at a small private school to go to a new "impersonal" (in her eyes) school; and her parents, while physically present, were emotionally distracted by the decision about whether to move. During this time, the despondent themes became more pronounced in her journal entries, but during much of that period, she appeared more independent and happy. Nineteen days later she committed suicide by hanging herself.

Marked self-depreciation and alienation. Suicidal youngsters frequently seem to have feelings of unhappiness about their value as individuals and their importance to others. Mattsson et al. found these feelings among 20 to 27 percent of the youngsters they studied. These self-deprecatory feelings often represent a sudden behavioral deterioration and/or marked change in mood and behavior. Other behavior problems are underfunctioning in school, mood changes, social withdrawal, bouts of weeping, sleep disturbance, somatic symptoms, and communication of suicidal ideas (Connell, 1972).

The suicide note left by a 17-year-old Chicago boy who shot himself illustrates his despair:

I'm sick and there is no obvious cure. God forgive me. I smoke and I cannot stop. I cannot control my diabetes. I steal. I lie. I'm failing in typing and trigonometry. I have been thrown out of physics class. My teachers are not to blame, they did their best. My parents, partly, they did not prepare me for life. I'm sorry for the troubles I'm causing. But my troubles will be over. Please have them sing the hymn "Amazing Grace" at my funeral.

We saw the same kind of self-depreciation in Vivienne's writing. The summer before Vivienne killed herself, her family spent the summer in Maine; while there, she attempted suicide. Around the same time, the family found out that Vivienne's older sister was pregnant, and Vivienne's suicidal gesture was not taken too seriously. At the end of that summer, she wrote a poem that poignantly illustrates her detachment and alienation.

Suggestibility. It has often been noted that when the topic of suicide is receiving public attention, the incidence of suicides increases. Known as the "Werther effect," this notion grew out of observations gathered in the late 1700s. In 1774, Goethe published a romantic novel entitled *The Sorrows of Young Werther*, a story about a gifted young man who shot himself in the head when despondent over unrequited love. The book was believed to have caused a wave of imitative suicides in impressionable young people, which caused authorities in several principalities to ban the book. Sociologist David Phillips tested the hypothesis that publicity increases suicides by comparing suicide rates after highly publicized suicides in the Los Angeles area to suicide rates when the topic was receiving less attention (Phillips, 1974). He found a significant correlation between the increase in suicides and the extent of publicity as measured by the length of news articles and circulation size of the newspaper. Additionally, Bollen and Phillips (1982) found an increase in suicides after suicide stories were broadcast on the evening television news. (Because of this phenomenon, the media have been encouraged to focus news accounts of suicides on the educational aspects—that is, on what can be done in the way of prevention rather than on the sensationalistic aspects.)

A poem written by Harriet Moore when she was 10 years old in reaction to the death of a classmate attests to the potence of suggestibility:

I hear them whispering—what is it?
"Lizzie Wescott—hush."
Where is she? Yesterday she was here—
So nice, so pretty, with curly hair—
Here at her desk, like me.
It's something awful—where is she?
"Hush—Lizzie Wescott is dead."
Dead.
What is it to be dead?

It's easy—anybody might do it—
Yes,—even me!

Why do I think of it all the time,
God?
Please take the thought from me—
I don't want to!
It's too dark for a little girl down there,
And too cold.

Take it away.
If I step on that crack in the sidewalk—I'll have to do it.
Oh, awful, if I should step on that crack!
Help me over it, God—surely you don't want me to do it!
Thank you!
Oh, help me!

Why am I running so fast—
Running away!
Oh, why did I see it—
That big blue bottle with Poison on it, and a skull—and two bones!
Now I'll have to do it—
It's right there—so near!
How can I help it now?

Fortunately, Harriet Moore did not succumb to the suggestion raised by her friend's suicide and did not find out firsthand what death meant to a young person. She grew up to be a poet and editor.

Rage, hostility, and a wish for revenge. Feelings of rage, hostility, and revenge are frequently mentioned as motivations for attempting or committing suicide. Hurry (1977) describes the treatment of Jessie, a suicidal adolescent girl whose family was "highly disturbed." Both her mother and father were repeatedly sadistic and sometimes abusive toward her. Jessie described her angry feelings toward them as "cold with hate." Her suicide attempt followed a particularly unpleasant family fight during which both parents physically attacked her. In treatment, she revealed that she had had fantasies about being a ghost and seeing her family and her therapist "grovelling" (p. 77). She imagined them beating their breasts and saying it was all their fault. She wanted them to experience public shame and neighbors to talk about what bad parents she had had. She also imagined her mother writing to the newspapers about what a bad analyst she had had, and hoped he would no longer be allowed to practice analysis. She described her home as the "gas chamber" and her mother looking at her "with such hate in her eyes." She also related during therapy how her father had attacked her and shouted that he would murder her while her mother "danced around and laughed" (p. 78).

Everstine and Everstine (1983) elaborate on this motive. They postulate that (1) suicide is intended to send a message from one person (the "victim") to another; (2) the suicide act is performed for the individual who is the intended recipient of the message; and (3) the primary content of the message is anger. Symbolically, the suicide "victim" is not the real victim—the real victim is the recipient of the suicide message. The recipient is placed in the "mythic role of murderer" (p. 211) and must bear the burden of guilt.

A distorted view of death. Besides these motivations for suicide, a number of authors note that many suicidal youngsters lack a mature understanding of death. It is consistently reported that children and adolescents do not really understand the finality of death. Many youngsters report thinking that death is temporary, the same as or at least similar to sleep. McIntyre and Angle questioned 597 children, ages 6 to 16, about death (Valente, 1984). Many of the younger children described death as a reversible event and denied the finality of death. Older youngsters reported believing in a spiritual continuation after death. Orbach, Gross, and Glaubman (1981) tell of an orphan boy who "hoped to meet his parents in heaven where they would continue to live again as if none of them had died," and of a young child who knew that God would give him "candies and send him back to earth on a special ray" (p. 185). They also describe a ten-and-a-half-year-old boy who planned to commit suicide so his parents could collect the insurance money to provide better medical services for his sick sibling and another youngster who believed that "it is good to be dead for it is like sleeping . . . I will lay in my grave and I will be warm" (p. 185).

Analyzing death fantasies of the youngsters in their sample of 11 children who had attempted or threatened suicide and who were between 6½ and 12½ years of age, Orbach, Gross, and Glaubman (1981) report that the fantasies reflected a belief that death is some sort of continuation of life, usually an improved and more satisfying experience. They note that these beliefs can coexist with more realistic views of the finality of death and can fluctuate with changes in life circumstances and inner changes.

Piaget (1923) observed that young children (up to 6 or 7 years) attributed life, or the concept of being alive, to anything that was active; youngsters between the ages of 7 and 11 cognitively knew that death was a final event, but only in adolescence was the concept mature affectively and cognitively. Nagy (1959) observes that until the age of 5, youngsters see death as temporary; between 5 and

9, the child understands that it is irreversible; after age 9, that it is an internal process that happens to everyone and is inevitable.

Family background. Characteristics of the families are important in considering why youngsters are suicidal. Studies report that suicidal youngsters come from broken homes or from unhappy families. Pfeffer (1981) studied 5 hospitalized inpatient suicidal youngsters of latency age and noted these family patterns: (1) power and authority relationships seemed to shift, making it difficult to determine who was in charge of whom; (2) conflict between the parents was open, and the threat of separation was ever-present; (3) parents projected their hostile and ambivalent feelings toward their spouses onto the suicidal youngster; (4) the suicidal child had a particularly close attachment with one of the parents; and (5) a rigid family system responded to change as a threat, was characterized by denial, secretiveness, and lack of open communication, and allowed the suicidal youngster no feeling of power.

Hurry (1977) illustrates the type of special relationship referred to by Pfeffer in the description of Jessie. In treatment, Jessie expressed her awareness that her mother could not perceive Jessie as having feelings of her own and independent from her mother's. As Jessie stated, "She probably picked me up if I was crying, but she would not see if I was hungry or needed my nappy changing: she probably grippled me and put me down again" (p. 68). The mother openly blamed Jessie for many of her own illnesses and frequently reminded Jessie that she had been sick every day for the nine months of her pregnancy. The mother also told Jessie how much her teeth had hurt when she was breast-feeding, then reassured Jessie, "You'll always be my little girl" (p. 68). Pfeffer also offers case material illustrating the family patterns, although her descriptions are briefer than those of some other authors.

The concept of the "expendable child" has also been offered as a possible explanation for youngsters' suicides. This hypothesis presumes "a parental wish, conscious or unconscious, spoken or unspoken, that the child interprets as their desire to be rid of him, for him to die" (Sabbath, 1969, p. 273). In this model the parents see the child as a threat to their well-being, and the child sees the parents as persecutors and oppressors. This causes the child to feel and think that he or she is going to be abandoned. Stresses associated with adolescence place additional strain on already troubled relationships. Youngsters who see themselves as expendable tend to come from financially marginal families, from families who fight about money and/or blame their monetary problems on the child. Rabkin (1978) relates an account of a suicidal youngster that illustrates this concept:

> I first knew I was cracking up when I was fourteen. I bit my hand as hard as I could and I drew blood. I called my mom and said, "Look! I need help." And she said, "There's a good movie on downstairs and we have company." At the time I really felt like a fool. But now, looking at it from a different perspective, I could boot her ass for her reaction.
>
> It wasn't long after that I made my first suicide attempt. I remember I was going with my mother and sister to a roadside stand to buy some corn. I had taken two bottles of sleeping pills before we left and I told my mother what I had done a few minutes after we got into the car. She said, "I hope you're happy. Now we can't go to get corn. We'll have to go to the hospital to have your stomach pumped." I said, "Well just forget it then." And she forgot it. I went home and slept it off. I guess the pills weren't too powerful. (quoted in Husain & Vandiver, 1984, p. 110)

Cultural factors. Cross-cultural studies have attempted to identify differences in cultures that have high suicide rates to cultures that have low suicide rates. Once isolated, these indices generate hypotheses about why suicides occur on a social or cultural level.

An example of this approach is McAnarney's (1979) study. She compared rates of suicide among adolescents in English-speaking countries and generated a number of hypotheses, critical factors she identified were family, religion, mobility and change, achievement orientation, and outlets for expressing aggression. Specifically, she found that in societies where family ties were close, suicide rates were lower, and, conversely, societies where family ties were not as tight had high suicide rates. She concluded:

Loss of the intact family, whether it is from the death of a parent or parents, divorce, separation, or the family's changing status, is an important variable in the histories of some contemporary

adolescents who take their own lives. One of the major tasks of adolescence is the acquisition of one's adult identity. In the presence of supportive families, teenagers usually pass through this developmental phase without major problems. If adolescents have lost one or both parents and do not have adequate parent substitutes, they may be severely compromised in their ability to complete this developmental phase without being vulnerable to impulsive, self-destructive behaviors to avoid confronting their failures. (McAnarney, 1979, pp. 767–768)

She also found that in cultures with low suicide rates, the majority of the people subscribed to a formal religion; conversely, where formal religion was not generally accepted, suicide rates were high. Catholic countries and Orthodox Jewish communities tended to have low rates, perhaps because both religions frown upon suicide. Table 13–3 lists suicide rates for selected countries.

Disorganized, transitional geographic areas also had high suicide rates, as did

TABLE 13–3
**Suicide Rates from Selected Countries During 1981, by Gender
(Rate per 100,000 population.)**

Country	Males Ages 15–24	All Ages	Females Ages 15–24	All Ages
Australia	17.6	16.4	4.5	5.6
Austria	33.6	42.1	6.8	14.5
Denmark	17.1	38.9	5.0	21.3
France	14.6	28.5	5.0	11.1
Germany, Fed. Rep.	21.2	29.6	6.4	14.4
Ireland	9.7	8.6	1.8	2.9
Israel	10.8	8.1	1.2	3.8
Japan	14.8	22.0	6.4	12.4
Netherlands	5.3	12.2	3.8	7.9
Norway	20.2	19.1	3.3	6.5
Poland	19.5	21.8	4.3	4.0
Sweden	14.3	24.6	4.1	10.6
Switzerland	33.5	33.6	10.2	14.4
United Kingdom	7.0	11.4	2.1	6.5
United States	19.7	18.0	4.6	5.7

Source: US Center for Health Statistics-Comparative International Statistics

highly mobile communities. Both variables appear to be particularly relevant to adolescents, who are in the developmental transition from childhood to adulthood and need support and guidance in adapting to change and the process of growing up.

Achievement-oriented cultures and cultures that suppress aggressive feelings also had higher suicide rates (McAnarney, 1979). These types of cultures pressure the individual to achieve; failure can therefore be painful. Youngsters who are struggling with many pressures often do not do well in school, which only compounds their personal problems and sense of worthlessness.

Mack and Hickler (1981) considered many issues in discussing the reasons that led Vivienne Loomis to commit suicide, one of which was the educational system Vivienne attended in her early years. They note:

But schools themselves are not entirely to blame. Societies generally design the educational systems they need and want. Our society seems to impose a business model on our schools. Students are placed in competitive situations with one another as though each individual were a profit-making organization. At a time when young people seek their own self-acceptance through friendships, we pit them against each other. In the stage when adolescents need to identify with adults, we subject most of them to large schools and impersonal and authoritative teachers. We take the unready and forming personality, full of its own uncertainties and doubts, and require proof of its "earning power." Our courses seem aimed at a "final product." (Mack & Hickler, 1981, pp. 164–165)

Cultures that do not sanction the expression of aggression exert different type of pressure on individuals. These cultures foster guilt about one's angry feelings, which also leads to feelings of worthlessness. Adolescence is a time of normal rebellion and faultfinding as a means of establishing a separate identity. Youngsters who lack so-cially acceptable means of expressing their feelings and needs may have trouble with this developmental process and may suppress and internalize their feelings.

Japan has a high suicide rate, and besides fitting some of the cultural criteria we have mentioned, the Japanese consider the dead to be divine, no matter how sinful they were during their lifetimes. Their sins are forgiven when they die, and they are worshipped as holy spirits. Many Japanese people who are experiencing financial, physical, or psychological problems consider death preferable to dependence on others. Another social value that may contribute to their high suicide rate is the parental expectation that children think like their parents and share their parents' joys and sorrows (Husain & Vandiver, 1984). According to Ohara (1963), parent-child suicides (with the mother killing the child and then taking her own life) accounts for 16 percent of the multiple suicides in Japan—a higher ratio than in most countries.

When considering these cross-cultural studies, one must remember that not all countries keep the same types of records, the same quality of records, or keep records at all. Data on suicide in some underdeveloped nations, are nonexistent; whereas countries like Sweden and Australia keep extensive and detailed records. The high rates found in those countries may be partly a function of good record-keeping. Countries in which suicide is considered an unacceptable method of dying may underreport more than other countries.

Referring to social and cultural influences, it is interesting to examine the suicide death rate for all ages over time. Variance in the rate appears to be at least partly a function of the social and economic times. Table 13–4, for example, shows that the suicide death rate decreased sharply during both World War I and World War II. Yessler (1968) notes that war provides individuals with a greater opportunity to discharge hostility or, alternatively, suicides may more often be counted as battle casualties. It is also interesting that suicide rates peaked during 1932, the middle of the Great Depression and a period of particular social and economic unrest.

ASSESSMENT OF SUICIDE POTENTIAL

The American Association of Suicidology (1977) identified five "danger signs" of someone at risk for committing suicide. They are:

TABLE 13–4
United States Suicide Death Rates (1900–1982)*

Year	SDR**	Year	SDR	Year	SDR
1982	12.2	1954	10.1	1926	12.6
1981	12.0	1953	10.1	1925	12.0
1980	11.9	1952	10.0	1924	11.9
1979	12.6	1951	10.4	1923	11.5
1978	12.5	1950	11.4	1922	11.7
1977	13.3	1949	11.4	1921	12.4
1976	12.5	1948	11.2	1920	10.2
1975	12.7	1947	11.5	1919	11.5
1974	12.1	1946	11.5	1918	12.3
1973	12.0	1945	11.2	1917	13.0
1972	12.0	1944	10.0	1916	13.7
1971	11.7	1943	10.2	1915	16.2
1970	11.6	1942	12.0	1914	16.1
1969	11.1	1941	12.8	1913	15.4
1968	10.7	1940	14.4	1912	15.6
1967	10.8	1939	14.1	1911	16.0
1966	10.9	1938	15.3	1910	15.3
1965	11.1	1937	15.0	1909	16.0
1964	10.8	1936	14.3	1908	16.8
1963	11.0	1935	14.3	1907	14.5
1962	10.9	1934	14.9	1906	12.8
1961	10.4	1933	15.9	1905	13.5
1960	10.6	1932	17.4	1904	12.2
1959	10.4	1931	16.8	1903	11.3
1958	10.7	1930	15.6	1902	10.3
1957	9.8	1929	13.9	1901	10.4
1956	10.0	1928	13.5	1900	10.2
1955	10.2	1927	13.2		

*Death rates are per 100,000 population annually.
**Suicide death rate (SDR) obtained from the National Center for Health Statistics, U.S. Dept. of Health, Education and Welfare and the Historical Statistics of the United States: Colonial times to 1957. U.S. Dept. of Commerce, Bureau of the Census.

- A suicide threat/statement or behavior indicating a wish or intention to die
- A previous suicide attempt
- Mental depression
- Marked changes in behavior and/or personality
- Making final arrangements (e.g., giving away prized possessions)

Several techniques are clinically useful in assessing potential for suicide, but none can stand alone. This type of assessment requires both careful and thorough examination of all aspects of the youngster's life as well as input from friends, the child, the parents, mental health professionals, and teachers. Tragically, it happens all too often after a youngster has committed suicide that people reveal they knew of the youngster's despair and suicidal thoughts, but, for a variety of reasons, did not share their knowledge with others.

Perhaps the most direct and accessible assessment technique is the clinical interview. Koocher (1974) observes that children are interested in discussing their ideas about death and will elaborate in great detail. Many adults, however, are reluctant to discuss the topics of suicide and death with youngsters for fear they will "put ideas in their head"— despite repeated assurance that these discussions do not provoke suicidal action and may in fact prevent a suicide. Certainly, teachers and other professionals should not necessarily raise this topic out of the blue, but any adult who suspects that a child's moods or behavior indicate preoccupation with death or dying should either talk to the youngster directly and privately or encourage another adult who has a close relationship with the youngster to talk to him or her.

After the interviewer establishes good rapport with the youngster, he should ask questions that help clarify the extent of suicidal ideation and behavior, the degree of alienation and depression, cognitive understanding of suicide and death, personality strength, and amount of available environmental support. Corder and Haizlip (1982) outline the types of questions to ask of the youngster and the parent when assessing suicide potential (see Table 13–5).

TABLE 13–5
Examples of Evaluation Questions for Children and Parents*

Child Questions**	Parent Questions
It seems things haven't been going so well for you lately. Your parents and/or teachers have said _____. Most children your age would feel upset about that.	Has any serious change occurred in your child's or your family's life recently (within the last year)?
Have you felt upset, maybe some sad or angry feelings you've had trouble talking about? Maybe I could help you talk about these feelings and thoughts.	How did your child respond?
Do you feel like things can get better or are you worried (afraid, concerned) things will just stay the same or get worse?	Has your child had any accidents or illnesses without a recognizable physical basis?
Other children I've talked to have said that when they feel that sad and/or angry they thought for awhile that things would be better if they were dead. Have you ever thought that? What were your thoughts?	Has your child experienced a loss recently?
What do you think it would feel like to be dead?	Has your child experienced difficulty in any areas of his/her life?
How do you think your father and mother would feel? What do you think would happen with them if you were dead?	Has your child been very self-critical or have you or his/her teachers been very critical lately?
Has anyone that you know of attempted to kill themselves? Do you know why?	Has your child made any unusual statements to you or others about death or dying? Any unusual questions or jokes about death or dying?
Have you thought about how you might make yourself die? Do you have a plan?	Have there been any changes you've noticed in your child's mood or behavior over the last few months?
Do you have (the means) at home (available)?	Has your child ever threatened or attempted suicide before?
Have you ever tried to kill yourself before?	Have any of his friends or family, including yourselves, ever threatened or attempted suicide?
What has made you feel so awful?	How have these last few months been for you? How have you reacted to your child (anger, despair, empathy, etc.)?

*These are modifications of Corder and Haizlip (1982).
**Words and phrasings should be changed to better fit the child and/or interviewer. Two things need to be accomplished during this questioning: (1) to gather more information about the child, and (2) to try to evaluate the parents in terms of their understanding, cooperation, quality of connection with their child, energy to be available to a child in crisis.
From "Suicidal Crises in Schools" by J. Davis, 1985, *School Psychology Review, 14.* Copyright 1985 by *School Psychology Review.* Reprinted by permission.

Davis (1985) suggests nine criteria to consider in interpreting the information obtained through interviews:

1. Degree of suicidal potential. Davis cites the five-point suicide continuum developed by Pfeffer, Conte, Plutchik and Jerrett (1980) that ranges from a = nonsuicidal to e = serious attempt (an attempt that would have killed the child or an attempt that the child clearly thought was lethal). On this scale, b = suicidal ideation, which is quite common and fairly normal, as long as the child is not obsessed with the thoughts; c = suicidal threats, such as "I'm going to hang myself"; and d = mild attempts that the child *believed* would not really be fatal.

2. Presence of a suicidal plan. Children who have thought about a realistic plan and have the means available to carry out the plan are at greater risk for actually committing suicide. Planning is relatively nonexistent in preoperational youngsters, however, and extremely impulsive youngsters are not likely to develop plans, even if they are cognitively capable of doing so.

3. Past suicide attempts. The child's past suicide attempts as well as the suicidal behavior of individuals close to the child should be carefully examined. Many children who commit suicide have made previous attempts and/or are from families in which suicide has been committed or attempted.

4. Presence of depression, hopelessness, feelings of worthlessness, resignation, or rage. These and other intense feelings are associated with suicide, and alcohol and drug abuse are frequent in suicidal youngsters.

5. Family background. Determining whether child abuse is present, whether or not family members are suicidal, and whether there have been significant losses, separations, or changes is of particular concern.

6. Precipitating events. Youngsters rarely commit suicide in reaction to only one stressful or disappointing event. Suicide is usually a response to an accumulation of disappointments—"the straw that broke the camel's back."

7. Response from support network. The child needs a *lifeline*—"one or more interested persons who want the patient to stay alive. An immobilized other, no matter how significant, is not a lifeline. In fact, if he is immobilized enough, he may unconsciously drive the patient to suicide" (Beebe, 1975, p. 38). The clinician must carefully assess the messages from lifeline to child, be they conscious or unconscious, or spoken or unspoken. Rare is the parent who would openly express a wish for a child to commit suicide, but an overburdened single parent or a parent enmeshed in the hostility of divorce may convey such a wish, or at least be immobilized.

8. Child's concept of death. As we have said, many youngsters who commit or attempt suicide have a distorted view of death. Many view death as a haven, a peaceful, positive process. More difficult to assess is that many youngsters have both a realistic understanding of death and a fantasized notion of it. Children with this attitude are at greater risk.

9. Ego functioning. Obviously, youngsters who have problems with reality testing and/ or impulsivity and who use more primitive defenses are at greater risk for committing suicide.

Other techniques for assessing suicidal risk include the Hopelessness Scale (Kazdin et al., 1983) mentioned earlier. Hopelessness has been empirically associated with suicidal behavior. The standard psychological assessment battery described in Chapter 5 is also useful in determining why a child feels suicidal and how he feels about himself. This assessment provides valuable information about personality strengths in general.

If an adult believes a child is at risk for committing suicide, the adult should not promise to keep the information confidential, but should inform the child that the information must be shared. Rather than betraying a confidence, this action is protective and therefore reassuring. When a child is suspected of suicide, hospitalization should be considered until the crisis is past.

TREATMENT OF SUICIDE ATTEMPTERS

Suicidal youth are a heterogeneous group; consequently, there are no unique interventions for dealing with them. The most appropriate interventions are those that are individualized to address personal problems as well as family and social problems.

Several issues of intervention merit attention. First, what should adults do when they suspect that a child is suicidal? How does one manage the child until more long-term, individualized help is obtained? Second, what can be done on a societal level to prevent the growing problem of suicide? Third, what can be done for the survivors to help them deal with their inevitable guilt, anger, and loss?

Managing Potentially Suicidal Youngsters

Most people find dealing with a potentially suicidal person a frightening responsibility. They fear they may be overreacting or that they will do the wrong thing. They are uncomfortable talking about why they are worried (superstitiously wanting to avoid naming the fear) and often do not know where to go for advice and direction. The worst alternative, however, is avoidance. When one has concerns about another's potential for suicide, one should not hesitate to convey these concerns to the child. During this conversation, the adult should convey concern for the child while also exploring how seriously suicidal the youngster may be. To assess the degree of seriousness, the adult should discuss with the child the topics we have outlined. At this point, assessment is part of treatment.

The adult may wish to involve parents, a mental health worker, or school counselor. Collaboration among several people is often helpful in assessing the child's current status. If there is any doubt that the child might be seriously suicidal, it is both wise and ethical for those who are untrained and inexperienced in managing suicide prevention to refer the child to professionals. Grave consequences can result from an untrained individual's either denying the seriousness of self-destructive behavior or trying to deal with the problem independently.

A referring professional should be specific in conveying his concerns about a child's suicidal potential. The referral source should share relevant information about current stressors, emotional state, and behavior, as well as information about relevant background and development. Too often school personnel refer youngsters without conveying their specific concerns, so the mental health professional may not focus on their concerns. Several hours with a youngster cannot compare to observations gained at school over long periods.

When mental health professionals believe a child is at high risk for committing suicide, they can admit the youngster to an inpatient facility where around-the-clock supervision and crisis counseling are available. Most inpatient programs have established procedures for dealing with suicidal youngsters, often called *suicide watches*, to insure that the child is not alone at any time and is under continuous surveillance. Pfeffer (1986) lists the functions a psychiatric hospital fulfills for suicidal children:

1. Protect the child from his own suicidal behavior

2. Remove the child from the environmental stressors that are currently aggravating the child

3. Conduct multimodality diagnostic assessments

4. Work to change the family equilibrium

5. Help the child get involved in the normal activities of daily living

6. Provide therapeutic contact with a variety of professionals around the clock

7. Coordinate and compile observations of the various therapies and therapists

8. Decrease the child's sense of isolation by encouraging participation in activities with peers, school, and recreational activities

9. Monitor treatment progress

10. Plan for a coordinated discharge

Therapeutic treatment in a hospital can be beneficial for suicidal children and their families, but the process of hospitalizing a child can be confusing and discouraging if one is not informed about how to proceed. Some school systems have negotiated contracts with local mental health officials so that when a potentially suicidal youngster is identified, specific persons are available as consultants to determine how best to manage the case. These people also function as collaborators in getting the child admitted to a hospital service, when that is necessary. These proactive, preventive arrangements can prevent the frustrating situation that occurred in Jon's case.

Jon's tenth-grade English teacher became concerned about Jon after reading an essay that to her sounded bizarre and depressed. She asked him to stay after class and expressed her concern, but he was not willing to talk. He denied feeling upset, said he didn't think the essay was any reason for concern, and seemed to want to get out of her class as quickly as possible. She did not insist that he talk further since he so clearly did not want to, so she reiterated her regard for him and let him go. She did, however, share her concerns with the school counselor, who began asking others in the school about Jon. The counselor discovered that Jon had indeed been having problems in recent months—his grades had dropped from As and Bs to Cs, Ds, and Fs, and it was alleged that he had made a fairly benign attempt at suicide. With these data, the counselor called Jon's parents, who were surprised and concerned. Jon, his parents, the counselor, and the school principal met to talk about their concern and plan an immediate referral to professionals. Alternatives were outlined and the parents selected whom they wished to see. They contacted the professionals, who did not have time in their schedules to see Jon immediately. Two other outpatient treatment facilities were approached; neither could take Jon immediately, so they decided to go to the emergency room of the hospital. There they were seen, and hospitalization was recommended; however, the hospital had no beds in the psychiatric wards, and hospital officials were unwilling to admit Jon to another service because they could not provide continuous observation. Another hospital was consulted, but they too were full. The family was sent back home, and admission was planned in four days.

Jon and his family survived, but the outcome could have been quite serious. Unfortunately, this kind of story is common. Professionals who are likely to refer to community agencies for help with suicidal youngsters are well advised to complete, and keep posted in a public place, an information sheet on community resources. With the information readily accessible, adults can act more quickly in an emergency.

Suicide prevention programs. Suicide prevention programs have been developed, although data regarding their effectiveness are not yet available. Suicide hotlines, crisis centers, inservice education, and educational literature about suicide have all been tried as means of preventing suicide.

Suicide hot lines and *crisis centers* are appearing all over the country. They are usually staffed by paraprofessionals who have received training in suicide prevention. The content in this training covers how to evaluate the lethality of intent, the probability of rescue, the client's history, and the severity of current stressors. Phone lines (hot lines) are established so that someone who is contemplating suicide can call to talk to a volunteer.

The effectiveness of these services is hard to evaluate. Weiner's (1969) comparison of suicide rates in Los Angeles County before and after a suicide-prevention program was instituted is an example of one study. He found no reduction in suicide rates concomitant with the service, and speculated that those who call a crisis line may not be the same group that actually commit suicide.

Suicide prevention workshops and educational literature have also been widely used. These interventions are directed toward both the professionals who might encounter youngsters contemplating suicide and the children themselves. The underlying assumption of the approach is that if a professional caregiver is educated about risk factors regarding suicide and is taught how to intervene, he will be more effective in identifying which clients may be at risk for committing suicide and more effective in dealing with a troubled client. Likewise, if youngsters learn about suicide, they may be more perceptive and effective in identifying friends and classmates who are at risk. One example of this type of approach is the curriculum developed by the American Association of Suicidology, intended for teachers to use in the classroom.

Its concept 1 is that "Natural death is part of human existence, growth and development—an integral part of life that gives it meaning. Suicide, however, is an act of self-destruction that involves an 'individual's tortured and tunneled logic in a state of inner-felt, intolerable emotion.' " The specific goals related to this concept can include:

- To identify one's feelings about his or her own death;

- To deal with those feelings;
- To understand the relationship between death and the quality of life;
- To examine one's own feelings and the feelings of others about the act of suicide.

These are some suggested activities for achieving these objectives:

- For class discussion, ask: Have you ever known someone who committed or attempted suicide? If so, what was your reaction? How did you feel and what were your thoughts? How did other people react?
- Distribute the questionnaire, "You and Death," prepared by Edwin Shneidman, Ph.D., that appeared in the August, 1970, issue of *Psychology Today*. Have the students complete the questionnaire and discuss it in class.
- Have students write their own death certificates, wills, and obituaries, and discuss the results.
- Have students sketch or describe their concepts of death or suicide, considering such questions as: Is death a person, place, condition, biological occurrence? What is death or suicide like? If death were a person, how would he or she look and feel? After discussion, have students come to conclusions about their perceptions of death and suicide.
- Allow 15 to 20 minutes for this writing assignment: A young student has decided that he or she will commit suicide within a week. What reasons can you give him or her for not going through with those plans?
- Ask students for the first word that comes to mind when they hear the words "death" and "suicide."
- For special assignments or extra credit, ask students to read *The Stranger*, by Camus, or *No Exit*, by Sartre. Ask, What view of death is presented? How does it agree or disagree with your own? Other readings on suicide can include *The Savage God*, by Alvarez, and *The Bell Jar*, by Plath.

Before teaching a unit about suicide, teachers should receive training on the topic. Most mental health clinics have staff professionals who are qualified and willing to provide such training; if not, the American Association of Suicidology is a helpful source of information.

A few school systems have developed *systemwide, school-based suicide prevention programs.* The Cherry Creek School District in Englewood, Colorado, provides one such model. As a result of concern from their mental health-team members about the high rate of self-destructive behavior among adolescents, this district conducted a survey to sample attitudes and knowledge about suicide and suicide prevention. Findings from the survey indicated that the respondents were generally not well informed about the severity of the problem, nor did they understand the role school personnel might play in preventing suicide. For example, in response to the question about the contributory role of the school in suicide, 50 percent of parents who responded felt the schools were a major contributing factor; among administrators, only 30 percent felt schools were a major contributing factor; 34 percent of the teachers felt schools played a major role; and 44 percent of the mental health workers felt schools were a major contributor (Barrett, 1982).

These data were a source of concern, because research suggests that, while schools do not cause a child to commit suicide, they can play a contributory role. Furthermore, schools can be instrumental in helping to prevent or reduce the number of suicides. Toward this end, a two-year pilot project was undertaken. It was considered effective, and has consequently been adopted as part of the school program.

The three components of the Cherry Creek School District Suicide Prevention Project were prevention, identification, and intervention. The prevention components consisted of five facets: (1) training school psychologists, social workers, nurses, counselors, and special education teachers in crisis intervention techniques; (2) training teachers to become better observers of self-destructive student behavior and how and when to refer students; (3) training parents to detect signs of depression and how to get help if needed; (4) conducting three classes about suicide prevention—causes, symptoms, and sources of help—for students enrolled in health education classes at the junior high level and in high-school freshman-orientation classes; and (5) initiating programs to help ease the entry of students who move into the schools from other districts.

The identification component involved teaching teachers, parents, peers, and youngsters how and when to refer themselves or a child for help. Students, teachers, and parents were trained to be sensitive to student products such as art and writing that reflected feelings of depression and alienation. The effectiveness of this component depends on the quality of training provided on how and when to refer for help.

The third component, intervention, was divided into three types: (1) ongoing individual counseling conducted by a trained member of the school staff or by a therapist outside the system (when therapy was conducted outside the school system, a member of the school staff was responsible for collaborating with the therapist; (2) eight one-hour stress management groups that covered information about the effects of stress, the causes of stress, and healthy ways for managing stress, such as assertiveness training, relaxation training, cognitive restructuring, and time management; and (3) divorce groups designed to give youngsters whose parents were divorced or separated opportunities to discuss their feelings and problems with other young-sters experiencing the same problems and with a mental health worker.

The individual components of this project were designed so that they might be used separately from the rest of the project components; however, the project director reported that implementation of the total project was more beneficial than implementation of only one or two components because the identification of high-risk students seemed to be a function of the number of project components in operation.

Careful attention was given to evaluating the effectiveness of individual components. The effectiveness of the interventions was evaluated by a number of different assessment devices, including pre- and posttesting of content covered in inservice workshops, attitude and information surveys among parents and students, and individual interviews with selected individuals. The measures generally reflected greater knowledge of and sensitivity to self-destructive behavior. One hundred ninety-one potentially self-destructive students were referred for assistance. Some sought help from professionals outside the school system, and in 96 percent of the cases, outside clinicians concurred that the referral was appropriate.

Although these efforts at evaluation are commendable, they leave unanswered questions. One can never know what would have been had a program not been instituted; however, it is not intrusive, it does not hurt participants, and it may well help them. Given the potential losses, preventive education efforts seem most appropriate.

Bereavement groups for the family and friends of a child who has committed suicide are another type of intervention that seems relevant to this topic. These groups have been established to help survivors share their feelings and gain support and help from each other. They developed after a series of pub-lished studies said that survivors wished they had been seen by a professional shortly after the suicide. As Danto (1977) points out, suicide survivorship is different from other types of death survivorship in that the bereavement is exacerbated by the social stigma attached to suicide and by the survivor's loss of self-esteem resulting from the inability to have prevented the death. Survivors are often obsessed with the notion that the suicide could have been prevented and that they failed the individual by not rescuing him; thus, the suicidal person's psychological problems become the burden of the survivors.

Bereavement groups are designed to help survivors cope with these feelings and adjust to the suicide. Hatton and Valente (1984) believe the groups typically have three phases, lasting an average of ten total sessions. The early sessions (typically three) are characterized by sharing and ventilating feelings. Facilitators help participants get a proper perspective on their feelings, and participants try to understand why the suicide occurred. Feelings of impotence at not having been able to prevent the suicide surface, and shock, disbelief, and guilt are examined. Discussions center around the survivors' thoughts and feelings about the suicide, how it happened, and how to better understand it. The middle phase (approximately five sessions) is concerned with "grief work." With support and reassurance from one another, survivors begin to gain a perspective on the loss. They ventilate hostility toward society in general, and their own anger at the dead person for committing suicide begins to surface. In the final phase (the last two meetings), the survivors show signs of having reached some level of resolution: they can remember happy times and can be more open about their anger. They are interested in making plans for the future and in moving ahead with their lives. These programs are important components of suicide prevention and treatment, because the *real* victims of suicide may not be those who kill themselves, but their survivors, who suffer longest.

School officials have occasionally conducted discussion and support groups for friends of a child who committed suicide. Trained personnel should be involved, and the focus should be on what can be done when one feels so "down." Properly conducted, these groups can be helpful.

(For more detailed information, you can write to the American Association of Suicidology Central Office, 2459 S. Ash St., Denver, CO 80222; the phone number is [303] 692–0985. This organization publishes a quarterly journal, *Suicide and Life-Threatening Behavior,* and a quarterly newsletter, *Newslink.*)

CONCLUSION

Childhood is characterized as a time of carefree happiness and security, but it is becoming increasingly apparent that for many, it is not so joyous. Suicide is the second or third leading cause of death between the ages of 14 and 22, and this rate appears to be staying at a high level. Several factors are predictive of being at risk for suicide: psychiatric problems, particularly those associated with depression and impulsive hostility; precipitating events, such as loss of a loved one or revenge; social problems, such as conflict in the family and impersonal, competitive schools; media attention to suicides; and immature cognition that leads to a distorted view of death. All have been associated with increased risk for suicide, but none are reliable, independent predictors.

Efforts to prevent suicide look promising. Suicide hot lines, crisis centers, schoolwide information programs, outpatient counseling for the child and family, and hospitalization of the child in crisis are common techniques whose effectiveness is supported by clinical observations.

REFERENCES

Alvarez, A. (1971). *The savage God.* London: Weidenfeld Nicholson.

American Association of Suicidology. (1977). *Suicide and how to prevent it.* West Point, PA: Merch, Sharp, and Dome.

Barrett, T. C. (1982). Cherry Creek Schools Title IV-C project director's manual and final project report—Intervention/Prevention: Seeking solutions to self-destructive behavior in children. Available from Dr. William W. Porter, Pupil Services, 4700 South Yosemite Street, Englewood, Colorado 80111.

Beebe, J. E. (1975). Evaluation of the suicidal patient. In E. P. Rosenbaum & J. E. Beebe (Eds.), *Psychiatric treatment: Crisis, clinic, and consultation.* New York: McGraw-Hill.

Bollen, K. A., & Phillips, D. P. (1982). Imitative suicides: A national study of the effects of television news stories. *American Sociological Review, 47,* 802–809.

Camus, A. (1955). *The myth of Sisyphus and other essays.* New York: Alfred A. Knopf.

Carlson, G. A., & Cantwell, D. P. (1982). Suicidal behavior and depression in children and adolescents. *Journal of the American Academy of Child Psychiatry, 21,* 19–25.

Cohen-Sandler, M. A., Berman, A. L., & King, R. (1982). Life stress and symptomatology: Determinants of suicidal behavior in children. *Journal of the American Academy of Child Psychiatry, 21,* 178–186.

Connell, H. M. (1972). Attempted suicide in school children. *Medical Journal of Australia, 1,* 686–690.

Corder, B., & Haizlip, T. (1982). Recognizing suicidal behavior in children. *Medical Times, 255–305.*

Danto, B. (1977). Project SOS: Volunteers in action with survivors of suicide. In B. Danto & A. H. Kutscher (Eds.), *Suicide and bereavement.* New York: MISS Information Corp.

Davis, J. (1985). Suicidal crises in schools. *School Psychology Review, 14,* 313–324.

Dulcan, M. K. (1985). Psychopharmacology in childhood and adolescence. *Psychiatric Annals, 15,* 64.

Durkheim, E. (1951). *Suicide: A study in sociology.* New York: The Free Press.

Eisenberg, L. (1984). The epidemiology of suicide in adolescents. *Pediatric Annals, 13,* 47–54.

Everstine, D. S., & Everstine, L. E. (1983). *People in crisis: Strategic therapeutic interventions.* New York: Brunner/Mazel.

Ferster, C. B. (1974). Behavioral approaches to depression. In R. J. Friedman & M. M. Katz (Eds.), *The psychology of depression: Contemporary theory and research.* New York: Holt, Rinehart & Winston.

Freud, S. (1955). *The standard edition of the complete psychological works of Sigmund Freud* (Vol. XVIII). London: The Hogarth Press.

Greuling, J. W., & DeBlassie, R. R. (1980). Adolescent suicide. *Adolescence, 15,* 589–601.

Hatton, C. L., & Valente, S. M. (1984). *Suicide: Assessment and intervention* (2nd ed.). Norwalk, CT: Appleton-Century-Crofts.

Hawton, K., & Osborn, M. (1984). Suicide and attempted suicide in children and adolescents. In B. B. Lahey & A. Kazdin (Eds.), *Advances in clinical child psychology* (Vol. 7). New York: Plenum Press.

Hurry, A. (1977). My ambition is to be dead. *Journal of Child Psychotherapy, 4,* 66–83.

Husain, S. A., & Vandiver, T. (1984). *Suicide in children and adolescents.* Jamaica, NY: Spectrum.

Jacobson, E. (1971). *Depression: Comparative studies of normal, neurotic and psychotic conditions.* New York: International Universities Press.

Jacobziner, H. (1965). Attempted suicides in adolescence. *Journal of the American Medical Association, 191,* 101–105.

James, N. (1984). Psychology of suicide. In C. L. Halton & S. M. Valente, *Suicide: Assessment and intervention* (2nd ed.). Norwalk, CT: Appleton-Century-Crofts.

Kazdin, A. E., French, N. H., Unis, A. S., Esveldt-Dawson, K., & Sherick, R. B. (1983). Hopelessness, depression, and suicidal intent among psychiatrically disturbed inpatient children. *Journal of Consulting and Clinical Psychology, 51,* 504–510.

Kazdin, A. E., Rodgers, A., & Colbus, D. (1986). The Hopelessness Scale for Children: Psychometric characteristics and concurrent validity. *Journal of Consulting and Clinical Psychology, 54,* 241–245.

Koocher, G. P. (1974). Talking with children about death. *American Journal of Orthopsychiatry, 44,* 404–411.

Kreitman, N., & Schreiber, M. (1979). Parasuicide in young Edinburgh women, 1968–75. *Psychological Medicine, 9,* 469–479.

Lawler, R. H., Nakielny, W., & Wright, N. A. (1963). Suicidal attempts in children. *Canadian Medical Association Journal, 89,* 751–754.

Lewinsohn, P. H. (1974). A behavioral approach to depression. In R. J. Friedman & M. M. Katz (Eds.), *The psychology of depression: Contemporary theory and research.* New York: Holt, Rinehart & Winston.

Lourie, R. S. (1966). Clinical studies of attempted suicide in childhood. *Clinical proceedings of the Children's Hospital of the District of Columbia, 22,* 163–173.

Mack, J. E., & Hickler, H. (1981). *Vivienne, the life and suicide of an adolescent girl.* Boston: Little, Brown.

Mattsson, A., Seese, L. R., & Hawkins, J. W. (1969). Suicidal behavior as a child psychiatric emergency: Clinical characteristics and follow-up results. *Archives of General Psychiatry, 20,* 100–109.

McAnarney, E. R. (1979). Adolescent and young adult suicide in the United States—A reflection of societal unrest? *Adolescence, 14,* 765–774.

McKnew, D. H., Cytryn, L., Efron, A. M., Gerson, E. S., & Bunney, W. E. (1979). Offspring of patients with affective disorders. *British Journal of Psychiatry, 134,* 148–152.

Miller, J. P. (1975). Suicide and adolescence. *Adolescence, 10,* 11–24.

Nagy, M. (1959). The child's view of death. In H. Feifel (Ed.), *The meaning of death.* New York: McGraw-Hill.

Ohara, K. (1963). Characteristics of suicides in Japan, especially of parent-child double suicide. *American Journal of Psychiatry, 120,* 382–385.

Orbach, I., Gross, Y., & Glaubman, H. (1981). Some common characteristics of latency-age suicidal children: A tentative model based on case study analyses. *Suicide and Life-Threatening Behavior, 11,* 180–190.

Otto, U. (1972). Suicidal acts by children and adolescents: A follow-up study. *Acta Psychiatrica Scandinavica, 233,* 5–123.

Pfeffer, C. R. (1981). The family system of suicidal children. *American Journal of Psychotherapy, 35,* 330–341.

Pfeffer, C. R. (1984). Clinical aspects of childhood suicidal behavior. *Pediatric Annals, 13,* 56–61.

Pfeffer, C. R. (1986). *The suicidal child.* New York: Guilford.

Pfeffer, C. R., Conte, H. R., Plutchik, R., & Jerrett, I. (1980). Suicidal behavior in latency-age children: An empirical study: An outpatient population. *Journal of the American Academy of Child Psychiatry, 19,* 703–710.

Pfeffer, C., Plutchik, R., & Mizruchi, M. S. (1983). Suicidal and assaultive behavior in children: Classification, measurement, and interrelations. *American Journal of Psychiatry, 140,* 154–157.

Phillips, D. P. (1974). The influence of suggestion on suicide: Substantive and theoretical implications of the Werther effect. *American Sociological Review, 39,* 340–354.

Piaget, J. (1923). *Language and thought of the child.* London: Routledge & Kegan.

Rabkin, B. (1978). *Growing up dead: A hard look at why adolescents commit suicide.* Nashville, TN: Abingdon.

Sabbath, J. C. (1969). The suicidal adolescent—expendable child. *Journal of the American Academy of Child Psychiatry, 8,* 272–289.

Shaffer, D. (1974). Suicide in childhood and early adolescence. *Journal of Child Psychology and Psychiatry, 15,* 275–291.

Shaw, C. R., & Schelkun, R. F. (1965). Suicidal behavior in children. *Psychiatry, 28,* 157–168.

Sheras, P. L. (1983). Suicide in adolescence. In C. E. Walker & M. C. Roberts (Eds.), *Handbook of clinical child psychology.* New York: John Wiley.

Valente, M. (1984). The history of suicide. In C. L. Hatton & S. M. Valente, *Suicide: Assessment and intervention* (2nd ed.). Norwalk, CT: Appleton-Century-Crofts.

Weiner, I. W. (1969). The effectiveness of a suicide prevention program. *Mental Hygiene, 53,* 357–363.

Weissman, M. M. (1974). The epidemiology of suicide attempts, 1960–1971. *Archives of General Psychiatry, 30,* 737–746.

Whitehead, P. C., Johnson, F. G., & Ferrence, R. (1973). Measuring the incidence of self-injury: Some methodological and design considerations. *American Journal of Orthopsychiatry, 43,* 142–148.

Yessler, P. G. (1968). Suicide in the military. In H. L. P. Resnick (Ed.), *Suicidal behaviors.* Boston: Little, Brown.

Often and often afterwards, the beloved Aunt would ask me why I had never told anyone how I was being treated. Children tell little more than animals, for what comes to them they accept as eternally established.

RUDYARD KIPLING
SOMETHING OF MYSELF, FOR MY FRIENDS
KNOWN AND UNKNOWN

A 7-year-old boy who had been sexually abused by his father since the age of two-and-a-half drew this haunting picture with chalk. The "person" is colored hot pink, with eyes and mouth outlined in red, and sits on a black base; the background is chartreuse.

CHAPTER FOURTEEN

Drug and Alcohol Abuse

Don McNeil
LESLIE COLLEGE

Alcohol is the primary drug abuse problem in the U. S. today.

The etiology of alcoholism is unknown, but its negative effects are considerable.

Apparently many sociocultural as well as biological factors contribute to the use of alcohol among children.

The incidence of children's experimentation with and use of drugs other than alcohol is high, and there are several negative psychological effects, and in some instances, health hazards.

Problems in school are usually present before the drug use begins.

Intervention strategies vary, depending on the pattern of abuse and whether medical assistance is needed.

Prevention efforts should be given a higher priority, and the educational system should be a primary target.

Children with one alcoholic parent have a high risk of developing a pattern of alcohol abuse themselves, and are at risk for developing other problems that may affect their school performance.

Serious neglect and abuse represent one of the greatest risks for children's physical and psychological development, risks greater than those of childhood disease and cancer.

Sexually exploited children are at high risk for developing severe emotional problems.

The probability of parents' abusing their children is affected by many ecological factors. Abusive parents are usually not mentally ill, but are likely to be socially isolated, suffer stress in their work and/or marriage, and are often themselves victims of child abuse.

Educational programs relating to sex education, parenting, and family life could help prevent child abuse.

THE EFFECTS OF alcohol and of child abuse are obviously of substantial concern to educators, since they so often both distort the course of development and inhibit children's ability to learn. The situation is further confused by the fact that these may often represent hidden problems of which the school is not, and may never be, aware. Both alcoholism and many forms of child abuse are often zealously guarded family secrets. Children who are victims may feel a sense of intense responsibility to keep the secret, and their sometimes overwhelming feelings of guilt, shame, fear, or anger can be expressed only through isolation or aggressiveness, uncompleted school work, or other manifestations that may not be at all clear to the teacher. Thus, the child whose parent was drunk and abusive in the morning before school may not have a good morning in the fourth-grade classroom, but is also unlikely to respond truthfully even if questioned by a sympathetic teacher.

In this chapter we will consider these social problems, along with their implications for development and learning, and discuss the services that may be important and ways that schools can help. There is a list of resources at the end of the chapter.

ALCOHOL ABUSE

Alcohol has many connotations in American culture. Over 68 percent of the adult population drinks, and those who drink spend roughly five percent of their annual budgets on alcohol (Kinney & Leaton, 1979). Alcohol is associated with celebrations, parties, and status on the one hand, and skid row, auto accidents, and domestic discord on the other.

While commercials and advertisements remind us of the association between alcohol and the good life, it has become painfully apparent that, for many people, the association turns sour. It is estimated that about ten million Americans are afflicted with alcoholism, and that some 36 million others are profoundly affected by their relationship to an alcoholic (Kinney & Leaton, 1979). Half of all fatal automobile accidents are related to alcohol, as are half of all police arrests (North & Orange, 1980). Alcohol plays a role in one quarter of all admissions to general hospitals, and is substantially related to suicide and homocide (Vaillant, 1983). Thus, it clearly represents the primary drug abuse problem in the United States.

Alcoholism is considered a serious disease, and, in the eyes of many, an incurable condition—even if one is able to stop drinking completely, the potential for abuse remains. Theories about the etiology of alcoholism range from biogenetic and psychodynamic concepts to sociological theories; presently the cause is unknown. Indeed, there probably is not one cause, but many factors. We do know, however, that being the child of an alcoholic puts one at high risk for abusing alcohol as an adult, which may demonstrate either genetic or modeling influences or both (Ackerman, 1983). There are also substantial differences in the alcoholism rates among different cultures and ethnic groups. In this country, for example, Jewish and Italian-American groups have very low rates of alcoholism, while the rate for Irish Americans is significantly higher (Vaillant, 1983). These differential rates probably represent both the place of alcohol in a given culture and the ways children are socialized into its use. In Italian-American culture, for example, alcohol use is usually associated with meals, and it is relatively rare for people to congregate just to drink. Taking food with alcohol also reduces the probability of intoxication. Drinking large amounts, or drunkenness, is generally frowned on, or considered deviant. Children are likely to be introduced to small amounts of alcohol, in the way of watered wine, at an early age and with their meals; alcohol is not treated as a mystery or as an indicator of adult status. Contrast this kind of socialization to that of the child from a different background who sees adults frequently drinking on Saturday afternoons or evenings, hears bragging about how much someone drank, watches a parent eagerly mix a drink to relieve anxiety or tension, and sees alcohol as a mysterious taboo for everyone except adults.

Thus, although we do not know the causes of alcoholism, some predisposing factors have been identified, including having an alcoholic parent and the attitudes and socialization practices surrounding alcohol in different cultural or ethnic groups. Since alcohol passes into the circulatory system directly from the blood vessels in the stomach, and thence to the brain, it is relatively fast-acting, so primary reinforcement may also play a role in the frequency of use. Researchers have recently found that one's expectations regarding the effects of alcohol are powerful determinants in the quality of the experience. For example, subjects told that they are drinking vodka and tonic become progressively louder, more boisterous or aggressive, and report feeling high, even if there is no alcohol at all in their drinks (MacDonald, 1984). What one learns about the expected effects of alcohol, along with the body's ability to tolerate relatively large amounts without getting sick, may also be factors in advancing spirals of abuse.

Alcohol is a central nervous system depressant which, in moderate amounts, tends to release one from normally present inhibi-

tions. In large amounts, it can lead to sleep or, in extreme cases, death. One can become psychologically dependent upon its effects, as in needing a drink to relax, or physically addicted, in which case withdrawal symptoms would follow sudden abstinence (Seixas & Youcha, 1985). There has been a good deal of discussion in the literature about the alcohol-prone personality, characterized by high dependency needs and impulsivity; however, there is little premorbid evidence to support this hypothesis. One of the few longitudinal studies available, a 40-year follow-up of men, seems to indicate that dependency and impulsivity stem instead from abuse of alcohol over a long period. Thus, the more one abuses alcohol, the more dependent and impulsive he becomes (Vaillant, 1983).

Youthful Alcohol Use and Abuse

In 1980, surveys showed that 5 percent of seventh grade boys used alcohol to the extent that they reported being drunk at least four times a year; 40 percent of high school seniors reported the same level of use (North & Orange, 1980). Over 75 percent of high school juniors said they had tried alcohol outside their homes and would drink occasionally (MacDonald, 1984).

The media—movies, television, magazine advertising—consistently present alcoholic beverages as an important part of the daily routine of people who are physically attractive, popular, and powerful. Professional athletes, surrounded by comrades and admirers, appear regularly in beer commercials. Beautiful women look with favor on young men who choose the right brand of wine. The most competent and attractive characters in the shows sponsored by these commercials often have drinks in their hands. These images, repeated over and over, carry a powerful message of the relationship between drinking and being a competent, attractive, and popular adult, ideas that are developmentally compelling for many adolescents. Although it is illegal in our society for most adolescents to buy alcohol, that very possession may, at least for a time, confirm their status as adults.

Besides the provocation from the larger culture for adolescents to be interested in alcohol, the majority of adolescents who drink regularly say they do so "because it makes me feel better" and because "my friends are doing it" (Tessler, 1981). Pressure from friends is indeed a powerful factor, and many adolescents report a feeling of isolation and of being different. Adolescent social activities are often organized around alcohol, and the fact that it is illegal and must also be hidden from many parents gives an added cachet to the "field party"; large groups congregate at night in an isolated field, equipped perhaps with a keg and several bottles of different kinds of liquor. Obtaining alcohol is seldom a problem.

Automobiles become a natural setting for drinking, with obvious dangers to the youths involved and anyone else on the highway. This drinking is usually unaccompanied by food and, since the drinking must remain secret, tends to take place rapidly, both of which increase the probability of intoxication (Vaillant, 1983). A 16-year-old boy who demolished the family car said he had had someone buy him two six-packs of beer, and that he had to drink them all since he didn't want to waste them and obviously couldn't take them home. And since he only had the car for two hours, he had to drink them quickly. Fortunately, only the car and a tree at the end of his parents' street were damaged.

Some adolescents progress from this secret and adventuresome drinking to drinking for pleasure, to forget about things that are troubling them, or to reduce anxiety and increase self-confidence in social situations. For some young people, this includes drinking at school and solitary drinking. Although there are no specific data, it is clear that there are a fair number of adolescent alcoholics. By most

counts of adolescent alcohol abuse, boys outnumber girls approximately two to one (North & Orange, 1980). Preadolescent children occasionally try alcohol, often in groups. Some children (often those with alcoholic parents) begin solitary drinking, and sometimes take alcohol to school and keep it in their lockers.

Tommy is an 11-year-old boy, the oldest child in a family living in constant turmoil because of the father's serious alcohol abuse. Tommy's father regularly sits in the living room during the evening with a bottle of whiskey and a glass, and drinks until he passes out. He usually spends the night in the chair. With Tommy, he has alternated between complete permissiveness, savage criticism, and verbal aggression. Although obviously bright, Tommy was failing nearly everything in school. One Saturday morning, Tommy went to a friend's house to watch cartoons, and took along a bottle of his father's vodka. The boys all sampled it. When the friend's mother got up and began to make breakfast for the boys, Tommy left and went out to a small woods nearby, where he drank the rest of the vodka. Feeling sick, he got up and headed for home, but passed out in a snowdrift. Fortunately, he was discovered by a man out walking his dog. He was taken to the local hospital, where he was admitted and treated for hypothermia. Later, Tommy said this was the third time he had taken alcohol from his home and drank until he passed out. Because of the crisis at the hospital, Tommy's father was able to seek help for his own alcoholism and drug problems, and the family entered family therapy; Tommy also received support in school through the special education resource teacher.

USE AND ABUSE OF OTHER DRUGS

Many of the factors we find in relation to alcohol also operate in children's and adolescents' use of other drugs. Children who grow up in our culture have many opportunities to observe adult use of drugs to alter their moods. One-half of the world's coffee supply comes into the United States, and tobacco use is still common (MacDonald, 1984). Psychotropic prescription drugs are in wide use; in 1982, seven of the top ten best-selling prescription drugs were tranquilizers or other psychotropics (Vaillant, 1983). Sleep drugs are advertised on television, and children hear about athletes and truck drivers who take speed.

After alcohol, marijuana is the most commonly used drug by adolescents. It is widely available in most communities, no longer restricted to cities and upper-middle-class suburbs. A 1980 survey by the National Institute for Drug Abuse showed 60 percent of high school seniors saying they had tried marijuana, and 35 percent had smoked it at least once within the 30 days preceding the survey. Slightly more than two percent of the regular users reported they had begun experimenting with the drug by the sixth grade, and an additional 12 percent began during junior high school. There is considerable controversy about the effects of marijuana on motivation, the so-called *amotivational syndrome*. Some people feel that regular users had little motivation before they started using marijuana, while others attribute the lack of motivation to the drug itself (Nystrom, Bal, & LaBrecque, 1979). In any case, some children and adolescents who use it regularly do poorly in school and may have reduced involvement in other activities. Adolescents often use marijuana in combination with alcohol, particularly wine and beer. Marijuana is not physically addictive, and there is little evidence to demonstrate psychological dependency, but there are apparently some health hazards.

Some adolescents also use barbiturates, tranquilizers, Quaalude, stimulants, cocaine, and LSD, although the percentages of high school seniors who use these drugs with any regularity are much lower than those for alcohol and marijuana—generally around two percent (National Institute for Drug Abuse, 1980). Mixing drugs to obtain exotic new effects has become increasingly popular. The most common danger in mixing is the combination of alcohol with barbiturates or tranquilizers (MacDonald, 1984). Table 14–1 lists the effects of the major legal, illegal, and prescription drugs.

As with alcohol, some adolescents move beyond experimentation and begin to use drugs for pleasure rather than curiosity, then begin to feel they need them to get through the school day. These students often feel unhappy about themselves and doubt their ability to succeed or even find meaning in school. For the great majority, their problems of functioning in school began before the drug use or abuse. They often form subcultures within the school, taking some pride in their designation as "druggies" or "burnouts," and become further isolated from peers and activities that would provide opportunities to function somewhat differently.

INTERVENTION AND PREVENTION

Intervention strategies differ depending on the pattern of abuse and whether medical assistance is needed. Alcoholics Anonymous can be helpful for older adolescents, and some AA chapters have special groups for adolescents. AA is a self-help organization with chapters in or near almost every community in the country. The groups have been extremely important for many thousands of people who have struggled to eliminate their dependence on alcohol, and are a major resource for anyone who works with adolescents or adults who are abusing alcohol. There are also a number of similar self-help groups available for those having difficulty with other drugs. In addition to AA chapters, Al-Anon is a self-help group for spouses or other relatives of alcoholics, and Alateen is a similar group for adolescents who live in alcoholic families. These groups can help adolescents or adults who are trying to deal with an alcoholic and at the same time keep their own lives in order.

TABLE 14–1
Major Drugs: Uses and Effects

Name	Street Name	Short-term Effects	Long-term Effects of Chronic Use
Legal Drugs			
Alcohol	Beer	Relaxation, euphoria	Brain and liver damage
	Wine	False confidence	Impotence
	Liquor	Talkativeness	Delirium
		Decrease in alertness and motor coordination	Withdrawal symptoms
Caffeine	Coffee	Wakefulness	Increased chance of
	Tea	Increased heartbeat	heart attack
	Cola		Withdrawal reactions
	No-Doz		
Illegal Drugs			
Hallucinogens		Altered state of perception	Medical evidence
LSD	Acid	Rapid mood changes	inconclusive
MDA	Love drug	Visual and sensory	May cause memory loss,
Mescaline	Cactus	distortion	insomnia, psychosis,
Peyote	Buttons	Heavy doses may cause	depression, loss of
Psilocybin	Magic mushrooms	panic, tremors, nausea	energy and ability
PCP	Angel dust	Psychotic states	to concentrate
Cannabis		Relaxation, euphoria	Contradictory
Hashish	Herb	Altered perception	studies/some report
Marijuana	Grass	Laughter	confusion, impairment
	Ganja	Anxiety, panic, confusion	to concentration and memory
Cocaine	Coke	Addictive	Economic disaster
	Snow	Can cause death	Hallucinations
	Toot		Paranoia
	Uptown		
Prescription Drugs			
Amphetamines/Stimulants		Decrease in appetite	Severe withdrawal
Benzedrine	Bennies	Feeling of being wired	Dependence
Dexedrine	Speed	Insomnia	Depression
Preludin	Uppers	Rise in blood pressure	Hallucinations
Ritalin	Uppers		
Barbiturates		Relaxation	Tolerance level increases
Nembutal	Yellow jackets	Loss of inhibition	with use but lethal dose
Phenobarbital	Purple hearts	Slurred speech	does not
Seconal	F-40's, Reds	Slow respiration	Severe withdrawal
Quaalude	Ludes	Large dose can be fatal	symptoms:
Optimil			anxiety, tremors, convulsions, insomnia
Narcotics		Drowsiness	Physical addiction
Codeine	Schoolboy	Mental clouding	Lethargy
Demerol	Demies	Overdose can be fatal	Irritability
Heroin	Smack, junk		Tremors
Methadone	Dollies		Panic
Morphine	M, Miss Emma		Chills
Opium	Blue velvet		
Percodan	Perkies		

Community mental health centers and alcoholism treatment programs usually offer family therapy services and therapy groups for adolescents who are abusing alcohol or other drugs. Schools may provide counseling or special education services, or sometimes placement in an alternative high school; many, if not most, students in trouble with alcohol or drugs feel they are failures in school and see little hope for changing their failure cycle. Educational programs that can provide a new sense of relatedness to other adults and some meaning to learning make a significant contribution to treatment. Some adolescents also benefit from intense involvement in different group experiences, such as a therapeutic camping program that integrates an Outward Bound experience with group problem solving (McNeil, 1975).

Because both adolescents and adults who become seriously involved with alcohol or other drugs can find it extremely difficult to change, prevention needs a much higher priority than it has had (Botvin, 1983). Because of its central place in society, the educational system is a primary target for developing large-scale prevention programs, which can be organized around three basic efforts.

The first approach is the development of effective alcohol and drug education programs that promote meaningful learning about alcohol in relation to the self and give young people the necessary information for making responsible decisions about drinking and drug use. A model for this approach is the CASPAR alcohol education program in Somerville, Massachusetts. CASPAR provides training for all teachers and other professionals in the school system. It also provides an alcohol-specific education program that begins in the early primary grades and goes through high school. Trained teachers provide instruction, as do a cadre of peer-group leaders—young people between the ages of 14 and 18 who have been carefully trained and are supervised by the CASPAR

staff. Their role is to run discussion groups of alcohol issues for various grade levels, following a carefully developed curriculum. The CASPAR Program also has strong ties with the community, including a citizen board of directors, and relationships with a variety of different youth service agencies, making possible a variety of treatment services for children or adolescents whose problems often come to light through the alcohol education program (Deutsch, 1982). Other communities have similar, comprehensive programs, and several published curricula are also available. Sources for further information about these programs are listed at the end of this chapter.

A second approach to prevention focuses more broadly on the development of personal and social competencies, offering help in applying these competencies to peer pressure and situations that call for decisions about alcohol and drug use. An example of this approach is a program called Life Skills Training (Botvin, 1983). In a series of group sessions, this program helps to enhance self-esteem, increase assertiveness, cope with anxiety, and relate more effectively with peers. The program is based on the assumption that problems with alcohol and drugs are often related to poor self-concept, anxiety about peer relations, and difficulty saying no. Preliminary results from this program are encouraging; the same program applied to preventing smoking has been quite effective (Botvin, 1983).

An even more comprehensive approach than these two would focus on developing support systems in school and involving parents constructively, to facilitate success and enhance adolescents' self-esteem. To have lost all interest in school, and to feel that one is without prospects and without hope in what society sees as the work of the adolescent—school—obviously makes one more vulnerable to the anxiety and anger that many adolescents describe in relation to their use of alcohol and drugs (Deutsch, 1982). For children or adolescents who have little support at home, or who are isolated and restricted to role models who themselves abuse alcohol, that vulnerability can be devastating. To conceptualize school as an alternative to these conditions, and to be able to move toward implementation, would be a substantial accomplishment in terms of both prevention and intervention.

High Risk: The Child with an Alcoholic Parent

As we have mentioned above, children who come from homes with an alcoholic parent have a high risk of developing a pattern of alcohol abuse themselves (Vaillant, 1983). They are also at risk for developing a number of problems that can affect their performance in school or their sense of self and personal adequacy. These are often hidden problems: the family with an alcoholic parent tends to use an amazing amount of denial, and to draw a veil of secrecy around the problem so no one else will know. Children in these situations often learn to use denial themselves; one high school girl, speaking of her alcoholic mother, said, "she really loves me; when she hit me in the head with a heavy glass ashtray, she took me to the hospital and stayed with me until the stitches were all in." These children may also live with daily ambiguity and unpredictability. Their parent may be warm and nurturing at one moment, then expansive, then hostile and aggressive. Alcohol abuse makes it difficult for a parent to be consistent in providing children's needs, particularly in relation to basics like food, nurturance, and stability (Seixas & Youcha, 1985).

Several studies have examined the roles children forge for themselves in families that live under these circumstances, roles that may well stay with children long into their adult years. Deutsch (1982) identifies four roles. The role of Family Hero is often taken by the oldest child in the family, who learns to control things by pleasing people and doing things for them. This child may do well in school, always acting obedient and cheerful, but fears that everything will fall apart if he doesn't do everything and finds it difficult to express his own needs. These children of alcoholics may be under intense pressure in adolescence, worrying about holding the family together and trying to redeem the family through performance in school or other areas.

The Scapegoat is the child who learns to express all the family's denied feelings of anger and disappointment and to gain the attention of the alcoholic parent by causing trouble. These children seldom do well in school and are quite disruptive. In a sense, they use their own failure to hold the family together. The Lost Child truly does become lost within the confusion of the family and the distraction that is constantly present with an alcoholic parent. The lost child presents a distinct learned helplessness, which generally characterizes school performance and behavior. These children just never quite get anything right.

The Mascot is usually the youngest child in the family, protected and overprotected by everyone, out of a sense of guilt or shame. This child usually learns to get needs met by manipulating others, and to reduce tension by constant activity and a kind of court-jester buffoonery. In school, this child makes a perfect candidate for the role of class clown.

These children need support and encouragement to break out of the role bonds that have developed so tightly within the alcoholic family, and to explore other parts of themselves. They need teachers who can respond to them as they are, not as they present themselves through the dramaturgical aspects of their roles. They may also need referral to counselors or special education teachers; growing numbers of community service agencies offer groups for children with alcoholic parents. Alateen groups also offer, for some children, a format in which they can recognize themselves in others and begin to explore alternative ways of being, with support from the group. The CASPAR Program described earlier has trained peer-group leaders, themselves from alcoholic families, to lead discussion groups. The children of alcoholics are at risk, and need alternatives to the confusion and denial they are likely to bring with them from home.

CHILD ABUSE AND NEGLECT

Although child abuse and, to a lesser extent, neglect have been the focus of concern and intense media coverage in the past several years, they are not a new problem. Mutilation and murder of infants and children, along with abandonment or neglect, have occurred throughout history. The first recorded case of child abuse intervention in this country was in 1874, when an 8-year-old girl was found beaten and chained to her bed. The intervenors found there was no law to protect her, and action was possible only after a group of citizens appealed to the state Society for the Prevention of Cruelty to Animals (Erikson, McEvor, & McClu, 1984). Two years later, the first Society for the Prevention of Cruelty to Children was formed in New York State, initiating a long period of citizen and professional advocacy for children's rights' protection. In the early 1950s, pediatricians began to use X-rays as evidence of bone fractures that could only be the result of abuse, and the term "battered child" was coined (Kempe & Helfer, 1980). The concept of abuse has since been expanded to include physical, emotional, or sexual abuse, along with neglect, and all fifty states have laws to protect children and mandate reporting of suspected abuse or neglect.

States vary widely in their legal definitions of abuse and neglect, as do professionals. Most professionals agree that the incidence of abuse and neglect is substantially greater than had been thought before 1970. Media

exposure and reporting laws have dramatically altered the number of cases that come to the attention of officials. For example, in Florida during 1970, there were 17 reported cases of child mistreatment; during that year, a reporting law was passed and a public relations campaign organized, and the next year, over 19,000 cases were reported. Although a National Child Abuse Center now collects statistics from around the country each year, the actual level of abuse and neglect is still unknown. In 1980 some 625,000 children were reported abused or neglected—nearly one of every 100 children (American Humane Association, 1981). Most agree that this is a low estimate; some believe the actual numbers would range upward from one million children a year. Using these figures, more than twice as many children were neglected as were abused. During 1980, 1,000 children were killed as a result of abuse. Another researcher estimates that three out of every 100 children are at risk for serious injury through abuse (Straus, Gelles, & Steinmetz, 1979). Boys are at slightly greater risk than girls, and those at greatest risk for serious physical harm are between the ages of birth and three years old (American Humane Association, 1981). Again, these figures are difficult to interpret, since no one knows how many cases of abuse or neglect go unreported, but it is clear that serious abuse or neglect represents one of the greatest risks for children's physical and psychological development—substantially greater than those of childhood disease and cancer.

Physical Abuse

Twelve-year-old Larry was admitted to a residential treatment center because of his consistent acting out at school and his severe difficulties in adjusting to several foster homes after being removed from his family when he was nine. Larry had been treated in emergency rooms on several occasions, the first time when he was seven months old, for broken bones, lacerations, burns (from cigarettes), and malnutrition. His father had left home shortly after Larry was born, and he had been physically abused and often isolated for long periods of time by his mother and, later, by an older brother who was given a good deal of responsibility for Larry's care. His mother had told him over and over that he was a bad kid, that he had "bad blood," and by the time he was removed from his home, he saw himself as so thoroughly bad that he played this role to the hilt in both schools and foster homes, forcing people to reject him. He became an expert in getting excluded from settings that were supposed to be good for him.

Larry's story sadly illustrates several important issues about physical abuse. Children are often abused over long periods of time, sometimes beginning in infancy. Although the abuse is normally hidden from outsiders, it is a family affair, and other family members may be involved. In the course of growing up, abused children must learn to give meaning to the violence and unpredictability of their lives, as all children learn to make some kind of sense of the world and their place in it. All too often, this means that abused children learn that they are bad, that they "had it coming," and that, on this basis, the adults around them are acting rationally. This perception, along with modeling violence and aggression as a way of dealing with problems, can create exceptionally challenging problems for schools and other settings where people attempt to work constructively with these children. Abused children's alternative way of coping may be withdrawal from any kind of human relationships, lack of trust, and seeking safety from their awful vulnerability through isolation.

Emotional Abuse

Some children may be trapped in similar patterns of abuse but never physically injured. Cases of emotional abuse are much less likely to be reported. Parents may consistently derogate children, frighten them, threaten them with abandonment, or be so wildly unpredictable in their responses that nothing seems to have any certainty.

Melinda is a 7-year-old girl who has been placed in a special education class for emotionally disturbed students; her behavior in the regular classroom ranged from stealing, lying, and fighting to threatening her second grade teacher with a pair of scissors. She is the middle of three children in a single-parent family; her mother has been diagnosed as manic-depressive. The mother has managed to meet all the children's physical needs and to adequately parent the oldest and youngest children, but her anger and unpredictability have focused on Melinda. A typical interaction between the two was for Mother to call Melinda to give her a hug and sit in her lap, then, in the midst of this, scream at her for being dirty, for being the worst child in the world, for ruining her mother's life, and so on. This might go on for 15 minutes, during which Mother would also tell her how ugly she was, how she smelled, how she wished Melinda would run away from home or be hit by a car. At school, Melinda now speaks in an obnoxiously loud voice, thrusts her face right next to the person she is talking to, is intensely envious of the other children and their belongings, and demands the teacher's total attention at all times.

Emotional abuse leaves no scars that can be detected by X-rays, but often leads to the same distorted learning about oneself and how others are likely to respond as does physical abuse. Many of the problem behaviors described in earlier chapters may be understood as the child's response to emotional abuse.

Sexual Abuse

Sexual abuse is usually defined as any form of sexual activity or exploitation between an adult and a minor child. This includes rape or intercourse, other forms of sexual activity or stimulation, or making pornographic movies or pictures involving children. Whether the child consents to the sexual activity is not at issue; by definition, children are presumed not to have the emotional or cognitive maturity necessary to actually consent to sexual activity. Reported abuse cases indicate more girls than boys as the targets of abuse, and although sexual abuse occurs even with infants, the highest risk period is between the ages of 9 to 12 (Mayer, 1983).

A substantial number of sexual abuse cases occur within the family; when those involved are directly related (father-daughter, brother-sister), it is called *incest*. Although the incest taboo in American culture is generally strong, there is no doubt that incest affects the development of many children. Estimates vary between 200,000 and ten million cases per year; the actual number is unknown, since most cases go unreported, and many adults who were abused as children have never told anyone (Mayer, 1983). Biological fathers are involved in 28 percent of reported sexual abuse cases occurring within the family, and it is estimated that nearly half of these men could be considered alcoholic (Erickson et al., 1984). Stepfathers and live-in boyfriends account for a larger percentage of sexual abuse cases within families; the rising divorce rate has brought more such families, and thus perhaps an increase in the numbers of children suffering exploitation (Mayhall & Norgard, 1983).

Patterns of abuse vary widely in both occurrence and significance for the child. Children exposed to one nonviolent sexual encounter outside the family may respond well to help in talking about it and a good deal of support from their parents. Children who have been raped or assaulted will require intensive individual and family therapy, along with supportive medical treatment (Kempe & Hefler, 1980).

Children for whom sexual exploitation occurs within the family are at high risk for developing severe emotional problems. Patterns of abuse generally take place over an extended period, often years. If a father or stepfather is involved, the exploitation may well occur with at least the silent collusion of the mother, and the child or adolescent may actually be holding the family together. Since children are both physically and emotionally dependent on their parents, exploitation robs them of both choice and protection. Their feeling trapped is a realistic perception; there may be no way out. It may seem to them that telling anyone will bring shame and economic ruin to the family, so denial and silence often ensue. Younger children may dramatically regress, show striking changes in eating patterns, and experience night terrors. Preadolescent or adolescent girls often consider themselves bad and shameful, and alternate between intense guilt and anger. They may act out in school, or seem passive and unmotivated, as if in a depression. A recent study of prostitutes in the San Francisco area found that two-thirds of the sample had been victims of incest or sexual abuse between the ages of three and sixteen (Silbert, 1982). Most psychotherapists who see adults are familiar with stories of childhood sexual abuse or incest and their debilitating effects on both self-concept and sexual development.

Sharon is a seventh grade girl who was referred by her school for a psychological evaluation. She was disruptive in school, talking loudly and responding to teachers' requests for quiet with giddy laughter, which often resulted in a trip to the principal's office. At other times she was very quiet, almost listless, and was failing three of her five subjects, primarily because she seldom completed her work. On evaluation, she expressed feelings of hopelessness, dislike of herself, and anxiety about loss of control. She wanted to do well academically and to stay in school, liked to draw, and was interested in learning to be a fashion designer. She saw no way that she could really change, however, and refused offers of counseling. Two months later she ran away from home; after several days she was picked up by the police and requested that she be jailed instead of taken home. Only then did she ask to talk to someone and, in halting terms, told her story of three years of sexual exploitation at home, both from her 18-year-old brother and from a man who sometimes lived with her mother. She had finally decided that she deserved a fresh start, but running away was the only alternative she could see.

Causes of Abuse

Most of us have a tendency to respond with both anger and sadness to a tale of abuse or neglect, and it is common to blame, punish, or dismiss parents as mentally ill. The causes of child abuse are not nearly so simple, however, nor will it advance our efforts at assistance and prevention to blame parents who may themselves be victims. Basically, abuse or neglect represents either a failure in development or breakdown of the ability to care for and nurture children. Children's needs for parenting include, at a minimum, physical care, safety and protection, emotional nurturance, and stimulation in relating to others and the world. The inability to provide these basics may result from any one or combination of different issues, but we can best understand it within an ecological or interactive context: by thinking about the strengths and vulnerabilities of the individual parent, and the capacity for either support or stress within the family and community environment. Thus, while we can identify no one cause for these serious and often tragic failures in parenting, we can look at different levels of the larger ecological system in which children develop and identify some risk factors that may increase the probability of abuse or neglect.

Beginning with the larger culture, society's values regarding children and their care tend to emerge as mixed messages. On the one hand, children are supposed to be valued, and good parents admired. In a high-tech, consumer society, however, we have yet to make a commitment to ensuring adequate nutrition, medical care, day care, and educational supports for all children. Some years ago, the Joint Commission on the Mental Health of Children, after a comprehensive survey of developmental supports for children throughout the country, concluded that it is a myth that America is a child-oriented society (Joint Commission Report, 1970). Since that report, there are more single-parent families and more children living below the poverty line (Simonds & Engleman, 1982).

The U. S. is also a violent society, and family life reflects that violence. Physical violence is still an acceptable method of disciplining children within the family. Most states allow corporal punishment in schools, making children the only group of citizens in our society for whom physical punishment is still a legal and acceptable response to nonconformity. Parents who have grown up with physical discipline at home and in school are likely to consider physical violence toward children legitimate. This model may, for some parents under some circumstances, blur the line between physical punishment and physical abuse.

Studies of abusing and neglecting families show that a very small percentage of abusive parents suffer from mental illness; probably about two percent of those parents would be diagnosed as psychotic, and about 10 percent as afflicted by alcoholism (Justice & Justice, 1976). Abusive parents tend to be more isolated socially; they tend not to have relationships of trust with their neighbors, but at the same time have some difficulty in being self-sufficient (Garbarino & Sherman, 1980). Stress also appears to be an important factor; psychosocial stressors such as difficult marital relationships and work problems seem to relate more to physical and sexual abuse, while neglect is more prevalent in families unable to cope with severe economic stress (Erickson et al., 1984).

Finally, we often find a history of abuse in the backgrounds of abusive parents. It is estimated that upwards of 25 percent of persons abused as children will become abusive parents (Mayhall & Norgard, 1983). Whether these parents are modeling their own parents, or are filled with anger at being cheated of their own childhoods, this cycle is extremely difficult for many people to break.

Ralph is a 37-year-old father of two boys, ages five and nine. As a child, he had been physically abused and neglected by both parents. His father abandoned the family when Ralph was five; shortly after his ninth birthday, he returned home from school to find the house stripped of all furniture, no curtains on the windows, a small pile of his clothes in the middle of the empty living room floor, and a note from his mother saying she was taking his two older brothers and moving across the country, and that he should go to his aunt's house, who lived in the next town. Now, with a good job and a snug house for his family, Ralph would become helplessly enraged when he saw his own children getting the very things that he wanted for them, but had not received himself. In the middle of his son's birthday party, he burned all the presents in the incinerator, threw the cake against the wall, gave his son a black eye, and then hit him with a belt to make him stop crying. Christmas and other celebrations brought similar disasters.

Role of the School

At least after the age of five, if not before, the school becomes a critical link in the array of services available for abused or neglected children. Schools are the one place in American society where all children are mandated by law to be present. Schools are also accountable by law to provide the screening, assessment, and other services required to identify and meet special education needs. Thus, nearly all children spend a significant amount of time in school, and teachers have far more opportunity to observe them under a variety of conditions than do any other professionals. If children are not making satisfactory adjustments to the school's expectations, services are in place to carefully examine a child's development status and home situation. Thus, in many ways, schools are in an ideal position to identify children who may be suffering from abuse or neglect.

All 50 states mandate reporting child abuse or neglect (Mayhall & Norgard, 1983).

Although laws vary from one state to another, many specifically mention teachers and other school personnel as reporters, meaning that a teacher is legally bound to report a case of suspected abuse or neglect within a certain period, often 24 hours, and that there may be a penalty for failure to report. Only one state does not grant immunity from lawsuits to anyone who reports in good faith (Erikson et al., 1984). Regular and special educators' sensitivity to abuse issues and their knowledge of current laws and policies in regard to reporting make a difference. After an inservice program in one city school system designed to sensitize teachers to abuse and reporting issues, the schools became the largest single source for reporting abuse or neglect cases (Mayhall & Norgard, 1983). Obviously, if suspected abuse is not reported, there can be no effort to change things for the child. It is not the teacher's responsibility to investigate; this is the second step of the process, and is handled by the local child protection agency. A report results in an investigation; if there are problems, some sort of intervention ensues that one hopes will provide support to the family and any needed protection for the child. Every school system should have a policy for reporting suspected abuse, and anyone who works for a school should learn the policy and what the related state and local laws specify. Child protection agencies and child advocacy centers often provide inservice education to school faculty, which is especially important because teachers are in an ideal position to observe children and their development over time. Many cases of abuse and neglect continue over long periods; the longer the time, the greater the risk of serious physical or emotional damage. The experience of most professionals who treat victims of abuse or neglect is that the earlier the problem surfaces, the more quickly and fully children respond to treatment. There are thus moral as well as legal reasons for educators to take their reporting responsibilities seriously.

Prevention of abuse and neglect is also an important issue for schools. There are two important aspects to the school's role in prevention; the first relates to its obvious function of providing education. Children growing up in the 1980s live in a society in which families and family support systems have changed radically over the past generation. The greater divorce rate means that many more children live in families headed by a single parent who must also work. Other children must deal with recombining families, or accepting new stepparents, or with live-in boyfriends or girlfriends. These situations can be good for children, but for a growing number of children, they also present conditions of greater family stress. One consequence for some children may be a lack of stable parenting models to which they will be able to reach back when they have their own children. Programs of sex education, parenting, and family life should address these issues, as well as issues of abuse and neglect, within the context of meaningful discussions about discipline, parenting responsibilities, children's needs at different ages, and ways that parents can learn to handle anger and frustration. Unfortunately, programs like these are somewhat controversial, because some people feel that schools should not intrude into the area of values—and discussions of family issues and child rearing certainly involve values. The alternative, however, is to accept the continuation of an already unacceptably high level of abuse and neglect for children in the next generation. Exploitation and destructive parenting are an intergenerational cycle that is difficult to break, and the schools represent an invaluable resource to begin to alter the cycle of abuse.

The second prevention issue for schools is that it provides the fabric of experience for learning to live with others. A school's hidden curriculum involves ways to handle nonconformity and conflict, ways to balance individual needs against the interests of the group, and the ways in which teachers provide protection, instruction, and comfort. Children with violent or neglectful parents will not benefit from violence or neglect in school. Currently, only four states have laws forbidding the use of corporal punishment in the schools. It is difficult to justify physical violence in schools at the same time the schools are attempting to teach children not to be violent; the sanctioned paddling of a student by an adult authority figure obviously implies that "might makes right." This is not to argue for permissiveness, but to suggest that an important way to learn to resolve conflict through negotiation and problem solving is within the context of a classroom. Children who experience violence at home, who watch it on TV, who see its effects daily in newspapers or perhaps down the street, should at least have the opportunity of watching and being a part of alternative ways for resolving conflict and dealing with feelings of frustration and anger.

RESOURCES

Information on Alcohol Abuse

Alcoholics Anonymous—World Services
P.O. Box 459, Grand Central Station
New York, NY 10017

Al-Anon Family Group Headquarters
P.O. Box 182, Madison Square Station
New York, NY 10010

National Clearinghouse for Alcohol Information
Box 2345
Rockville, MD 20852

National Council on Alcoholism
733 Third Avenue
New York, NY 10017

National Institute on Alcohol Abuse &
  Alcoholism
5600 Fishers Park Lane
Park Carver Building
Rockville, MD 20852

Information about Curricula for Alcohol Education Programs

Alcohol Specific Curricula: A Selected List
National Institute on Alcohol Abuse and
Alcoholism
Rockville, MD 20852

Decisions About Drinking (Grades 3–12)
By D. Mills, C. Deutsch, & L. DiCicco
CASPAR Alcohol Education Program
226 Highland Ave.
Somerville, MA 02143

Information on Child Abuse or Neglect

Children's Division
American Humane Association
P.O. Box 1266
Denver, CO 80201

Education for Parenthood: A Primary Prevention
Strategy for Child Abuse & Neglect
(Report #93)

Education Policies and Practices Regarding Child
Abuse & Neglect (Report #85)
Available from Education Commission of
the States, 300 Lincoln Tower Bldg.,
1860 Lincoln, Denver, CO 80295

Guidelines for Schools: Teachers, Nurses,
Counselors and Administrators (Child Abuse)
Children's Division
American Humane Association
P.O. Box 1266
Denver, CO 80201

Incest Survivors, Anonymous
P.O. Box 5613
Long Beach, CA 90800

National Committee for Prevention of
Child Abuse
Suite 510
111 East Wacker Drive
Chicago, IL 60601

Victims of Incest Can Emerge
Grand Junction, CO 81501

Books on Alcohol Problems

Al-Anon Family Groups. (1977). *What's Drunk,
Maura?* Al-Anon Family Group Headquarters,

P.O. Box 182, Madison Square Station, New
York, NY 10010 (For elementary age children)

AIMS Instructional Media Services. *All Bottled Up.*
626 Justin Avenue, Glendale, CA 91201 (Short
animated film for children)

Black, C. (1979). *My Dad Loves Me, My Dad Has a
Disease.* ACT: Newport Beach, CA (Nonfiction
for elementary age children)

Brooks, Catherine. (1981). *The Secret Everybody
Knows.* Operation Cork, 4425 Cass Street, San
Diego, CA (Nonfiction for adolescents)

Figueroa, R. *El Secrito De Pablito.* National Association of Children of Alcoholics, 31706 Coast
Highway, Suite 201, South Laguna, CA 92677 (A
bilingual book about alcoholism in the family)

Hornik, Edith. (1984). *You and Your Alcoholic Parent.* National Council on Alcoholism (For adolescents)

Melquist, Elaine, *Pepper.* National Council on Alcoholism (For young children)

Seixas, Judith. (1977). *Alcohol: What It Is, What It
Does.* Greenwillow Books, New York, NY (Basic
facts for elementary children)

Seixas, Judith. (1979). *Living with a Parent Who
Drinks Too Much.* Greenwillow Books, New
York, NY (For older elementary and adolescent
students)

Summers, J. (1966). *The Long Ride Home.* Westmin-
ster Press, Philadelphia, PA (Fiction for early
adolescents)

Typpo, M., & Hustings, J. *An Elephant in the Living
Room.* National Association for Children of Alcoholics, 31706 Coast Highway, Suite 201, South
Laguna, CA 92677 (A story about denial in an
alcoholic family)

Woititiz, J. (1984). *Adult Children of Alcoholics.*
Health Communications, Pompano Beach, FL

Films on Child Abuse

A Time for Caring: The School's Response to the
Sexually Abused Child. Lawren Productions,
Inc., P.O. Box 666, Mendocino, CA 95460 (For
inservice training for school personnel)

Lift a Finger: The Teacher's Role in Combating
Child Abuse & Neglect. Consortium C, 1750
Seamist Box 863, Houston, TX 77008 (Slide/tape
presentation for teacher inservice training)

Parenting: Growing With Children. Film Fail Communications, 10900 Ventura Blvd., Studio City,

CA 91604 (For adolescents or parent training groups on abuse prevention)

Soft Is the Heart of a Child. Gerald T. Rogers Productions, Inc., 5225 Old Orchard Road, #6, Skokie, IL 60077 (Film for adolescents)

Teenage Parents. CRM, McGraw-Hill Films, 110

Fifteenth Street, Del Mar, CA (Documentary)

Who Do You Tell? MTI Teleprograms, 3710 Commercial Avenue, Northbrook, IL 60062 (For school-age children—how to deal with problems of exploitation or abuse)

REFERENCES

Ackerman, R., (1983). *Children of alcoholics: A guidebook for educators, therapists, and parents* (2nd ed.) Holmes Beach, FL: Learning Publications.

American Humane Association. (1981). *National analysis of official child neglect and abuse reporting.* Denver, CO: Author.

Black, C. (1981). *It will never happen to me: Children of alcoholics as adults.* Denver, CO: M. A. C.

Botvin, G. (1983). Prevention of adolescent substance abuse through the development of personal and social competence. In T. Glynn, et al. (Eds.), *Preventing adolescent drug abuse: intervention strategies.* NIDA Research Monograph #47. Rockville, MD: National Institute for Drug Abuse.

Deutsch, C. (1982). *Broken bottles/broken dreams: Understanding and helping the children of alcoholics.* New York: Teachers College Press.

Erikson, E., McEvor, A., & McClu, B. (1984). *Child abuse and neglect: A guidebook for educators and community leaders.* Holmes Beach, FL: Learning Publications.

Garbarino, J., & Gillian, G. (1980). *Understanding abusive families.* Lexington, MA: Lexington Books.

Johnson, V. (1973). *I'll quit tomorrow.* New York: Harper & Row.

Joint Commission on the Mental Health of Children. (1970). *Crisis in child mental health.* New York: Harper & Row.

Justice, B., & Justice, R. (1976). *The abusing family.* New York: Human Sciences Press.

Kempe, C., & Helfer, R. (1980). *The battered child* (3rd ed.). Chicago: University of Chicago Press.

Kinney, J., & Leaton, G. (1978). *Loosening the grip: A handbook of alcohol information.* St. Louis, MO: Mosby.

Korbin, Jill. (1981). *Child abuse and neglect: Cross-cultural perspectives.* Berkeley: University of California Press.

MacDonald, D. (1984). *Drugs, drinking and adolescents.* Chicago: Year Book Medical Publishers.

Mayer, A. (1983). *Incest.* Holmes Beach, FL: Learning Publications.

Mayhall, P., & Norgard, K. (1983). *Child abuse and neglect: Sharing responsibility.* New York: John Wiley.

McNeil, D. (1975). *Boys with problems grow into manhood.* Hawkins, TX: Dallas Salesmanship Club Therapeutic Company Program.

North, R., & Orange, R. (1980). *Teenage drinking.* New York: Macmillan.

Nystrom, F., Bal, A., & LaBrecque, V. (1979). Substance abuse. In J. Noshpits (Ed.), *Basic handbook of child psychiatry* (Vol. 2). New York: Basic Books.

Polansky, N., Hally, C., & Polansky, N. (1981). *Damaged parents: An anatomy of child neglect.* Chicago: University of Chicago Press.

Seixas, J., & Youcha, G. (1985). *Children of alcoholics: A survivors' manual.* New York: Crown Publishers.

Silbert, M. (1982). *Delancy Street study: Prostitution and sexual assault.* San Francisco: Delancy Street Foundation.

Simonds, J., & Engleman, M. (1982). *America's children and their families: Key facts.* Washington, DC: Children's Defense Fund.

Smith, P., & Bohnstedt, M. (1980). *Child victimization study highlights.* Sacramento, CA: Social Research Center, American Justice Institute (NCCAN) 90-C-1870.

Straus, M., Gelles, R., & Steinmetz, S. (1979). *Behind closed doors: Violence in the American family.* Garden City, NY: Doubleday/Anchor.

Tessler, D. (1981). *Drugs, kids and schools: Practical strategies for educators and other concerned adults.* Santa Monica, CA: Goodyear.

Vaillant, G. (1983). *The natural history of alcoholism.* Cambridge, MA: Harvard University Press.

Among the other books were a primer, some child's readers, numerous picture books, and a great dictionary. All of these he examined, but the pictures caught his fancy most, though the strange little bugs which covered the pages where there were no pictures excited his wonder and deepest thought.

EDGAR RICE BURROUGHS
TARZAN OF THE APES

The 11-year-old learning disabled boy who drew this picture is bright, attractive, and athletic, but by the time his specific disabilities were identified in fourth grade, he had acquired emotional problems. He has little self-confidence, is unwilling to speak in class, and does not like to disclose his feelings. He drew a football player—his "successful self"—but the immature figures and handwriting belie his success.

CHAPTER FIFTEEN

Learning Disabilities and Emotional/ Behavioral Problems

Lynne Feagans
FRANK PORTER GRAHAM CHILD DEVELOPMENT CENTER
UNIVERSITY OF NORTH CAROLINA AT CHAPEL HILL
CHAPEL HILL, NORTH CAROLINA

Many emotionally disturbed and behaviorally disordered children also have learning problems (estimates range from 30 percent to 70 percent). Determining which is the predominant problem can be difficult.

Defining a learning disability is a controversial problem.

Learning disabled youngsters constitute a large, heterogeneous group that is overrepresented by boys, working class families, and children who score below normally achieving children on standardized achievement and intelligence tests and often demonstrate attentional problems.

Although the definition in P.L. 94–142 for learning disabilities excludes children with emotional disturbance, many learning disabled youngsters display mild to moderate problems in social relations and emotional stability.

Determining which techniques are most effective with learning disabled youngsters has been an elusive process. Deficit treatment approaches have been disappointing. Investigators are evaluating the effectiveness of teaching organizational strategies and cognitive behavior modification techniques to learning disabled children.

Longitudinal studies indicate that learning disabilities do not disappear; rather, many of these children develop behavioral and social problems that complicate their adult adjustment.

THE TERM *LEARNING DISABLED* has been used to describe a heterogeneous population of children who display persistent school achievement problems that are not easily explained by poor intellectual abilities. The term was first adopted in the 1960s to describe children who had previously been described with these labels: dyslexia, school phobics, minimal brain dysfunction, neurological handicap, perceptual handicap, underachievers, specific reading disability, and specific underachievement (Clements, 1966; Epstein, Cullinan, Lessen, & Lloyd, 1980). These labels reflect the diversity of the many professional fields that deal with these children in clinics, hospitals, and schools. The theoretical and educational orientations also reflect the professional traditions, resulting in both biological and psychological explanations for various learning disabilities. Thus, the available information often appears conflicting, which results in some disagreement about exactly what constitutes a learning disability.

Despite the controversies about definition, this disability has been identified in a growing number of children, and the number of professionals involved in research and service has increased comparably. Although the incidence of learning disabilities among children is, as defined by the federal government, the second largest handicap, it is not clear how it might overlap with other handicapping conditions, especially emotional disturbance and behavior disorders.

HISTORY

The history of learning disabilities is less well known than the history of other exceptionalities. Although the term was coined only recently, the roots of this disability can be traced back to the early part of the century, overlapping the areas of mental retardation and emotional disturbance.

Kurt Goldstein's work (1939) was the cornerstone of the early theoretical work in learning disabilities. His study of brain-injured soldiers during World War I resulted in the description of behavioral characteristics of his patients. To this day, these characteristics remain behaviors associated with learning disabled children, although many are reminiscent of behaviors associated with emotional or behavioral problems:

- *Forced responsiveness to stimuli*—responding indiscriminantly to all stimuli in the environment, thus easily distractible from a task by irrelevant stimuli
- *Figure-ground confusion*—inability to sort out central parts from incidental parts of a task, or unable to focus on target stimuli and disregard background stimuli
- *Perseveration*—repetitive action without obvious purpose and apparent inability to stop these actions easily (thought to be caused by person's constant attention and reattention to a stimulus)
- *Hyperactivity*—constant gross motor and fine motor movements that appear aimless and are difficult to control
- *Meticulousness*—rigidity in routine activities and in placement and arrangement of objects in the environment (may be result of attempt to control an environment that seems overwhelming)
- *Catastrophic reaction*—emotional breakdown caused by inability to deal with chaotic environment

Strauss and Werner (1942) later used Goldstein's framework to study mentally retarded children. They distinguished two kinds of retardation: endogenous and exogenous. *Endogenous retardation* was retardation inborn in the child and not a result of brain injury. *Exogenous retardation* was the result of some brain insult before, during, or after birth. Werner and Strauss found that exogenous children exhibited many more of the Goldstein behavioral characteristics than did the endogenous children. They inferred that many so-called "exogenous" children had neurological injury even when medical information did not warrant that conclusion. This led to much controversy, from which terms such as *minimal brain damage* emerged (denoting both learning and behavioral problems).

From this initial work, Strauss and his colleagues developed educational environments for brain-injured children that were conducive to learning (Strauss & Lehtinen, 1947; Strauss & Kephart, 1955). They reduced irrelevant stimuli in the environment and made learning materials as salient as possible to minimize distractibility. The environments for these children were in fact stark; Strauss had no pictures on the walls, teachers dressed in drab colors, children were spaced at a distance from one another, and desks faced the bare walls. At this point, there was no distinction between a pure learning problem and a pure emotional disorder.

Cruickshank took the information about exogenously retarded children and applied it to intellectually normal children who displayed some of the same behavioral characteristics (Cruickshank, Bentzen, Ratzeburg, & Tannhauser, 1961). Although Cruickshank pioneered grouping children by behavioral style rather than intelligence, his work was often misconstrued as making the distinction between learning/emotional disorders and mental retardation (Cruickshank, 1977). Cruickshank, like Strauss, created stark learning environments which, it was hoped, would help the children in their learning.

While the pioneers in learning disabilities were focusing on control of the environment, psychiatrists were also seeing children who displayed similar characteristics. Many articles appeared in the 1950s and 1960s describing the learning inhibitions displayed by emotionally disturbed children. Their distractibility and lack of attention in learning were described as symptoms of their underlying emotional problem. Pearson said about the inattentive child, "The distractibility of a particular child is usually considered to be due to either the strength of instinct representations or to the developmental weakness of the ego's function in centering attention" (1952, p. 336). Thus, psychiatry and the field of learning disabilities began to diverge in their diagnosis and treatment of such children. As Forness and Cantwell stated as recently as 1982, "an attention deficit disorder may be seen as primarily a learning disability by a special education teacher, while a psychiatrist may consider it under the behavior-disorder rubric" (p. 52).

Beginning in the late 1950s and early 1960s, a host of prominent investigators emerged in the field of learning disabilities, including Marianne Frostig, Samuel Kirk, Helmer Myklebust, and Joseph Wepman. These people made major contributions to our understanding of learning disabilities through their innovative theories and interventions, which were based on deficits in basic cognitive processes. At this point, refinements on the definition of learning and emotional disorders forged a wedge between the two syndromes that remains today. The field of learning disabilities focused on cognitive/perceptual deficits, with minimal attention to behavioral/emotional problems.

Marianne Frostig (Frostig & Horne, 1964) created a popular program for perceptual motor training. She felt that perceptual problems were neurologically based and at the root of reading disabilities. Her program came under severe criticism in the early 1970s because, although the children in her program gained in perceptual motor ability, they failed to show gains in reading (Hammill & Larsen, 1974).

Samuel Kirk (Kirk, McCarthy, & Kirk, 1968) based his program on his test instrument, the Illinois Test of Psycholinguistic Abilities (ITPA), which grew out of Charles Osgood's conceptual model of language functioning. Kirk envisioned three dimensions of language processing: the communication level, the psycholinguistic level, and the organizational level. His test reflected these dimensions and produced differential profiles for children that indicated deficit areas. Although theoretically appealing, the instrument has not been able to predict academic outcomes well or to help formulate effective interventions based on test results (Hammill & Larsen, 1974).

Helmer Myklebust also conceptualized language as a key element in learning disabilities, especially in the reading process. He developed an LD screening instrument called the Pupil Rating Scale (PRS) (1971) that the classroom teacher fills out. The instrument contains five areas of functioning—auditory comprehension, spoken language, orientation, motor coordination, and personal-social behavior—and is still popular as a general screening device.

Joseph Wepman created a model for expressive language disorders that examined the complex operations involved in receiving, integrating, and transmitting information (Wepman, Jones, Boch, & Van Pelt, 1960). The model helped in identification of certain language disorders because it allowed for greater precision in differentiating information processing skills.

These theorists helped us understand the cognitive and language characteristics of learning disabilities, but often overlooked the obvious social and emotional aspects associated with learning problems. Indeed, it has often been difficult to find learning disabled children who do not also have some social or emotional problem (Hallahan & Kauffman, 1976). Thus, many of the programs, especially in the public schools, drew on the programs and services for emotionally handicapped children (Fagan, Long, & Stevens, 1975). Practitioners found that, for the appropriate teaching techniques to work for those children, they had to attend to their social and emotional problems at the same time. Thus a tradition arose in the field of learning disabilities in which learning problems are seen in the context of more global social and emotional problems. Whether the learning problems or the social/emotional problems are primary is not an issue for the practitioner, except during diagnosis. Once the child was placed in a classroom, each aspect of his problem needed to be addressed (Rutter, 1974). Although this tradition prevailed in the 1950s and 1960s, more recently with newer legislation, the categorical approach to exceptionalities has diminished the integrative approach to teaching learning disabled children. In addition, the accountability movement, in which parents and administrators have demanded proof that a child is progressing in a special program, has forced teachers to use a more direct method of remediation to help LD children. Helping them perceptually or linguistically was not transferring to work in the classroom; thus, the 1970s brought a "back to básics" approach in learning disabilities. This approach was largely atheoretical in orientation and based on direct instruction in the academic deficit, regardless of etiology. Children were grouped for instruction based on behavioral characteristics, not by etiology or identifiable handicap.

ISSUES REGARDING DEFINITION

As many as 30 percent of the school children in the U. S. experience extreme academic difficulty that is not easily explained by constitutional factors such as intelligence and physical handicaps, nor by exogenous variables, including home stability and parent education (Epstein, Cullinan, Lessen, & Lloyd, 1980). Such children have often been called *underachievers* and form the pool from which children with learning disabilities are identified. Although many investigators have tried to separate learning disabilities from other kinds of exceptionalities, including emotional disorders, agreement as to definition has been a major problem. Even with Public Law 94–142 in 1975, the Education for All Handicapped Children Act, what constitutes a learning disability and whether there should be some limit on the number of children diagnosed for special education remain unsettled. The federal definition reflects the diversity of opinion by excluding other handicaps without specifically defining a learning disability. Therefore, professionals in the field have been left to sort out many definitional issues without strict federal guidelines. Under PL 94–142, this definition still stands:

"Specific learning disability" means a disorder in one or more of the basic psychological processes involved in understanding or in using language, spoken or written, which may manifest itself in an imperfect ability to listen, think, speak, read, write, spell, or to do mathematical calculations. The term includes such conditions as perceptual handicaps, brain injury, minimal brain dysfunction, dyslexia, and developmental aphasia. The term does not include children who have learning problems which are primarily the result of visual, hearing, or motor handicaps, of mental retardation, or emotional disturbance, or of environmental, cultural, or economic disadvantage. (Federal Register, Dec. 29, 1977, p. 65083)

This definition is in many ways similar to that of behavior disorders, because behavior disordered children must also be failing to progress in school as the first criterion for eligibility. After this criterion has been met, it is often difficult to discriminate between an attention deficit (which would classify a child as learning disabled) and a more severe behavioral problem that would classify the child as emotionally/behaviorally disordered.

In addition to the definition, PL 94–142 states that a child identified as learning disabled must meet the following criteria:

(a) A team may determine that a child has a specific learning disability if:
  (1) The child does not achieve commensurate with his or her age and ability levels in one or more of the areas listed in paragraph (a) (2) of this section, when provided with learning experiences appropriate for the child's age and ability levels; and
  (2) The team finds that a child has a severe discrepancy between achievement and intellectual ability in one or more of the following areas:
      (i) Oral expression;
      (ii) Listening comprehension;
      (iii) Written expression;
      (iv) Basic reading skill;
      (v) Reading comprehension;
      (vi) Mathematics calculation; or
      (vii) Mathematics reasoning.
(b) The team may not identify a child as having a specific learning disability if the severe discrepancy between ability and achievement is primarily the result of:
  (1) A visual, hearing, or motor handicap;
  (2) Mental retardation;
  (3) Emotional disturbance; or
  (4) Environmental, cultural or economic disadvantage. (Federal Register, Dec. 29, 1977, p. 65083)

Because these criteria are loose and lend themselves to interpretation by local and state agencies, prevalence rates vary tremendously from one area of the country to another.

The disorders mentioned in the federal definition contain as many as 100 characteristics associated with learning problems (Federal Register December 29, 1980, p. 65083), some of which are common among many of the studies. Hallahan and Kauffman (1976) identify five major areas of agreement among theoretical and research papers: (1) academic retardation, (2) an uneven pattern of development, (3) equivocal central nervous system dysfunction, (4) exclusion of mental retardation as well as emotional disturbance, and (5) exclusion of environmental disadvantage. These authors, however, challenge the legitimacy of the last two characteristics on the basis of logic. They see no reason that a child from a disadvantaged background could not suffer from a learning disability, and use the same argument with respect to mentally retarded and emotionally disturbed children.

As one might surmise, excluding behavioral problems is not possible in many cases because learning and behavioral problems occur together in many children. It has been estimated that between 30 and 80 percent of children with behavior problems also have learning problems (Cullinan, Epstein, & Lloyd, 1983). Thus, because of the federal guidelines, children with more emotional/behavioral problems than learning problems are identified as emotionally handicapped, while children with more learning than emotional problems are identified as learning disabled. The separation persists even though theory and research continually show that the two disorders overlap (Kessler, 1966; McKinney & Feagans, 1983; Bryan & Bryan, 1978). For instance, in an epidemiological study, Rutter, Tizard, and Whitmore (1970) showed that children with both behavioral problems and a reading disability had more in common with children with a pure reading disability than with children with a pure behavioral disorder.

The three remaining areas of agreement allow enormous latitude as to which types of children can be classified as learning disabled. Most professionals consider children who are behind academically in relation to ability, who display an uneven pattern of abilities, and who show so-called soft neurological signs to be learning disabled.

The greatest impact of PL 94–142 has been not in the definition of learning disabled children, since the definition is so controversial, but on service delivery. The law gives each handicapped child the right to appropriate services in the least restrictive environment. It requires an Individualized Education Plan (IEP) for every handicapped child. This aspect of the law may have been the most important part of the legislation, because for the first time accountability was demanded. The law specifies that a team of experts, including the parents, prescribe specific educational objectives and placement for each student and that the IEP be updated yearly. Teachers must fully inform parents as to the objectives and report the child's progress to the parents over the school year.

The specification required by the IEP has drastically changed the way we conduct special education. Although the initial paperwork involved in implementation overwhelmed most teachers and administrators, most school systems have streamlined the process to make it more manageable. In the meantime, the law has created greater parent and student involvement in the educational process and has helped special educators face the accountability issue head on. This has led, in most cases, to better and more individualized instruction for all special children.

CHARACTERISTICS

Although we can characterize learning disabled children in a variety of domains, we will concentrate on only a few areas. Background and demographic characteristics will circumscribe the population and demonstrate some of the salient features of this group. The children's intellectual status is linked to identification and cognitive functioning, and we will discuss academic skills in relation to intelligence and different kinds of academic performance. We will also consider a variety of learning and behavioral characteristics, including classroom behavior, social/emotional problems, language, perceptual development, and neurological functioning.

Background and Demographic Characteristics

When we talk about learning disabled children, whom are we really talking about? In fact, we are talking about a large, heterogeneous group, about whom we lack much information as to the exact nature of their many problems. One large-scale examination of the background characteristics of learning disabled children found that most research studies are inconsistent and lacking in descriptions of the children (Keogh, Major, Omori, Gandara, & Reid, 1980). There are only a few background characteristics of which we can be absolutely sure, and many that need much more research.

We know that many more boys than girls are identified as learning disabled; the ratio of boys to girls ranges from 3 to 1 to about 6 to 1, so boys are certainly at greater risk for developing learning problems. We also know that most learning disabled children are of elementary school age. This fact probably reflects identification procedures more than anything else. It also reflects the emphasis of research and interventions, which do not emphasize identifying or treating the preschool or adolescent child. (The same is true for emotional/behavioral handicaps.)

Other characteristics are less well known. For instance, it had been thought that learning disabled children came predominantly from middle-class families and that they were mostly white. Although this may have been true 20 years ago, it has become less and less true. Recent studies show a growing representation of minority groups and a growing spread in socioeconomic status (SES). In large, urban samples, the children identified as LD come predominantly from working class families and represent all strata of socioeconomic status. Birth and early experience problems are thought to contribute to learning disabilities, but no prospective studies have actually indicated that this is the case. In addition, preschool and health histories are often not indicative of problems, although children are later identified at school entry to have problems. Family attitudes and beliefs have not generally been implicated in learning disabilities, although there is a possibility that learning disabled children tend to come from larger families and are more often later born. All these characteristics need further verification.

Intellectual Status

Measuring intelligence in children with learning disabilities as well as using intelligence test subtest scores for identification have been important both theoretically and practically. Research shows that these children score lower, as a group, on intelligence tests compared to normal children (Feagans & McKinney, 1981; Farnham-Diggory, 1978). This finding has not been part of the conventional folklore, which often portrays the learning disabled child with above-average intelligence. Although some learning disabled children score well on intelligence tests, the usual child with LD scores from 5 to 10 points below the average.

Besides the total intelligence score, there also has been interest in the pattern of abilities displayed on the tests as indicating an uneven pattern of development. The Wechsler scales, which contain a number of verbal and nonverbal subtests, have been widely used for this purpose. In fact, Wechsler (1958) suggested that examining the spread between the lowest and highest subtest scores might indicate particular problems. This approach has been called the *examination of subtest scatter*. Exaggerated patterns of strengths and weaknesses on the tests may suggest an uneven pattern of development as well as neurological dysfunction. Although the use of subtest scatter is widespread, it has not reliably predicted learning disabilities nor differentiated these children from others (Bryan & Bryan, 1978; Feagans & McKinney, 1981). Cronbach (1960) has said "Indices representing 'scatter' of subtest scores—e.g., the range from highest to lowest subtest scores—are worthless as diagnostic signs." Many studies now indicate that the subtest scatter found within a population of learning disabled children is not different from that found in normal achievers (Huelsman, 1970; Kender, 1972). In one study of WISC-R performance, Feagans and McKinney (1981) did not find more scatter in normal achievers than in learning disabled children; both the normal and learning disabled groups exhibited scatter scores comparable to a large-scale study of the WISC-R based on a heterogeneous sample of children (Kaufman, 1976).

So there are two major findings with respect to intelligence. Learning disabled children score consistently below normally achieving children on intelligence tests, but still within the normal range. Learning disabled children also display a pattern of subtest scatter that does not clearly differentiate them from normally achieving children. Given the first finding, we might predict that learning disabled children will not perform as well academically as children with an average IQ. Thus, when considering a diagnosis of LD, it has been of concern to professionals to examine the discrepancy between expected level of achievement based on IQ and the child's actual level of achievement.

Academic Functioning

Children identified as learning disabled are usually first noticed by the classroom teacher who perceives that they do not profit from regular classroom instruction. Although academic retardation can be distributed among many academic areas, the primary area of difficulty that teachers see is in reading and language arts; many fewer learning disabled students have problems with mathematics (Hallahan & Kauffman, 1976; McKinney & Feagans, 1983). This is often the case with emotionally disturbed or behavior disordered children also. As Wood (in press) describes the eligibility criteria of such children, they must first give evidence of unsatisfactory academic progress along with some behavior problem. Again we see the close link between learning disabled and emotionally disturbed/behavior disordered children.

Although teachers and professionals usually suspect a discrepancy between intelligence and achievement, some learning disabled children appear to perform academically only slightly below their potential as measured by intelligence tests. These children do not show a discrepancy between intelligence and achievement; they may be identified for other reasons, including emotional or neurological difficulties. The majority of these children perform well below expected levels given their intellectual ability, but we often find this pattern in both language arts and math, even though teachers do not often perceive the double academic deficiency. It also occurs with mild behavioral problems (McKinney & Feagans, 1984). It is more common to find that learning disabled children have pervasive academic and attention problems rather than a specific deficit in such areas as spelling or writing with no other discernible problems.

IQ/achievement discrepancies. More and more states are adopting strict criteria formulas for documenting a discrepancy between intelligence and achievement, in the hope of serving a smaller and more disabled population of children. Of the variety of formulas in use, all have strengths and weaknesses. Some examples will help us understand the difficulties in finding the "perfect" formula.

Many states use a grade-discrepancy formula; in this case, a child must show an IQ within the normal range but performance below grade level by some degree, perhaps at least one year. This formula is easy to calculate, but has many drawbacks; for one thing, it does not take into account the child's age. A child who had failed two grades would be judged as comparable to other children in his grade who were two years younger. To qualify by this grade discrepancy formula, a child who had already failed two grades would have to be at least an additional grade behind. In addition, falling one year behind in elementary school is far more disabling than being one year behind in high school, which the formulas also fail to take into account. Other, more statistically sophisticated formulas may solve problems like these but present other problems. Recent research indicates that the formulas do not even identify the same children and that we know little about the real validity of using different formulas (Cone & Wilson, 1981).

Reading deficits. Both the medical and educational communities consider that the most severe problem for learning disabled children is in reading. This disability affects all areas of academic functioning. Terms such as *dyslexia* and *reading retardation* have been used to describe these children, and many specific subtypes have been proposed to label the process and etiology. Both cross-sectional and longitudinal studies suggest that academic retardation in reading causes learning disabled children to, at worst, fall progressively further behind their peers, or, at best, to maintain the loss that was documented at the time of identification (McKinney & Feagans, 1984). Remedial programs, at least in the public schools, have so far been unsuccessful in early remediation.

In general, two types of reading problems are associated with learning disabilities, and there is much dispute over which is the primary problem. First, some children have trouble understanding and interpreting the written code; that is, they have trouble associating a sound with a letter, and, later, in sounding out words. This is called a *decoding* or *reading recognition* problem. We see decoding problems in many young learning disabled children, and the causes may be multiple. Some children may have perceptual or auditory problems, while others may simply have problems in the translation between oral and written language.

The second aspect of reading is *comprehension*—understanding what is being read and being able to paraphrase or answer questions about the material. A large number of learning disabled children have problems with comprehension. Many children are considered reading disabled because, although they can read adequately, they forget or do not understand what they read. This reading comprehension problem is much more evident in older LD children who have learned how to decode but still have significant problems learning in school. Detecting comprehension problems is often more difficult than detecting decoding problems because comprehension problems may be more subtle. For instance, some children have problems understanding causal relationships that are not always apparent from answers to questions about a reading passage.

Both the decoding and comprehension areas are important for the acquisition of reading skill and, although learning disability theorists argue about the primacy of one skill over the other in defining the central problem, practitioners often find that children have both kinds of deficits over the early elementary school years.

This academic retardation is a persistent problem without easy remedies. A learning disability, although considered a mildly handicapping condition, is more than a passing phenomenon, and one that continues to affect children throughout the school years. Unfortunately many professionals and parents often minimize the long-term academic and social consequences because of the children's other perceived competencies. Studies of adolescent learning disabled children indicate that the increasing demands at the secondary level actually produce more numerous and more varied school problems, including academic, social, and emotional problems (Deshler, Warner, Schumaker, & Alley, 1983). In a long-term follow-up of learning disabled children as adults, Werner and Smith (1977) found that of all childhood handicaps, learning disabilities resulted in the most maladjustment in adulthood.

The basic source of the problems for these children may encompass a wide range of developmental processes, including spatial and perceptual discrimination of letters, auditory discrimination, language processing, attention, and information processing. Investigators originally concentrated on both visual and auditory discrimination as well as the inability to control irrelevant stimuli (Birch & Belmont, 1965; Frostig, 1972; Orton, 1937). Psychiatrically oriented clinicians focused on learning inhibitions and various other psychiatric syndromes that could cause reading problems (Pearson, 1952). Recent attention, however, has focused on oral language deficits (Wiig & Semel, 1976) and information processing problems (Torgesen, 1980), some of which we will discuss.

Social/Emotional Disorders

Although the federal definition of learning disabilities excludes children with a primary diagnosis of emotional disturbance, many learning disabled children display mild to moderate problems in social relationships and emotional stability (Hallahan & Kauffman, 1976). It is thought that the school failure that usually accompanies learning disabilities exacerbates these social/emotional problems. Yet, it is still unclear whether social/emotional problems occur along with learning disabilities or whether they may help to create or are the result of learning disabilities. Studies of children with emotional handicaps consistently find that socially and emotionally disturbed children display many of the same academic problems that are associated with learning disabilities, so it has

often been difficult to determine some children's primary disability.

Learning disabled children are described as socially less desirable than normally achieving children (Bryan & Bryan, 1983). In a series of studies of sociometric ratings (ratings by all children in a class of how popular other children in the class are), LD children are consistently rated as less desirable peers. Observational studies also show that LD children are not more aggressive or inappropriate with peers, but that subtle problems do occur in their use of language in social situations. These subtle but somewhat inappropriate verbal strategies may contribute to their poorer peer status (Bryan, Donahue, Pearl, & Sturm, 1984). Although the subtle differences are difficult to code objectively, subjective judgments by adults of LD and normal children show that LD children are rated as less socially appropriate. These studies were done by having naive adults watch videotapes of LD and normal children interacting; afterwards, the adults rated each child's behavior and affect without knowing which children were normal and which LD.

Given all these somewhat negative findings about the social status and affect of learning disabled children, it is not surprising that they also rate themselves more poorly. In assessments of self-concept, learning disabled children rate themselves more poorly than their peers rate themselves (Reid & Hresko, 1982). This rating seems to correlate highly with their academic performance in the classroom; so we again face the question of whether school failure is the cause or effect of these social/emotional problems.

There is a close link between social/emotional difficulties and learning disabilities. Although the social/emotional difficulties may not be primary to the major learning disability, they often pose a serious problem for intervention with these children. For a teacher to deal with them effectively, techniques for academic difficulties alone may not work. Being sensitive to and using techniques that are effective with emotional and social problems may be necessary before remediation of the academic problem can begin.

Neurological and Behavioral Disorders

Academic failure is often the stimulus for diagnosing learning disabilities, and since it is not easily explained, there has been much speculation about etiology. It was first thought that subtle neurological problems were involved, because of some of the similarities between these children's reading problems and the problems of brain-injured adults. Several leaders in the field argued this relationship persuasively (Orton, 1937; Strauss & Werner, 1942). Their influence was so pervasive that, even without sound research evidence, a 1957 medical definition of dyslexia read "an inability to read understandingly due to a central lesion" (Dorland, 1957). There is now much less reliance on neurological explanations, but research and speculation continue.

Neurological hypotheses can be divided into two major types: direct measurement of neurological processes and indirect measurement of inferred neurological processes. Both areas have used neurological explanations in the past, but the area of indirect measurement has come to use fewer neurological explanations and more behavioral and psychological ones.

Measurement of direct neurological processes. Children who are referred to clinics for evaluation of learning problems are often seen by a medical team for measurement of brain-wave patterns, including auditory and visually evoked potentials and regional cerebral blood flow while the children engage in a variety of cognitive activities (Rosenthal, 1977). These approaches have yielded suggestive findings in the way of some neurological abnormalities, yet most of these studies are based on flawed methods and the samples are unrepresentative of the larger learning disabled group. As Cole (1978) explains, many of the studies have not used proper control groups and were unable to relate the degree of abnormality to academic problems. In addition, a variety of EEG findings, using similar EEG procedures, suggests an absence of a specific neurological syndrome (Cole, 1978; Routh & Roberts, 1972).

Still, neurological research is a burgeoning area in which new techniques often outstrip our knowledge of how to use them effectively. This is often the case because theories of how measurements of brain activity relate to actual behavior and how behaviors relate to academic progress and learning await meaningful formulation.

Indirect measurement of inferred neurological problems. By far the most prevalent type of neurological research concerns indirect indices of neurological dysfunction. These indices include measurements of behavior that are thought to have a neurological basis. They range from perceptual and gross motor problems to hyperactivity and attention deficits. For instance, problems in perceptual discrimination, gross motor coordination, and eye-hand coordination were thought to be directly linked to reading problems and to have a minor neurological dysfunction as an etiology. The work of Frostig (1972) became a hallmark of neurological mechanisms and a basis for treatment programs for perceptual motor problems. However, this work has now been largely discounted as the cause of learning disabilities. Although there seems to be a small number of children with such disorders, an even smaller number can be linked to reading and writing problems; and even those perceptual problems that are correlated with reading and writing problems do not seem to be helped by perceptual motor training (Bryan & Bryan, 1978; Epstein et al., 1980).

Another early hypothesis was the mixed dominance theory (Orton, 1937). Experiments were conducted to determine if learning disabled children used the anatomically preferred side of the brain in a bizarre manner by being left-eyed and right-handed or something similar. This mixed dominance was thought to give rise to reading problems. Recent evidence gives little credibility to this relationship (Belmont & Birch, 1965).

Based on the seminal work of Strauss and Werner (1942), much of the behavioral work in learning disabilities has focused on problems of attention and hyperactivity. The early work likened learning disabled children to brain-injured children. This analogy has been discarded, but there has been a burst of studies on the behavioral characteristics of learning disabled children. Many studies indicate that learning disabled children are less task-oriented and more distractible compared to normal classmates in the classroom (Bryan & Bryan, 1978; McKinney & Feagans, 1984). These studies indicate that learning disabled children are not disruptive or aggressive, but that teachers must constantly remind them to return to their work. Longitudinal studies of LD children's classroom behavior show that on-task behavior does improve over the years, but so does that of normal classmates. Therefore, relative to their normal peers, they still appear to be off-task. The problem with attention has been so overwhelming for many LD children that it has often been dubbed the "overriding disability" (Hallahan & Kauffman, 1976).

Experimental studies of attention have focused on the "incidental learning task" developed by John Hagen (1967). This task taps what we call *selective attention* in learning. Selective attention is the ability to focus on and process the critical information in a task for learning or problem solving while disregarding extraneous information in the task that does not help in learning or problem solving. In selective attention tasks, children are shown stimulus cards; each card contains two objects, such as an animal and a toy. The children are asked to remember the animal

and disregard the toy. During the course of the task, the experimenter places the cards face down on the table and the children are asked where a particular animal stimulus has been placed in the facedown array. The number the child gets correct is called the *central recall score*. The children are then asked to remember the pairings of stimuli on the cards, which is irrelevant to the main task. The number the child remembers is his *incidental recall score*. Normal children show good incidental learning until the end of elementary school, at which time they seem to shift and focus only on the central objective of the task, receiving high central recall and low incidental recall scores. Experiments with learning disabled children show that they have deficits in selective attention and remember irrelevant information that often interferes with learning (Hallahan, 1975).

Hyperactive children, although closely related to poorly attentive children, exhibit more severe behavioral problems, including more and unproductive gross motor activity. Although a small fraction of the total learning disabled group, these children are a particular problem because their behavior is often disruptive in school and at home. Consequently, much attention has focused on helping hyperactive children adjust to school, independent of possible learning problems.

The typical learning disabled child is not usually hyperactive, but may still present maladaptive classroom behavior. This maladaptive behavior has not generated interest in etiology, but rather in the relationship to academic problems. Distractibility and ineffective teacher interaction are negatively correlated with academic progress, implicating the behaviors themselves as a cause of poor learning (Feagans & McKinney, 1981; McKinney, Mason, Perkerson, & Clifford, 1975).

Maladaptive behaviors characterize many learning disabled children, and both the medical and educational communities are concerned with these behaviors. Although hyperactivity may be medically treatable, other kinds of behavior problems, including problems in distractibility and inappropriate social behavior, have not been amenable to medical intervention. Many learning disabled children exhibit behavioral problems, but we don't know how many learning disabled students exhibit these problems, what the etiology is, and what specific effect the behaviors have on learning.

Cognitive Processes

Although all the areas we have discussed involve cognitive processes, we have emphasized only static characteristics or traits. A *process* is an ongoing cognitive activity applied to solve a problem, to control behavior, or to reflect upon knowledge. Thus, cognitive processes, in some global way, account for the problems of learning disabled children. For instance, instead of saying that a perceptual-motor deficit is causally implicated in reading problems in a static way, cognitive theorists try to specify the ongoing mechanisms that mediate learning in general. The theorists are not interested in a static characteristic like IQ, or a static etiology like neurological abnormalities. They are interested in developing theories that capture the strategies children use to process information. There has also been emphasis on the interaction of a number of processes in producing an outcome. With the advent of sophisticated statistical techniques, research in learning disabilities has focused on multivariable causal explanations.

Recent research in learning disabilities has been directed toward processes that cut across various areas of functioning, taking the form of information processing approaches. These approaches are based on basic cognitive research in psychology and in computer simulation experiments on human problem solving. One model of this kind in the area of human memory has generated hypotheses and research in learning disabilities (Atkinson & Shiffrin, 1968). They dis-

tinguished between structural features of memory that are more or less preset by brain anatomy and physiology and control processes that are under voluntary control. Short-term memory for random material may be fixed, for example, but the strategies for remembering information, such as grouping like words or objects by categories and rehearsing the material before recall, are under voluntary control. Evidence has accumulated that LD children are less strategic and organized in their approaches to cognitive tasks; they do not effectively use control processes. This finding has led many to describe learning disabled children as "inactive learners." Research in memory most consistently supports this hypothesis (Torgesen, 1980).

In one task (Torgesen & Goldman, 1977), children were asked to watch as the experimenter pointed to a series of pictures in a particular sequence. After a delay, the children were asked to recall the sequence. During the delay, the experimenter looked for evidence of control processes or strategies the children used to help them remember. Looking for whispering or lip movements that indicated rehearsal, they found that LD children used fewer of these strategies and also remembered fewer correct sequences than normal children. Another study evaluated other strategies (Torgesen, 1977). Children were asked to study 24 pictures of 24 common objects that could be grouped into four conceptual categories. While the experimenter was out of the room, the children studied these 24 pictures to remember them at a later time. During the study period, good readers moved the pictures around more, rehearsed the picture names more, and were less distracted from the task compared to poor LD readers.

Experiments like these have been replicated often and indicate that LD children fail to use strategies that could help them remember and learn. Mentally retarded children also lack these strategies, but there seems to be a difference between the two groups (Belmont & Butterfield, 1969). When both mentally retarded and learning disabled children are explicitly taught control processes (strategies), MR children improve memory performance but are still inferior to normal children. On the other hand, LD children improve dramatically and perform like normal children when they are taught appropriate strategies. They are said to have a larger "zone of potential" than MR children. This evidence is the reason that the "inactive learner" hypothesis has gained such popularity. It seems that learning disabled children are basically competent, but fail to use strategies spontaneously to help them learn, either because of poor attention to the task or poor overall organizational structures.

Language. Language deficits appear in as many as 50 percent of the children with learning disabilities (Marge, 1972). Brain-injured adult models suggested both expressive and receptive language problems for learning disabled children, and many models like those of Kirk and Mykelbust suggest areas of language deficits for LD children.

By far the greatest research in learning disabled children's language has been the area of syntax and semantics. Syntactic knowledge includes the ability to understand the abstract rules of word combination and inflections (*grammar*) of language, independent of the memory of words and sentences. Semantic knowledge includes the ability to understand the meanings of words and to interpret these meanings within the context of the grammar of the language. A variety of tests tap these skills, including the Northwestern Syntax Screening Test (Lee, 1969), the Illinois Test of Psycholinguistic Abilities (Kirk, McCarthy, & Kirk, 1968), and the Wiig-Semel Test of Syntactic-Semantic Knowledge (Wiig & Semel, 1974). All these tests are based on the assumption that deficits in these areas of language are necessarily predictive and/or related to school or learning

problems. Although differences have been found between learning disabled and normal children using these tests, reviews indicate that most tap only a general language factor and most are poorly standardized (Sommers, Erdige, & Peterson, 1978).

A variety of studies with LD children have examined whether there are really specific deficits in syntax and/or semantics. Vogel (1974) found that normal and dyslexic boys in the second grade did differ on a battery of syntactic and morphological tests. The battery consisted of nine different measures of abilities, from sentence repetition to sentence completion procedures; Vogel found that dyslexics performed more poorly on seven of the nine measures. Similarly, a series of studies by Wiig and her associates have found consistent differences between learning disabled and normal children at a variety of grade levels on syntactic, morphological, and semantic tasks (Semel & Wiig, 1975; Wiig, Lapointe, & Semel, 1977; Wiig, Semel, & Abele, 1981; Wiig, Semel, & Crouse, 1976).

As part of this research, they developed a test of syntactic-semantic development, requiring children to understand the cognitive semantic content of sentences as well as the syntactic structure. They found that LD grade-school children and adolescents differed markedly in their understanding of these structures in comparison to normally achieving children (Wiig & Semel, 1976).

Although differences have been found between normal and LD children in syntactic and semantic knowledge, the deficits have not been linked to reading. It may be that these deficits are implicated in school performance at a higher level.

Other approaches have also been fruitful in the area of language, especially in looking at language beyond the sentence level, at the discourse level. The original work of Bartlett and others (Bartlett, 1932; Schank & Abelson, 1977) indicates that text and thematic materials have an inherent structure characterized by a hierarchal framework. The child learns this structure through repeated contact with narrative or text material. Thus, incoming information in the form of stories or narratives is processed by this established hierarchy of expectancies. Learning disabled children are less able to recall the important elements of text material and to make inferences (Feagans & Short, 1984; Feagans, 1983). A less developed hierarchy of expectancies has been useful in explaining language processing deficits in learning disabled children, especially with school-based materials (Hansen, 1979).

TREATMENT

Effective treatment is elusive. Many techniques, programs, and approaches have been briefly popular but almost all have proved disappointing. There were originally a variety of focused, one-deficit treatment approaches. The Frostig perceptual-motor program and materials and the Doman-Delacato developmental program both generated initial appeal only to show little or no successful transfer to school functioning (Hallahan & Kauffman, 1976; Cole, 1978). These kinds of interventions were based on the premise of a neurological deficit or disorganization which, when corrected, would allow the child to function normally.

Cruickshank, Bentzen, Ratzeburg, and Tannhauser (1961) hypothesized that learning disabled children were unable to block out external, irrelevant stimuli during learning tasks. The researchers developed an intervention program that provided quiet rooms with no distracting pictures on the walls and a structured curriculum. Evidence tends to support the contention that the children attended more closely to their tasks under these optimal conditions, but most follow-up studies did not show increases in achievement.

Passage of Public Law 94–142 brought a different focus to interventions. Teachers and administrators are accountable for the yearly goals set for each child, so treatments are generally based not on etiological considerations but on practical school-oriented needs. Teachers must specify what elements of classroom activity are particularly difficult for the learning disabled child and initiate specific behavioral and teaching techniques to help this immediate problem. Although the atheoretical approach may have been initially ineffective, it has forced researchers to face the practical problems of school learning. Better and sounder theories of intervention are now being tested that can be applied to all children with academic difficulties, including emotionally handicapped children.

For instance, Hallahan and his colleagues have been using cognitive behavior modification techniques (CBM) developed by Donald Meichenbaum (1977) to help learning disabled children stay on task. These techniques require that the child be aware of the nature and result of the intervention because cognitive behavior modification calls for self-instruction (verbalization), self-monitoring, and self-feedback. This is based on the theoretical work of Vygotsky (1962), who emphasized the role of language in controlling behavior. Although cognitive behavior modification can be applied to a wide variety of behaviors in school, it has been used mostly to teach on-task behavior during individual self-instruction of academic skills such as handwriting, spelling, and reading. Studies with learning disabled children have been positive, and gains have been maintained over several months (Hallahan, Kneedler, & Lloyd, in press). It is too early to evaluate the long-term effects or relate this intervention to other areas of academic functioning, but the results look promising.

A related approach focuses on teaching learning disabled children organizational strategies, no matter what the material. They are taught to approach work systematically with strategies for completion and retention. Deshler et al. (1983) say this approach has been particularly effective with older learning disabled children. Based on the "inactive learner hypothesis," organizational strategies indicate that the field of learning disabilities is finally understanding the many links between theory and practice.

Both cognitive behavior modification and strategic training depend on the child's awareness of the process that is being imposed upon him. The child becomes an integral part of the delivery and evaluation of the technique. This active participation in itself may be the most important element of success. The techniques also help the child organize his world and help the teacher structure the learning environment. Thus, it may not be the specific technique that helps these children, but the child's ability to respond to his own performance by using certain organizational strategies.

In general, medical interventions seem less impressive. Drugs such as Piracetam are being tested in hopes of increasing left-hemispheric functioning. Although some animal studies look promising, clinical application is not yet feasible. Thus, treatment of learning disabilities has not been characterized by drug use except in the area of hyperactivity. Ritalin (methylphenidate) and related drugs have been used extensively with hyperactive children to reduce their activity levels, although use is declining.

Treatment programs of all kinds for learning disabilities have not generally been effective in preventing academic problems. The few longitudinal studies indicate that LD does not go away. Werner and Smith (1977) studied children who were at risk for school and social problems because of perinatal problems, emotional disturbance, and learning disabilities. Follow-up into adulthood showed that the learning disabled children had improved the least of all the groups. Four out of five continued to have serious academic problems compounded by truancy and aggressive behavior. Contact with community services was nine times that

seen for normal children. There thus appear to be emotional and social as well as academic problems associated with learning disabilities, and these social problems seem to increase over time (Bryan & Bryan, 1978).

The area of learning disabilities has been floundering for many years in search of effective intervention strategies. Emphasis on improving academic performance has been at the expense of developing social/emotional programs. Only recently has attention been paid to the children's emotional and social lives, and now intervention strategies are attempting to foster development or remediate problems. Adelman and Taylor (1986) list twelve steps for helping learning disabled children solve interpersonal problems and enhance motivation. These techniques have immediately been taken up by LD specialists, because of the overwhelming need for effective remediation strategies in the social/emotional area.

The new techniques are broader-based than previous intervention strategies; it appears that effective programming calls for focusing the intervention on the whole child, including academic and social/emotional functioning. The fields of learning disabilities and emotional/behavioral disturbance may need to join forces to teach each other effective techniques for learning and social/emotional adjustment.

CONCLUSION

Learning disabilities are a large and growing field within education, psychology, and medicine. The problem of definition will be grappled with in the future, as funds for education become increasingly scarce and there is further pressure to differentiate learning disabilities from general underachievement. Although the underlying causes of learning problems are not well understood, recent advances have helped us understand some of the processes that cause children to have learning problems in school. Our goal now is to conceptualize and test more comprehensive intervention and prevention programs that will help the child's entire functioning. A large segment of children have persistent problems in school, and we are only beginning to understand why they have these problems and how to remediate them.

REFERENCES

Adelman, H. S., & Taylor, L. (1986). *An introduction to learning disabilities.* Glenview, IL: Scott, Foresman.

Atkinson, R. C., & Shiffrin, R. M. (1968). Human memory: A proposed system and its control processes. In K. W. Spence & J. T. Spence (Eds.), *The psychology of learning and motivation* (Vol. II). New York: Academic Press.

Bartlett, F. C. (Ed.) (1932). *Remembering: A study in experimental and social psychology.* Cambridge: Cambridge University Press, 1932.

Belmont, L., & Birch, H. G. (1965). Lateral dominance, lateral awareness, and reading disability. *Child Development, 34,* 57.

Belmont, J. M., & Butterfield, E. C. (1969). The relations of short-term memory to development and intelligence. In L. P. Kipsett & H. W. Reese (Eds.), *Advances in child development and behavior* (Vol. 4). New York: Academic Press.

Birch, H. G., & Belmont, L. (1965). Auditory-visual integration, intelligence, and reading ability in school children. *Perceptual and Motor Skills, 20,* 295.

Bryan, T. H., & Bryan, J. H. (Eds.) (1978). *Understanding learning disabilities* (2nd ed.). Sherman Oaks, CA: Alfred.

Bryan, T. H., & Bryan, J. H. (1983). The social life of the learning disabled youngster. In J. D. McKinney & L. Feagans (Eds.), *Current topics in learning disabilities* (pp. 57–85). Norwood, NJ: Ablex.

Bryan, T., Donahue, M., Pearl, R., & Sturm, C. (1984). Learning disabled children's conversational skills: The "TV Talk Show." *Learning Disability Quarterly, 4,* 13–22.

Bryan, T., & Wheeler, R. (1972). Perception of children with learning disabilities: The eye of the observer. *Journal of Learning Disabilities, 5,* 484.

Clements, S. D. (1966). *Minimal Brain Dysfunction in Children* (NINDS Monograph No. 3). Washington, DC: Government Printing Office.

Cole, G. S. (1978). The learning-disabilities test battery: Empirical and social issues. *Harvard Educational Review, 48,* 313.

Cone, T. E., & Wilson, L. R. (1981). Quantifying a severe discrepancy: A critical analysis. *Learning Disability Quarterly, 4,* 359–371.

Cronbach, L. J. (1960). (Ed.) *Essentials of psychological testing* (pp. 192–213). New York: Harper & Row.

Cruickshank, W. M. (1977). *Learning disabilities in home, school, and community.* Syracuse, NY: Syracuse University Press.

Cruickshank, W. M., Bentzen, F., Ratzeburg, F., & Tannhauser, M. A. (1961). *A teaching method for brain-injured and hyperactive children.* Syracuse, NY: Syracuse University Press.

Cullinan, D., Epstein, M. H., & Lloyd, J. W. (1983). Learning disorders. In *Behavior disorders of children and adolescents.* Englewood Cliffs, NJ: Prentice-Hall.

Deshler, D. D., Warner, M. M., Schumaker, J. B., & Alley, G. R. (1983). Learning strategies intervention model: Key components and current status. In J. D. McKinney & L. Feagans (Eds.), *Current topics in learning disabilities* (Vol. 1). Norwood, NJ: Ablex.

Dorland's Illustrated Medical Dictionary (23rd Ed.). (1957). Philadelphia, PA: Saunders.

Dorval, B., McKinney, J. D., & Feagans, L. (1982). Teacher interaction with learning disabled children and average achievers. *Journal of Pediatric Psychology, 17,* 377–380.

Epstein, M. H., Cullinan, D., Lessen, E. I., & Lloyd, J. (1980). Understanding children with learning disabilities. *Child Welfare, 59* (2).

Fagen, S. A., Long, N. J., & Stevens, D. J. (1975). *Teaching children self-control: Preventing emotional and learning problems in the elementary school.* Columbus, OH: Merrill.

Farnham-Diggory, S. (1978). (Ed.) *Learning disabilities: A psychological perspective* (pp. 1–47). Cambridge, MA: Harvard University Press.

Feagans, L. (1983). Discourse processes in learning disabled children. In J. D. McKinney & L. Feagans (Eds.), *Current topics in learning disabilities* (Vol. 1). Norwood, NJ: Ablex.

Feagans, L., & McKinney, J. D. (1981). The pattern of exceptionality across domains in learning disabled children. *Journal of Applied Developmental Psychology, 1,* 313.

Feagans, L., & Short, E. J. (1984). Developmental differences in the comprehension and production of narratives by reading disabled and normal children. *Child Development, 22,* 1727–1736.

Forness, S. R., & Cantwell, D. P. (1982). DSM-III psychiatric diagnosis and special education categories. *The Journal of Special Education, 16,* 49–62.

Frostig, M. (1972). Visual perception, integrative functions and academic learning. *Journal of Learning Disabilities, 5,* 1.

Frostig, M., & Horne, D. (1964). *The Frostig program for the development of visual perception: Teacher's guide.* Chicago: Follett.

Goldstein, K. (1939). *The organism.* New York: American Book.

Hagen, J. W. (1967). The effect of distraction on selective attention. *Child Development, 38,* 685–694.

Hallahan, D. P. (1975). Distractability in learning disabled children. In W. M. Cruickshank and D. P. Hallahan (Eds.), *Perceptual and learning disabilities in children: Vol. 2. Research and theory.* Syracuse, NY: Syracuse University Press.

Hallahan, D. P., & Kauffman, J. M. (Eds.) (1976). *Introduction to learning disabilities.* Englewood Cliffs, NJ: Prentice-Hall.

Hallahan, D. P., Kneedler, R. D., & Lloyd, J. W. (1983). Cognitive behavior modification techniques for learning disabled children: Self-instruction and self-monitoring. In J. D. McKinney, & L. Feagans (Eds.), *Current topics in learning disabilities* (Vol. 1). Norwood, NJ: Ablex.

Hammill, D. D., & Larsen, S. C. (1974). The effectiveness of psycholinguistic training. *Exceptional Children, 41,* 5–14.

Hansen, C. L. (1979). Chicken soup and other forms of comprehension. In J. E. Button, T. C. Lovitt, & T. D. Rowland (Eds.), *Communications research in learning disabilities and mental retardation* (pp. 1–31). Baltimore, MD: University Park Press.

Huelsman, C. B. (1970). The WISC subtype syndrome for disabled readers. *Perceptual and Motor Skills, 30,* 535.

Kaufman, A. S. (1976). A new approach to the interpretation of test scatter on the WISC-R. *Journal of Learning Disabilities, 9,* 160.

Kender, J. P. (1972). Is there really a WISC profile for poor readers? *Journal of Learning Disabilities, 5,* 397.

Keogh, B. K. (1983). Individual differences in temperament: A contributor to the personal-social education competence of learning disabled children. In J. D. McKinney, & L. Feagans (Eds.), *Current topics in learning disabilities* (Vol. 1). Norwood, NJ: Ablex.

Keogh, B. K., Major, S. M., Omori, H., Gandara, P., & Reid, H. P. (1980). Proposed markers in learning disabilities research. *Journal of Abnormal Child Psychology, 8,* 21–31.

Kessler, J. (1966). *Psychopathology of childhood.* Englewood Cliffs, NJ: Prentice-Hall.

Kirk, S. T., McCarthy, J., & Kirk, W. (1968). *Illinois Test of Psycholinguistic Abilities* (Rev. ed.). Urbana: University of Illinois Press.

Lee, L. (1969). *The Northwestern Syntax Screening Test.* Evanston, IL: Northwestern University Press.

Marge, M. (1972). The general problem of language disabilities in children. In J. V. Irwin & M. Marge (Eds.), *Principles of childhood language disabilities.* Englewood Cliffs, NJ: Prentice-Hall.

McKinney, J. D., & Feagans, L. (1983). Adaptive classroom behavior of learning disabled students. *Journal of Learning Disabilities, 16,* 360–367.

McKinney, J. D., & Feagans, L. (1984). Academic and behavioral characteristics: Longitudinal studies of learning disabled children and average achievers. *Learning Disabilities Quarterly, 7*(3), 251–256.

McKinney, J. D., Mason, J., Perkerson, K., & Clifford, M. (1975). Relationship between classroom behavior and academic achievement. *Journal of Educational Psychology, 67,* 198–203.

Meichenbaum, D. (1977). *Cognitive-behavior modification: An integrative approach.* New York: Plenum Press.

Myklebust, H. R. (1971). *Pupil Rating Scale for Learning Disabilities.* New York: Grune & Stratton.

Orton, S. (1937). *Reading, writing, and speech problems in children.* New York: W. W. Norton.

Pearson, G. H. J. (1952). A survey of learning difficulties in children. In *Psychoanalytic study of the child* (Vol. 7). New York: International Universities Press.

Reid, D. K., & Hresko, W. P. (1982). *A cognitive approach to learning disabilities.* New York: McGraw-Hill.

Rosenthal, J. H. (Ed.) (1977). *The neuropsychopathology of written language.* Chicago, IL: Nelson-Hall.

Routh, D. K., & Roberts, R. D. (1972). Minimal brain dysfunction in children: Failure to find evidence of a behavioral syndrome. *Psychological Reports, 31,* 307.

Rutter, M. (1974). Emotional disorder and educational underachievement. *Archives of Disease in Childhood, 49,* 249–255.

Rutter, M., Tizard, J., & Whitmore, K. (1970). *Education, health and behavior.* London: Longman.

Schank, R. C., & Abelson, R. P. (Eds.) (1977). *Scripts, plans, goals and understanding: An inquiry into human knowledge structures.* Hillsdale, NJ: Erlbaum.

Semel, E. M., & Wiig, E. H. (1975). Comprehension of syntactic structures and critical verbal elements by children with learning disabilities. *Journal of Learning Disabilities, 8,* 53–58.

Sommers, R. K., Erdige, S., & Peterson, M. K. (1978). How valid are children's language tests? *The Journal of Special Education, 12,* 393–407.

Strauss, A. A., & Kephart, N. C. (1955). *Psychopathology of the brain-injured child: II. Progress in theory and clinic.* New York: Grune & Stratton.

Strauss, A., & Lehtinen, L. (1947). *Psychopathology and education of the brain injured child.* New York: Grune & Stratton.

Strauss, A. A., & Werner, H. (1942). Disorders of conceptual thinking in the brain injured child. *Journal of Nervous and Mental Disease, 96,* 153–172.

Thomas, A., & Chess, S. (Eds.) (1977). *Temperament and development.* New York: Brunner/Mazel.

Torgesen, J. K. (1977). The role of non-specific factors in the task performance of learning disabled children: A theoretical assessment. *Journal of Learning Disabilities, 10,* 27–35.

Torgesen, J. K. (1980). The use of efficient task strategies by learning disabled children: Conceptual and educational implications. *Journal of Learning Disabilities, 13,* 364.

Torgesen, J., & Goldman, T. (1977). Verbal rehearsal and short-term memory in reading-disabled children. *Child Development, 48,* 56–60.

Vogel, S. A. (1974). Syntactic abilities in normal and dyslexic children. *Journal of Learning Disabilities, 7,* 47–53.

Vygotsky, L. S. (1962). *Thought and language.* Cambridge, MA: MIT Press.

Wechsler, D. (1958). *The measurement and appraisal of adult intelligence* (4th ed.). Baltimore, MD: Williams and Wilkins.

Wepman, J. M., Jones, L. V., Boch, R. D., & Van Pelt, D. (1960). Studies in aphasia: Background and theoretical formulations. *Journal of Speech and Hearing Disorders, 25,* 323–332.

Werner, E. E., & Smith, R. S. (1977). *Kauai's children come of age.* Honolulu: The University Press of Hawaii.

Wiig, E. H., Lapointe, C., & Semel, E. M. (1977). Relationships among language processing and production abilities of learning disabled adolescents. *Journal of Learning Disabilities, 10,* 292–299.

Wiig, E. H., & Semel, E. M. (1974). Logico-grammatical sentence comprehension by learning disabled adolescents. *Perceptual and Motor Skills, 35,* 863–866.

Wiig, E. H., & Semel, E. M. (Eds.) (1976). *Language disabilities in children and adolescents.* Columbus, OH: Merrill.

Wiig, E. H., Semel, E. M., & Abele, E. (1981). Perception and interpretation of ambiguous sentences by learning disabled twelve-year-olds. *Learning Disability Quarterly, 4,* 3–12.

Wiig, E. H., Semel, E. M., & Crouse, M. B. (1976). The use of English morphology by high-risk and learning disabled children. *Journal of Learning Disabilities, 6,* 457–465.

Wood, F. (in press). Issues in the education of behaviorally disordered students. *Monographs in severe behavioral disorders.*

Wong, B. Y. L. (1979). Increasing the retention of main ideas in learning disabled children through the use of questions. *Learning Disability Quarterly, 2,* 43.

Name Index

Subject Index

ABOUT THE AUTHORS

Betty C. Epanchin, Ed.D., is the director of research and evaluation at Wright School, the North Carolina Re-Education Center, and an assistant clinical professor at the University of North Carolina at Chapel Hill. She received both her master's and doctorate degrees at Duke University. She has worked as a teacher, therapist, and director of the educational programs in a psychiatric hospital for children and adolescents and as a consultant to public school teachers who work with mainstreamed, behavior disordered children and to educators in mental health programs. She has written books and articles that deal with teaching and managing children with emotional problems.

Randall William Evans, Ph.D., directs a transitional program for the head injured in Durham, North Carolina, and is an adjunct assistant professor at the medical school of the University of North Carolina at Chapel Hill. He is a practicing clinical neuropsychologist who earned a master's degree in clinical psychology from Trinity University in San Antonio, Texas, a Ph.D. from United States International University in San Diego, and a postdoctoral, interdisciplinary research fellowship at the Biological Sciences Research Center. His major research interests have been in the areas of neuropsychiatry and psychopharmacology, and he has published a number of articles and chapters on these topics.

Lynne Feagans, Ph.D., is a professor in the Department of Individual and Family Studies, College of Human Development, Pennsylvania State University. She earned her Ph.D. from the University of Michigan with an emphasis in developmental psychology and linguistics. After completing a year of postdoctoral training at the Child Development Institute at the University of North Carolina at Chapel Hill, she accepted a post as a senior investigator and research professor at the Frank Porter Graham Child Development Center and clinical associate professor in the Special Education Program. She has written numerous books, articles, and grants on learning disabilities and language.

C. Thomas Gualtieri, M.D., is an associate professor of psychiatry and Director of the Neuropsychiatry Research Program at the Biological Sciences Research Center at the University of North Carolina at Chapel Hill School of Medicine. He graduated from Columbia University Medical School, completed an internship at McGill University and a residency in psychiatry at UNC-CH. He writes books, articles, and grants on attention deficit disorders and pediatric psychopharmacology.

Charles Rush Keith, M.D., is an associate professor of psychiatry at Duke University Medical Center and a supervisor in child analysis with the Washington Psychoanalytic Institute. He attended medical school at Kansas University and completed his residency in psychiatry at the Menninger School of Psychiatry. He completed his child psychiatry training at Duke University and his child psychoanalytic training at the Washington Psychoanalytic Institute. Author of articles and chapters on clinical practices and diagnostic issues, he currently spends much of his time training clinicians, providing clinical service, and consulting with schools.

Donald McNeil, Ph.D., is a professor of special education at Leslie College and a psychologist in private practice in the Boston area. He earned his Ph.D. from the University of Michigan and completed a postdoctoral fellowship at Berkeley. For the past several years he has specialized in work with children who are having problems with alcohol and drug abuse and with children who come from families of alcoholics. He also regularly consults with schools about understanding and dealing with child abuse, alcohol, and drug abuse in children and adolescents, and in families with alcoholic parents.

Lynne B. Monson, Ph.D., is a behavioral scientist at Dynamics Research Corporation in Wilmington, Massachusetts. She earned her Ph.D. in special education from the University of North Carolina at Chapel Hill with an emphasis in the social development of handicapped youngsters. Before moving to New England, she held the position of Assistant Professor in the Department of Educational Psychology at Rutgers University, during which time she conducted numerous studies on perception and communication effectiveness.

James L. Paul, Ed.D., is a professor of special education at the University of North Carolina at Chapel Hill. He earned an Ed.D. at Syracuse University, an M.A. from George Peabody College, and an M.A. from Scarritt College. He has held administrative, clinical, and research positions while pursuing his interests in advocacy, emotional disturbance, and the humanities in relation to exceptional children. He is the author of books, articles, and grants that deal with teaching emotionally disturbed children, advocacy, teacher training, theories of emotional disturbance, parents of handicapped children, and the humanities in relation to exceptional children.

Paula K. Shear, B.A., a graduate of Dartmouth College, worked as a research assistant in the Department of Psychiatry of the medical school of the University of North Carolina at Chapel Hill. She is currently working on her Ph.D. in clinical psychology at the University of California at San Diego.

Rune J. Simeonsson, Ph.D., is a professor of special education and school psychology at the University of North Carolina at Chapel Hill. He earned a Ph.D., an M.A., and an Ed.S. from George Peabody College and an M.A.T. from the University of Chattanooga. He has held clinical and research posts in the Departments of Pediatrics, Psychiatry, and Psychology at the University of Rochester and the University of Nebraska medical schools. He has written books, journal articles, and grants, and his major research interests are early childhood development, pediatric psychology, and developmental disabilities.